AF756065

# Private International Law

Sai Ramani Garimella · Stellina Jolly
Editors

# Private International Law

## South Asian States' Practice

Springer

*Editors*
Sai Ramani Garimella
Faculty of Legal Studies
South Asian University
New Delhi
India

Stellina Jolly
Faculty of Legal Studies
South Asian University
New Delhi
India

ISBN 978-981-10-3457-2 ISBN 978-981-10-3458-9 (eBook)
DOI 10.1007/978-981-10-3458-9

Library of Congress Control Number: 2016960188

© Springer Nature Singapore Pte Ltd. 2017
This work is subject to copyright. All rights are reserved by the Publisher, whether the whole or part of the material is concerned, specifically the rights of translation, reprinting, reuse of illustrations, recitation, broadcasting, reproduction on microfilms or in any other physical way, and transmission or information storage and retrieval, electronic adaptation, computer software, or by similar or dissimilar methodology now known or hereafter developed.
The use of general descriptive names, registered names, trademarks, service marks, etc. in this publication does not imply, even in the absence of a specific statement, that such names are exempt from the relevant protective laws and regulations and therefore free for general use.
The publisher, the authors and the editors are safe to assume that the advice and information in this book are believed to be true and accurate at the date of publication. Neither the publisher nor the authors or the editors give a warranty, express or implied, with respect to the material contained herein or for any errors or omissions that may have been made.

Printed on acid-free paper

This Springer imprint is published by Springer Nature
The registered company is Springer Nature Singapore Pte Ltd.
The registered company address is: 152 Beach Road, #22-06/08 Gateway East, Singapore 189721, Singapore

# Foreword

Private international law has come of age for some years now. Today, it is a vital and vibrant area of law, the practical importance of which cannot be overstated. Long gone seem those times when Prof. Prosser could, then perhaps validly, yet certainly famously and often referred to, describe private international law as "a dismal swamp, filled with quaking quagmires and inhabited by learned but eccentric professors who theorise about mysterious matters in a strange and incomprehensible jargon".[1]

While I used this quote, like many others, as juxtaposing quip in speeches and papers, I never subscribed to Prof. Prosser's description of private international law. In an era dominated by global trade liberalisation agendas, unbridled competition for foreign investment, and the high mobility of people, the days where the preponderant part of transactional and personal relationships are mono-jurisdictional are clearly waning; contrariwise, the number of such relationships connected to more than one jurisdiction is rising sharply. The resulting immense practical utility of the rules and principles of private international law, and their clear ubiquity, impressed upon me very early in my career the enormous value of this area of law.

Yet, when Prof. Prosser, in the very next sentence following his famous observation, exhorted that "[t]he ordinary court or lawyer is quite lost when engulfed or entangled in" (see note 1) private international law, this still seems to ring surprisingly true. Too often remain the rules and principles of private international law overlooked, misunderstood and misapplied. Too frequent appears the struggle with questions such as which court is competent, which law would apply and how can a foreign judgment be recognised and enforced in a particular jurisdiction.

The importance of finding answers to these questions is immediately apparent. Derived from the proper application of the rules and principles of private international law, the answers will allow a layperson to better understand its legal position in a multijurisdictional setting. They will guide the transactional lawyer when

[1]W.I. Prosser 'Interstate Publication' (1953) 51 Michigan Law Review 959, p. 971.

drafting contracts, and they enable the litigator to advise clients on strategic decisions important to conducting a case in court. More specifically, the certainty around the competency of a court can reduce the instances of costly satellite litigation, potentially even in multiple fora. Clarity around the questions of the applicable law, whether as a result of parties exercising consensually choices at the transactional stage, or due to the existence of a clear set of promulgated rules, will reduce instances of surprises such as the unavailability of a certain anticipated remedy or a lower than expected amount of compensation. And in cases where the successful litigant seeks to vindicate rights established by judicial process, being able to predict not only whether the court's judgment will be recognised and enforced in a foreign jurisdiction, but also the process which must be followed so that recognition and enforcement will occur, is essential in the sense that it gives purpose to litigation. In other words, without being able to have a judgment recognised and enforced in a foreign jurisdiction, regardless whether due to a genuine bar to enforcement, or because the process is cumbersome, inefficient and time consuming, and prohibitively expensive, there is no point in commencing litigation in the first place.

Seen collectively, the rules and principles of private international law allow individuals, businesses, their legal advisers and the courts alike to predict with certainty and clarity the outcome of cross-border transaction or questions relating to multijurisdictional personal relationships. They are fundamental to ensuring access to justice and to strengthening the rule of law at a global level, especially when they are combined with legal and administrative procedures that are streamlined, speedy, efficient and cost-effective.

It is thus only befitting that we see an increased focus on the rules and principles of private international law as an important tool of global normative ordering among private relationships. This focus is important to anyone confronted with transactional or personal relationships that is connected to more than one jurisdiction, and is discernible in at least three ways: first, domestic legislative reform agendas pay particular attention to the multilateralisation of transactions and relationships, such as Australia's reform efforts in the area of commercial transactioning, a reform which I have had the privilege to conceive, develop and accompany at its early stages. Second, it can also be seen in the continued strong interest in the work of the Hague Conference on Private International Law, including its core conventions, which, first convened by Dutch lawyer and diplomat Tobias M C Asser in 1893, pursues its mandate to progressively uniform private international law through developing and adopting treaties and, more recently, soft law options. And, third, this focus is also evidenced by the strong attention given to this area of law in scholarly discourse.

This book is an important contribution to this discourse. First, it concentrates on South Asia as geographical region. Thus, this book provides insights into a region, and, more specifically, jurisdictions such as Nepal and Afghanistan that are not always easily accessible for, and which are accordingly less understood by, jurists in other regions, also because they are an intricate mix of statutory and case-based law, influenced and shaped by religious teachings. These insights evidence two important issues: first, the importance of private international law is not confined to some particular well-known regions such as Europe, East Asia or the Americas, but it extends truly globally. Second, there is an emerging, but still underdeveloped appreciation of the subject matter in South Asia. Thus, this book is a strong testament that increased reform efforts within the region are needed, and that these will be vital to ensuring that countries in the region are better integrated in, and can reap greater benefits from, global trade, foreign investment and people's movement.

Second, this book brings together the breadth and depth of private international law, ranging from cross-border family law to complex commercial issues, also including matters pertaining to cross-border civil procedure. It does so very skilfully, striking a balance between essays that contribute very valuably to policy discussions on the one hand, while also including in-depth legal discourses on very specific topics. I note that the selected essays are highly relevant not only to readers in the region. Rather, they are topical for a global audience, covering topics that are highly prevalent. It is particularly important that they embrace subjects that are emerging, highly complex and not without controversy, such as international commercial surrogacy in India.

Naturally, I am delighted to see that many of the essays draw on, discuss, and emphasise the relevance and importance of the conventions and other instruments of the Hague Conference on Private International Law to ameliorating, or even solving, some of the issues besetting individual jurisdictions and, thus, the region more broadly. Drawing on my own significant experience with these conventions and instruments, they certainly offer solutions based on internationally agreed best practices and their implementation, and subsequent application improves certainty, clarity, efficiency and effectiveness in cross-border situations. Many of these instruments are most suitable in South Asia, and I can commend their consideration.

I commend Dr. Garimella and Dr. Jolly to this excellent book, a truly important contribution to the development of private international law, not only in South Asia, but globally.

November 2016

Thomas John
ACIArb, Legal Counsel
Hague Conference on Private International Law
The Hague
The Netherlands

# Acknowledgement

It's not a mere ritualistic statement, but a heartfelt thanks to many people who have been with us through the last year's journey and also to the new friends who have come aboard for this project. The conception of this book came out of our experience of teaching the courses of Private International law and International Commercial Arbitration at the South Asian University. The curious questions and the energetic discussion with the young minds in the classroom gave the first thoughts for this book to be conceptualised. As it reaches this stage of fruition, there are many who rendered assistance and encouragement.

The editors extend their special gratitude to Mr. Thomas John for the valuable foreword. His contribution has enriched the value of the book.

The editors would like to thank all the contributors who willingly contributed to this volume in spite of their busy schedule. The editors wish to place on record the suggestions and comments of the reviewers for this edited collection. Professors and members of bar and bench from the countries of this region have enriched this work with their comments, suggestions and sometimes help with the resources that formed part of this book. We also would like to thank the entire Springer team, especially Sagarika Ghosh and Nupoor Singh for their encouraging response to our project and the constant cooperation and for ensuring an expedited publication process.

Special thanks are expressed to Dr. Kavita A. Sharma, President, South Asian University for her enthusiastic response and kind encouragement for this project. The editors acknowledge Prof. Sasanka Perera, Vice President, South Asian University, and Prof. Santosh C. Panda, Vice President, South Asian University for encouraging South Asian academic collaboration. This book project is inspired by this endeavour of the university to encourage South Asian academic collaboration.

The editors thank Prof. Yogesh Tyagi, Vice Chancellor, University of Delhi. Initial discussions between the editors and Prof. Tyagi provided the much-needed clarity on the project. The editors also record their gratitude to Dr. V.G. Hegde, Associate Dean, and our colleagues at the Faculty of Legal Studies, South Asian University, for their continued encouragement.

Its not a mere tradition to invoke the blessings of our teachers, but a bounden duty to thank them for their continued interest and constant encouragement in our academic endeavours. The editors record their gratitude to Prof. Veer Singh, Former Vice Chancellor NALSAR, Hyderabad, Prof. P.S. Jaswal, Vice Chancellor Rajiv Gandhi National law University, Patiala, Prof. A. Lakshminath, Vice chancellor, Chanakya National Law University, Patna, Prof. R. Venkata Rao, Vice chancellor, National Law School of India University, Bangalore.

The editors take this opportunity to acknowledge the research assistance rendered by Ms. Shachi Singh who has assisted us with extensive research on few chapters in this collection. We also acknowledge the research assistance of Mr. Yesheswi Mann, Mr. Ashraful M.Z. and Mr. Roopak V., Ms. Niroshika Sajeewani Liyana Muhandiram and the copyediting assistance provided by Ms. Snigdha Penumarthy.

The past year has been tiring, and this book would not have been possible with out the help of our family, especially our angels Pranava and Agastya for putting with our long hours of work. You help us move ahead in our life, professional and personal. Without you, we aren't anything.

# Contents

# Editors and Contributors

## About the Editors

**Dr. Sai Ramani Garimella** works as an assistant professor at the Faculty of Legal Studies, South Asian University, New Delhi, India. She is trained at the International Chamber of Commerce (ICC) Summer programme in International Commercial Arbitration. Her research interests are in legal theory and in private law as represented in private international law, international commercial arbitration, international dispute settlement and comparative constitutional law. She has published numerous articles in the area of private international law and has also written a textbook on private international law for undergraduate courses in Indian universities entitled "Private International Law" (Central Law Publications, 2014). She was an invited faculty speaker at the Institute of Security Studies, University of Hamburg, at the Indian Institute of Corporate Affairs, Government of India. She also serves on the editorial board of various journals, including the Journal of Law and Conflict Resolution.

**Dr. Stellina Jolly** is an assistant professor at the South Asian University (SAU), New Delhi, India. Her teaching interests include international environmental law, conflict of laws and bio-ethics. She has worked with Rajiv Gandhi Foundation, Delhi, India, on a research project to develop indicators for "Rule of Law" for states in India. She is a part of the Expert Group on National Consultation on Rule of Law project in the National Law University (NLU), Delhi. Her publications include articles in the European-Asian Journal of Law and Governance, UNESCO Journal of Bio-Ethics, International Journal of Public Law and Policy and the International Journal of Juridical Sciences. She has been a part of the editorial board of peer-reviewed journals, including the Indian Journal of Human Rights, the International Journal of Bioethics, the NUJS International Journal of Legal Studies and Research and the Kuwaiti Journal of Health Care Management. She has been a visiting professor at the Indian Institute of Public Administration (IIPA), the Indian Society of International Law (ISIL) and the NLU Delhi.

## Contributors

**Sarmad Ali, Advocate, Lahore High Court, Pakistan** is LLM and LLB (Hons) from the Northumbria University at Newcastle Upon Tyne, UK. He enrolled as an advocate in 2010 and got the right to audience in the High Court in 2012. He is an Honorary Advisor to Ombudsman Punjab, Pakistan. He is a regular columnist on legal matters to newspapers including Dailytimes—Pakistan.

**Dr. Ijaz Ali Chishti, Supreme Court of Pakistan** is the superintendent of Supreme Court of Pakistan, Islamabad, mandated to assist the Supreme Court through research conducted on the legal issues relevant to a particular case. He holds a Ph.D. in Law in International Commercial Arbitration for which he was a research scholar at Colombia Law School, in 2013. He has been a visiting law faculty to various institutions including International Islamic University, Islamabad. He has published commentary on Supreme Court Rules, 1980 published by Federal Law House, Islamabad-Lahore edition, 2009, for which he was awarded commendation certificate. He has contributed to Annual Supreme Court Report 2004, published by the Supreme Court of Pakistan and also to the Pakistan Law Journal.

**Dr. Sai Ramani Garimella, Assistant Professor, Faculty of Legal Studies, South Asian University, New Delhi, India** holds a doctoral degree in Law from Osmania University, India, and is a member of the Faculty of Legal Studies, South Asian University, New Delhi, an inter-governmental organisation of the countries of the SAARC region. Her research interests are in legal theory and in private law as represented in legal theory, private international law, international commercial arbitration, international dispute settlement, comparative constitutional law, social exclusion studies, feminist writings, theories and commentaries on gender rights regimes with reference to South Asia and the South Asian diaspora. Her recent publications in the area of private international law include *The Enforcement of Multi-tier Dispute Resolution Clauses—Contemporary Judicial Opinion* (2016, IIUMLJ, 24(1), 157–191); *The Balco Rationale—A Shift to the Territoriality Principle in International Commercial Arbitration* (2014, CNLU LJ, 4(1), 26–36); *Third Party Funding in International Arbitration—Issues and Challenges in Asian Jurisdictions* (2014, AALCO Journal of International Law, 3 (1), 45–60); *Emerging Public Policy Contours: Is Indian Arbitration moving closer to the Asian Scenario?* (2013, AALCO Journal of International Law, 2(1), 55–70). She has also written a text book in private international law for undergraduate course in Indian universities entitled *Private International Law*, Central Law Agency, Allahabad, India.

**Md Sanwar Hossain, Barrister-at-law, Advocate Supreme Court of Bangladesh** was called to the Lincoln's Inn, Barrister-at-Law in 2007. He is an Advocate at the Supreme Court of Bangladesh since 2010, and was formerly the in-house legal counsel and the General Counsel of The Hong Kong and Shanghai Banking Corporation, Bangladesh.

Sanwar Hossain heads the chambers, S Hossain & Associates in Dhaka, Bangladesh. The firm has extensive clientele amongst local and multinational business corporations and individuals, and non-resident Bangladeshi members. The firm is also the Bangladesh retainer for many English law firms like HRS Family Law Solicitors, UK, Barrister Hossain was awarded LLB (hons) Degree from University of Wolverhampton, UK, and the Bar Vocational Course (PG Diploma) from Northumbria University, New Castle Upon Tyne, UK.

**Dr. Stellina Jolly, Assistant Professor, Faculty of legal Studies, South Asian University, New Delhi** works at the Faculty of Legal Studies, South Asian University (SAU), New Delhi, a collaborative effort of SAARC countries. Her teaching interests include international environmental law, and conflict of laws and bio-ethics. Her recent research is related to a project of developing indicators for "Rule of Law" for states in India supported by the Rajiv Gandhi Foundation, Delhi —Friedrich Naumann Institute, Germany. She also completed a research project on regulatory reform, supported by Rajiv Gandhi Foundation. Her research appeared as published articles in *European Asian Journal of Law and Governance, UNESCO Journal of Bio Ethics, International Journal of Public Law and Policy, International Journal of Juridical Sciences*, etc. Her recent publications include a chapter on responsibility to protect in disaster in Prof. Amita Singh's forthcoming edited volume "The Emerging Threshold of Disaster Law" (Routledge), and the paper "Access and Benefit Sharing under Nagoya Protocol and Sustainable Development: A Critical Analysis" (2015, *AGORA International Journal of Juridical Sciences*). She is associated with a few journals as a member of their editorial board such as the *Indian Journal of Human Rights*, *International Journal of Bio Ethics*, *NUJS International Journal of Legal Studies and Research*, and *Kuwaiti Journal of Health Care Management*. She has been associated with the Indian Institute of Public Administration, Indian Society of International Law and the National Law University Delhi as a visiting faculty.

**M.P.S. Kaushani Pathirana, Lecturer in law, Department of Private and Comparative Law, Faculty of Law, University of Colombo, Sri Lanka** has earned her masters from the University of Colombo after graduating from the same university. She has research interests in family law and the Sri Lankan legal system. She has worked as the research assistant on a study titled 'Comparative Study of Conservation Easements Applicable in United State of America and Servitude Rights Applicable in Sri Lanka and their effect on Sustainable Development'. This research project was in collaboration with University of Wisconsin Law School, Madison, USA. She is a life member of the Bar Association of Sri Lanka and an associate member of the Sri Lanka Association of Improving Higher Education Effectiveness (SLAIHEE).

**Prof. Maimul Ahsan Khan, Professor of Law, University of Dhaka, Bangladesh** specialises in jurisprudence, Islamic law, international institutions, international commercial law, Islam and muslim culture, political science, comparative human rights, and religious and Middle Eastern and South Asian studies. His teaching assignments include, amongst universities in Bangladesh and USA, University of Illinois-UIUC (1998–2002) and University of California-Davis and Berkeley (2002–2006). He served as a national consultant for an EU funded study to develop a "Tractability System in the Fruits and Vegetable Sectors in Bangladesh". A Fulbright Fellow in USA from 1998 to 2000, he has authored many books such as 'Human Rights in the Muslim World: Constitutionalism, Fundamentalism, and International Politics' (Carolina Academic Press, 2003), 'Islamic Jurisprudence and Women's Rights: Relevance to Modern Trade and Business' (The Nahar Light Foundation, Dhaka, 2009), 'The Basics of Jurisprudence: Law, Politics, and Morality' (Law's Empire Publications, Dhaka, 2010), 'The Vision and Impact of Fethullah Gulen: A New Paradigm for Social Activism' (Bluedome Press, New York, 2011), 'Islamic Financing and Banking: From Traditional Views to Arab Spring' (Lincoln University College, Malaysia, 2012).

**Justice Saleem Marsoof, PC** is currently the Chairman Law Commission of Sri Lanka, an Attorney-at-law of the Supreme Court of Sri Lanka, and was formerly with the Attorney General's Department of Sri Lanka for three decades, rising from the post of State Counsel to that of Additional Solicitor General. He was awarded silk in recognition of professional eminence in 1998.

Justice Marsoof was appointed as the president of the Court of Appeal in March 2004 and was elevated to the office of Judge of the Supreme Court in 2005, which position he held till he retired from judicial service in 2014. During this period, he has held office as Acting Chief Justice of Sri Lanka on numerous occasions and has functioned as a member of the Board of Management of the Judges' Institute of Sri Lanka as well as a member of the Judicial Service Commission.

Justice Marsoof also pursued his academic research interests and has held a few teaching stints as a visiting lecturer of law at the University of Colombo and the Sri Lanka Law College. He has also served as a member of the faculty of the Indian Judicial Academy in Bhopal, India. He has been an active member of the incorporated Council of Legal Education of Sri Lanka and currently serves as a member of the Faculty Board of the Law Faculty at the University of Colombo, and as a resource person for the ICLP Arbitration Centre. He is a also non-resident judge of the Supreme Court of Fiji.

**Wali Mohammed Naseh, Professor of Law, University of Kabul** is a professor with the Faculty of Law and Political Sciences, Kabul University, Afghanistan. He specialises in commercial law, private international law, conflict of law, and bankruptcy law. He holds an LLM from University of Washington School of Law,

Seattle, WA, USA, and is pursuing doctoral research from Frankfurt University, Germany. He has been a part on the Legal Advisory Board to the President of Afghanistan, advising the Afghan President on legal issues especially pertaining to laws, regulations and presidential decrees. He has been a consultant with USAID, reviewing and commenting on the draft of trademarks law, civil procedure law, criminal code and commercial procedure law, and aligning the above-mentioned laws and regulations with TRIPS and other international documents regarding intellectual property in the context of Afghanistan. He was part of legal advisory board, Ministry of Commerce and Industries, Afghanistan, and was involved in legislative capacity-building in the areas of Commercial Arbitration Law, Commercial Mediation Law, Business Partnerships Law, Law on Business Corporations and Limited Liability Companies, Trade Marks Law, Patent Law, Agency Law, Antitrust Law. He has been a legal consultant to Italian Embassy in Afghanistan, 2009, commenting on the Draft Labour Law. He has authored a few textbooks for LLB and LLM students approved by Kabul University. Some of the titles include 'Private International Law', a textbook for law students published in 2013, 'Bankruptcy in Commercial Law' in 1998, and Legal Aspect of Nationality in 2000.

**Gandhi Pandit, Associate Professor of Law, Tribhuvan University, Nepal** is also the founding partner of Gandhi and Associates, a leading corporate law firm in Nepal. He holds an LLM from Columbia University and an MCL from Delhi University, India. He has more than three decades of work experience as a practitioner of law in Kathmandu, New York, and in teaching law in Nepal Law Campus. He has been a consultant for ADB, World Bank, US Aid, Aus Aid and other donor agencies.

**Avdhesh Pant** graduated from the prestigious NALSAR University of Law, Hyderabad, India, in the year 2013. He returned to Nepal to practice corporate law in the chambers of Gandhi and Associates, Kathmandu. He also holds a masters degree in business law from National Law University, Delhi, India, wherein one of his core areas of research was on dispute resolution. He also supervises the corporate law department at Gandhi and Associates, Kathmandu.

**Dr. Markus A. Petsche, Associate Professor, Legal Studies Department, Central European University, Budapest, Hungary** was awarded the doctoral degree for his thesis on 'The Growing Autonomy of International Commercial Arbitration' by the European University Institute at Florence in 2004. During his doctoral research, he won Austrian Federal Ministry for Education and Science Scholarship and the European Union Scholarship. His recent publication on the subject is the *Punitive Damages in International Commercial Arbitration: A Conflict of Laws Lesson, 30 J.Int.Arb. 31–47 (2013).*

Markus Petsche's main fields of academic interest include international arbitration and litigation, alternative dispute resolution, conflict of laws, international business transactions and comparative law. He has authored one book and numerous law review and journal articles on related issues. He also holds visiting appointments at Singapore Management University's School of Law, and the Sorbonne-Assas International Law School—Asia. Prior to embarking on an academic career, Markus Petsche was a deputy counsel at the Secretariat of the International Court of Arbitration of the International Chamber of Commerce, and an associate in the international arbitration department of Gide Loyrette Nouel's Paris office. In this latter capacity, he represented corporate and governmental clients in commercial and investment disputes conducted under the rules of the ICC, ICSID and UNCITRAL. Markus Petsche is a panelist at the Kuala Lumpur Regional Center for Arbitration and acts as arbitrator and mediator in international business disputes.

**Mohammed Abdur Razzak, Barrister and Solicitor, Law Society of Upper Canada, Ontario, Canada; Advocate, Bangladesh Bar Council** is a licensed Notary Public. He did his articling in Lexpand Professional Corporation, supervised by Gardiner Roberts LLP. At the Ontario courts, his work is in the areas of separation agreement, marriage contracts, divorce proceeding, matrimonial property, spousal and child support, child custody and access issues. He also holds a few briefs in commercial litigation. Razzak practiced as a lawyer in Bangladesh, in the chambers of Mr. M. Amir-Ul Islam, Barrister-at-Law and at Amir & Amir Law Associates. Razzak was a Chevening scholar for LLM in international commercial law at the University of Nottingham's School of Law in UK. His research entitled "Judicial Interpretation of "Foreign Jurisdiction Clause" in a Contract—Calls for Review: in the Context of Bangladesh" was published in *India Law Journal,* June, 2009, Vol. II. He has also worked as a leading member of a team nominated by the firm to conduct two research projects, namely "Lex Mundi/World Bank-Yale-Harvard Corporate Governance Project", 2003–4, and "Bangladesh-Corporate Governance ROSC Assessment—P07129656" 2003–4, organised by the World Bank Group in collaboration with the Yale School of Management, USA, Harvard University, USA and Lex Mundi, USA.

**Srijana Regmi** is a Nepalese lawyer currently working with a legal consulting company based in Warsaw, Poland. Ms. Regmi was till recently employed as a Legal Officer at the Ministry of Law, Justice and Parliamentary Affairs, Nepal. Before moving to Warsaw, she was also teaching law undergraduates at Chakrabati Habi Educational Academy's College of Law, Kathmandu, Nepal. She writes for journals and newspapers on contemporary legal issues. Ms. Regmi has worked for various national as well as international law firms. Her prior work experiences also includes freelance legal advising and research consultation on her SSRN page. Her recent publication has been 'Corporate Criminal Liability: Associated Theories And Justifications' *Business Law Journal,* Nepal, 2014.

**Sameer Sattar, Barrister (Lincoln's Inn); Advocate (Bangladesh Bar)** graduated from the Queen Mary, University of London, and completed his Masters in International Business Law from University College London. He has been designated to the ICSID panel of arbitrators. His representative publications include 'Enforcement of arbitral awards and public policy: Same concept, different approach—Resolving international business disputes by ADR in Asia' (*TDM*, 5, 2011)

Sameer advises private companies, state entities and sovereign states on a wide range of contentious and non-contentious matters. He has worked on and appeared in several high-value international commercial arbitrations. He also advises on public international law and related dispute resolution issues, such as the protection of international investments under bilateral and multilateral investment treaties and concession contracts, state sovereignty over natural resources and issues of diplomatic protection.

**Dr. Prakash Shah, LLB (LSE) LLM (LSE) Ph.D. (SOAS), Reader in Culture and Law, Queen Mary University of London** specialises in legal pluralism, religion and law, ethnic minorities and diaspora in law, immigration, refugee and nationality law, and comparative law with special reference to South Asia. Dr. Shah was a lecturer at SOAS, University of London from 1993, and a lecturer at the University of Kent at Canterbury from August 2000. He joined Queen Mary, University of London in 2002, where he is now a Reader in Culture and Law. Some of his recent publications include 'Family, Religion and Law' (Ashgate, Farnham, 2014), 'Transnational family relations in migration contexts: British variations on European themes' in Satvinder Juss (ed.), *The Ashgate research companion to migration law, theory and policy* (Ashgate, Farnham, 2012), 'When South Asians marry trans-jurisdictionally: Some reflections on immigration cases by an 'expert'', in Livia Holden (ed.), *Cultural expertise and litigation: Patterns, conflicts, narratives* (Routledge, London, 2011), and a podcast during the RELIGARE Expert Seminar: Unregistered Marriages and Alternative Dispute Resolution in European Legal Systems (2012), amongst others.

FSV please note, the word 'expert' is within single quotes and after that the single quote of the title name closes.

**Ms. Molshree A. Sharma, Attorney and Partner at Mandel, Lipton, Roseborough and Sharma, Ltd., Greater Chicago area, USA** is a family law practitioner in Chicago, Illinois, advising on custody and visitation issues. Her areas of expertise are family law, adoption law, complex financial settlements, litigation and custody. She has been awarded the distinction of being an Illinois Super Lawyer in 2013 and 2015. She further received the Distinguished Service Award from Chicago Volunteer Legal Services and the Chicago Bar Association Award for Pro Bono Services.

Molshree's research is published in the *Illinois Bar Journal* and also as a chapter on changing strategies in family law for West Law/Thompson Reuters. Her current research is on a law review article on the issues of defenses to the return of the child in the Hague Convention on Child Abduction and Protection. She also has been a panelist and expert on the Hague Convention on Child Abduction and Protection in the USA, India, her recent speaking assignments include a talk at the Foreign Ministry in Ethiopia on Private International Law.

**Dr. Vandana Singh, Assistant Professor of Law, USLLS, Guru Gobind Singh Indraprastha University, Delhi, India** holds a doctoral degree in law, from the University of Delhi, Delhi, India, and is working as an assistant professor of Law at the USLLS, Guru Gobind Singh Indraprastha University, Delhi, India. Her areas of specialisation are intellectual property rights, alternative dispute resolution, private international law and consumer law. She has co-authored the book 'Case Laws on Medical Negligence: Consumer Case Laws' (Series I), Department of Consumer Affairs, Government of India, in association with IIPA. Her research papers have been published in leading international journals. She has co-authored three monographs on private international law, insurance law and economic law, for the International Encyclopedia of Laws, published by Wolters Kluwer, Law and Business. She has also contributed a chapter in the Toshiyuki Kono (ed.), *Intellectual Property and Private International Law: Comparative Perspectives* (Hart Publication, Oxford, 2012).

**Dr. Poomintr Sooksripaisarnkit, LLB (Thammasat), LLM (International Commercial Law), Ph.D. (Leicester), MCIArb, CEDR & HKMAAL Accredited Mediator, AFNI, Senior Lecturer, Australian Maritime College, University of Tasmania** is a senior lecturer with Australian Maritime College, University of Tasmania. Previously, he was an assistant professor at the School of Law, City University of Hong Kong, and the associate director of the Hong Kong Centre for Maritime and Transportation Law, City University of Hong Kong. His research interests lie in the fields of insurance law (marine-and non-marine), admiralty and maritime law, carriage of goods by sea, international sales of goods carried by sea, private international law (commercial conflict of laws) and aspects of international arbitration (relevant to private international law). He is on the Executive Committee of the Hong Kong Insurance Law Association Limited (HILA) and the Hong Kong Maritime Association Limited (HKMLA). His recent publications include a chapter contribution. 'Jurisdiction and Applicable Law' in the forthcoming Mary Thomson (ed.), *Maritime and Practice in Hong Kong* (Sweet & Maxwell Asia) and an article co-authored with Daryl YH Lee 'Identifying Choice of Law in Maritime Torts—Yet Still a Challenge for Courts in Hong Kong' (*University of San Francisco Maritime Law Journal*, 26(2), 2014).

**Prof. Vasanti Nimushakavi, NALSAR University of Law, Hyderabad, India** attended the College of Law at the Osmania University, Hyderabad, from where she obtained her doctoral degree in constitutional studies. Her interest in advocacy-based research is reflected in her work on issues related to disability rights, indigenous people's rights, gender rights and clinical legal education. In 2012, she surveyed the *Chenchu* tribe in Andhra Pradesh spread across 6 districts in Andhra Pradesh in terms of their financial inclusion within the larger framework of social exclusion. Gender studies hold a special interest for her and she worked on the legal regime concerning financial inclusion of women as the RBI Chair Professor at the Council for Social Development, Hyderabad. Her representative publications include 'Addressing Paid Domestic Work: A Public Policy Concern' (*Economic and Political Weekly,* 46(43), 2011), 'Resurrecting/Renegotiating Labour Rights in a Globalising World: Critical Theory and Contract Labour' (*NALSAR Law Review*, 3(1), 2006), amongst others.

**Rose Wijeyeskera, Department of Private Law, Faculty of Law, University of Colombo, Sri Lanka** is a senior lecturer in the Faculty of Law, University of Colombo, Sri Lanka at the university, and a researcher in women's rights law, children's rights law, family law and legal philosophy. She is the director of the women's rights law course in the Master of Laws Programme at the Faculty of Law. She was a member of the Family Law Reform Committee appointed by the Ministry of Justice, Sri Lanka, and also works as a consultant and trainer, particularly in the area of Women's Rights, for many government and non-government organisations. Her research has been cited, amongst others, in the CFR-OECD Working Paper on child marriages entitled "Fragile States, Fragile Lives" and is available as "*Assessing the Validity of Child Marriages Contracted During the War: A Challenge in Post-War Sri Lanka,*" *Annual Research Symposium, University of Colombo, 2011*, http://www.cmb.ac.lk/?page_id=2782.

**Prof. Bruno Zeller, Professor of Law, University of Western Australia, Crawley WA, Australia** specialises in transnational commercial law and is the author of the seminal work—'*Four-Corners* – The Methodology for Interpretation and Application of the UN Convention on Contracts for the International Sale of Goods' (2003), amongst a host of research work in the form of books, chapters in edited collections and journals. His recent research includes 'The CISG and the Battle of the Forms' in Larry A. DiMatteo (ed), *International Sales Law: A Global Challenge* (Cambridge University Press, 2013) and 'Attorneys' Fees—Last Ditch Stand?' in *Villanova Law Review 761* (58(4), 2013). He is also an adjunct professor at Murdoch University, Perth; fellow of the Australian Institute for Commercial Arbitration, Panel of Arbitrators—MLAANZ; visiting professor at Humboldt University, Berlin; and a visiting professor Stetson Law School, Florida. Professor Zeller is an international law consultant with Michael Bula Solicitors.

# Introduction

Individual interactions are increasingly witnessing their scope and presence beyond a single jurisdiction. Globalisation has been a significant fillip to this increase—a collateral effect of transjurisdictional interactions in domains like family law issues, transnational commerce has been the evident presence of the foreign element in the disputes. This foreign element could be either related to jurisdiction, choice of law or the applicable law and the enforcement of the result of the dispute resolution. The foreign element manifests itself as a dispute within the breach of contractual relationships, validity of marriage and divorce brought to question in foreign courts, transnational sale of goods, tortious incidents, increased skilled and non-skilled labour movement across continents, inter-country child abduction, same sex marriages, inter-country adoption, surrogate motherhood, etc. The domain area of conflict of laws/private international law has grown beyond its traditional concern —identification of the forum to decide the dispute, the applicable law and the enforcement of foreign court orders. Today, the domain traverses these fundamental issues with much alacrity, but more importantly, it has, through a concerted and sustained effort, attempted law-making activity through international conventions and soft law instruments in areas much beyond the breaches in contracts and issues arising from broken family relationships. The domain area address questions of cross-border insolvency of corporate institutions, intellectual property rights, internet commerce, amongst others. The focus, however, is steadfast to the basics—ensures fairness in the application of law and procedure in national courts while handling disputes with varied foreign element.

Private International law explains the methods that could be adopted to address contradictions between different legal systems when seized upon an issue having its implications across territorial boundaries and by logical extension, the legal systems. The primordial questions before a domestic court in matters having a foreign element are—(1) When can the domestic court's jurisdiction be called upon—the specific circumstances which give the jurisdiction to the court, (2) In the event of the above question being answered in affirmative—will the domestic court apply the Indian law completely, or will it apply the appropriate foreign law, and

(3) When a foreign judgment is recognised in the domestic jurisdiction and will the court order execution of a foreign decree.

Most countries have developed their own jurisprudence related to issues having a foreign element, and they have viewed private international law as a branch of municipal law. Often these laws have revealed fundamental differences on the same issue. The subject of private international law emerges as a consequence of the fact that the laws of states are diverse and contradictory. Consequentially, there were concerted international efforts, institutional and scholarly, to explore and devise rules that help courts in different jurisdictions decide upon the applicable law in disputes having foreign element. A robust collection of scholarly writing continues to help courts across jurisdictions in identifying the proper law for that dispute. Contemporaneously, there are increasing efforts to work towards harmonisation of private international law. Foremost amongst these harmonisation and codification efforts are those fronted by the Hague Conference on Private International law (HCCH) and European Union through conventions and regulations.

While these codification efforts have contributed to ushering in clarity on a few aspects of the domain area, desirable certainty especially with regard to issues that are recent entrants into the domain area remained elusive. The South Asian Countries are no exception to this legal predicament. South Asia provides an expanding yet underdeveloped terrain for the study of this subject. The research, study and practice of private international law in South Asia are stagnated, as reflected in the dearth of case law and paucity of academic writings. Neither has there been an attempt to showcase a south Asian perspective on private international law. While the forces of globalisation have ignited an expansion of economic interaction intra-South Asia as well as the region's interaction with the rest of the world, absence of a mature private international law system has exposed a gaping hole in the legal infrastructure necessary to facilitate international transactions in South Asia. Private international law is still in its infancy in South Asia, despite increasingly being called upon to address new legal challenges.

This book examines the development of private international law in South Asian countries. It is presented as a compendium of essays on contemporary issues authored by academics and practitioners in the field. There are a few research statements from outside the region, addressing contemporary discourse within this knowledge domain. The chapters address diverse and crucial issues affecting South Asian legal systems' understanding of private international law with a view to bringing this subject to the centre stage of private international law discourse globally as well as within the South Asian region. The compendium is an effort towards infusing and sustaining research in the domain of private international law in South Asia.

This book addresses the three major threads of private international law—jurisdiction, choice of law and enforcement—within each of the South Asian countries in the domain areas of family law and commercial law. South Asian nations have often presented a mixed response towards the conflict of laws questions. Often an evolutionary pattern of fashioning a rule system is visible—a combination of rules and features borrowed from English and European systems and a few indigenously developed rules highlighting their unique practices, often founded within the religious law. For example, Afghanistan has a civil code that specifies the law applicable to non-nationals—the rights and obligations of non-nationals. Nepal is preparing a legislative statement on the applicable law issues, demonstrating a clear shift from its earlier position which required commercial contracts, enforceable in Nepal, have Nepalese law as applicable law. This research effort aims at presenting these unique features of State practice in disputes with foreign element being addressed within the legal systems of this region.

The research in family law domain addresses the traditional research areas of the institution of marriage, divorce and also some of the contemporary concerns that are affecting nations of this region—inter-country child retrieval, surrogacy and the country statement on accession to the Hague Conventions related to this domain. In commercial law, the research addresses the concerns with regard to choice of law issues in transnational contracts and also enforcement of foreign judgment/arbitral awards in the nations of this region.

To put together, a compendium of essays reflecting on a subject of law existing in a region is an uphill task as the essays need to traverse jurisdictions affected by such legal rules. The difficulty is inflated further by the necessity of traversing untrammelled paths and treading less-chartered areas of this knowledge domain in a setting of difficulties in access to materials, lack of translated texts, lack of authoritative judicial statements, amongst others.

This book is organised into twenty-one chapters arranged into four parts. Each chapter begins with a brief abstract and statement of the problem, and the structure of the chapter is specially written to facilitate a reader who has no background in the subject and for easy reference. The first part of this book consists of a few introductory chapters not specifically focusing on South Asia. These chapters highlight important aspects of the contemporary discourse within this knowledge domain related to the three main aspects of private international law.

Chapter "South Asian Legal Systems and Families in Foreign Courts: The British Case" deals with the reception and acceptance of South Asian legal systems and family law in foreign courts. The chapter, through cases being litigated mainly in the UK (with some reference to the EU), describes the engagement with the local courts when legal activity that has taken place in South Asian countries appears for question and/or litigation. Private international law theory, including its resort to choice of law frameworks, has so far been unable to accommodate the complex transnational movements and the consequent personal decision making that is involved in the process of transjurisdictional activity. Narratives related to personal experiences, often gendered, derived from reported and unreported case material that the author could access have been used to explain the complexities that arise from the decision on reception of foreign law by a foreign court. These narratives also discuss the ways of manoeuvring within and around official legal systems. Countries of this region, forming the largest of the diaspora groups in the world, also demonstrate the common pattern of carrying their personal law to other jurisdictions, thus presenting an even stronger case for recognition of foreign law.

Chapter "Choice of Law in International Commercial Arbitration" deals with the choice-of-law rules applied by arbitral tribunals with regard to (i) the determination of the applicable law in the absence of a choice of law by the parties, (ii) the interpretation and supplementation of the law chosen by the parties and (iii) the application of mandatory norms. With regard to point (i), the chapter analyses Article 4(1)(b) of the Rome I Regulation on the Law Applicable to Contractual Obligations and Article 28(2) of the UNCITRAL Model Law on International Commercial Arbitration which allows arbitrators to determine the applicable law on the basis of the conflict rule of their choosing. Regarding point (ii), the chapter deals with situation where arbitrators are entitled to apply non-national law such as general principles of law, the UNIDROIT Principles of International Commercial Contracts, or principles common to the parties' legal systems. The discussion on point (iii) relates to the specific provisions of Rome I Regulation that prescribe rules regarding the application of the mandatory norms of both the forum and other relevant jurisdictions.

Chapter "The Hague Convention on Choice of Court Agreements—Should the European Union's Footsteps Be followed?" deals with the Hague Convention on the Choice of Court Agreements, 2005 drafted under the auspices of the Hague Conference on Private International Law. The chapter draws upon the experience of the States that are signatories to the Convention and critiques the scope and the comparative advantages and disadvantages of the Convention. The chapter explores the possibility of suggesting accession to the convention for countries of Asia, South Asia in particular.

Part II introduces the readers to a few important issues in transnational family law in South Asian countries. Although this book has attempted to maintain continuity between the issues, it addressed a concern in the shape of sparse literature resources on the subject and little documentation of judicial opinion has hindered the absolute continuity of the topics.

Chapter "Conflict of Laws—State Practice in Afghanistan" introduces the reader to the landscape of private international law in Afghanistan. The chapter primarily focuses on the following:

- issues concerning personal status—marriage, divorce, inheritance, will and alimony;
- conflict of laws with regard to property law, movable and immovable;and
- examine the statutory provisions related to applicable law with regard to commercial disputes. Owing to an absence of case law, the chapter appears as a descriptive analysis of statutory provisions.

Chapters "Cross-Border Divorce Regime in Bangladesh" and "Cross-Border Divorce—Sri Lankan State Practice" discuss the legal issues concerning cross-border divorce. The continuity would enable readers to look at the similarities and dissimilarities in South Asian jurisdictions in matters of cross-border divorce. Chapter "Cross-Border Divorce Regime in Bangladesh" presents an overview of procedural and substantive legal aspects dealing with cross-border divorce in Bangladesh with a primary focus on Muslim Divorce Laws. The acceptability of a

Bangladeshi law-based divorce in countries like USA, UK, Australia, Canada and EU has also been discussed; there is a suggestion for Bangladesh's engagement with the Hague Conventions in family law. The author shares his experience as a practitioner in representing clients who had to face multitude of legal hurdles in cross-border divorce and shares the practical and legal obstacles and ambiguities.

Chapter "Cross-Border Divorce Decrees—Recognition in India and Public Policy Considerations" examines the position of Indian courts with regard to the matrimonial relief of divorce by examining public policy considerations that Indian courts have used. The chapter examines the public policy exception within the private international law and attempts to mainstream gender concerns into Private International Law through public policy. It focuses on the enforcement of foreign judgements in matters of divorce under Hindu law in the judicial system in India.

Chapter "Foreign Judgments in Matrimonial Disputes—Recognition in Nepal and Public Policy Considerations" attempts a descriptive as well as a methodical analysis of the existing scenario related to private international law in Nepal. The chapter includes a narrative of the legal framework as well as judicial opinion on the subject. The primary focus of the chapter consists of a detailed narrative with an analysis of the opinion in the *Sabina Pandey* judgment, the landmark case on private international law in Nepal. The subject matter of the case relates to the recognition and enforcement of foreign judgment in Nepal. The chapter also introduces the readers to a descriptive and analytical study of the draft law on private international made as per the judicial pronouncement in *Sabina Pandey*. The draft law consists of provisions related to jurisdiction, choice of law and recognition and enforcement of foreign judgment.

Chapter "Cross-Border Divorce—Sri Lankan State Practice" focuses on issues centred on residence versus domicile, and the existence of jurisdiction in Sri Lankan courts to dissolve a marriage contracted abroad, choice of law issues in the context of divorce in regard to matrimonial unions with a cross-border element, whether foreign judgments on divorce can be recognised enforced by the Sri Lankan courts.

India has become a major surrogacy market, and the issue of cross-border surrogacy opens up a pandora box of legal issues in the form of question of legal parentage and nationality. Chapter "Cross-Border Surrogacy: Indian State Practice" deals with cross-border surrogacy and legal position with regard to India. Through a narrative on the judicial opinion and the Indian Assisted Reproductive Bill 2014, the chapter analyses the Indian legislative position and response of Indian judiciary to this legal fiasco.

Chapters "Inter-Country Child Abduction—Indian Legal Response"–"Inter-Country Child Abduction—Sri Lankan Legal Response" address one of the contentious issues of private international law within South Asia and in contemporary times. International marriages are becoming increasingly common as immigration and vast diasporas become a reality. As a result, the development of a body of private international family law has been crucial to resolving the inevitable issues that arise. A significant issue is that of child custody where parents may not only be of different nationalities but also may live or be present in different countries for what become crucial periods of time. Inquiry related to identification of the jurisdiction for adjudicating the custody matter must precede an inquiry into custody and best interest of the child. To avoid competing jurisdictions and purposeful wrongful removal of children by a parent attempting to divest the other parent of any custody rights, the Hague Convention on the Civil Aspects of International Child Abduction serves as the comprehensive body of law that first establishes which country has the right to adjudicate custody. Within Pakistan and India have not, as yet, acceded to the Hague Convention. On the contrary, Sri Lanka having many similarities with its neighbors is, however, a party to the Convention and has also legislated in fulfilment of the Convention obligations.

There has been a strong push by practitioners for India to sign the convention. Further the Indian Law Commission in its report of 2009 concluded that India must accede to the convention and sign it rather than become a haven for parental kidnapping. This is, however, controversial for a number of reasons where realities of spousal abuse, fraudulent marriages and lack of ability to litigate are cited. Further, so far, the judiciary in India has been extremely quick to adjudicate custody disputes even when the child has not resided in India for any substantial period or arguably has been "wrongfully removed" as per standards of the convention. Chapter "Inter-Country Child Abduction—Indian Legal Response" explores the Indian case law for ascertaining the reasons that explain the judicial opinion in these cases. The chapter highlights the merits, the significance and the disadvantages arising from signing the convention and especially the specific realities of developing nations.

Chapter "Inter-Country Child Abduction—Pakistan's Legal Response" continues the discussion thread of Chapter "Inter-Country Child Abduction—Indian Legal Response" and highlights the position of Pakistan—a non-signatory to the Hague Convention. Taking note of the immense importance of cross-border family law issues, recently, the Pakistan Government has expressed its commitment to accede to Hague Convention. The chapter puts together a discussion on the need for Pakistan's accession to the Hague Convention, and/or enactment of a law addressing international child abduction.

In the context of the objectives of Sri Lanka's Hague Convention enabling legislation, Civil Aspects of International Child Abduction Act, 2001, Chapter "Inter-Country Child Abduction—Sri Lankan Legal Response" analyses the Sri Lankan pre-legislation and post-legislation legal position in respect of parental obligations, duties and responsibilities of the Central Authority, and the procedural aspects including jurisdiction. The judicial opinion on inter-country child abduction is documented and analysed in the context of the nation's international obligations and the municipal law, and the relevance and applicability of foreign judgments in local courts. The impact of the 2001 legislation is also assessed for its comparative advantage over the Reciprocal Enforcement of Judgments Ordinance, 1921 and of 1935.

Part III of this book deals with commercial aspects discussed within the domain of private international law, specifically focussing upon issues concerning International Arbitration and State Practice of South Asian Jurisdictions.

Chapter "Conflict of Laws—State Practice of Bangladesh" presents the jurisprudence of Bangladesh in respect of foreign jurisdiction and proper law clauses in a contract and the enforcement of foreign judgments in Bangladesh, in the context of the civil procedure law of Bangladesh. It highlights the few theoretical constructs that have been derived from the judicial opinion and compares them with similar such constructs in other common law jurisdictions.

Chapters "Issues of Jurisdiction, Choice of Law and Enforcement in International Commercial Arbitration: A Bangladesh Perspective"–"Issues of Jurisdiction, Choice of Law and Enforcement in International Commercial Arbitration: A Pakistan Perspective" deal with issues concerning 'law governing jurisdiction, choice of law and enforcement in international commercial arbitration' in Bangladesh, India, Nepal, Pakistan and Sri Lanka, respectively. This would ensure the much-needed continuity of the discussion on the topic thereby enabling the reader access a comparative perspective between South Asian jurisdictions. Chapter "Issues of Jurisdiction, Choice of Law and Enforcement in International Commercial Arbitration: A Bangladesh Perspective" focuses on the provisions of the Arbitration Act, 2001 concerning the enforcement of foreign arbitral awards in Bangladesh. Chapter "Enforcement of Foreign Arbitral Awards in Bangladesh: The Law, Its Implementation and Challenges" approaches the enforcement of arbitral award in Bangladesh in a comparative manner with the primary focus on public policy exception to enforcement of arbitral awards.

Chapter "Issues of Jurisdiction, Choice of Law and Enforcement in International Commercial Arbitration: An Indian Perspective" on International Commercial Arbitration in India will focus on the following cases laws—*NTPC v. Singer AIR 1993 SC 998, Bhatia International v Bulk Trading SA [2002] 4 SCC 105*, and *Bharat Aluminum co. v. Kaiser Aluminum Technical Services Inc 2012 9 SCC 552.* This chapter would further explore the lack of clarity that prevails in the understanding of governing law in the context of the judicial statement in *Enercon (India) Ltd And Ors vs Enercon Gmbh And Anr [Civ. App. 2086/7 of 2014]* Chapters "Issues of Jurisdiction, Choice of Law and Enforcement in International Commercial Arbitration: A Nepal Perspective"–"Issues of Jurisdiction, Choice of Law and Enforcement in International Commercial Arbitration: A Srilankan Perspective" continue the discussion on the state practice on International Arbitration and elaborate the legal position relating to jurisdiction, choice of law and the enforcement of foreign arbitral awards in Nepal, Pakistan and Sri Lanka, respectively.

The next chapter in the book addresses an emerging issue of private international law. The chapter analyses the applicability of principles of private international law in India within the Intellectual Property Rights-related disputes. The chapter discusses the relationship between the law on intellectual property rights and the private international law with the help of principle of territoriality, the subject-matter of jurisdiction, and the applicable law. It also attempts to document the judicial opinion in India in disputes related to Intellectual Property Rights having a foreign element. The analysis of the judicial opinion is supplemented with a suggestion to legislate upon the applicable rule structure as well as take notice of the increasing presence of arbitration of intellectual property-related disputes in transnational contracts.

Part IV of this book presents guidance for nations of South Asia in addressing Private International Law issues within their respective jurisdictions. Chapter "Private International Law in South Asia—A Few Pointers for Harmonization" attempts to construct a road map founded upon a recognition of the immediate and increasing necessity of harmonising the practice of the nations of this region in this domain area with their neighbours in the immediate neighbourhood and beyond. The chapter exemplifies through the practice of a few other regional groups the need for increased harmonisation of the legal platforms for the countries of this region.

A reader approaching the subject from a European perspective and witnessed a codified and matured private international law jurisprudence may be surprised at the paucity of case law-related material evidenced within the chapters. As noted earlier, the subject of private international law is in its nascency in the region—statutory law and case law is in the evolutionary process, hence much underdeveloped. It is also a manifested fact that there was no documented judicial opinion or secondary resources such as scholarly writing with regard to an issue that concerns the chapter and yet has to be referenced only with a description of the statutory provision. Hence, the chapters could reveal a limited description of the nuances of the law. This book attempts to put together a discussion on some of the contentious issues of private international law relevant to South Asian region. In terms of the coverage and scope of the area, this book is only a beginning, and hopefully, a significant one.

# Part I
# Contemporary Discourse on Private International Law—Some Strands

# South Asian Legal Systems and Families in Foreign Courts: The British Case

**Prakash Shah**

**Abstract** This chapter discusses some salient features of the private international law framework applicable in Britain and compares it with that of the European civil law countries where different assumptions apply. It then provides a brief overview of the South Asian comparative backdrop against which some questions which come up in British and other European legal systems can be set, including the basic feature of personal laws which is the norm in South Asia but exceptional for Europe. It discusses the how South Asians in Europe have formed communities that result from immigration over several decades, including how that has conditioned the types of private international law questions raised and how recent developments associated with Muslims question previously favoured models of multiculturalism. Lastly, there is a focus on how the development of unofficial sharia fora in the UK, within a larger comparative context, is complicating and potentially undermining the existing model of private international law.

**Keywords** South Asia · Legal systems · Foreign courts · Family law · *Sharia*

## Introduction

The focus of this chapter is on the experience of cases being litigated mainly in the UK, but with some reference to other European countries, when legal activity that has taken place in South Asian countries comes up for question. In the background are a number of related developments visible through reported case law as well as through less visible resources acquired through the writer's own experience as an expert witness in British courts and tribunals. Private international law theory, including its resort to choice of law frameworks, has so far been unable to accommodate the complex transnational movements and the consequent personal decision making that is involved in the process of trans-jurisdictional activity. To these can be added the comparative law problems taking the form of smoke and mirrors games of what exactly South Asian legal systems allow and don't allow

P. Shah (✉)
Queen Mary University of London, London, UK
e-mail: prakash.shah@qmul.ac.uk

© Springer Nature Singapore Pte Ltd. 2017 
S.R. Garimella and S. Jolly (eds.), *Private International Law*,
DOI 10.1007/978-981-10-3458-9_1

partly because of their recognition of personal laws in the sphere of the family. What has generally been referred to as 'forum shopping' is a reality but it is far more nuanced than capable of being explained merely by the seeking of the most appropriate or profitable forum. There are also problems within Western jurisdictions such as the UK that impose a stricter dividing line between official and unofficial practices and recognize only the former as legitimate. The emergence of *sharia* fora in the UK and elsewhere has focused the mind on the role of unofficial institutions as well as the capacity of official legal systems to contain Muslim legal alterity in particular. These complexities are discussed through the use of reported and unreported case material, the latter gleaned through the writer's own work as an expert witness, where stories can be related of the personal experiences, which are also gendered, and ways of maneuvering within and around official legal systems. This chapter characterizes the current state of play as a possible stage in the eventual collapse of the boundary currently maintained by private international law to contain Muslim legal difference.

## 1 Britain in Europe: The Basic Recognition Framework

It is widely known that European legal systems employ the mechanism of private international law by which they grant recognition to claims with a 'foreign' element. This mechanism differs from country to country, but the basic approach as outlined in the relevant texts is recognition via private international law.[1] Private international law diminishes in importance the more established and settled a population becomes and its foreignness recedes. In recent years, especially in the domain of family relations, questions of Muslim law arise frequently and in an unprecedented way in European courts.[2] Although other laws from South Asia have also arisen in courts, it has been much less so than for Muslim law. For reasons that have not been appropriately analysed yet, it is also particularly for Muslims that current discussion about legal pluralism occurs in Western countries that are not only about 'foreign law' in the sense conceived of in private international law, although they may overlap with the latter. Given continuous immigration and trans-jurisdictional behaviour, questions of how 'foreign law' can be recognised in European legal systems remain prominent and should continue to do so given there

[1]Mathias Rohe, *Muslim Minorities and the Law in Europe: Chances and Challenges* (Global Media Publications, 2007).

[2]Elisa Giunchi (ed), *Muslim Family Law in Western Courts* (Routledge, 2014); Rubya Mehdi, Werner Menski and Jørgen S. Nielsen (eds), *Interpreting Divorce Laws in Islam* (DJØF Publishing 2012); Rubya Mehdi and Jørgen S. Nielsen (eds), *Embedding Mahr (Islamic dower) in the European Legal System* (DJØF Publishing 2011); Prakash Shah, Marie-Claire Foblets and Mathias Rohe (eds), *Family, Religion and Law: Cultural Encounters in Europe* (Ashgate 2014).

is no real alternative conceptual framework being provided to that of private international law. My own suggestion that a 'comity of peoples' rather than a 'comity of nations' should be the basis of any such reformulation has not been picked up by other scholars, although, in an increasingly transnational world, some such conceptualisation may yet provide a basis for an alternative.[3] Thus, the recognition of legal and cultural alterity and its accommodation tends to be seen as a matter of working out the best way of using *existing legal methods or mechanisms*, even though current official legal frameworks are not able to 'contain' the complexity of legal pluralism, but end up distorting the experiences of migrants and transnationals.

A key difference between those continental European jurisdictions, which have a civil law basis to their rules on private international law, and the British common law approach is that the former rely far more on the nationality link and attempt to apply the relevant foreign law in their court systems too. Unlike in most continental European countries, nationality is used in the UK as a connecting factor only in some cases, while domicile, with all its slipperiness, is still used as a basic point of departure to determine capacity to enter into certain legal relations such as polygamous marriage.[4] For British courts, this approach of *applying* the foreign law is not familiar except where contracts specify an applicable law while giving jurisdiction to British courts.[5] More usually, however, the law of the forum (i.e. English or Scottish law) has to be applied to the substantive claim. Foreign law is not 'applied' in the sense it is in civil law countries but is merely noticed as a 'fact' which helps assess the validity of legal relationships concluded in other jurisdictions. This key difference between some civil and common law countries means that in the former set of countries foreign law has a stronger position as part of the official law, while jurisdictions like the ones in Britain apply the law of the forum, thus according the mere status of 'fact' to a foreign law. In turn, this difference lies behind some important developments in Anglospheric common law jurisdictions, discussed further below. Although treaties increasingly feature in Europe as part of the applicable rule complex, this is far less so in Britain that relies on the common law approach and reforming legislation. However, treaty law may be relevant when the UK is also a party to a multilateral convention (e.g. the Hague Convention on Protection of Children and Co-operation in respect of Intercountry Adoption 1993, to which both the UK and India are parties since 2003); takes part in an arrangement as part of the EU legal system (e.g. the Brussels Convention on jurisdiction and the enforcement of judgements in civil and commercial matters); or is party to some other arrangement with Commonwealth countries (e.g. on the enforcement of

[3]Prakash Shah, 'Transnational Family Relations in Migration Contexts: British Variations on European Themes' in Satvinder Juss (ed), *The Ashgate Research Companion to Migration Law, Theory and Policy* (Ashgate 2013).

[4]For example, Prakash Shah, 'Attitudes to Polygamy in English Law' (2003) 52 ICLQ 359.

[5]For example, see *Shamil Bank of Bahrain EC v Beximco Pharmaceuticals Ltd.* (No. 1) [2004] 1 WLR 1784.

judgments with Pakistan and India, which seems increasingly relevant in practice today).

Outside of those countries of origin that apply a secular form of law in the context of family relations on the broad European model (which the larger countries in South Asia do only exceptionally, since they use religion-based personal laws), the focus tends to be on 'religious' rules and justifications and their accommodation to find a *modus vivendi*. Although it is true that 'custom' remains relevant for legal recognition within South Asian family laws too,[6] it is not well understood, is generally confused with religion and, being often apprehended in the narrowly-constrained, colonial sense, it tends to be much underplayed by lawyers. The formal rule framework of private international law—involving questions about the applicable law, the capacities of parties, and whether to recognise or apply the foreign law—seems to play an important role, but one which is not necessarily conducive to finding the best or the most just solution to the problem or dispute that parties are faced with. For many decades official authorities in the fields, say of immigration, housing and social welfare have also intervened in families that have some legal relations of a transnational character, which means that concerns of a public law nature are often at stake.

An accepted means of excluding the application or recognition of foreign law is referred to as the public order (or 'public policy' in British usage) exception. This can be used to exclude the foreign law although, in practice, it is not used as an exception but is routinely applied, especially to exclude ways of entering into legal relations under Muslim law or consequences flowing therefrom. Addressing the question slightly differently, but not inconsistently, Bowen and Rohe say as follows,

> The definition of what offends *ordre public* in what other people do thus not only reveals current French, German, or British notions about the limits of the morally acceptable, but also may be used to render concrete a general sense of a "clash of civilizations." It is with respect to Islam that this last function of *ordre public* emerges most notably in current jurisprudence.[7]

While it is by default within the domain of judicial practice, public order is increasingly used by legislatures to circumscribe judges in being able to decide the limits of what is acceptable and what is not. This restricts judicial discretion and, to that extent, judges have to conform to legislated assessments of what public order requires. For example, from the 1970s, British judges were already constrained by legislation demanding that only divorces obtained abroad through "judicial or other proceedings" may be recognised by English courts, effectively preventing judges from recognising non-state forms of divorcing, which affects the Muslim *talaq* in

[6]Werner F. Menski, *Hindu Law: Beyond Tradition and Modernity* (Oxford University Press 2003).

[7]John R. Bowen and Mathias Rohe, 'Juridical Framings of Muslims and Islam in France and Germany' in John R. Bowen, Christophe Bertossi, Jan Willem Duyvendak, Mona Lena Krook (eds), *European States and their Muslim Citizens: The Impact of Institutions on Perceptions and Boundaries* (CUP 2013) 143.

particular,[8] although not only, since Hindu custom divorces have also run into problems.[9] Similar reforms have occurred more recently in Belgium too.[10] In effect, the judicial sense of justice based on an evaluation of the situation as judges might see it in individual cases is being substituted for a more rigid rule based system which is likely create more, not fewer, problems in practice. If the latter approach has the attraction of having greater legal certainty, it is a dubious one, because legislation creates its own uncertainties. Private international law is anyway hedged around with many other uncertainties, making it impossible for parties to rely on any rule without doubts creeping in and for lawyers to clearly advise when advance planning is needed or once relationships have run into problems and disputes reach the courts. However, even judges are not always minded to settle cases based on individuated evaluation but on rigid antipathy for particular foreign legal institutions and, again, the Muslim *talaq* divorce runs into problems among judges in several European countries.[11] Indeed, as Bowen and Rohe also indicate in the quote cited above, when judges are confronted by practices that they discover do not conform to the dominant prevailing framework of family relations in their states, they tend not to recognise or apply them. This reinforces my hypothesis that public order or public policy is not deployed *exceptionally* but *routinely* to limit recognition to foreign, particularly Islamic legal institutions.

## 2 Euro-South Asian Comparisons in Family Regimes

All these modes of recognition and exclusion presume what Griffiths refers to as the 'weak' form of legal pluralism, whereby the legal agent is and should be the state, which is also presumed to be dominant. Meanwhile, the wider dimensions of 'strong' legal pluralism, i.e. the presence of more than one legal order in a social field, tend to be missed out.[12] This is an area where a lot of uncertainty prevails and, although presupposing the state as central ('legal centralism') has elicited critical writing, notably by Menski,[13] the idea of the primacy of a state law able to determine matters of intimate family relations remains in place. It would be odd if it were otherwise given that all European states still maintain the façade of state

[8]David Pearl and Werner Menski, *Muslim Family Law* (3rd edn, Sweet & Maxwell, 1998).

[9]Werner F. Menski, 'Life and Law: Advocacy and Expert Witnessing in the UK' in Livia Holden (ed), *Cultural Expertise and Litigation: Patterns, Conflicts, Narratives* (Routledge 2011).

[10]Mathias Rohe, 'Family and the Law in Europe: Bringing Together Secular Legal Orders and Religious Norms and Needs' in Prakash Shah, Marie-Claire Foblets and Mathias Rohe, *Family, Religion and Law: Cultural Encounters in Europe* (Ashgate 2014) 63–64.

[11]Ibid., 64.

[12]John Griffiths, 'What is legal pluralism?' (1986) 24 Journal of Legal Pluralism and Unofficial Law 1.

[13]Pearl and Menski (n 8); Werner F. Menski, 'Muslim law in Britain' (2001) 62 Journal of Asian and African Studies 127.

intervention in family life among citizens too. It is a façade because, in the UK at any rate, the state is increasingly withdrawing from intervention in family life by limiting access to legal aid funds and encouraging private ordering.[14] Except for Greece,[15] European states do not follow the colonial model of personal laws, which has been preserved, with some reforms, by the South Asian post-colonial countries, which anyway function within a cultural background that supports the usually much looser state interventions in family life. In fact, the differences between the South Asian models of personal laws and the prevailing European models often create problems of understanding, especially given the rather myopic view of comparative law prevalent in European law schools.[16] The large-scale ignorance of these comparative aspects, which actually exists on both sides of the European-South Asian legal-cultural divide, means that when lawyers enter into legal practice they are not competent to advise about them and fictitious assumptions often dominate, while academic experts may well take different positions on a single point, leaving judges with another problem to solve. The resultant distortions overlap with the additional distortions created by the framework of private international law, premised as it is on a particular, Western view of the link between persons and the legal systems of origin or transit, and of the way courts should decide about the 'reception' of that link in their legal systems.

It might help if any legal reform either to personal laws or to private international laws within South Asian countries takes place only after such matters have been considered thoroughly and it is by no means the case that European models, once widely thought as worthy of emulation but now increasingly under question, are suitable for that. Unfortunately, original thinking in the realm of law, and family law in particular, and the commensurate predisposition to consider problems in an original way for South Asian contexts, is in short supply among scholars within South Asia as well as abroad. The longstanding and periodically revived idea of enacting a uniform civil code in India may therefore be a face-saving measure ostensibly to eliminate the visibility of palpably separate personal laws and the quite retrograde treatment of Muslim women and children. However, it needs proper consideration whether a code based on a European model, which is probably what is desired, is any solution to the culture specific requirements of a country like India. Although European in origin, the prospect of a uniform civil code today raises the spectre of *Hindutva*, although nobody is able to explain how such a modern uniform civil code would be 'Hindu' in content.[17]

Modernist reforms of Pakistani Muslim law under the military-rule induced Muslim Family Laws Ordinance 1961 also appear to have been clawed back by the

---

[14]Gillian Douglas, 'Who Regulates Marriage? The Case of Religious Marriage and Divorce' in Russell Sandberg (ed), *Religion and Legal Pluralism* (Ashgate 2015) 61–64.

[15]Konstantinos Tsitselikis, *Old and New Islam in Greece: From Historical Minorities to Immigrant Newcomers* (Brill 2012).

[16]Werner Menski, *Comparative Law in a Global Context: The Legal Systems of Asia and Africa* (2nd ed. Cambridge University Press, 2006) 25–81.

[17]Menski (n 16) 252, Mathias Rohe, *Islamic Law in Past and Present* (Brill 2015) 401–402.

reassertion of non-official religious rules and customary practices.[18] Meanwhile, the near-disappearance of official non-Muslim family laws in Pakistan and Bangladesh, either by ignoring the legal status needs of those minorities or by colluding in their ethnic cleansing and other violations, seems like an unjustifiable contemporary version of *dhimmi* status. Such mistreatment is spreading to parts of India such as West Bengal. It speaks volumes about the actual treatment of non-Muslim minorities under Muslim dominance, belying the much-touted tolerance and peaceful nature of Islam. The current Indian government's promise to allow Hindu refugees a place in India responds to those very concerns. Although the old customary Hindu law is supposed to have survived in Pakistan, as Menski has noted, it is "being studiously ignored", it is "hoped that the Hindu personal law might just become irrelevant", as "an unwanted and unreformed colonial relic".[19] Hindus in Pakistan thus face problems of recognition of marriages leading to potential abuses and inaudible Islamisation, while requisite legislation tabled in 2014 has not received approval. Knowing that Ahmadis are not recognised as Muslims in Pakistan, in *R v M* the High Court in London moved to recognise Ahmadi marriages given that they are treated as falling out of reach of Pakistani Muslim law, thereby also having no statutory law to which they can point.[20] Matters take a quite different turn in Europe where, in some countries, notably Britain, Muslims are prone to denounce any circumscription of their associational and religious freedoms. Effectively, these are demands that *sharia* rules be observed in many spheres of life. Although their starting position as not long-present communities of recent migrant origin is different to the once-dominant Indian Muslims, there are echoes of the staunch Muslim resistance to any reforms in Indian personal law.[21] Any pan-South Asian conversation about private international laws in connection with the domestic legal systems, which would inevitably now also involve large South Asian populations in other continents and regions of the world too, have to take on board these problems.

## 3 Immigration and Multiculturalism

As South Asian countries have been the key source of migration for Britain since the 1950s, and increasingly there are South Asians settled in several European pockets, there are obvious transnational connections. Much of the case law in

[18]Pearl and Menski (n 8) 48, Nausheen Ahmed, 'Family Law in Pakistan: Using the Secular to Influence the Religious' in Elisa Giunchi (ed), *Adjudicating Family Law in Muslim Courts* (Routledge, 2014).

[19]Menski (n 6) 187n, 210n, 292–293n.

[20][2011] EWHC 2132 (Fam).

[21]Pearl and Menski (n 8) 45–46; Sylvia Vatuk, 'The Application of Muslim Personal Law in India: A System of Legal Pluralism in Action' in Elisa Giunchi (ed), *Adjudicating Family Law in Muslim Courts* (Routledge, 2014) 52–53; Rohe (n 17) 398–407.

Britain that dealt with questions of private international law was itself generated within an immigration control context, and immigration cases continue to feature strongly. Often immigration law and practices of control have added further requirements as regards, say, the relationship between married partners or the adoption of children to what was already a complex field of law. Earlier, racial considerations were given as the reason for the legislation of the 1960s that laid the foundations for control of immigration from the British Commonwealth, with the non-white Commonwealth identified as the target. That legislation was ratcheted up to limit the immigration of South Asians being driven away from East African countries. However, the need to control immigration from societies that were *culturally and religiously* so different was emphasised more so from the early 1970s and, for Britain, this meant South Asian countries. The case law generated from the immigration context in the 1970s features Pakistanis as the main group who were engaged in family reunification at the time, while case law (as well as changes in the legislation and immigration rules) from the 1980s saw the prevalence of Bangladeshis who were engaged in family reunification in a major way at the time.[22] Such patterns of immigration have not subsided although regions of origin may have diversified much more since the older days of mainly Commonwealth immigration. The basis that South Asian family reunification (and family formation) laid for the development of an unprecedentedly plural Britain also laid the foundation for the legal problematizing of culturally different family forms, as the prospects of a plural society were not always welcomed despite the famed British tolerance and official backing for multiculturalist policies. Underage marriage, adoptions, polygamous marriage, marriages of convenience, forced marriages, and *talaq* divorces began to see light of day in the case law both within as well as beyond the immigration law context. As South Asian settlement advanced, cases increasingly issued from private litigation between spouses or between housing and welfare authorities and individuals and their families. Newer South Asian groups have also been added with Sri Lankans, Afghans, and Nepalis now represented.

That there are segments of society, particularly among the Muslim South Asians, joined by coreligionists from Somalia and West Asia, who follow a different sense of civility and do not mingle and mix well with other sections of British society, have borne out the fears of those who predicted problems way back in the 1970s, today formulated in terms of anxieties about segregation and lack of social cohesion. The idea of multiculturalism that Roy Jenkins famously expressed as Home Secretary 50 years ago, as a contemporary version of British toleration, is no longer the favoured catchword and doubts about it are expressed across Europe as a failed model.[23] Folk wisdom also puts such complained-of living patterns down to the

[22]Satvinder S Juss, *Discretion and Deviation in the Administration of Immigration Control* (Sweet & Maxwell, 1997).

[23]Steven Vertovec and Susanne Wessendorf, *The Multiculturalism Backlash: European Discourses, Policies and Practices* (Routledge, 2010), Claire L. Adida, David D. Laitin and Marie-Anne Valfort, *Why Muslim Integration Fails in Christian-heritage Societies* (Harvard University Press, 2016).

importation of *sharia*, often conveyed through the geographical idiom of '*sharia* zones'. Rightly or wrongly, such living patterns contribute to the spectre of Islamist terrorism, with particular concerns about Pakistan as a laboratory, training ground and exporter of terror activities within South Asia and beyond. The discovery that groups of Muslim, mainly Pakistani men across the UK are involved in criminal activity, including the trapping of young women into sexual exploitation, does nothing to alleviate concerns about lack of adherence to norms of British civility. Negative demographic measures such as the disproportionate presence of Muslim men in British prisons, higher unemployment, higher levels of reliance on social welfare, and educational under-achievement among Muslims are not unnoticed,[24] and could well mirror the pattern in South Asia.

On the one hand, this developing profile has led to the tightening of immigration controls against those coming from countries, notably Pakistan, seen as most prone not to integrate well into British society. As a result, various requirements have been added to qualifications for immigration, residence and nationality status such as minimum age of entry for spouses (out of concerns for early and forced marriage), income, and English language ability,[25] with Muslim groups showing the least likelihood of acquiring English language ability. Although not strictly matters of private international law, these add to basic qualifying criteria and give a different tinge to how 'foreignness' is determined under British law and certainly cannot be ignored as part of the landscape. On the other hand, British legal systems have also been drawing up other types of legal and administrative measures to control and even criminalise unwanted conduct such as forced marriages.[26] UK law has not yet equated the making of marriages between cousins to forced marriage but Danish law already does so, effectively disqualifying such marriages for immigration purposes.[27] It is known, however, that Pakistanis are likely to engage in consanguineous marriages, leading to severe health problems for offspring.[28]

---

[24]Muslim Council of Britain, *British Muslims in Numbers: A Demographic, Socio-economic and Health profile of Muslims in Britain drawing on the 2011 Census* (MCB, January 2015). http://www.mcb.org.uk/muslimstatistics/, accessed 16 January 2016.

[25]Helena Wray, 'Moulding the Migrant Family' (2009) 29(4) Legal Studies 592; Prakash Shah, 'Trans-jurisdictional Marriage and Family Reunification for Refugees in the United Kingdom' (2010) 9(2) İstanbul Kültür Üniversitesi Hukuk Fakültesi Dergisi 94–100.

[26]Ralph Grillo, *Muslim Families, Politics and the Law: A Legal Industry in Multicultural Britain* (Ashgate 2015) 59–91.

[27]Anika Liversage and Mikkel Rytter, 'A Cousin Marriage Equals a Forced Marriage: Transnational Marriages between Closely Related Spouses in Denmark' in Alison Shaw and Aviad Raz (eds), *Cousin Marriages: Between Tradition, Genetic Risk and Cultural Change* (Berghahn 2015).

[28]Khola Hasan, 'The Medical and Social Costs of Consanguineous Marriages among British Mirpuris' (2009) 29(3) South Asia Research 275.

## 4 South Asians and *Sharia*: Official, or Not?

*Sharia* has been mentioned, but more needs to be said about it because of the identification of Britain as a European hub for the building of unofficial *sharia* institutions. Somewhat like the *Dar-ul Qaza* movement in India, and similar institutions in North America,[29] these bodies are known in the UK as "*sharia* councils" although they are often dubbed "*sharia* courts" by the press. They too are a factor in the way Muslims organise their legal lives and somewhat complicates how Muslims use private international law mechanisms. Since men and women enjoy completely asymmetrical opportunities for divorce under Islamic law, the main function of these *sharia* councils appears to be to respond to women who want to end their marriages.[30] It is sometimes said that there is a link between the existence of these bodies and the fact that official British courts will *not* issue Islamic divorces. However, the Indian example shows that this hypothesis is not quite complete. The fact is that Indian courts are able to issue '*sharia*' divorces given the application of Muslim personal law officially in India and yet the *Dar-ul Qaza* movement seeks to keep matters of family law away from the official courts and in the hands of the *ulema*.[31] So the Indian example shows that there is distrust of the non-Muslim judges who, especially since the *Shah Bano* case[32] some thirty years ago, have been making inroads into the allegedly sacrosanct status of Muslim personal law and that forms part of the background to how the *ulema* have been developing an alternative framework.

Still, after a series of reported "obnoxious fatwas",[33] the Supreme Court of India's decision (7 July 2014) in the *Vishwa Lochan Madan* public interest litigation petition confirmed that decisions of a *Dar-ul Qaza* cannot have official effect. According to the court, they do not constitute a "parallel judicial system", and are therefore not illegal, illegitimate and unconstitutional, as the petitioner had claimed. This very briefly reasoned judgement by the Indian Supreme Court underplays that "it is possible for social pressure to reach a degree that makes implementation of rulings inevitable".[34] Would an English Court then be free not to recognise the marriage of Muslim woman who marries after being divorced by a *Dar-ul Qaza* in India? At present that question receives a positive answer because, according to the applicable English legislation, the Family Law Act 1986, section 46 (1) and (2), it would not be seen as "effective under the law of the country in which it was obtained". That situation would anyway be consonant with the non-recognition in

---

[29] Julie Macfarlane, *Islamic Divorce in North America: A Shari'a Path in a Secular Society* (Oxford University Press, 2012), Anna C. Korteweg and Jennifer A. Selby, *Debating Sharia: Islam, Gender Politics, and Family Law Arbitration* (University of Toronto Press, 2012).

[30] Grillo (n 24) 18–19.

[31] Pearl and Menski (n 8) 45n; Vatuk (n 21) 50–53; Rohe (n 17) 391–396.

[32] A.I.R. 1985 S.C. 945.

[33] See Rohe (n 17) 365–366.

[34] Ibid. 394.

the UK of marriages that take place subsequent to "non-proceedings" *talaq* divorces in South Asia generally (although the qualifying rules under section 46 (1) and (2) differ for 'proceedings' and 'non-proceedings' overseas divorces respectively). However, this question of recognition of various styles of *talaq* divorces, which affects all those South Asian Muslims who try to function trans-jurisdictionally, constitutes a critical and recurrent question in British (and European) courts and tribunals. To that extent, Muslims can expect continued trouble, as European fora remain suspicious of the evident privileging by Islamic law of the male right to divorce as well as the possibilities of divorcing by non-formal means.

Distrust of official courts and tribunals which are observed among Muslims in India were confirmed recently when the *Jamiat-Ulama-i-Hind* submitted in a public interest litigation case that Muslim personal law could not be scrutinised by the Indian Supreme Court.[35] Such distrust may also be present in the UK context whereby the *ulema* keep open and enable the prospect of a more 'Islamic' solution to women's divorce. Non-registered marriages are officially not valid if they take place in the UK although, with some exceptions, they would be recognised in British legal systems if they have taken place in a jurisdiction where they are valid, which would include all South Asian countries. These rules of thumb will not necessarily prevent marriages getting into recognition problems if they are conducted by telephone, by proxy, or are polygamous or temporary. Meanwhile, UK-formed *nikah*-only marriages, which appear to be a significant proportion of Muslim marriages,[36] would not come under the matrimonial jurisdiction of the official courts if they run into trouble, although courts and social welfare authorities can still exercise vigilance over children. For non-Muslim South Asians in Britain, the non-registration phenomenon seems to be an insignificant issue and, by all accounts, such cases are rare, although sometimes surfacing through case law.[37] Some continental jurisdictions, such as France, Belgium, and the Netherlands demand registration prior to any religious marriage although, originating at a time when the civil authorities in these European states sought to establish a jurisdiction in family matters that would precede church jurisdiction, it is broadly unheard of that there is any real enforcement of such provisions today. Courts in Turkey, which also used actively to criminalise unregistered, so-called *imam nikahı* marriages, now take a less strident position, a sign of the turn to Islamisation. British legal systems, meanwhile, simply tolerate unregistered marriages, by treating them as cohabitation arrangements, while the courts are still refusing to extend general recognition to such marriages *as marriages*.[38] To unmake such unregistered marriages *sharia* councils in the UK, and those in other countries as far as they exist,

---

[35]'Muslim personal law founded on Quran, SC can't question it: Jamiat' *Times of India*, February 6, 2016.

[36]Grillo (n 24) 41–47.

[37]*Chief Adjudication Officer v Kirpal Kaur Bath* [2000] 1 FLR 8 CA; *Gandhi v Patel* [2002] 1 FLR 603.

[38]Douglas (n 14); Grillo (n 24) 41–47.

may therefore be seen as a useful 'Islamic' port of call, although reports of misogynistic attitudes among *ulema* will not endear them to many Western-educated women.

The author has suggested elsewhere that the rise of *sharia* councils and similar tribunals in the Anglospheric countries as compared to the continental 'civil law' jurisdictions may have some relationship to the differently structured systems of private international law in either type of legal system.[39] The Anglospheric 'common law' countries tend to rely on the *lex fori* in dealing with disputes in their courts and, as noted, they use private international law in a more limited sense to determine the validity of legal relationships that have been formed (or unmade) abroad. In this sense, they provide little space for *sharia* based arguments to surface in the courts unless it is to persuade the courts that they should take notice of a cultural or religious tinge bearing upon a particular practice. Meanwhile, the continental 'civil law' countries, at least presumptively, seek to apply the foreign law to a dispute. Sometimes this can have unexpected consequences as in the rejection by French authorities of a full-fledged civil law adoption on the ground of the Algerian nationality of the child and the prohibition of adoption within Islam as his personal status law. Such a refusal was held to be compatible with France's human rights obligations by the European Court of Human Rights.[40]

This case provides us the opportunity to make a detour on adoption and related concerns. In that context, it indicates a view entrenched in some jurisdictions that nationality determines personal status law and thus a Muslim child could not lawfully be an adoptee. British legal systems meanwhile take a different position, making it unlikely that such the adoptive parent would have been refused an adoption on those grounds. Instead, we see English law making a concession to the Islamic norms against full adoption in its general law by providing for a neutral-sounding 'special guardianship' through section 115 of the Adoption and Children Act 2002, meant especially (but not only) for "some minority ethnic communities, who have religious and cultural difficulties with adoption".[41] This is evidently not restricted to Muslims but could apply for example to those observing the traditional African prohibitions on full adoption. It remains open to question how such a special guardianship made for a Muslim child would be respected in another country perhaps where the personal status law prohibits adoption and may raise particular questions for South Asian countries. This indication of the softer approach at official level for in-country child rearing responsibility allocation, however, contrasts with the official resistance to the recognition of traditional forms of adoption according to South Asian customs, notably under Hindu personal law, or the traditional forms of guardianship among Muslims, if they take place in a

[39]Prakash Shah, 'Shari'a in the West: Colonial Consciousness in a Context of Normative Competition' in Elisa Giunchi (ed), *Muslim Family Law in Western Courts* (Routledge, 2014) 16–17, 20.

[40]*Harroudj v France*, Application no. 43631/09.

[41]*S (A Child)* [2007] EWCA Civ 54, remarks of Wall J at paras. 11 and 42 referring to the White Paper of 2000.

South Asian country.[42] Some residual judicial discretion in such matters has even ensured that should the 'adoptive' parents take action on their own and decide to bring a child into the UK jurisdiction, judges may be willing to decide in their favour. This recounts the case of a child being adopted by custom in Azad Kashmir and brought to the UK and the court supporting the parents over the objections of the social services who tried to stick to the stricter Islamic non-adoption line.[43]

The above-mentioned French case on adoption also underlines how private international law can act to hold some foreign nationals under a form of Islamic law in these civil law countries. It provides endorsement, in an awkward way, of what Rohe says of how Islamic law has a strong position in the areas of family law and inheritance, which are often determined in Germany and in other European countries on the nationality of the persons involved rather than by their domicile.[44] By contrast, British and other Anglospheric legal systems have provided a more fertile ground for *sharia* councils and similar fora to emerge as part of the unofficial landscape and deal most often with issuing certificates of divorced status for Muslim women. There are active attempts to involve *sharia* councils and like fora in more than just family matters. Reported cases reveal transnational activity in this regard[45] as well as a consciousness of developments in other jurisdictions, such as the negative focus on *sharia* tribunals in Ontario, which can in turn determine how matters are played out in the UK.[46]

A proper consideration of the use by women of *sharia* councils should also keep in mind that especially when marriages are arranged between cousins or close kin,[47] incompatibility between them may be underplayed given other priorities around marriage making, and when a relationship fails those around the couple may insist that the parties reconcile. Men can use the *talaq* option if they are bold enough to go against wishes of kinsfolk, while *sharia* councils may well provide a means for women to get out of such marriages. In this way, they can use the 'Islamic' imprimatur from such councils as a trump card to show to their kinsfolk that *ulema* accept that the marriage has failed and should be ended. This kind of problem does not surface in the on-going scrutiny of *sharia* councils by parliamentarians, the government and the media. Researchers have not yet gone into the specific question of how kinship structures and their role in marriage making influences decisions to have recourse to *sharia* councils. The tendency among Muslims to conceptualise

[42]Prakash Shah, 'Transnational Hindu law Adoptions: Recognition and Treatment in Britain' (2009) 5(2) International Journal of Law in Context 107.

[43]Werner F. Menski, 'Life and Law: Advocacy and Expert Witnessing in the UK' in Livia Holden (ed), *Cultural Expertise and Litigation: Patterns, Conflicts, Narratives* (Routledge 2011).

[44]Rohe (n 1) 19, 90.

[45]*Bhatti v Bhatti* [2009] EWHC 3506 (Ch), concerning Ahmadi transnational arbitration through their own system.

[46]*Jivraj v Hashwani* [2011] UKSC 40, concerning Shia Ismaili litigation and designed to ensure a safe playing field in the UK for their Conciliation and Arbitration Boards.

[47]Alison Shaw, 'Kinship, Cultural Preference and Immigration: Consanguineous Marriage among British Pakistanis' (2001) 7 Journal of the Royal Anthropological Institute 315.

family matters in terms of their religious doctrines rather than as an outcome of customary processes and kinship relations (often consigned to the state of pre-Islamic paganism) prevents much sense being made out of these questions even by researchers.[48] Meanwhile, current research shielding Muslim women who use *sharia* councils by centring on their agency will not do much to salvage the role of institutions that have acquired a bad name publicly and which, in any case, can be seen as party to the subordination of women.[49] While it is known that women dissatisfied with individual *sharia* councils may shop around to see what sort of response they obtain from other similar bodies, there is a more intricate if somewhat haphazard and contingent mixing of the official and unofficial laws in what appears to be the process of securing the maximum from the legal options available. More research is required on this issue to examine closely just how the different legal orders are being accessed and utilised. Accounts of individual cases are already emerging.[50] Many such cases, which reveal some kind of 'interlegality' between the official and unofficial levels, have a transnational dimension too which makes them important from the perspective of those thinking about problems from a private international law perspective.

One such case where the author was an expert witness during 2013–14 involved a marriage contracted between a woman from Muzaffarnagar in Uttar Pradesh, India and a man of Pakistani origin living in Britain. Interestingly, they had had a telephone *nikah* based on which the woman obtained entry as a spouse to the UK. This was certainly odd because, if one examines the guidance on the recognition of marriage and divorce issued by the UK's Immigration Services Directorate, there is a clear statement that "a telephone marriage celebrated whilst one of the parties is in the United Kingdom will not be valid as telephone marriages are not valid in this country". Notwithstanding that rule, the wife was somehow admitted to the UK as a spouse. After some ten years of marriage and the birth of four children, she sought a divorce and she managed to obtain a religious divorce from the Islamic Judiciary Board U.K. (IJB) based in Birmingham (operated by the *Markazi Jamiat Ahl-e-Hadith*, and most likely drawing support and funding from Saudi Wahhabis). During those proceedings the husband cooperated and agreed to the divorce implying that he accepted the existence of a marriage. He could not have done otherwise as he had helped in the woman's admission to the UK and had four children with her. To an Islamic judge, it would appear incongruous that he would deny being married to her and the alternative would be to regard their relationship as being tantamount to *zina*.

Yet the wife did not stop there and wanted to pursue the issue of financial provision in the official family court. Issues such as deciding on financial provision

---

[48]Prakash Shah, 'In Pursuit of the Pagans: Muslim Law in the English Context' (2013) Vol. 45(1) Journal of Legal Pluralism 58.

[49]Samia Bano, *Muslim Women and Shari'ah Councils: Transcending the Boundaries of Community and Law* (Palgrave Macmillan, 2012) expresses this tension well.

[50]John Bowen, 'How Could English Courts Recognize Shariah?' (2011) 7 Univ. of St. Thomas LJ 411, discussing *Uddin v Choudhury* [2009] EWCA Civ 1205.

and those related to children are not generally dealt with by *sharia* councils. The official courts remain attractive because of the high potential awards that can be expected from them especially if a marriage lasts some years. The husband then began to deny the validity of the marriage, arguing that he had been compelled to enter into the marriage and that the wife had not been free to enter into a marriage with him because, at the time, she was already married to someone else. The author was at this point called in as an expert witness. There was evidence that the previous marriage of the wife had broken down prior to her marriage with the defendant husband. This author also stated in his report, and later in court, that both as a matter of private international law and as a matter of English law there were grounds on which the judge could uphold its validity. Otherwise, the court would be going against the presumption in both Islamic and English law that there was a marriage on the basis of cohabitation and the four children of the couple, the fact that both would have had to collaborate to facilitate the wife's admission to the UK, and that the husband had already accepted he was married while cooperating with the *sharia* council's decision on divorce. Unfortunately, the author is unaware of the family court judge's ruling in the case. The trail often runs cold once lawyers have what they want from an expert witness.

## 5 Conclusion

This chapter discussed some features of the private international law framework applicable in Britain, comparing it to that prevailing in European civil law countries where different assumptions apply. Most interestingly, for the present discussion, the difference between the two models is characterized by the recognition of foreign law as a fact in the former, whereas in the latter there are attempt to apply the foreign law, thus potentially maintaining South Asians, and others, in a foreigner category for longer. The brief overview of the comparisons of family law regimes in South Asia shows in particular how the retention in post-colonial South Asia of personal law systems leads to more complicated scenarios which European legal systems find difficult to grapple with and often end up distorting further. This does not mean that the distinction between official and unofficial is not maintained in South Asia too. The recent development of *Dar-ul Qaza* shows, on the one hand, how difficult it remains for the state to retain control of the legal field. On the other hand, for those states, like Bangladesh and Pakistan, that engaged in a studied neglect and even persecution of non-Muslim minorities, the personal law field has evidently failed to accommodate the concerns of these non-dominant groups. The larger Euro-South Asian comparative canvass demonstrates that whether Muslims live as significant non-dominant populations or as dominant groups, there is lacking a spirit of mutual accommodation and adjustment in the legal field, whereby Muslim-only concerns and the spreading of a Muslim-centric framework by which also non-Muslim others ought to live are prioritized. In the British and wider

European context the effects of this are being felt as these countries begin to withdraw concessionary multiculturalist frameworks.

There are suggestions that, like in India, Muslims in the UK are developing a parallel court system. Although this seems an exaggerated position to adopt given the current situation and evidence, the prospect of a number of *sharia* councils functioning more like courts, and thus involving themselves in more than merely declaring the marital status of Muslim women, may not be a very distant prospect in the UK either. The Indian experience reveals that the *ulema* have placed emphasis on the *Dar-ul Qaza* because they have taken the position that the Indian legal system, being secular and Hindu dominated, cannot rightly be submitted to by Muslims. There have been signs for several decades that Muslims, especially women, are taking recourse to the secular British courts. Those courts are able to furnish remedies to them that would not be available to them in an Islamic forum. Muslim women can use the British court system to secure advantages that would not be available to them under any interpretations of Islamic law, which obviously remains quite male centred. The case cited above is not the only one of its kind that the author dealt with where men make an effort, often in alliance with their families, to avoid divorced women gaining access to a portion of the property they may have shared during a marriage. Often this takes the form, as also in the case above, of denying the validity of marriage, a line of argument that lawyers may encourage given that more funds can be gained from pursuing legal arguments that ultimately prove to be without much weight.

As the welfare state recedes further and men are made more liable to support families they might otherwise take less interest in, there could well be greater resentment in future against submitting to British legal systems. Some of the evidence cited in this chapter shows that already the distinction between what properly belongs to the realm of private international law and what is raised merely as a matter of cultural or religious rights before the legal system in the UK may be collapsing. Perhaps this will eventually be replaced by *first* greater pressure on British legal systems to accommodate Muslim alterity to a much higher degree and *second*, and arguably in tension with the first, the building of autonomous institutions that cover a greater range of legal areas to avoid submitting to the British courts. Thus, the attempt to contain Muslim alterity through private international law, which is currently widely advocated by European scholars, is bound to crumble. Having said that, there are also simultaneous efforts being made so that official law is less accessible to persons with modest means and the longer-term effects of such developments could mean that parallel Islamic court systems may fill the vacuum thereby created.

# Choice of Law in International Commercial Arbitration

**Markus A. Petsche**

**Abstract** The choice-of-law rules applied by arbitral tribunals differ in several respects from the approaches followed by domestic courts. Those differences arise in connection with three distinct choice-of-law problems: (i) the determination of the law applicable absent a choice of law by the parties, (ii) the interpretation and supplementation of the law chosen by the parties, and (iii) the application of mandatory norms. As far as item (i) is concerned, arbitration-specific choice-of-law rules typically grant arbitrators more freedom than ordinary conflict-of-laws norms. In relation to international sale of goods transactions, for example, Article 4(1)(b) of the Rome I Regulation on the law applicable to contractual obligations provides for the application of the law of the country where the seller has his habitual residence (unless the contract is more closely connected with another country), while Article 28(2) of the UNCITRAL Model Law on International Commercial Arbitration allows arbitrators to determine the applicable law on the basis of the conflict rule of their choosing. Under the arbitration laws of several countries, arbitrators are even entitled to apply non-national law such as general principles of law, the UNIDROIT Principles of International Commercial Contracts, or principles common to the parties' legal systems. With regard to item (ii), arbitral tribunals may similarly resort to non-national legal sources when interpreting, or filling the gaps of, the applicable domestic law. This was expressly contemplated by the drafters of the aforementioned UNIDROIT Principles according to whom the Principles "may be used to interpret or supplement domestic law" (see Preamble). As to item (iii), the conflict rules of codifications such as the Rome I Regulation lay down specific rules regarding the application of the mandatory norms of both the forum and other relevant jurisdictions. The former cannot be transposed to international arbitration due to the absence of a "forum" of international arbitral tribunals. The latter, while not directly applicable, may be taken into account by arbitral tribunals. However, it is more likely that arbitral tribunals will view the question of the application of specific mandatory norms from the angle of possible enforcement problems that may result from the non-application of those norms.

M.A. Petsche (✉)
Legal Studies Department, Central European University, Budapest, Hungary
e-mail: PetscheM@ceu.edu

© Springer Nature Singapore Pte Ltd. 2017

S.R. Garimella and S. Jolly (eds.), *Private International Law*,
DOI 10.1007/978-981-10-3458-9_2

**Keywords** International Arbitration · Choice law · Mandatory rules · Rome I Regulation

## Introduction

International commercial arbitration proceedings give rise to a variety of choice-of-law issues. Those notably relate to the determination of (i) the law governing the arbitration agreement[1]; (ii) the law governing the arbitration proceedings[2]; (iii) the law applicable to the merits (the applicable substantive law)[3]; and—to the extent that this question is properly framed as a choice-of-law issue—(iv) the law governing the arbitration award (or its enforceability).

This contribution examines the specific question of the determination of the applicable substantive law in the absence of a choice of law by the parties. The significance of this topic derives from the fact that the relevant rules and approaches differ quite dramatically from those applicable and/or followed in the context of international litigation. Indeed, as will be explained in this paper, arbitral tribunals typically enjoy considerably broader discretion than State courts in the determination of the applicable law.

## Structure of the Chapter

This study discusses the two principal dimensions (or aspects) of such arbitral discretion. Section 2 explores choice-of-law discretion, i.e. the fact that arbitral tribunals enjoy considerable freedom in the determination of the applicable domestic law. Section 3 deals with the ability of arbitral tribunals to apply transnational rules, rather than a specific domestic law. While the former relates to the question of *how* arbitral tribunals may determine the applicable domestic law, the latter pertains to the question of *what* it is that they may apply.

---

[1]For in-depth analysis of this issue, see, e.g., Julian D. M. Lew, 'The Law Applicable to the Form and Substance of the Arbitration Clause' in Albert Jan van den Berg (ed.) *Improving the Efficiency of Arbitration Agreements and Awards: 40 Years of Application of the New York Convention*, ICC Congress Series Volume 9 (1999)114; Klaus Peter Berger, 'Re-examining the Arbitration Agreement: Applicable Law—Consensus or Confusion?' In Albert Jan van den Berg (ed.), *Arbitration 2006: Back to Basics?*, ICCA Congress Series Volume 13 (2007) 301; Dongdoo Choi, 'Choice of Law Rules Applicable for International Arbitration Agreements' (2015) 11 Asian Int'l Arbtn J 105.

[2]On this topic, see, e.g., Gabrielle Kaufmann-Kohler, Identifying and Applying the Law Governing the Arbitration Procedure—The Role of the Law of the Place of Arbitration in ICCA Congress Series Volume 9 (n 1) 336.

[3]On this issue, see, e.g., Wolfgang Kühn, 'Express and Implied Choice of the Substantive Law in the Practice of International Arbitration' in Albert Jan van den Berg (ed.), *Planning Efficient Arbitration Proceedings: The Law Applicable in International Arbitration*, ICC Congress Series Volume 7 (1996)380; Marc Blessing, 'Choice of Substantive Law in International Arbitration' (1997) 14(2) J of Int'l Arbtn 39; Abdul F. Munir Maniruzzaman, Choice of Law in International Contracts—Some Fundamental Conflict of Laws Issues, Journal of International Arbitration, Volume 16 (1999), Issue 4, p. 141.

# 1 Discretion of Arbitral Tribunals in the Determination of the Applicable Domestic Law

## *1.1 Recognition of Arbitral Discretion in Arbitration Conventions, Laws, and Rules*

Virtually all contemporary legal instruments in the area of international commercial arbitration provide for broad arbitral discretion in the determination of the applicable substantive law absent a choice of law by the parties. Three principal approaches can be distinguished: (i) requiring (or, perhaps more appropriately, allowing) arbitral tribunals to apply a closest-connection test; (ii) allowing arbitral tribunals to have recourse to the conflict-of-laws norms that they consider "appropriate"; and (iii) enabling arbitral tribunals *directly* to apply the law or rules of law that they consider appropriate without the need to refer to any particular choice-of-law rule (the *voie directe* method).

Examples illustrating the first approach notably include Swiss and German arbitration laws. Under Swiss Law, failing a choice of law by the parties, arbitral tribunals "*shall decide the case according to the rules of law... with which the case has the closest connection.*"[4] Under German law, absent a determination by the parties, arbitral tribunals "*shall apply the law of the State with which the subject-matter of the proceedings is most closely connected.*"[5]

The second approach has notably been followed in the European Arbitration Convention of 1961, the UNCITRAL Model Law, and the English Arbitration Act. Under the European Convention, absent a choice of law by the parties, the arbitrators "*shall apply the proper law under the rule of conflict that [they] deem applicable.*"[6] The Model Law and English Act similarly refer to the application of "*the law determined by the conflict of laws rules which [the tribunal] considers applicable.*"[7]

The third and last approach can be illustrated by French law, as well as various institutional arbitration rules. Under the French Code of Civil Procedure, failing a relevant determination by the parties, arbitral tribunals "*shall decide the dispute in accordance with the rules of law [they] consider[...] appropriate.*"[8] Similarly worded provisions can be found in the ICC, LCIA, and VIAC Rules.[9]

All of these approaches entail a degree of discretion in the determination of the applicable substantive law that is (far) superior to any discretion that domestic courts may enjoy. In the specific context of the EU, for example, courts are bound

---

[4]Swiss Private International Law Act Art. 187(1).

[5]German Arbitration Act Sect. 1051(2).

[6]European Convention on International Commercial Arbitration Art. VII(1).

[7]Model Law Art. 28(2); English Arbitration Act S. 46(3).

[8]French Code of Civil Procedure Art. 1511.

[9]ICC Rules Art. 21(1); LCIA Rules Art. 22(3); VIAC Rules Art. 27(2).

by the provisions of the Rome I Regulation[10] which lays down a number of specific choice-of-law norms pertaining to different categories of contracts including, inter alia, contracts for the sale of goods, contracts for the provision of services, and franchise and distribution agreements.[11] Only in exceptional circumstances may courts depart from these specific rules.[12]

## *1.2 Specific Methodological Approaches Followed by Arbitral Tribunals*

This Section discusses some of the principal methods applied by arbitral tribunals when determining the applicable substantive law in the absence of an agreement between the parties including (i) the application of the conflict norms of the arbitral seat; (ii) the cumulative application of domestic conflict norms; and (iii) the application of general principles of choice of law.

### 1.2.1 Application of the Domestic Conflict Norms of the Place of Arbitration

Contrary to the other two methods examined below, this particular approach does not involve the exercise of any arbitral discretion. It is discussed in this Section because it played and continues to play a rather significant role in arbitral practice. Under this approach, arbitral tribunals apply the conflict norms of the seat, i.e. those conflict norms that the courts of the seat are bound to apply. These conflict norms can be qualified as the "general" conflict norms of the country of the seat and can be contrasted with the "specific" conflict norms contained in that country's arbitration law, if any.

The following cases will serve as illustrations for this particular method. In CAC case No. 44/70,[13] an arbitral tribunal seated in the Czech Republic heard a dispute between a Claimant of unidentified nationality and a group of Austrian Respondents. It decided to apply Czech law to the merits of the dispute on the grounds that the Czechoslovak Statute on International Private and Procedural Law No. 97/1963 (i.e. the conflict norms of the seat) mandated the application of this law.[14]

---

[10]Regulation (EC) No. 593/2008 of the European Parliament and of the Council of 17 June 2008 on the law applicable to contractual obligations (Rome I).

[11]Regulation Art. 4(1).

[12]See Regulation Arts. 4(3), 4(4).

[13]CAC case No. 44/70, 9 January 1975 in Pieter Sanders (ed.), Yearbook Commercial Arbitration (hereinafter, the Yearbook) 1977, Vol. II, 142.

[14]Ibid.

In joint ICC cases No. 2977, 2978, and 3033 (the well-known *Götaverken* case),[15] an arbitral tribunal having its seat in Paris heard a dispute between a Swedish shipyard and a Libyan State entity. The arbitral tribunal held that the substantive applicable law had to be determined "*either by an international convention or by the conflicts (sic!) of laws rules of France, as the country of the place of arbitration.*"[16] It ultimately based its decision to apply Swedish law primarily on French conflict rules and the weight allocated by these rules to the place of construction, the place of delivery, and the place of payment.[17]

In ICC case No. 5460,[18] a sole arbitrator sitting in London heard a dispute between an Austrian franchisor and a South African franchisee. With regard to the determination of the law governing the merits he observed that: "*The place of this arbitration is London, and on any question of choice of law I must therefore apply the relevant rules of the private international law of England.*"[19] He held that under those conflict norms, South African law was the "proper law" of the contract.[20]

Similar approaches have also been adopted in more recent arbitral awards. In ICC case No. 12112,[21] for example, a sole arbitrator sitting in Switzerland heard an investment dispute between two EU Claimants and a non-EU State. The parties' contract provided for the application of the laws of the State party and, when giving effect to this provision, the sole arbitrator did so on the grounds that the Swiss conflict norms (i.e. the conflict norms of the seat) recognized the validity of such a choice, noting that "*the lex fori [was]... decisive to the determination of the applicable law*".[22]

Finally, in ICC case No. 13756,[23] a sole arbitrator sitting in Sweden heard a dispute between an US agent and a Russian principal. As regards the law applicable to the contract, he noted that the parties had agreed on the application of the Hague Convention on the Law Applicable to Agency Agreements, which led to the application of the law of the State of Michigan.[24] As regards the contract's formal

---

[15]*AB Götaverken v. General National Maritime Transport Company (GMTC)*, as legal successor of Libyan General Maritime Transport Organization (GMTO), Award, ICC Case Nos. 2977, 2978 and 3033, 1978 in Yearbook 1981, Vol. VI, 133.

[16]Ibid., 136.

[17]Id, 137.

[18]*Austrian franchisor v South African franchisee*, Final Award, ICC Case No. 5460, 1987, Yearbook 1988, Vol. XIII, 104.

[19]Ibid., 106.

[20]Id.

[21]First Investor, in liquidation (EU country), Second Investor (EU country) v Ministry of Agriculture (Non-EU country), Final Award, ICC Case No. 12112 in Yearbook 2009, Vol. XXXIV, 77.

[22]Ibid., 81.

[23]Agent (US) v Principal (Russian Federation), Final Award, ICC Case No. 13756, 2008 in Yearbook 2014, Vol. XXXIX, 118.

[24]Ibid., 120.

validity, however, the arbitrator resorted to the conflict norms of the 1980 Rome Convention on the Law Applicable to Contractual Obligations on the grounds that this Convention was in force in the place of the arbitral seat (Sweden).[25]

### 1.2.2 Cumulative Application of Domestic Conflict Norms

One method whereby arbitral tribunals make use of their discretion in the determination of the applicable substantive law consists of the *cumulative* application of the conflict norms involved. What conflict norms are "involved" will be a matter for the arbitral tribunal to decide but those norms are typically considered to include those of the parties' respective legal systems and, frequently, those of the seat. The applicability of this method requires, of course, that the conflict norms concerned be identical or, at least, that they point towards the same domestic law. This approach can therefore only be applied where there is convergence between the relevant conflict norms.

The following examples will usefully illustrate this method. In ICC case No. 6281[26] a sole arbitrator sitting in France heard a dispute between an Egyptian buyer and a Yugoslav seller. As regards the determination of the applicable substantive law, the arbitrator examined Egyptian, Yugoslav, and French conflict norms.[27] Those norms provided for different connecting factors (place of signing of the contract; place of principal office of the seller; habitual residence of the seller) but they all led to the application of Yugoslav law.[28]

In ICC case No. 7319[29] a sole arbitrator sitting in an unidentified location heard a dispute arising out of an agreement for the distribution of goods in Ireland (the distributor was presumably Irish and the manufacturer French). In his determination of the law governing the merits, the sole arbitrator decided to apply "*both the Irish and the French rules of conflict, given that these are the only ones having a direct connection with the parties and the dispute*."[30] The arbitrator held that French and Irish conflict norms were similar in their recognition of the closest-connection test and concluded that Irish law was applicable to the merits.[31]

Lastly, in a Stockholm Chamber of Commerce case,[32] an arbitral tribunal seated in Stockholm heard a dispute between a Chinese seller and a US buyer. In its

[25]Id.

[26]*Egyptian Company (buyer) v Yugoslav Company (seller)*, Final Award, ICC Case No. 6281, 26 August 1989 in Yearbook 1990, Vol. XV, 96.

[27]Ibid., 97.

[28]Id, 98.

[29]*Manufacturer v Distributor*, Partial Award, ICC Case No. 7319, 1992, in Yearbook 1999, Vol. XXIV, 141.

[30]Ibid., 145.

[31]Id.

[32]*Licensor and buyer v Manufacturer*, Interim Award and Final Award, 17 July 1992 and 13 July 1993, in Yearbook 1997, Vol. XXII, 197.

decision on the applicable substantive law, the arbitral tribunal reviewed possible choice-of-law approaches and observed that, in the case at hand, it was "*immaterial which doctrinal method is employed because the center of gravity rule is common to all conflict-of-laws systems which may be resorted to (including the Chinese, United States and Swedish conflict-of-laws systems).*"[33] The tribunal ruled that Chinese law was applicable.[34]

### 1.2.3 Application of General Principles of Choice of Law

Another method consists of the application of *general principles* of choice of law. In theory, the application of such an approach should raise difficult threshold questions as to what norms enjoy sufficiently broad acceptance in order to constitute general principles. In practice, arbitral tribunals applying this method have been largely undisturbed by this question. They have based their findings either on limited comparative analysis or on the fact that the norms at stake were enshrined in international instruments (without paying particular attention to the ratification or acceptance statuses of those instruments).

In ICC case No. 1512[35] for example, a sole arbitrator sitting in Switzerland heard a dispute between a Pakistani guarantor and an Indian beneficiary. The parties' agreement provided for the application of Indian law. The arbitrator decided to give effect to such a choice on the grounds that "*few principles [were] more universally admitted in private international law than that... according to which the law governing the contract is that which has been chosen by the parties*".[36]

ICC case No. 6149[37] involved a dispute between a Jordanian and a Korean party submitted to an arbitral tribunal having its seat in Switzerland. The arbitral tribunal based its decision to apply Korean law to the merits of the dispute primarily on the cumulative application of the conflict norms concerned.[38] However, it then went on to clarify that this decision was "*further supported by some other general principles prevalent in modern conflict of laws*",[39] specifically those contained in the 1955 Hague Convention on the Law Applicable to International Sale of Goods and those contained in the 1980 Rome Convention on the Law Applicable to Contractual Obligations.

---

[33]Ibid., 203.

[34]Id.

[35]*Indian Company v Pakistani Bank,* Award, ICC Case No. 1512, 1971 in Yearbook 1976, Vol. I, 128.

[36]Ibid., 130.

[37]*Seller v Buyer*, Interim Award, ICC Case No. 6149, 1990 in Yearbook 1995, Vol. XX, 41.

[38]Ibid., 53.

[39]Id, 54.

Finally, in ICC case No. 6527[40] an arbitral tribunal sitting in France heard a dispute between a Turkish seller and a buyer of unidentified nationality. In its determination of the applicable substantive law, the tribunal rejected the approach whereby arbitral tribunals are bound by the conflict norms of the seat and considered it "*more appropriate to apply the general principles of international private law as stated in international conventions, particular (sic!) those in the field of the sale of movable goods.*"[41]

## 1.3 Explanation of Arbitral Discretion

### 1.3.1 Absence of an Arbitral Forum (and of an Arbitral Lex Fori)

The easy answer to the question of why arbitral tribunals enjoy conflict-of-laws discretion is that such discretion is provided for in the applicable arbitration laws and rules. But why do these laws and rules afford arbitral tribunals discretion? One explanation for this legislative and institutional approach is that arbitral tribunals, unlike domestic courts, do not have a forum. The very same idea also underlies the criticism that is sometimes addressed to the use of the concept of arbitral "seat"[42] which some consider unduly to equate the relationship that an arbitral tribunal entertains with the place of arbitration with the link that exists between a domestic court and its home jurisdiction.

Domestic courts necessarily have a forum. This is due to the fact that such courts constitute judicial organs of a particular state (the forum state) and that they derive the entirety of their powers from the law of that state. As is frequently noted in this connection, courts therefore have a duty to apply the law of the forum (the lex fori), including the forum's conflict-of-laws norms.

Traditionally, there has been a tendency to assimilate arbitral tribunals to state courts and to consider that the place of arbitration (or arbitral seat) is the equivalent of a judicial forum. Proponents of this "localized" approach to international commercial arbitration have advocated, to varying extents, the applicability of the law of the forum, including its choice-of-law rules.[43]

---

[40] *Buyer v Seller*, Final Award, ICC Case No. 6527, 1991 in Yearbook 1993, Vol. XVIII, 44.

[41] Ibid., 46.

[42] Although this author has some sympathy for this criticism, the term arbitral "seat" is used as a synonym for "place of arbitration" throughout this contribution.

[43] For a classic article taking such a position, see F.A. Mann, 'Lex Facit Arbitrum' in P.Sanders (ed.) *Arbitration: Liber Amicorum for Martin Domke* (The Hague, Martinus Nijhoff, 1967) 157.

In the contemporary context, such views are generally considered as obsolete. Critics of the traditional approach point out that arbitral tribunals are not judicial organs of any state and that they do not therefore have a *lex fori* which they would be bound to apply.[44] As has been shown, the vast majority of arbitration statutes implicitly adopt this view insofar as they do not require arbitral tribunals to apply the general conflict norms of the place of arbitration.[45]

### 1.3.2 Predictability and Legitimacy of Choice-of-Law Determinations

The second explanation for arbitral discretion pertains to the interests that the conferral (or recognition) of such discretion is intended to serve. Unlike the first explanation, it does not rely on any presumably "inherent" characteristics of the arbitral process. Rather, it relates to the objectives underlying the adoption of norms providing for arbitral discretion or, viewed from the perspective of the parties, to the advantages that such discretion offers. This author submits that those advantages consist of enhanced predictability and legitimacy of arbitral choice-of-law determinations.

Parties to a transaction have a basic interest in the predictability of the rules applying to their legal relationship. Those rules include the conflict of laws norms that a court or tribunal will apply in order to determine the applicable substantive law. The fact that the parties failed to determine the applicable law in their contract does not call into question the relevance of predictability since such a failure is typically attributable to the parties' inability to reach an agreement, rather than to perceived irrelevance of the issue of the applicable law.

Even though it may seem contradictory, limited arbitral discretion may adversely affect the predictability of arbitral choice-of-law determinations. Limited arbitral discretion could result from the adoption of narrowly-tailored[46] conflict norms specific to international arbitration (virtually nonexistent in practice). It may also stem from approaches that seek to extend the applicability of the forum's general conflict norms (i.e. the conflict norms applicable to courts) to the field of international arbitration. As has been shown above, a number of arbitral tribunals have followed this approach, even in recent years.[47]

[44]See, e.g., N. Blackaby, C. Partasides et al., Redfern and Hunter on International Arbitration (Oxford 2015), § 3.212.

[45]See supra 1.1.

[46]"Narrowly-tailored" conflict norms for the purposes of the present contribution are conflict norms that use specific connecting factors (such as residence, domicile, place of performance, place of signing, etc.) to determine the applicable law.

[47]See supra 2.2.1.

But why does limited discretion undermine predictability? The answer is that limited discretion *may* diminish predictability whenever the conflict norm that the arbitral tribunal applies, if any, is unpredictable for the parties. This may be the case where that conflict norm is peculiar to one or a few jurisdictions only and/or where that conflict norm differs from the conflict norms applied in the parties' respective home jurisdictions.

An example will be useful to illustrate this point. A seller from country A enters into a contract with a buyer from country B. Under the conflict rules of both country A and country B, sale of goods transactions are governed by the law chosen by the parties and, absent such a choice, by the law of the seller. The arbitral tribunal seated in country C applies C's general conflict norm which provides for the application of the law of the buyer. Such a choice-of-law determination is not predictable for the parties (unless they are familiar with the private international law of C).

The same example can also be used to show how increased arbitral discretion may enhance predictability. Assume that, rather than being (or considering itself to be) bound by the general conflict norms of C, the arbitral tribunal has (or considers itself to have) broad discretion and chooses to apply the law of the seller. Such a result is arguably more predictable for the parties than the application of the law of the buyer (unless the parties are familiar with the private international law of C and expected its application by the arbitral tribunal).

In practice, as has been explained above, such an outcome (i.e. the application of the more predictable law of A in our scenario) can be achieved either by *cumulatively* applying the conflict norms of the parties or by applying *general principles* of choice-of-law (under the—perhaps questionable—assumption that the rule providing for the application of the law of the seller constitutes such a principle). As far as the former method is concerned, it is worth noting that, under the cumulative method, the conflict norms of the seat need not necessarily be included in those norms that the tribunal applies cumulatively (although this was done in at least two of the three cases examined above).

Increased arbitral discretion may enhance not only the predictability, but ultimately also the legitimacy of arbitral choice-of-law determinations. For present purposes, a legitimate choice-of-law ruling is understood as a decision that the parties accept as fair and correct. Both the cumulative method and the application of general principles are likely to encounter a high level of acceptance from the parties. This is due to the fact that both approaches normally entail the application of the conflict norms applied in the parties' home jurisdictions.

# 2 Right of Arbitral Tribunals to Apply Transnational, Rather Than Domestic, Law

## *2.1 Legislative Recognition[48] of the Right of Arbitral Tribunals to Apply Transnational Law*

The recognition of the right of arbitral tribunals to apply transnational law absent a choice of law by the parties requires acceptance of two ideas. The first such idea is that arbitral tribunals should not be under an obligation to apply a conflict-of-laws rule (or reasoning). In fact, as long as arbitral tribunals have to resort to a particular conflict norm (and despite the fact that they have broad discretion to decide what conflict norm they wish to apply), they will inevitably have to apply a particular domestic law.

The second idea, which does not necessarily follow from the acceptance of the first one, is precisely the recognition of the right to apply transnational rules, rather than a specific domestic law. In those instruments that do recognize such a right, arbitral tribunals are not required to apply a particular "law", but are authorized to apply the "rules of law" which they consider appropriate. While the former expression confines the scope of arbitral discretion to domestic laws, the latter is generally regarded as permitting the application of transnational law.

It is fair to say, however, that the majority of texts in the field of international commercial arbitration do not grant arbitral tribunals such a right. Amongst those more "conservative" instruments are the European Arbitration Convention, the English and German acts, and the Model Law.[49] Those instruments invariably require arbitral tribunals to apply a conflict norm (typically the conflict norm they consider appropriate), the application of which necessarily leads to the application of a particular domestic law.

Amongst the more "permissive" legal instruments are French and, possibly, Swiss law, as well as various sets of institutional rules. Under French law, absent a choice of law by the parties, arbitral tribunals can directly apply the "rules of law" which they consider appropriate.[50] The rules of the ICC, the LCIA, and the VIAC

---

[48]The right of arbitral tribunals to apply transnational law absent a choice of law by the parties has also been recognized by the domestic courts of various countries. Those courts have enforced arbitration awards based on transnational law and rejected allegations that the application of such rules would be in violation of international public policy or otherwise incompatible with the rules governing the enforcement or setting aside of arbitral awards. For reasons of space, this judicial recognition of the right of arbitral tribunals to apply transnational law cannot be examined in this contribution. For scholarly discussion, see, e.g., David Rivkin, 'Enforceability of Arbitral Awards Based on *Lex Mercatoria*' (1993) 9 Arbtn Int'l 67; Markus Petsche, 'The Application of Transnational Law (*Lex Mercatoria*) by Domestic Courts' (2014) 10(3) J of Priv. Int'l L 489, 503–505.

[49]European Convention on International Commercial Arbitration Art. VII(1); English Arbitration Act Sect. 46(3); German Arbitration Act Sect. 1051(2); Model Law Art. 28(2).

[50]French Code of Civil Procedure Art. 1511.

confer similar discretion upon arbitral tribunals.[51] Whether this can also be said about Swiss law is questionable since the PILA, although it allows the application of "rules of law", simultaneously provides for a closest-connection test. While it is arguable that such a test necessarily leads to the application of a particular domestic law, authoritative Swiss writers take the opposite view.[52]

## 2.2 *Application of Transnational Law in Practice*

This Section provides a few examples illustrating how and when arbitral tribunals have applied transnational law in the absence of a choice of law by the parties. Since it cannot possibly examine the application of all forms or branches of transnational law, it focuses on three categories of decisions: (i) those where arbitral tribunals have decided to apply the rules that are common to the parties' legal systems (the so-called *tronc commun*); (ii) those where they have decided to apply the CISG as a manifestation of transnational law (and not because it would be applicable under its own rules); and (iii) those where arbitral tribunals have applied the UNIDROIT Principles.

### 2.2.1 Application of the *Tronc Commun*

Under the doctrine of the *tronc commun*[53] arbitral tribunals apply the rules that are common to the parties' respective legal systems. Sometimes the application of the tronc commun is agreed by the parties.[54] Other times it is the result of an independent decision of arbitral tribunals. As is easily understood, this method has practical limitations since it can only effectively be applied where the relevant rules are indeed identical or at least similar. In practice, the necessity to engage in legal comparison between the rules of two or more legal systems may give rise to various complications.

[51]ICC Rules Art. 21(1); LCIA Rules Art. 22(3); VIAC Rules Art. 27(2).

[52]See Anya George, Georg von Segesser, 'Swiss Private International Law Act (Chapter 12), Article 187 [Decision on the merits: applicable law]' in Loukas A. Mistelis (ed.) *Concise International Arbitration* (2nd edn, Kluwer 2015) 1225, 1228.

[53]See, e.g., Mauro Rubino-Sammartano, 'Le "tronc commun" des lois nationales en présence (Réflexions sur le droit applicable par l'arbitre international)' (1987) Revue de l'Arbitrage 133; Bertrand Ancel, 'The Tronc Commun Doctrine: Logics and Experience in International Arbitration' (1990) 7(3) J of Int'l Arbtn 65.

[54]In ICC case No. 2272, for example, the parties had agreed that "the arbitrators shall decide, seeking to bring into agreement the rules of Belgian law and of Italian law which govern this matter." See *Italian claimant A v Belgian respondent B*, Award, ICC Case No. 2272, 1975 in Yearbook 1977, Volume II, 151.

A number of arbitral tribunals have applied the *tronc commun* absent a choice of law by the parties. In ICC case No. 2886, for example, an arbitral tribunal hearing a dispute involving a commercial agency agreement decided to apply the rules common to the agent and the principal (the rules common to German and Yugoslav law).[55] In ICC case No. 5103, the arbitral tribunal decided to apply the rules common to French and Tunisian law in a dispute involving several European buyers and Tunisian sellers.[56]

### 2.2.2 Application of the CISG as Part of Transnational Law

In a large number of (sale of goods) cases where the parties failed to select the applicable law, arbitral tribunals have applied the CISG on the basis of the CISG's provisions governing its own applicability. In other cases—those that we are concerned with here—arbitral tribunals have chosen to apply the CISG because they considered it to form part of the general principles of international commercial law (which are included in the broader concept of transnational law), resort to which they deemed appropriate in the cases submitted to them. In those cases, the arbitral tribunals concerned did not, therefore, examine whether the CISG's applicability requirements were met. On the contrary, they sometimes expressly or implicitly stated that this was not the case.

In ICC case No. 7331, for example, an arbitral tribunal having its seat in Paris heard a dispute between a Yugoslav and an Italian party.[57] In its determination of the applicable substantive law, the tribunal first observed that it was "*not bound to apply any particular national law.*"[58] It then went on to state that "*general principles of international commercial practice... should govern the dispute*" and that such principles were "*most aptly contained in the United Nations Convention on Contracts for the International Sale of Goods*".[59] En passant, it noted that this solution was particularly appropriate in light of the fact that both Yugoslavia and Italy were signatories to the Convention.[60]

In ICC case No. 8502 another arbitral tribunal sitting in Paris heard a dispute between a Vietnamese seller and a Dutch buyer.[61] The tribunal considered that the reference in the contract to the Incoterms and the UCP 500 reflected the parties' "*willingness to have their Contract governed by international trade usages and customs.*"[62] It decided that depending on the circumstances, it would refer either to

[55]Collection of ICC Arbitral Awards 1974–85, 332.

[56]Collection of ICC Arbitral Awards 1986–90, p. 361.

[57]An excerpt of the award is available at: http://www.unilex.info/case.cfm?id=140.

[58]Ibid.

[59]Id.

[60]Id.

[61]An excerpt of the award is available at: http://www.unilex.info/case.cfm?id=395.

[62]Ibid.

the CISG or to the UNIDROIT Principles on International Commercial Contracts as instruments codifying such usages and customs.[63]

In ICC case No. 8817 an arbitral tribunal seated in Paris heard a dispute between a Danish and a Spanish party.[64] When determining the law governing the merits, it noted that the appropriateness of the applicable rules depended on their "*presence in the legal systems of both parties*."[65] It found that such considerations supported the application of the CISG since both Denmark and Spain were Contracting Parties at the time of its ruling (although that had not been the case at the time of the conclusion of the contract).

Finally, in ICC case No. 9474 an arbitral tribunal with an undisclosed seat heard a dispute between parties of similarly undisclosed nationalities.[66] In the absence of a choice of law by the parties, the tribunal suggested applying "*the general standards and rules of international contracts*",[67] which the parties accepted. It held that such standards and rules could be found in a variety of instruments including the Principles of European Contract Law, the UNIDROIT Principles, and the CISG.[68] It decided to refer to the rules contained in these instruments depending on their relevance for deciding particular issues submitted to it.[69]

### 2.2.3 Application of the UNIDROIT Principles

According to their drafters, the UNIDROIT Principles may serve three distinct purposes:

(i) they may constitute the applicable substantive law;
(ii) they may be used to interpret or supplement the applicable law; and
(iii) they may serve as a legislative model.[70]

As regards the first of these three functions, the drafters expressly envisioned that the Principles may not only be chosen by the parties, but also be applied where the parties failed to specify the applicable law.[71]

---

[63]Id.

[64]An excerpt of the award is available at: http://www.unilex.info/case.cfm?id=398.

[65]Ibid.

[66]An excerpt of the award is available at: http://www.unilex.info/case.cfm?id=716.

[67]Ibid.

[68]Id.

[69]Id.

[70]UNIDROIT Principles of International Commercial Contracts (2010), Preamble.

[71]Id. The Preamble states that the Principles "may be applied when the parties have not chosen any law to govern their contract." For a recent overview of the application of the UNIDROIT Principles in practice, see Michael Joachim Bonell, 'Symposium Paper: The *UNIDROIT Principles of International Commercial Contracts*: Achievements in Practice and Prospects for the Future' (2010) 17 Austl Int'l LJ 177.

The following cases will illustrate this particular function of the UNIDROIT Principles. In ICC case No. 10422, an arbitral tribunal with an undisclosed seat heard a dispute between a European manufacturer and a Latin-American distributor.[72] The parties had not selected the applicable law but had agreed that such law should be "neutral" vis-à-vis the parties. The arbitral tribunal read this requirement of neutrality as supporting its decision that "*general principles and rules of international contracts*" should apply.[73] It ultimately decided to apply the UNIDROIT Principles, considering that those Principles represented, with some exceptions, "*a restatement of the rules which business persons engaged in international trade consider to be (sic!) meet their needs and expectations.*"[74]

In ICC case No. 11265, an arbitral tribunal having its seat in the Netherlands heard a dispute between parties of unidentified nationalities.[75] As far as the determination of the applicable substantive law was concerned, it considered, first of all, that the application of a particular national law was inappropriate in light o the fact that the case presented significant links with several countries (including Bermuda, Rwanda, and Tanzania).[76] It further observed that neither of the parties was opposed to the application of a-national or transnational law and that one of the parties had expressly requested the application of the UNIDROIT Principles.[77] On the basis of these considerations, it held that the Principles should apply.[78]

In a case decided under the rules of the Russian Chamber of Commerce and Industry,[79] an arbitral tribunal hearing a dispute between a Russian and a Hungarian party decided to apply the UNIDROIT Principles on the grounds that those Principles reflected the "*most common approaches of the majority of national legal systems in regulating problems of international commercial transactions.*"[80] It also noted that the Principles were "*broadly applied in international commercial practice and widely used by [the] international business community*".[81]

Lastly, in ICC case No. 13012, an arbitral tribunal with an unidentified seat heard a dispute between a US and a French party.[82] When addressing the question of the applicable substantive law, the tribunal approvingly cited earlier decisions rendered by ICC arbitral tribunals declining to apply a particular domestic law,

---

[72]An abstract of the award is available at: http://www.unilex.info/case.cfm?id=957.

[73]Ibid.

[74]Id.

[75]A French-language excerpt is available at: http://www.unilex.info/case.cfm?id=1416.

[76]Ibid.

[77]Id.

[78]Id.

[79]Award in case No. 100 of 30 October 2009. An abstract of the award is available at: http://www.unilex.info/case.cfm?id=1550.

[80]Ibid.

[81]Id.

[82]An excerpt of the award is available at: http://www.unilex.info/case.cfm?id=1409.

notably on the basis of considerations of neutrality.[83] It also referred to decisions of tribunals that, for similar reasons, opted for the application of the UNIDROIT Principles. It therefore decided to apply the Principles, along with what it referred to as "*the fundamental rules of the Lex Mercatoria*" and commercial usages.[84]

## 2.3 Rationale Underlying the Application of Transnational Law

Arbitral tribunals apply transnational law because they perceive it to offer certain advantages or benefits when compared to domestic laws. This Section will explore the two most significant such advantages, namely (i) the *neutrality* of transnational law and (ii) its particular *suitability* as a set of norms governing international business transactions.

### 2.3.1 Neutrality

Neutrality of the applicable substantive law refers to the fact that the application of a particular law does not put any party at a disadvantage. Neutrality in this sense is not related to the actual *substance* of the applicable law, i.e. the way in which that law balances the parties' respective rights and obligations (substantive neutrality). Not only would an assessment of such substantive neutrality be virtually impossible, but it is also rather unlikely that the balance struck in a particular domestic law should significantly differ from the one prevailing under transnational law.

Neutrality for present purposes can therefore be characterized as *practical*, rather than *substantive*. It requires that the parties be placed on an equal footing in relation to factors such as (i) familiarity with the applicable law; (ii) access to relevant legal authorities; (iii) ability to understand applicable legislation and case law in their original language; and, more generally, (iv) costs incurred in the performance of legal research, to name just the principal ones. Neutrality also has a *psychological* aspect, i.e. it requires that the parties subjectively feel that they are not disadvantaged as a result of the application of a particular substantive law.

Where a court or arbitral tribunal is bound to apply a particular domestic law, neutrality may be compromised. Assume, for example, that a Spanish supplier enters into a contract with an Indian distributor and that the parties fail to agree on the law governing their contract. A dispute arises and the arbitral tribunal hearing the dispute needs to decide the issue of the applicable substantive law. In most cases, it will decide to apply either Indian or Spanish law, i.e. the law of one of the

---

[83]Ibid.

[84]Id.

parties.[85] This evidently undermines the achievement of neutrality since the party whose law is found to be applicable will frequently be in a better position in relation to the practical issues listed above.

An alternative option for the arbitral tribunal would be to apply the law of a third country, say English law or French law. While such a choice is indeed likely to ensure neutrality, it would lead to a situation where the application of a particular law is inconvenient, rather than convenient, for both parties. In other words, the choice of the governing law preserves equality but at the cost of putting both parties in an equally undesirable situation.

The application of transnational law offers a superior solution to the problem of neutrality. Like the application of the law of a third country, it ensures that none of the parties is, a priori, better off in terms of the above-mentioned practical considerations pertaining to the applicable law.[86] Unlike the application of the law of a third country, the application of transnational law does not, in principle, generate particular inconveniences for any party, especially where the arbitral tribunal decides to resort to a particular transnational law codification such as the UNIDROIT Principles.

Arbitral case law confirms that considerations of neutrality are crucial for the parties and play a significant role in the choice-of-law decisions of arbitral tribunals. In ICC case No. 10422 referred to above, the parties had been unable to agree on the applicable law, but had stipulated that such law should be "neutral".[87] The arbitral tribunal decided that the UNIDROIT Principles should apply.[88] In ICC case No. 13012 discussed above, the arbitral tribunal similarly emphasized the importance of neutrality. Quoting from the award rendered in ICC case No. 7110, it observed that the parties' choice to submit disputes to arbitration could be regarded as an implicit agreement to subject such disputes to a neutral substantive law.[89]

### 2.3.2 Suitability as a Set of Rules Governing International Business Transactions

A number of scholars have highlighted that domestic laws do not provide an adequate normative framework for international business transactions. Berger, for example, considers that the application of domestic law amounts to a "nationalization of international commercial cases" and that such a phenomenon is

---

[85]A court established in one of the Member States of the EU, for example, would in principle apply Indian law since Art. 4(1)(f) provides for the application of "the law of the country where the distributor has his habitual residence".

[86]Ole Lando, 'The *Lex Mercatoria* in International Commercial Arbitration' (1985) 34(4) ICLQ 747, 748 (stating that the parties "plead and argue on an equal footing" and that "nobody has the advantage of having the case pleaded and decided by his own law").

[87](n 72).

[88]Ibid.

[89](n 82).

"irreconcilable with the interests of the international commercial community."[90] This "dilemma of international commercial law"[91] is due to the fact that domestic law (whether statutory or judge-made) is generally adopted with the sole or principal aim of regulating domestic legal relationships without taking into account the specificities of international transactions.

There are two principal reasons why domestic laws may be inappropriate in an international context. Firstly, they may unduly interfere with party autonomy, i.e. the parties' freedom of contract. The case law of the German Federal Court on the validity of clauses contained in standard forms is illustrative in this respect. Under this case law, a large number of such clauses (e.g., exclusions or limitations of liability; penalty clauses) are void not only in consumer contracts but also in contracts concluded between merchants, including international ones.[92]

Secondly, domestic laws may contain unpredictable rules and may therefore lead to unpredictable outcomes. This may occur when the relevant rule of domestic law is one that is applied only in one or a few jurisdictions. Illustrative examples notably include the rule of the Scandinavian Sale of Goods Act which requires the buyer immediately to notify the seller upon arrival of the goods in order to preserve his right to bring a claim based on late delivery[93] and domestic provisions providing for unusually short limitation periods.[94]

Recourse to transnational law allows arbitral tribunals (and the parties to the dispute) to avoid the application of such undesirable domestic rules. As is well known, transnational law consists of norms and usages that are widely applied or followed at the international level. It is therefore extremely unlikely that isolated or restrictive domestic norms such as those at issue in the German and Scandinavian examples referred to above could ever be regarded as rules of transnational law.

## 3 Conclusion

In the absence of a choice of law by the parties, international arbitral tribunals enjoy broad discretion when determining the applicable substantive law. Such discretion pertains not only to the particular *method* by which arbitral tribunals may determine the applicable domestic law, but also to the *nature* of the rules that they may choose to apply (as has been seen, arbitral tribunals are frequently authorized to apply transnational rules). This arbitral discretion is enshrined in the vast majority of arbitration laws and rules and is regularly relied upon in arbitral practice.

[90]Klaus Peter Berger, *The Creeping Codification of the New Lex Mercatoria* (2nd rev. edn, Kluwer 2010) 19–20.

[91]Ibid., 19.

[92]Id, 28–29.

[93]Lando (n 86) 753.

[94]Ibid., 748.

Evidently, arbitral discretion in the determination of the applicable substantive law is not a per se objective. Rather, it constitutes a tool to achieve other, more vital, aims. On the one hand, as has been explained, broad discretion allows arbitral tribunals to ensure the predictability and legitimacy of their choice-of-law decisions. On the other hand, as has also been highlighted, it assists arbitral tribunals in enhancing the neutrality and suitability of the applicable rules.

# The Hague Convention on Choice of Court Agreements—Should the European Union's Footsteps Be Followed?

**Poomintr Sooksripaisarnkit**

**Abstract** The Hague Convention on the Choice of Court Agreements ('Convention') drafted under the auspice of the Hague Conference on Private International Law was concluded on 30 June 2005. It was ratified by Mexico on 26 September 2007. With the ratification by the European Union on 11 June 2015, the Convention has come into force on 1 October 2016. Therefore, the question is whether other countries should follow the European Union's footsteps in ratifying and giving effect to this Convention. This chapter will consider the said question.

**Keywords** Foreign judgments · Enforcement · Hague convention on choice of court agreements · Hong kong

## Introduction

The Hague Convention on the Choice of Court Agreements (hereinafter, the Convention) drafted under the auspices of The Hague Conference on Private International Law was concluded on June 30th, 2005. Mexico, European Union ratified the Convention, Singapore ratified the Convention in June 2016, while the United States[1] and the Ukraine have signed the Convention. This work, as its title indicates, seeks to question whether the international community, not only the Hong Kong SAR, should consider ratifying the Convention. Writing in 2010, Marta

LLB (Thammasat), LLM (International Commercial Law), PhD (Leicester), MCIArb, CEDR & HKMAAL Accredited Mediator, AFNI, Lecturer in Maritime Law, Department of Maritime and Logistics Management, Australian Maritime College, University of Tasmania. Formerly Assistant Professor, School of Law, City University of Hong Kong.

[1]The USA signed the Convention on 19th January 2009. See The Hague Conference on Private International Law, 'Status Table 37: Convention of 30 June 2005 on Choice of Court Agreements'.https://www.hcch.net/en/instruments/conventions/status-table?cid=98, accessed 07 September 2015.

P. Sooksripaisarnkit (✉)
Department of Maritime and Logistics Management, Australian Maritime College, University of Tasmania, Launceston, TAS, Australia
e-mail: poomintr@icloud.com

© Springer Nature Singapore Pte Ltd. 2017

S.R. Garimella and S. Jolly (eds.), *Private International Law*,
DOI 10.1007/978-981-10-3458-9_3

Petergás, the First Secretary of the Hague Conference on Private International Law, stated that many countries were actively considering ratifying the Convention.[2] In the Hong Kong SAR, there were two public consultations in 2004 and 2007, to discuss the ratification of the Convention. There's been a mixed response; the Convention found little favour with the Hong Kong Bar Association.[3] The response from the professional organization in the Hong Kong SAR would be contrasted to Singapore, who has ratified the Convention. Other countries have not yet made their intention explicit.

**Structure of the Chapter**

The chapter, arranged in three parts, discusses the two primary objectives of the Convention as clearly stated in the Preamble:

- to affirm the effectiveness of exclusive choice of court agreements between parties to commercial transactions, and
- to ensure judgments from the courts whose jurisdictions conferred by such agreements will be recognised and enforced.

The first part attempts to critique the key provisions of the Convention dealing with the effectiveness of the exclusive jurisdiction agreement. The second part discusses the key provisions relating to the recognition and enforcement of judgments. The third part provides evaluative consideration as to whether the Convention should be ratified.

## 1 Analysis of Key Provisions on the Effectiveness of the Exclusive Jurisdiction Clause

The Convention concerns itself with the "exclusive jurisdiction" clause, which allows parties to confer jurisdiction on the courts of one of the State Parties to the Convention, to the exclusion of any other court that is otherwise competent to deal with the dispute.[4] What constitutes the "exclusive jurisdiction" clause is defined in Article 3:

---

[2]Marta Petergás, 'The Brussels I Regulation and The Hague Convention on Choice of Court Agreements' (2010) *ERA Forum* 19, 20–21.

[3]The Government Information Centre, 'Press Releases: LCQ15: The Hague Convention on Choice of Court Agreements'. http://www.info.gov.hk/gia/general/201406/25/P201406240828.htm, accessed 07 September 2015.

[4]However, the Contracting State may recognize and enforce the non-exclusive jurisdiction agreement by way of declaration mechanism provided for in Article 22(1) of the Convention: "A Contracting State may declare that the courts will recognize and enforce judgments given by courts of other Contracting States designated in a choice of court agreement concluded by two or more parties that meets the requirements of Article 3, paragraph (c), and designates, for the purpose of deciding disputes which have arisen or may arise in connection with a particular legal relationship, a court or courts of one or more Contracting States (a non-exclusive choice of court agreement)".

For the purposes of this

(a) 'exclusive choice of court agreement' means an agreement concluded by two or more parties that meets the requirements of paragraph c) and designates, for the purpose of deciding disputes which have arisen or may arise in connection with a particular legal relationship, the courts of one Contracting State to the exclusion of the jurisdiction of any other courts;
(b) a choice of court agreement which designates the courts of one Contracting State or one or more specific courts of one Contracting State shall be deemed to be exclusive unless the parties have provided otherwise;
(c) an exclusive choice of court agreement must be concluded or documents

  (i) in writing; or
  (ii) by any other means of communication which renders information accessible so as to be enable for subsequent reference…

The definition in Article 3(a) seems broad and simplistic. It does not seem to take into account the reality of the complexity in contractual drafting, thereby leaving the existing uncertainty surrounding the interpretation whether a jurisdiction clause is exclusive or non-exclusive. What does the phrase 'to the exclusion of the jurisdiction of any other courts' in Article 3(a) mean? This is a matter of construction of the contractual clause,[5] which is not always straightforward. For example, the issue came under consideration of the United States Court of Appeals, Tenth Circuit, in *K & V Scientific Co Inc. v Bayerische Motoren Werke Aktiengesellschaft* (hereinafter, the *BMW*).[6] The case involved a clause in a confidential agreement: "Jurisdiction for all and any disputes arising out of or in connection with this agreement is Munich. All and any disputes arising out of or in connection with this agreement are subject to the laws of the Federal Republic of Germany".[7] Initially, the District Court found the clause to be clear in language, in that it reflected the parties' intention to have their dispute resolved solely only in the courts in Munich.[8] Hearing an appeal the United States Court of Appeals, Tenth Circuit, disagreed with this conclusion, finding the clause to be of a non-exclusive nature. "In particular, the clause referred only to jurisdiction, and does so in non-exclusive terms (e.g. there is no use of terms "exclusive", "sole" or "only")".[9] The emphasis is placed on the existence of the word *exclusive* or alike which, as shall be seen further below, at odds with cases in other jurisdictions. Differently, in *Wall Street Aubrey Golf, LLC v Aubrey*,[10] before the United States Court of

[5]Sir Lawrence Collins and the others (eds), *Dicey, Morris and Collins on The Conflict of Laws Volume 1* (14th edn, Sweet & Maxwell 2006) para 12.092.

[6]314 F.3d 494 (10th Cir. 2002).

[7]Ibid., 496.

[8]Ibid., 497.

[9]Ibid., 500.

[10]189 Fed.Appx. 82 (2006).

Appeals, Third Circuit, the clause in issue contained in a lease agreement provided: "This Lease shall be construed in accordance with the laws of the Commonwealth of Pennsylvania, with venue laid in Butler County, Pennsylvania".[11] It was argued that the clause dictated the choice of law. As far as the choice of jurisdiction is concerned, the phrase 'with venue laid in Butler County, Pennsylvania' did not pinpoint a particular court.[12] However, the court found the clause to have an exclusive nature because linguistically, the word 'shall' encompasses the whole clause and this indicates the mandatory nature. Secondly, the phrase 'does not logically allow for the possibility of any other venue'.[13] More recently, in the United Kingdom, the Court of Appeal in *Compania Sud Americana de Vapores v Hin-Pro*[14] was tasked with the burden of interpreting a clause in the bill of lading[15]:

> This Bill of Lading and any claim or dispute arising hereunder shall be subject to English law and the jurisdiction of the English High Court of Justice in London. If, notwithstanding the foregoing, any proceedings are commenced in another jurisdiction, such proceedings shall be referred to ordinary courts of law. In the case of Chile, arbitrators shall not be competent to deal with any such disputes and proceedings shall be referred to the Chilean Ordinary Courts.

As such, it would be possible to determine the clause in question to be a non-exclusive one, given the second sentence of the clause. However, the Court of Appeal reached a contrary conclusion. It took into account a linguistic analysis. First, the phrase 'shall be subject to' suggests the imperative nature and this should be read in relation to both the choice of law and the choice of jurisdiction.[16] As to the problematic phrase, 'if notwithstanding the foregoing', Christopher Clarke LJ explained[17]:

> …the use of the phrase 'if *notwithstanding the foregoing*, any proceedings are commenced in another jurisdiction' in the second sentence is…a recognition that the first sentence requires litigation in England as a matter of contract. I do not regard it as realistic to interpret it as meaning 'notwithstanding that advantage is not taken of the option for English jurisdiction'. If the first sentence made English jurisdiction optional, the phrase 'notwithstanding the foregoing' would be unnecessary…I would read the phrase as if the clause read: 'If notwithstanding the parties' agreement that all claims or disputes arising under the bill of lading shall be determined in accordance with English law and by the English court'.

He explained further that the second or third sentences of the clause intended to be applicable when the English law and the English jurisdiction cannot be invoked,

---

[11] Ibid., 85.

[12] Ibid.

[13] Ibid., 85–86.

[14] [2015] EWCA Civ. 401; [2015] 2 Lloyd's Rep. 1.

[15] Ibid., [4].

[16] [2015] EWCA Civ. 401; [2015] 2 Lloyd's Rep. 1. [61].

[17] Ibid., [67] (Italics followed the original text).

for example, when the matter is subject to a compulsory regime of an international convention, or when the dispute is brought up in certain jurisdictions where the exclusive jurisdiction clause is not recognised.[18]

In Hong Kong, the Deputy Judge Reyes SC stated *obiter* in *Hwoo Huang Linda v Fu Being San*[19] in relation to a jurisdiction clause: "…When there is any need to institute legal proceeding, the two parties agree to seek adjudication in the court inside the United States".[20] He held that the clause is a non-exclusive one as the parties did not designate the *specific* courts in the United States of America. In his reasoning,[21]

> The US is comprised of state and federal jurisdictions. Literally read, the forum clause enables a dispute to be brought before any US state court or federal court, whether or not such court was a convenient forum and whether such court had a significant or trivial link to the parties or their business. If the clause is viewed thus, it is hard to see how the parties could have intended to confer exclusive jurisdiction *en bloc* to any US courts whatsoever.

There are many such instances in many jurisdictions where Courts had to engage in semantic analysis of the jurisdiction clause. An inclusion of the word 'exclusive' still left the jurisdiction for court's determination.[22]

Reviewing case authorities, especially those decided in the United Kingdom, Briggs observed that there are four approaches in dealing with the jurisdiction clause, adopted, albeit, inconsistently. The first approach allowed a presumption of the clause being exclusive, rather than non-exclusive.[23] The Convention's draftsmen favoured this approach, evident in Article 3(b). Yet, in view of the author, this presumption is problematic as discussed in the following pages. The second approach allows a presumption in favour of the exclusive nature if the named forum would have jurisdiction anyway, and hence clause itself is not useful.[24] The third approach does not resort to any presumption. Instead, the court takes it purely as a matter of construing the language employed.[25] The fourth approach is that "where the parties submit *disputes* to the jurisdiction of a court, that court was intended to have exclusive jurisdiction, but where they submit *themselves* to the court's jurisdiction is not exclusive".[26] The fourth approach needs elucidation, especially, through case law.

[18]Ibid., [68].

[19]HCA 4888/2001; [2013] 1 HKLRD 259.

[20]HCA 4888/2001; [2013] 1 HKLRD 259 [7].

[21]Ibid., [44].

[22]Adrian Briggs, *Agreements on Jurisdiction and Choice of Law* (Oxford University Press 2008) para 4.11.

[23]Ibid., para 4.13.

[24]Id.

[25]Id.

[26]Id.

The first approach would be considered at the outset, since it is similar to the Convention's approach to the term 'exclusive'. Briggs explained the rationale supporting the first approach as being the parties' need for certainty on the forum of their dispute resolution. Such certainty cannot be found in the non-exclusive jurisdiction clause.[27] However, the essential question is when exactly the presumption is to be invoked. This question is asked because "the word used, commercial sense, and the documentary and factual context are, and should be, normally enough to determine the meaning of a contractual provision".[28] Moreover, "[t]he proper interpretation of the contract must exist at the time it is made, and not change. It cannot come and go as the parties' fortunes wax and wane. It cannot be unknowable and shrouded in fog until after the event".[29] Therefore, the judge can be satisfied with the meaning of the jurisdiction clause through the process of interpretation. In that sense, he will find the clause at the end to be unambiguous and hence there is no need to resort to the presumption available in the Convention at all. In contrast, the judge may exercise judicial inactiveness by by-passing the interpretation exercise and resort to the presumption whenever he feels the clause is prone to interpretation. However, doing so would be much against intuition, as it means the judge acts in ignorance of the parties' intention. Naturally the presumption is rebuttable, but the party wishing to challenge this will have the difficult task of proving 'the parties have provided otherwise' as the evidence of negotiating the jurisdiction clause which may not always be documented, especially if such jurisdiction clause is contained in a standard form contract of one of the parties. Indeed, the Singapore Academy of Law even went to point out implication on costs in training up lawyers on how the presumption works.[30]

It is also the presumption that received serious objection from the Hong Kong Bar Association. The Hong Kong Bar Association in its response to the Consultation Paper of the Department of Justice[31] was of the view that this presumption went too far.[32] It referred to two examples given in the 'Explanatory Report on the Preliminary Draft Convention on Exclusive Choice of Court

[27]Id, 4.14.

[28]*Hin-Pro* (n 14) [69] quoting *K/S Victoria Street v House of Fraser (Stores Management) Ltd and Others* [2011] EWCA Civ. 904; [2012] Ch. 497, [68].

[29]Ibid., [73].

[30]The Singapore Academy of Law, 'Report of the Law Reform Committee on the Hague Convention on Choice of Court Agreement 2005' (March 2013). http://www.sal.org.sg/Lists/Law%20Reform%20Committee%20Reports/Attachments/38/01%20LRC%20Hague%20Convention%202005.pdf, accessed 19 July 2016. See in particular paragraph 6.

[31]The Hong Kong Bar Association, 'Consultation Paper on the Hague Convention on the Exclusive Choice of Court Agreements Submission of the Hong Kong Bar Association' (7 November 2007). http://www.hkba.org/whatsnew/submission-posutuib-papers/2007/20071107.pdf, accessed 19 July 2016.

[32]Ibid., para 22.

Agreements' ("Explanatory Report") of two clauses which are deemed to have an exclusive nature: "The Courts of State X shall have jurisdiction to hear proceedings under this contract" and "Proceedings under this contract shall be brought before the courts of State X".[33] The Hong Kong Bar Association pointed out that the former clause does not deny the possibility of the courts in other states to have jurisdiction. Deeming such clause to be an exclusive jurisdiction clause is 'artificial and unfair'.[34] There is no further elaboration of its attack on this point from the Hong Kong Bar Association. However, the author believes that this argument is forceful. As pointed out earlier, the presumption, which is rebuttable in nature, only invites technical arguments on the construction. This unnecessarily consumes the court's time. As Briggs maintained,[35]

> For every general argument in favour of interpreting an ambiguous jurisdiction agreement as exclusive, another points in the opposite direction. The answer is that the court must ascertain the meaning of the words used assuming commercial sense on the part of the contracting parties, and without under assistance or presumption in favour of one or another conclusion: did they agree that the proceedings in question could or would not be brought?

Therefore, the utility of the presumption is questionable because ultimately, it is the court's task of construing the clause in any event.

Indeed, the Hong Kong Bar Association had expressed its concerns on clause 2 (2) of the draft convention (equivalent to Article 3(b) of the Convention) that the language of which is "too sweeping and at variance with the position in common law…"[36] because the common law threshold on the exclusive jurisdiction clause is "whether the agreement obliges the plaintiff to litigate in the jurisdiction stated therein".[37] It referred to the judgment of the Court of First Instance in *T & K Electronics Ltd v Tai Ping Insurance Co. Ltd.*[38] This case involved a jurisdiction agreement in the cargo insurance contract which provided: '*This insurance is subject to English jurisdiction*'.[39] Stone J adopted the approach of the English Court of Appeal in *Sohio v Gatoil.*[40] The *Sohio* case involved the sale and purchase

[33]Id, para 20 referring to the Hague Conference on Private International Law, 'Explanatory Report on the Preliminary Draft Convention on Exclusive Choice of Court Agreements' (Preliminary Document No.25 of March 2004 drawn up for the attention of the Special Commission of April 2004 on Jurisdiction, Recognition, and Enforcement of Foreign Judgments in Civil and Commercial Matters). http://assets.hcch.net/wop/jdgm_pd25e.pdf, accessed 19 July 2016.

[34]Ibid., para 21.

[35]Briggs (n 22) para 4.16.

[36]The Hong Kong Bar Association, 'The Hong Kong Bar Association's Submission on the Consultation Paper on the Draft Hague Convention on Exclusive Choice of Court Agreements' (13 February 2004). http://www.hkba.org/whatsnew/submission-position-papers/index.html, accessed 19 July 2016, para 11.

[37]Ibid.

[38][1998] 1 HKLRD 172.

[39]Ibid., 174.

[40]Ibid., referring to *Sohio Supply Co v Gatoil (ISA) Inc.* [1989] 1 Lloyd's Rep. 588.

of crude oil.[41] The jurisdiction clause contained in the standard terms and conditions provided: "Under the jurisdiction of the English courts without recourse to arbitration".[42] The Court of Appeal found the question as to whether such clause connoted an exclusive nature is purely a matter of construction.[43]

> The question is one of the construction of this contract and nothing more. It is…part of the matrix background, or surrounding circumstances, whichever term one chooses to use, that *this was a* contract made between sophisticated business men who *specifically chose their words as to English jurisdiction for the purpose of this contract...*To my mind, *it is manifest that these business men intended that the clause to apply to all disputes that should arise between them.* I can think of every reason why they should choose that some Court, in this case the English Court, should have exclusive jurisdiction.[44]

Adopting the approach in the *Sohio* case, Stone J in the *T & K Electronics* case reached a different conclusion despite the parties in the case before him being well-established commercial entities. Stone J considered as well the analysis of Mr. Justice Hobhouse (as he then was) in *S & W Berisford v New Hampshire.*[45] In the *S & W Berisford* case, the cargo insurance policy contained the clause: "This insurance is subject to English jurisdiction".[46] Hobhouse J considered the clause to be only declaratory in nature.

> [T]he words used are inapt to create any obligation. *If an obligation is intended it could easily have been so stated in clear words.* The provision appears in the underwriters' printed form of policy which is issued to the assured…The primary relevance of the clause must be to actions to be brought by the assured against the underwriter. To construe this wording as requiring the assured to sue only in England is to go beyond the natural meaning of the words actually used…It is a statement to the assured, who may be foreign, that the rights that he has under the policy are capable of enforcement in the English Courts…Such a clause, even though creating no obligation to sue only in England is a contractual acknowledgment of the jurisdiction of the English Courts and a contractual agreement to the invocation of that jurisdiction.[47]

With respect, the author could not see how the clause in the *S & W Beresford* case can be drafted in any clearer manner to reflect the intention to oblige the parties to refer their disputes to the English jurisdiction, apart from perhaps adding the word *exclusive* or alike. Despite the exact same clause in the factual situation of the *T & K Electronics* case, Stone J found the clause not to have a declaratory nature, but instead a permissive nature.[48] In reaching such a conclusion, he relied primarily on overwhelming connecting factors from the factual situations of the case towards

---

[41] *Sohio* (n 40) 589.

[42] Ibid., 590.

[43] Id, 591.

[44] Ibid., 591–592 [Staughton LJ] (emphasis added).

[45] *S & W Berisford Plc and NGI International Precious Metals Inc v New Hampshire Insurance Co.* 1990 1 Lloyd's Rep. 454 referred to in *T & K Electronics* (n 38) 175–176.

[46] Ibid., 456.

[47] Id, 458 [Hobhouse J].

[48] *T & K Electronics* (n 38) 175.

Hong Kong.[49] This permissive nature, as he explained, "…the clause in question is no more than a contractual acknowledgment of English jurisdiction, and that it does not *oblige* the invocation of such jurisdiction…"[50]

Neither Hobhouse J in *S & W Berisford* nor Stone J in *T & K Electronics* opined on the factors distinguishing a declaratory or a permissive clause from a clause exclusive in nature. The Convention's definition of the exclusive jurisdiction clause is not helpful to the interpretation. Once again, the deeming provision is likely to lead to the same result; the courts will have to come to the interpreting exercise in any event due to arguments raised by the parties.

The fourth approach identified in Brigg's categorization above leads to a doubt on the Convention's scope being wide enough to encompass such a matter or not. Fawcett explained this approach that "[t]he court has to determine whether the jurisdiction clause is to be interpreted in a transitive sense (i.e., it contemplates the submission of disputes to the chosen forum) or in an intransitive sense (i.e., the parties merely submit themselves to the jurisdiction of the chosen forum)".[51] However, as Fawcett noted, it is not always conclusive to say that the clause, construed in a transitive sense, is an exclusive jurisdiction clause.[52] Such distinction between transitive and intransitive interpretations was made in a number of cases referred to by Briggs[53] while Fawcett[54] referred to *Continental Bank v Aeakos Compania* (hereinafter, the *Continental Bank*)., [55] These cases will be discussed chronologically since they are valuable in light of insufficiency of the Convention's definition.

The first case to be considered is *British Aerospace Plc v Dee Howard Co*[56] (hereinafter, the *BAe*) involving an agreement between an English company and a Texan company. The agreement contained the following clause,

> This agreement shall be governed by and be construed and take effect according to English law and the parties hereto agree that the courts of law in England shall have jurisdiction to entertain any action in respect hereof and that in the event of such proceedings being commenced each party shall forthwith notify to the other an address in England for the service of documents.[57]

---

[49]Ibid.

[50]Id, 176.

[51]James Fawcett, 'Non-exclusive jurisdiction agreements in private international law' [2001] LMCLQ 234, 236.

[52]Ibid.

[53]Briggs (n 22), see in particular at footnote 23 in page 113.

[54]1994 1 Lloyd's Rep. 505.

[55]Fawcett (n 51) 236.

[56][1993] 1 Lloyd's Rep. 368.

[57]Ibid., 370.

Waller LJ identified a few factors to consider the above clause as exclusive.

- the clause is of transitive nature in that the parties "submitting disputes to the English Court as opposed to the parties simply submitting themselves to the jurisdiction of the English Court".[58] This is supported by the phrase 'any action' in the clause, which means "*all* actions".[59]
- it is pointless for the parties to agree to the English jurisdiction as well as the English law without conferring exclusive jurisdiction to the English court
- the last part of the clause provided only for the service of documents in England and not elsewhere.[60]

His interpretation is reinforced by the word 'shall', according to him, "is apposite to create the language of obligation".[61] As can be observed, Waller LJ made a fine distinction between the parties submitting *disputes* to the English Court and the parties submitting *themselves* to the English Court, only the former could make a jurisdiction clause exclusive. Briggs, commenting upon the distinction, observed

> The difference between 'the parties submit' and 'the parties submit their disputes' eludes most minds. It is true that the former suggests that the verb is reflexive, and that the parties submit something, disputes, to the court. It is unclear what the point of that observation might be. The idea that the parties submit themselves to the jurisdiction of a court for something *other* than a dispute is surreal.[62]

The broad language of Article 3 of the Convention unfortunately does not assist with the interpretation of the clause of such kind as in the *BAe* case. Hence, the interpretation is left to the courts in each jurisdiction. English precedents lay down certain guidance on the interpretation of the clause. Different jurisdictions may likewise have different sets of rules or principles as to the method of interpretation.

*Continental Bank* involved a type of jurisdiction agreement, which is not uncommon in financing transactions. The clause provides:

> Each of the Borrowers...hereby irrevocably submits to the jurisdiction of the English Courts and hereby irrevocably nominates Messrs... London...to receive service of proceedings in such Courts on its behalf but the Bank reserves the right to proceed under this Agreement in the Courts of any other country claiming or having jurisdiction in respect thereof.[63]

Despite the lack of language to suggest that the parties were submitting *disputes*, the clause was interpreted to have the transitive nature. The reason given was that "the clause contemplated submission of disputes to the English Courts",[64]

---

[58]Id, 375.

[59]Id (italics followed the original text).

[60]Id.

[61]Id.

[62]Briggs (n 22) para 4.14 (Italics followed the original text).

[63]*Continental Bank* (n 54) 507.

[64]Ibid., 508.

supported by the place for the service of documents.[65] With respect, there appears to be no logical explanation between the fine distinction made by Waller LJ in the *BAe* case and the interpretation of the clause before Steyn LJ in the *Continental Bank* case. It is inexplicable why every clause providing for the parties submitting themselves to a jurisdiction cannot be construed likewise, as the disputes are anticipated in that jurisdiction.

However, the latter part of the clause in the *Continental Bank* proved to be more problematic. Steyn LJ explained that the clause only obliged the borrower, not the bank, to submit disputes to the English Courts.[66] This type of clause leads to uncertainty as far as the scope of application of the Convention is concerned. It was suggested in the Explanatory Report that such a clause falls outside the ambit of Article 3.[67] The given example was: "Proceedings by the borrower against the lender may be brought exclusively in the courts of State X; proceedings by the lender against the borrower may be brought in the courts of State X or in the courts of any other State having jurisdiction under their own law".[68] The Explanatory Report stated

> It might be thought that such an agreement would be covered by the Convention when the proceedings were brought by the borrower, but not when they were brought by the lender. However, this would produce unacceptable results. Assume, in the above example, that the lender brings proceedings in State Y. They would not be covered by the Convention, and the courts of State Y would be entitled to hear them. If the borrower then brought proceedings in State X, those proceedings would be covered; so the courts of State X would have to hear them even though the case was already pending in State Y. Moreover, a judgment given by the courts of State X would have to be recognised under the Convention in State Y, even if the courts of the latter had already given judgment in the proceedings brought by the lender, since there is [so far] no provision…regarding conflicting judgments.[69]

However, the explanation was changed in the subsequent Explanatory Report.[70] The drafters (Professors Masata Dogauchi and Trevor C. Hartley) preferred leaving the interpretation of such a clause open-ended depending on the point of time when the clause comes to be construed. They explained,

> Many lawyers would consider that, under Article 3(a), the question whether an agreement is exclusive must be determined at the time of its conclusion. In other words, it must be exclusive irrespective of the party bringing the proceedings. On the other hand, however,

[65]Ibid.

[66]Id, 509.

[67]The Explanatory Report (n 33) paras 49–50.

[68]Ibid., para 49.

[69]Id, para 50.

[70]The Hague Conference on Private International Law, 'Preliminary Draft Convention on Choice of Court Agreements: Explanatory Report' (Preliminary Document No. 26 of December 2004 drawn up for the attention of the Twentieth Diplomatic Session on Jurisdiction, Recognition, and Enforcement of Foreign Judgments in Civil and Commercial Matters). http://assets.hcch.net/upload/wop/jdgm_pd26e.pdf, accessed 19 July 2016.

> the question will arise for decision only when proceedings are brought. Consequently, it would be possible to wait until that occurs before answering it. If this latter approach were taken, the answer might depend on which party brought the proceedings. If they were brought by the borrower, the agreement would not be covered by the Convention, since the lender would remain free to bring proceedings elsewhere. If he did so, Convention would not preclude the court from hearing them. The Convention would also not apply if the lender brought proceedings in a court other than that designated in the agreement. If, on the other hand, the lender brought proceedings in the designated court, the agreement would, from that moment onwards, become exclusive, since the borrower would not be entitled to bring them in any other court.[71]

While it is true to say that the question of interpretation comes after the initiation of proceedings it is unacceptable that the jurisdiction agreement with undetermined status has existed long before the proceedings. Above all, parties' contractual intention must be referred to at the time the contract was entered into.[72]

The Convention provides limited guidance on the applicable law to determine whether the clause in dispute is the exclusive jurisdiction agreement, bearing in mind rules on contractual interpretation may differ from country to country. The language of Article 6(a) which provides the court of the other state to decline its jurisdiction in favour of the named forum, unless the agreement is null and void under the law of the chosen forum seems to hint the interpretation, should be made in accordance with the law of the named forum. However, the usual approach would be that this is a matter for the law governing the contract to which the said jurisdiction agreement forms part.[73] Regardless of which law is applicable, further complication is inevitable for it is trite rule that a foreign law is a question of fact.[74]

Apart from Article 6(a), there are also other grounds where the court of the state other than the named forum may not decline its jurisdiction in favour of the named forum. Of note is Article 6(c), "giving effect to the agreement would lead to manifest injustice or would be manifestly contrary to the public policy of the State of the court seized". This exception does not seem to alter the common law position. When proceedings are sought to be initiated in Courts of the state other than that of the named forum, the court exercises discretion to decide on stay of the proceedings. In *Aratra Potato Co. Ltd and Another v Egyptian Navigation Co* (hereinafter, *The El Amria*)[75] the Court attempted to identify the criteria for the exercise of such discretion.

---

[71]Ibid., para 72.

[72]"An agreement, though supported by consideration, is not binding as a contract if it was made without any intention to create legal relations". Edwin Peele, *The Law of Contract* (13th edn, Sweet & Maxwell 2011) para 4.001.

[73]Adrian Briggs, 'Crossing the river by feeling the stones: Rethinking the law on foreign judgments' (2004) 8 S'pore YBK of Int'l L 1, 6.

[74]James Fawcett and Janeen M. Carruthers, *Cheshire, North & Fawcett Private International Law* (14th edn, Oxford University Press 2008) 111.

[75][1998] 1 Lloyd's Rep. 119, 123–124.

(a) In what country the evidence on the issues of fact is situated, or more readily available, and the effect of that on the relative convenience and expense of trial as between the [forum] and the foreign Courts;
(b) Whether the law of the foreign Court applies and, if so, whether it differs from [forum] law in any material respects;
(c) With what country either party is connected; and how closely;
(d) Whether the defendants genuinely desire trial in the foreign country, or are only seeking procedural advantages; and
(e) Whether the plaintiffs would be prejudiced by having to sue in the foreign Court because they would: (i) be deprived of security for their claim; (ii) be unable to enforce any judgment obtained; (iii) be faced with a time-bar not applicable in [forum]; or (iv) for political, racial, religious or other reasons be unlikely to get a fair trial.

A combined reading of the above-mentioned criteria appears to produce the result equivalent to the question of manifest justice or injustice. Yet, the Convention does not seem to lay down criteria for considering this issue of manifest justice.

The Convention does not apply to the exclusive jurisdiction agreements contained in all types of contracts. As stated in the Preamble, the purpose of the Convention is to promote "uniform rules on jurisdiction and on recognition and enforcement of foreign judgments in civil or commercial matters". Hence, it is not surprising to see agreements where one of the parties is a natural person and employment contracts excluded from the scope of the Convention, as per Article 2 (1). There is also a long list of further excluded agreements in Article 2(2). The exclusion of some of these agreements is doubtful, and indeed, arguable.[76]

The Hong Kong Bar Association raised particular doubts to the issue of intellectual property rights.[77] In this regard, one should be reminded of Article 2(2)(n) where "the validity of intellectual property rights other than copy rights and related rights" is excluded from the scope of the Convention. In discussing the scope of this exception, the Hong Kong Bar Association referred to what they called the '*Mozambique Rule*'.[78] The term is a reference to a non-intellectual property case of *The British South Africa Company v The Compania de Mocambique and Others.*[79] This rule was affirmed in the context of intellectual property in *Tyburn Productions Ltd v Conan Doyle.*[80] However, these cases must be read in the context of the recent decision of the United Kingdom Supreme Court in *Lucasfilm Ltd v Ainsworth.*[81] As one would recall, the judgment in the *Mozambique* case dealt with the action for trespass to foreign land. The House of Lords found the matter cannot be tried in the

[76]See for example the maritime exceptions pursuant to Article 2(2) (*f*) and (*g*) in Craig Forrest, 'The Hague Convention on Choice of Court Agreements: The Maritime Exceptions' (2009) 5 J of Priv. Int'l L 491.

[77](n 31) para 13.

[78]Ibid.

[79]1893 A.C. 602.

[80]1991 Ch. 75.

[81][2011] UKSC 39; 2012 1 A.C. 208.

English courts.[82] In the *Tyburn* case, a descendant of Sir Arthur Conan Doyle threatened to forbid the plaintiff company from distributing in the USA, a film among which characters were Sherlock Holmes and Dr. Watson.[83] The plaintiff company sought declaration before the court in the United Kingdom to deny her right on the ground that she obtained neither a copyright nor right under an unfair competition nor right in trade mark under the laws of the USA.[84] Reviewing certain authorities, Vinelott J came to the conclusion that the rule in the *Mocambique* case is extended likewise to the case before him and hence the issue, the potential breach of the copyright law of the USA, cannot be tried in England.[85]

The ruling in the *Mocambique* case came to be scrutinized again in the *Lucasfilm* case, a case involved alleged infringement of copyrights in the 'Imperial Stormtrooper helmet' used in the film *Star Wars*.[86] The allegation was made against Mr. Ainsworth and his company who made those similar helmets, some of which sold in the United States of America.[87] Reviewing authorities from other jurisdictions and observing that the ruling in the *Mocambique* case has recently been undermined,[88] the Supreme Court of the United Kingdom overruled the *Tyburn* case.[89] It explained,

> …in the case of a claim for infringement of copyright of the present kind, the claim is one over which the English court has jurisdiction, provided there is a basis for in personam jurisdiction over the defendant, or to put it differently, the claim is justiciable…[90]

The Court observed that the *Mocambique* rule remained good law only for questions related to the title to or the property right in the foreign land.[91] In the area of the intellectual property rights, the United Kingdom Supreme Court saw the possibility that the *Mocambique* rule may remain applicable to patents.[92]

---

[82]"But in respect of a trespass to land situate abroad there was no right of action, for an alleged right which the Courts would neither recognise nor enforce did not constitute any right at all in point of law". *Mocambique* (n 79) 629 (Lord Herschell L.C); "But wherever the place was material, as the unvarying current of authorities establishes that it was in all controversies relating to land, the defendant right might traverse the place, and, even if he did not, if it appeared in proof that the place was out of England, the plaintiff was nonsuited" at 632 (Lord Halsbury).

[83](n 80) 78–79.

[84]Ibid., 80.

[85]Id, 88.

[86](n 81) [1].

[87]Ibid., [3]–[4].

[88]Id, [69].

[89]Id, [110].

[90]Id, [105].

[91]Id.

[92]Id, [106].

It could be predicted that the *Lucasfilm* decision would be followed in Hong Kong where common law rules are enforced in Hong Kong[93] and the decisions from the English courts remain highly influential. It could then be said that the concerns of the Hong Kong Bar Association be addressed the other way around. The question to the Convention would be why the validity of intellectual property rights, except perhaps for patents, has to be excluded at all. The draftsmen of the Convention only attribute the distinction between copyrights and other intellectual property rights to the outcome of the negotiation.[94] However, it remains that the concerns of the Hong Kong Bar Association at the relevant time are likely to be no longer justified.

The above analysis of the key provisions on the effectiveness of the exclusive jurisdiction agreements reveals that the weakness of the Convention is in the subject-matter of the Convention itself, i.e. what constitutes the 'exclusive jurisdiction agreement'? The broad definition provided by the Convention will certainly open the floodgate of litigation on this seemingly technical point.

## 2 Analysis of the Key Provisions Relating to the Recognition and Enforcement of Judgments

For the purpose of the recognition and enforcement of judgments, a judgment is 'international' if it is enforced in a foreign court apart from the court in the country that rendered the judgment.[95] A dispute non-international at the time of the original judgment could become international at the time of recognition and enforcement of the judgment in another State.[96] Singapore viewed the Convention's scheme on recognition and enforcement of judgments as its defining feature. The Singapore Academy of Law observed,

> Singapore stands to gain from potential wider enforceability of its court judgments and the facilitation of enforcement of its judgments in Convention countries which otherwise would not recognise Singapore judgments…If more complex cross-border commercial cases are attracted to the Singapore courts, then Singapore stands to gain further opportunities to

[93]Article 8 of the Basic Law of The Hong Kong Special Administrative Region of the People's Republic of China: "The laws previously in force in Hong Kong, that is, the common law, rules of equity, ordinances, subordinate legislation, and customary law shall be maintained, except for any that contravene this Law, and subject to any amendment by the legislature of the Hong Kong Special Administrative Region".

[94]The Hague Conference on Private International Law, 'Convention of 30 June 2005 on Choice of Court Agreements: Explanatory Report by Trevor Hartley & Masato Dagauchi: Off-print of the Proceedings of the Twentieth session Tome III Choice of Court Agreements'. https://assets.hcch.net/upload/expl37final.pdf, accessed 20 July 2016, paragraph 33.

[95](n 3) Art.1(3).

[96](n 94) para 11.

develop its own commercial law as well as to contribute to international law jurisprudence on the interpretation of the Convention.[97]

While the Academy recommended a 'wait and see' approach,[98] Singapore perceived the benefits from ratifying the Convention, as it is in conjunction with its recently-established judicial organ, the Singapore International Commercial Court (SICC). Ratifying the Convention "will make the SICC a more attractive dispute settlement option as a neutral litigation venue".[99] The driving force was also partly trade implication,[100] and the fact of EU's ratification of the Convention. The combination of these factors led Singapore to ratify the Convention.

The provisions on the recognition and enforcement of judgment can be regarded as the strength of the Convention since the Convention provides an almost unchallengeable status to the judgment rendered by the named forum, so to support the sanctity of the exclusive jurisdiction agreement. According to Article 8:

(1) A judgment given by a court of a Contracting State designated in an exclusive choice of court agreement shall be recognised and enforced in other Contracting States in accordance with this chapter. Recognition or enforcement may be refused only on the grounds specified in this Convention.
(2) Without prejudice to such review as is necessary for the application of the provisions of this chapter, there shall be no review of the merits of the judgment given by the court of origin. The court addressed shall be bound by the findings of fact on which the court of origin based its jurisdiction, unless the judgment was given by default.
(3) A judgment shall be recognised only if it has effect in the State of origin, and shall be enforced only if it is enforceable in the State of origin.
(4) Recognition or enforcement may be postponed or refused if the judgment is the subject of review in the State of origin if the time limit for seeking ordinary review has not expired. A refusal does not prevent a subsequent application for recognition or enforcement of the judgment.
(5) …

The Hong Kong Bar Association expressed few concerns on the definition of 'judgment'. Article 4(1) of the Convention defines this term widely as:

In this Convention, 'judgment' means any decision on the merits given by a court, whatever it may be called, including a decree or order, and a determination of costs or expenses by the court (including an officer of the court), provided that the determination relates to a

[97](n 30) para 5.

[98]Ibid., para 7.

[99]Singapore Ministry of Law, 'Singapore Ratifies Hague Convention on Choice of Court Agreements' (Press releases, 2 June 2016). https://www.mlaw.gov.sg/content/minlaw/en/news/press-releases/singapore-ratifies-hague-convention-on-choice-of-court-agreement.html, accessed 20 July 2016.

[100]Yeo Tiong Min, 'International Litigation in Asia: Will the Hague Choice of Court Convention Make Any Difference?' http://www.jsil.jp/annual_documents/2013/1012224.pdf, accessed 20 July 2016. See in particular para 18,Yeo observed that Singapore's eight major trading partners were China, European Union, Hong Kong, Indonesia, Japan, Malaysia, South Korea, and the United States.

decision on the merits which may be recognised or enforced under this Convention. An interim measure of protection is not a judgment.

The argument raised is that the broad definition inevitably encompasses "non-monetary judgments granting more unconventional remedies".[101] It should be noted that, in Hong Kong, by the Foreign Judgments (Reciprocal Enforcement) Ordinance (Cap. 319), in S.3(2)(b), it is clearly stated that a judgment provides for the sum of money to be payable. This is also the case under the traditional common law if the judgment is made in courts of foreign countries that have no reciprocal arrangement with Hong Kong.[102] The Hong Kong Bar Association noted that such a broad definition of 'judgment' resembles that of the 'Brussels I Regulation' adopted in the European Union.[103] The same definition is used in the 'Brussels Recast Regulation'.[104] Pertinent to this, it must be noted that in Canada, the enforcement of non-monetary judgment has been allowed.[105]

In *Pro Swing Inc v Elta Golf Inc*,[106] the Supreme Court of Canada faced the question, whether the consent decree and the contempt order of the United States District Court for the Northern District of Ohio Eastern Division relating to the alleged copyright infringement should be recognised and enforced.[107] Despite disagreement as to whether the consent decree and the contempt order in question should be enforced, judges of the Supreme Court of Canada were unanimous that the traditional common law approach should be expanded to encompass non-monetary judgments.

> I agree that the time is ripe to revise the traditional common law rule that limits the recognition and enforcement of foreign orders to final money judgments. However, such a change must be accompanied by a judicial discretion enabling the domestic court to consider relevant factors so as to ensure that the orders do not disturb the structure and integrity of the Canadian legal system.[108]

---

[101](n 31) para 25.

[102]Graeme Johnston, *The Conflict of Laws in Hong Kong* (2nd edn, Sweet & Maxwell 2012) para 9.015; Collins and the others, *Dicey, Morris & Collins on The Conflict of Laws* (n 5) para 14–020.

[103](n 31) para 25 referring to the Council Regulation (EC) No.44/2001 of 22 December 2000 on jurisdiction and the recognition and enforcement of judgments in the civil and commercial matters. See in particular Article 32 which provides: "For the purpose of the Regulation, 'judgment' means any judgment given by a court or tribunal of a Member State, whatever the judgment may be called, including a decree, order, decision or writ of execution, as well as the determination of costs and expenses by an officer of the court".

[104]Regulation (EU) No. 1215/2012 of the European Parliament and of the Council of 12 December 2012 on jurisdiction and the recognition and enforcement of judgments in civil and commercial matters, see in particular Article 2.

[105]Trevor C. Hartley, *International Commercial Litigation: Text, Cases and Materials on Private International Law* (Cambridge University Press 2009) 391.

[106]2006 2 S.C.R. 612.

[107]Ibid., [2]–[3].

[108]Id, [15] [Deschamps J].

McLachlin CJ identified certain restrictions to the recognition and enforcement of such non-monetary judgments. First, general exceptions to the enforcement of foreign judgments that exist in monetary judgments, including defenses that foreign judgment was obtained by fraud, and that the foreign judgment was against public policy and natural justice, should equally exist.[109] The foreign judgment must be final and clear.[110] Lastly, the foreign judgment will not be enforced if it relates to foreign public law or criminal law.[111] Both Deschamps J and McLachlin CJ cited the passage in the earlier case to justify such expansion.[112] The quoted speech of La Forest J read[113]:

> The world has changed since…19th century England. Modern means of travel and communications have made many of these 19th century concerns appear parochial. The business community operates in a world economy and we correctly speak of a world community even in the face of decentralized political and legal power. Accommodating the flow of wealth, skills and people across state lines has now become imperative. Under these circumstances, our approach in the recognition and enforcement of foreign judgments would appear rise for reappraisal.

Perhaps, it might be due to the context of the case that the decree or the order sought to be enforced in Canada came from a court in the United States of America. The Supreme Court of Canada did not have in mind potential problems raised by the Hong Kong Bar Association. The balance of academic commentators appears to welcome such an expansion of the traditional common law approach. Pitel argued that most remedies available in common law countries are not much different in nature. Even in the case of exotic or unfamiliar remedies, the forum court can simply characterize them, and work with help derived from the closet domestic analogy, and this would indeed benefit from some understanding of the role the remedy plays in the foreign legal system.[114] Even if this means that the forum court has to study the foreign judgment, this additional task does not make the refusal to enforce in any way become a legitimate reason.[115] It would also be less burdensome for the forum court than if it does not enforce the foreign non-monetary judgment and the claimant has to re-litigate again in the forum.[116] The Supreme Court of Canada seems to take a slightly different approach, from that of the European Union where it requires the foreign non-monetary judgment to be final—something that

[109]2006 2 S.C.R. 612 [90].

[110]Ibid., [91].

[111]Id [100].

[112]Id [7] and [78] citing *Morguard Investments Ltd v De Savoye* 1990 3 S.C.R. 1077, 1098.

[113]Id.

[114]Stephen G.A. Pitel, 'Enforcement of foreign non-monetary judgments in Canada (and beyond)' (2007) 3(2) J of Priv. Int'l L 241, 247.

[115]Ibid.

[116]Id.

does not exist in the European context.[117] Oppong suggested that this finality requirement must be read in the context of non-monetary judgment. "A defining characteristic of some non-money judgments is that they are interlocutory, and hence not final judgments…It is important that finality be interpreted within the context of non-money judgments…"[118] He further explained,

> The finality requirement serves three principal purposes. First, it enables the enforcing court to know precisely what it is agreeing to recognise and enforce. Second, it serves to protect the party against whom the order is enforced from the injustice than [sic] can result from future variations of the order. Finally, it removes the risk of undermining public confidence that might arise if the enforcing court recognizes and enforces the foreign order only to have it changed or even cancelled. Where none of these purposes is undermined by the enforcement of a non-money judgment, its interlocutory nature should not hinder enforcement.[119]

The Singapore Academy of Law noted the 'judgments' in the Convention encompasses non-monetary judgments, which was not viewed as a serious problem. Non-monetary judgments "could be used to create an issue estoppel on the validity and enforceability of the underlying contractual obligation, and the judgment creditor could then sue for specific performance in the Singapore court on that basis".[120] The author is inclined to agree that the judicial system of the Hong Kong SAR should be opening up to foreign non-monetary judgments considering the position of this city as an international financial centre. The fact that the European Union maintained the enforcement of non-monetary judgments in the Brussels Recast seems to suggest that giving effect to such judgment does not bring serious problems in practice. In Hong Kong, perhaps the accession to the Convention will facilitate such development. To this extent, the author does not agree with the concern of the Hong Kong Bar Association.

Despite the Convention giving relatively definite obligations to the forum to recognise and enforce judgment from the named forum in the exclusive jurisdiction agreement, Article 9 provides grounds for refusing to recognise and enforce such judgments. These grounds are well-familiar to lawyers in common law jurisdictions. These include when the judgment is null and void according to the court of the named forum,[121] when there is a problem with the capacity of the parties or one of the parties pursuant to the law of the forum court,[122] or when there are defects in certain documents relevant to the claim,[123] or such recognition or enforcement will

---

[117]Richard Fentiman, *International Commercial Litigation* (Oxford University Press 2010) para 18.44.

[118]Richard Frimpong Oppong, 'Canadian Courts Enforce Foreign Non-Money Judgments' (2007) 70 MLR 670, 677.

[119]Ibid., 678.

[120](n 30) para 55.

[121](n 3) Art.9(a).

[122]Ibid., Art.9(b).

[123]Id, Art.9(c).

be against the public policy of the forum,[124] or else there was an issue of *res judicata* or estoppel.[125] However, the contentious issue, according to the Hong Kong Bar Association, is in Article 9(d) "the judgment was obtained by fraud in connection of a matter of procedure", especially when this is read in conjunction with Article 8(2).[126] It maintained the position in the Convention and contrasts with the established common law principles in *Owen Bank Ltd v Bracco.*[127]

The facts of the *Bracco* case should be revisited here. The case arose out of the loan purported to be made by an individual, Mr. Bracco, and his company from the bank. The jurisdiction agreement contained in the loan documents stated the High Court of St. Vincent and the Grenadines.[128] There was an argument by Bracco and his company as to the signature contained in the loan documents, but the judge at St. Vincent and the Grenadines held for the bank.[129] Before the trial in the St. Vincent and the Grenadines, nevertheless, the issue of the authenticity of the signature had been raised before the court in Italy.[130] The bank tried to enforce the judgment of the court in St. Vincent and the Grenadines in the United Kingdom. The matter came before Sheen J. who allowed the judgment to be enforced.[131] Bracco and his company challenged this order alleging among other things that the judgment from the court in St. Vincent and the Grenadines was obtained by fraud.[132] At the interval between the judgment of the Court of Appeal was handed down and the appeal to the House of Lords was raised, the court in Italy reached the conclusion that the loan documents were indeed forgeries.[133] In the judgment of Lord Bridge of Harwich, with whom the other Law Lords concurred, the possibility of overruling the earlier authorities in *Abouloff v Oppenheimer & Co*[134] and in *Valala v Lawes*[135] was denied.[136] Lord Bridge of Harwich quoted in particular the passage of Lindley LJ in the *Valala* case,[137]

> …if the fraud upon the foreign court consists in the fact that the plaintiff has induced that court by fraud to come to a wrong conclusion, you can reopen the whole case even although

---

[124] Id, Art.9(e).

[125] Id, Arts. 9(f), 9(g).

[126] (n 31) paras 45–48.

[127] Ibid., referring to *Owen Bank Ltd v Bracco and Another* 1992 2 A.C. 443.

[128] *Bracco* (n 127) 449.

[129] Ibid., 450.

[130] Id.

[131] Id, 451.

[132] Id.

[133] Id, 482.

[134] (1882) 10 Q.B.D 295.

[135] (1890) 25 Q.B.D. 310.

[136] *Bracco* (n 127) 489.

[137] Ibid., 486 citing *Valala* (n 135) 316–317.

> you will have in this court to go into the very facts which were investigated, and which were in issue in the foreign court.[138]

With respect, the author doubts the attempt to link Article 8(2) and Article 9(d) together was correct. Article 8(2) deals with the usual situation when the judgment from the named forum is enforced in the other state. The court of that state does not have to enquire into the merits of the judgment. One of the defenses to such enforcement is when the judgment was obtained by fraud as per Article 9(d). Nothing in the language of this particular provision suggests that the court where the judgment is enforced cannot review the judgment on the merits, except perhaps the phrase "in connection of a matter of procedure" at the end of Article 9(d). But again, the language is not explicit enough to the exclusion of the possibility of reviewing the foreign judgment upon the merits when fraud is alleged. Instead, the draftsman of the Convention appears to suggest that the fraud on substance can also be raised for non-recognition.

> Fraud as to the substance could fall under the public policy exception in Article 9(e). The Convention deals with procedural fraud as a separate ground of non-recognition because there may be some legal systems in which public policy cannot be used with regard to procedural fraud.[139]

Therefore, it does not seem that the Convention altered the position in the *Bracco* case.

## 3 Conclusion: Should the European Union's Footsteps Be Followed?

The European Union has a long tradition of judicial co-operation among Member States as represented by the Brussels Regime. Within the European Union, there is also a judicial body, the European Court of Justice, who provides interpretations of European instruments, so there is a high level of uniformity across the European Union. Against this background, a shift to adopt the Convention seems to be a less complex matter.

However, looking at the international community more broadly, with different degrees of judicial co-operation, judicial chauvinism remains in some countries, and with no particular judicial body with supreme authority to ensure the Convention will be interpreted in the same direction, it does not take long for one to predict that the Convention will face hiccups during the early stage of implementation. The review of the key provisions has revealed uncertainties, sometimes due to the drafting technique itself. The major flaw lies in the way in which the very subject matter of the Convention, the exclusive jurisdiction agreement, is defined. The

---

[138] Ibid.

[139] (n 94) see at page 831, Footnote 228.

author predicts that such a broad definition will open a floodgate of litigations in different Member States of what constitutes an exclusive jurisdiction agreement. It will take time for courts in different jurisdictions to come to a plausible definition or an agreed guideline. However, this phenomenon should not be viewed in a very pessimistic light. Indeed, almost every newly introduced piece of legislation invites litigations at the early stage of implementation. No piece of legislation is perfectly drafted, which is more so the case for international conventions with prolonged negotiations among different States with different judicial systems.

The Convention sets and facilitates the mechanism for recognition and enforcement of foreign judgment, which would encourage international trade and investment, which in turn becomes the strength of the Convention. Being encouraged by this strength, Singapore decided to ratify the Convention, to also promote its Singapore International Commercial Court. The Convention, if adopted, will open up the possibility for many common law jurisdictions to revisit current restrictions on enforcing only foreign monetary judgments. This is only to be supported in light of almost free movement of persons.

The Hong Kong Bar Association represents one voice against the Convention. However, closer examination suggests that not all objections raised were valid and indeed some points represented overly anxious views of certain members of legal professions.

The whole scheme of the Convention with focus on the 'State Parties' of the Convention seems to demand almost a universal ratification for it to be effective, which is a challenging task. Nevertheless, on balance, the author believes that the ratification of the Convention would be beneficial for the international community.

# Part II
# Private International Law in South Asia—States' Practice in Family Law

# Conflict of Laws—State Practice in Afghanistan

**Wali Mohammed Naseh**

**Abstract** Afghanistan as a civil law based country has a codified set of Private International Law rules related to concerns arising from personal status, property, martial disputes and the law related to commercial disputes. This chapter showcases and analyses the n legal system, the provisions of the Afghan Civil Code, Afghan Commercial Code and other related laws that address the conflict of laws scenario in disputes related to matrimonial relief, movable and immovable property and the applicable law on commercial disputes. The chapter attempts to discuss the unique features of the private international law in Afghanistan.

**Keywords** Private international law · Civil law · Applicable law · Sharia · Civil code · Commercial code

## Introduction

Conflict of laws, as part of Private International Law, comes into existence when there are foreign elements involved in a dispute before a court. According to Afghanistan's Private International Law (hereinafter referred as APIL), a dispute is characterized as a matter of foreign element firstly when such foreign element is related to the personality of a person or the nationality of the country that he or she belongs to. The second element is related to the action of a person and finally, when the asset or property is located outside of Afghanistan or located within the Afghanistan territory but leased by a foreigner.[1] Therefore, the existence of a

[1]The Constitution of the Islamic Republic of Afghanistan 2004, Article 41(1) does not permit foreigners to have immovable property in Afghanistan. English version is available at: http://www.embassyofafghanistan.org/page/constitution, accessed on 3 March 2016.

W.M. Naseh (✉)
University of Kabul, Kabul, Afghanistan
e-mail: walinaseh@hotmail.com

© Springer Nature Singapore Pte Ltd. 2017

S.R. Garimella and S. Jolly (eds.), *Private International Law*,
DOI 10.1007/978-981-10-3458-9_4

foreign element in a legal dispute is necessary to bring the case under the subject matter of Private International Law. Furthermore, the authority and jurisdiction of national courts and recognition and enforcement of a foreign judgment are vital issues for a legal system to address.

**Structure of the Chapter**
This chapter is arranged in five sections. The introduction to the legal system of Afghanistan is followed by a discussion on the legal provisions related to jurisdiction. The third section discusses the principles of choice of law with regard to contract, personal status and property, followed by a discussion of the legal provisions related to recognition and enforcement of a foreign judgment in Afghanistan including the institutional mechanism for such enforcement. The chapter concludes with a critique on the existing legal structure.

## 1 Afghanistan's Legal System—An Overview

Afghanistan, a civil law country, has a mixed legal system the formation of which goes back to 19th century. In 1885 Afghanistan's first "code of state procedure and ethics" called the *Asas al- quzat* (Fundamental for judges) was adopted. The purpose of this code was to provide a guideline and instruction for judges based on the *Hanafi* School of Islamic jurisprudence.[2] However, the modernization of Afghanistan's legal system started after the adaption of the 1930 Constitution. The Constitution was based on Islamic values; however, it identified some legislations and regulations that could be codified. Following the adoption of the 1930 Constitution, new laws dealing with administrative issues of government, as well as criminal, commercial and civil issues were enacted. During the codification of these laws, Afghanistan drew inspiration from the laws of Turkey, Germany, Switzerland, Egypt and France. Religious values and national traditions co-exist with positive law.[3] In addition to the formal written positive laws and Islamic law (*sharia*), the customary law on informal dispute resolution is another component of the legal system of Afghanistan. Article 130 of the Constitution of Afghanistan (the 2004 Constitution) states

> While processing the cases, the courts apply the provisions of this Constitution and other laws. When there is no provision in the Constitution or other laws regarding ruling on an

[2]Carol Wang, 'Rule of Law in Afghanistan: Enabling a Constitutional Framework for Local Accountability' (2014) 55(1) HIJ 217.

[3]Abdul Satar Sirat, 'The Modern Legal System of Afghanistan An Introduction to the Study of Comparative Law' (1968) 16(4) AJCL 563.

> issue, the courts' decisions shall be within the limits of this Constitution and in accordance with the *Hanafi* jurisprudence and in a way to serve justice in the best possible manner.[4]

The sources of Afghanistan's Private International Law are statutory law, Islamic law, customary law and judicial precedent. However, these sources are not uniformly applied for different types of issues that arise in private international law matters. With regard to personal status, property and contracts, the first and primary source is Afghanistan's Civil Code (ACC). Articles 16–35 of the Civil Code deal with applicable law concerning disputes that contain foreign element. They have been transplanted from the Egypt Civil Code's (Article 10–28) because of religious and cultural commonalities between the two countries.[5] Where a possible dispute scenario has not been articulated in the Code, courts apply the *Hanafi* jurisprudence, as per the constitutional mandate. In disputes related to the commercial transactions, the applicable law would be based on different hierarchy. Article 2 of Afghanistan Commercial Code, 1955 states,

> Commercial disputes are to be settled in accordance with the agreements and in their absence; disputes are to be determined and settled by reference to the meaning and implication of existing commercial laws. In the absence of a law, local customs (those that are commonly recognized, consented to, and used) are applied. Local customs and practices are preferred to general custom. In the absence of any of the above – mentioned methods, any other laws which might apply to the dispute are used.[6]

Thus the hierarchy of applicable law in Commercial disputes is—the contract, commercial laws, local customs and finally other laws such as Civil Code provisions. However, the personal status of foreigners, according to APIL, is subject to the law of nationality. The disputes regarding to estates and property issues, movable and immovable, are subject to the law of *lex loci rei sitae*.

## 2 Jurisdiction

Addressing the conflict of authority is the first step for solving the disputes in conflict of laws.[7]

---

[4]Afghanistan 2004 Constitution (n1) Official Gazette, Issue No 818, 2004, Art. 130. Dari version is available at: http://moj.gov.af/content/files/Pages/OfficialGazetteIndex_D-header.htm http://icoic.gov.af/fa/page/992, accessed 3 April 2016.

[5]Abdul Aziz Mohammad Kamal, *Al-Taqnin Fi Zoo Al-Qaza Wa Al-Feqa* (1st volume, Egypt 1980) 132 (Arabic text).

[6]Afghanistan Commercial Code, Official Gazette, Issue No 89, 1955, Art. 2 Dari version is available at: http://moj.gov.af/content/files/Pages/OfficialGazetteIndex_D-header.htm, accessed on 4 April 2016.

[7]Nezamuddin Abdulah, *Private International Law* (3rd edn, Saeed Publication 2011) 157 (Dari text).

The laws that regulate the jurisdiction of courts in Afghanistan are the Law on Organization and Jurisdiction of Judiciary Branch of Afghanistan (LOJJB)[8], the Civil Procedure Code and the Commercial Procedure Code.[9]

Foreigners (non-Afghan nationals) have the right to refer to national courts and submit their claim before the domestic courts. The Law on the Organization and Jurisdiction of Judiciary Branch of Afghanistan (LOJJB)[10] states: "the judiciary may resolve all disputes between and among persons, legal entities including the State in accordance with law".[11] The entities could be explained to include a person who is not a citizen of Afghanistan. Consequently, all foreigners have the right to refer to Afghan courts to resolve their disputes. Further, Article 6 stated that every person, notwithstanding any distinction, could petition the Afghan courts.

Apart from the LOJJB, the Civil Procedure Code (CPC)[12] and the Afghanistan Commercial Procedure Code[13] specified the civil and commercial courts designated to hear a claim that has a foreign element. In the context of Afghan legal and judicial system, jurisdiction refers to an Afghan court's authority to hear and determine a dispute and make a judgment.[14] Conflicts of jurisdiction between the Civil and Commercial Procedure Codes are resolved in accordance with Article 31 (2) of LOJJB—jurisdiction and authority would be decided by a nine-judge High Council of Supreme Court.[15]

The Civil Procedure Code conferred jurisdiction on the civil court to hear disputes where either of the disputing parties is not citizens of Afghanistan. Article 95 of the

[8]Afghanistan Law on Organization and Jurisdiction of Judiciary Branch LOJJB. Official Gazette, Issue No. 1109, 2013. The purpose and scope of this law is to regulate the organization, structure, duties and responsibilities of Afghanistan Judiciary branch. Dari text available at: http://moj.gov.af/content/files/Pages/OfficialGazetteIndex_Dheader.htm, accessed on 10 March 2016.

[9]In the legal system of Afghanistan based on Art. (61) of LOJJB there are special courts that are dealing with special cases and issues—family court, dealing with family issues, commercial courts which are dealing with commercial issues, civil courts which are dealing with civil issues such as land and Juvenile Court.

[10]The purpose and aim of this law is to manage the affairs related to the organization of the judiciary, duties and powers of the Supreme Court, Primary and Appeal Courts and judges of the Islamic Republic of Afghanistan. Official Gazette, Issue No 1109, 2013. Art. 1.

[11]LOJJB (n 8) Art. 3.

[12]Afghanistan Civil Procedure Code, Official Gazette, Issue No 722, 1990. The purpose and scope of the Civil Procedure Code is related to the proceedings in civil cases and judgments in the courts of the Republic of Afghanistan. See also Official Gazette, issue No 722, 1992, Art. 1.

[13]Afghanistan Commercial Procedure 1955, The purpose and scope of the Commercial Procedure Code is to regulate and resolve all those disputes that arise with commercial transactions is the duty of three courts (primary, secondary and supreme court) and is subject to the provisions of this law.

[14]Mohammad Jaffar Langrodi. *Legal Terminology* (6th edn, Ganj-e-Danish publication, 1998) 485 (Persian text).

[15]LOJJB (n 8) Art. 31.

CPC states: "Hearing of the claims related to foreign citizens residing in Afghanistan shall be within the jurisdiction of the courts of the Republic of Afghanistan".[16] According to this Article the Afghan Civil Court has jurisdiction in disputes involving a foreigner, domiciled or residing in Afghanistan. However, the Civil Procedure Code has provided no definition/criteria for residence. The terms domicile and residence have been used interchangeably. Few instances of such usage are:

- Article 81, Civil Procedure Code used the term residence instead of domicile. It states: "Civil claims are resolved in the defendant's place of residence. In case the defendant possesses multiple residences, civil claims against him/her are heard in such court in whose jurisdiction the defendant resides while making the claim.[17]
- Article 15 of Afghanistan's Civil Code[18]—residence is defined as the place where a person is usually settled down whether it is a permanent domicile or temporary.[19]
- Article 7 of Commercial Procedure Code defined the legal residence as a place that a person willingly chooses for his/her permanent residence.[20]

Further, the methodology for ascertaining the residence/domicile of natural and legal persons has not been determined by the domestic laws and regulation.[21]

Article 10, Commercial Procedure Code confers jurisdiction on the commercial court of the place of residence of a person, in the absence of a legal domicile in Afghanistan.[22] This rule is equally applicable to disputes with foreign element. A general principle of private international law that courts at the forum exercise jurisdiction if the defendant is residing within their territorial jurisdiction of if it is possible that summons could be served on him. The Afghan Commercial Procedure Code also recognizes this principle of jurisdiction of the court that defendant's legal residence is located in.

---

[16](n 12) Art. 95 (Dari text).

[17]Ibid., Art. 81.

[18]It was enacted in 1355/1977. It has 2416 Articles with regards to civil issues. Dari text is available at: http://moj.gov.af/content/files/Pages/OfficialGazetteIndex_D-header.htm, accessed 12 January 2016.

[19]Afghanistan Civil Code, Official Gazette, Issue No 353, 1355/1977, Art. 51 (Dari text).

[20](n 13) Art. 7.

[21]Nezamuddin Abdulah, (n 7) 68.

[22]"Against people, who do not have legal residence in Afghanistan, lawsuit will be filed in a court that it has jurisdiction over the place of their residence. If their residence is unknown, the claim shall be filed with the court that has jurisdiction over the defendants' property, sureties or disputed property otherwise the claim shall be filed with Primary Commercial Court of Kabul". According to this Article the domestic court authority and jurisdiction has been determined based on the three criteria: the first one is "legal residents" the second criteria is "the place and location of a defendant property" and finally the Primary Commercial Court of Kabul. This hierarchy is applicable merely concerning to commercial disputes. Article 10 of Afghanistan Commercial Procedure Code, Official Gazette, Issue No 1–4, 1334/1955, Non official translation.

> Considering the provisions of this chapter, the commercial lawsuits shall be resolved in a court where the defendant resided legally. If there are several defendants and one plaintiff or several disputes (but related to each other), the lawsuit should be filed with the court related to one of defendants' residence.[23]

Furthermore, Article 7 defines the legal residence as a permanent residence.[24] Therefore in the Afghan legal system the distinction between domicile, legal residence and permanent residence is unclear.

An important feature exclusive to the APIL is the usage of a new criteria—optional residence. Article 96 of the Civil Procedure Code stated that in a claim related to a foreign citizen who did not have a place of residence in Afghanistan, the courts of the Republic of Afghanistan have jurisdiction to hear such a claim in the following situations:

- The foreigner has an optional residence in Afghanistan[25]
- The subject of the contract or the place of performance is Afghanistan
- the claim related to a demand for division/assignment of bequeathed property has commenced in Afghanistan
- the whole or part of the bequeathed properties is located in the Republic of Afghanistan.[26]

Afghanistan has not acceded to any of the Hague Conventions in Private International Law.[27] However, there are illustrations of inspiration from these Conventions, especially in commercial and civil transactions. For instance, the Law on Commercial Contract and Selling Property 2014[28] has recognized the importance of a contractual choice of court clause. Article 87 deals with the international commercial contracts. It permits the parties to solve their dispute that emanates from the contract and permits them to refer to one of their country's commercial

---

[23](n 12) Art. 6.

[24]A Legal Residence is a place that a person willingly chooses for his/her permanent residence. Commercial Procedure Code, (n 13) Art. 7.

[25]Optional residence (residence of choice) has not been defined in the legal system of Afghanistan but it has been used in the legal terminology of Afghanistan. For instance it has been used in Article 54 of Civil Code of Afghanistan, 1977, as following: "a person may have an optional residence for a specified legal activity". However, scholars define the optional residence as a place that a person selects a place for residing there and that place will be counted as a center for their main affairs. See: Said Jalaladdin Madani, *Private International Law* (3rd edn, Jangal Publication, Tehran 1384/2005) 124 (Persian text).

[26]Ibid.

[27]http://www.hcch.net/index_en.php?act=states.nonmember, accessed on 13 January 2016.

[28]Article 4 explains the scope and application of the law as follows: (1) the provisions of this law are applicable on the following issues, unless the agreement stipulated otherwise: 1—agreements that have been concluded between Afghan citizen inside of Afghanistan. 2—Agreements that have been concluded between Afghan Citizens and foreign nationals inside of Afghanistan. 3—Agreements that have been concluded between foreign nationals inside of Afghanistan. Generally this law is applicable on commercial contract in the national and international level. Non official translation of the provision.

courts.[29] Further, Article 4 specified that the Afghan court has the authority to hear the disputes related to contracts between Afghan citizens inside Afghanistan, Afghan citizens and foreign citizens inside Afghanistan, and, foreign citizens inside Afghanistan.

Sub-section (2) of Article 4 of the law also states

> parties can agree to manage their contract based on the law of other country or international applicable conventions, in case of dispute, the Afghan courts are obliged to resolve the case according to the selected law.[30]

Party autonomy extends to the choice of jurisdiction in favour of Afghan court. It needs to be mentioned that the agreement on jurisdiction is valid only in commercial and civil transactions. It is not applicable with regards to family law matters as they are determined by Islamic rules and Islam-designated institutions.

## 3 Choice of Law

### *3.1 Commercial Transactions*

Freedom to choose the governing law enables the parties to find the better solution for their transaction according to the law, which may serve better the party to resolve the future and possible disputes.[31] Problems arise when such choice of law is not clearly identifiable, or when more than one law has been chosen to apply to different clauses of the contract. In such scenario, identification of the law chosen to govern the disputes is the primordial task of a lawyer in an international commercial contract.

National courts consider the following criteria for applying the choice of law in conflict of laws-related disputes

- Whether the case is subject of national or international rules,
- How the other national law is related to the subject-matter,
- Avoiding from uncertainty, unpredictability and inconsistency of the outcome, and
- Considering the facilities for the applicability and functionality of the selected law or laws.[32]

Choice of law identification is based on the following four sources of rules and principles.

[29]Afghanistan Law on Commercial Contracts and Selling Property. Official Gazette, Issue No 1150, 2014 Art. 87 Dari version is available at: http://moj.gov.af/content/files/Pages/OfficialGazetteIndex_D-header.htm, accessed 28 December 2015.

[30]Ibid., Art. 4.

[31]Nezamuddin Abdulah (n 7) 187.

[32]Daniel CK Chow & Thomas J. Schoenbaum, *International Business Transactions* (1st edn, ASPEN 2005) 27, 29.

(a) Parties' Choice of law
(b) *Lex loci solutionis*
(c) *Lex loci contractus*
(d) *Lex nationalis* and *lex domicilii*[33]

The issue of choice of law has been reflected into the Commercial Code of Afghanistan, Civil Code and lately in the Law on Commercial Contract and Selling Property. The following paragraphs briefly assesse the mentioned principles.

### 3.1.1 Choice of Law—Afghanistan's Commercial Code, 1955

Enacted with 945 Articles in 1955, the Afghanistan's Commercial Code articulated various issues related to commercial contracts including the choice of law. Article 2 enumerated the sources and the hierarchy of the applicable sources of law concerning the commercial disputes,

> Commercial disputes are to be settled in accordance with content of a contract and in case of lack of such contract, disputes will be determined and settled by reference to the meaning and implication of existing commercial laws. In the absence of a law, the issue will be settled based on the commercial customs (those that are commonly recognized, consented to, and used). In the absence of any other of the above – mentioned methods, any other laws that might apply to the dispute are used.[34]

However, there are a few mandatory laws applicable irrespective of the parties' choice of law—these are laws and regulations that are most closely connected to the contract such as labor law.[35]

Commercial disputes would be defined and resolved according to the agreement and contract that parties have concluded. The law as identified and agreed by the parties would be legally binding and explain all the terms of the contract. There is no distinction between the express and implied choice of law. If the parties have not expressly made choice of law, the court would refer to the contents of contract for deriving the intention of the parties with regard to choice of law.[36]

According to Article 2 the second source is the Commercial Laws. It means that if the parties have not identified the governing law for the substantive dispute and there is no identification of law governing the dispute resolution process the parties shall refer to the Commercial Laws to resolve the disputes. Substantive provisions of the Commercial Code applicable to domestic contracts would also be applicable

[33]Wali Mohammad. Naseh, *Private International Law* (4th edn, Saeed Publication 2015) 269 (Dari text).

[34](n 13) Art. 2.

[35]Nasrullah Stanikzai & Wali Mohammad Naseh, *Commercial Law* (2nd edn, Saeed Publication 2013) 37 (Dari text).

[36]Nezamudin Abdullah (n 7) 117.

to contracts with foreign element. It could therefore be concluded that Article 2 has acknowledged the essential principle of party autonomy, especially in contracts with a foreign element.

### 3.1.2 Choice of Law—Afghan Civil Code

Afghan Civil Code Part Three entitled Application of Law from View Point of Place[37] stipulated the different issues pertaining to conflict of laws. Article 27 of the law has specifically been allocated for the applicable law on the contract and it has selected three options, as it states: "With respect to obligations arising from contracts,

- the law of the state in which the parties to the contract reside shall be applicable.
- in case they do not reside in the same country, the law of the state in which the contract is completed shall be applicable, provided that the parties to the contract have not agreed to application of a specific law, or evidence does not point to the fact that the parties to the contract did not think of application of another law.

However, with respect to contracts about immovable property, the law of the locality [*lex rei sitae*] on immovable property is applicable."[38] The Article is silent about the scope of chosen law—whether the chosen law covers all aspects of the contract between the parties as it has been articulated within the Article 9 of the Hague Convention on Principle on Choice of Law in International Commercial Contract, hereafter (Hague Convention). Article 9 of the Convention states: "If the law chosen by the parties shall govern all aspects of the contract between the parties, including but not limited to-

(a) Interpretation;
(b) Rights and obligations arising from the contract;
(c) Performance of contract and consequences of non-performance, including the assessment of damage;
(d) The various ways of extinguishing obligations, and prescription and limitation period;
(e) Validity and consequences of invalidity of the contract;
(f) Burden of proof and legal presumptions;
(g) Pre-contractual obligations."[39]

Paragraph I (e) does not preclude the application of any other governing law supporting the formal validity of the contract. There seems to be consistency between the Afghan Civil Code and the Hague Convention,

[37]Articles 16–35.

[38](n 19) Art. 27.

[39]Hague principle of Choice of Law in International Commercial Contracts, 2015. http://www.hcch.net/index_en.php?act, accessed 12 February, 2016.

With respect to conditions relating to the form of contracts, provisions of the law of the state in which the contract is completed shall be applicable.[40]

Articles 32[41]and 35[42] of the Civil Code expressly provide for reading the rules of private international law in a dispute involving a foreign element. Similar to Article 11of the Hague Principles of Choice of Law, the Afghan Civil Code, in disputes with related to choice of law permits reference to the general principles of Private International Law. Therefore, if there is no resolution about the conflict of law, applying Article 32 of the Civil Code, the judge could refer to the general principles of private international law provided that those general principles are not in contrary to the public order of Afghanistan. It is pertinent to recall here Article 11of the Hague Principles of Choice of Law-

1. These Principles shall not prevent a court from applying overriding mandatory provisions of the law of the forum which apply irrespective of the law chosen by the parties.
2. The law of the forum determines when a court may or must apply or take into account overriding mandatory provisions of another law.
3. A court may exclude application of a provision of the law chosen by the parties only if and to the extent that the result of such application would be manifestly incompatible with fundamental notions of public policy (public order) of the forum.
4. The law of the forum determines when a court may or must apply or take into account the public policy (public order) of a State the law of which would be applicable in the absence of a choice of law.

These Principles shall not prevent an arbitral tribunal from applying or taking into account public policy (public order), or from applying or taking into account overriding mandatory provisions of a law other than the law chosen by the parties, if the arbitral tribunal is required or entitled to do so.[43]

The second option for the determination of the applicable law in a contract is the law of the country where the contracting parties have their own residence or

[40]Ibid.

[41]Article 32 states: "If there is no provision in the foregoing Articles of this Act with respect to contradiction in laws, rules of private international law shall be applicable." This Article recognizes the general rules of Private International Law to solve or define a dispute. However, it is not clear how to define the private international law's rules and who will make decision which rules are counted as an international rules. In addition this Article provides a wider range of authority for a court to solve a civil case that has a foreign element.

[42]Article 35 states: "Provisions of foreign law in cases defined in this Part shall be applied to the extent that they are not repugnant to public order or standards of decency in Afghanistan." This Article limits the applicability of a foreign law or any other law that have been selected by the parties. A foreign law or a selected law only will be applicable that it is not in contrary to the public order of Afghanistan.

[43]HPCL, 2015 Art. 11. http://www.rechtsanwaltskammer-duesseldorf.de/assets/Uploads/Aktuelles/Rechtswahl.pdf, accessed 10 May 2016.

domicile[44] or *lex domicili*. In the absence of a chosen applicable law to govern their dispute, the law of the country where they reside would be the alternative applicable law. A third option with regard to applicable law on contract is the law of *lex loci contractus*. In such case if the parties are resident in different countries, the applicable law based on Article 27 of Afghan Civil Code[45] is the law of the country where the contract is concluded, *lex loci contractus*.

Therefore, the applicable law with regard to the contractual rights and obligations in moveable property under the Afghan Civil Code is:

(1) The law chosen by the parties
(2) In case of no express/implied choice of law, the law of the country of parties' residence/domicile
(3) the law of the country where the contract has been concluded would be applicable.[46]

With regard to immoveable property Article 27 specifies that the contract shall be subject to the law of locality of immoveable property or *lex rei sitae*.[47] The applicable law in disputes with regard to immovable property is the *lex situs*—law of the place where the property is situated.

### 3.1.3 Choice of Law Based on the Law on Commercial Contracts and Selling Property (LCCSP)

The Law on Commercial Contracts and Selling Property, 2014 (LCCSP) regulates the commercial contracts specifically from national and international points of view. Article 4 of the law explains the scope of the applicable principles of the law in

[44]Afghan Commercial Code in Articles 51–53 stipulates the domicile issues "Residence is the place where a person is usually reside there, whether it is a permanent resident or a temporary". Also article 7th of the Law of the Procedure for Getting the Right define the residence as follow: "the local resident according to this law are: 1—the place where a person live there more than one year. 2—The place where a person has a non interim official duty. 3—The place where a person has a commercial and business there. 4—Any other places that the laws have recognized those places as the place of resident of a person". See the official Gazette issue no 786/2000.

[45]Afghan Civil Procedure Code, (n12) Article 27 states that: (2) In case they do not reside in the same country, the law of the state in which the contract is completed shall be applicable, provided that the parties to the contract have not agreed to application of a specific law, or evidence does not point to the fact that the parties to the contract did not think of application of another law.

[46]Abdulwahed Afzali and Mohammad Ishaq Rahimi, *Private International Law* (1st edn, Meezan Publication 2011) 348 (Persian text).

[47]Afghan Civil Procedure Code (n 12) Art. 27(3) With respect to contracts on immovable property, the law of the locality of the property is applicable. http://www.asianlii.org/af/legis/laws/clotroacogn353p1977010513551015a650/, accessed 10 May, 2016.

general.[48] Subsection 2 of Article 4 acknowledges the freedom of choice of law in a commercial contract as it states: "(2) parties can agree to prepare their contract based on the law of other country or international applicable conventions, in case of dispute, the Afghan courts are obliged to resolve the case according to the selected law".[49] The Article thus allows the contracting parties choose a foreign law as the applicable law and have any such contractual disputes heard by the Afghan courts.

## 3.2 *Choice of Law with Regard to State Contracts*

With regard to issue of choice of law in contracts involving State or Governmental agencies, Afghanistan law specifies the same rules as are applicable to disputes involving private contracting parties. Two provisions of the Procurement Law of Afghanistan, 2015[50] discuss the possible issues with regard to choice of law in State contracts. Article 34 of the law states:

> the import of goods with the way of transfer, measurement of responsibility with regard to risk of loss, delivery, transport insurance, and export and import formalities, internationally recognized trade terms shall be applied to as provided in the procurement contract.

Article 51 articulates the dispute settlement of a procurement contract as follows in the dispute resolution of procurement contracts, the execution of the contract, delay, payments, duties and another related issues that will be determined in the

---

[48]Article 4 of the law describes the scope of the law as follows: "This Law shall apply to:
1—Any Contract between Afghans domiciled in Afghanistan;
2—Any Contract between an Afghan and a foreign citizen in Afghanistan;
3—Any Contract between foreign citizens in Afghanistan;
4—Any immovable contracts which is located in Afghanistan between Afghan citizens and
4—Any Contract under the provisions of this Law".

[49]LCCSP. Official Gazette, issue No 1150, 2014. Art. 4.

[50]This law has been enacted pursuant to the provision of Article 75, section 4 of Afghan Constitution to regulate the public procurement of goods, services and coordination of works, both domestic and foreign, for administrations, institutions, and mixed companies. Therefore, according to Article 4 of the law the scope of this law are: The entities, municipalities and other units funded under government budget are required to procure goods, works and services in accordance with the provisions of this Law, except in cases as mentioned below:

(1) where procurement of goods, works and services requires confidentiality to ensure the interests and protection of the nation;
(2) where the procurement rules of an international institution conflict with this Law, the government may, taking into consideration the agreement in accordance with the mentioned rules, agree to procure the goods works or services funded in accordance with the provisions of the agreement;
(3) Afghan government entities located abroad shall conduct procurement in accordance with rules and procedures of the host country and as per provisions of Article 91 of this Law, unless agreed otherwise. Procurement Law, Art. 51.

contract.[51] A concerted reading of these two provisions would allow an interpretation that irrespective of the nature of the legal personality of the contracting parties, the same rules would be applicable.[52]

## 3.3 *Choice of Law—Personal Status*

Personal status issues refer to individual's private relationship with others.[53] Status means a person's legal conditions, whether personal or proprietary; the total sum of a person's legal rights, duties, liabilities, and other legal relations or any particular group of them separately considered. It also denotes a person's legal condition regarding personal rights but excluding property relation.[54] Moreover, the term status itself originally signified nothing more than the position of a person before the law. Therefore, every person has a status.[55] Mohammad Walid Jarhi in his book titled "Civil Appeal" defines the personal status

> Personal status are those attributes that distinct a human from others and those attributes includes the being male or female, single or married, divorced, parent, children, minor, competence, inheritance and so on.[56]

In private international law, the issues concerning personal status are numerous and on the rise. The people from different cultural background and religions travel to different parts of the world and issues of marriage, divorce, and inheritance and will come to the fore.[57] The next sections of this chapter analyze the issues of marriage, divorce and inheritance from Afghanistan's private international law perspective and will address the question of the applicable law with regards to those issues in conflict of laws.

### 3.3.1 Applicable Law in Marriage

Afghanistan's Civil Code defined marriage as a contract between man and woman with the object to establish a family, creating rights and obligations for both parties.[58] A matrimonial contract, though distinct from a commercial contract, creates a

---

[51]Afghanistan Law on the Procurement, Official Gazette, Issue no 1186, 2015, Art. 51. Dari version available at: http://moj.gov.af/content/files/Pages/OfficialGazetteIndex_D-header.htm, accessed on 13 February 2016.

[52]Nejad Ali Almasi, *Conflict of Laws* (3rd edn, Aagah publication, 2008) 81 (Persian text).

[53]Naseh (n 33) 217.

[54]Bryan A. Garner, *Black's Law Dictionary* (8th edn, Thomson West 2006) 674.

[55]Ibid., 1447.

[56]Mohammad Walid Jarhi, *Civil Appeal* (1st edn, Maktabturjal Alqozat, 2000) 334 (Arabic text).

[57]Wali Mohammad Naseh, *Private International Law* (4th edn, Saeed Publication, 2015) 216 (Dari text).

[58](n 19) Art. 60.

contractual status between the husband and wife.[59] With respect to marriage a basic distinction is followed in legal discussion regarding material and formal requirements.[60] Material/substantive aspects are considered to be of considerable significance to marriage and include capacity, religion etc.[61] Formal aspects include matters of procedure, such as the duration of public notice, the number of witnesses whose presence is required at the marriage ceremony etc.[62] According to Article 19 of the Afghan Civil Code the condition and qualification of a marriage is subject to the law of states of each parties. It states, "With respect to substantive conditions of the validity of marriage, laws of the state of each spouse are applicable; and as regards conditions pertaining to the form of marriage, will be determined by the law of the place of celebration of marriage".[63]According to APIL, the substantive/material issues of marriage are subject to the law of nationality of parties to marriage. The formal aspect of marriage is governed by *lex loci celebrations.*[64]

Article 28 of the Civil Code explicitly acknowledges the application of the *lex fori* rule on the procedure and formality of all issues that happen within the jurisdiction of Afghan courts.[65] It states that with respect to conditions relating to the form of contracts, provisions of the law of the state in which the contract is completed shall be applicable. According to the existing laws Marriage is a "contract" and consequently the law of the state where the contract has been concluded will govern the form and procedure aspect. Likewise, Article 30 of the Civil Code more specifically, admits the form of an action should be subject to the law of the state in which the action happens. The Article states: "With respect to specialized rules and all affairs pertaining to the conduct of duties, provisions of the law of the state in which the suit is filed, or in which the conduct has taken place, shall be applicable".[66] The purpose of this Article is to provide guidance with regards to formality and procedures. It accepts general principles of international law rule that a transaction should comply with the legal formality of the place where the transaction occurred and will be regarded valid in all the jurisdictions where it has been presented for question. This rule is called *locus regit actum.*[67] Additionally, the Supreme Court of Afghanistan in 2011 implemented a manual

[59]Cheshire and North, *Private International Law* (13th edn, Butterworths, London, 1997) 704.

[60]Dicey Morris & Collins, *The Conflict of Laws* (14th edn, Sweet & Maxwells 2006) 285.

[61]R.H. Graveson, *Conflict of Laws* (7th edn. Sweet & Maxwell Ltd, London 1974) 251.

[62]Ibid.

[63](n 19) Art. 19.

[64]Abdulwahed Afzali and Mohammad Ishaq Rahimi, *Private International Law* (1st edn, Meezan Publication 2011) 316 (Persian text).

[65](n 19) Art. 28.

[66]Ibid., Art. 30.

[67]Garner (n 54) 960.

called Marriage Registration and Certificate for Foreign Citizens.[68] Article 7 of the manual has articulated the formalities and procedure for the registration of a foreign marriage in Afghanistan's court. It specifies that in a marriage between a foreign Muslim and an Afghan citizen, the Ministry of Foreign Affairs would utilize the diplomatic channels in Afghanistan to gain information on the personal marital status of such foreign Muslim citizen.[69] Article 9 of the Manual specified that in the event one of the parties to the marriage contract is a foreign non-Muslim (a follower of a religious book), their marriage would be certified in a confession letter *(Iqrar khat).*[70]

Formal equality of the spouses and other substantial issues are decided according to the governing law of the marriage. However exclusively the law of husband will govern the consequences and effects of marriage. Paragraph one of Article 20 of Afghan Civil Code states:

> With respect to effects of marriage including financial affairs, the laws of the state of which the husband is a citizen at the time of the marriage contract shall be applicable.[71]

However, the meaning and definitional aspects of "effects" and "financial affairs" have not been clarified. According to Islamic Law the personal effects of a marriage is the intercourse between wife and husband.[72] Financial affairs are interpreted to cover for providing the living place and basic necessities for wife in the form of alimony.[73] Article 118 of Afghan Civil Code specifies the law on alimony to the wife: "The alimony of the wife shall consist of food, clothes, residence and medical treatment in proportion to the financial power of the husband".[74] The quantum of alimony is based on the financial capacity of husband.[75]

### 3.3.2 Applicable Law in Divorce

Article 135 of Afghan Civil Code defined divorce as dissolution of matrimonial relationship between husband and wife through words that clearly imply the manifestation of divorce.[76] The husband or an authorized court according to the

[68]Supreme Court of Afghanistan, Manual for Marriage Registration and Certificate for Foreign Citizens, Qaza Journal, 1st issue, 2011.

[69]Ibid., Art. 7.

[70]Ibid., Art. 9.

[71](n 19) Art. 20.

[72]Wali Mohammad Naseh (n 33) 230.

[73]Article 115[t] of Afghanistan Civil Code articulates this issue: "The husband shall provide a suitable residence for his wife". According to this Article a husband must provide a suitable accommodation for his wife.

[74]Ibid., Art. 118.

[75]Abdul Aziz Mohammad Kamal, *Al-Taqnin Fi Zoo Al-Qaza W Al-Feqa* (1st volume, Egypt 1980) 139 (Arabic text).

[76](n 19)Art. 135.

provision of Afghan Civil Code shall issue divorce.[77] Article 16 Afghan Civil Code deals with all issues pertaining to conflict of laws in divorce proceedings. It states: "In case of ascertaining legal relations in which the laws are contradictory, provisions of the law of Afghanistan shall be applicable."[78] The law specifies that determination of a legal relationship is on the basis of Afghan legal system. As regards the applicable law in divorce proceedings Article 20(2), Afghan Civil Code prescribes: "With respect to divorce, laws of the State of the husband at the time of the divorce shall apply."[79] In 2001 a Russian woman married a Frenchman in Japan. In 2013 both husband and wife got the nationality of Germany. In 2014 they came to Afghanistan and were working in an international NGO. There was a marital dispute with regard to legal separation (*enfesal*) between them and they approached the first primary family court in Kabul. According to Article 20(2) of Afghanistan Civil Code, the substantive issues with regard to legal separation were decided upon the law of husband at the time of divorce. The applicable law was traced on the basis of husband's nationality at the time of filing of the divorce petition and is not determined on the basis of husband's nationality at the time of marriage.[80]

Afghan Civil Code is silent with respect to the applicable law governing procedural matters in divorce. However, Article 30 of the Civil Code explicitly acknowledges the application of the *lex fori* rule on the procedure and formality of all issues that happen within the jurisdiction of Afghan courts.[81] Therefore, the procedural aspects of divorce and legal separation are also subject to the jurisdiction of the court where the divorce petition is filed.[82] Accordingly, formality and procedure for the dispute resolution in divorce will be subject to *lex fori.*

### 3.3.3 Applicable Law for Inheritance and Wills

Legal system of Afghanistan considers inheritance and will substantively two co-related issues articulated in one Article in the Civil Code.[83]

The law of inheritance, *lex successionis*, is the law that regulate matters related to inheritances rights, obligations and properties of deceased person after his death. In other words, "inherit as a verb is an action to receive property and rights from an ancestor under the laws of intestate succession upon the ancestor's death."[84] Questions regarding inheritance in the domain of private international law arise

[77]Ibid.
[78]Ibid. Art. 16.
[79]Ibid. Art. 20.
[80]Naseh (n 33) 239.
[81](n 19) Art. 30.
[82]Mohammad Nasiri, *Private International Law* (1st and 2nd Volume, Agha Publication 2005) 197 (Persian text).
[83](n 19) Art. 25.
[84]Garner (n 54) 799.

when the deceased person's nationality and properties are under different national jurisdictions. Similar to Egypt, Afghanistan recognized the law of the State where the deceased held nationality at the time of his death as the applicable law.[85] However, it should be noted that countries such as USA and UK adopted principle of *lex domicile* of deceased person applicable with regard to succession rights pertaining to movable property.[86]

According to Article 2103 of Afghan Civil Code a will constitutes taking action against a property in a way that it would become effective after the death of the bequeather.[87] A will is made in word or in writing; in case the bequeather is unable to write or speak, he or she may employ customary signs. There is no restriction on the religious beliefs of bequeather and bequeathed. The legal validity of a will depends upon the capacity of bequather, consent of the person who make the will and the person included in the will. Further the time that the will was made, should be known and specified.[88]

There are two diverse theoretical explanations regarding the applicable law with regard to inheritance and will:

The unitary principle states that inheritance is subject to one law, which is the state law of deceased person. According to this principle regardless of the distinction between moveable and immovable property law, *lex personality* of ancestor is applicable.

The principle of division of patrimony or left property calls for the law to make a distinction between movable and immovable properties. Movable property should be subject to the State law of deceased person. Regarding immovable property the law of *lex loci rei sitae* should be the applicable law in the inheritance issues.[89] Article 25 of Afghan Civil Code follows the first approach as far as governing law of inheritance and wills are concerned. It states

> With respect to established provisions relating to inheritance, testament, and other actions effective after death, the laws of the state of which the bequeather, the executor of the will, or the person who, while dying, effected the action, shall be applicable.[90]

When the patrimony is immovable property and located outside of Afghanistan Article 26 of Civil Code explicitly states that the rule of *lex loci rei sitae* is applied on immovable property and will not be considered inconsistent with Article 25 of the Civil Code.

---

[85](n 19) Art. 25.

[86]Cheshire and North (n 59) 704.

[87](n 19) Art. 2103.

[88]Mahmmod Saljuqi, *Private International Law: Conflict of Laws Vol.2)* (Dadgustar Publication. 1998) 310 (Persian text).

[89]Naseh (n 33) 247.

[90](n 19) Art. 25.

Regarding the formal aspects concerning testamentary succession, the Afghan legal system stipulates the law of the place where the will was drafted as the applicable law. Article 25(2) of the law states

> With respect to formal provisions on will, provisions of the law of the testator at the time of making the will, or provisions of the law of the place wherein the will was completed shall apply.[91]

However, with regard to inheritance the Afghan Civil Code is silent and has provided no provision about the applicable law on the procedural aspects of inheritance. Guidance can be sought from Article 30 of the Civil Code also which regulates that procedural issue of inheritance is subject to the *lex fori*.[92]

## *3.4 Choice of Law in Property Transactions*

The legal regime on property-related transactions makes a clear distinction between movable and immovable property. Afghan Civil Code Article 478 defined movable and immovable property.

> Immovable things are that which have fixed base and their transportation would be impossible without destroying them. Things which are not of this characteristic are deemed as movables.[93]

In a property-related that has a foreign element, the primary concern of the court is the characterization of the property, movable or immovable. The determination of the applicable law is founded upon such characterization. The immovable property is subject to the law of *lex loci rei sitae* while the rights over the movable properties are not necessarily subject to the law of *lex rei sitae*.[94] APIL accepted the law of *lex loci rei sitae* as a general principle of applicable law pertaining to immovable and moveable properties. Article 26 of the Civil Code describes the applicable law on both moveable and immovable property

> With respect to possession, ownership and other real rights, the law of the place wherein the real estate is located shall apply, and with regard to movables, the law of the place wherein the movables were present at the time of occurrence of events resulting in acquisition or loss of the right shall apply.[95]

---

[91]Ibid., Art. 25.

[92]Abdulwahed Afzali and Mohammad Ishaq Rahimi, *Private International Law* (1st edn, Meezan Publication 2011) 336, 7 (Persian text).

[93](n 19) Art. 478.

[94]Cheshire and North (n 59) 924.

[95](n 19) Art. 27.

The reasons for the acceptance of the law of *lex loci rei sitae* are

- State's sovereign interest in eminent domain right over the property that is part of the geographical area of the country despite being owned and possessed by a foreign citizen.
- Conservation of the rights of proprietor of the property.

To ensure clarity in the possession and transactions of immoveable property it needs to be registered in the relevant offices of the state.[96]

## 4 Recognition and Enforcement of a Foreign Court Judgment

The legal system of Afghanistan recognizes the validity of the documents that have been prepared in a foreign country.[97] Articles 307 and 308 of Civil Procedure Code recognize the documents[98] that have been prepared outside of the country.

> The documents prepared outside the country can be valid when the said documents have been prepared and signed by one of the political missions of the Republic of Afghanistan and the Ministry Foreign Affairs has officially recognized its accuracy.[99]

Article 308 applies to the validity of translated documents that have been prepared in a foreign language.

> If resort is made to a document that has been prepared in a foreign language, the person resorting to such a document is obligated to present the original document simultaneously with its certified translation to the court. If the translation of the document is not accepted by the opposing party or by the court, a new translation of the document is made by the court at the expense of the person presenting it….[100]

Article 162 of the Commercial Procedure Code is relevant to this scenario.

> Those documents that have been prepared outside Afghanistan are legally valid only when they have been prepared and attested in accordance with the provisions of Article 32 of this law.[101]

Article 32 of Commercial Code deals with the letter of grant of power of attorney prepared outside Afghanistan

[96]Afzali and Rahimi, (n 92) 346.

[97](n 19) Art. 307.

[98]The concept of "document" that has been used in this context embraces a broader meaning that a judgment is also one type of documents.

[99]Afghanistan Civil Procedure Code, Official Gazette, issue No 722, 1990, Art. 307.

[100](n 12) Art. 308.

[101]Ibid., Art. 162.

> Power of attorney letters, which are prepared outside Afghanistan, are recognized only if they have been prepared in a diplomatic mission or consulate or have been attested by them.[102]

While the Code has not given a definition for the term documents[103] it has, however, categorized them as official documents and conventional documents.[104] The concept of documents from a legal point of view embraces the deeds, agreements, title papers, letters, receipts and other written instruments used to prove a fact.[105] A decision of Court is considered to be part of the official documents. Law on Procedure of Obtaining the Rights (LPOR)[106] Article 10 states that the obtainable documents are:

- Documents that have been prepared and issued by the authorized court and registered with the judicial branch without the doubt of being forged/forgery.
- Documents that have been prepared in the embassies or consulates of Afghanistan outside of the country.
- Foreign countries court decisions between a citizen of Afghan and a citizen of another country which have been finalized based on general principle of private international law and have been verified by Afghanistan Ministry of Foreign Affairs, and
- Any other documents that have been given a legal and judicially validity.[107]

A decision of a foreign court would be enforced in Afghanistan in the following circumstances.

- The verdict has been issued by the related authority and ratified by the Ministry of Foreign Affairs.
- It is final and conclusive.
- The decision should be registered.
- There is no suspicion of forgery or lack of certainty with regard to the verdict.
- The verdict is in conformity with the general principle of Private International Law.[108]

---

[102]Ibid., Art. 32.

[103]Nasrullah Stanekzai, Wali Mohammad Naseh et al., *Commercial Procedure Law* (IDLO, Kabul, 2009) 36.

[104](n 19), Art. 991 and 995.

[105]Garner (n 54) 519.

[106]The purpose and scope of this law is to regulate the affairs related to the ways for obtaining and getting the civil and commercial rights and privileges of natural and legal persons over another natural and legal persons. The Civil and Commercial rights of a natural and legal person over another natural and legal person will be obtained based on the *Hanafi* jurisdiction and provision of this law. All law departments of ministry of Justice, in capital and provinces, are obliged to apply the provisions of this law. Ministry of Justice, Law on Procedure for Getting the Rights LPGR Official Gazette, issue No 798, 1379/2000.

[107]Law of Procedure for Obtaining the Rights Official Gazette, Issue No 786, 1998, Art. 10 (Dari text).

[108]Nezamuddin Abdulah(n 7) 158.

Article 10, LPOR seems to be consistent with Article 9 of the Hague Convention on Choice of Court Agreement[109] which states the circumstances wherein the recognition or enforcement of a judgment may be may be refused

(a) The agreement was null and void under the law of State of the chosen court, unless the chosen court has determined that the agreement is valid;
(b) A party lacked the capacity to conclude the agreement under the law of the requested State;
(c) The document that was the cause of the claim in the proceedings or an equivalent document, including the essential elements of the claim,
    (i) Was not notified to the defendant in sufficient time in such a way as to enable him to arrange for his defiance, unless the defendant entered an appearance and presented himself without contesting the notification in the court of origin, provided that the law of the State of origin permitted notification to be contested; or
    (ii) Was notified to the defendant in the requested State in a manner that is incompatible with fundamental principle of the requested State concerning service of documents;
    (d) The judgment is obtained by fraud in connection with a matter of procedure;
    (e) Recognition or enforcement would be manifestly incompatible with the public policy of the requested State, including situations where the specific proceedings leading to the judgment were incompatible with fundamental principle of procedural fairness of the State;
    (f) The judgment is inconsistent with a judgment given in the requested State in a dispute between the same parties; or
    (g) The judgment is inconsistent with an earlier judgment given in another State between the same parties on the same cause of action, provided that the earlier judgment fulfills the conditions necessary for its recognition in the requested State.[110]

It could thus be inferred that Afghanistan follows the generally accepted legal principles with regard to enforcement of foreign judgments.

The provisions of Civil Procedure Code recognize the documents and judgments that have been issued by a foreign court or authority. However there is an absence of explicit and direct provision in the civil and commercial laws pertaining to enforcement of foreign court judgment. The situation was sought to be rectified by the Supreme Court, which set a precedent with regards to the enforcement of a foreign court judgment.[111]

---

[109]HCCCA, 2005.

[110]HCCCA 2005, Art. 9.

[111]Naseh (n 33) 192.

Afghanistan's Supreme Court pronounced a judgment in its response to a request forwarded by Kabul Primary Court.[112] The subject matter related to the validity of the dissolution of a marriage (separation) that had taken place between two Afghan couples outside of the country. The Court held that if the dissolution of marriage had been ordered outside Afghanistan by a foreign court and declared final and conclusive, the case being decided in the absence of husband, the husband if not satisfied with the issued verdict of the court, can present his objection in the appeal court of his related province. But if the verdict is decided in the presence of husband and the decision is finalized based on the law of the *lex fori*, in such condition according to the Article 10 of the Law on Procedure of Obtaining the Rights, the judgment would be final and enforceable in Afghanistan.[113]

The judgment clarified the substantive requirement of foreign judgment before it could be enforced in Afghanistan. It could be concluded that a judgment of a foreign court would be enforced in Afghanistan provided that the judgment has the following criteria:

- The court should declare the judgment valid according to applicable law of Afghanistan, *lex fori*. An enforcement order shall be made only when the foreign court judgment is consistent with the Afghan law.
- A competent court should have pronounced it. Else, it's unenforceable. For instance, in the legal system of Afghanistan there is a distinction between commercial transactions and civil transactions.[114] In this regard if commercial court hears a case the nature of which substantively belongs to civil issues, the result and judgment made by commercial court will not be applicable.
- The enforcement of judgment shall not be in contrary to public order.[115] A foreign law is not contrary to a state's public policy merely because it is different or because the state has not legislated on the matter. It means that the judgment

[112](n 12), Art. 79, Kabul Primary Court has jurisdiction over all cases that happen in its jurisdiction. As it states: "Civil claims at the trial stage shall be decided by the city, municipal, district or sub-district courts, except in situations where the law provides otherwise". Moreover, according to Article 81 of Civil Procedure Code, Kabul Primary Court had jurisdiction over the case as it states: "Civil claims are resolved in the defendant's place of residence. In case the defendant possesses multiple residences, civil claims against him/her are heard in such court in whose jurisdiction the defendant resides while making the claim. In this case as Kabul was the defendant place of resident therefore the Kabul Primary Court referred the case to the supreme court for finding the legal source. could you explain in brief what is the jurisdiction of court in Afghanistan in the context of Kabul Primary court.

[113]Afghanistan Supreme Court, 'Jurisprudence no 2323/1388/81388,' Qaza Legal and Judicial Monthly Journal, (2009) 3(4) 32 (Dari text).

[114]Naseh (n 33) 192.

[115]Article 35 of Afghan Civil Code recognizes the public order as a basic element and impediment for the implementation of a foreign law. Article 35 states: "Provisions of the foreign law in cases defined in this part shall be applied to the extent which is not repugnant to public order, or standards of decency in Afghanistan." Non official translation of Afghan Civil Code.

is not in conformity with the society values, morality and religious values of Afghanistan.[116]

- The judgment shall be based on a valid law in existence. If the verdict is according to the law, which has no authority over the specific issues, or the law has already been revoked; it will not have any effect in the third country. For instance, a judgment will be refused where civil code was applied in the place of commercial code.
- The issued judgment shall not be contrary to the recognized international commitments of Afghanistan.[117]

Afghanistan has in recent times signed some bilateral agreements in commercial and transportation areas with different countries. One of them is the Agreement between Government of Afghanistan and Republic Government of Turkey on International Land Transportation in 2009. Article 24 of this agreement authorizes both countries' courts to hear the disputes that happen within their territories. It states that the court of each side of the contract shall resolve the disputes derived from the land transportation within the limitation of territory of each contracting party.[118]

The agreement between the governments of Afghanistan and Qatar Kingdom with regard to transportation of labor signed in 2009 authorized the local courts of Qatar to hear the dispute has explicitly been accepted. It States that disputes between employer and employee arising out of the labor contract would be submitted to the authorities of Ministry of Labor and Social Affairs of Qatar for amicable resolution and failing which the dispute would be referred to judicial authorities.[119] These agreements are indicative of the growing acceptance of the authority and judgments of a foreign country in Afghanistan.

## 4.1 *Institutional Mechanisms for the Enforcement a Foreign Judgment*

The Institutional mechanism responsible for enforcing a foreign judgment has not been sufficiently and explicitly dealt under Civil and Commercial Procedure Codes as well as other laws and regulations detailing the enforcement of a foreign judgment. Law on Procedure of Obtaining the Rights (LPOR) specifies the procedure for enforcement of domestic decrees and judgments. According to the provisions of

---

[116]Afzali and Rahani (n 92) 268, 9 (Persian text).

[117]Naseh (n 33) 190.

[118]Agreement between Government of Afghanistan and Republic Government of Turkey on International Land Transportation, Official Gazette Issue No 985, 2009 (Dari text).

[119]Agreement between Afghanistan and Qatar Kingdom, Official Gazette, Issue no 982, 2009. According to the agreement the judgment of Qatar court will be enforceable in Afghanistan (Dari text).

this legislation, the Law Department (*Hoqoq*) of Ministry of Justice entrusted with the responsibility to enforce the commercial and civil judgments of the authorized courts. Article 24(2) deals with the compulsory enforcement of the related court. The Law Department of the Government of Afghanistan proposed compulsory enforcement of the court orders pertaining to property. The authorized court has been entrusted with this responsibility.[120] Moreover, Article 5 specified that the help of the police may be sourced by the Law Department for the enforcement of a judgment.[121] It should be mentioned that the Law Department is the only institutional mechanism for the enforcement of every judgment in Afghanistan including civil and commercial cases. However, the criminal cases are not subject to this arrangement.[122] In the absence of an explicit institutional mechanism dealing with enforcement of foreign judgments it is only an inference that similar arrangement could be applied with regard to foreign judgments.

## 5 Conclusion

Despite the myriad ways in which the position of conflict of laws has been existing in Afghanistan, there was little attempt to institutionalize it, as in the West. Afghanistan as a civil law country has its own legal specifications. The conflict of laws issues of choice of court and choice of law have been reflected in a limited sense within the legal system of Afghanistan. Choice of court issues has been dealt, minimally, within LCCSP. The various laws of Afghanistan have recognized choice of law principles in contracts. Therefore, applicable law concerning contracts is founded on the principle of party autonomy. However regarding to personal status such as marriage, divorce, inheritance and will there is no choice of law and applicable law has already been determined by the legal system of Afghanistan, based on the nationality of a person. The law regarding property rights, moveable a immovable, follows the principle of *lex situs*. The applicable law on procedure and formality is the *lex fori.* However the Afghan Civil Code and Commercial Code are silent on the scope of the contract, the interpretation of contract and the assessment of damages caused by a breach of contract. The legal system of Afghanistan has not stipulated the difference between national domicile and international domicile as well as between place of resident and domicile. There is a dire need to clarify the definition and criteria for both national and international domicile as well as the place of residence.

[120] Afghanistan Law on Procedure of Obtaining the Rights Afghanistan Law on Procedure of Obtaining the Rights, Official Gazette, issue no 786, 1378/1999, Art. 24 (Dari text).

[121] Ibid., Art. 5.

[122] Marie Noelle, Payam Shahrjerdi, Wali Mohammad Naseh et al., *Private International Law-Basic Principle* s (Vol.1) (IIPEC, Kabul 2012) 249 (Dari text).

The law on the recognition and enforcement of a foreign judgment lacks clarity. There is no institutional mechanism for the enforcement of a foreign judgment. These issues need immediate and sustained legislative activity and law reform process of the legal system in Afghanistan.

The characteristics of a legal system that significantly addresses private international law issues are clear and unambiguous provisions concerning choice of court agreements, choice of law and recognition and enforcement of foreign judgments. Though, Afghanistan's Private International Law has addressed conflict of laws issues, in a restricted manner, law reform efforts need to be attempted as an immediate priority to ensure that the increased inter-personal and commercial engagement between Afghan population and the rest of the world encounters less friction from the legal system. The growth of Afghanistan's Private International law could be made robust by acceding to the Hague Conference on Private International Law.

# Cross-Border Divorce Regime in Bangladesh

**Sanwar Hossain**

**Abstract** About 40 Million Bangladeshi citizens live in foreign countries; many of whom were married in Bangladesh under Bangladeshi laws and when they decide to divorce they face a dilemma in choosing the legal regime for their divorce procedure. This chapter focuses on divorce procedures for Bangladeshi citizens married under the laws of Bangladesh who are now living abroad. The current domicile or citizenship of these people are varied as they have either become foreign national or have attained dual citizen or still holding Bangladeshi citizenship. The chapter describes the available divorce procedure for them and the procedure to resolve related matters in Muslim marriage, child custody, child support, distribution of marital property etc. The primary legislation of divorce registration in Bangladesh; The Muslim Family Laws Ordinance 1961 is to a large extent silent regarding cross border divorce procedures. However the simple procedure for Muslim Divorce in Bangladesh attracts the concerned population to choose Bangladeshi regime. The acceptability of divorce under Bangladeshi laws in the countries like USA, UK, Australia, Canada and EU countries have also been discussed as well as Bangladesh's association with Hague Conference on Private International Law in family matters convention. The author of the chapter from his experience in representing the non-resident Bangladeshi clients shares the practical legal obstacles and ambiguities.

**Keywords** Cross-Border divorce · Recognition of divorce · Family law ordinance · Divorce procedure

S. Hossain (✉)
Supreme Court of Bangladesh, Dhaka, Bangladesh
e-mail: sanwar@shossainandassociates.com; shossainlaw@hotmail.com

© Springer Nature Singapore Pte Ltd. 2017

S.R. Garimella and S. Jolly (eds.), *Private International Law*,
DOI 10.1007/978-981-10-3458-9_5

**Introduction**
Over the last four decades the search for a better life and employment prompted millions of Bangladeshis to migrate to different countries of the world such as the Middle East, Malaysia, Singapore, U.S.A, U.K, EU Countries, Australia, Canada etc. Many of the migrants preferred to marry in Bangladesh and have had their marriages registered under the laws of Bangladesh even after the acquisition of nationality/citizenship in foreign jurisdictions. Many non-resident Bangladeshis also contracted matrimonial relationship with foreigners. It is not unusual that non-resident Bangladeshis married within Bangladesh face difficulties with regard to non-recognition of their marriage within the foreign jurisdictions. The scenario is further compounded when non-resident Bangladeshis obtain divorce in foreign jurisdictions for marriages contracted within Bangladesh. The increase in cross border marriage and divorce has significant implications for the society and the legal system. These scenarios occupy an important space of the discourse of family law and private international law in Bangladesh today.

**Structure of the Chapter**
The focus of this chapter is on the cross-border divorces and their recognition in Bangladesh. For this purpose, the first part of this chapter presents a narrative on the legal regime on divorce within the Bangladeshi jurisdiction. The chapter confines itself to the law of divorce among the Muslims. The second part of the chapter discusses the Muslim Family Laws Ordinance 1961 and its implications in terms of execution and enforcement of divorce procedure. The third section of this chapter addresses the procedure for recognition and enforcement of foreign divorce judgments/decrees in Bangladesh. This section of the chapter also articulates Bangladesh's need for accession to the Hague Convention.

## 1 Legal Regime on Divorce in Bangladesh

The law and procedure governing matrimonial issues including divorce in Bangladesh is premised on religious norms and hence its method of documentation is essentially different. It is codified for the Muslims[1] and Christians.[2] The Hindu,

[1]The Muslim Family Laws Ordinance 1961 is the only legislation that incorporates the Muslim divorce procedure.

[2]The Divorce Act 1869 codified the Christian Divorce system in Bangladesh. Section 10 of the Act provides grounds upon which parties to a Christian marriage may repudiate dissolution of marriage.

Buddhist and the people practicing other religions do not have any codified law governing the divorce procedure. As per the religious norm practised by the Hindus in Bangladesh, there is no provision for divorce.[3] The Hindus and the Buddhists can, however, apply for judicial separation[4] in the Family Court established under the provisions of the Family Courts Ordinance, 1985.[5] A Family Court is presided by, either a Senior Assistant Judge or an Assistant Judge. If an individual is not satisfied with the order of the Family Court, an appeal can be preferred to the District Judge's Court.[6] After the establishment of the Family Court under the 1985 Ordinance, experts and public alike questioned its scope and applicability. In *Krishnapada Talukder*[7] the Court had to consider whether a Hindu woman could file a case against her husband under the Family Court Ordinance 1985. A bench of the High Court Division (HCD) of Bangladesh Supreme Court held that the Family Courts have the jurisdiction to entertain, adjudicate and dispose of any matter arising between two Muslim litigants only.[8] However, the HCD reversed its position some days later in *Nirmal Kanti Das*.[9] It held that persons irrespective of religious faith can apply to the Court on family-related disputes stated under the 1985 Ordinance. In 1997, the Court strengthened this position in *Pochon Rikkssi Das*[10] removed all the perplexities and declared the applicability of the ordinance to all religious faiths.

---

[3]Bangladesh enacted the Hindu Marriage Registration Act in 2012. The Government of Bangladesh is also considering a Hindu Divorce Registration Act. The move is being debated within and beyond the Hindu community. One of the apprehensions of the opponents of the move is that the enactment of such a law may give rise to divorce numbers among the Hindu community.

[4]The concept of legal separation is different in the context of Hindu family laws in Bangladesh. In no situation can a person belonging to Hindu religion file a suit for marriage dissolution. However, under the Hindu Women's Right to Separate Residence and Maintenance Act, 1946 a Hindu woman has the right to obtain limited remedy in respect of separate residence and maintenance. In such case, the woman claiming the rights has to prove the grounds.

[5]The Family Courts were established due to the failure of the traditional civil court in Bangladesh to deal successfully all the family matters. The objective of this 1985 law was to provide quick, effective and amicable disposal of some specific family matters.

[6]Section 17 (1) of the 1985 Ordinance reads: Subject to the provisions of sub-section (2), an appeal shall lie from a judgment, decree or order of a Family Court to the Court of District Judge.

[7]*Krishnapada Talukder v Geetasree Talukder* (1994) HCD, 14 BLD 415, see also Zahidul Islam Biswas, 'The Confusions And Uncertainties Thwarting Family Courts In Bangladesh' (2006) 10 Bangladesh Journal of Law 97.

[8]Section 5 of the Family Courts Ordinance 1985 provides that:-

Jurisdiction of Family Courts—Subject to the provisions of the Muslim Family Law Ordinance, 1961, a Family Court shall have exclusive jurisdiction to entertain, try and dispose of any suit relating to, or arising out of, all or any of the following matters, namely—Dissolution of marriage; Restitution of conjugal rights; Dower; Maintenance and guardianship.

[9]*Nirmal Kanti das v Sreemati Biva Rani*, (1994) HCD 14 BLD 413.

[10]*Pochon Rikkssi Dasv KhukuRani Dasu and Others* (1998) AD 50 DLR 47.

The Christian community could deposit their applications for divorce with the Church. In case the Church refuses to award a divorce, an aggrieved party may resort to the High Court Division, where such divorce proceedings takes place on the basis of mutual agreement. In the absence of such a mutual agreement, the spouse pleading for divorce must prove sufficient ground for divorce as listed in the codified law on divorce for Christians.[11]

## *1.1 Law Relating to Divorce in Islam*

The dissolution of marriage under Islamic law could be effected in two ways—in the event of death of either spouse, or by divorce. The Muslim divorce law emanates from the Holy Quran. The Holy Quran says:

> If they disagree and must part, Allah (The God) will provide abundance for all from His all reaching bounty. For Allah is He who cares for all and is wise.[12]

Mustafa Kamal CJ, in *Hefzur Rahman*,[13] stated the Bangladeshi position on Muslim divorce law in the following words:

> When a divorce proceeds from the husband, it is called *talaq*, when affected by mutual consent it is called *Khula* or *Mubara'at*. The Muslim Family Laws Ordinance, 1961 has given statutory recognition to a wife's right of divorce (*talaq-i-taufiz*) in exercise of her delegated power to divorce, as also to dissolution of marriage otherwise than by *talaq*. There are different modes of *talaq*. In the case of *Talaq Ahsan* (most proper), a single pronouncement is made during a *tuhr* (period between two menstruations) followed by abstinence from sexual intercourse up to three following menstruations, at the end of which *talaq* becomes absolute. In the case of *Talaq Hasan* (proper) three pronouncements are made during successive *tuhrs*, there being no sexual intercourse during any of the following three *tuhrs*. In the case of *Talaq-ul-bidaat* or *Talaq-i-badai* (which is popularly called *Bain*

---

[11]The Divorce Act, 1869 s 10: Any husband may present a petition to the District Court or to the High Court Division, praying that his marriage may be dissolved on the ground that his wife has, since the solemnization thereof, been guilty of adultery. Any wife may present a petition to the District Court or to the High Court Division, praying that her marriage may be dissolved on the ground that, since the solemnization thereof, her husband has exchanged his profession of Christianity for the profession of some other religion, and gone through a form of marriage with another woman; or has been guilty of incestuous adultery, or of bigamy with adultery, or of marriage with another woman with adultery, or of rape, sodomy or bestiality, or of adultery coupled with such cruelty as without adultery would have entitled her to a divorce mensa et toro, or of adultery coupled with desertion, without reasonable excuse, for two years or upwards.

[12]Surah *An-Nisa*, *Ayat* (verse) 130, Holy Quran.

[13]*Hefzur Rahman v Shamsun Nahar and another* [1999] AD, 4 BLC 14 (AD).

*talaq* in Bangladesh) either three pronouncements are made during a single *tuhr* in one sentence or three separate sentences or a single pronouncement is made during a *tuhr* clearly indicating an intention to dissolve the marriage irrevocably. This form of *talaq* is not recognised by the *Shafi*[14] and *Shia* Schools of Thought, but the Muslim Family Laws Ordinance, 1961 recognises "pronouncement of *talaq* in any form whatsoever".[15]

The observation of Mustafa Kamal CJ clearly expound the types of divorce which is accepted under the legal system of Bangladesh.

## *1.2 Statutory Law on Divorce*

### 1.2.1 Pre-independence

In the Indian sub-continent, during the pre-1947 partition period, the legal regulation of divorce did not assume prominence and the only legislation regulating divorce was in the form of Dissolution of Muslim Marriages Act, 1939 (hereinafter, the DMMA).[16] Following partition in 1947, legal reforms made a slow start. In 1961, the legislature ushered in the strongly contested Muslim Family Laws Ordinance (hereinafter, the Ordinance) to "provide for procedures and mechanisms for divorce" and provided certain procedural safeguards to women as far as the divorce proceedings are concerned.[17] The Ordinance was based on the recommendations of the Rashid Commission set up on the basis of the protests by women's associations.[18] Ordinance specified rules related to marriage, divorce, maintenance and other ancillary matters.[19]

[14]*Shafi'iyyah* was the third school of Islamic jurisprudence, and was named after *Muhammad ibn Idris al-Shafi'i* (767–819). The sources of legal authority are the *Qur'an* and the *Sunnah*. *Ijma'* and *Ijithihad* (community customs and thought of scholars) are of lesser authority. The scholar must interpret the ambiguous passages of the *Qur'an* according to the consensus of the Muslims, and if there is no consensus, according to *qiyas*. http://www.philtar.ac.uk/encyclopedia/islam/sunni/shaf.html, accessed 01 August 2016.

[15](n 13).

[16]The Act intended to consolidate and clarify the provisions of Muslim law relating to suits for dissolution of marriage by women married under Muslim law and to remove doubts as to the effect of the renunciation of Islam by a married Muslim woman on her marriage tie.

[17]Karin Carmit Yefet, The Constitution and Female-Initiated Divorce in Pakistan: Western Liberalism In Islamic Garb, (2011) 34 Harvard Journal of Law & Gender 553, 578, See Muslim Family Laws Ordinance 1961.

[18]Elisa Giunchi, *Adjudicating Family Law in Muslim Courts*, (Routledge, 2013) 71.

[19]Ibid., Also see, Martin Lau, *The Role of Islam in the Legal System of Pakistan* (Brill 2006).

## 1.3 Post Independence

### 1.3.1 Muslim Family Laws Ordinance 1985

In the post-independence setting, the Muslim Family Laws Ordinance 1961[20] continues to be the most prominent legislation governing divorce among Muslims. However it was supplemented in procedural matters by the Family Court Ordinance 1985[21] and The Muslim Marriages and Divorces (Registration) Act 1974 which was enacted to regulate the functions of Muslim Marriage and Divorce Registrars and finalize different forms and certificate templates.[22] With regard to divorce, the Family Law Ordinance 1961 explained the types of *talaq* recognized and deemed acceptable in Bangladesh. The intense hostility of the *ulemas* towards the Commission's recommendations relating to divorce, forced the framers of the Ordinance to ignore the idea of court intervention in divorce.[23] The Ordinance discusses the procedure to be followed for the divorce. Section 7 of 1961 Ordinance provides the process to be followed in case of *talaq*

> *Talaq*: (1)Any man who wishes to divorce his wife shall, as soon as possible after the pronouncement of *talaq* in any form whatsoever, give the chairman notice in writing of his having done so, and shall supply a copy thereof to the wife.
>
> (2) Who ever contravene the provisions of sub-sec (1) shall be punishable with simple imprisonment for a term, which may extend to one year or with fine, which may extend to [ten thousand taka] or both.
>
> (3) save as provided in sub-sec (5), a *talaq*, unless revoked earlier, expressly or otherwise, shall not be effective until the expiration of ninety days from the day on which notice under sub-section (1) is delivered to the chairman.
>
> (4) Within thirty days of the receipt of notice under sub-section (1), the chairman shall constitute an arbitration council for the purposes of bringing about reconciliation between the parties, and the arbitration council shall take all steps necessary to bring about such reconciliation.

---

[20]Muslim Family Laws Ordinance 1961 introduced important changes in the Anglo-*Muhammedan* law of the Indian sub continent, in the geographical areas of present Pakistan and Bangladesh. See generally Lucy Carroll, 'The reception of the Muslim Family Laws Ordinance, 1961, in a Bangladeshi village: a critique of Jean Ellickson, 'Islamic institutions: perception and practice in a village in Bangladesh' (1978) 12(2) Contributions to Ind. Soc. 279. Munir Muhammad, 'Talaq and the Muslim Family Law Ordinance, 1961 In Pakistan: An Analysis' (2011) 1 Spectrum of Int'l L 16. http://papers.ssrn.com/sol3/Papers.cfm?abstract_id=1925704, accessed 10 June 2016.

[21]Family Courts Ordinance 1985, The Act intended to establish Family Courts, prescribe jurisdiction and procedure for the same.

[22]The Muslim Marriages and Divorces (Registration) Act 1974, section 6 prescribes the conditions for registration of divorce, section 6. (1) states A Nikah Registrar may register a divorce effected under Muslim Law within his jurisdiction on application being made to him for such registration. (2) An application for registration of a divorce shall be made orally by the person or persons who has or have effected the divorce.

[23]Munir Muhammad (n 20) 17.

(5) If the wife be pregnant at the time *talaq* is pronounced, *talaq* shall not be effective until the period mentioned in sub-section (3) or the pregnancy, whichever be letter ends.

(6) Nothing shall debar a wife whose marriage has been terminated by *talaq* effective under this section from re-marrying the same husband, without an intervening marriage with a third person, unless such termination is for the third time so effective.

Co-existent with the other traditional types of divorce recognised in *Hefzur Rahman (Md) v Shamsun Nahar Begum and another*[24] the Islamic law practiced in Bangladesh allows *Talaq-e Tawfiz* (delegated power to divorce).[25] The 1961 Ordinance explicitly states that this method of *talaq* could be perfectly exercised in Bangladesh under the 1961 Ordinance.[26] Factually, there is no prohibition to practice any kind of Islamic divorce in Bangladesh as the Muslim Family Laws Ordinance, 1961, recognizes all types of divorce. Section 7(1) of the MFLO 1961:

Any man who wishes to divorce his wife shall, as soon as may be after the pronouncement of talaq in any form whatsoever, give the Chairman notice in writing of his having done so, and shall supply a copy thereof to the wife.

The construction of this provision, and more specifically the phrase "after the pronouncement of *talaq* in any form whatsoever" allows an inference to be drawn that in Bangladesh all types of Islamic divorce is permissible.

Muslim divorce procedure in Bangladesh does not require a court proceeding as such. This is a feature inherited from the Ordinance in its original version in the undivided Pakistan. The divorce process under the Ordinance is in the form of an administrative reconciliation. The concerned local government institution i.e. the City Corporation, Municipality Corporation or Union Council depending on the place of residence of the divorcing spouses sets up an arbitration council to resolve differences between the spouses.[27] The reconciliation effort does not precede the pronouncement of *talaq*, it only follows it.[28] The Arbitration Council[29] is required to formed within thirty days of the receipt of written notice of pronouncement of *talaq*[30]

[24](n 13).

[25]According to section 8 of the Muslim Family Laws Ordinance, 1961, "Where the right to divorce has been duly delegated to the wife and she wishes to exercise that right, or where any of the parties to a marriage wishes to dissolve the marriage otherwise than by *talaq*, the provisions of section 7 shall, *mutatis mutandis (?)*, and so far as applicable, apply."

[26]Muslim Family Laws Ordinance 1961, (n 17) S. 8.

[27]Ibid., S. 2(b).

[28]Munir Mohammed, (n 20) 17.

[29](n 17) Muslim Family Laws Ordinance, 1961, section 2(a) provides the composition of Arbitration Council. According to this section an arbitration council consists of the Chairman and a representative of each of the parties to a matter dealt with in this Ordinance and where any party fails to nominate a representative within the prescribed time, the body formed without such representative shall be the Arbitration Council.

[30]Ibid., Sub section (4) of the section 7 of Muslim Family Laws Ordinance 1961 stated that within thirty days of the receipt of written notice of pronouncement of *talaq* the Chairman will constitute an Arbitration council with a view to reconciliation among the parties.

by the Chairman/Mayor of the local council as per his wish.[31] The effect of the *talaq* remains ineffective for the next ninety days, during which the Arbitration Council attempts to reconcile the couple.[32] The Arbitration Council issues letters to both the spouses requesting them to attend reconciliation meeting either personally or through a representative.[33] The law does not empower the Arbitration Council to enforce the attendance of any spouse. The Arbitration Council cannot provide any decree of divorce, prevent the talaq by the husband even if it is highly arbitrary, or reject any divorce; it can only delay the divorce with the hope that some reconciliation might take place between the parties.[34] Upon the expiration of ninety days from the receipt of the notice[35] the arbitration council records an Order stating that reconciliation could not be achieved and hence the matter is closed. It is important to mention here that the reconciliation period of ninety days will start form the date of the receipt of the notice by the Chairman not from the date when it was written.[36] However, if parties agree to reconcile then the parties need to submit an affidavit/undertaking to that effect. The affidavit needs to be notarised[37] along with an application to withdraw the divorce.[38] Once the arbitration council receives such application it records the depositions of the spouses and issues an Order of withdrawal of divorce.[39] However, this is a simple practice undertaken by Dhaka City Corporation and other local Government organizations having power to act as the Arbitration Council as per the Muslim Family Laws Ordinance 1961 and no explicit statutory provisions are provided. In the absence of an explicit system requiring notification of *talaq* revocation, the Muslim Family Laws Ordinance provided no restrictions on divorce nor increased the likelihood of a woman receiving provisions for maintenance following divorce. Hence, in practice, while the institution of marriage became formalized under this law, the institution of divorce was relatively minimally regulated and the husband maintained complete rights to unconditional divorce.[40]

---

[31]Muslim Family Laws Rules 1961, Rule 5.

[32]Ibid. S. 7(1), (4); see, Yefet (n 17) 579.

[33]Rule 6 of the Muslim Family Laws Rules, 1961 provides that the chairman shall, by order in writing, call upon each such party shall, within seven days of receiving the order, nominate in writing a representative and deliver the nomination to the chairman or send it to him by registered post.

[34]*Abdus Sobhan Sarkar v Md Abdul Ghani* [1973] HCD, 25 DLR (HCD).

[35]Muslim Family Laws Ordinance 1961, S. 7(3).

[36]*Shafiqul Islam and others v State* [1994] 46 DLR 700.

[37]Notaries Ordinance 1961, S. 8(1) (a) and (g).

[38]This is a practice undertaken by Dhaka City Corporation and other local Government organizations having power to act as the Arbitration Council as per the Muslim Family Laws Ordinance 1961 but there is no codified provision to support that.

[39]Muslim Marriage and Divorce (Registration) Rules 2009, The Muslim Marriage and Divorces (Registration) Rules, 2009 are framed to determine the qualifications for appointment of a Marriage Registrar, fees payable to a Marriage Registrar and any other matter ancillary thereto.

[40]Attila Ambrus, Erica Field and Maximo Torero, 'Muslim Family Law, Prenuptial Agreements and the Emergence of Dowry in Bangladesh' (2010) 125(3) The Quarterly Journal of Economics 1349.

If the divorce notice is not withdrawn within three months the divorce is deemed to be final.[41] The Marriage and *Nikah* Registrar[42] issues a divorce certificate[43] and *Talaqnama*.[44] Under section 7 of the Ordinance a *talaq* must be duly registered—the husband must submit written notice of divorce to the Chairman of the regional Union Council and to his wife.[45] The Ordinance is silent as to the legal consequences of a failure to provide notification of the *talaq*.[46]

It should be noted that under section 24(1) of 'Muslim Marriages and Divorces Registration Rules, 1975' and section 8 of 'Muslim Family Law Ordinance, 1961, if the right to divorce is delegated to the wife in the *Nikahnama* the wife can affect the divorce by exercising her right to divorce on any one or more of these eight grounds:

(i) the whereabouts of husband is unknown for four years;
(ii) negligence or failure to provide her maintenance for two years and taking an additional wife without her consent;
(iii) imprisonment for seven years or upwards;
(iv) failure to perform marital obligation for three years;
(v) impotence of husband at the time of marriage and continues to be so;
(vi) husband's insanity for two years or leprosy or virulent venereal disease;
(vii) child marriage before the age of eighteen or repudiation before the age of nineteen;
(viii) husband's cruel dealings.

The prescribed procedure for execution of divorce involves, firstly, the pronouncement of "*Talaq*", the next stage involves service of the divorce *notice* through the registered post to the spouse and the designated local government institution, followed by registration of that "*Talaq*" with any authorised Muslim

[41]The period of 90 days will start from the day on which notice is delivered to the chairman and not from the day on which the divorce (*Talaq*) is pronounced. Therefore, if husband takes 10 days time to serve notice under sub section (1) of the 1961 Ordinance then it will be 100 days. However, it was held in *Sayed Ali Nawaz Gardezi v Lt Col Md Yusuf* [1963] SC, 15 DLR (SC) case that sub section (1) of the 1961 Ordinance requires the husband to give a notice of having pronounced *talaq*.

[42]Muslim Marriages and Divorces (Registration) Act 1974, establishes *Nikah* registrar for the purpose of registration of Marriage and Divorce.

[43]Muslim Marriages and Divorce Registration Act 1974, S. 9. It is a certificate issued under Muslim Marriage and Divorce (Registration) Rules 2009.

[44]*Talaqnama* is the Divorce paper, see generally, T Hashmi, *Women and Islam In Bangladesh* (Springer 2000) 10.

[45](n 17) Muslim Family Laws Ordinance 1961 S. 7(1).

[46]Ibid. section 7(1) of the MFLO only requires the husband to give notice "as soon as may be after the pronouncement of talaq." It seems that husbands could simply circumvent the law by not registering their divorces, as the law remains silent on the consequences of non-compliance (other than threatening such husbands with relatively insignificant punishments); See Yefet (n 17) 579.

*Nikah* and Divorce registrar. The Apex Court in a few significant statements emphasized upon the importance of the service of divorce notice.[47]

In *Shafiqul Islam and Others* v *State*[48] Zakia (complainant) was married to Shafiqul Islam (petitioner) on 28 August 1989. Soon after the marriage the petitioner demanded dowry from the complainant and her guardians. When she failed to meet petitioner's demand, she was sent to her father's house. Since then the petitioner neither ensured her return to the matrimonial home nor cared for her well-being despite repeated efforts of conciliation by her and her guardian. On 18 November 1992 the Senior Assistant Judge of the Family Court adjourned the case with a direction that the parties should try to come to a compromise. The petitioner allegedly, on the same date, demanded 3 lakh Taka (the currency of Bangladesh) for taking her back. Then she lodged the complaint under section 4 of the Dowry Prohibition Act, 1980. The petitioner submitted before the honourable High Court Division that even if the alleged demand of 3 lakh Taka dowry proved to be true, such demand could not come under section 4 of the Dowry Prohibition Act, 1980, as it was not made during the subsistence of their marriage, as the divorce notice was given on 26 April 1992. By then ninety days for reconciliation under section 7 (3) of the Muslim Family Laws Ordinance expired. The Court clarified the requirement of 90 days waiting period and held that

> Ninety days reconciliation period is to start from the date of the receipt of the notice by the Chairman, and not from the date when it was written *Talaq*, which are not in conformity with the conditions prescribed in section, will not be considered to be effective.[49]

In *Aktar v AHM Mohsin*[50] a Muslim wife *Dilruba Aktar* (hereinafter, complainant) lodged a complaint against her husband *AHM Mohsin* (hereinafter, respondent) under section 6(5) of Muslim Family Laws Ordinance, 1961. They were married on 29 August 1987 and lived together as husband and wife for three months. The Respondent, thereafter, sent the complainant to her father's house and neither took her back, nor cared for her. Respondent contracted a second marriage on 13 March 1988 without the permission of the complainant and the Chairman of the *Union Parishad*. Respondent argued that he married the complainant under pressure from her and others, and he had divorced *her* on 12 September 1987 So on 13 March 1988 the complainant was no more his wife and marrying second time on 13 March 1988 without the permission of the complainant and the Chairman was not a violation of section 6(5) of the Ordinance, 1961. Under section 7(1) of the

---

[47] *Abdul Aziz v Razia Khatun* (1969) 21 DLR; *Sayed Ali Nawaz Gardezi v Lt Col Md Yusuf* [1963] SC, 15 DLR (SC); *Ataul Hoque (Md) v Anwar A Karim* [1999] AD, 4 BLC (AD) See Hossain, Kamrul "In Search of Equality: Marriage Related Laws for Muslim Women in Bangladesh". (2003) 5(1) Journal of International Women's Studies, 96–113. http://vc.bridgew.edu/jiws/vol5/iss1/6, accessed 3 June 2016.

[48] (n 36).

[49] Ibid.

[50] [2004] 55 DLR 568.

Ordinance, 1961 a man divorcing his wife, in any form whatsoever, shall issue his wife a notice in writing, and also a copy of the same to the Chairman. According to the High Court Division the *Talaq* to the claimant was characterised as a disputed *Khula Talaq* on 12 September 1987 as the "amount of money" respondent claims to have paid to claimant while divorcing her did not match the testimony of a witness of the divorce.[51] Hence a notice to council before the second marriage was held to be mandatory. The court noted that contracting a second marriage before the finalisation of divorce or during the subsistence of marriages allowed only with the permission of the council.[52] Section 6(5) of the Ordinance prescribes punishments to those who has entered into a second marriage during the subsistence of existing marriage without the permission of the council.[53]

The enactment of Muslim Family Law Ordinance 1961 and the subsequent legislations was intended to provide much needed substantial and procedural clarity to the entire divorce process among Muslims, However lack of clarity persists relating to type and form of divorce and modalities for the same.

An Islamic form of divorce or *Talaq* is *khula*. The Muslim Marriage and Divorce Registrars established under Muslim Marriages and Divorces (Registration) Act 1974[54] have been validating the execution of divorce pronounced in the *khula talaq* for long time. As per the practise in *Khula talaq* the husband and wife sign the government registry book together and the divorce is executed instantly. Even in the Rules issued by the Government there is a prescribed form of *Khula Talaq*, helping a derivation that such divorce is recognized by the Government. However the law does not clearly exempt the requirement of service of notice and 90 days waiting time for completing divorce proceedings under *Khula talaq*.[55] It is often used by Non-Resident Bangladeshis as this form of *Talaq* is instant and thus a male non-resident Bangladeshi could remarry quickly without having to wait for 90 days. However it is to be noted that a female is required to wait 90 days to remarry even in *Khula Talaq*. Many such Bangladeshis residing in Australia who divorced their spouse through *Khula talaq* and then remarried and applied for immigration for their current spouse found their applications rejected because the Immigration Department of Australia perceived the law as being that even for *khula talaq* service of divorce notice and waiting for ninety days is not exempted. They

---

[51]Ibid.

[52]According to section 6 of the Family Court Ordinance 1985 any person who wants to contract another marriage during the subsistence of an existing marriage shall have to obtain first permission his existing wife permission from the arbitration council. Without which the subsequent marriage will be illegal and liable to punishment.

[53](n 17) Muslim Family Laws Ordinance 1961, s 6(5).

[54]Ibid. Under section 4 of the Act The government give licenses to such number of persons to be called *Nikha* Registrars to perform the registration of marriage and divorce performed under Muslim Law.

[55]Ibid., section 7(3) of the Muslim Family laws Ordinance 1961 requires a mandatory 90 days notice. The ordinance does not make an exception in favour of Khula Talaq.

had to withdraw their application for immigration for their spouse, execute the divorce again, then remarry and make the application again, such process resulted in immense expense of and ushered legal uncertainty.[56]

## 2 Divorce Procedure for Non-resident Bangladeshi Muslims

For applicants of *Talaq* or divorce who are living outside Bangladesh, the procedure for divorce is similar as discussed above and they can pronounce *Talaq* in the country they are living in and sign the divorce notice and post it to the spouse and relevant local government institutions.[57] For the registration in the office of a Muslim Marriage and Divorce Registrar, a power of attorney has to be executed by the applicant of divorce in favour of any relative staying in Bangladesh. The Power of Attorney Act 2012 (hereinafter, the POA Act) and the Power of Attorney Rules 2015 (hereinafter, the Rules 2015) specified the required procedure for executing a power of attorney (hereinafter, the POA) outside Bangladesh, which is to be used inside Bangladesh.[58] While it is not mentioned in the statutes related to divorce or power of attorney that an applicant of divorce can register a divorce in Bangladesh through a duly appointed attorney by executing a POA from outside Bangladesh, it has not been explicitly prohibited or barred. The implementation of POA executed abroad is a protracted process involving the notarisation in the native country, attestation by Bangladesh Embassy or High Commission, re-attestation of Ministry of Foreign Affairs, Dhaka Bangladesh, stamping of special Revenue stamp by the Government Treasury Office.

POA is, however, not required if the applicant for divorce would wish to travel to Bangladesh to serve the divorce notice. It is not necessary for the applicant to be present in Bangladesh for the subsequent 3 months statutory waiting period. While there is no legislation or judicial opinion on divorce executed through a POA, it is accepted by Muslim Marriage and Divorce Registrars. Where the spouses are either living or domiciled outside Bangladesh, the divorce notice is to be served at the last known address of the spouse or the parental home of the spouse. Such address could also be the address outside Bangladesh, where the spouse was living at the time of the notice.

There are very few reported case law references regarding cross-border divorce in Bangladesh. The rule regarding choice of the law that governed the divorce of non-resident Bangladeshis stated that the personal law of the husband would

---

[56]These are the cases where author was involved as Counsel.

[57](n 17) Muslim Family Laws Ordinance 1961, S. 2(b).

[58]Power of Attorney Act 2012 and Power of Attorney Rules 2015. https://resource.ogrlegal.com/power-of-attorney-rules-2015-published/, accessed 4 June 2016.

determine the applicable law. In an old case *Emperor v Maha Ram*,[59] involving the marriage of a Bangladeshi Muslim male to a Christian female solemnised according to Muslim rituals celebrated in Muslim form, the Court held that the applicable law with regard to a divorce application would be the *lex loci celebrationis* and the personal law of the husband, for the marriage as well for the dissolution of the marriage.

In *Mrs. Marina Jatoi v Nuruddin K Jatoi*[60] Marina (hereinafter, appellant) a Christian girl domiciled in Spain and *Nuruddin Jatoi* (hereinafter, respondent) a Pakistan-domiciled Muslim and a Bar student in London, were married at a registrar office in London under the British law. Following marital discord, the appellant applied to the Magistrates' Court in London for maintenance under the Matrimonial Proceedings Act, 1960. In 1963, the appellant obtained a maintenance order, then registered in Pakistan and confirmed by the Karachi District Magistrate's Court. The appellant applied to the District Magistrate, Karachi for enforcement of the Order. The respondent opposed this application enforcement and sent a *Talaq* notice to appellant on 1 July 1965 and one to Union Council Chairman to give effect to the divorce under section 7 of the Ordinance.[61] Following a 90-day notice period the respondent applied to the District Court making an argument that as per Muslim law, the husband was not obliged to pay maintenance to the ex-wife beyond the three month period (known as *Iddat* period) after the *talaq* became irrevocable.

The Hon'ble Court observed that according to the rules of Private International Law, the *lex loci celebrationis* has nothing to do with the questions of divorce, which is a matter governed by the *lex domicile* of the parties at the time of the suit. This may well be different from the law that governed the solemnization of the marriage.[62] According to S. A. Rahman J.

> If the Muslim husband is married to a Christian woman in a form recognized by Muslim law, or to a non-Christian woman, there is no reason why section 7 (b) of Muslim Family Law Ordinance would not apply.[63]

Thus as per Bangladeshi laws, irrespective of the law governing the solemnisation of marriage, divorce laws are based on the domicile of the parties. Hence under the 1961 Ordinance Muslim Marriage and *Nikah* registrars are empowered to execute divorce proceedings on marriages celebrated and registered outside Bangladesh.

---

[59][1918] 45 Ind. Cas 519.

[60][1967] PLD SC 580.

[61]Muslim Family Laws Ordinance 1961, S. 7.

[62](n 60).

[63]Ibid.

# 3 Recognition of Foreign Divorce Judgments/Decrees in Bangladesh

There has been an increasing incidence of non-residents Bangladeshis opting to file divorce proceedings in their country of residence in foreign jurisdictions. Such divorce proceedings could result in a formal divorce decree or ancillary relief relating to transfer of properties in Bangladesh from one spouse to another, sale of property and distribution of sales proceeds etc.

Under Bangladeshi Law, the provisions of the Code of Civil Procedure, 1908 (hereinafter, the CPC) govern execution of decrees, foreign as well as domestic.[64] Under the Code there are two ways of enforcing a foreign judgment.

a. **Through an execution petition u/s 44A**

According to section 44A of the CPC, judgments of foreign courts can directly be executed in Bangladesh, where the judgment has been pronounced by a court in a country with which Bangladesh has a reciprocal agreement. The section provides that decrees of any of the Superior Courts of any reciprocating territory are executed as a decree passed by the domestic Court.[65] The section provides

## *3.1 Execution of Decrees Passed by Courts in the United Kingdom and Other Reciprocating Territory*

The CPC, 1908 specifies the following procedure for execution of decrees ordered by the Courts in the United Kingdom and other territories under reciprocity.

(1) Where a certified copy of a decree of any of the superior Courts of any reciprocating territory has been filed in a District Court, the decree may be executed in Bangladesh as if it had been passed by the District Court.[66]
(2) Together with the certified copy of the decree shall be filed a certificate from such superior Court stating the extent, if any, to which the decree has been satisfied or adjusted and such certificate shall, for the purposes of proceedings under this section, be conclusive proof of the extent of such satisfaction or adjustment.[67]
(3) The provisions of section 47 shall as from the filing of the certified copy of the decree apply to the proceedings of a District Court executing a decree under this section, and the District Court shall refuse execution of any such decree, if

[64]Civil Procedure Code 1908.
[65]Ibid., S. 44A.
[66]Ibid., S. 44A(1).
[67]Ibid., S. 44A(2).

it is shown to the satisfaction of the Court that the decree falls within any of the exceptions specified in clauses (a) to (f) of section 13.[68]

b. **Enforcement through a suit application**

Currently Bangladesh does not have a reciprocal agreement with any country. Therefore, in case the decree does not pertain to a reciprocating territory or a Superior Court of a reciprocating territory as notified by the Government in the Official Gazette, the decree is not directly executable in Bangladesh. In that case a fresh suit will have to be filed on the basis of such a decree. In the fresh suit, the said decree will be treated as another piece of evidence against the defendant.[69]

However in either situations mentioned above the foreign decree has to pass the test of section 13 CPC which specifies certain exceptions under which a foreign judgment becomes inconclusive and is rendered in-executable or unenforceable in Bangladesh.[70] Under the section a foreign judgment becomes inconclusive and consequently unenforceable in the following circumstances:

(a) where it has not been pronounced by a Court of competent jurisdiction;
(b) where it has not been given on the merits of the case;
(c) where it appears on the face of the proceedings to be founded on an incorrect view of international law or a refusal to recognise the law of Bangladesh in cases in which such law is applicable;
(d) where the proceedings in which the judgement was obtained are opposed to natural justice;
(e) where it has been obtained by fraud;
(f) where it sustains a claim founded on a breach of any law in force in Bangladesh.[71]

The provisions of the sections apply to both plaintiffs as well as defendants. A competent court must be competent according to the place, it is constituted and also in the international sense decided on the basis of private international law.[72] Only a judgment where both the parties gave evidence and have a fair opportunity to defend becomes a judgment on merits.[73] A judgment in a matter where one disputant party did not have an opportunity to present his/her case would be against natural justice.

[68]Id, S. 44A(3).

[69]Ibid., section 14 of the Civil Procedure Code stipulates that "The Court shall presume upon the production of any document purporting to be a certified copy of a foreign judgment, that such judgment was pronounced by a Court of competent jurisdiction, unless the contrary appears on the record; but such presumption may be displaced by proving want of jurisdiction."

[70]Mahmudul Islam, Neogi Probir, The *Law of Civil Procedure, Vol 1, Commentary on the Code of Civil Procedure and the Civil Courts*, (Dhaka' Mullick Brothers 2012).

[71]Ibid., S. 13.

[72]Mahmudul Islam, (n 70) 120–121.

[73]Ibid., 126.

In matters relating to matrimony and custody, the law of the place must govern which has the substantial connection with the spouse and marriage.[74] Mahmudul Islam in his book points out that the courts in Bangladesh can not enforce a foreign judgment, which is in violation of the law of Bangladesh, and cite Indian cases of *Satya v Teja*[75] and *Narasimha Rao v Venkata Lakshmi.*[76] The cases suggest that as far as the recognition of foreign divorce are concerned, Bangladesh courts will follows the below condition laid down in these cases

(1) The divorce obtained outside should be in accordance with the substantive law in India
(2) Procedure followed in those divorces should be in accordance with natural justice[77]

In *Abdul Jalil and ors. v Mrs. Sharon Laily Begum* Jalil[78] the case involved the efforts of a mother armed with a foreign custody order in her favour to enforce the same in Bangladesh. However the court with out looking into the legal aspects of the enforcement of the foreign custody order, awarded custody of the children to the mother and observed "It is now settled that the term 'welfare' must be read in the largest possible sense as meaning that every circumstance must be taken into consideration and the court must do what under the circumstances a wise parent acting for their true interests of the child would do or ought to do. The moral and religious welfare of the child must be considered as well as its physical well-being" An explicit case on the point of recognition of foreign judgments have not been decided by the courts in Bangladesh.

A significant reason for the difficulty in enforcement of a foreign divorce decree in Bangladesh is because of its non-participation in the codification in this area attempted by the Hague Conference on Private International Law. The Conference has become a center for international judicial and administrative cooperation, by taking on new roles, implementing and monitoring the Conventions and providing education and assistance. It is to be noted that Bangladesh is neither a member state nor a signatory of Hague Conference on Private International Law in any of its convention relating to family matters.[79] This leads to a situation where the

---

[74]Ibid.

[75]1975 AIR 105.

[76]1991 SCR (2) 821.

[77]Kondaiah Jonnalagadha, 'Jurisdictional Issues in Enforcement of Foreign Divorce Decrees in India; An Analysis' in Bimal P Patel (ed) *India and International Law: Introduction* (Martinus Nijhoff Publishers, 2008) 469–486, 475.

[78]*Abdul Jalil and others v. Mrs. Sharon Laily Begum Jalil* (APPELLATE DIVISION) Civil Appeal Nos. 56–59 of 1995, see Faizunnessa Taru 'Is joint custody compatible with the Islamic law? A discussion on child custody in Bangladesh as well as different contemporary countries of the world, (2016) 21 (3) IOSR-JHSS 61–69, 66.

[79]Convention on the Recognition of Divorces and Legal Separations (adopted 1 June 1970, entered into force 24 August 1975); Convention on Celebration and Recognition of the Validity of Marriages (adopted 14 March 1978, entered into force 1 May 1991); Convention on the Law

enforcement of foreign judgments is completely left to be decided by domestic forum. Case laws reveals that Courts in Bangladesh has not pronounced on the application of these principles as far as the question of recognition of foreign divorce decrees are concerned. This inertia could be explained as revealed from cases that most of the non-resident Bangladeshis prefers to obtain divorce in Bangladesh even after becoming the citizens or resident in another country.

## 3.2 *Recognition of Bangladeshi Divorce Judgments/Decrees in Foreign Jurisdictions*

Case law suggests that the attitude of the courts and legal frame exhibits considerable diversity and has undergone substantial changes over the course of time. The United States judicial system recognise the divorce that take place in Muslim countries when they have been conducted in accordance with the formalities of that jurisdiction.[80] They insist on some substantial connection with the forum in which the divorce was granted and the parties to the case either in the form of domicile, nationality or residence.[81] Divorce proceedings executed in Bangladesh are being recognized in foreign jurisdictions due to the fact that the applicants of the divorce were married under the laws of Bangladesh and that the marriage had been recognized by that particular foreign jurisdiction. The case of *Ashfaq v Ashfaq*[82] involves the question of validity of Pakistani Muslim divorce. Husband and wife were married according to the Pakistani matrimonial laws in 2007. In 2009 the husband under the Pakistani law obtained a divorce by pronouncing '*talaq*'. The facts reveal that husband had dual US-Pakistani citizenship and wife was a Pakistani citizen. Wife argued before the US court that Pakistani divorce is unconstitutional, as it did not confirm with due process of law. Courts however denied the claim of wife on the basis of comity of nations.[83]

---

(Footnote 79 continued)

Applicable to Matrimonial Property Regimes (adopted 14 March 1978, entered into force 1 September 1992); Convention on the Law Applicable to Maintenance Obligations (adopted 2 October 1973, entered into force 1 October 1977).

[80]Julie Macfarlane, *Islamic Divorce in North America: A Shari'a Path in a Secular Society* (Oxford University Press 2012) see generally. Prakash Shah, Distorting Minority laws, Religious and European Minority legal Systems, in Prakash Shah, Marie-Claire Foblets (eds) *Family, Religion and Law: Cultural Encounters in Europe*, (Routledge, 2015), 25. John, R. Bowen, 'How Could English Courts Recognise Sharia' (2010) 7(3) University of St Thomas Law journal, 411–435.

[81]Macfarlane, ibid.

[82]*Fariha Ashfaq v Mohammed Ashfaq* No. 01-14-00329-CV, Court of Appeal, Texas, April 28, 2015, 11.

[83]Robert Epstein, 'Recent Texas Cases Involving the Recognition of Foreign Divorce'. http://www.texasdivorceattorneyblog.com/2015/05/03/recent-texas-cases-involving-the-validity-of-foreign-divorce/, accessed 4 July 2016.

With regard to English Courts a distinction between "procedural" *talaq* and the classical form of "bare" *talaq* is made.[84] A procedural *talaq* is recognised in UK if the parties to the divorce have substantial connection with the place of divorce at the relevant date of divorce in the form of habitual residence or domicile.[85] In contrast, for a bare *talaq* to be recognized two conditions have to be followed,

(1) It has to be effective in the country where divorce is pronounced,
(2) The parties to the divorce were domiciled in that country, or if only one of the parties was domiciled in that country, the other parties' domicile should recognize the bare *talaq*.[86]
(3) No recognition will be entertained if one of the parties has been habitually resident in the UK throughout the period of one year immediately preceding the pronouncement.[87]

A Divorce granted in Bangladesh following the formalities under 1961 ordinance would fall under the category of 'procedural talaq'.

In the Chancery Court of Claiborne County, Mississippi Mrs. Suraiya Begum Haque filed for divorce from Dr. Abu Saeed Mohammed Zahurul Haque,[88] Dr. Haque counter-claimed for divorce and also asserted that the parties were already divorced pursuant to a divorce obtained in Bangladesh. He claimed that lower court erred in refusing to recognize the divorce granted in Bangladesh. The Mississippi Court observed, "enforcement of foreign national judgments in our courts is governed by the principle of comity. The principle of comity is similar to full faith and credit except that it is not governed by Federal statutes and that its application rests in the discretion of the trial judge."[89] The Court on the facts of the case felt that Bangladesh divorce was made exparte and against public policy. The Court also observed that it is permissible to maintain an alimony action in a Mississippi Court when the divorce decree was obtained in a foreign jurisdiction. This is regardless of the recognition of Bangladeshi divorce.[90] The decision indicates with clarity to the recognition of Bangladeshi divorce provided the procedural and substantive requirements are complied with.

---

[84]Family Law Act (United Kingdom) 1986. http://www.legislation.gov.uk/ukpga/1986/55/pdfs/ukpga_19860055_en.pdf, accessed 4 July 2016, See David Paul, 1995 Noel Coulson Memorial Lecture, The application of Islamic law in the English Courts. https://www.library.cornell.edu/colldev/mideast/isllaw.htm, accessed on 4 August 2016.

[85]Ibid., S 46(1).

[86]Ibid., s 46(2).

[87]Id, s 46(2)(c).

[88]*Haque, Abu Saeed Mohammad Zahurul v Suraiya Begum Haque Appeal* No. 12177, 1993.

[89]Id.

[90]Id.

### 3.3 *Muslim Women and 'Islamic Divorce' in England*

A significant concern with recognition of foreign divorces was that the English Court had no jurisdiction to deal with ancillary matters unless it itself dissolved the marriage. The outcome of recognizing a foreign divorce, whether or not it was based on judicial process or extra-judicial process, was that the courts in England would be deprived of the jurisdiction to order monetary relief to the divorced spouse/wife. This predicament was more pronounced in the case of divorce based on '*talaq*' as Muslim law recognizes neither division of matrimonial assets nor alimony on divorce.[91] A wife is entitled to her dower and three months maintenance at the time of divorce.[92] The Bangladeshi law does not recognize the idea of matrimonial property.[93] Before the Family Ordinance 1961, the Muslim women belonging to *Hanafi* school of jurisprudence had no institutionalised mechanism to apply for arrears of maintenance.[94] The new Ordinance conferred the power on Arbitration Council to deal with the question of arrears of maintenance. However, it only dealt with maintenance for married women, and not for divorced women.[95] The situation encouraged the Bangladeshi males in England to dissolve the marriage by *Talaq* rather than petitioning for divorce in the English Courts.

The above concern was addressed by law reforms under Part III of the Matrimonial and Family Proceedings Act, 1984 of the UK.[96] This statute empowered the English Courts to grant financial relief to one or other spouse even in cases where the English Court had not dissolved the marriage.[97] In the case of enforcement of ancillary relief, the same principles and provisions dealing with

---

[91]Lucy Carroll, 'Muslim Women and 'Islamic Divorce' In England' (*WLUML*, 1998). http://www.wluml.org/node/304, accessed 4 July 2016.

[92]*Md Hefzur Rahman v Shamsun* Nagar begum [1999] AD, 51 DLR (AD); Sharmin Aktar, 'Protecting Divorced Muslim Women's Rights through Maintenance: A Comparative Analysis Based on the Present Legislative Reforms among the Muslim Community' (2012) 3 Northern University Journal of Law.

[93]Matrimonial property, or 'matrimonial assets,' is property acquired by either or both married spouses during their marriage, and includes the matrimonial home(s).

[94]Dr. Faustina Pereira, 'Post Divorce Maintenance for Muslim Women and the Islamist Discourse' (*WLUML*, 2000). http://www.wluml.org/node/334, accessed 4 July 2016.

[95]Ibid.

[96]Matrimonial and Family Proceedings Act 1984.

[97]Section 15, part III of the Matrimonial and Family Proceedings Act 1984 provides that-the court shall have jurisdiction to entertain an application for an order for financial relief

(a) either of the parties to the marriage was domiciled in England and Wales on the date of the application or was so domiciled on the date on which the divorce, annulment or legal separation obtained in the overseas country took effect in that country; or
(b) either of the parties to the marriage was habitually resident in England and Wales throughout the period of one year immediately before the application or
(c) parties to the marriage has beneficial interest in possession in a dwelling-house situated in England or Wales which was at some time during the marriage a matrimonial home of the parties to the marriage.

enforcement of foreign judgment under CPC will apply. With regard to the enforcement of foreign ancillary relief in matters of divorce, the possibility of refusal to enforce the same on grounds of public policy are more, since the Bangladeshi laws differ considerably with regard to matrimonial property and alimony.[98] Drawing a comparison with Indian jurisprudence reveals that through section 125 of the Code of Criminal Procedure in India[99] and the Supreme Court decision in *Bai Tahira v Ali Hussain Chothia*[100] the law of India granted equal protection with regard to maintenance to a divorced wife irrespective of her religious faith.[101] In recent times it has been noticed that where both the spouses are living abroad and specially where the spouses are living in a country where ancillary reliefs for wife is higher than Bangladesh, the spouses agree to execute divorce in Bangladesh and settle financial deals on mutual agreement on the basis of ancillary relief legal regime of their foreign resident jurisdictions.

## 4 Conclusion

The legal regime for divorce in Bangladesh is founded upon the religious faith of individuals. For the Muslims and Christians there are codified laws and for the Hindus, Buddhist and the people belonging to other faiths, there is no codified law. Recently, The Hindu Marriage Registration Act has been enacted and the Government of Bangladesh is considering a Hindu Divorce Registration Act. However the Act has not been welcomed by all sections of the Hindu community as they foresee a rise in divorce among Hindu community if such law were to be enacted. The Muslim Family Law Ordinance provides that the husband shall notify the local official of his pronouncement of *talaq*, provides for quasi-judicial procedures and intends to empower local councils to impose barriers on arbitrary divorce. This provision is also applicable to non-resident Bangladeshis opting divorces at their domicile. The provisions of the Code of Civil Procedure, 1908, govern the recognition and enforcement of foreign decrees. However the judicial decisions governing the recognition and enforcement of foreign divorce decrees are completely absent in Bangladesh. The legal recognition and enforcement of Bangladeshi divorce in foreign jurisdictions was beset with doubt initially. One of the problems with non-recognition of Bangladeshi divorces was that the foreign courts had no jurisdiction to deal with ancillary matters unless it itself dissolved the marriage. This predicament was more pronounced in the case of divorce based on

[98]Private International Law, Muslim laws and Gender Equality, The Adjudication of Mahr in Scandinavian, English and French Courts, 92. https://www.duo.uio.no/bitstream/handle/10852/21802/86632.pdf?sequence=1, accessed on 3 August 2016, the author cites the example of Pakistan to prove the point.

[99]Code of Criminal Procedure 1973.

[100]AIR 1979 SC 362.

[101]Lucy Carroll, 'Pakistani and Indian *Talaq*s in English Courts' (1981) 23(4) J Ind. L Inst. 589.

*talaq* as Muslim law recognizes neither any concept of division of matrimonial assets nor alimony on divorce. This situation has been remedied though legal reforms in many foreign jurisdictions. However absence of clarity persists in cross-border divorce matters. A clear legislation or amendment in existing laws is necessary to address the increasing cross-border divorce matters. Bangladesh should also consider membership of the Hague Conference on Private International Law as well as acceding to the Conventions related to family law to ensure that the marriages and divorces executed in Bangladesh and under the law of Bangladesh have recognition in other jurisdictions.

# Cross-Border Divorce Decrees—Recognition in India and Public Policy Considerations

**Vasanti Nimushakavi**

**Abstract** The framework of Private International Law is based on the premise of choice of law in matters that are considered private or personal. Private persons may determine the law that applies to them and may seek remedies in forums that are available for the law chosen. The right to agency, consent and contract which are fundamental to private law are also libertarian values intrinsic to public law. The critique of private law from a feminist perspective has focused on the need to mainstream gender concerns into public and private law. Gender mainstreaming has led to an increased concern for gender issues as part of public policy. One of the controversies in the private law domain has been with regard to adding the ground of irretrievable breakdown of marriage in Indian Law. Thus while an irretrievable breakdown of marriage is a valid ground for divorce in many jurisdictions it is not a ground under Indian law although there have been judgments which have suggested that this might be added as a ground by the legislature. The Indian Judiciary has been reluctant to recognise a foreign court's judgment and has held women who do not want to submit to the jurisdiction of foreign courts may invoke that domestic jurisdiction. In this context Indian law is clearly not in tune with many other jurisdictions. This paper will examine the position of Indian courts with regard to the matrimonial relief of divorce by examining public policy considerations that Indian courts have used.

**Keywords** Private international law · Cross border divorce · Public policy · Gender mainstreaming · Recognition of cross border divorce

V. Nimushakavi (✉)
NALSAR University of Law, Hyderabad, India
e-mail: vasanthi_nkavi@yahoo.com

© Springer Nature Singapore Pte Ltd. 2017

S.R. Garimella and S. Jolly (eds.), *Private International Law*,
DOI 10.1007/978-981-10-3458-9_6

## Introduction

Recognition of cross-border divorce decrees has yet to be satisfactorily settled in India. The Hon'ble Supreme Court, in *Y. Narasimha Rao and othrs v Y. Venkatalakshmi and anr*[1] held that a decree of a foreign court not in consonance with the matrimonial laws applicable to the parties shall not be recognized in India. The Supreme Court in this case used the ground of public policy as the justification for non-recognition of a foreign decree in India. However, the Hon'ble Supreme Court has differed from this position in various other judgments.

The 65th Law Commission report on recognition of foreign divorces[2] (hereinafter, the Report) proposed significant reforms in family laws and also proposed draft legislation on the recognition of cross border divorce decree which was based on the English law. Following the 219th report on the need for family law legislation for Non-resident Indians,[3] (hereinafter, the 219th Report) the Marriage Laws (Amendment) Bill, 2013 proposing amendments to the Hindu Marriage Act, 1955[4] and the Special Marriage Act, 1954[5] was introduced but has yet not been approved by the Parliament.[6]

The Report suggested that the principle of habitual residence should govern the recognition of foreign divorce decrees. The 219th Report recommended that the dissolution of marriage on the ground of irretrievable breakdown of marriage should be introduced following the decision in *Y. Narasimha Rao.*[7]

The general principle of Private International Law is that the law of the forum where the parties are domiciled/habitually residing at the time of the petition shall be the applicable law and the forum of that particular jurisdiction shall be the proper

---

[1]*Y. Narasimha Rao and othrs versus Y. Venkatalakshmi and anr* 1991 SCC (3) 451.

[2]Government of India, Law Commission of India, 'Sixty-fifth Report on Recognition of Foreign Divorces', April 1976. http://lawcommissionofindia.nic.in/51-100/report65.pdf, accessed 20 April 2016.

[3]Government of India, Law Commission of India, 'Need for Family Law Legislations for Non-resident Indians', 219/2009. http://lawcommissionofindia.nic.in/reports/report219.pdf, accessed 20 April 2016.

[4]India being a secular country does not have a uniform code for the family matters including marriage, divorce and custody. These matters are governed either by statutes through customary or religious laws of the parties involved. In general, religion is the essential factor determines the applicable law of marriage. For instance, all the matters pertaining to marriage or divorce shall be governed under the Hindu Marriage Act 1955 provided the parties to the marriage are Hindus. An exception to the above rule is the Special Marriage Act, 1954 enacted in order to regulate inter-religious marriages. For details see, the Hindu Marriage Act, 1955;

The Special Marriage Act, 1954.

[5]The Special Marriages Act was enacted to regulate marriage between persons who belong to different religions. For Details See, The Special Marriage Act, 1954.

[6]The Marriage Law (Amendment) Bill, 2013 (As passed by the Rajya Sabha) Bill No. XLI-C of 2010. http://www.prsindia.org/uploads/media/Marriage%20Laws/Marriage%20Laws%20Bill%20as%20passed%20by%20RS.pdf, accessed 24 April 2016.

[7]*Y. Narasimha Rao* (n 1).

forum. The Report of the Law Commission of India adheres to the above stated principle. But the courts in India have refrained from adopting this principle and have largely relied on the ground of public policy as envisaged in the decision of the Supreme Court in *Y. Narasimha Rao*.

This chapter proposes to examine the decision of Hon'ble Supreme Court in the *Y. Narasinha Rao* on two counts: whether the ground of public policy is rightly invoked in this case? And whether the rule applied by the Supreme Court has any unintended and adverse consequences for women?

**Structure of the Chapter**

This chapter examines the position of Indian courts with regard to matrimonial relief in cross-border divorces by examining public policy considerations that Indian courts have applied in recognition proceedings of such decisions. The first part of the chapter presents an overview of the definition of public policy and its applicability in the private international law regime, in general. The second section traces the issues involved in enforcement of foreign judgments in India with specific reference to the applicability of the ground of public policy. The third section of the paper attempts to analyze the jurisprudence of the Indian courts, especially the invocation of public policy as a methodology to further the interests of women in the context of matrimonial reliefs.

## 1 Public Policy and Private International Law

> An English court will refuse to apply a law which outrages its sense of justice or decency. But, before it exercises such power, it must consider the relevant foreign law as a whole.
>
> Scarman J[8]

Public policy remains an important part of Private International Law. Two clearly discernible strands evolved

- In a negative sense of exclusion of applicable foreign law according to the rules of private international law, and
- In a positive sense that certain rules of public law may be of paramount importance without any consideration of whether or not foreign law is applicable.[9]

Public policy is perceived as a 'safety net' to choice of law rules, rules governing the recognition and enforcement of foreign decrees as well as a doctrine that defines 'the outer limits of the tolerance of differences that are implicit in these rules.[10] Its

[8] *In the Estate of Fuld (No 3)* (1968) 699.

[9] Lipstein K., 'The Hague Conventions on Private International Law, Public Law and Public Policy' (1959) 8(3) ICLQ 506.

[10] Alex Mills, 'The Dimensions of Public Policy In Private International Law' (2008) 4(2) J. Priv. Int'l L. 201.

use has been criticized as being uncertain, vague, unpredictable and as giving excessive discretion to the courts for using it as a ground to exclude applicable law in a given situation.[11] Scholars have also supported the application of the exception of public policy and the positive role that it plays particularly in the cross-border divorce and separation cases.[12]

## 1.1 *The Hague Convention, 1970 and the Public Policy*

The Hague Convention on Recognition of Divorces and Legal Separation, 1970 attempted to facilitate the recognition of divorces and legal separation obtained in different states. It applies to recognition in one contracting State of divorces and legal separations obtained in another contracting State which follows judicial or other proceedings officially recognized in that State and are legally effective there.[13]

Divorces and legal separations shall be recognized if at the date of institution of proceedings in that State, the respondent has a habitual residence there or the petitioner is habitually resident and has been so resident for a period of one year immediately before the submission of the petition or is habitually resident and the spouses last habitually resided there,[14] or both spouses were nationals, or the

[11]*Richardson v Mellish* (1824), 2 Bing. 252 130 E.R. 294 [Burrough, J].

[12]Jan L Neels, 'The Positive Role Of Public Policy In Private International Law and the Recognition of Foreign Muslim Marriages' (2012) 28(2) S. Afr. J. on Hum. Rts. 219.

[13]The Convention on the Recognition of Divorces and Legal Proceedings, 1970 Article 1.

The present Convention shall apply to the recognition in one Contracting State of divorces and legal separations obtained in another Contracting State which follow judicial or other proceedings officially recognized in that State and which are legally effective there. The Convention does not apply to findings of fault or to ancillary orders pronounced on the making of a decree of divorce or legal separation; in particular, it does not apply to orders relating to pecuniary obligations or to the custody of children.

[14]Ibid, Article 2.

Such divorces and legal separations shall be recognized in all other Contracting States, subject to the remaining terms of this Convention, if, at the date of the institution of the proceedings in the State of the divorce or legal separation (hereinafter called "the State of origin")

(1) the respondent had his habitual residence there; or
(2) the petitioner had his habitual residence there and one of the following further conditions was fulfilled—
    (a) such habitual residence had continued for not less than one year immediately prior to the institution of proceedings;
    (b) the spouses last habitually resided there together; or
(3) both spouses were nationals of that State; or
(4) the petitioner was a national of that State and one of the following further conditions was fulfilled—
    (a) the petitioner had his habitual residence there; or
    (b) he had habitually resided there for a continuous period of one year falling, at least in part, within the two years preceding the institution of the proceedings; or

petitioner was a national and either had his habitual residence there or was present in the State when such a petition was filed. The term habitual residence could include domicile if the concept of domicile is used as a test of jurisdiction in that particular State i.e. the state of origin.[15]

In case of a cross petition, a divorce or legal separation following upon the cross petition shall be recognized provided it falls within the ambit of either Article 2 or Article 3.[16] Where a legal separation has been converted into a divorce in the State of origin, the recognition of divorce shall not be refused on the ground that the conditions stated in Article 2 or 3 were not fulfilled at the time of the institution of the divorce proceedings provided that the terms of this Convention were fully complied with at the time of the institution of the legal separation proceedings.[17] Where the respondent had appeared in the proceedings, the judiciary of the State where such recognition is sought shall be bound by the findings of fact on which jurisdiction was assumed.[18]

Article 6 also provides that recognition shall not be refused on the ground that the internal law of the State where such recognition is sought would not allow

---

(Footnote 14 continued)

(5) the petitioner for divorce was a national of that State and both the following further conditions were fulfilled—
   (a) the petitioner was present in that State at the date of institution of the proceedings and
   (b) the spouses last habitually resided together in a State whose law, at the date of institution of the proceedings, did not provide for divorce.

[15]Ibid. Article 3.

Where the State of origin uses the concept of domicile as a test of jurisdiction in matters of divorce or legal separation, the expression "habitual residence" in Article 2 shall be deemed to include domicile as the term is used in that State. Nevertheless, the preceding paragraph shall not apply to the domicile of dependence of a wife.

[16]Ibid. Article 4.

Where there has been a cross-petition, a divorce or legal separation following upon the petition or cross petition shall be recognized if either falls within the terms of Articles 2 or 3.

[17]Ibid. Article 5.

Where a legal separation complying with the terms of this Convention has been converted into a divorce in the State of origin, the recognition of the divorce shall not be refused for the reason that the conditions stated in Articles 2 or 3 were no longer fulfilled at the time of the institution of the divorce proceedings.

[18]Ibid. Article 6

Where the respondent has appeared in the proceedings, the authorities of the State in which recognition of a divorce or legal separation is sought shall be bound by the findings of fact on which jurisdiction was assumed. The recognition of a divorce or legal separation shall not be refused

(a) because the internal law of the State in which such recognition is sought would not allow divorce or, as the case may be, legal separation upon the same facts, or,
(b) because a law was applied other than that applicable under the rules of private international law of that State. Without prejudice to such review as may be necessary for the application of other provisions of this Convention, the authorities of the State in which recognition of a divorce or legal separation is sought shall not examine the merits of the decision.

divorce or legal separation on the same facts. It states further that the authorities of the State where recognition is sought shall refrain from examining the case on its merits.

The exceptions to the recognition of decrees are found in Article 7.[19] A contracting State may refuse to recognize a decree if, amongst other reasons, if the respondent was not given proper notice, or not afforded a sufficient opportunity to present her case,[20] if it is incompatible with an earlier decision,[21] or if it is manifestly incompatible with their public policy.[22] It is important to note here that the Hague Convention allows for a public policy exception to recognition of divorces but does not attempt to explain or illustrate the possible essential components of this exception.

## *1.2 The Law Commission of India: Sixty-Fifth Report on Recognition of Foreign Divorces*

The Law Commission of India in its Report discussed the applicability of the exception of public policy in various jurisdictions. The Report commented that a foreign judgment could be addressed and assailed on three grounds—collateral, direct and equitable.[23] While the rules of conflict of laws could operate with regard to a collateral attack, fraud and the ground of public policy would fall under equitable grounds. A direct address to set aside a judgment for error would be part of the original proceeding. The report distinguished both fraud and non-application of principles of natural justice from the ground of public policy.[24]

---

[19]Ibid, Article 7.

Contracting States may refuse to recognize a divorce when, at the time it was obtained, both the parties were nationals of States which did not provide for divorce and of no other State.

[20]Ibid, Article 8.

If, in the light of all the circumstances, adequate steps were not taken to give notice of the proceedings for a divorce or legal separation to the respondent, or if he was not afforded a sufficient opportunity to present his case, the divorce or legal separation may be refused recognition.

[21]Ibid, Article 9.

Contracting States may refuse to recognize a divorce or legal separation if it is incompatible with a previous decision determining the matrimonial status of the spouses and that decision either was rendered in the State in which recognition is sought, or is recognized, or fulfils the conditions required for recognition, in that State.

[22]Article 10.

Contracting States may refuse to recognize a divorce or legal separation if such recognition is manifestly incompatible with their public policy ("*order public*").

[23]Report (n 2) 99.

[24]Report (n 2) 101.

The Report observed that while the two grounds may occur separately, however, they might be pleaded in the same instance too. To explain such pleading, the Report identified an instance—wrongful pleading before the foreign court by the petitioner about the whereabouts of the respondent being unknown.[25]

It also noted with approval the distinction that Winfield drew between what a law ought to be and public policy—it is not concerned with what law ought to be but the community's perception of its requirements at any specified time.[26]

The author observes that the Report discussed the holistic view of public policy as barring the application of foreign law on the ground that it conflicts with the fundamental moral, ideological, social, economic or cultural standards of the forum, as well as necessity required the unconditional and absolute application of domestic law. Further it may also be invoked when the principle of a foreign legal rule conflicts with the law of nations or the state's international commitments or the requirements of justice as recognized by the international legal commitment. Thus public policy stands above the literal text of the law and it is well known that it varies in time and space as well as with the sense of justice of the judge.[27]

This positive aspect of public policy is also reiterated by Jan Neels who argued that public policy not only has a negative aspect, i.e. the refusal to invoke the law that is applicable to the dispute, but a positive role in the sense of ensuring that principles of public law such as non-discrimination are respected.[28]

## 2 Enforcement of Foreign Judgments in Matters of Divorce Under the Hindu Law in India

The law relating to the recognition of a foreign divorce decree is to be found in various statutes such as the Code of Civil Procedure 1908 (hereinafter, the CPC), the Indian Contract Act, 1872, the Indian Succession Act 1925, the Indian Divorce Act 1869, and the Special Marriage Act 1954 as well as in the Supreme Court judgments. Section 13 of the Code of Civil Procedure specifies,

> A foreign judgment shall be conclusive as to any matter thereby directly adjudicated upon between the same parties or between parties under whom they or any of them claim litigating under the same title except,
> (a) where it has not been pronounced by a Court of competent jurisdiction;
> (b) where it has not been given on the merits of the case;

[25] Ibid, 115.

[26] Id, 102.

[27] Id, 110.

[28] Neels (n 13) 222.

(c) where it appears on the face of the proceedings to be founded on an incorrect view of international law or a refusal to recognize the law of India in cases in which such law is applicable;
(d) where the proceedings in which the judgment was obtained are opposed to natural justice;
(e) where it has been obtained by fraud;
(f) where it sustains a claim founded on a breach of any law in force in India.[29]

Foreign courts assume jurisdiction on the basis of either domicile, habitual residence or real and substantial connection to the forum. Such assumption of jurisdiction for domiciliary reasons could also be based upon a misrepresentation of the facts before the forum. In *Satya v Teja Singh*[30] (hereinafter, *Satya*) the forum court in the US assumed jurisdiction on such misrepresentation of facts by the respondent-husband and ordered divorce, often referred as 'mail-order divorce'.

The rules of Private International Law on domicile—the wife adopts the husband's domicile—has created difficulties, arising from the fact that in many cases the divorce was granted by the foreign court without notice to the party or a contest. In many cases the deserted spouse, often the wife, approached the Indian courts for relief. In absence of a law relating to domicile, India adopted the principles of private international law.

Since the position on domicile of the wife was unclear, the Indian Supreme Court invoked the public policy exception to refuse recognition of a foreign divorce decree. A perusal of the judicial opinion reveals contradictions in the rules applied specifically in the invocation of the public policy exception. The High Courts and the Supreme Court have not indicated the precise manner in which they seek to invoke the public policy exception. Invoking the public policy exception *Y. Narasimha Rao*[31] refused to recognize a foreign judgment and in addition laid out new rules. However, subsequent decisions do not reveal a consistent application of the public policy exception. Further, this decision is in contradiction with the decision in *Satya*.[32] The following section analyzes these decisions to map the application of the public policy exception. These decisions are classified into two categories based on time line i.e. those before the decision in *Y. Narasimha Rao*[33] and those after.

## 2.1 *Decisions Before* Y. Narasimha Rao

The decisions before *Y. Narasimha Rao* relied on the domicile principle along with the accepted principles of private international law such as the principle of *animus*

[29]CPC, s 13.
[30]AIR 1975 SC105 http://judis.nic.in/supremecourt/imgs1.aspx?filename=6180.
[31]*Y. Narasimha Rao* (n 1).
[32]*Satya* (n 30).
[33]*Y. Narasimha Rao* (n 1).

*manendi* i.e. clear intention of the parties, fraud as to jurisdiction, and the law of the place which has the closest concern with the well being of the spouses and off-spring.

In *Jagir Kaur and Another v Jaswant Singh*[34] the appellant-wife filed for maintenance on the ground that the respondent-husband had married another woman and refused to maintain her and their daughter. Upon notice the respondent filed for exemption from personal appearance. The Magistrate Court assumed jurisdiction and granted maintenance, which was confirmed in the revision application. The High Court, however, held that the magistrate court did not have jurisdiction.

The Supreme Court, on appeal, noted the fact that the parties had resided together within the jurisdiction of the magistrate court at the time of filing of the petition, as required under Section 488 (8) CPC. The Court held that temporary residence with *animus manendi* i.e. clear intention, sufficed residence within the meaning of the provisions of the sub-section (8) related to maintenance to the wife and children.[35]

In *Sankaran Govindan v Lakshmi Bharathi*[36] the family of an England-domiciled person applied to the Indian court to contest a decision of the High Court of Judicature at England[37] in an intestate succession dispute. On claims by the applicant's family of an expression of intent to return to India by the applicant and hence his assets ought to be governed by Indian succession law, the Court explained that domicile referred to the present intention[38] of permanent residence. The Court on an appreciation of the evidence concluded that claims of intention of return to India not established. Denying the allegations of fraud practiced on the English Court, the Supreme Court rejected the allegation and upheld the jurisdiction of the English court.[39]

In *Satya*[40] the Supreme Court addressed the issue of limping marriages. In this case, the respondent-husband moved to the United States leaving behind the appellant-wife domiciled in India. He filed for divorce in the court at Nevada. In an uncontested case the Nevada court granted a divorce decree. On a petition of maintenance in the Indian court, the respondent presented the divorce decree as a defense against payment of maintenance. He appealed against the maintenance order of the Lower Court in the High Court, which held, relying on the *Le Mesurier v Le Mesurier*[41] rule, that the Nevada court being the last domicile of the parties

---

[34]AIR 1963 SC 1521 http://judis.nic.in/supremecourt/imgs1.aspx?filename=3600.

[35]Ibid, 08.

[36]AIR 1974 SC 1764 http://judis.nic.in/supremecourt/imgs1.aspx?filename=6276.

[37]Ex. 56 order.

[38]*Sankaran* (n 36) 09.

[39]Ibid, 22.

[40]*Satya* (n 30).

[41](1895) AC 517.

(wife's domicile attached to the husband's domicile) had jurisdiction. On appeal, the Supreme Court opined

> The answer to the question as regards the recognition to be accorded to the Nevada decree must depend principally on the rules of our Private International Law. It is well-recognized principle that 'private international law is not the same in all countries'. There is no system of private international law, which can claim universal recognition.[42]

It further held that comity, public policy and morals could be factors that influence decisions of recognition of a foreign divorce decree, reiterating that the foreign law must not offend against our public policy.[43]

The Court held that fraud vitiated the jurisdiction of the court[44] and the rules of private international law clearly prohibited a person from taking advantage of the jurisdiction by deceiving the court on facts. When the fraud was obvious from the facts of the case, the rules of domicile or matrimonial law, as evident in the lower courts' orders, were inapplicable.

In *Smt. Surinder Kaur v Harbax Singh Sandhu*[45] the Supreme Court of India applied the domicile principle. The disputants married in India and left for England and were domiciled there, a son was born in England. The husband was convicted of an attempt to get his wife killed but on the intervention of the wife he was granted probation. During the period of probation he took his son after making a false declaration that his passport was lost and reached India. The wife obtained a Ward of the Court order in England under section 41 of the Supreme Court Act, 1981. She applied for custody in India. The respondent-husband contested claiming to be the natural guardian to the child.

Refusing to apply the matrimonial law the Court decided in favour of the rule of domicile. It held that in the instant case the intention of the parties to establish a matrimonial home in England where they last lived together and where the wife had obtained custody order would be the factor that attributed to jurisdiction to the English courts.

Some of the other private international law rules applied by the Indian courts include

- real and substantial connection test
- false representations as to jurisdictional facts
- petitioner habitually resident in the foreign jurisdiction and the grounds of divorce were homologous to the grounds available in the matrimonial law
- the parties being resident in India on the date of application to the court entailed jurisdiction of the Indian courts.[46]

---

[42] *Satya* (n 30) 05.

[43] Ibid, 14.

[44] Ibid, 03.

[45] 1984 AIR SC 1224.

[46] See, for example, *Dipak Banerjee v Sudipta Banerjee* 1987 CALLT 491(HC).

In *Marggarate Maria Pulparampil Nee ... v Dr. Chacko Pulparampil and Ors*[47] the Kerala High Court in a *habeas corpus* petition by a mother for the custody of children, had to decide its jurisdiction to order upon the custody of children who are Indian nationals, born of an Indian father, who are now present in India; whether it should honour the German court's order to grant custody to the mother based on a foreign decree. The Kerala High Court accepted the foreign decree as an order passed by a competent court having jurisdiction to grant the relief. It used the principle of a real and substantial connection to determine that the foreign court had jurisdiction even if domicile was not satisfied.

> Assuming without deciding – we are not at all certain that the decision should be that way – that the father had not acquired a German domicile of choice, and therefore the father, the mother, and the children were of Indian domicile, a competent German Court will have jurisdiction to pass a decree for divorce or custody of the children on the ground that the petitioning spouse had a real and substantial connection with the country of that Court or that the children were ordinarily resident in that country. This is a rule or principle that has been adopted by English Courts in very recent times and it seems to us that this trend manifests an important and necessary development of the law.[48]

In *Maganbhai Chhotubhai Patel v Maniben*[49] the High Court applied the principle of false representation as to jurisdictional facts. The case involved the husband moving to USA for further studies leaving behind in India his family of wife and children. A few years later he communicated with his wife for a divorce on consensus. He eventually obtained a divorce from a court in Mexico. The wife filed for maintenance in a Civil Court in India. The husband denied liability to maintain his wife as he had obtained a divorce from her.

The High Court held that the petitioner obtained the divorce decree in Mexico misleading the Mexican Court regarding his residence, when, he had no domicile there and his attempt to establish his residence was only for the purpose of the divorce decree. Referring to S. 13(e), CPC the Court held the judgment obtained on false representation of jurisdictional facts as inconclusive. The Court ordered maintenance to the wife commensurate with the income of the husband.

In *Mrs. Anoop Beniwal v Dr. Jagbir Singh Beniwal*[50] the Court ruled in favour of recognition of the foreign court jurisdiction on the grounds of homologous provisions in the matrimonial law of the parties, the Hindu Marriage Act. The husband moved to Iran and was joined by his wife, but she returned to India. He then moved to the UK, and while his wife was visiting him served a divorce notice; she received emergency legal aid in the UK. The pleadings of the husband in the English court claimed it impossible to continue in the relationship owing to the wife's behavior, a ground for divorce within The Matrimonial Causes Act.

---

[47]AIR 1970 Ker 1.

[48]Ibid, 7.

[49]AIR 1985 Guj 187.

[50]AIR 1990 Del. 305.

On an application by the wife, the Delhi High Court ruled in favour of the English court's jurisdiction on grounds of habitual residence. Holding the English law ground of behavior of the spouse as being similar to the ground of cruelty under the matrimonial law of the parties, the Court recognized the divorce decree of the English court, reiterating that the exceptions set out in S. 13, CPC were not found in the instant case.

The decisions before *Y. Narasimha Rao* followed the principles of private international law without relying on public policy as a ground for refusal of recognition of a foreign divorce decree. There is certainly no precedent to hold that public policy meant that only Indian courts had jurisdiction to dissolve a Hindu marriage.

## 2.2 *The Decision in* Y. Narasimha Rao[51]

The disputants were married for three years before the first appellant, the husband of the first respondent before the Supreme Court, filed for the dissolution of marriage in the court at the place of their marriage as well as in Louisiana where they had last resided together. He filed another petition for dissolution of marriage in the Circuit Court St. Louis Country, Missouri, the USA claiming that he has been a resident of the State of Missouri for 90 days or more immediately preceding the filing of the petition. The wife filed a reply in the Missouri Court raising objections on the maintainability of the petition and stated that her reply was without prejudice to her contention that she was not submitting to the jurisdiction of the court.

The Missouri Court granted a decree for dissolution of marriage on the ground of irretrievable breakdown of marriage even though the wife was not present before the court. The first appellant then married the second appellant. The respondent filed a complaint of bigamy against the appellants. The Magistrate Court discharged the appellants from the allegations of the offence of bigamy on the basis of the decree of dissolution of marriage but the High Court set aside the discharge on the ground that the foreign decree was not proved properly as a photocopy of the judgment of a foreign court was not evidence under the Indian Evidence Act. The Supreme Court dismissing the appeal held that the judgment of the foreign court was without jurisdiction as it was not the place where the marriage was solemnized, neither was it the place where the parties last resided (jurisdiction of the forum) nor was the respondent residing within its jurisdiction. Further irretrievable breakdown of marriage, the ground of divorce in the instant case, was not a ground of dissolution of marriage available under the law applicable to the parties i.e. the Hindu Marriage Act.

---

[51] *Y. Narasimha Rao* (n 1).

The Supreme Court held that the Missouri court's judgment un-enforceable in India.[52] It held the foreign judgment as not being conclusive, a requirement under the CPC.[53]

The Supreme Court held that the jurisdiction assumed by the foreign court as well as the grounds on which the relief is granted must be in accordance with the matrimonial law of the parties. It outlined a few exceptions:

(1) the matrimonial action is filed in the forum where the respondent is domiciled/habitually resident/has permanent residence and the relief is granted on a ground available in the matrimonial law of the parties
(2) respondent voluntarily and effectively submitted to the jurisdiction of the forum as discussed above and contested the claim which is based on a ground available in the matrimonial law of the parties;
(3) respondent consented to the grant of the relief although the jurisdiction of the forum is not in accordance with the provisions of the matrimonial law of the parties.[54]

The Court opined that matrimonial law rule ensured fairness and equity without causing injustice as well as rescuing the institution of marriage from the uncertain maze of the rules of private international law of different jurisdictions.[55] It further observed that this rule ensured certainty and therefore conformed to the exception of public policy. Significantly, it protected women and freed them from the tyrannical rule of domicile, i.e. the wife's domicile follows that of the husband.

Matrimonial law rule is in variance with the proposal of the Law Commission of India outlined in the Report. Section 4 of the Recognition of Divorces and Legal Separations Bill, which is appendix 1 of the Report, provided for recognition of a decree as valid if either spouse was habitually resident of that country and not on the basis of the availability of a remedy under the matrimonial law that the parties were married under.[56]

However, the 219th Report, taking note of the difficulty in the recognition of foreign divorce decrees in India and extensively relying upon the decision in *Y. Narasimha Rao*, recommended the introduction of the ground of irretrievable breakdown of marriage be introduced in the Hindu Marriage Act, 1955 and the Special Marriage Act, 1954[57] so that Indian law would have homologous grounds as in other jurisdictions.

---

[52]Ibid, 835.

[53](n 29).

[54]*Y. Narasimha Rao* (n 1) 834,5.

[55]Ibid, 834.

[56](n 2), The Recognition of Divorces and Legal Separations Bill Section 4

(1) The validity of a foreign divorce or legal separation shall be recognized if, at the date of the institution of the proceedings in the country in which it was obtained:

  (a) either spouse was habitually resident in that country; or
  (b) either spouse was a national of that country; or
  (c) both spouses were domiciled in that country.

[57](n 3) 24.

## 2.3 *Decisions Post-*Y. Narasimha Rao

Post-*Y. Narasimha Rao* some High Courts have followed the ratio of that decision while others applied concepts already existing in S. 13, CPC such as violation of principles of natural justice, fraud as to facts and even the domicile rule. There was also a suggestion that the recognition of a foreign divorce decree be statutorily prohibited.[58] This section of the chapter discusses the ratio of the decisions post-*Y. Narasimha Rao*.

In *Y. Narasimha Rao* the respondent had filed a criminal complaint alleging that the respondent had committed the offence of bigamy. Although the Court did not expressly pronounce the second marriage as adulterous, it allowed the magistrate to proceed with the case of bigamy alleged against the respondents. The Court also observed that there was a delay of ten years and hence directed the magistrate to dispose of the petition expeditiously.

However, in *Mrs. Veena Kalia v Dr.Jatinder Nath Kalia*[59] the Delhi High Court ruled the second marriage adulterous. The husband obtained a divorce decree in an uncontested action in 1975 from the Supreme Court, Nova Scotia, Canada. The wife filed for maintenance from the Court in Nova Scotia through a letter application, which was successful; however she did not receive the maintenance ordered from 1978 to 85. The wife applied for a divorce decree in India claiming that since she could not present her case and the Canadian court made an ex parte order it is not valid. The husband contesting this claim stating that accepting the maintenance ordered by the Canadian court in effect meant acceptance of the divorce decree ordered by the foreign court.

The High Court, despite being informed of the estranged relations between the parties, held the second marriage of the respondent as a nullity for being an adulterous one. The Court refused to recognise the decree obtained in Canada holding that the principles of natural justice were not followed as the wife could not contest the divorce and the divorce was granted on the ground of irretrievable breakdown that is not a ground under the Hindu Marriage Act, 1955. The Delhi High Court then granted the decree of divorce that the wife claimed along with permanent alimony. Although it discussed the *Satya* and the *Narsimha Rao* decisions it specifically held in favour of non-recognition of the foreign divorce decree for non-compliance of the principles of natural justice are not followed.[60]

In *Harmeeta Singh v Rajat Taneja*[61] the plaintiff-wife invoked the jurisdiction of the Delhi High Court under the Hindu Marriage Act, after the defendant-husband initiated proceedings in the Superior Court, State of Connecticut, U.S.A. The High Court restrained the defendant from litigating the dispute in US, however he pursued the litigation and obtained a decree ex-parte. Adopting the ratio of

[58]*Neerja Saraph v Jayant V. Saraph* 1994 SCC (6) 461.

[59]AIR 1996 Delhi 54.

[60]Ibid, para 6.

[61]102(2003) DLT 822.

*Y. Narasimha Rao* the High Court held that the foreign domicile of the parties was not established and hence the divorce proceedings in the foreign country not binding on the parties. The forum of convenience was India, as the wife could not pursue the case in the foreign country. The Court did not rely on public policy but on the rule of domicile and forum of convenience.

Conversely, the Punjab and Haryana High Court in *Rupak Rathi v Anita Chaudhry*[62] extended the ratio of *Y. Narasimha Rao* by adding a requirement to the rule set out in that case—the consent of the respondent to the jurisdiction of the foreign court (Brentford County Court, United Kingdom) The disputants were domiciled within the jurisdiction of the foreign Court, the decree passed by the foreign court dissolving the marriage between the parties by divorce is binding on the parties.

Drawing strength from the averment submitted by the *amicus curiae* the Court considered the plea of the petitioner in the instant case for an exclusive application of exception (iii) to the matrimonial law rule[63] as outlined in *Y. Narasimha Rao*.

> (iii) where the respondent consented to the grant of the relief although the jurisdiction of the forum is not in accordance with the provisions of the matrimonial law of the parties.[64]

The Court accepted the averment of the *amicus* and similar argument on behalf of the Respondent that the entire paragraph [20] of the decision in *Y. Narasimha Rao* had to be contextualized and not the exclusive reading of each of the exception. Such contextualized reading of the matrimonial law rule and the exceptions to it would require the enforcing jurisdiction to consider whether the reliefs granted were in accordance with the matrimonial law of the parties. The High Court in this case observed that there is no mention of the grounds on which the relief may be granted. It observed that if the third rule were read such that it meant that the matrimonial law of the parties was not applicable, it would defeat the rule. The Court held that exception (iii) applied to consent-based decree obtained on foreign soil on the grounds similar to the Hindu Marriage Act and not otherwise.[65]

In *Sondur Gopal v Sondur Rajini*[66] the Supreme Court adopted a contrarian position stating that Hindu Marriage Act applied only to persons domiciled in India. The appellant-husband and the respondent were married in India under the Hindu Marriage Act. They moved to Sweden and acquired citizenship. Further they moved to India before relocating to Sydney. The wife and children arrived in Mumbai on a visit visa. The wife filed a petition for judicial separation. On appeal against the lower court order the Supreme Court was asked to consider whether the Mumbai Court had jurisdiction in the case because the husband claimed to be a Swedish citizen living in Australia. Rejecting the plea of the appellant with regard to the Australian domicile,

---

[62](2014) 175 (2) PLR 407.

[63]*Y. Narsimha Rao* (n 1) 834.

[64]Ibid, 834.

[65]*Rupak* (n 60) [18].

[66](2013) 7 SCC 426 http://judis.nic.in/supremecourt/imgs1.aspx?filename=40556.

the Supreme Court held that the domicile of origin, India, continues till a new domicile is acquired, and in the instant case such acquisition could not be established. Therefore the Hindu Marriage Act continued to be applicable to the parties for any matrimonial relief. The Court further observed that extra-territorial operation of law per Ss. 1(2) and 2(1) is saved not because of the nexus with Hindus but Hindus domiciled in India —Hence, 1955 Act will apply to a Hindu outside the territory of India only if such a Hindu is domiciled in the territory of India.[67]

In *Mrs. M.v Mr. A*[68] the Bombay High Court hearing the appellant-wife in a divorce petition held that Indian court had jurisdiction in matters relating to a marriage solemnized abroad and registered under s 18(3) of the Foreign Marriage Act, 1969. Faulting the Trial judge's dismissal order the High Court explained the domicile principle as requiring a three-year pre-application stay in the country, not short term casual visits, for exercising jurisdiction.[69]

The Madras High Court in *Balasubrahmanyam Guhan v Hemapriya*[70] held that the matrimonial law rule applied to the parties. Here the respondent had filed a suit for declaration of divorce decree of the Scotland court as ultra vires, unsustainable, illegal, unenforceable and without jurisdiction; and for a consequential injunction restraining the petitioner herein from enforcing the said decree or claim any rights under the said decree. The High Court held that the foreign judgment, affected by the exceptions under S. 13, CPC would cease to be conclusive as to any matter thereby adjudicated upon and will be open to collateral attack on the grounds mentioned therein.[71] In the instant case, the foreign court made an ex parte order, hence the Indian court held it not to have jurisdiction.

Contrarily, the Bombay High Court held the Hindu Marriage Act, 1955 inapplicable in case the parties were not domiciled in India. In *Kashmira Kale v Mr. Kishore Kumar Mohan Kale*[72] the disputants, US residents, married in India and returned to the United States. In a divorce application by the wife in the US court, the husband moved the Indian court claiming matrimonial residence in Pune; his application was granted. On appeal by the petitioner-wife the Bombay High Court held that since the parties were domiciled in the United States and the decree was passed on merits, there has been conformity with s 13 CPC. Further the court decided in favour of the US court's territorial jurisdiction as it was the place of their last residence together. The Court further held the Hindu Marriage Act, 1955 inapplicable since the parties were not domiciled in India[73] thus differing from the opinion in *Sondur.*[74]

---

[67]Ibid, 17, 19.

[68](1993) DMC 384.

[69]Ibid. [4].

[70]MANU/TN/0165/2005.

[71]Ibid. [49].

[72]II (2010) DMC 854.

[73]Ibid. [30].

[74]*Sondur* (n 66) 17.

In *Mrs. Indira Sonti v Mr.Suryanarayan Murty Sonti*[75] the petitioner approached the Indian courts for maintenance against the defendant who was domiciled in the United States. The Petitioner, after marriage to the defendant, joined him in the United States. The alleged instance of cruelty and desertion took place in the United States. The Petitioner had initially approached the Delaware Court in United States for maintenance but could not proceed as no decree for divorce was filed. The question was whether Indian Courts had the jurisdiction to entertain a petition for maintenance. The Delhi High Court relied on Section 20, CPC, which granted a legal right to the wife to initiate proceedings in the place of her residence when she is living separately from the husband.[76]

In *Hemavathi Shivashankar v Dr. Tumkur S Shivashankar*[77] the High Court held that since the petitioner had instituted further proceedings before the American Courts over a period of several years and has derived the benefit of the decree of divorce, she had impliedly accepted the decree of divorce and submitted to the jurisdiction of the forum, although, the jurisdiction of that forum was not in accordance with the provisions of the matrimonial law of the parties.[78]

The criss-cross pattern of adjudication on matrimonial actions reflects the varied rules that were invoked in these suits. The decisions in *Sondur, Kale and Hemavathi* have not applied the matrimonial law rule in matters of cross border divorce while *Rupak Rathi* and *Balasubrahmanyan Guhan* have done so.

## 3 Legal Pluralism, Private International Law and Gender Perspectives

Legal pluralism, as John Griffiths defined it, is the presence in a social field of more than one legal order. As an idea it is juxtaposed against 'legal centralism', which is the idea that law is and should be the law of the State, uniform for all persons and

[75] II (2013) DMC 71.

[76] CPC, Section 20.

Other suits to be instituted where defendants reside or cause of action arises.

Subject to the limitations aforesaid, every suit shall be instituted in Court within the local limits of whose jurisdiction—

(a) the defendant, or each of the defendants where there are more than one, at the time of the commencement of the suit, actually and voluntarily resides, or carries on business, or personally works for gain; or
(b) any of the defendants, where there are more than one, at the time of the commencement of the suit actually and voluntarily resides, or carries on business, or personally works for gain, provided that in such case either the leave of the Court is given, or the defendants who do not reside, or carry on business, or personally work for gain, as aforesaid, acquiesce in such institution; or
(c) the cause of action, wholly or in part, arises.

[77] 2013(1) Kar.LJ 231.

[78] Ibid, 22.

exclusive of all other laws, and administered by a single set of state institutions.[79] Margaret Davies has comprehended legal pluralism as emphasizing the non-systemic and disorderly nature of our normative relationships. She also notes that feminist theory has critiqued the public/private divide as a means by which legal culture masks its participation in hegemonic forms of power and the understanding of legal cultures as not the product of social and political processes but as embedded in it.[80]

Feminist legal theory has also critiqued the nature and concept of law by invoking an analysis of power as well as socio-political context. While the liberal feminist theory of law focused on a rights-based paradigm for women within the existing law, structural feminist theory has questioned the nature of law as not accommodative of feminist concerns. Cultural invocations in law have led to debates on the success or failure of multiculturalism to provide enough space for a feminist understanding of the law. The debates on locating women's rights within their specific cultures as against a universal understanding of rights has allowed for complex understanding of rights to be articulated.

John Murphy alluded to the need to acknowledge cultural values particularly for immigrants, when they seek to have marriages performed in foreign countries and recognised in the United Kingdom. He observed that English Courts by invoking a non-specific use of public policy, were viewed as as imposing a cultural imperial ism.[81] He argued that to acknowledge cultural values would be the first step to rationalize the decision. Thus a child-wife seeking recognition of her marriage must be allowed to state that the legal culture to which she belongs allowed such a marriage as valid and the court might want to consider her claim instead of simply invoking public policy to refuse recognition of such marriages.

Private International Law recognizes legal pluralism. Its rules are structured such that the plurality of laws is seen as lateral rather than hierarchical. The superiority of any norm is not established. The first step in resolving disputes in private international law is the recognition that there is a conflict of laws and there are rules to determining which law would apply in a given conflict, implying that for different conflicts, different rules and laws would apply.

Karen Knop, Ralf Michaels and Annelise Riles propose an approach based on conflict of laws style towards issues involving women's rights that provides new insights quite distinct from insights that are already available from a public law perspective.[82] For a long time, public law in terms of constitutional law, international human rights law has been used to understand and advocate for legal rights of

---

[79]John Griffiths, 'What is Legal Pluralism?'. http://www.jus.uio.no/smr/english/research/areas/diversity/Docs/griffiths_what-is-legal-pluralism-1986.pdf, accessed 11 May 2016.

[80]Margaret Davies, 'Pluralism and Legal philosophy' (2006) 57 N. Ir. Legal Q. 577.

[81]John Murphy, 'Rationality and cultural pluralism in the non-recognition of foreign marriages', (2000) 49(3) ICLQ 643.

[82]Karen Knop, Ralf Michaels and Annalise Riles, 'From Multiculturalism to Technique: Feminism, Culture, and the Conflict of Laws Style' (2012) Cornell Law Faculty Publications, 1307/2012. http://scholarship.law.cornell.edu/facpub/1307, accessed 24 December 2015.

women. Knop, Michaels and Riles propose a shift of focus from the larger frame of public law to the more specific and limited frame of private international law to address the issues of women's rights particularly at a time when different strands in the feminist approach are calling for a more location specific understanding of women's rights. The argument is that the specific and narrow focus of private international law allows for questions of culture and human rights to be addressed in a more non-western and non-universal manner. The understanding of the rules of private international law as technique allows for an examination of issues not in terms of establishing a superior norm but in terms of selecting a suitable norm. The apparent indeterminacy of laws in private international law can be viewed as its strength rather than as a failing.

Applying this understanding to the issue of recognition of cross border divorce decrees, the rules of Private International Law along with domestic law on the recognition of foreign decrees provide for an appropriate framework for adjudication of these matters. It is evident from the cases discussed that none of the cases really warranted the use of the public policy exception. All the cases including *Y. Narasimha Rao* could be adjudicated upon using the rules of Private International Law and the Code of Civil Procedure, 1908. The invocation of public policy in the context of recognition of foreign divorce decrees has not added any new element to the discourse but in fact has made the law more rigid and capable of being interpreted to harm the interests of parties particularly women.

Since the *Y. Narasimha Rao* decision explicitly invoked the social context of women who are put to hardship by the outrageously fraudulent conduct of their spouses, the issue is closely related to whether the rules of private international law are just towards women. It is widely acknowledged that they are not so.[83] A majority of the cases discussed clearly portray the unfair rule of domicile of the wife, which is deemed to follow that of the husband. The underlying premise of these cases is also that when the wife is not living with her husband should her domicile determine the adjudication of her rights or should other considerations also be entertained.

The working paper of the Council of Europe on equal opportunities for men and women notes that discrimination is frequent in terms of women's personal status, in family law and in private international law. It recommended that there was a need for a new protocol on gender equality to ensure that the remaining discrimination against women both in the field of national law as well as private international law can be finally eliminated.[84]

Thus while public policy continues to be a useful principle in the context of eliminating discrimination against women, its use in India in the context of recognition of foreign divorce decrees may have unintended consequences. There is a suggestion to amend the law on divorce for inclusion of the ground of

[83]Law Commission of India (n 2) 87, Y. Narasimha Rao (n 1) 834.

[84]Doc 11177 6 February 2007, Respect for the principle of gender equality in civil law, Report, Committee on Equal Opportunities for Women and Men, Rapporteur: Ms. Svetlana Smirnova. http://assembly.coe.int/nw/xml/XRef/X2H-Xref-ViewHTML.asp?FileID=11635&lang=EN, accessed 12 May 2016.

irretrievable breakdown of marriage. Courts have also taken the line that a marriage solemnised under the Hindu Marriage Act, 1955 could only be dissolved in India and on grounds available under that law. Such reasoning does not address the discrimination in terms of the domicile principle for women or any of the other forms of discrimination in the law that women face. It in fact might be another barrier to those women who may be married under the Hindu Marriage Act but are domiciled in other countries. To require them to maintain petitions in Indian Courts under Indian Law certainly is not a desirable proposition of law.

The afore-discussed mapping of Indian jurisprudence reveals that the principle of domicile has been widely prevalent, before and after the *Y. Narasimha Rao* case. Necessity has been an important reason for recognizing the domicile rule. The rule has been interpreted flexibly to hold that Indian as well as foreign courts have jurisdiction to decide a matter depending on whether domicile is proved or not. In *Satya* the Court observed that the marriage was a limping one, one that was valid in the foreign jurisdiction but not in India and hence Indian Courts have jurisdiction in matters such as maintenance.

In cases like the *Neerja Saraph*[85] a blatant abuse of international law, the option with the court is always to examine if the domicile of the wife has changed and whether the domicile of the husband has been established as being of a foreign country.

Contrary to the domicile rule, Supreme Court of India in *Y. Narasimha Rao* and the High Courts adopted the reasoning of matrimonial law rule that stated that foreign courts have no jurisdiction to adjudicate on divorce petition, since only Indian courts have the jurisdiction. This position conflicts with the domicile rule in Private International Law, as well as having negative consequences for women. When the court in this case wants all divorces to be filed in India, it is also imposing this rule on women who might have acquired a foreign domicile and would rather proceed under that law. In *Mrs. M vs. Mr. A.*[86] the petitioner wife filed for divorce in India although the marriage was solemnized in Houston U.S.A.

Women in different situations invoked different rules to claim reliefs from courts. For instance in *Hemavathi Shivshankar*[87] the petitioner-wife pleaded the matrimonial law to apply, in *Kashmira Kale*[88] the petitioner-wife pleaded for the domicile rule to apply. Similarly, in *Surinder Kaur*[89] *or Marggarate Maria Pulparampil,*[90] women had approached a foreign court and had obtained orders for the custody of their children who had been abducted and brought to India.

Many of the cases including *Y. Narasimha Rao* could have been decided using the fraud on the court principle, which is a well-recognised principle of private

[85]*Neerja* (n 58).

[86]*Mrs. M* (n 68).

[87]*Hemavathi* (n 77).

[88]*Kashmira Kale* (n 72).

[89]*Surinder* (n 45).

[90]*Marggarate* (n 47).

international law and forms part of the principle of natural justice. Decrees that violate these must be held to be void and there was no need to invoke public policy as a distinct principle.

In the place of allowing for a flexible interpretation of rules, to impose either the irrevocable breakdown of marriage as a ground for divorce, or to hold that the matrimonial law will prevail notwithstanding the domicile of the parties would lead to greater hardship and injustice to women. The gendered understanding of law is not only to provide unilateral measures but also to facilitate the use of the law to their advantage.

That said, public policy per se has been used in few of the cases. It is only in *Y. Narasimha Rao* that one finds that public policy has been used to modify the domicile principle to bring in matrimonial law. In *Rupak Rathi* the court seemed to extend the matrimonial law rule even in cases of consent of the parties. The invocation of public policy is not required in cases of fraud or violation of principles of natural justice. It could be used as in the case of South Africa and France to bring in questions of public international law such as issues of discrimination or racism, or leave it undefined to be decided by courts in exceptional cases rather than equate public policy to the grant of divorce on the ground of irretrievable breakdown of marriage. The use of public policy in the *Y. Narasimha Rao* decision does not add anything to the rules of private international law. All the rules used whether it is the matrimonial law rule, or the domicile rule or the exceptions such as fraud or violation of principles of natural justice find place in the rules of private international law.

If there is a dominant motive behind this judgment it is to protect the rights of women who are deceived and abandoned by their spouses. That is the only discernable public policy that can be served in many ways rather than only the matrimonial law rule.

## 4 Conclusion

The Courts in India have played a protective role in using the rules of private international law as well as public policy to secure justice to women in many of these cases. The main concern of the courts has been to protect women, the most vulnerable section of the society unchain them from tyrannical rules like the domicile of the wife following that of her husband, or that husband's domicile alone determines the jurisdiction in a matrimonial dispute. In this endeavor they have in many cases used the domiciliary rule and alternately looked at questions of fraud, lack of respect for principles of natural justice. The authority of the courts to give effect to the matrimonial laws is an important element of their jurisdictional powers and must be retained by these courts. This is quite in conformity with the recommendations of the 65th Report that limping marriages were not necessarily unfair to the parties. It could serve several purposes. It might be necessary to allow recognition in certain forums and not in the others. The rule of certainty of giving effect to the foreign decree is to be weighed against the issue of ensuring justice to the parties. This however must not lead to denial of the domiciliary principle that might be the better rule in certain situations as demonstrated in a few cases cited above.

The protection of rights of women such as custody or maintenance will not be secured merely by introducing the ground of irretrievable breakdown of marriage. In fact, by this move it is possible that a foreign divorce decree will automatically be granted recognition since it is a homologous ground while ignoring the larger issues of fraud, desertion, and even questions of domicile and jurisdiction. This paper strongly recommends the drafting of a law on the recognition of foreign divorce decrees in line with the recommendations of the Law Commission's Sixty Fifth Report on Recognition of Foreign Divorces.

# Foreign Judgments in Matrimonial Disputes—Recognition in Nepal and Public Policy Considerations

**Srijana Regmi**

**Abstract** Private international law is a relatively less developed domain in Nepal. There is no specific legislation governing private international law. Over the past few years, however, the judiciary of Nepal has witnessed a number of cases regarding recognition of foreign judgments, exclusively concerning matrimonial issues. In this backdrop, this chapter discusses the situation of recognition of foreign judgments vis-à-vis matrimonial cases in Nepal. Beginning with an overview on the historical development of private international law in Nepal, the chapter proceeds on to discuss existing legislations governing issues involving foreign elements and judicial decisions on the recognition of foreign marriages and divorces in Nepal. The chapter then makes a descriptive narration of the draft law on private international law and an analysis of the provisions related to matrimonial matters in the draft. An attempt to provide recommendation on improvising the draft law vis-à-vis matrimonial issues has also been made.

**Keywords** Private international law · Public policy · *Sabina pandey* judgment · Nepal draft civil code · Foreign divorce recognition

## Introduction

One of the first cases involving foreign element was brought before the court of Nepal more than five decades ago.[1] The case addressed the question of application of foreign law in deciding a case by a domestic court of Nepal when the defendant was a foreign national. The case was decided as though it was a purely domestic case and the association of foreign element in the case and the issue of conflict of laws were completely overlooked. Justice Prakash Bahadur K.C., however, in his

[1] *Tung Sumsher JBR v Indian Airlines Corporation* [1967] 1 NKP 165 (SC).

S. Regmi (✉)
RMS Legal Consulting, Warsaw, Poland
e-mail: srrizana@gmail.com

© Springer Nature Singapore Pte Ltd. 2017



S.R. Garimella and S. Jolly (eds.), *Private International Law*,
DOI 10.1007/978-981-10-3458-9_7

separate opinion comprehensively discussed the issue of Private International Law and its relevance in the case. This separate opinion introduced the legal/judicial system of Nepal to the notion of Private International Law, and is thus considered a milestone in the development of Private International Law in Nepal.

Subsequent cases concerning issues of private international law were reported a few times after that, although sparingly[2] and thanks to the above-mentioned separate opinion, the association of foreign elements in these subsequent cases was acknowledged and the cases were decided from the perspective of Private International Law.

The last few years have seen important developments in private international law in Nepal, although more significantly in the area of recognition of foreign judgment. The number of cases involving recognition of foreign judgment, particularly matrimonial cases has risen sharply in Nepal and therefore the jurisprudence of Nepal in Private International Law has largely been in the recognition of foreign judgments.

Justice Balram KC in a recent case[3] involving recognition of a foreign divorce judgment stated as follows:

> Whether courts of a country should recognize judgments of foreign courts is an important question of law. Even though every nation is sovereign and has exclusive jurisdiction over people residing as well as property located within its territory, such concept of exclusive jurisdiction is not viable in today's era of interdependence. In today's world nations cannot ignore decisions of foreign courts relying on the principle of territorial sovereignty.[4]

As pointed out by Justice Balram KC, although each sovereign nation is able to unilaterally decide upon the enforcement of foreign judgments, the importance of giving recognition to foreign judgments cannot be undermined in the context of globalized world. The territorial rationale for non-recognition—the forum cannot trust any foreign judgment in the same manner in which it trusts local judgments—no longer holds validity. Foreign judgments are checked upon various criteria for validity to hold them enforceable.[5]

Nepal does not have any legislation regarding recognition of foreign judgments, or private international law for that matter. The first attempt to legislate was made few years ago by including a chapter on private international law in the draft civil code. The draft code, more than five year old now, is awaiting presentation to the Nepalese Parliament. The delay in the procedure has been due to the postponement of pending work in favour of Constitution-making process.

---

[2] *Minadevi Rana* et al. *v Shanta Sumsher J B* R [1972] 1 NKP 69 (SC); *Uma Sundari Devi v Basanta Kunwara* [1972] NKP (SC).

[3] *Sabina Pandey v Pushkarraj Pandey* [2011] 3 NKP 387 (SC) (hereinafter, the *Sabina Pandey*).

[4] *Sabina* (n 3) 3 (Translation by author, Original text in Nepali).

[5] PR Barnett, Res judicata, Estoppel and foreign judgments; the preclusive effects of foreign judgments in private international law (1st end Oxford University Press 2001) 36–37; JHC Morris, The Conflict of Laws (3rd edn, Stevens and Sons 1984) 110–125; Dieter Martiny, "Recognition and Enforcement of Foreign Money Judgments in the Federal Republic of Germany", (1987) 35 AJCL 721–759.

**Structure of the Chapter**

The chapter is divided into four parts. The first part consists of a general description of the development of private international law in Nepal. This part makes an overall account on the existing legal framework of Nepal with respect to Private International Law as well as a methodical study on emergence of Private International Law though judicial decisions.

The second part discusses the specific area of matrimonial disputes involving foreign elements decided by the courts of Nepal. This part makes a comprehensive analysis of the *Sabina Pandey* concerning the recognition and enforcement of foreign divorce judgment. It also highlights inconsistencies in the decisions of the courts regarding recognition (or non-recognition) of foreign matrimonial judgments through a comparative study of the decided cases.

The third part makes a descriptive narration of the draft law on private international law in Nepal, especially the provisions of the draft law concerning jurisdiction, choice of law and the recognition and enforcement in matrimonial cases.

The last part of the chapter makes a critical analysis of the provisions of the draft law related to matrimonial matters and provides recommendations for improvement.

## 1 Development of Private International Law in Nepal

Nepal adopted a unitary system of governance until the new constitution[6] introduced federalism in the country.[7] Although the structure of state and distribution of state power has been conceptualized in the constitution,[8] it is yet to be realized in application.

Nepal's early systems for the administration of justice were based on Hindu beliefs.[9] The first modern legal code, The General Code[10] adopted in 1853 was largely influenced by Hindu religious scriptures and customary practices. After

[6]The new Constitution made by the Constituent Assembly was promulgated in 20 September 2015.

[7]The Constitution of Nepal 2015 Art 4(1).

[8]Ibid., Arts 56–60.

[9]Purna Man Shakya, 'Challenges and Prospects of Federalism in Nepal' (2013). http://reliance.com.np/relian/wp-content/uploads/2013/07/Challenges-and-Prospects-of-Federalism-in-Nepal.pdf.

[10]The General Code, 1853 (Muluki Ain in Nepal) was the first modern codified law of Nepal. It draws its inspiration from the Napoleon Code. It's revised version, The General Code, 1963 is a codification of various civil and criminal laws of Nepal and is still in force. In hierarchy, it has the same status as Acts, however it consists of various Chapters (for example, Chapter on marriage, Chapter on general transaction, Chapter on Homicide, e.c.t.) and the provisions are not numbered as 'Section' but as 'Number'. For instance, the legal provision referring to intentional homicide is quoted as—'The General Code, chapter on Homicide, no. 13', denoting that number 13 of the chapter contains provision relating to intentional homicide.

being declared as a secular nation,[11] the legal system has less to do with religion and culture. Nepal does not have a separate personal law, however the law gives due regard to traditions and customs that have been in practice.[12]

Nepal's courts are arranged in three tiers—District courts are the courts of first instance, courts of appeal being the intermediate courts and the Supreme Court. There are also a few specialized tribunals, and certain administrative officials have quasi-judicial powers. Court procedures in Nepal correspond more closely with English common law traditions than with continental civil law traditions.[13] The courts usually apply adversarial procedure and follow a system of binding case law.[14]

With Nepal opening its market for foreign investment, Nepalese businesses contracting internationally, Nepalese citizens migrating to different parts of the world, entering into marital relations and having residence there, foreign nationals residing and having business in Nepal, disputes arising in the courts of Nepal are no longer purely domestic. Globalization has ensured that countries can neither refuse to hear cases involving foreign subjects or objects nor refuse to give recognition to disputes decided by foreign courts.

Absence of a comprehensive legislation on private international law addressing all the three strands—jurisdiction, choice of law and recognition and enforcement of foreign judgments—has had its causation in the difficulties relating to constitutional development process. Further, such causation could also be attributed to absence of indigenous scholarship in this knowledge domain. In the absence of the comprehensive legislation and secondary sources, when the cases involving foreign element were presented before the Nepalese courts, the identification of legal questions and elaboration on issue of private international law was left to judges. In some earlier cases involving foreign element, the court was not able to identify the case as that of private international law and would decide cases without taking private international law in consideration, resulting in unjust verdicts.[15] Although that was more than five decades ago, problems in identifying foreign elements in cases, deciding them without considering principles of private international law[16] as well as inconsistency in comprehending some issues[17] still exists now.

While it is recognized that one of the merits of the unwritten conflict of law rules is their relative flexibility and adaptability, in the absence of sufficient guidance on

[11]The Interim Constitution of Nepal, 2008 declared Nepal as a secular nation.

[12]The General Code 1963, Chapter on Etiquette, no. 10.

[13]Johanna Bond, 'Nepal' in H.M. Kritzer (eds). Legal Systems of the World: A Political, Social and Cultural Encyclopedia (ABC-CLIO 2002).

[14]James Michel et al., 'Nepal Rule Of Law Assessment Final Report' (2009, USAID).

[15](no. 1).

[16](no. 3).

[17]*Tenji Lama v Yangji Lama* [2014] CA 196.

the identification of the prerequisites for application of these unwritten rules[18] they would be of little help to countries like Nepal where the basic understanding of the concept of private international law is very minimal. Legislation would at the very least provide private international law with the advantages of a structure, uniform terminology and clear methodology and greatly improve the consistency of court decisions.

Presently, there is no explicit law governing private international law in Nepal. Although there are a few legislations that define the status of foreigner in various civil and family matters such as acquiring and inheriting property,[19] having immovable property registered in one's name,[20] and adoption.[21] According to the chapter on *Adal* (Etiquette) under the General Code, a foreigner can obtain immovable property by virtue of succession or partition, nevertheless, cannot register such property in his/her name. Such person is entitled to sell or otherwise transfer such property to a citizen of Nepal.[22] The law of Nepal permits a foreigner to adopt a Nepalese child so long as the law of the country of such a foreign national provides that an adopted child has the same legal rights as a birth child.[23] The law of Nepal also recognizes the jurisdiction of courts of Nepal in cases concerning transaction between a Nepalese citizen and a foreigner carried out in a foreign country. A foreigner creditor who has obtained a deed meeting the requirements of the law of Nepal is entitled to sue the Nepalese debtor in the courts of Nepal.[24]

The Arbitration Act of Nepal, 1999 details the method for enforcement of foreign awards, including the exceptions to such enforcement. According to the provision, a foreign arbitral award shall not be implemented in Nepal

(a) if the settled dispute cannot be settled through arbitration under the laws of Nepal or
(b) the implementation of the award is detrimental to the public policy.[25]

An attempt to legislate in the domain of private international law has been made by including a chapter on private international law in the Draft Civil Code (hereinafter, the Code). The chapter lays down rules relating to jurisdiction, applicable law, the recognition and enforcement of foreign judgments. Whether the provisions of the chapter are sufficient to meet the objective behind the enactment is certainly a matter to be discussed, nevertheless, the enacting of the Code with a chapter

[18]Aude Florini, 'The Codification of Private International Law: the Belgian Experience' (2005) 54 ICLQ 499–519.

[19]The General Code 1963, Chapter on Etiquette, no. 3.

[20]Ibid.

[21]The General Code 1963, Chapter on Adoption, nos. 12A, 12B.

[22](no. 20).

[23]Ibid.

[24]The General Code 1963, chapter on General Transaction, no. 34.

[25]Arbitration Act 1999, s 34.

dedicated to private international law should be considered a decent stride to start with.

Nepal is yet to accede to the international conventions on private international law.[26] Further such Conventions need to be ratified and transformed into the domestic law of Nepal. The Treaty Act of Nepal provides that in case a domestic law of Nepal contradicts with international law, the provisions of international law will prevail.[27] This provision has largely remained merely as a theory. No case can be filed in the court on the basis of international law and courts of Nepal cannot decide a dispute merely by taking reference of a rule of international law. A relevant domestic legislation needs to be referred to. However, it is preferable to have a domestic legislation than international law in terms of freedom to tailor the provisions to suit its needs and interests and to make amendments whenever deemed necessary.

## 2 Judicial Opinion on Private International Law—Few Instances

The first reported case of Nepal involving foreign element was *Tung Sumsher v Indian Airlines Corporation.*[28] Following an accident of an aircraft belonging to Indian Airlines Corporation, which resulted in the death of all the passengers, Tung Sumsher, the grandfather of the children who travelled on the aircraft filed a suit against Indian Airlines claiming compensation for the loss of their lives. The Corporation was registered in India pursuant to Indian law. The aircraft in question was flying within Nepal. The compensation was claimed as per Indian Air Act since there was no relevant legal provision under Nepalese law. The Court reached its verdict without considering any rule of private international law and held that the Indian law and the Warsaw Convention referred to in the Indian law were not applicable in the cases brought before the court of Nepal. However, Justice Prakash Bahadur KC, in his separate opinion recognized the case as one involving foreign element and thus of private international law. He opined that the courts of a country might apply law of another country to decide cases involving conflict of law

[26]Convention of 14 March 1978 on the Law Applicable to Matrimonial Property Regimes, Convention of 14 March 1978 on Celebration and Recognition of the Validity of Marriage, Convention of 1 June 1970 on the Recognition of Divorces and Legal Separations are of particular relevance with respect to matrimonial issues. Given the swift increment in cases related to recognition and enforcement of foreign judgments, Convention of 15 April 1958 concerning the recognition and enforcement of decisions relating to maintenance obligations towards children, Convention of 1 February 1971 on the Recognition and Enforcement of Foreign Judgments in Civil and Commercial Matters and Supplementary Protocol of 1 February 1971 to the Convention on the Recognition and Enforcement of Foreign Judgments in Civil and Commercial Matters hold significant importance in the context of Nepal.

[27]Nepal Treaty Act 1990, s 9(1).

[28](n 1).

situation.[29] The importance of this opinion is derived as being the pioneering statement on the subject of private international law and thus of precedent value.

Few years later in the case of *Minadevi v Shanta Sumsher*[30] the Supreme Court held that it did not have jurisdiction to decide issues regarding immovable property situated in a foreign country for reasons of non-enforceability of its decision. The plaintiff had filed a property suit where a part of the claimed property was immovable property situated in India. The Court however decided on issues concerning the property situated within Nepal. In the case *of Uma Sundari Devi*[31] the Court reiterated its holding in *Minadevi* stating that in the absence of any agreement between the countries, the issue of immovable property should be decided according to the law of the country where the property is situated (Nepal, thus subscribes to the principle of lex situs in disputes related to immovable property).

Although these first few cases related to private international law were filed in the courts of Nepal during the 1960s, the necessity of legislating on the subject matter was largely overlooked, probably because of a negligible incidence of cases involving foreign element. The number of cases on private international law, especially those involving matrimonial issues, are in escalating for the past couple of years. Issues regarding commercial transactions and other corporate matters are heard of occasionally, and a yet judicial decision is yet to be pronounced.

## 3 Private International Law in Matrimonial Disputes

The discussion on Private International Law issues came up in the Nepalese Court when a Spanish national, Maria Victoria, married to a Nepalese citizen, filed a polygamy complaint against her husband.[32] She claimed that her husband Mr. Kami Sherpa married a Nepali woman while he was still married to her. Mr. Sherpa however claimed that they had already been divorced in Spain according to Spanish law. The court had to decide if the divorce case in Spain would be recognized in Nepal or not. The defendants, apart from the claim of divorce, also denied the allegation of having married another woman. Since polygamy is a criminal offence in Nepal, the prosecutors' failure to prove the alleged marriage beyond a reasonable doubt led to the defendant's acquittal. The court did not address the issue of recognition of foreign judgment.

Few years later, Maria filed a writ petition before the Supreme Court of Nepal against the Immigration Department for cancelling her spouse Visa.[33] Apparently,

---

[29] *Tung Sumsher* (n 1) separate opinion Justice Prakash KC.

[30] *Minadevi* (n 2).

[31] *Uma* (n 2).

[32] *Maria Victoria Subirana Rodrigage v Kami Sherpa* et al. [2006] CA.

[33] *Maria Victoria Subirana Rodrigagev Immigration Department Kathmandu* et al. [2011] 11 NKP (SC).

she had filed a case in the District court claiming her share in her husband's property according to Nepalese matrimonial law. Her husband submitted an application to the Immigration Department to have her Spouse Visa cancelled on account of the fact that they have already been divorced hence Maria no longer being entitled to the Spouse Visa. The Court held the decision of the Immigration Department to cancel her Spouse Visa valid and thereby recognized the divorce case decided by the court of Spain. In doing so, it stated that even though there is no law in Nepal regarding the enforcement of foreign judgment, the judgment rendered by an independent judiciary of a sovereign nation should be taken in judicial notice by the court of Nepal. However, in light of principles of fair trial and due process, the Court issued an order to the Immigration Department to grant her a Visa till the property case she filed to the District Court has been decided. The Court also shed light on the necessity to have a clear rule defining the status of judgments by courts of a country and said that it draws the attention of the government to make appropriate laws in Nepal on the recognition of foreign judgments.

Less than a year later, the *Sabina Pandey*[34] was decided by the full bench of Supreme Court. In analyzing if the divorce obtained in the United States would be recognized in Nepal, the Supreme Court made a detailed discussion on the issue of enforcement of foreign decisions, in general as well as in the specific case. The Court refused to recognize and enforce the judgment made by the Oklahoma District Court on three grounds namely lack of jurisdiction, denial of fair trial and due process, and public policy.

In 2014, the Court of Appeal heard another application involving the recognition of foreign divorce judgment.[35] The petitioner filed a lawsuit before the District Court of Nepal claiming a share on her husband's property. It was later found out that a Canadian court had earlier granted the couple divorce on an application by the wife. The District Court relied heavily on the *Sabina* judgment to hold the foreign divorce case unrecognizable and decided in favor of the petitioner.

The Court of Appeal however found that the District Court made an erroneous interpretation of the Supreme Court's ruling in *Sabina*. The Court of Appeal held that the Supreme Court in *Sabina* refused to recognize the foreign divorce judgment on the ground that Sabina, the defendant in the divorce case was neither the domicile of the USA nor submitted to the jurisdiction of the US court therefore US court lacked jurisdiction in the decided case. The Supreme Court also based its decision of non-recognition on the fact that Sabina was not present in the USA at the time and the divorce case against her was decided irrespective of her absence throughout the proceeding hence violating principles of fair trial and due process. The Court of Appeal also reiterated that the court in *Sabina* was in favor of the recognition of foreign judgment in general, but refused recognition in the particular cases because of some exceptions. The Court of Appeal noted in the instant case the fact that that Mrs. Lama herself had filed the divorce case and the proceedings were

---

[34]*Sabina* (n 3).

[35]*Tenji* (n 17).

carried out in the presence of both the parties and their legal representations. The court restated the importance of recognizing the judgment of the courts of a country by another and held that not recognizing such judgments would undermine the established principles of private international law as well as the doctrine of finality of judgment.

Recently in a similar case, the District court gave its judgment in *Srijana Ranjitkar v Kiran Kumar Ranjit et al.*[36] involving a foreign divorce. The wife filed a divorce against the husband in the US court and a divorce agreement was reached between the couple. She then filed another case in the court of Nepal claiming share in his property. The divorce agreement had a provision that the issue of interests on real ad movable property of the parties is not under the jurisdiction of Maryland Courts and such interest shall not be affected by the agreement. The Court of First Instance decided that the applicant was entitled to her share in the husband's property, however it did not state whether it recognized the judgment on divorce made by the court of Maryland. The Court held that since the petition claiming the share in property was filed before the divorce agreement (yet after the divorce case was filed), and since according to the law of Nepal, women have right to husband's property even after divorce, unless they explicitly renounce it, the petitioner is entitled to the share in the property. The judgment is full of errors from various points of views which hopefully the court of Appeal would correct, nevertheless, the court of Nepal once again failed to discuss the issue of private international law in a case which calls for it.

## *3.1* Sabina Pandey—*The Landmark*

The judgment in the *Sabina Pandey* is a pioneering decision it was the first matrimonial case involving the issue of private international law; the Supreme Court issued a directive order to the government to enact a legislation on private International law in Nepal.

Sabina Pandey filed a case to the District Court of Nepal claiming for her share in her husband, Mr. Pushkarraj Pandey's property. According to the divorce law of Nepal, when a divorce case is filed in a court of Nepal, the court first needs to decide on the matter related to wife's share in the husband's property and only after decreeing upon the wife' share in the property can the court decide on the divorce case.[37]

While the case was still pending in the court of Nepal, the Oklahoma court gave its final verdict on the divorce case in the favor of Mr. Pandey. The Kathmandu District Court decided that Ms. Pandey's claim to her husband's property cannot be sustained given she was no longer his wife after the divorce. The court of Appeal

[36][2016] DC 162.

[37]The General Code 1963, chapter on Husband and Wife, no. 4A.

upheld the District court's decision. The case was appealed to the Supreme Court. The question of whether or not should the court recognize the divorce case decided by the Oklahoma District court was crucial in order to determine if Ms. Pandey had a valid claim over her husband's property.

In analyzing the possibility of recognition of the US court ordered divorce, the Supreme Court wrote extensively on the issue of enforcement of foreign decisions, in general as well as in the specific case. The Court refused to recognize and enforce the judgment made by the Oklahoma District Court on three grounds namely lack of jurisdiction, denial of fair trial and due process, and public policy.

The Supreme Court held that the Court of Oklahoma could not exercise jurisdiction over Ms. Pandey in the divorce case as she did not have domicile in the USA. Although initially she had intention to stay in the USA, following the differences with the husband, she had returned to Nepal thereby no longer having domicile in the USA. The court noted the denial of the Oklahoma court's jurisdiction by Ms. Pandey and the fact that she had not submitted to the same.

The Court further reiterated the fact that Ms. Pandey had returned back to Nepal from the USA due to conflicts with her husband on various matters, one of them being his unwillingness to support her financially, it was thus impossible for her to be able to be present for the hearing of the case. Citing Article 24(1) of the ICCPR, the Court held that not being able to be present in the hearing amounted to denial of right to fair trial. Furthermore, the Court held that recognition of judgment in such situation (absence of jurisdiction and fair trial) could amount to denial of access to justice, which would be against public policy.

The ratio of *Sabina* seems to have been misunderstood in the cases that followed. Since the court refused to recognize foreign judgment, the *Sabina Pandey* decision has been viewed as a precedent for non-recognition of foreign judgment in absence of a national legislation or a bilateral agreement. Lower courts have relied on the judgment of *Sabina* to deny recognition without considering the grounds on which refusal to recognize in *Sabina* was made. Furthermore, the ground of public policy as well was comprehended in a different way than was intended by the court to mean.

## 3.2 *Non Recognition of Foreign Judgments in* Sabina *and Public Policy*

The *Sabina Pandey* was heard by the division bench of the Supreme Court before it was reviewed by the full bench. The division bench had refused to recognize the decision on the basis of public policy. In doing so, the division bench held that the divorce law of Oklahoma is different than that of Nepal and the judgment on the divorce case made by the Oklahoma District Court against the national of Nepal, domiciled in Nepal on grounds other than stipulated in the divorce law of Nepal cannot be recognized, thus meaning the application of matrimonial law of the parties.

The Court went on to state that matrimonial disputes including divorce are categorized under criminal cases by the law of Nepal and the law of Nepal has determined grounds on which divorce can be granted as well as the procedures to be followed for deciding the case.[38] Moreover, in the situation where the respondent has not consented on getting divorced, recognizing the divorce judgment made by the Oklahoma Court on different grounds than stipulated in Nepalese law would be against public policy of Nepal.

During the proceedings before the full bench, the Court deliberated upon the public policy concerns in the recognition of the foreign judgment. In talking about public policy as a ground of non-recognition, the Court acknowledged the importance that the legal system of Nepal gives to women's right to property, especially the right of wife to have share in husband's property. The US law according to which the divorce case was decided by the Oklahoma District Court does not recognize such right of the wife and therefore recognizing such decision will be against the public policy of Nepal. The court also highlighted that *lexi domicili* of Sabina and *lex loci celebrationis* of the marriage is the law of Nepal.

Apart from the women's right to property, the Court in *Sabina Pandey* also identified access to justice as a component of public policy of Nepal. It held that since the petitioner was contesting the jurisdiction of the Oklahoma District court in the divorce case and was not present during the proceedings, denying jurisdiction of the court in Nepal to hear her claim would amount to denial of justice, which would be against the public policy of Nepal. Access to justice as a matter of public policy however was brought up not with respect to enforcement of foreign judgment but vis-à-vis jurisdiction on the domestic case.

Refusal to recognize foreign judgment in *Sabina Pandey* was also because of the lack of jurisdiction of the foreign court and denial of fair trial. The public policy exception to recognition and enforcement as interpreted by the Court cannot be considered on its own without taking note of the other factors. In fact the court laid more importance to the issue of submission to the jurisdiction of the foreign court. The court in *Sabina* therefore refused to recognize the foreign divorce case not on the ground that the law applied by the foreign court in making the decision did not have the same grounds for granting divorce thereby not recognizing women's right to property in the same extent alone, but because the defendant did not submit to the jurisdiction of the court, thereby not consenting to the application of US divorce law in her case.

Public policy as a ground of non-recognition as held in *Sabina Pandey* has to be understood with respect to the ground of non-submission. It is the refusal to submit to the jurisdiction of the foreign court that gave rise to situation where the recognition of the foreign judgment made in accordance to a foreign law would be against public policy. While the divorce law of Nepal requires that the wife in a

[38] n(37) s 1, 1A.

divorce case should be provided with her share in the husband's property while deciding a divorce application, a woman submitting to the jurisdiction of a foreign court and thereby consenting to the application of foreign law in the divorce case waives such right provided under Nepalese law.

The public policy exception as explained in *Sabina Pandey* is not applicable in cases where the party who is seeking the non-recognition actually submitted to the jurisdiction of the foreign court and thus accepted the competence of the foreign court to decide the case as well as agreed on the applicability of foreign law.

Post-*Sabina Pandey*, a number of similar cases have been filed in the courts of Nepal. In the case of *Srijana Ranjitkar*[39] the District Court relied on the principle of public policy to grant the divorced wife right to her husband's property irrespective of the fact that the wife-petitioner had acquired the nationality of the USA. In applying the public policy exception to recognition and enforcement, courts need to consider, *inter alia* the degree to which the parties have affiliated themselves with the forum.[40] In cases where the party against whom the recognition/enforcement is sought has sufficiently affiliated themselves with the forum, the foreign judgment is usually recognized.

Public policy is violated only if recognition or enforcement of the foreign-country judgment would clearly injure the public health, the public morals, or the public confidence in the administration of law, or would undermine "that sense of security for individual rights, whether of personal liberty or of private property, which any citizen ought to feel."[41] The Supreme Court in *Sabina Pandey* did not clarify on the meaning of public policy. The draft law was expected to provide some guideline on the scope of the public policy exception but it failed to do so.

## 4 Draft Civil Code on Private International Law

As an attempt to enact a law on private international law, legislators included a chapter on private international law in the Draft Civil Code 2067 (Nepali Calendar) (hereinafter, the Code). The objective behind the drafting of a new civil code was to reform and codify existing laws concerning civil matters. Although the initiation of the drafting of the civil code had begun before the Supreme Court issued an order to enact on private international law, it is quite apparent from the structure as well as the substance of the chapter on private international law that it was added to the code to comply with the Court's order. The chapter begins with the scope of application clause—it mentions that the chapter would be applicable to issues of

[39](n 36).

[40]Charles W. Mondora, 'The Public Policy Exception, "the Freedom of Speech, or of the press" and the uniform foreign-Country Money Judgments Recognition Act' (2008) 36 Hofstra L. Rev. 1139.

[41]*Hunt v BP Exploration Co. (Libya) Ltd* 580 F. Supp. 304 (1984).

private law involving foreigners, foreign objects or any act carried out in a foreign country.[42] It specifies rules relating to jurisdiction, choice of law, and recognition and enforcement of foreign judgment. The chapter made a detailed explanation of the provisions regarding choice of law. The chapter has one overriding rule according to which where any agreement to which Nepal is a party exists, the agreement will apply in spite of any contrary stipulation anywhere in the chapter and one residual rule which provides that matters not included in this chapter shall be decided on the basis of local law of Nepal and in absence of that, general principles of Private International law.

## 4.1 *Jurisdiction*

The Code suggests the basis of personal jurisdiction over persons as nationality and residence. It provides that the courts of Nepal have jurisdiction to hear cases between foreign nationals residing in Nepal or between a foreign national and a Nepalese, concerning subject matters regulated by the laws of Nepal. Regarding *jurisdiction in rem*, courts of Nepal are competent to hear cases regarding immovable property situated in Nepal, inheritance of property located in Nepal and belonging to a foreigner who was residing in Nepal at the time of death and disputes vis-à-vis any property located in Nepal between parties, at least one of them being a foreigner.

## 4.2 *Applicable Law*

Provisions relating to applicable law deal with specific topics such as property, marriage, adoption, guardianship, divorce, contract, and tort and determine connecting factors to determine the applicable laws in each area. Domicile as a connecting factor is absent. Nationality of the concerned person is the key connecting factor determining the applicable law in cases relating to personal and proprietary relationships between members of a family. Other connecting factors are habitual residence, current residence, country of registration in case of corporation and so on.

### 4.2.1 Marriage

The chapter suggests two scenarios where the problem of conflict of laws is likely to arise in cases of marriage,

(a) marriage involving a Nepalese citizen in a foreign country and
(b) marriage involving a foreign citizen in Nepal.

---

[42]Draft Civil Code 2015, no. 713.

In either of the situations, the law of the nationality of the parties shall determine the capacity of the parties to marriage and the *lex loci celebrationis* would determine the formal validity of the marriage.

> Any Nepali citizen getting married in a foreign country shall have the capacity to marry as required by the law of Nepal and the marriage shall comply with the formality as the law of the country of celebration requires.[43]

Similarly, in a marriage between foreigners or a foreigner and a Nepali citizen, the parties should comply with the rules of their respective country of nationality vis-à-vis capacity to marry and with the law of Nepal vis-à-vis formality of marriage.[44] However, in both the cases, if the marriage is celebrated within the territory of the foreign Embassy or consular office, the law of the particular country shall determine the formality of the marriage.

The rule of *lex loci celebrationis* to determine the formality of a marriage has been a fairly accepted rule of private international law.[45] Lord Dunedin in the case of *Berthiaume v Dastous*[46] stated "if there is one question better settled upon than any other in international law, it is that regards marriage-putting aside the question of capacity-*locus regit actum*".[47] The Hague Convention on Celebration and Recognition of the Validity of Marriages, 1978 stated that the formal requirements for marriages shall be governed by the law of the State of celebration.[48]

The question of capacity however has been a contending issue with different theories proposing varied connecting factors.[49] The most widely accepted theory is the theory of ante-nuptial domicile according to which the legal capacity of each party's country of domicile before the marriage determines the legal capacity of the parties to enter into marriage.[50] The provision of the Code in respect of legal capacity seems to be based on this theory as well, except that the connecting factor is not the domicile of the parties but their nationality.

---

[43]Draft Civil Code 2015, no. 721.

[44]Ibid.

[45]*Brook v Brook* (1861) 9 HLC 193; *Forbes v Forbes* (1854) 69 ER 145, *Johnson v Hazen* (1914) 43 NBR 154.

[46][1930] AC 79, 83.

[47]Ibid.

[48]Convention on Celebration and Recognition of the Validity of Marriages, 1978, Art 2. https://assets.hcch.net/docs/8e321c1a-9151-4608-a8a1-6dbee0f92cfd.pdf, accessed 29 July, 2016.

[49]JHC Morris, The Conflict of Laws (3rd edn, Stevens and Sons 1984) 159. There have been two rival theories on what law governs capacity to marry. According to the first theory, it is determined by the ante-nuptial domicile of the couple. The second theory states that the basic presumption is that the capacity is governed by the law of the husband's domicile but this presumption is rebutted if it can be inferred that the parties at the time of the marriage intended to establish their home in a certain country and they did in fact do so within a reasonable time.

[50]The Law Reform Commission, 'Report on Private International Law Aspects of Capacity to Marry and Choice of Law in Proceedings for Nullity of Marriage' (1985). http://www.lawreform.ie/_fileupload/Reports/rPrivateNullityofMarriage.html; *Pugh v Pugh* (1951) 2 All ER 680; *Brook v Brook* (1861) 9 HLC 193.

While nationality is easier to ascertain than domicile because it does not depend upon subjective criteria like intention, the criteria of domicile identifies a genuine connection of an individual to a particular country and hence, its laws. Having nationality as a connecting factor might give rise to difficulty in cases where individuals possess dual nationality. Nevertheless, the civil code has provided a solution by stipulating that in such situations, the law of the country of nationality where the person has habitual residence or in absence of such, the country of nationality to which he/she has the closest connection will be the applicable law.[51] The Code has however failed to anticipate situations where the habitual residence, or country with close connection for that matter, of the person concerned may be a third country, of which he/she is not a citizen. Another problem with nationality as a connecting factor arises if the court needs to determine whether the individual is a citizen of a certain country. Unlike domicile, *lex fori* can never say if a person is a citizen of a particular country or not, only the law of the concerned country can do vso.[52]

According to the Code, after the marriage, the marital relation and other consequences following the marriage shall be governed, in case both the spouse have the same nationality, by the law of the country of nationality and if they do not, the law of the country of habitual residence and if the country of habitual residence is not the same for both the parties, by the law of the country of current residence. If the consequence of marriage cannot be determined on any of these bases, the law of country where the marriage was celebrated will be applied in deciding the matter.[53]

The Code had deviated from its approach of nationality as the key connecting factor in matrimonial causes in cases of separation. According to the code, the issue of separation shall be governed by the law of the country of habitual residence of the couple. In cases where such country is not the same, by the law of the country where they were last residing habitually and if such country cannot be determined, by *lex fori*.[54]

### 4.2.2 Divorce

The only provision that the Code contains on divorce is the recognition and enforcement of foreign divorce judgments. It does not mention anything about the applicable law in divorce cases. From the clause on jurisdiction, it could be assumed that the courts of Nepal have jurisdiction in divorce cases (a) between foreigners residing in Nepal, (b) between a Nepali citizen and a foreigner, and (c) where the defendant is a foreigner residing in Nepal. On account of the residual rule, the applicable law in divorce cases involving private international law filed

[51]Draft Civil Code, 2015 no. 737.

[52]JHC Morris (n 49) 10.

[53]Draft civil code, 2015, no. 723.

[54]Ibid., no. 727.

before the courts of Nepal will always be the domestic law of Nepal, irrespective of the nationality of the parties to the divorce case.

The provision of choice of law to be applicable in divorce cases seems ironical given that the division bench of the Supreme Court in *Sabina Pandey* in refusing to recognize a foreign divorce judgment had based its decisions *inter alia* on the grounds of granting divorce being different in the foreign law than in the law of Nepal. The court had inferred that since the marriage was celebrated according to the law of Nepal, such law that provides different grounds for divorce could not dissolve it. Not only has the draft code mentioned that all divorce cases filed before the court of Nepal shall be decided according to the domestic law of Nepal, it also mentions that foreign divorce cases decided in accordance to the law of that country will be recognized and enforced in Nepal, thereby differing with the court's analysis.

## 5 Recognition and Enforcement of Foreign Judgment

There is only one clause in the Code concerning recognition and enforcement of foreign judgments. It states that divorce between Nepalese citizens or between Nepali citizen and a foreigner decided by a foreign court on the basis of the *lex fori* will be recognized and enforced by the courts of Nepal. The provision related to the applicable law governing capacity and formality of marriage specifies that marriage celebrated contrary to the provisions of this will not be recognized in Nepal. The Code is silent regarding the recognition and enforcement of other foreign judgments. Noting that the Supreme Court of Nepal ordered a directive to the government to legislate upon private international law rules the case of *Sabina Pandey* such legal provision could have either been an honest mistake or an ironical oversight. It is expected that the provisions on recognition and enforcement would be revised.

The Code's provision related to recognition and enforcement of foreign divorce decrees/orders is not far-reaching, as it requires recognition and enforcement of foreign judgments without mentioning any exceptions. Recognition and enforcement of foreign decisions without limitations is not a sound legislative methodology. Such recognition and enforcement entails an examination of several issues, including the jurisdiction of the foreign court to give the judgment, the finality of the judgment, and compliance with the principles of natural justice and due process, compatibility of the foreign judgment with public policy of the recognizing country.[55]

---

[55]Matthew B. Berlin, 'The Hague Convention on Choice of Court Agreements: Creating an International Framework for Recognizing Foreign Judgments' (2006) 3 BYU Int'l L. & Mgmt. Rev. 43; Susan L. Stevens, 'Commanding International Judicial Respect: Reciprocity and the Recognition and Enforcement of Foreign Judgments' (2002) 26 Hastings Int'l & Comp. L. Rev. 115.

The Code under the non-applicability clause mentions that in cases where the application of the provisions of the specified provisions of the Code would be against public order,[56] the same would not be applicable. This clause seems to provide a general exception to the applicability of the provisions of the specified provisions, which by derivation can be interpreted as an exception to the recognition of foreign judgments. A further reading of the clause however makes it clear that this particular exception is only intended for provisions regarding applicable law. The succeeding sub-clause states that in the event of the scenario exemplified in the sub-clause manifesting, the issue would be governed on the basis of other linking criteria and if such criteria cannot be determined, in accordance to the domestic law of Nepal.

## 5.1 Analysis of the Draft Civil Code

The Draft Civil Code is a significant step towards the development of private international law in Nepal. The law however needs a serious revision before its enactment.

The Code provides residence in Nepal as a sufficient ground for assuming jurisdiction over a foreigner. While it can be generally presumed that a court of a country has jurisdiction *in personam* over individuals who are present within its territory, the presumption is refuted if the defendant refuses to submit to the jurisdiction of the court. Mere residence in a particular country cannot render a person subject to the jurisdiction of its courts. Residence as an absolute ground to assume jurisdiction without any exception sounds problematic. Further, the Code does not stipulate submission as a ground of assuming jurisdiction.

There is no provision for courts to decline to hear a case on *forum non conveniens* grounds.[57] The Code has attempted to incorporate the concept of *lis alibi pendens* to some extent. Although the courts cannot per se refuse to assume jurisdiction in a case on ground of *lis alibi pendens*, courts can withhold a case where any case between the same parties on the same subject matter is pending in a foreign court and the decision of the court is likely to affect the case being heard by the court of Nepal. However, parties need to request the court for such withholding.

Regarding the choice of law in matrimonial disputes, the Code provides for applicable law in cases of marriage and separation. Divorce is mentioned but only with reference to recognition of foreign judgments. It is necessary that the Code covers various other aspects of matrimonial cases. For example, the law provides for legal capacity for marriage to be governed by the law of nationality and legal

---

[56]Draft Civil Code, 2015, s 751 para 6.

[57]The Code however has a provision that with respect to cases pending in the court of Nepal in which one party is a foreigner, if both the parties jointly submit in writing that the court of the nationality of the foreigner will be better suited to hear the case, the court shall allow for the case to heard by the foreign court. Draft Civil Code, no. 738.

formality by *lex loci celebrationis*. Yet, the law does not clarify as to which issues are considered as pertaining to capacity and which issues to formality. Parental consent, for instance is considered as an aspect addressed by the law governing formal validity in some countries while others consider it an issue of capacity.

With respect to divorce cases, the Code needs to specify with clarity the connecting factor in the determination of the applicable law. The Code in its existing form specified that all divorce cases involving foreign element would be decided by the local law of Nepal irrespective of the domicile or nationality of the parties which is likely to be problematic. For instance, the domestic divorce law of Nepal is based on the traditional concept of status of men and women in family/society and is therefore quite lenient towards the wife vis-à-vis right to the husband's property. Notwithstanding the grounds for the divorce, the wife to be divorced is entitled to share in husband's ancestral property. This may give rise to problems like forum shopping and non-recognition of judgments.

The provisions on choice of law do not address the issue of *renvoi*- it is unclear whether *renvoi* is applicable or excluded. The Code does not clarify whether the law of foreign country means its domestic law or the whole system of law, including private international law. With nationality as a major connecting factor in the draft law and majority of the legal systems stipulating domicile as the key connecting factor, the applicable law would be different if foreign law would mean its domestic law or whole system of law. For instance, the court of Nepal is faced with an application for decision on the validity of a marriage involving a national of country X domiciled in Nepal, where the dispute relates to her marriageable age. The draft law requires that the question pertaining to marriageable age is to be determined by the law of nationality, X and the conflict of law rules of X provides that it is governed by the law of the country of domicile and if choice of one law would render the marriage valid and the other void, the only question to be decided by the court is the applicable law. In the absence of the definition of foreign law, one party to the dispute would argue that foreign law means foreign domestic law thus concluding the marriage as void while the other would claim that it means whole legal system and hence the marriage is valid.

The provision related to recognition and enforcement of foreign judgment is very insignificant in the Code. It only requires for the recognition and enforcement of foreign divorce judgments, and to some extent, marriage. The position with regard to other family law-related issues is undetermined. If a court has to decide on the recognition of foreign judgments in cases other than these, there is pretty much no assistance it can except from the draft law, if it were to be passed as legislation as it is.

Besides, exceptions to recognition and enforcement of foreign judgments need to be included in the draft law. The decision of the Supreme Court in *Sabina Pandey* can be a good reference while drafting provisions regarding the exceptions. The court had refused to recognize foreign judgment on the grounds of absence of jurisdiction, fair trial lacunae and public policy and its obiter dicta had mentioned other grounds, which need to be considered while deciding on the recognition of foreign judgments.

The Hague Conventions on Private International Law could be used as a reference for revisions of the provisions of the Code. Although Nepal is not a member of the Hague Conference, taking into consideration its provisions and incorporating them as far as practicable in the local law would be a wise step to contribute towards promoting harmonization of conflict of law rules as well as ensure wider recognition of the decisions rendered by Nepalese courts.

## 6 Conclusion

Private international law has seen an increased presence in Nepal's courts in the last decade, especially since the *Sabina Pandey* decision. In the last 6 years there were four important decisions in matrimonial law issues having a foreign element, and others are awaiting appeal or final judgment. Although the Supreme Court issued a directive to the government to enact necessary legislation on private international law almost six years ago, that directive has not been implemented as yet, leaving the courts to take help from the unwritten conflict of laws rules borrowed from other jurisdictions while deciding cases of private international law. Lack of specific legislation has resulted in conflicting court decisions there by creating uncertainty in the law on the subject.

The Code with a chapter on private international law is a welcome step, but needs to be significantly revised to cover all the issues related to private international law, especially recognition of foreign judgments. The Code needs a serious revision before being enacted in order to ensure its efficacy.

# Cross-Border Divorce—Sri Lankan State Practice

M.P.S. Kaushani Pathirana

**Abstract** The increased number of Non Resident Sri Lankans and international marriages have given rise to a host of cross-border legal problems. The current chapter discuses one of the contentious areas of Sri Lankan family law dealing with cross-border divorce. The chapter elaborates the Sri Lankan legal system to understand the different personal law applicable to questions of marriage. The paper will focus on the statutory and the judicial approach developed towards the recognition of cross border divorce under Sri Lankan legal system. The chapter will also look at the three important strands of Private International Law in the form of Jurisdiction, choice of law and enforcement of foreign judgment. The chapter will also focus on Sri Lanka's association with Hague Conference on Private International Law in the sphere of matrimonial matters.

**Keywords** Conflicts of laws · Public policy · Foreign divorce recognition · Divorce laws · Sri Lanka · Personal laws

## Introduction

The definition of 'Marriage' upon which the concept of marriage was established and applied in the common law has been borrowed from a definition of marriage set out by the English courts in *Hyde v Hyde.*[1]

> ....that marriage as...... defined as the voluntary union for life of one man and one woman, to the exclusion of all others.[2]

In countries like Sri Lanka, India and most of the developing countries that have once been under the British colonial rule (except the former British possessions in

[1] *Hyde v Hyde* [1866] Lr 1 P&D 130.
[2] Ibid. 133.

M.P.S. Kaushani Pathirana (✉)
Department of Private and Comparative Law, Faculty of Law,
University of Colombo, Colombo, Sri Lanka
e-mail: kaushipathirana@gmail.com; kaushani.law@cmb.ac.lk

© Springer Nature Singapore Pte Ltd. 2017

S.R. Garimella and S. Jolly (eds.), *Private International Law*,
DOI 10.1007/978-981-10-3458-9_8

the Caribbean) dual matrimonial regimes have been recognized. In some countries, similar to Sri Lanka, there are poly-matrimonial regimes. Sri Lanka has mainly three legal regimes governing matrimonial relationships; the General Law, the Kandyan Law and the Islamic Law. Each of these systems provides their own peculiar matrimonial regimes.[3] A monogamous regime originated from a Christian colonial power and a polygamous regime founded upon the local religions and customs are made available to the inhabitants of each of these territories.[4]

The private international law applied in Sri Lanka corresponds to the principles and rules recognized by the English courts, subject to the modifications by statutes.[5] English principles governing domicile of origin and of choice are applicable in Sri Lanka.[6] The rules of civil procedure were embodied in the Civil Procedure Code of 1889; it was replaced by the Civil Procedure Code (Amendment) Law of 1977.

**Structure of the Chapter**

This chapter attempts to address the current legal framework on the divorce proceedings of Sri Lanka and its application on matrimonial issues that have a foreign element. The chapter will further discuss the jurisdiction-related issues in divorce proceedings in conflict of laws of Sri Lanka and jurisdictional issues in actions for the decree of nullity; the situation related to personal laws of Sri Lanka; choice of law in divorce proceedings and the position with regard to conflict of laws rules applicable in the Sri Lankan law; recognition and enforcement of foreign divorce judgements, decrees and public policy; and Sri Lanka's engagement with the Hague Conventions.

## 1 The Legal System of Sri Lanka

The legal system of Sri Lanka could be arranged into two categories—the common Law i.e. Roman-Dutch Law(civil) and the Customary Law. There is, further, a third category, the statutes, that refers to subject-matters that are addressed, either within the Common Law or the Common Law Personal Law. The Roman-Dutch Law in British times came to be applied in all situations in which there was no relevant statute and in case of those Ceylonese (people belonging to Ceylon, the colonial name of Sri Lanka) subject to the special/personal laws, where those laws were inapplicable or silent.[7] The customary laws are personal as well as territorial. For

[3]Lakshman Marasinghe, 'The Abeysundere Decision- Polygamy v. Bigamy: An area for reform' (2005) 41 Meezan-Law Students' Muslim Majlis, 94.

[4]Ibid., 94.

[5]Cheshire, North & Fawcett, *Private International Law*, (14th Edition, Oxford University Press).

[6]*Annakedde v Myappen* [1932] 33 NLR 198; *Thevagnana Sekeran v Kuppammal* [1934] 36 NLR 337.

[7]L.J.M. Cooray, *An Introduction to the Legal System of Sri Lanka*, (A Stamford lake Publication, 2009) 11.

instance, the Kandyan Law is applicable to all residents of Kandy, and also whose ethnicity is Sinhalese. It does not apply to Sinhalese who are not resident of the Kandy province. However, the impact on the Common Law system derived from the English Law has had a much greater influence on the Laws of Sri Lanka than the Roman-Dutch Law. Yet, the Roman-Dutch Law remains the residuary or the common law of Sri Lanka. Needless to say, the Common Law has been modified in many directions, expressly and by necessary implication by our statute law and also by the judicial decisions.[8] The influence of English law is extensively apparent in the procedural law of Sri Lanka. The Criminal Procedure Code of 1898, which was the same as the Indian enactment, was replaced by the Administration of Justice Law of 1973 and which in turn was replaced by the Code of Criminal Procedure Act of 1979.[9] The rules of civil procedure which were embodied in the Civil Procedure Code of 1889 were derived from the rules of Indian procedural law, English Rules of Court and the New York Civil Procedure Code was replaced by the Civil Procedure Code (Amendment) Law of 1977.[10]

## 1.1 The Diversity of Personal Laws in Sri Lanka

The existing personal laws of Sri Lanka are multi-ethnic since the population of Sri Lanka is composed of Sinhalese, Tamils and Muslims and a few other ethnic groups like Moors, Brugher (of Eurasian descent). The personal laws that exist in Sri Lanka are the Kandyan Law, The Thesawalamai and the Muslim Law.[11]

The Kandyan Law applies as a personal law to a category of Sinhalese who are deemed to be Kandyans. Although the Sinhala laws are now called Kandyan Law, it was so termed only in the 19th century, by the Europeans, as the Kandyan Kingdom was the only region that exclusively applied the Sinhala laws as the law of the land.[12] Many writers pointed out that the so called 'Kandyan law' was the applicable law in the Kandyan provinces.[13] Being the territorial law, it applied to all residents of the Kandyan provinces. The legal distinction between Kandyan Sinhalese and Low Country Sinhalese was established in the cases of *Williams*

[8]Ibid.

[9]Cooray (n 7) 12.

[10]Ibid.

[11]S.W.E. Goonesekere, The Application of the Personal Laws in Sri Lanka, (1985) FESTSCHEIFT M.C. Sansoni, 77.

[12]L. Marasinghe & S. Scharenguivel, *Compilation of Selected aspects of the Special laws of Sri Lanka* (2015, Vijitha Yapa Publications) 3.

[13]Modder, Hayley etc., Ibid., 3–4, However, it is clear that certain sections of the Sinhala population of the Maritime provinces were governed by the Dutch law, it is unlikely that the Portuguese or the Dutch actually attempted to apply *in toto* their own laws to the Sinhalese of the maritime Provinces. (Ralph Peiris, *Cleghorn Minute*, (1953) 3 Royal Asiatic Society Journal 125–152.

*v Robertson*[14] and *Wijesinghe v Wijesinghe*,[15] where it was held that the Kandyan law was applicable only to Kandyan Sinhalese settled in the Kandyan provinces, and therefore a low-country Sinhalese, though settled in Kandyan provinces is not governed by the Kandyan Law. While the Court did not, in these two cases, define the applicability of the Kandyan Law, it made few illustrative statements; such statements were however visible in later decisions.[16]

*Thesawalamai* applies as a personal law only to those Tamils, also called as Malabar inhabitants of the Jaffna Peninsula, who established a permanent home in the Northern Province and as a territorial law of the lands situated in the Northern Province, regardless of whether the owners reside there or not.[17] The primary source of the *Thesawalamai* is the *Thesawalamai* Code, which is a compilation of the customs of Jaffna in 1707 and it received statutory recognition by the Regulation No. 18 of 1806.[18]

The Muslim Law is considered as the personal law the religious law applies to all Muslims, either by birth or conversion, who are inhabitants of Sri Lanka. The Muslims of Sri Lanka belonged to different ethnicities during the colonial era.[19] In 1806, after the colonization of Sri Lanka by the British, the special laws (the *Shaffie* law) of the Muslims of the province of Colombo were codified[20] and then applied throughout the country as the Muslim Law of the country, despite the existence of other sects.[21] The personal law of the Muslims is now codified into a few legislations and Ordinances,[22] the content of the law that was codified was largely drawn from the traditional law of the Shaffie sect; the Muslim Marriages and Divorce Act (hereinafter, the MMDA) states that the law of the sect shall be applicable to the members of that sect.[23] Sri Lankan courts have consistently held that since the

---

[14][1886] 8 SCC 36.

[15](1891) 9 S.C.C. 199.

[16]*Kapuruhamy v Appuhamy* [1910] 13 NLR 321; *Mudiyanse v Appuhamy* [1913] 16 NLR 117, *Punchihamy v Punchihamy* [1915] 18 NLR 294.

[17]Goonesekere (n 11) 86, *Spencer v Rajaratnam* [1913] 16 NLR 321, 322, see further, N. Selvakkumaran, 'The applicability of Thesawalamai: Sivananalingam v Sunderalingam' (1991) 7 Colombo LR 148.

[18]Cooray (n 7) 143.

[19]The Ceylon Moors (of Arab descent), the Coast Moors (of Indian descent) and the Malays who were brought to Ceylon by the Dutch and British from Indonesia, Malaysia, and Sumatra to serve as soldiers. In addition, the Borahs and the Memons also form part of the Muslim community. These communities are North Indian business communities who settled in Sri Lanka during the British period. Further see, L. Marasinghe, S. Scharenguivel, *Compilation of Selected aspects of the Special laws of Sri Lanka* (2015, Vijitha Yapa Publications) 255–265.

[20]Marasinghe, Scharenguivel (n 12) 260.

[21]There are a few Muslims who follow the Hanafi sect, as well as a very small group of Shiites from the Imamiyah School. Ibid., p. 260.

[22]Muslim Marriage and Divorce Act No. 13 of 1951; Muslim Intestate Succession and Wakf Ordinance No. 10 of 1931, Muslim Mosques, Charitable Trusts and Wakf Act No. 51 of 1965.

[23]Muslim Marriage and Divorce Act No 13 of 1951, Section 16 and 98(2); See Saleem Marsoof, 'The Muslim Marriage Law Applicable in Sri Lanka' (2006) Law College LR 33, 34.

Muslims in Sri Lanka largely belong to the *Shaffie* sect, the *Shaffie* doctrine is generally applicable in the matters relating to rights and obligations of the parties in their marriage and divorce. The party should be presumed to be *Shaffie* unless there is evidence to prove otherwise.[24] The scope of application of the Muslim Law in Sri Lanka is limited; it is applicable to the Muslims in the areas of marriage, divorce, succession and charitable trusts.[25]

For the population not covered by the above-mentioned personal laws, such as Non-Kandyan Sinhalese, Tamils not governed by the *Thesawalamai* etc., are governed by the General law of the land i.e. Roman-Dutch Law.[26]

## *1.2 The Divorce Law of Sri Lanka*

In the general law of Sri Lanka, the grounds for divorce, judicial separation and nullity of marriage set out in the statutory law—substantive and procedural laws—are equally applicable to men and women without any distinction. The Marriage Registration (General) Ordinance[27] specified

> No marriage shall be dissolved during the lifetime of the parties except by judgement of divorce a *vincula matrimonii* pronounced in some competent court.[28]

A prominent feature of the statutory grounds for divorce applicable in modern Sri Lanka is the synchronized application of the two widely differing criteria for the dissolution of a marriage. On the one hand, the Marriage Registration (General) Ordinance[29] requires proof of adultery subsequent to marriage, malicious desertion or incurable impotency to cease a marriage and on the other hand, the amended Civil Procedure Code[30] enacts that a decree of judicial separation may be converted to a decree of divorce after the lapse of two years and that a mere separation a *mensa at thoro* for a period of seven years is sufficient to find an action for divorce.[31]The basic difference between the diverse systems of law operating in the country also become clear on an examination of the subject of dissolution of

---

[24]*Mangandi Umma v Lebbe Marikkar* [1908] 10 NLR 1; *Marikkar v Marikkar* [1916] 18 NLR 446.

[25](n 22).

[26]Goonesekere (n 11) 77–83.

[27]Marriage Registration (General) Ordinance No. 19 of 1907 (Cap. 112).

[28]S. Ponnambalam, *Law and the Marriage Relationship in Sri Lanka*, (2nd revised edition, Stamford lake Publication, 2011) 311.

[29]No. 19 of 1907.

[30]Civil Procedure Code, No. 02 of 1889 (as amended).

[31]*Muthurani v Thuraisingham* [1984] 1 SLR 381.

marriage.[32] The grounds for divorce under the general law Roman-Dutch Law apply to the people who are governed by Tesawalamai.

The Kandyan Law and the Muslim Law recognize eligibility for matrimonial relief on the grounds of breakdown of marriage and both laws permit the parties to get divorce on mutual consent. However, the grounds for the grant of matrimonial relief differ under the common law; matrimonial relief can be obtained on matrimonial fault consequent on the repudiation of the basic obligation of marriage. Matrimonial relief can also be availed under the relevant provisions of the Kandyan Law and the Muslim Law in accordance with a very simple, convenient procedure.[33]

The grounds for divorce under Kandyan Law as described in the Kandyan Marriage and Divorce Act (hereinafter, the KMDA)[34] are adultery by wife after marriage, adultery by husband coupled with incest or gross cruelty, complete and continued desertion for a continuous period of 2 years by either of the spouses, inability to live happily together, of which actual separation from marital home for a period of one year.[35] It is significant to note that the adultery of the husband without the offence of incest or gross cruelty is not a ground for divorce for a Kandyan wife to obtain divorce from her husband. This provision within the substantive law appears to be discriminatory. Further, the divorce mutual consent of both parties or inability to live in cordiality (which ground could be proved by separation for one year) are also allowed under the Kandyan Law.[36] No case need to be instituted and the parties can appear before an administrative officer and obtain a divorce by making representations.[37]

The option of divorce by mutual consent is also a feature of the Muslim Law of Sri Lanka.[38] However, under the Sri Lankan Muslim Law, there are noticeable differences between the grounds on which a wife could obtain divorce from her husband, and the grounds available for the husband to obtain divorce from his wife. A Muslim husband has an inherent right to divorce his wife without giving any reason to the Court (preliminary *Kathii/Quazi* courts) and the court also has no jurisdiction to refuse the request of the husband. On the other hand, when a Muslin wife seeks a divorce against her husband, she should satisfy the court by proving the husband's faults or the ill-treatment meted out her by the husband. If a Muslim wife needs to obtain a divorce from her husband when there is no fault or ill treatment on his part, she has to get the husband's consent for divorce and she also has to pay compensation to him. Under the Muslim Law too, a husband unilaterally

[32]N. Samarasundera, *Women and Domestic Law and Life in Sri Lanka and the SAARC Countries* (Godage International Publishers, 2011).

[33]Ibid.

[34]No. 44 of 1952.

[35](n 34) S. 32.

[36]Ibid.

[37]Ibid., Ss 32(2)(f), 33.

[38](n 23).

declaring *talaq* is entitled to a divorce from his wife. A judicial trial is not required, but a procedure for bringing reconciliation between the parties is available.[39]

There is, however, a possibility to prove 'fault' of adultery, malicious desertion or incurable impotency under the common law and obtain a divorce or a judicial separation.[40] However, this relief is available only through a court action. The Muslim Law of Sri Lanka permits a Muslim woman to obtain divorce from her husband only on the grounds of cruelty of the husband; in comparison with the Marriage Registration (General) Ordinance and Kandyan Law, such ground of divorce is not available for non-Muslim women. However, the above-mentioned narrative on Muslim law illustrates the difficulty of obtaining divorce for a Muslim women, as compared to a Muslim man. A perusal of the above mentioned provisions show that the law is discriminatory towards women.

It would be clear from the foregoing that there are basic differences between the Kandyan Law, the Muslim Law, and the General Law with regard to the grounds for matrimonial relief as well as in the procedure to obtain relief. Samarasundera suggested law reform especially with regard to the procedure to claim matrimonial relief.[41]

Nonetheless, in the present law, divorce by mutual consent is almost available for those who are governed by the General Law. Consequently, it is easy to obtain a divorce when the defendant agrees not to contest the case. Although collusion is not an impediment, in reality, there is the possibility of a case succeeding even under collusion.[42] This position, it would appear, has not changed under the amended Civil Procedure Code. The practice of gaining a divorce under mutual agreement is not illegal and is considered a legitimate process.

## *1.3 Special/Personal Laws on Divorce in Sri Lanka*

Sri Lanka has three matrimonial law regimes derived from customary law as well as common law—the General Law, Kandyan Law and Muslim Law. A legal regime for monogamous marriages acquired from a Christian colonial power and a legal regime for polygamous marriages founded upon the local religions and customs are made available to the inhabitants of each of these territories.[43] Where such a duality in the matrimonial regimes exists mutation from one system to another was made possible.

[39](n 23) S. 27.

[40]General Marriage Ordinance Section 19, Administration of Justice (amendment) Law, Section 267(1).

[41]Samarasundera (n 32).

[42]Ibid.

[43]Marasinghe (n 3) 94.

The laws relating to divorce under the Kandyan customary law were based on a concept which is a mixture of fault-based and non fault-based systems, whereas the grounds of divorce in General Law are based purely on matrimonial fault. The law relating to Kandyan divorce is now contained in the KMDA. A divorce under this Act is available only to the spouses who were married under the KMDA.[44] Marriage between a Kandyan man and a foreign woman or a foreign man and a Kandyan woman should be solemnized under the Marriage Registration (General) Ordinance and not according to the KMDA.[45]

With reference to the MMDA[46] of Sri Lanka, there is no difference in the applicability of the Muslim Law, irrespective of the person being a Muslim by birth or is a convert to Islam. This situation is adopted in the case of *Christopher Abeysundera v Nataliya Abeysundera*[47] wherein the petitioner converted into Islam and married again, within four weeks of his divorce application in the first marriage being rejected. However, in this case the conversion to Islam was not accepted, as the Court saw that as a colourable conversion, to gain advantage of a regime that allowed polygamy.

It may be recalled here that the dual matrimonial regime dates back to 1876 when the colonial administration enacted the Matrimonial Rights Ordinance.[48] This was the precursor to the General Marriage Ordinance of today. In that 1876 Ordinance and the current General Marriage Ordinance, Section 2 excluded the application of its provisions to the Mohammedans. It comes from the colonial days to introduce into the colony of Ceylon a dual matrimonial regime.[49] Further, in 1886 the Mohammedan Marriage Registration Ordinance[50] was first enacted. The 1886 ordinance has been to codify the existing Mohammedan law of the time.

An important decision on the dual matrimonial regime and the applicability of personal laws is the *King v Perumal*[51] decision. It is pertinent to recall the facts of this case. A Hindu Tamil domiciled in British India, and went through a ceremony that constituted a valid marriage at the place of domicil, went through a marriage with a Burgher lady in Kandy province in Ceylon, where he has since acquired residence. In an action for bigamy under the Penal Code of Ceylon, he claimed that the *Tesawalmai* Code permitted polygamy.[52] The Court held that the accused,

---

[44]Marasinghe, Scharenguivel (n 12) 36.

[45]KMDA (n 34) Ss 2&3.

[46]MMDA (n 23).

[47]*Abeysundere v Abeysundere* [1998] 1 Sri LR 185.

[48]Matrimonial Rights Ordinance No. 15 of 1876.

[49]Marasinghe (n 3) 95.

[50]Mohammaden Marriage Registration Ordinance No. 8 of 1886.

[51]*King v Perumal* [1912] 14 NLR 496 (Supreme Court of Ceylon).

[52]Ibid. 497.

Perumal was domiciled in British India, and underwent a marriage ceremony with rituals that confirmed the valid marriage under the Hindu law of his region. Further the Court held that the *Tesawalamai* code was not applicable in the case of the accused as he was not a resident of the area of the law's application, nor did he have any descent in the Northern regions of the country where the law was applicable.[53] The Supreme Court proceeded to hold that polygamy as being obnoxious to public policy of Ceylon.[54]

The universal validity of the law of domicile in Private International Law was recognized as governing a person's capacity to marry. But it was held to be subservient to the domestic law of Ceylon—the law of the place of his residence. The Court, therefore, refused to accept the contention of the accused's counsel that the private international law rule of domicile ought to be applicable, holding further that polygamy being prohibited by the Municipal law of Ceylon, made contracting a second marriage violative of the law, and hence the conviction was affirmed. The rule of domicile was refused to be recognized, because there was no express exception to the rule of polygamy available under the law applicable to the accused, unlike the Muslim law where such express exception was available.

What is grievous and unpardonable is that the court in 1998 in *Abeysundre*[55] ignored the abundance of authority that there was, but perhaps not made available to the court, since the watershed decision of *Sinha Peerage*[56] especially the principle that notwithstanding the fact that a marriage may be potentially polygamous at its inception, it could subsequently become converted or mutated into a monogamous marriage[57] at a later stage. If the court had examined those decisions, referred to the above, the error of jurisprudence, it would have become abundantly clear. *Abeysundere* gives the appearance of a pre-1946 decision, delivered in 1998, as if the development of the law between 1946–1998, had been a mere mirage.[58] As Prof. Marasinghe commented[59] dual matrimonial regimes allow for the co-existence of monogamy and polygamy, with both the regimes resulting in valid marriages that continue to co-exist. This co-existence allows for an inference that a person, therefore, could move from one regime to another. One of the methods by which such a movement may take place is by conversion. The point that needs emphasis is that in a dual matrimonial regime the second polygamous marriage does materialise into a valid marriage, valid according to the polygamous law and therefore by definition, there could not be conviction for bigamy. However, while

---

[53]Id, 497–498.

[54]Id, 499.

[55](n 47).

[56][1946] 1 All ER 348.

[57]M.L. Marasinghe, 'Polygamous Marriages and the Principle of Mutation in the Conflict of Laws' (1978) 24 McGill LJ 394, 398.

[58]Marasinghe (n 3) 95–96.

[59]Prof. Lakshman Marasinghe, Abeysundere vs. Abeysundere: Monogamy, Polygamy and Bigamy – A Conundrum, The Island, 8th April 1998, 9th April 1998 and 11th April 1998.

the *Abeyesundere* decision may help in discouraging colourable conversions to take advantage of the personal law features, it also stands as a decision overlooking the precedent on the subject in Sri Lanka[60] as well as the incorporation of change by recognizing the validity of polygamous unions in claims made under the personal law where such unions were valid, elsewhere in the world.[61]

## 2 Jurisdiction in Divorce Proceedings in Conflict of Laws of Sri Lanka

In considering the jurisdiction related issues in the matrimonial actions of Sri Lanka, it is necessary to recall the position of the common law—jurisdiction is based on domicile of the disputants at the time of the initiation of proceedings.[62] The basis of the rule vesting exclusive jurisdiction in the court of common domicile is considered as the 'status theory', which is also consistent with the rule of the unity of domicile.[63] Some factors that could help reach a decision on domicile are

- that the parties changed their domicile before the proceedings, or
- that one or both of the parties are not resident in the court's jurisdiction at the time of commencement of the action, or
- that the matrimonial offence was committed outside the court's jurisdiction, or
- that the offence committed is not a ground for divorce in the place of its occurred, or
- that the marriage was solemnized outside the court's area that will not affect the jurisdiction of the court to entertain a petition for divorce.[64]

Nevertheless, the basis of the Sri Lankan courts' jurisdiction in a divorce matter having a foreign element is the 'residence' as specified in Section 09 of the Civil Procedure Code.

Subject to the pecuniary or other limitations prescribed by any law, action shall be instituted in the court within the local limits of whose jurisdiction

(a) a party defendant resides; or [emphasis added]
(b) the land in respect of which the action is brought lies or is situated in whole or in part; or
(c) the cause of action arises; or
(d) the contract sought to be enforced was made.

---

[60]In *Attorney General v Reid* (67 NLR 25) the Privy Council held that a person belonging to a non-Islam religion, converts to Islam and marries a person belonging to that faith during the subsistence of the first marriage contracted before conversion to Islam, as not guilty of bigamy.

[61]See for example, *Shahnaz v Rizwan* [1965] 1 Q.B. 390 [Winn J.].

[62]Ponnambalam (n 28) 370.

[63]*Le Mesurier v Le Mesurier* [1895] A.C. 517, 539–540, 541.

[64]Ponnambalam (n 28) 371.

## 2.1 The Decision of Le Mesurier and Its Impact

A seminal decision on jurisdiction has been the ratio of the court in *LeMesurier v Le Mesurier*[65] (hereinafter, the *LeMesurier*). The moot question for decision was whether the Sri Lankan courts possessed jurisdiction to dissolve a marriage between a British national and a French lady. The marriage had been solemnized in England and from the date of their marriage until the commencement of the action for divorce upon the allegation of adultery, the spouses had lived in Ceylon. The appellant contended that though residing in Ceylon, he had retained his English domicile of origin. When the appellant instituted the action before the District Court of Matara, the defendant argued that the District Court had no jurisdiction to entertain the suit. However, the District Court judge ruled for existence of jurisdiction to proceed in the suit by virtue of the Civil Procedure Code[66] and granted *decree nisi* to become absolute in four months unless good cause was shown against it.

The Supreme Court, nevertheless, reversed the decision of the District judge on the reasoning that the courts of Ceylon had no jurisdiction to dissolve a marriage between a British and a European national resident in the island. Ponnambalam commented that the Chief Justice and the Acting Puisne Judge opined that by virtue of the Royal Charter of 1801[67] British and European residents in the island were to be governed by the law of England.[68]

On appeal to the Privy Council, however, it was observed by their Lordships that the Charter of 1801 was revoked and annulled by the Ceylon Charter of Justice in 1833 and that there had been no legislation regulating the jurisdiction of the courts of Ceylon in matrimonial causes arising between the British and European spouses. They concluded that subsequent to the Charter of 1833, those kinds of spouses resident in Ceylon were governed by the Roman-Dutch Law, which was introduced to the island by the Royal Proclamation of 1799. Their Lordships had to then decide whether the Roman-Dutch law permitted the District Court to dissolve a marriage contracted in England between the British who still retain their English domicile, but reside within the forum. Their Lordships cited *Brodie v Brodie*[69] and *Jack v Jack*,[70] as well as other English and Scottish judgements and concluded that there could be no satisfactory canon of international law regulating jurisdiction in divorce cases, which was not capable of being enunciated with sufficient precision to ensure practical uniformity in its application. Further, it was commented that the Court concluded that according to international law, the domicile for the time being of the married couple affords the only true test of jurisdiction to dissolve their

[65]*Lemesurier v Le Mesurier* [1895] 1 NLR 160.

[66]Civil Procedure Code, No. 2 of 1889, S. 597.

[67]Section 53.

[68]Ponnambalam (n 28) 372–373.

[69](2 S & T 259).

[70]*Jack v Jack* 24 Sess. Ca. 2nd Series 467 cited in *Le Mesurier v Le Mesurier* [1895] 1 NLR 160, 169.

marriage.[71] Therefore it could be surmised that the persons domiciled in Sri Lanka alone despite residence abroad could obtain a divorce in Sri Lanka.

The *Lemesurier* court cited Lord Penzance in *Wilson v Wilson*[72]

> It is the strong inclination of my own opinion that the only fair and satisfactory rule to adopt on this matter of jurisdiction is to insist upon the parties in all cases referring their matrimonial differences to the courts of the country in which they were domiciled. Different communities have different views and the laws respecting matrimonial obligations, and a further different estimation of the causes that would justify an order divorce. It is both just and reasonable; therefore, that the differences of married people should be adjusted in accordance with the law of the community to which they belong, and dealt with by the tribunals which alone can administer those laws. An honest adherence to this principle, moreover, will preclude the scandal which arises when a man and woman are held to be man and wife in one country, and strangers in another.[73]

In order to cure the hardship caused by the above mentioned legal situation, the Indian and Colonial Jurisdiction Act of 1926 was enacted. This legislation was made applicable to Ceylon by the Ceylon Divorce Jurisdiction Order in Council by virtue of which the Supreme Court of Ceylon was granted the original civil jurisdiction to make decrees for dissolution of marriage when the parties were British subjects domiciled in England or Scotland on grounds for which a dissolution of a marriage may be granted by the High Court in England according to the law for the time being in force.[74]

The Supreme Court of Ceylon was vested with the jurisdiction to dissolve a marriage only where it was proved that the petitioner resided in Ceylon at the time of presenting the petition; and that the parties had last resided together in Ceylon and that either the marriage was solemnized in Ceylon, or the adultery or crime complained of was committed in Ceylon.[75] The alternative requirement that the marriage should have been solemnized in Ceylon was held to have no application to suits on grounds other than 'adultery, cruelty or crime'.[76]

In *Wooldridge v Wooldridge*[77] the petitioner in an action for dissolution of marriage on the allegation of desertion, pleaded the jurisdiction of the Ceylon Court on the basis of the matrimonial domicile, despite the marriage being solemnized outside the jurisdiction of Ceylon. The Supreme Court had to decide whether this fact had the effect of denying the Ceylon court's jurisdiction. According to Keuneman S.P.J., under the new proviso for Section 1 of the Indian and the

[71]Ponnambalam (n 28) 373.

[72](1872) L.R. 2 P. & M. 435.

[73]*Le Mesurier* (n 65) 176; See also *Case v Case* 37 T.L.R 499; *Wright v Wright* [1903] 9 N.L.R 516.

[74]Ponnambalam (n 28) p. 373.

[75]Ibid., 374.

[76]*Wooldridge v Wooldridge* [1945] 46 NLR 516.

[77][1945] 46 NLR 516.

Colonial Divorce Jurisdiction Act of 1926[78] there are two conditions necessary to prove in all suits for the dissolution of marriage,

(i) the plaintiff ought to be Ceylon at the time of presenting the petition, and
(ii) that the parties to the marriage must have last resided together in Ceylon.

The Law also has a special provision for suits where a dissolution of marriage is pleaded on ground of 'adultery, cruelty or crime' and in such suits; there is the further requirement that the marriage must have been solemnized in Ceylon or that the 'adultery, cruelty or crime' must have been committed in Ceylon. Hence, in *Wooldridge*, the court held that there was no statutory bar to the granting of a decree of dissolution of marriage.[79]

In *Morris v Morris*[80] the petitioner was a native and a permanent resident of Ceylon while her husband was a European, domiciled in England, and the Supreme Court of Ceylon was held to have jurisdiction to entertain the petition for divorce.

In *Annakedde v Meyappen*[81] the petititioner applied for the dissolution of marriage on the grounds of malicious desertion by her husband while the defendant claimed divorce on the ground of the wife's adultery. The defendant was an Indian Tamil who had come to Ceylon as a child of six years with his mother. He had remained in Ceylon and had never been to India. He married in Ceylon and claimed that he knew no other home than Ceylon and that as such, he had a Ceylon domicile. Garvin S.P.J. held on the above evidence that the defendant had a Ceylon domicile, and that consequently the court had jurisdiction to entertain the petition for divorce.

The position in the modern law of Sri Lanka, however, is different as the Ceylon Independence Act of 1947 specified,

> No court in Ceylon shall by virtue of the Indian and Colonial Jurisdiction Acts 1926 and 1940, have jurisdiction in or in relation to any proceedings for a decree for the dissolution of a marriage, unless those proceedings were instituted before the appointed day, but, save as aforesaid and subject to any provisions to the contrary which may hereafter be made by any Act of the Parliament of the United Kingdom or of Ceylon, all courts in Ceylon shall have the same jurisdiction under the said Acts as they would have had if this Act had not been passed.[82]

## 2.2 Asokan V Asokan *and the Consequences*

The *Le Mesurier* ratio prescribed the primacy of the domicile as the determinant factor and that ratio lead to the derivation that the people domiciled in Sri Lanka,

[78]As amended in 1940.

[79]Ponnambalam (n 28) 375.

[80](1938) 40 NLR 246.

[81](1932) 33 NLR 198.

[82]Ceylon Independence Act, S. 3(1).

even if resident abroad, obtain a decree of divorce only in Sri Lanka and that the people who were domiciled abroad could not obtain a decree of divorce within the jurisdiction of Sri Lanka. However, this position was distinguished in the case of *Asokan Nee Kandasamy v Asokan*[83] (hereinafter, *Asokan*).

In the case of *Asokan*, plaintiff (wife) and defendant (husband) were married in India. The parties lived in India, however, the plaintiff had to vacate the matrimonial home owing to the matrimonial fault, i.e. constructive malicious desertion of the defendant. A divorce suit was filed in the District Court of Colombo where the plaintiff now lives. It was decided that the plaintiff is entitled to present a plaint in the District Court of Colombo as she resides within the jurisdiction of the courts in terms of Section 597 of the Civil Procedure Code. Malicious desertion is a valid ground for dissolution of marriage, according to the law applicable in Sri Lanka as set out in Section 19 of the Marriages (General) Ordinance. Jurisdiction is not affected by the fact that the malicious desertion took place in India and the fact that the husband is domiciled in India.[84]

Section 19 of the General Marriage Ordinance read with Section 24 of the Judicature Act and also with Section 3 of the Judicature Amendment Act No. 71 of 1981, reveals that divorce jurisdiction is exercisable by the District Court irrespective of where the marriage was contracted. The decision of *Le Mesurier* as distinguished and decided in the *Asokan* case states the current legal position on jurisdiction of the courts in cross border divorce matters.

## 2.3 *Jurisdictional Issues in Actions for the Decree of Nullity*

Cheshire observed that since the decree of nullity is merely declaratory in effect,[85] the plaintiff should be able to bring an action in any court he or she pleases. Ellison Kahn[86] pointed out that the object of pleading for a decree of annulment of a void marriage is to establish by a judgement in rem, in which the proper law is applied, that there was never a valid marriage. Case law on the subject provides several alternative criteria for determination on questions related to jurisdiction.

(i) The court of the area of celebration of the marriage
(ii) The court of the area of common domicile at the institution of proceedings
(iii) The court of the area of plaintiff's domicile at the institution of proceedings
(iv) The court of the area of defendant's domicile at the institution of proceedings

---

[83][1994] 1 SLR 413.

[84]Ibid.

[85]G.C. Cheshire, *Priavte international Law*, (Oxford, 1947) 447; Ponnambalam (n 28) 377.

[86]H.R. Hahlo, *The South African law of husband and wife*, with an appendix by Ellison Khan (Cape Town: Juta, 1975): Ponnambalam (n 28) 377.

For an annulment of a voidable marriage the court of the husband's domicile, that is, the common domicile at the institution of proceedings has jurisdiction.

In *Navaratnam v Navaratnam*[87] the plaintiff, of Ceylon domicile, sued the defendant, who, until her marriage had an Indian domicile, for a declaration that the marriage solemnized between them was null and void on the ground that the defendant gave birth to a child about three months after the marriage and that the plaintiff was unaware that the defendant was pregnant and that the plaintiff has no access to the defendant before marriage. The marriage took place in India and the defendant remained in India and never came to Ceylon. The Action was instituted in the District Court of Jaffna. Keunaman S.P.J. in the Supreme Court approved and followed the decision in *Inverclyde v Inverclyde*[88] where it was held that a decree obtained on the ground of impotency dealt with a marriage which was voidable only and not void. Keunaman, S.P.J. went on to hold that in an action for nullity decree, the marriage being valid/voidable as on the date of the application of the decree, the domicile of the wife is that of the husband, and hence the Ceylon Court could exercise jurisdiction.

## 3 Choice of Law in Divorce Proceedings and Conflict of Laws in Sri Lanka

While there is no exclusive statutory provision, *Asokan* decision offered explanation of the applicable law by interpreting several legislation. The case mentioned that Section 19 of the Marriage (General) Ordinance read with Section 24 of the Judicature Act, and also with Section 03 of the Judicature (Amendment) Act No. 71 of 1981, reveals that divorce jurisdiction is exercisable by the District Court irrespective of where the marriage was contracted.

Section 597 of the Civil Procedure Code states as follows:

> Any husband or wife may present a plaint to the family court within the local limits of the jurisdiction of which he or she, as the case may be, resides, praying that his or her marriage may be dissolved on any ground for which marriage may, by the law applicable in Sri Lanka to his or her case, be dissolved. [Emphasis added]

According to this provision the plaintiff who resides in Sri Lanka is entitled to present a plaint to the District Court of Sri Lanka. All grounds for divorce stated in the Marriage Registration (General) Ordinance are applicable in Sri Lanka to dissolve the marriage in question. Nowhere in the above mentioned section it is stated

[87] *Navaratnam v Navaratnam* [1945] 46 NLR 361.

[88] 2 [L.R. 1931 Probate 29].

that only a marriage contracted within Sri Lanka can be dissolved, by filing a plaint as contemplated in that section. In other words, this section does not preclude a marriage contracted outside Sri Lanka to be dissolved on any ground, by laws applicable in Sri Lanka under Section 19 of the Marriage Registration Ordinance.

Section 19 of the General Marriage Ordinance is as follows;

19(1) No marriage shall be dissolved during the lifetime of the parties except by judgement of divorce a vincula matrimonii pronounced in some competent court.

19(2) Such judgment shall be founded either on the ground of adultery subsequent to the marriage, or of malicious desertion, or of incurable impotency at the time of such marriage.

19(3) Every court in Sri Lanka having matrimonial jurisdiction is hereby declared competent to dissolve a marriage on any such ground.

An analysis of the said section with Section 597 of the Civil Procedure Code reveals that no restriction is imposed to the effect that only adultery or malicious desertion, or incurable impotency at the time of the marriage should be a ground that took place in Sri Lanka in order that a party be entitled to get a divorce on one of such grounds. If a party succeeds in establishing one of such grounds, then he or she is entitled to get a divorce from the Court.[89]

Further, Section 597 of the Civil Procedure Code does not prohibit a court from entertaining a plaint where the matrimonial fault took place outside of Sri Lanka. This section read with Section 19 of the Marriage Registration Ordinance does not preclude a competent District Court to entertain a plaint where it appears from the plaint that the party resides within its local jurisdiction and alleges a ground for divorce as contemplated in Section 19 of the Marriage Registration Ordinance.[90]

Sri Lankan courts, in distinction from the general principles of Private International Law, held the applicable law to be the law of the place of the residence. Such a conclusion is totally undeserved in the light of the principles of Private International Law. In the case of *Mendis v Perera*[91] the meaning of residence was stated as, according to the Section 9, Civil Procedure Code, the place where the applicant before the court has his family establishment and home, and not a mere place of business. In *Mendis* case, the arguments presented in the case of *Fatima Begum v Sakina Begum*[92] were cited, where it was held that the words 'dwelling' and 'residence' were synonymous with domicile and home and meant that place where a person had fixed his permanent home, to which, whenever he was absent, he had the intention of returning; however, this ratio was not followed.

---

[89]*Asokan* (n 83).

[90]Ibid.

[91]13 NLR 41.

[92](1875) ILR 1 All 51.

According to the Sri Lankan law, only a mere residence is enough to fulfil the legal requirements in the event of the cross-border divorce matters. However, the definition of residencê given by the Sri Lankan Courts is greatly inconsistent with the rules of Private International Law where the emphasis is on domicile. There are different kinds of domiciles in Private International Law: domicile of origin, domicile of choice and domicile of dependent person such as domicile of children, married women, and persons of unsound mind. Domicile is defined in *Lord v Colvin*[93] as,

> The place is properly the domicile of a person in which he has voluntarily fixed the habitation of himself and his family, not for a mere special and temporary purpose, but with a present intention of making it his permanent home, unless and until something (which is unexpected or the happening of which is uncertain) shall occur to induce him to adopt some other permanent home.

Morris observed that a person may be domiciled in a country which is not and never has been his home; a person may have two homes but he can only have one domicile.[94]

There are different views on distinguishing the domicile from the residence. In some of the cases, it was stated that domicile is the permanent residence of a person [Emphasis added]. However, in other cases, it was stated that domicile is different from the residence and needs to be decided according to the intention of the person. However, there are five general principles which have been created by the courts on domicile.[95]

1. No person can be without a domicile.[96]
2. One person cannot have two domiciles.[97]
3. Domicile signifies connection with a single system of territory law and it does not necessarily indicate a system that prescribes identical rule for all classes of persons.[98]
4. An existing domicile is presumed to continue until it is proved that a new domicile has been acquired by one person.[99]
5. For the purpose of a rule of conflict of laws, domicile of a person is to be determined according to the English and not the foreign concept of domicile.[100]

---

[93] *Lord v Colvin* [1859] 4 Drew. 366, 376.

[94] J.H.C. Morris, *Conflict of Laws*, (4th ed. By J.C McLean, Sweet & Maxwell, 1993) 126.

[95] Cheshire (n 5) 155–156.

[96] *Bell v Kennedy* [1868] LR 1 Sc & Div 307; *Udny v. Udny* [1869] L.R 1Sc. & Div.441.

[97] *Mark v Mark* [2005] UKHL 42 at 37, [2006] 1 AC 98.

[98] Cheshire (n 5) 156.

[99] *Winans v A.G* [1904] AC 287; *Re Fynn* (No.1) [1968] 1 WLR103; *IRC v Bullock* [1976] 1 WLR 1178.

[100] *IRC v Duchess of Portland* [1982] Ch. 314 at 318–319.

Moreover, if a person resides in several countries, the dual or multiple residence of domicile of choice can be acquired in one country, if that can be shown as the main residence. This was established in *Plummer v IRC.*[101]

Therefore, it is suggested that Sri Lankan courts should consider in their respective decisions to define the residence in consonance with the Private International Law understanding of that term considering the principles that distinguish domicile with residence.

## 4 Recognition and Enforcement of Foreign Divorce Judgements/Decrees and Public Policy Considerations

A precise legislative enactment on enforcement of foreign divorce judgements, decrees and maintenance orders is a significant lacuna in the Sri Lankan Law. The law of Sri Lanka recognizes the enforcement of foreign money judgements by two statutes: Enforcement of Foreign Judgments Ordinance No. 4 of 1937 and Reciprocal Enforcement of Judgments Ordinance No. 41 of 1921.

Enforcement of Foreign Judgements Ordinance No. 4 of 1937, which is an Ordinance to make provision for the Enforcement in Ceylon (now Sri Lanka) of judgements given in countries which accord reciprocal treatment to judgements given in Ceylon, for facilitating the enforcement in other countries of judgements given in Ceylon and for other purposes in connection with the matters aforesaid. Although this Ordinance remains in the legislative enactments, it has not been brought into operation in terms of Section 2 thereof, which provides that this Ordinance shall come into operation on such date as the Minister may appoint by Order published in the Gazette.[102]

Reciprocal Enforcement of Judgments Ordinance No. 41 of 1921 (hereinafter, the Reciprocal Ordinance) is an Ordinance to provide for the enforcement in Ceylon (now Sri Lanka) of judgements obtained in the Superior Courts of the United Kingdom and of the other Parts of Her Majesty's Realms and Territories. This Statute is presently in force. The rules can be made by the Judges of the Supreme Court under the provisions of Section 5 of the Reciprocal Enforcement of Judgments Ordinance.

The Reciprocal Ordinance defines, in Section 2 thereof, the term Superior Court in the United Kingdom to mean the High Court in England or Northern Ireland and the Court of Session in Scotland and the term United Kingdom to mean the United Kingdom of Great Britain and Northern Ireland. Judgements entered by Courts in some foreign countries can be enforced under the Reciprocal of Enforcement of Judgments Ordinance. The countries covered by the Reciprocal Enforcement of

[101] *Plummer v IRC* [1988] 1 AER 97, [1988] 1 WLR 292.

[102] F.J & G. De Saram, 'Sri Lanka- Enforcement of Money Judgments'. http://www.jurispub.com/Sri-Lanka-Enforcement-of-Money-Judgments.html, accessed 20 March 2016.

Judgments Ordinance are United Kingdom of Great Britain, Northern Ireland, Hongkong, Mauritius, New South Wales, Straits Settlements; Tanganyika, Uganda, Victoria, Federation of Malaya, Australian Capital Territory, Northern Territory of Australia, New Zealand (including the Cook and Nicue Islands) and the Trust Territory of Western Samoa, Queensland, Western Australia, South Australia and Tasmania.[103]

In *Alagappa Chettiar v Palaniappa Chettiar*[104] it was held that where a person who applied for the registration of a judgement in his favour under the Reciprocal Ordinance failed to comply with the requirement of Section 3 of the rules framed under the Ordinance regarding essential statements in the affidavit on which the application was based, it could not be made good by an inquiry under Section 384 of the Civil Procedure Code. Further it was mentioned that under Section 3 of the Reciprocal Ordinance, the Court should have conducted an inquiry and followed the procedure prescribed in Chapter XXIV of the Civil Procedure Code.[105]

In *Plexus Cotton Ltd. v Dan Mukunthan*[106] the learned Judge of the District Court refused to register the judgement of the High Court of Justice in England under the Section 3(1) and 3(2) of the Reciprocal Ordinance on the basis that the respondent was not served with the summons. The Court of Appeal of the view that the District Court has no jurisdiction to go into the merits of the case and direct to proceed to register the judgement under the Ordinance.[107] In *Lalwani v Indian Overseas Bank*[108] the Court pointed out that, since the requirement of reciprocity must only be established when the initial order is made, its disappearance by the repeal of the reciprocal legislation in a particular jurisdiction will not affect the validity of the extension order in favour of that jurisdiction.

---

[103]http://www.neelakandan.lk/Compendium%20of%20Law/Legal_Systems_in_Sri%20Lanka.php , accessed 01 May 2016.

[104]*Alagappa Chettiar* et al. *v. Palaniappa Chettiar* 42 NLR 47.

[105]Chapter XXIV of the Civil Procedure Code described the Summary Procedure and Section 384 is included in this Chapter; See, *Vaitalingam v Murugesu* 34 NLR 79; *Shamji Gordhandas & Co. v Ramanathan & Co* 20 NLR 129.

[106]*Plexus Cotton Ltd. v Dan Mukunthan* CA/1865/2005 decided on 13.1.2012.

[107]See further on the application of Section 3 of Reciprocal Ordinance, *Marchant Heyworth & Swift Ltd. v Usoof* [1955] 57 NLR 217; In the case of *Worman & Co. v Noorbhai* 15 NLR 355, the Court decided that the judgment of the foreign court is not binding on the defendant if he is not resident or domiciled in the relevant foreign court and if he did not appear in the case or submit himself to the jurisdiction of the court. A foreign court is defined in the Civil Procedure Code as a Court situate beyond the limits of, and not having authority in Ceylon (Section 5).

[108]*Lalwani v Indian Overseas Bank (*1998) 3 SLR 197, further see, *Associated Newspapers of Ceylon Ltd. v Prins Gunesekere* (2000) 2 SLR 323.

## 5 Sri Lanka's Engagement with the Hague Conventions on Marriage and Divorce

The Hague Conference was established as a permanent intergovernmental organisation in 1955, to further its global mission to work towards the progressive unification of the rules of Private International Law, as well as of providing international co-operation in civil and commercial matters.

Sri Lanka was recently admitted as a member state of the Hague Conference. Prior to its membership, Sri Lanka actively followed the work of the Hague Conference as an observer. It has, since, acceded to the Hague Conventions on the protection of children and co-operation in respect of inter-country adoptions, service abroad of judicial and extra-judicial documents in civil and commercial matters and the taking of evidence.[109]

However, Sri Lanka is yet to accede to conventions in the domain of matrimonial laws.

## 6 Conclusion

Marriage is considered as one of the vital institutions to carry forth the society, which may also lead to many conflicts of law among the countries. To diminish the challenges of such a situation, a country should establish its own Private International Law rules. In the matters relating to matrimonial issues, Private International Law established its own principles i.e. *Lex loci celebrationis* and *Lex domicilii*, and these common law principles are applicable in different countries.[110] When considering the position of India, in the event of the formal validity of the marriage, it would be governed by *lex locai celebrationis*.[111] Nevertheless, the situation of Sri Lanka is complex, owing to the absence of the clearly defined statutory law or and not much guidance from the judiciary. *Asokan* decision demonstrated a shift from the traditional understanding of domicile as the determinant factor of jurisdiction given in the *Le Mesurier*; however, the position on residence as the jurisdictional factor is not very clear. When interpreting Section 597 of the Civil Procedure Code together with Section 19 of the Marriage (General) Ordinance read with Section 24 of the Judicature Act, and also with Section 03 of the Judicature (Amendment) Act No. 71 of 1981, it can be noticed that the divorce jurisdiction with a foreign element is decided on the basis of the residence, which is inconsistent with the principles of Private International Law.

---

[109]http://www.priu.gov.lk/news_update/Current_Affairs/ca200108/20010822Private_International_Law.htm, accessed 20 March 2016.

[110]J.H.C. Morris, *The Conflict of Laws* (Sweet & Maxwell Ltd. London, 2005) 187, Cheshire, North & Fawcett, *Private International Law*, (14th Edition, Oxford University Press).

[111]*Noor Jehan Begum v Eugene Tscenko* AIR 1941 Cal 582.

Further the definition for residence is not in consonance with the concept of habitual residence. Habitual residence is a concept without various legal artificialities of domicile, such as the doctrine of revival, and analogies with that concept are not appropriate.[112] Habitual residence for the purpose of divorce jurisdiction under Section 5(2) of the Domicile and Matrimonial Proceedings Act 1973 of England need to be the lawful residence and the problem is it also can be acquired by a person who is in England illegally, as the issue of denial of domicile could be unhelpful in private law matters.[113] Additionally it could be observed that the flexibility or rigidity that is found in the different personal laws under different situations do affect and influence the cross-border divorce matters in Sri Lanka. It is essential to harmonize the Private International Law principles applicable in Sri Lanka with the standards of practice suggested by international community and institutions like the Hague Conference on Private International Law, without unduly compromising upon the fundamental rights of all persons within the Constitution of Sri Lanka.

---

[112]Cheshire (n 5) 185.

[113]*Mark v Mark* [2006] 1 AC 98.

# Cross-Border Surrogacy: Indian State Practice

**Stellina Jolly**

**Abstract** Cross-Border surrogacy helps couples, with difficulties of child conception, avail of a medical alternative. The National Commission for Women, India has highlighted the increasing availability of medical services for surrogacy and India's emergence as a surrogacy market, almost to an unofficial value of US$1 billion. Contemporary legal position on surrogacy, across the world, is diverse. Such diversity presents much challenge to private international law dealing with issues of determination of legal parentage and nationality for the child born. The Hague Conference on Private International Law has been, since 2011, working towards developing legal resources involved in exploring a solution to the issue. This chapter attempts to present the legal structure in India, minimal though it is, affecting cross-border surrogacy arrangements. It also contextualizes the discussion on the cases where children born to foreign citizens through surrogacy were left to face legal battle to determine nationality and parentage.

**Keywords** Cross border surrogacy · Conflict of laws · Public policy · Nationality · Parentage · Draft assisted reproductive technology bill · India

## Introduction

In October 2015, the Supreme Court of India expressed concern over the misuse, legal imbroglio and the country becoming an attractive destination for surrogacy.[1] The Court sought clarification from the government on the legal questions including the primary concern of legal parentage in surrogacy. The Court was concerned with the rights of multiple parties involved in the scenario including woman who donates her egg for commercial surrogacy, surrogate mother and intended mother.

[1] 'Supreme Court asks Centre to bring commercial surrogacy within the ambit of law', Indian Express, (Oct 15, 2015). http://indianexpress.com/article/india/india-newsindia/supreme-court-asks-centre-to-bring-commercial-surrogacy-within-ambit-of-law/, accessed 19 December 2015.

S. Jolly (✉)
Faculty of Legal Studies, South Asian University, New Delhi, India
e-mail: stellinajolly@sau.ac.in

© Springer Nature Singapore Pte Ltd. 2017

S.R. Garimella and S. Jolly (eds.), *Private International Law*,
DOI 10.1007/978-981-10-3458-9_9

The Surrogacy (Regulation) Bill 2016, approved by the Union Cabinet in August 2016, is to be tabled in the Parliament. The Bill bans commercial surrogacy and shuts the door on many categories of commissioning parents for availing surrogacy. It prohibits married couples with biological or adopted children, single people, live-in partners and homosexuals from opting for surrogacy.[2]

This chapter focuses on the Draft Assisted Reproductive Technology (ART) (Regulation) Bill, 2014—the version available in the public domain, and attempts to differentiate with the latest 2016 Bill wherever relevant. The ART Bill 2014 prohibited foreigners from availing the surrogacy services in India.[3] The move was unexpected, as the ART industry positioned India as a center for medical fertility.[4] Estimates suggest that around 20% of the intended parents seeking surrogates are foreigners.[5] The Governmental initiative was motivated by the intention to prevent the exploitation of poor women,encouraged to act as surrogates for economic reasons. Further, and importantly, the legal reasons that necessitated the move were the many existing protracted litigation and absence of clarity on determination of legal parentage and nationality.

The infamous case of *Jan Balaz*[6] highlighted a situation where a child was born in India but had 'no country to belong'.[7] 'No country to belong', the word reflects the concerns that this chapter attempts to address through an analysis of India's legal landscape.[8]

---

[2]Sunil Prabhu, 'Big Changes in India's Surrogacy Rules: Your 10-Point Guide' (NDTV, 24 August 2016). http://www.ndtv.com/india-news/cabinet-clears-surrogacy-bill-bans-foreigners-from-renting-wombs-1449590.

[3]The Assisted Reproductive Technology (Regulation) Bill, 2014, India. http://www.prsindia.org/uploads/media/draft/Draft%20Assisted%20Rproductive%20Technology%20(Regulation)%20Bill,%202014.pdf, accessed 28 November 2015.

See http://www.dhr.gov.in/latest%20Govt.%20instructions%20on%20ART%20Surrogacy%20Bill.pdf, accessed 28 November 2015.

[4]The rough estimates peg the number of surrogates' birth to more than 3000 in the last decade. See Usha Rengachary Smerdon, 'Crossing Bodies, Crossing Borders: International Surrogacy Between the United States and India,' (2008) 39 Cumb.L.Rev. 15, 22; Amrita Pande, 'Transnational Commercial Surrogacy in India: A Gift For Global Sisters?' (2011) 23 Reprod. Bio. Med, 618.

[5]The study by the Confederation of Indian Industry (CII) states the number of foreign intended parents who visited India in 2012 to be around 10000. http://www.thehindu.com/news/cities/Delhi/art-bill-may-close-surrogacy-doors-for-foreigners-unmarried-people/article7793884.ece, accessed 01 December 2015.

[6]*Jan Balaz v Anand Municipality & Ors* (2010) AIR Guj 21.

[7]'Born in India, Nowhere to Belong' The Times of India (online edn, 18 September 2009). http://www.timesnow.tv/Born-in-India-no-where-to-belong/articleshow/4334611.cms, accessed 2 January 2016, see Annika Tombleson, 'Contracting the new Delhi Belly: Responding to the practice of International Surrogacy' a dissertation submitted to Faculty of Otago. http://www.otago.ac.nz/law/research/journals/otago043937.pdf, accessed 03 August 2016.

[8]Ibid.

Consider the scenario of a child born to a German couple through an Indian surrogate mother. On childbirth, the Governmental institutions in India recognized the parenthood of the German couple listing them as the child's legal parents on the birth certificate. The child would not be granted Indian citizenship as being not legally the child of an Indian national. Germany does not recognize surrogacy and will not accept German couple as the legal parents of the child, leaving the child stateless.

**Structure of the Chapter**

Part one of the chapter deals with the conceptual dimensions associated with surrogacy. It also discusses the importance of India as an emerging surrogacy services destination. Part two deals with conflict of laws, issues associated with surrogacy, including those related to nationality and parentage and discusses the development of legal landscape of surrogacy in India, including the judicial opinion. The chapter does not deal with the ethical aspects arising out of surrogacy. The chapter explores the inadequacies of India's legal response to the cross border surrogacy conundrum. Part three attempts to discuss the codification efforts of 'The Hague Conference on Private International Law' (HCCH) on surrogacy and India's association.

## 1 Surrogacy: Some Conceptual Dimensions

The word 'surrogate' is derived from the Latin term '*surrogatus*', denoting a substitute or alternative. In the context of medical surrogacy it means some one carrying pregnancy in the place of another.[9] The Supreme Court of India in the *Baby Manji*[10] decision defined surrogacy in similar terms as a method of reproduction, whereby a woman substitutes another for the purpose of gestating and giving birth to a child she will not raise but hand over to a contracting party.

Based on the reproductive methods, surrogacy could take various forms.[11] In partial surrogacy, the intended mother does not have a genetic connection with the surrogate child.[12] In full surrogacy, surrogate mother is made pregnant through in vitro fertilization and the ovum does not belong to the surrogate mother.[13]

[9]Law Commission of India, Need for Legislation to Regulate Assisted Reproductive Technology Clinics as well as Rights and Obligations of Parties to a Surrogacy, (No. 228 of 2009 para 1.3. See Chandra Smith, Surrogacy and India (2011). http://ssrn.com/abstract=1762401, accessed 03 June 2016.

[10]*Baby Manji Yamada v Union of India and Another* (2008) 13 SCC 518.

[11]Claudia Carr, *Unlocking Medical Law and Ethics*, (Routledge, 2014) 263.

[12]Ibid., See Vasanti Fadva, 'Surrogacy, Issues and Complexities', in Susan Golombok et al. (eds), *Reguating Reproduction*, (Cambridge University Press 2015) 126, 164.

[13]Ibid., See Jyoti Bhakare, 'Surrogacy- A Reality Eclipsed by Ethical, Social, Legal Issues-Indian Perspectives' (2011) 2 IJLJ 80.

Surrogacy can either be commercial or altruistic. An altruistic arrangement exists when a surrogacy is based on human emotions and non-monetary considerations.[14] Commercial surrogacy is primarily driven by monetary consideration.[15]

## *1.1 India—The Emerging Surrogacy Services Destination*

The earliest recorded incidence of surrogacy in India was in 1994.[16] The indication of its popularity as a medical phenomenon is visible from the increasing availability of medical services offering artificial insemination, IVF and surrogacy.[17] Economic factors are the driver, the cost being a third of its cost in the developed world.[18] This coupled with willing surrogates have catapulted India as a leader in surrogacy market.[19] The advanced medical facilities available in India act as an additional incentive for foreign couples seeking surrogates.[20] The city of Anand in Gujarat is known as the hub of surrogacy in India.[21]

Surrogacy raises certain critical ethical and legal issues.[22] An initial fleeting glance at surrogacy gives an impression that surrogacy is an attractive option for all the interested parties—monetary security to surrogate mother and prospect of parenthood to the infertile couples.[23] However, this is far from reality. It has been

[14]Examples of altruistic could be as when one sister carries a baby for another purely out of love. Carol Sanger, 'Developing Markets in Baby-Making: In the Matter of Baby M', (2007) 30 Harv. J. L & Gender 67, 75; Janet L. Dolgin & Lois L. Shepered, *Bio Ethics and the Law*, (3rd edn, Aspen, 2013) 69.

[15]Katarina Trimmings and Paul Beaumont, 'General Report on Surrogacy' in Katarina Trimmings and Paul Beaumont (eds), *International Surrogacy Arrangements: Regulation at the International Level* (Hart Publishing, 2013) 444.

[16]M.L. Dhar, 'Need to Regulate Indian Surrogacy Industry'. http://pib.nic.in/newsite/efeatures.aspx?relid=72127, accessed 02 January, 2016.

[17]Ibid., See also, Anil Malhotra and Ranjit Malhotra 'All Aboard For the Fertility Express' (2012) 38 CLB 31.

[18]Law Commission (n 9) para 1.7.

[19]Ibid.

[20]Id.

[21]Jwala D. Thapa, 'The 'Babies M': The Relevance Of Baby Manji Yamada V. Union of India (UOI) and In the matter of Baby "M", (2011) 2 JILS 83, 86.

[22]Ethical Issues include questions of depersonalized parenthood, emotional issues of surrogate mother, informed consent, and possible adverse psychological effects on the child; See, Bonnie Steinbock, *Legal and Ethical Issues in Human Reproduction* (Ashgate 2002) 66; Paula Gerber, Katie O'Byrne, *Surrogacy, Law and Human Rights* (Routledge 2016); Anu, Kumar P, Inder D, Sharma N. 'Surrogacy and Women's Right to health in India: Issues and Perspectives', 2013(57) IJPH 65.

[23]Pikee Saxena, Archana Mishra, and Sonia Malik, 'Surrogacy: Ethical and Legal Issues', (2012) 37(4) Indian J Community Med, 211, 213.

observed that poverty and illiteracy are the two major factors that force the women to act as surrogates. This forced consent driven by circumstances cannot be interpreted as an expression of their reproductive liberty forcing many writers to call it as reproductive colonialism.[24] Given the fact that most of the females who agree to be surrogates belong to economically backward classes, the fear of exploitation is not unfounded. There is also fear that the entire process of parenthood and reproduction gets depersonalized, which could eventually affect the values and bonding in family relationships and people may misuse it for the fulfillment of their vested interests.[25]

## 1.2 Legal Status of Commercial Surrogacy in India

The legal position of surrogacy in India and its constitutional validity is far from clear. It is pertinent to recall the legal position in the United States where there is a constitutional guarantee to reproductive autonomy,[26] the contours of the right encompass not only the right to reproduction, avoid reproduction[27] but also the right *to reproduce* with the assistance of technology. Any limitation on this right is analyzed with the strictest scrutiny.[28]

The Constitution of India guarantees certain fundamental rights to its citizens and non-citizens as well.[29] Relevant to this narrative on surrogacy arrangements are Article 21 and 23 of the Indian Constitution. Article 21 of the Indian Constitution guarantees right to life and liberty to its citizens and non-citizens.[30] The facets of Article 21 has been substantially expanded through judicial activism to include

---

[24]Alison Bailey, 'Reconceiving Surrogacy: Toward a Reproductive Justice Account of Indian Surrogacy', (2011) 26(4) Hypatia 715. The author addresses the feminist viewpoints on surrogacy.

[25]In a typical surrogacy agreements a separation of genetic, gestational, and social parenthood appears and the consequences of that is difficult to gather. Lori B. Andrews, *Between Strangers: Surrogate Mothers, Expectant Fathers, & Brave New Babies,* (Harper & Row, 1989) 101; Donald DeMarco, *Biotechnology and the Assault on Parenthood,* (Ignatius Press, 1991) 75; Sonia Allan, 'The Surrogate in Commercial Surrogacy: Legal and Ethical Considerations', in Paula Gerber, Katie O'Byrne (eds) *Surrogacy, Law and Human Rights* (Routledge 2016).

[26]*Skinner v Oklahoma,* (1942) 316 U.S. 535. Court held that laws permitting the compulsory sterilization of criminals are unconstitutional if the sterilization law treats similar crimes differently.

[27]*Roe v Wade* (1973) 410 U.S. 113.

[28]John. A. Robertson, *Children Of Choice: Freedom and the New Reproductive Technologies* (Princeton University Press, 1994) 136.

[29]Constitution of India 1950, Part III—Fundamental Rights.

[30]Ibid., Article 21 Protection of life and personal liberty No person shall be deprived of his life or personal liberty except according to procedure established by law.

right to privacy,[31] right to livelihood etc.[32] Right to reproductive autonomy has not been explicitly mentioned under the Indian Constitution.

In *B. K. Parthasarthi v Government of Andhra Pradesh*[33] the Andhra Pradesh High Court declared "the right of reproductive autonomy" of an individual as a facet of his "right to privacy,"[34]—the judiciary cautioned against undue interference and limitations on procreation.[35] Whether the contours of this right include surrogacy still need to be answered. In linking surrogacy and reproductive freedom the major concern would be the arrangement that should be applicable to surrogacy, including adoption or a pure commercial contract.[36] However, fundamental rights are not absolute and Article 21 mandated restrictions on life and liberty based on fair procedures established by law.[37] Further it is quite possible that a court could find a surrogacy contract unenforceable on public policy grounds and unconstitutional under Article 23 of the Indian Constitution, which prohibits forced labour and trafficking in human beings.[38] Surrogacy being a contractual arrangement to transfer a baby in future, it could be interpreted as sale of baby for consideration thus qualifying as trafficking.

Surrogacy being a contractual arrangement for a medical process, the enforceability of such surrogacy agreements raises a few difficulties. Currently India lacks a comprehensive legislation dealing with surrogacy. The ART Bill 2014 defines "surrogacy" as an agreement between the commissioning couple, and the surrogate mother, availing the assistance of reproductive technology.[39] It mandates a binding

---

[31] *R. Rajgopal v State of Tamil Nadu* (1994) 632, Court held (1) the right to privacy is implicit in the right to life and liberty guaranteed to the citizens of this country by Article 21. It is a 'right to be let alone'. A citizen has a right to safeguard the privacy of his own, his family, marriage, procreation, motherhood, childbearing and education among other matters.

[32] *Olga Tellis v Bombay Municipal Corporation*, (1986) AIR SC 180, a case concerning the right of pavement dwellers, court opined that the right to livelihood is born out of the right to life.

[33] Law Commission (n 9) para 1.9.

[34] Ibid., Apoorva Mishra, 'Surrogacy Transaction – A Perspective on the Constitutional and Contractual Aspects (2015) 3(1) NLUJ LRev 134, 138. http://www.nlujodhpur.ac.in/downloads/lawreview/7.pdf, accessed 02 March 2016.

[35] Ibid.

[36] A.M. Capron, M.J. Radin, 'Choosing family Law over Contract Law as a Paradigm for Surrogate Motherhood' in Lawrence O. Gostin (eds) *Surrogate Motherhood: Politics and Privacy* (Indiana University Press, 1990) 59.

[37] Judiciary has repeatedly advised on the procedure established by law being fair. See, Manor Mate, 'The Origins of Due Process in India: The Role of Borrowing in Personal Liberty and Preventive Detention Cases', (2010) 28 BJIL 216, 247. http://scholarship.law.berkeley.edu/cgi/viewcontent.cgi?article=1381&context=bjil, accessed 03 March 2016.

[38] Usha Rengachary Smerdon, 'India' in Katarina Trimmings and Paul Beaumont (eds), *International Surrogacy Arrangements: Regulation at the International Level* (Hart publishing, 2013) 187; The Constitution of India 1950 Article 23(1).

[39] (n 3) Section 2 (Zs).

surrogacy agreement between the parties[40] ensuring that such an agreement is enforceable under the Indian Contract Act.[41]

However there are inherent challenges in perceiving a surrogacy arrangement as a contract. The Indian Contract Act categorizes contract as general contracts, special contracts, and specific contracts. It could be difficult to identify the specific category for a surrogacy contract. Further all categories of contract have to satisfy the requirements of Section 10 of the legislation—the conditions of a valid contract.[42]

Section 23 elaborates the circumstances for holding a contract illegal for unlawful object and consideration. They include activities forbidden by law; agreements, which are immoral or opposed to public policy or an activity if permitted, would defeat provisions of other laws.[43] The term "if permitted, would defeat the provisions of law" could be interpreted in the context of surrogacy as contravening provisions of adoption laws. Section 17(1) of the Hindu Adoption and Maintenance Act 1956, prohibited any kind of payment as a consideration in the adoption process.[44] Such prohibition was to discourage child transfers for monetary consideration. In surrogacy the basis of agreement is to transfer a child in future. The object of both the process being same, the said provision may be invoked to question the payment of compensation to the surrogate mother in any form.

What would be the stated dicta of the judiciary if a surrogate mother refused to relinquish her parental rights over the baby?[45] Could the contract be equated with a general commercial contract and the surrogate mother be forced to perform the

---

[40]Ibid., Section 60(1).

[41]The Law relating to contracts is contained in Indian Contracts Act 1872; See, Jennifer Rimm, 'Booming Baby Business: Regulating Commercial Surrogacy in India' (2014) 30 J Int'l L 1429.

[42]Ibid., Section 10 "All agreements are contracts if they are made by the free consent of parties competent to contract, for a lawful consideration and with a lawful object, and are not hereby expressly declared to be void. Nothing herein contained shall affect any law in force in India, and not hereby expressly repealed, by which any contract is required to be made in writing or in the presence of witnesses, or any law relating to the registration of documents; See Apoorva Mishra, (n 33) 134.

[43]Ibid., Section 23 The consideration or object of an agreement is lawful, unless—It is forbidden by law; or is of such nature that, if permitted it would defeat the provisions of any law or is fraudulent; of involves or implies, injury to the person or property of another; or the Court regards it as immoral, or opposed to public policy. In each of these cases, the consideration or object of an agreement is said to be unlawful. Every agreement of which the object or consideration is unlawful is void.

[44]Adoption under Indian law is governed differently for different religious groups. Adoption is not permitted for according to the personal laws of Muslims and Christians Hindu Adoption and Maintenance Act 1956, consolidates the law relating to adoption practiced among Hindus. Section 17(1) of the Act prohibits monetary considerations in adoption.

[45]Some scholars point out that surrogacy agreement relinquishing all the surrogate's rights is legally binding and enforceable. Charles P. Kindregan, Danielle White, 'International Fertility Tourism: The Potential for Stateless Children in Cross-Border Commercial Surrogacy Arrangements', (2013) 36 Suffolk Transnat'l L Rev. 527.

contract? Would it not violate the public policy provisions of the nation?[46] The addition of public policy dimension changes the entire landscape of cross border surrogacy. Public policy principles in many nations specify a defined stand on surrogacy, often founded upon their cultural, social, political, economic structure and religious beliefs. The most prominent public policy argument in the context of surrogacy is the purpose and object of the institution of family and parenthood. For the traditionalist, the procreation and rearing of offspring cannot be achieved through surrogacy and it will violate public policy.[47]

In the celebrated case of *Jan Balaz*[48] the Gujarat High Court opined that commercial surrogacy is never considered to be illegal in India. It found support from the Law Commission of India Report.[49] The Report had suggested that surrogacy agreement will continue to be governed by contract among parties, which will contain all terms requiring surrogate mother's consent to bear the child, reimbursement of all expenses for carrying the child, willingness to hand over a child to commissioning parents etc.[50] Till now the issue of direct enforceability of surrogate agreements has not directly arisen in the courts in India.

## 2 Private International Law Issues Arising Out of Cross Border Surrogacy Arrangements and Indian Legal Landscape of Surrogacy

Private international law concerns itself with disputes involving a foreign element.[51] It addresses fundamental issues of jurisdiction, applicable law and recognition and enforcement of judgments.[52] The complexities of the cross border surrogacy in determining issues of nationality and legal parentage were clearly acknowledged by the Council of the Hague Conference on Private International Law in 2010.[53] Experts' Group on Parentage/Surrogacy at the HCCH recognized that the absence of uniform approach with respect to the establishment and contestation of parentage can lead to conflicting legal problems for children and families, including uncertain paternity or maternity, immigration problems,

---

[46]Justice B.S. Chauhan, 'Law, Morality & Surrogacy- with Special Reference to Assisted Reproductive Technology' (2012) 3(4) Nyaya Deep 3, 4.

[47]Jerry Menikoff, *Law and Bioethics: An Introduction*, (Georgetown University Press 2002) 88.

[48]*Jan Balaz* (n 6).

[49]Law Commission (n 9).

[50]Id, 22 para 3.5.

[51]CMV Clarkson, Jonathan Hill, *The Conflict of Laws*, (4th edn, Oxford University Press, 2006) 1.

[52]Ibid.

[53]HCCH, Conclusion and Recommendations adopted by the Council on General Affairs and Policy of the Conference (5–7 April 2011). http://www.hcch.net/upload/wop/genaff_concl2011e.pdf, accessed 01 March 2016.

uncertain nationality or statelessness of the child, abandonment including the lack of maintenance.[54]

The primary legal issue in surrogacy arrangements is the identification of the parent. Section 112 of The Indian Evidence Act deals with the determination of paternity and presumption of legitimacy of a child born during wedlock.[55] The objective is the maintenance of the privacy of family life and also to protect the child from the social stigma of illegitimacy.[56] The primary presumption of legitimacy and paternity in case of surrogate child holds in favour of the surrogate mother and her husband and not to the intended parents. The presumption of paternity operates only in case of married couple and if the surrogate is an unmarried woman, the surrogate mother will be considered to be the legal parent. However according to the ART Bill 2014 unmarried woman is prohibited from becoming a surrogate.[57]

Surrogacy also brings forth the issue of nationality. Nationality was recognized as a basic human right in various conventions including the Universal Declaration of Human Rights and the United Nations Convention on the Rights of the Child.[58] In India the Citizenship Act, 1955, recognizes nationality based on birth and descent.[59] As per the Act, a surrogate child born in India can be considered to be a

[54]Report of the February 2016 Meeting of the Experts Group on Parentage/Surrogacy, Preliminary Document No 3 of February 2016 for the attention of the Council of March 2016 on General Affairs and Policy of the Conference, available https://assets.hcch.net/docs/f92c95b5-4364-4461-bb04-2382e3c0d50d.pdf, accessed 03 February 2016. Indian participation was also recorded.

[55]Evidence Act 1872, consolidates the rules governing admissibility of evidence in the Indian courts of law.

[56]Avtar Singh, *Principles of the law of Evidence* (Central law Publications, 2013); Section 112 of Indian Evidence Act 112. Birth during marriage, conclusive proof of legitimacy The fact that any person was born during the continuance of a valid marriage between his mother and man, or within two hundred and eighty days after its dissolution, the mother remaining unmarried, shall be conclusive proof that he is the legitimate son of that man, unless it can be shown that the parties to the parties to the marriage had no access to each other at any time when he could have been begotten.

[57]ART Bill (n 3) Section 60(5) Surrogate mother shall be an ever married Indian woman with minimum twenty three years of age and maximum thirty five years of age and shall have at least one live child of her own with minimum age of three years.

[58]Universal Declaration of Human Rights (adopted 10 December 1948 UNGA Res 217 A (III) (UDHR) article 5; United Nations Convention on the Rights of the Child (adopted 20 November 1989 UNGA Res 44/25 (UNCRC) article 7.

[59]Citizenship Act 1955, India, Citizen by birth (Sec. 3) Every person born in India On or after the 26th January, 1950, but before 1st July, 1987, on or after the 1st day of July, 1987 (but before 2nd Dec. 2004), either of whose parents is a citizen of India at the time of his birth; On or after 3rd December, 2004 where–(a) Both of his parents are citizens of India; or (b) One of his parents is a citizen of India and the other is not an illegal migrant at the time of birth shall be a citizen of India by birth. A person shall not be a citizen of India by birth if at the time of his birth—(a) his father possesses such immunity from suits and legal process as is accorded to an envoy of a foreign sovereign power accredited to the President of India and is not a citizen of India; or (b) his father is an enemy alien and the birth occurs in a place then under occupation by the enemy.

citizen of India as the factum of birth relates to Indian surrogate mother. This provision was followed by the High Court in *Jan Balaz*.

In the absence of a direct legislation to govern surrogacy, the Indian Council of Medical Research (ICMR) Ethical Guidelines for Biomedical Research on Human Subjects, 2000[60] contains certain provisions to regulate surrogacy.

- Surrogacy is an arrangement in which a woman agrees to carry a pregnancy that is genetically unrelated to her and her husband, with the intention to carry it to term and hand over the child to the genetic parents with whom she enters into a contract for surrogacy.[61]
- The intending parents should have a preferential right to adopt the child subject to six week's postpartum delay for necessary maternal consent.
- Genetic parent's claim for the custody of the child in it's best interest through adoption would be, to establish that the child is theirs through genetic (DNA) fingerprinting.[62]
- It conferred right on the surrogate mother to decide on the abortion based on medical grounds and in such a case the intending parents cannot demand the money and expenses already paid.[63]

ICMR Guidelines, 2005 addressing the control of malpractices by the ART clinics, supplemented these guidelines.[64] These national guidelines are non-statutory, and hence, not binding.

## 2.1 *ICMR Guidelines on Surrogacy*

Surrogacy could be an option for parents for whom it would be physically or medically impossible/undesirable to carry a baby to term.[65] The term 'normally' denotes the situations where surrogacy could be resorted for medical reasons. In order to avoid legal conflicts with respect to parentage the guidelines suggest that a

---

[60]Ethical Guidelines for Biomedical Research on Human Subjects, ICMR, 2000. http://icmr.nic.in/ethical_guidelines.pdf, accessed 03 February 2016.

[61]Ibid.

[62]Id.

[63]Id; In India Medical Termination of Pregnancy Act 1971 regulates procedures of abortion. An abortion can be performed before 12 weeks of pregnancy; t abortion could be performed up to 20th week with the consent of two medical practitioners. Abortion is permitted for reasons including danger to woman's physical or mental health, substantial risk of physical or mental disability to foetus, pregnancy resulting from sexual assault, threat to socio economic conditions.

[64]ICMR National Academy of Medical Sciences (India). National guidelines for accreditation, supervision and regulation of ART clinics in India. New Delhi: Ministry of health and family welfare, Government of India; 2005.

[65]Ibid., Section 3.10.2.

surrogate mother cannot be genetically related to the child.[66] The birth certificate shall be in the name of the genetic parents.[67] Third-party donor and a surrogate mother must relinquish in writing all parental rights concerning the child.[68] Under the guidelines, the child born out of surrogacy is presumed to be the legitimate child of the commissioning couple, born within the wedlock, with consent of both spouses, and with all the attendant rights of parentage, support and inheritance.[69]

There appears to be some contradiction in the rules. Guidelines mandate that the sperm/egg donor shall not have any legal parental rights with the child,[70] at the same time guidelines also dictate that the birth certificate shall be issued in the name of the genetic parents.[71] It could be that only the commissioning father was the genetic parent, as happened in *Baby Manji*. It could also be that the commissioning couple is not genetically linked to the child.

The Guidelines provide that the genetic parents must adopt a child born through surrogacy unless they can establish through genetic (DNA) testing that the child is theirs.[72] The problem is that Hindu Adoption and Maintenance Act 1956 does not allow non-Hindus to adopt a Hindu child. The Juvenile Justice Act, 2000 amended in 2006 allowed adoption for non-Hindus.[73] The Act, however, is applicable only to abandoned/orphaned children.[74] In a typical case of surrogacy, as in *Baby Manji*, one of the commissioning parents being genetically linked to the child, the adoption law in India is silent on the possibility of adopting one's own child. The law also does not allow parents a choice of a specific child for adoption.[75] It has been argued

[66]Id, Sec 3.5.4.

[67]This provision makes it very much clear that the intended parents only would be the legal parents of the child with all the attendance rights, parental responsibility etc.

[68]Ibid., Sec 3.5.5.

[69]Id, Sec 3(16)(1).

[70]Id, Sec 3.16.1.

[71]Ibid., Sec 3.5.4.

[72]Ibid., Sec 3.10.

[73]The Juvenile Justice (Care and Protection of Children) Act, 2000 is the fundamental law for juvenile justice in India. The Act provides for a special approach towards the treatment, punishment of juvenile delinquency and adequate rehabilitation.

[74]Akhileshwar Pathak, 'The Surrogacy Law Conundrum' (2016) Indian Institute of Management, Ahmedabad WPS. http://www.iimahd.ernet.in/assets/snippets/workingpaperpdf/1717570592016-01-01.pdf, accessed 03 March 2016; The Juvenile Justice (Care and Protection of Children) Act, 2015 repealed the Juvenile Justice (Care and Protection of Children) Act, 2000. The adoption process was streamlined. Central Adoption Resource Authority (CARA) is given the responsibility to act as a nodal agency to perform its function. Separate chapter (VIII) on Adoption provides for detailed provisions relating to adoption. Processes have been streamlined with timelines for both in-country and inter-country adoption including declaring a child legally free for adoption. http://pib.nic.in/newsite/PrintRelease.aspx?relid=134513.

[75]http://www.surrogacylawsindia.com/faq.php?id=%2010&menu_id=73, accessed 10 January 2016. See Guidelines Governing Adoption of Children, 2015, Ministry of Women and Child Development, Section 10 Selection of a child by the prospective adoptive parents.

(1) The seniority of the prospective adoptive parents shall be from the date of registration in the Child Adoption Resource Information and Guidance System. (2) On the basis of seniority, the

that, alternatively, the intended parents could petition for guardianship under the Guardians and Wards Act 1890.[76]

The ICMR Guidelines provided several protections to the surrogate. A surrogate mother should not be over 45 years of age.[77] No woman may act as a surrogate more than thrice in her lifetime.[78] The surrogate mother would also be entitled to a monetary compensation from the couple for agreeing to act as a surrogate; the exact value of this compensation should be decided by discussion between the couple and the proposed surrogate mother.[79] Form U attached with the ART Bill 2010 prescribes the modalities and the timeframe for such payment.[80] The Guidelines, thus, ensured the agreement for surrogacy legally enforceable.

The 2005 Guidelines did not aver to the nationality-related issues where the commissioning parents were not Indian citizens. The surrogate mother is not considered to be the legal parent of the child born, as she has to relinquish all her parental rights with respect to the child. Therefore not having Indian parents, child born in India out of cross border surrogacy is not the national of India under the

(Footnote 75 continued)

prospective adoptive parents shall be given an opportunity to view the photographs, child study report and medical examination report up to six children, in their preference category if any, in one or more specialised adoption agencies through the Child Adoption Resource Information and Guidance System. (3) After viewing the photographs, child study report and medical examination report of the child or children, the prospective adoptive parents may reserve one child within a period of forty eight hours for possible adoption and the rest of the children would be released through Child Adoption Resource Information and Guidance System for other prospective adoptive parents in the waiting list. (4) The specialised adoption agency will get the details of the prospective adoptive parents referred from the Child Adoption Resource Information and Guidance System site and fix appointment with the prospective adoptive parents to assess the suitability of the prospective adoptive parents by an Adoption Committee, consisting of its adoption in charge or social worker, pediatrician or visiting doctor and one official from the District Child Protection Unit. (5) The specialised adoption agency shall also organise a meeting of the prospective adoptive parents with the child. (6) The entire process of matching shall be completed within a maximum period of fifteen days from the date of reserving the child. http://www.wcd.nic.in/sites/default/files/adoption%20guidelines2015_1.pdf, accessed 03 June 2016.

[76]Guardians and Wards Act 1890, India Personal Laws of Muslim and Christians do not recognize adoption. The people belonging to such faiths can only take the child in Guardianship under the provisions of Guardian ship and Wards Act 1890. The statue does not deal with adoption but deals with guardian ship. The process makes the child a ward and child does not have automatic inheritance rights. Debaditya Roy, 'Adoption under Juvenile Justice Act: A Clarion Call to Secularism'. http://www.legalserviceindia.com/article/l327-Adoption-under-Juvenile-Justice-Act.html, accessed 12 January 2016.

[77]ICMR (Guidelines) (n 63) Se 3.10.5.

[78]Ibid., Sec 3.10.8.

[79]Id, Sec 3.5.4.

[80]The Assisted Reproductive Technology (Regulation) Bill 2010 Form U 1st installment which will not be less than 75% of the total amount, of Rs................ at the time of embryo transfer. 2nd installment of Rs.................. at .................. months after the embryo transfer, if the pregnancy is established. 3rd installment of Rs............. at the time of handing over the child to the patient in the presence of two witnesses.

Indian law.[81] The Gujarat High Court judgment in *Jan Balaz* is significant here. The High Court ruled that given the present legal framework, it has no other option but to hold that the babies born in India to the gestational surrogate are citizens of this country.[82] An appeal, against this judgment, is pending in the Supreme Court.

Regulating commercial surrogacy gained much legislative thought and effort—ICMR drafted another regulatory instrument—The Assisted Reproductive Technology (ART) (Regulation) Bill & Rules—2008. It was subject to much modification and the 2010 version imposed severe restrictions on foreigners from hiring Indian surrogates and the process could be allowed only in situations where their country's legal system recognized surrogacy and the child born through such surrogacy arrangement would be conferred with citizenship as a child of the commissioning couple.[83] The draft ART Bill, 2014 prohibited foreigners from availing the surrogacy services in India. The new surrogacy Bill 2016 has further extended the categories of people who are prohibited from availing surrogacy services.

## 2.2 *Salient Features of ART Bill 2014*

### 2.2.1 Institutional Requirements

A National Advisory Board and State Advisory Board for overseeing and regulating and setting standards in relation to surrogacy shall be constituted.[84] The Bill mandates registration of all ART clinics and banks with a state level authority and on a National Registry.[85] It suggested few general duties for ART clinics and banks.[86] The new Surrogacy (Regulation) Bill, 2016 also proposes the establishment of Surrogacy Regulation Board at central and state level.[87] The details regarding the structure of this institution are awaited.

---

[81]Ibid. Sec, s 3.5.5.

[82]*Jan Balaz* (n 47).

[83]The Assisted Reproductive Technology (Regulation) Bill 2010 The ART Bill). Sec 19 Further, the party seeking the surrogacy must ensure and establish to the assisted reproductive technology clinic through proper documentation (a letter from either the embassy of the Country in India or from the foreign ministry of the Country, clearly and unambiguously stating that (a) the country permits surrogacy, and (b) the child born through surrogacy in India, will be permitted entry in the Country as a biological child of the commissioning couple/individual).

[84]ART BILL 2014 (n 3) Sec 3(3), 17(1) & 22.

[85]Ibid., Sec 36.

[86]Id, Ch 1.

[87]"Surrogacy bill gets the Cabinet nod", The Hindu, August 31, 2016.

### 2.2.2 Permission and Restrictions on Surrogacy

The ART Bill 2014 positioned the process of surrogacy as a binding and enforceable contract.[88] It legalized commercial surrogacy, and granted the surrogate mother the right to claim compensation.[89] It thus allowed the surrogacy contract to be treated similar to other contracts under the Indian Contract Act, 1872.

The 2014 Bill detailed the mode of contacting surrogate and allowed ART clinics to advertise to seek surrogacy.[90] Surrogate mother is required to relinquish all her parental rights over the child or children.[91] It implied complete termination of visitation, intervention in the health, education and well being of the child.

However, the ban on commercial surrogacy envisaged under the new Surrogacy (Regulation) Bill, 2016 is likely to adversely impact the surrogacy activity in the country. It would be interesting to see the judicial response to the Bill taking into account the commercial dynamics.[92]

### 2.2.3 Rights and Duties of Parties in Relation to Surrogacy

The ART Bill 2014 and the new Surrogacy (Regulation) Bill 2016 allowed surrogacy only for Indian couples. The Bill 2014 defined commissioning couple as a married man and woman, in effect closing the opportunity for homosexuals and people in live-in relationships.[93] The conditions required to be fulfilled by the commissioning couples includes,

- a valid and subsisting marriage for a considerable period of time, and
- submit a certificate authenticating that the woman was unable to conceive.[94]

[88]Ibid., Sec 60 (1).

[89]Id, Sec 60 (2).

[90]Id, Sec 60(7).

[91]Id, Sec 60 (4).

[92]NDTV (n 2).

[93]The earlier Draft bill 2010 allowed single parents; married and unmarried couple can also have children using a surrogate mother. Article 32(1) bill defines couple as two persons living together and having sexual relationships which is legal in India. This makes it doubtful whether gays and lesbians can engage in surrogacy. It should be noted that *Naz Foundation v. Union Of India, a public interest Litigation was filed* in the Delhi High Court challenging the constitutionality of Section 377 of the India Penal Code, which makes it illegal to engage in any "unnatural" sexual act, defined as sex other than heterosexual intercourse. The Court found in favour of the petitioner and held that Section 377 was unconstitutional. On Appeal Supreme court of India held for retention of Section 377 IPC, which prohibits unnatural sex even between consenting adults in private on the ground of public morality.

[94]Ibid., Sec 60(21)(a)(i–ii).

It explicitly stipulated, "surrogacy for foreigners in India shall not be allowed[95] but surrogacy shall be permissible to Overseas Citizen of India (OCIs), People of Indian Origin (PIOs), Non Resident Indians (NRIs) and a foreigner married to an Indian citizen,[96] upon submission of a 'Medical Visa for surrogacy'.[97] An additional condition[98] imposed upon NRIs, PIOs and a foreigner married to an Indian is the appointment of a local guardian legally responsible for taking care of the surrogate during and after the pregnancy, till the child or children are delivered to the commissioning couple or the local guardian.[99] The new Surrogacy (Regulation) Bill, 2016 provided complete ban on OCI and PIOs from availing surrogacy.[100]

The ART Bill 2014 proposed an insurance scheme, which could be used for the protection of the child.[101] Further, it imposed a duty on the commissioning couple to legally accept the custody of the child or children irrespective of any abnormality.[102] They are also required to submit a certificate indicating that the child born is genetically related to them and they will not involve the child in any kind of pornography or pedophilia.[103]

Further the commissioning parents must ensure, through proper documentation (a letter from either the embassy of the country in India or from the appropriate Government Authority), that their country allowed surrogacy and the child born through surrogacy in India shall be permitted entry into that country as any biological child of the commissioning couple.[104] If the OCI, NRI or foreigner married to an Indian seeking surrogacy fails to take delivery of the child, the local guardian would be legally obligated for the upkeep of the child and hand the child or children over to an adoption agency.[105] On custody to the adoption agency, the child would be granted Indian citizenship.[106]

---

[95]Id, Sec 60(11)(a) The earlier Draft bill 2010s 34(7) had only put certain restrictions on foreigners seeking surrogacy. All foreigners seeking infertility treatment in India will first have to register with their embassy. The notarized statement will then be handed over to the treating doctor. The foreign couple will also state whom the child should be entrusted to in case of an eventuality such as a genetic parent's death.

[96]Id, Sec 60(11)(a) Surrogacy for foreigners in India shall not be allowed but surrogacy shall be permissible to Overseas Citizen of India (OCIs), People of Indian Origin (PIOs), Non Resident Indians (NRIs) and foreigner married to an Indian citizen.

[97]Ibid., Sec 60(12) A foreigner married to an Indian citizen shall have to come on a 'Medical Visa for surrogacy (MED-S)' when they come to India for commissioning surrogacy;.

[98]id, Sec 60(21)(a)(1)&(11) The requirements pertains to a subsisting marriage and the medical inability to conceive.

[99]Id, Sec 60(21)(a)(III).

[100](n 87).

[101]Id, Sec, 60(21(a)(1V).

[102]Id, Sec, 60(11)(b).

[103]Id, Sec 6017(b).

[104]Id, Sec 60(21)(b).

[105]Id, Sec 60(21)(c)(i).

[106]Id, Sec 21(ii).

The ART Bill 2014 and the new Surrogacy (Regulation) Bill 2016 specify penalties for the commissioning couple upon failure to take the custody of the child without any genuine reason.[107] The ART Bill 2014 also specified that foreign couples carry a certificate from the ART clinic regarding the custody and fulfillment of the contractual requirements.[108]

The new surrogacy Bill 2016, which has received the cabinet consent, has completely banned foreigners and even overseas Indians from availing surrogacy. The step with regard to OCI and NRI is a step backward when India is attempting to draft legislations to promote the ties between diaspora and the country of origin.

### 2.2.4 Surrogate Mother

The ART Bill 2014 as well as the new surrogacy (Regulation) Bill 2016 allowed Indians to act as surrogate only in India.[109] Indian woman will not be sent abroad to act as a surrogate. Provision for compensation has been envisaged to the family of surrogate in addition to the fixed amount for surrogacy in case of any mishap or death.[110] The written consent of surrogate mother's spouse is mandatory.[111] Surrogate mother needs to be a married Indian woman with minimum twenty-three years of age and maximum thirty-five years of age. She should also have at least one live child of her own who should be at least three years of age.[112]

The Bill 2014 prescribes that no woman shall act as a surrogate for more than one successful live birth in her life[113] and if she is already having a natural born child, the interval between two deliveries should not be less than two years. Surrogate mother shall be subjected to maximum three cycles of medications while she is acting as surrogate mother.[114] The 2014 Bill 2014 made a distinction on the amount of compensation paid to a surrogate mother by an OCI, PIO and NRI and foreigner married to an Indian citizen and the amount to be paid by an Indian commissioning couple.[115] Under the new Surrogacy (Regulation) Bill 2016 a

[107]Ibid., Sec 60(21)(c)(d).

[108]Id, Sec 60(21)(c)(1)(g).

[109]Id Section (25) Only Indian citizens shall have a right to act as a surrogate, and no assisted reproductive technology bank or assisted reproductive technology clinic shall receive or send an Indian woman for surrogacy abroad.

[110]Id, Sec (29) In case of death of surrogate mother after the conception is established and till she is declared free from all diseases and disorders resulting because of pregnancy, an appropriate compensation should be given to the family of surrogate in addition to the amount fixed at the time of agreement for her services as surrogate.

[111]Ibid., Sec 60(19)(b).

[112]Id, Sec 60(5).

[113]Id, Sec 60(5)(a) The earlier draft ART bill 2010 Section 34(5), A woman could be a surrogate for five live births which was reduced under the current Bill.

[114]ART Bill 2014 (n 3) Sec 60(5)(b).

[115]Ibid., Sec 31.

woman will be allowed to become a surrogate mother only for altruistic purpose and under no circumstances money shall be paid to her, except for medical expenses.[116] The move could be challenged as violative of right to livelihood guaranteed under Indian constitution.[117]

### 2.2.5 Legal Parentage

The ART Bill 2014 provides that the child born to a married couple through the use of assisted reproductive technology shall be presumed to be the legitimate child of the couple and shall have identical legal rights as a biological child of the couple.[118] Divorce of the commissioning couple after they have consented for the assisted reproductive technology but before the child or children were born has no effect on the rights of the child.[119] The birth certificate would be issued in the name of commissioning parents.[120] The intending parents, therefore, be able to register as parents, as it is also provided that a donor shall relinquish all parental rights over the child, which may be conceived from his or her gametes.[121] This provision overcomes the complicated requirements of adoption by declaring the intended parents to be the child's legal parent. However the new surrogacy (Regulation) Bill 2016 merely promises that parentage will be decided thorough a legal and transparent process.[122]

### 2.2.6 Nationality

The ART Bill 2014 specified that a child born to commissioning parents who are OCI, PIOs NRIs and a foreigner married to an Indian would not be an Indian citizen. He/she would be entitled to Overseas Citizenship of India under Section 7A of the Citizenship Act, 1955.[123] However, where the commissioning parents refuse to take the custody of the child, the local guardian will be legally bound to take care of the child or hand over the child for adoption. In such cases child will be granted Indian citizenship.

---

[116](n 87).

[117]See Delhi Transport Corporation *D.T.C v Mazdoor Congress and Others*, AIR 1991 SC 101, *M. J. Sivani & Ors. v State of Karnataka & Ors*, (1995)6 SCC 289

In Nov 2015 a group of surrogate mothers has approached the Supreme Court against Government move to ban foreigners from availing surrogacy as it violate their right o livelihood.

[118]The ART Bill, 2014, 61(1) The new Bill only permits married couple to adopt the method of surrogacy which was not the case under earlier versions of ART bill. Art Bill 2010 provided that a child born to an un married couple or single parent will be deemed to be the legitimate child of those parents respectively Section 35(2) &35(3).

[119]Ibid., Sec 61(3).

[120]Id, Sec 61(6).

[121]Id, Sec 58(3).

[122](n 87).

[123]ART BILL 2014, (n 3) Section 61(7).

The 2014 Bill and the new 2016 Bill prohibit foreigners from availing surrogacy. To prevent any kind of issues of citizenship and nationality arising out of surrogacy, the Union Home Ministry has instructed Indian missions and foreigners regional registration offices (FRRO) not to grant visa to couples intending to visit India for surrogacy.[124] This was in contrast to the earlier medical visa rules prescribed for surrogacy.[125] Both the Bills are seen as a setback for commissioning parents and the surrogate mothers in India as the fertility 'industry' is now valued at $1 billion.[126]

# 3 Judicial Opinion on Cross-Border Surrogacy Arrangements

## *3.1* Jan Balaz *Case*

Jan Balaz and his wife came to India and entered into a surrogate contract with one Marthaben Immanuel Khristi.[127] Twin boys were born out of surrogacy. Anand Nagar Palika issued a certificate of birth to the children as per the provisions of

---

[124]Guidelines for Commissioning of Surrogacy in India

"With effect from 3rd November, 2015, the Ministry of Home Affairs vide its Circular No. 25022/74/2011-F.I (Vol.III) dated 3rd November, 2015 has conveyed WITHDRAWAL of granting Medical Visa to Foreign Nationals intending to visit India for commissioning of Surrogacy and the provisions applicable to OCI/PIO cardholders hence forth. As such,

(i) No Visa will be issued by any Indian Mission/Post to foreign nationals intending to visit India for commissioning surrogacy.
(ii) No permission will be granted by Foreigners Regional Registration Officers (FRROs)/ Foreigners Registration Officers (FROs) to Overseas Citizen of India (OCI) cardholders to commission surrogacy in India." http://www.cgisf.org/page/display/291/26, accessed 2 February 2016.

[125]In 2012 A medical surrogacy VISA for surrogacy arrangement could be granted on the fulfillment of the following conditions:

(a) The foreign couple are duly married and a subsistence marriage for two years.
(b) A letter from the Embassy/ministry of the foreign country should state that the country recognizes surrogacy and the child/children born will be permitted entry into their country as a biological child of the couple commissioning surrogacy.
(c) The treatment should be done only at one of the registered ART clinics recognized by ICMR. (The list of such clinics will be shared with MEA from time to time)
(d) The couple should produce a duly notarized agreement between the applicant couple and the prospective Indian surrogate mother. http://mha1.nic.in/pdfs/Surrogacy-111013.pdf, accessed 03 March 2016. See also Anil Malhotra, *Surrogacy in India: A Law in the Making*, (Universal law Publishers, 2013).

[126]Bindu Shajan Persppadan, A setback for surrogacy in India? November 29, 2015, The Hindu, http://www.thehindu.com/opinion/op-ed/a-setback-for-surrogacy-in-india/article7927730.ece, accessed March 2016.

[127](n 47).

Registration of Birth and Deaths Act, 1969.[128] The birth certificate showed the name of the mother as Marthaben Immanuel Khristi, the surrogate mother.[129]

The High Court of Gujarat addressed the issue of citizenship of a child born in India to a surrogate mother, an Indian national, whose biological father is a foreign national. Counsel for the petitioner submitted that since both the children are born in India, they are Indian citizens by birth as per Section 3 of the Citizenship Act, 1955.[130]

The Court opined that in the absence of any legislation to the contrary, it was inclined to recognize the gestational surrogate who has given birth to twins as the legal mother of the twins.[131] It pointed out that factum of birth of the babies has been established and that too in India to an Indian mother. Egg donor is also reported to be an Indian woman; either way the mother of the babies is an Indian national. Even if the children are described as illegitimate children born out of marriage in this country to an Indian national and hence, they are entitled to get citizenship by birth.[132]

The High Court observed,

> the only conclusion that is possible is that a gestational mother who has blood relations with the child is more deserving to be called as the natural mother. She has carried the embryo for full 10 months in her womb, nurtured the babies through the umbilical cord.[133]

The Court never referred to the ICMR Guidelines, 2005 and the ART Bill, 2008, pending, then, in the Indian Parliament. The Court's pronouncement recognizing surrogate mother as the legal parent in surrogacy could create complications for child custody, maintenance etc. The Union of India has appealed against the decision.[134] The Supreme Court explored the possibility of adoption on humanitarian grounds by Central Adoption Research Authority of India.[135] Germany offered to issue visa to the children for the purpose of adoption in Germany.[136] As a

---

[128]Registration of Births & Deaths is mandatory according to the provisions of registration of Births & Deaths Act, 1969. It is mandatory register every birth/stillbirth and death to the concerned department within 21 days of its occurrence. The Government accordingly has put in place and codified system for registration of Birth, with the Registrar General at the Centre and the Chief registrars in the States, running through district registrars to the village and town registrars at the local level.

[129]http://blog.indiansurrogacylaw.com/gujarat-high-court-rules-on-surrogacy-case/, accessed 02 January 2016.

[130](n 47).

[131]Ibid.

[132]Id.

[133]Id.

[134]G R Hari, 'Jan Balaz Update', Web Blog of Indian Surrogacy Law Center. http://blog.indiansurrogacylaw.com/german-couple-case-surrogacy-india/, accessed 4 January 2016.

[135]Usha Rengachary Smerdon, (n 38) 233.

[136]Ibid. 27.

result the children were finally issued with German visas and the couple were allowed to adopt the children under German laws. The children lived in India till May 2010 for two years after their birth.[137]

## 3.2 *Baby* Manji Yamada v Union of India[138]

Baby Manji was born under a surrogacy agreement entered into by Dr. Yuki Yamada and Dr. Lkufumi Yamada of Japan.[139] The sperm had come from the intending father Dr. Lkufumi Yamada, but egg from an anonymous donor. Matrimonial discord between the couple resulted in their divorce and the wife refused to honour the agreement.[140] The child was born in Anand and the Municipality issued a birth certificate stating the name of genetic father only.[141] The genetic father Dr. Lkufumi Yamada desired to take custody of the child, but several legal problems had to be tackled before he could take the custody of the child.[142] The legal option before him was to adopt the child but it would have resulted in a long and protracted procedure. Meanwhile, an NGO called Satya filed a petition in the Rajasthan High Court seeking to prevent Manji from being taken out of India.[143] The grandmother of the baby Manji, Ms. Emiko Yamada flew from Japan to take care of the child and filed a petition in the Supreme Court under Article 32 of the Constitution.[144] Court ruled in favour of grandmother holding surrogacy to be legal in India. Following this, The Japanese Embassy granted Manji a one-year Japanese visa on humanitarian grounds and Manji's grandmother was able to take her to Japan.[145]

The point to be noted is that in the absence of a concrete legislative measure, the professional association of obstetricians and gynecologists, JSOG, applies an

---

[137]Hari Ramasubramanian 'German Couple All Set to Take Twins to Homeland' India Surrogacy Law. http://blog.indiansurrogacylaw.com/tag/jan-balaz/, accessed 04 January 2016; See generally, Marit Melhuus, *Problems of Conception: Issues of Law, Biotechnology, Individuals and Kinship*, (Berghahn Books, 2012), 84.

[138]*Baby Manji Yamada* (n 10).

[139]Ibid.

[140]Id.

[141]Id.

[142]Mark Henaghan, 'International Surrogacy Trends: How Family Law is Coping' (2013) Australian Journal of Adoption 1, 6. http://www.nla.gov.au/openpublish/index.php/aja/article/view/3188/3713, accessed 04 March 2016.

[143]Ibid.

[144]Id.

[145]Id.

industry-wide prohibition on surrogacy.[146] The conservative stand of JSOG was clearly evident when they held the surrogacy contracts are not ethically tolerable on the eve of the first surrogate child in Japan.[147]

## 3.3 *Israeli Gay Couple Case*

The case concerned the surrogacy agreement entered by a gay couple from Israel with a surrogate mother in India.[148] The surrogacy was performed using one of the partner's sperm and an anonymous donor's egg.[149] Israel regulates the practice and bars gay couples from contracting surrogacy arrangements.[150] It refused to grant citizenship to the twins born out of this surrogacy citing public policy reasons.[151] Hearing the petition the District Court of Jerusalem, which initially did not give an approval for conducting paternity test,[152] later consented for the paternity test, taking into account the best interests of the children.[153] Paternity test confirmed the genetic link between the intending father and the child forcing the Israeli authorities to grant passports to the children.[154] The case pointed at the bias against homosexuals becoming parents in Israel and highlighted the public policy dimension.[155]

These cases clearly represent the legal conflicts between jurisdictions and the plight of parties involved in cross border surrogacy arrangements.

---

[146]Stellina Jolly, 'Surrogacy and Family Ties: A Comparative Analysis of Indian and Japanese Legal frame work' (2010) 2 University of Legal Studies Journal, 299.

[147]Ibid.

[148]Mark Henaghan (n141).

[149]Ibid.

[150]Zoe MeleoErwin, Barbara Katz Rothman, 'Choice and justice; Motherhood in a Global Context' in Lorna Davies, Rea Daellenbach, Mary Kensington (eds) Sustainability, *Midwifery and Birth* (Routledge, 2010) 45.

[151]Mumbai: Wait gets longer, docs upset in Israeli twins case. http://www.ndtv.com/cities/mumbai-wait-gets-longer-docs-upset-in-israeli-twins-case-417582, accessed 24 February 2016.

[152]The Israel High Court on 11-03-2016 orders Israel to recognize gay adoption of child born through surrogacy. http://www.jpost.com/National-News/High-Court-orders-Israel-to-recognize-gay-adoption-of-child-born-through-surrogacy-339655, accessed 3 February 2016.

[153]Sharon Shakargy, Israel, in Katarina Trimmings, Paul Beaumont, (eds) *International Surrogacy Arrangements: Legal Regulation at the International Level*, 1st, (Hart publishing, Oxford, 2013) 244.

[154]Ibid.

[155]Anindita Majumdar, 'The Rheotoric of the Womb, The Representation of Surrogacy in India's Popular Mass Media', in Sayantani Das Gupta, Shamita Das Dasgupta (ed), *Globalization and Transnational Surrogacy in India: Outsourcing Life* (Lexington Books 2014) 114.

## 4 Hague Codification Attempt and Role of India

The Hague Convention on Protection of Children and Co-operation in Respect of Inter-country Adoption, 1993[156] is presently the closest international instrument germane to the issue of surrogacy and can be of assistance in clarifying knotty legal issues involved in surrogacy. India has acceded to the above convention.[157] It was debated whether to invoke the provisions of adoption convention to surrogacy related issues, but the general legal opinion seems to be against extending the adoption convention in case of surrogacy.[158] The HCCH is at present examining the legal issues arising out of cross border surrogacy including legal parentage and nationality.[159] The Group identified the jurisdictional issues in the context of legal parentage arising from (1) birth registration; (2) voluntary acknowledgment of legal parentage; or (3) judicial proceedings.[160] Regarding applicable law, the group merely acknowledged the divergence of opinion between the application of *lex fori* and foreign law.[161] The Group is currently continuing its engagement to harmonize rules on the recognition of foreign parentage, decisions and also examining the role of public policy.[162]

## 5 Conclusion

The ART Bill 2014, while having the virtue of instituting and clarifying clinical procedures and supporting the rights of infertile couples to access ARTs,[163] cannot be considered to be progressive as it overlooks the practical realities associated with

[156]Convention on Protection of Children and Co-operation in Respect of Inter-country Adoption, *opened for signature* May 29, 1993, S. TREATY DOC. No. 105-51, 1870 U.N.T.S. 167.

[157]India is party to the Hague Adoption Convention. India's Central Authority is Central Adoption Resource Authority - Ministry of Women and Child Development.

[158]June 2010 meeting of a Hague Special Commission on surrogacy, this Convention was rejected as an appropriate regulatory instrument for international surrogacy; See also Seema Mohapatra, Adopting an International Convention on Surrogacy-A lesson from inter Country adoption Feb 7 2016, Symposium: Cross Border Health Care: The Movement of Patients, Providers and Diseases, Loyola University School of Law-Chicago, 2015. http://papers.ssrn.com/sol3/papers.cfm?abstract_id=2617896, accessed 3 January 2016; Carolyn McLeod and Andrew Botterell, 'A Hague convention on contract pregnancy (or "surrogacy"): Avoiding ethical inconsistencies with the Convention on Adoption' (2014) 7(2) Special Issue on Transnational Reproductive Travel International Journal of Feminist Approaches to Bioethics 219–235.

[159]Report of the Experts Group Hague (n 54) para 4. India is an active participant in the Hague surrogacy project.

[160]Ibid.

[161]Id.

[162]Id.

[163]Maya Unnithan, 'Thinking through Surrogacy legislation in India, Reflections on Relational Consent and the Rights of Infertile Women', (2013) 1(3) Journal of Legal Anthropology 287.

cross border surrogacy in India. The Bill 2014 and new surrogacy (Regulation) Bill 2016 only recognizes the rights of the infertile couple to access surrogacy and completely ignore the rights of single parents. Both 2014 and 2016 Bill prohibits foreigners from availing the service of surrogacy. This makes a marked shift from the position articulated by ART Bill 2010 that allowed foreigners to access surrogacy with a requirement to follow the medical visa rules. Surrogacy is an economic and social reality. The "best interest of the child" standard should govern all surrogacy regulation and surrogates need to be protected against exploitation. While the 2014 and 2016 Bills emphasize accountability of the ART banks and ensure reduction in the malpractices associated with surrogacy, the 2016 Bill attempts to end the surrogacy-fertility industry. The economic implications of such a move need to be assessed. Policy makers need to remember that in a liberal democracy, with its emphasis on the right of individuals, new modes of reproduction should be permitted unless there is evidence that such practice causes harm to others.

# Inter-country Child Abduction—Indian Legal Response

**Molshree A. Sharma**

**Abstract** As the world shrinks and people travel all over the world to work and live so do they establish families and roots where they go. International marriages are becoming increasingly common as immigration and vast diasporas' becomes a reality of the world. As a result, the development of a body of private international family law has been crucial to resolving the inevitable issues that arise. A significant issue is that of child custody where parents may not only be of different nationalities but also may simply live or be present in different countries for what become crucial periods of time. Before, the issue of custody and best interest of the child can even be addressed the first matter of inquiry is which country can rightfully adjudicate the custody matter. To avoid, competing jurisdictions and purposeful wrongful removal of children by a parent attempting to divest the other parent of any custody rights, the Hague Convention on the Civil Aspects of International Child Abduction serves as the comprehensive body of law that first establishes which country has the right to adjudicate custody which is crucial as stated above, to avoid, multiple jurisdictional fights, and entanglement of politics on what become emotional issues of nationhood, cultural standards for children and issues surrounding parental kidnapping. There has been a strong push by practitioners for India to sign the Convention. To be a part of the global community, the case is made, that India must be seen as a place where standard international Conventions especially as they relate to child custody will be honoured. In fact the Indian Law Commission in 2009 completed its report authored in part by Justice Lakshmanan, concluded that India must accede to the Convention and sign it rather than become a haven for parental kidnapping. This is however controversial for a number of reasons where realities of spousal abuse, fraudulent marriages and lack of ability to litigate are cited. Further, so far, the judiciary in India has been extremely quick to adjudicate custody disputes even when the child has not resided in India for any substantial period or arguably has been "wrongfully removed" per standards of the Convention. The chapter will explore the case law

M.A. Sharma (✉)
Mandel, Lipton, Roseborough and Sharma, Ltd., Chicago, USA
e-mail: MSharma@mandellipton.com

© Springer Nature Singapore Pte Ltd. 2017

S.R. Garimella and S. Jolly (eds.), *Private International Law*,
DOI 10.1007/978-981-10-3458-9_10

generated specifically in the Indian case law and also changes in it, while at the same time explore what reasons Court's have applied to resolve these issues.

**Keywords** Inter country child abduction · Recognition of foreign custody order · Welfare of the child · Hague abduction Convention

## Introduction

With the opening up of the international boundaries for trade and commerce, transnational transactions and other sorts of interactions amongst people belonging to different nationalities has increased manifold. Some of the factors which one looks for while choosing the most suitable avenue for employment or investment are predictability of laws, comity of courts, returns, cultural similarities etc. As individuals travel to several new destinations for economic reasons; friendship, marriage and family ties develop as a collateral consequence. Hence, today's globalized world witnesses a considerable increase in the number of transnational marriages i.e. marriage between a citizen of one country with that of the other country.

This phenomenon has in turn given rise to several private international law issues, including the question of choice of jurisdiction or applicable law in matters of divorce, judicial separation, custody of children etc. Children born out of such unions are in particular at a major risk due to legal uncertainty as to their nationality and citizenship status because of existing differences in private international law rules of countries. The current scenario, requires uniform private international law norms with regard to the issue of divorce, custody and inheritance at the international level in order to secure the legal rights of children born out of cross-border marriage arrangements.

One of the significant issues that concern children born out of transnational marriages is the issue of parental child abduction. It arises mainly at the time of custody disputes. Here, one of the parent abducts the child and takes him/her to the country of one's own (parent's)nationality. This creates a serious trouble for the other parent seeking custody of the child in a different jurisdiction. The consequences of which are bore by the child so abducted, the parent who is away from the said child, the family members and also society at large.

A major step to address the above issue, culminated in the form of the Convention on Civil Aspects of Child Abduction (hereinafter, the Convention).[1] The Convention provides for expeditious return of a child internationally abducted by a parent from one member country to another. With the rapid increase in the number of international parental child abduction cases, there has been a subsequent

[1]The Convention on the Civil Aspects of International Abduction, (concluded 25 October 1980, entered into force 1 December, 1983). T.I.A.S No. 11,670.

increase in the number of countries becoming party to the Convention. Presently, ninety-four countries are signatories to the Convention.[2]

**Structure of the Chapter**

The present chapter shall provide a brief overview of the Convention beginning with defining its key terms. Specifically, I shall discuss the manner in which the jurisprudence regarding the term "Habitual Residence" has developed over the time and resulted in different interpretations. While this ensures some flexibility which can be important where it is hard to determine habitual residence, the unintended consequence is that there lacks a uniform approach resulting in enormous litigation and delay in decisions, and not to forget, the issue at hand of course is time sensitive. In the next part of the chapter, I shall examine the accepted defenses listed in the Convention that may result in a child not being returned even when removed from their habitual residence. Further, I will expand on the varying and somewhat inconsistent Indian case law where a child has been removed which has at best been extremely inconsistent and underscores the need for implementation of the recommendation by the Indian Law Commission in 2009 for India to accede to the Convention. Finally, I would provide a brief conclusion summarizing the current approach of Indian courts.

## 1 Brief Overview of the Convention

The Convention defines international parental abduction of children as the wrongful removal of a child from a place of habitual residence.[3] The welfare of the child is the central concern of the Convention, and the entire text and scope of the Convention emphasizes that, the return of the child to her place of habitual residence is the only way to ensure the best interest and welfare of the child.[4] The Convention is based on the conviction that wrongful removal is extremely harmful to the well being of a child whose relationship with the left behind parent is jeopardized and in addition may also result in severe trauma experienced by a child being uprooted from her home environment to place with a different culture, language and norms.[5]

[2]Status table: Convention of 25 October 1980 on the Civil Aspects of International Child Abduction. Hague Conference on Private International Law. https://www.hcch.net/en/instruments/conventions/status-table/?cid=24, accessed 22 July 2016.

[3]The Convention (n 1), art 4.

[4]L. Girdner, Introduction in L. Girdner and P. Hoff ed. *Obstacles to the Recovery and Return of Parentally Abducted Children: Final Report*, (Washington, DC: U.S. Department of Justice, Office of Justice Programs, Office of Juvenile Justice and Delinquency Prevention, 1994) 1.

[5]The Convention (n 1) Introduction.

The Convention requires signatory countries to accede to jurisdiction regarding any matter of custody to the Court of the child's habitual residence.[6] Simply put, the Convention provides that the habitual residence of the child shall be the connecting factor based on which the issue of jurisdiction of a court shall be determined in the member countries. The wrongful taking of a child, to another country, cannot be the basis for establishing jurisdiction of the courts of country where the child has been abducted to.[7]

The Convention defines a child as a person aged 16 and less.[8] The basic purpose of the Convention, in addition to ensuring rights of access of parents is to prevent the harm of international abduction and subsequent retention of the abducted child by providing a settled procedure to facilitate the return of the child to their place of habitual residence.[9] The idea explaining this Convention is twofold

- it ensures the prompt return of the child to her country of habitual residence and a right to a relationship with both parents, support continuity in the child's life,
- ensure that the issue of custody of the child is decided by the appropriate Court, which is most likely to have access to the relevant evidence.[10]

Importantly, the requirements of the Convention ensure that there is a deterrent to abductors thereby preventing the creation of havens for abductions so that the child is not a pawn to be used in the dispute between the parents. This stringent feature of the Convention requiring acquiescence to removal and retention and the return of the child to its habitual residence has an exception articulated in Article 13 founded upon the likelihood of such return causing physical or psychological harm or any other intolerable situation, which again implies that the main purpose of the Convention is to return the child to a jurisdiction best equipped to resolve issues of custody and therefore ensure the best interest of the child. Specifically, Article 13 states that the child must not be returned if "there is a grave risk that his or her return would expose the child to physical or psychological harm or otherwise place the child in an intolerable situation."[11]

However, it is important to note here that the Convention merely seeks the return of the child as a return of the status quo prior to wrongful removal.[12] It does not attempt to decide the merits of a custody case.[13] In fact, the premise is that the appropriate Court, with access to relevant evidence, is best suited to decide the

[6]The Convention (n 1).

[7]Ibid., art 1, 4.

[8]Ibid., art 4.

[9]Ibid.

[10]Barbara E. Lubin, 'International Parental Child Abduction: Conceptualizing New Remedies Through Application of the Hague Convention', (2005) 4 (2) Wash. U. Global Stud. L. Rev. 415, 421.

[11]The Convention (n 1) art 13.

[12]Ibid., art 16.

[13]Ibid., art 19.

merits of the custody case and not a Court in a jurisdiction where the child's ties are minimal and may be limited to simply that the one parent may originate from said place.

## *1.1 The Convention Terminologies*

The following paragraphs state the meaning of the seminal terms and concepts of this Convention.

(i) **Habitual Residence**

The Convention mandates the return of a wrongfully removed child to his/her "habitual residence". The Convention does not specifically define the term habitual residence; rather it is interpreted as the plain meaning of the term that is the ordinary residence of the child. Within the context of the Conventions, the word habitual residence could be assumed to be the place where the child was residing at the time of abduction. Clearly the determination of habitual residence is a question of fact and the Court reviews evidence regarding the history of the child's location till the time of abduction, based on facts like the place where the family ordinarily lived, worked, the school attended by the child, the intention of the parties and so on.

A 1989 Convention case from the United Kingdom, *In Re Bates*,[14] frequently cited in the United States, stated:

> It is greatly to be hoped that the courts will resist the temptation to develop detailed and restrictive rules as to habitual residence, which might make it as technical a term of art as common law domicile. The facts and circumstances of each case should continue to be assessed without resort to presumptions or pre-suppositions.[15]

Courts in the United States have noted that the Convention does not provide a definition of "habitual residence."[16] To illustrate the varying applications of the term habitual residence and the complexity of the issue, it is interesting to note that in the United States there has been a deep division between the different Circuit Courts on the subject. Specifically, the Ninth Circuit Court of Appeals has said the decision to not include a definition of "habitual residence" in the Convention "has

---

[14]*In Re Bates*, No. CA 122.89, 1989 WL 1683783 (UK) High Court of Justice, Family Division Court, Royal Court of Justice (1989).

[15]Ibid., 9, 10.

[16]*See, e.g., Nicolson v Pappalardo, 605 F.3d 100, 103-04 (1st Cir. 2010) Gitter v Gitter, 396 F.3d 124, 131 (2d Cir. 2005);*

*Silverman v Silverman, 338 F.3d 886, 897 (8th Cir. 2003), cert. denied, 540 U.S. 1107 (2004); Mozes v Mozes, 239 F.3d 1067, 1071 (9th Cir. 2001)*

*See also* Linda Silberman, 'Hague Convention on International Child Abduction: A Brief Overview and Case Law Analysis', (1994) 28 FAM. L.Q. 9, 20 ("The Convention does not provide a definition of habitual residence, but identifying the State of habitual residence is critical.").

helped courts avoid formalistic determinations but also has caused considerable confusion as to how courts should interpret 'habitual residence.'"[17]

The 6th circuit explained that in determining habitual residence it was concerned solely with a focus on the child and past experience, rejecting much consideration of the parent's intentions and plans as irrelevant. In *Freidrich v. Freidrich*[18] the mother, Jeanne was a US citizen stationed in Germany where she had a child with a German national who was a bartender on the base. After three years, the parties' marriage fell apart and Jeanne left with their German born son Thomas for the United States. The Court held that the child's habitual residence was Germany even though the mother may have only been in Germany temporarily. Specifically, even though the mother was in Germany for a limited duration as part of military duties, her intention was never to establish residency in Germany. The Court understood this but instead of considering her intentions, the decision relied on the principle of that the experience of the child was paramount. The child had lived in Germany his entire life, had relatives, social ties in Germany and understood the language there. Despite the fact, that it was obvious that the mother was simply stationed Germany for a temporary period of time as a result of being in the military and therefore, was not planning on living in Germany, the Court focused on the child's history and not the intention of the parents. The third circuit on the other hand, in *Feder v Evans-Feder*[19] has stated that the parents shared intentions along with the child's circumstance must be considered whereas the Ninth Circuit in the case of *Mozes v Mozes*[20] has held that the principal focus of the Court's analysis should be the shared intention of the parents.

## 1.2 Wrongful Removal or Retention

Wrongful removal of the child from her habitual residence occurs where

a. It is in the breach of rights of custody attributed to a person, an institution or any other body, either jointly or alone, under the law of the State in which the child was habitually resident immediately before the removal or retention; and
b. At the time of removal or retention or removal those rights were actually exercised, either jointly or alone, or would have been so exercised but for the removal or retention.[21]

[17] *Holder v Holder*, 329 F.3d 1009, 1015 (9th Cir. 2004).
[18] Ibid.
[19] *Feder v Evans-Feder*, 63F.3d 217 (3rd Cir. 1995).
[20] *Mozes v Mozes*, 239 F.3d 1067 (9th Cir. 2001).
[21] The Convention (n 1) art 3.

## 1.3 Defenses to Removal

Once a parent makes a prima facie case that there has been a wrongful removal of the child from their country of habitual residence, the other parent, against whom the case for such removal has been made, under Articles 13 and 20 of the Convention has the ability to prevent return of the child based on certain defenses.[22] These are:

a. **Exercise of custody rights**: There has been a very liberal interpretation of the exercise of custody rights. For example under *Friedrich v Friedrich*[23] a father who paid child support and visited the child five times a year was determined to have been exercising custody rights.
b. **Acquiescence or consent to the removal**: This would generally take an affirmative act such as relinquishment of custody, written statement, or consistent attitude of acquiescence such as delay in asserting a claim especially when there has been a lapse of over a year since the removal.
c. **The child is of sufficient maturity and age and objects to being returned**: Clearly this is a fact-based analysis and it could be one of the significant factors that the court would consider in determining whether to order a return of the child to the habitual residence.
d. **The child is well settled in their new environment**: While the Convention does not define "well settled" significant evidence must be provided about the child's connections to the new country and the most often the Court will only consider this defense only if any claim by the left behind parent was asserted after a year since the child was first removed.
e. **Grave Risk of Physical or Psychological Harm to the Child**: Courts would not order a return of the child if it could be demonstrably shown that the child is at grave risk of physical and psychological harm at the habitual residence. For example in the case of *Lopez v. Alcala*[24] the Court denied this defense when the mother could not show by clear and convincing evidence that the father had ever psychologically or physically harmed the children; the living conditions in their habitual residence in France was not intolerable. On the other hand a court found that a suicidal and abusive father, evidence of sustained and uncontrolled rage would expose the children to a grave risk of harm if they were to return to Peru.[25]
f. Under Article 20 of the Convention,[26] a Court is not bound to return the child if the parent proves that the return of the child would result in a violation of fundamental principles of human rights and freedoms. This has rarely been

[22]Ibid., art 13–22.

[23]Freidrich (n 18), 1397.

[24]*Lopez v Alcala*, 547 F.Supp.2d (M.D. Fla. 2008).

[25]*Acosta v Acosta*, 2013 WL 3970239 (8th Cir. (Minn.) 2013).

[26]The Convention (n 1), art 20.

invoked and is almost never successful. Courts have often rejected this defense and limited its application only to prevent gross violation of human rights. In one such instance where the defense was recognized when a mother removed her children from Israel to her native country of Spain, of which both she and the child were citizens. The Court in Spain denied return to Israel as the father had obtained in Israeli Courts, an Order of sole custody and a finding that the mother was "Moredet" which status meant, she was a rebellious wife resulting in a complete negation of her parental rights and status in the Israeli community.[27]

It must be emphasized that the defenses to the wrongful removal of a child from habitual residence are extremely difficult to prove. Since the purpose of the Convention itself is to ensure the prompt return of a child to her country of habitual residence, with the understanding that the Court with the best evidence to adjudicate the merits of the case is that located in the child's habitual residence, there must be clear and convincing evidence for a Court to not Order the return of the child based on the above defenses. Further, it is obvious that the Court must conduct a fact intensive analysis on a case-by-case basis as there are so many varying situations and no settled agreement on what is considered "intolerable" or what is "abuse". Cultural standards, the child and parents specific circumstances are all factors that inform the Court's analysis.

## 2 Indian Legal Framework and Jurisprudence Relating to Inter-country Child Abduction

The term custody has not been defined under any Indian statute. The Hindu Marriage Act, 1955; Hindu Succession Act, 1956 and the Hindu Adoption and Guardianship Act in the form of personal laws govern issues of guardianship of the child.[28] Guardians and Wards Act is a secular legislation regulating questions of guardianship and custody for all children within the territory of India, irrespective of their religion.[29] India has not acceded to the Convention, hence Indian Courts have often resorted to these statutes to disputes involving custody and guardianship of minors, born or settled abroad.

[27]In Re S, Auto de 21 abril de 1997, Audiencia Provincial.

[28]The Law Commission of India, "The Guardians and Wards Act 1890 and Certain Provisions of The Hindu Minority and Guardianship Act 1956", Report No. 83, (April 1980). http://lawcommissionofindia.nic.in/51-100/Report83.pdf, accessed 28 July 2016.

[29]The Guardians and Wards Act, 1890.

The Indian Law Commission Report in 2009,[30] authored by Justice Ramakrishna recommended India to become a signatory to the Convention. The Report observed

> Owing to the advent of technology with the establishment of easier and economic forms of travel and communication, national boundaries have increasingly become irrelevant for the purposes of cultural exchanges. The globe has shrunk to an extent that cultural taboos do not hold back anybody to go in search of greater achievements. This brings in a package of both desirable and undesirable effects. Every employment opportunity especially the ones established under the modern technological umbrella comes with a lot of responsibility and financial benefits with the aftereffect being increasing independence of individuals and ego inflations, which paves the way for undesirable familial problems.[31]

Further the Report found that as a natural repercussion to the above reality the Indian Courts had been faced with multiple cases where a parent has sought relief and filed for a *Habeas Corpus* petition for the return of a child alleged to have been wrongfully removed.[32] However, the report noted that there has been an absence of settled pattern in the opinions rendered, resulting in a lack of predictability as well as uncertainty and unintended wider consequences of the same.[33]

A review of case law illustrates this lack of clarity on the ascertainment of legal rights in such situations. While in the case of *Smt. Surinder Kaur Sandhu v Harbax Singh Sandhu*[34] and also in the case of *Mrs. Elizabeth Dinshaw v Arvind M. Dinshaw*,[35] the Supreme Court exercised summary jurisdiction in returning the minor children to their "habitual residence". In the case of *Dhanwati Joshi v MadhavUnde*,[36] the Supreme Court held that the order of a foreign court will only act as a factor when considering the return of the minor child or custody matters as India is not a signatory to the Convention and therefore not bound by the terms of the treaty. In fact, the Court further held that the welfare of the child is of paramount importance and therefore instead of applying summary jurisdiction held that the Court within whose jurisdiction the child is removed may consider the question of what is best for the child's well being.[37]

This precedent was reiterated in the case of *Sarita Sharma v Sushil Sharma*[38] where the children were both American citizens and the parents resided in Texas, USA. The Texas Court had granted custody rights to the father Sushil subject to the mother Sarita's rights of visitation. Without informing the Court or Sushil, Sarita

[30]Law Commission of India. 'Need to accede to the Hague Convention on the Civil Aspects of International Child Abduction (1980)', Report No. 218, March 2009. http://lawcommissionofindia.nic.in/reports/report218.pdf, accessed 20 July 2016.

[31]Ibid., para 1.1.

[32]Ibid.

[33]Ibid., para 2.15.

[34]*Smt. Surinder Kaur Sandhu v Harbax Singh Sandhu*, AIR 1984 SC 1224.

[35]*Mrs. Elizabeth Dinshaw v Arvand M. Dinshaw*, AIR 1987 SC 3.

[36]*Dhanwati Joshi v Madhav Unde*, (JT 1997(8) SC 720.

[37]Ibid., para 31.

[38]*Sarita Sharma v Sushil Sharma*, (2000) 2 JT (SC) 258.

unilaterally removed the children from Texas to India. Armed with an Order of sole custody from the District Court of Texas, Sushil filed a writ of Habeas in the Indian High Court, which was granted. Sarita then appealed to the Supreme Court which reversed the High Court decision and reiterated that the Texas decision was only one factor that the Court had to consider, and that despite the Texas Order, the Court observed that the welfare of the children was its paramount concern.[39] The Court noted that it found that it was not in the welfare of the children to be returned to their habitual residence of Texas. The Court opined that Sushil was in the habit of drinking excessively. Further, the Court noted that he had been violent towards Sarita.[40] The Court further determined that he was not in a good position to take care of the children as he had little support system and was also responsible for his aged mother who was at least 80 (eighty) years of age and resided with him.[41] Finally, the Court decided that a female child should live with her mother and because one of the children was a daughter, it followed that she should stay with Sarita and therefore the siblings were not separated the son should also live with Sarita.[42]

The Court opined in favor of the concept of comity of Courts and the principle that jurisdiction is best with the Court with the most access to evidence of relevant facts and the most significant ties.[43] Even though the children had resided for most of their lives in the United States, had been educated there, were part of a community, had friends and their most significant connections to Texas, were American citizens, that despite it being clear that both parents were residents of Texas and the mother had wrongfully removed the children, the Indian Court held that it was in a better position to make substantive custody decisions, in the light of welfare of the children.[44]

Interestingly, in contrast to this judgment, in the case of *Shilpa Aggarwal v Aviral Mittal*[45] the Court upheld the return of the minor to the UK, which happens to be his habitual residence and the country of citizenship. Shilpa did not return with the child after leaving for a vacation to India. The Supreme Court noted that comity of courts and welfare of the child could be competing interests; nevertheless since there was no perceived threat to the welfare of the child,[46] it affirmed the High Court's denial of writ petition for protection of child holding that UK would be the proper forum to exercise substantive jurisdiction relating to custody.[47] The Court

[39]Ibid., 264 see Siberman, (n 36) 11.

[40]Ibid., 264 and 265.

[41]Ibid.

[42]Id.

[43]Id.

[44]Id.

[45]*Shilpa Aggarwal v Aviral Mittal & Anr*, (2010) 1 SCC 591.

[46]Ibid., para 23.

[47]Ibid., para 30.

stated emphatically that the "Domestic courts cannot be guided entirely by the fact that one of the parents violated an order passed by a foreign court."[48]

Subsequently, in the case of *Ruchi Majoo v Sanjeev Majoo*[49]; one of the spouse namely Ruchi Majoo came to India with her children, after the couple experienced marital discord. The Superior Court in California had Ordered Ruchi to appear before the Court. Ruchi did not and had instead filed her own action in Delhi High Court. The father of the child questioned the jurisdiction of the Delhi High Court based on the fact that the children were not ordinary residents of Delhi i.e. as a whole of India.[50] The Supreme Court of India, on further appeal essentially held that the comity of Courts was a consideration of the Court but the Court was not bound to enforce a foreign Order.[51] The Court opined that the best interest of the child and the child's welfare was the most important matter for the Court. Further, the longer the child was in India, the greater the need for an elaborate inquiry about the welfare of the child rather than a summary inquiry. Even if a parent had removed the child in violation of a foreign Order and of the Court in whose jurisdiction the parties had set up home and lived, the Court would give the foreign Court's order due consideration but the Court emphasized that it is entitled and indeed duty-bound to examine the matter c, if any, only as an input for its final adjudication.'[52]

## 2.1 A Shift in Precedence—The Surya Vadanan Case

A recent Supreme Court judgment however leans heavily towards accession to the concept of comity of Courts. In the case of *Surya Vadanan and Mayura Vadanan*[53] authored in February 2015, the Court upheld the return of the parties' two minor children to the United Kingdom for a determination of custody by the UK courts. In the present case the father had become a naturalized citizen of the United Kingdom and after marriage, the mother Mayura had also obtained British citizenship.[54] The two girls were born in the United Kingdom and therefore were British citizens. Experiencing marital discord, Mayura took the children to India, advising Surya, that she and the children were going on a vacation. She purchased round trip tickets, although she later claimed that the only reason for that was economic. There was evidence that she had not advised the children's schools in the United Kingdom that

[48]Ibid., para 25 and 26.

[49]*Ruchi Majoo v Sanjeev Majoo* (2011) 6 SCC 479.

[50]Ibid.

[51]Ibid., para 33.

[52]Ibid., para 63 and 67.

[53]*Surya Vadanan v State of Tamil Nadu*, (2015) 5 SCC 450.

[54]Ibid., para 4 and 5.

they would not return.[55] In fact, Surya when realizing his wife was not planning to come back went to stay with her in Coimbatore and rather than have the children's education interrupted acquiesced to their admission in a local school, with an intent to attempt an amicable resolution with Mayura. In fact, unaware that she had already filed a Petition for divorce in Tamil Nadu, he lived with her at his in law's house. Unable to resolve the differences between them, Surya returned to the UK in September of 2012 when he was served with summons to appear in family court of Coimbatore. He filed his own divorce action in the U.K. and provided evidence that he had paid the private school tuition of his daughters in the U.K. and the schools were unaware the children would not return.[56] The U.K. High Court ordered the immediate return of the children and that the mother lodge her and the children's passports and any other travel documents with the Tipstaff.[57] Despite the fact that Mayura's filed a petition against Surya first, the first substantive order was that of the U.K. High Court. Specifically, Mayura filed a petition for divorce prior to Surya. Therefore, the first legal action taken between the parties' was by Mayura in India. However, even though Surya filed for relief in the UK after Mayura had already filed a divorce petition in India, the U.K. High Court, entered a ruling regarding custody prior to the Indian Court, therefore, the first substantive ruling was that of the U.K. Court.[58]

Having obtained a substantive Order from the U.K. High Court, Surya petitioned the Madras High Court by filing a writ of Habeas Corpus but was denied relief. Instead the Madras High Court, in contravention of the U.K. High Court order, exercised jurisdiction and made custody determinations, setting aside the legal rights of the parents or habitual residence of the children but rather found that the welfare of the children was of paramount importance. Further, since the mother was taking care of them and since she was their mother/legal guardian her custody of them could not be in any manner considered illegal or wrongful. Even though, the Court was aware that the mother had decided to stay with the children in India without Surya's consent and the parties had never agreed to her permanent removal of the children to India, the Court declined to find that her behavior was wrongful. On an appeal by the husband to the Supreme Court the High Court's judgment was reversed. The Hon'ble Court's opinion was founded upon the principle of comity of courts.[59] The Supreme Court opined that the lower court erroneously considered the principle of comity of courts and best interest of the child as "contrasting principles of law" whereas in fact the only way they were contrasting were as contrasting of both having to be applied to the fact based analysis of the case[60]:

[55]Ibid., para 6.

[56]Ibid., para 3.

[57]*Tipstaff's Office, Royal Courts of Justice, Strand, London.*

[58]*Surya Vadanan v* (n 53) para 14.

[59]Ibid., para 30.

[60]Ibid., para 31.

The opinion states, "These principles have been referred to 'contrasting principles of law' but they are not 'contrasting' in the sense of one being the opposite of the other but they are contrasting in the sense of being different principles that need to be applied in the facts of a given case."[61] The Court then further opined that the "most intimate contact" doctrine or "closest concern" doctrine could not be ignored simply because it may lead to an uncomfortable outcome at times. The Court stated "It is not appropriate that a domestic court having much less intimate contact with a child and having much less close concern with a child and his or her parents (as against a foreign court in a given case) should take upon itself the onerous task of determining the best interests and welfare of the child.[62] A foreign court having the most intimate contact and the closest concern with the child would be better equipped and perhaps best suited to appreciate the social and cultural milieu in which the child has been brought up rather than a domestic court."[63] Next, the Court was impressed by the fact that there had only been an interim or interlocutory order passed by the U.K. Court. This left Mayura the opportunity to seek custody of the children and the Court to determine her as the custodial parent in a final order. The Court distinguished this from the *Mckee* case where the Canadian Court was faced with a final Order of the California Court and not an interim Order.[64]

Court stated "In this appeal, we are not concerned with a final adjudication by a foreign court—the principles for dealing with a foreign judgment are laid down in Section 13 of the Code of Civil Procedure. In passing an interim or an interlocutory order, a foreign court is as capable of making a prima facie fair adjudication as any domestic court and there is no reason to undermine its competence or capability.[65] If the principle of comity of courts is accepted, and it has been so accepted by this court, we must give due respect even to such orders passed by a foreign court. The High Court misdirected itself by looking at the issue as a matter of legal rights of the parties. Actually, the issue is of the legal obligations of the parties, in the context of the order passed by the foreign court."[66] If an interim or an interlocutory order passed by a foreign court has to be disregarded, there must be some special reason for doing so. No doubt we expect foreign courts to respect the orders passed by courts in India and so there is no justifiable reason why domestic courts should not reciprocate and respect orders passed by foreign courts."[67]

Further the Court noted that the children had been born and raised in the United Kingdom, both parents had become naturalized citizens, worked for gain in the United Kingdom, purchased immovable property and the children had been

---

[61]Ibid.

[62]Ibid., para 32.

[63]Ibid., para 53.

[64]Ibid., para 54.

[65]Ibid.

[66]Ibid.

[67]Ibid., para 55.

educated there.[68] Therefore, the Court in some sense did an analysis of habitual residence mirroring the analysis completed by Courts in signatory countries.

While the case is indeed heartening for those who support India's accession to the Convention, the dicta of the Court leaves the window open for Courts to simply consider the foreign Court judgment and disregard it as a mere factor. For example, while the Supreme Court ultimately acceded jurisdiction to the U.K. Court, the rationale used was that the U.K. Court had only entered an interlocutory order, which meant, that the U.K. Court could still order the mother final custody. This is indeed troubling, as the Convention outlines that the Court with jurisdiction to decide custody is that of the habitual residence of the child, that is the Court the with the most intimate information, and that a child should not be abducted simply to establish a new jurisdiction regardless of whether the order is interlocutory or final. In fact, a final Order should have more if not the same weight as a temporary one. Further, the Court noted, that Mayura had not obtained a substantive order first, rather in fact Surya had. The Supreme Court takes pains to explain that the matter would have been different if Mayura had been first to obtain a substantive custody order from an Indian Court. The principal of the Convention of course is exactly the opposite that rather base decisions on who wins the race to the Courthouse and gets there first, the analysis must be based on which Court has jurisdiction based again on the child's habitual residence. To encourage a parent to rush to a Court in a foreign jurisdiction, to obtain a substantive order, even if it means taking the child without consent, would only encourage parental kidnapping and forum shopping.

The Court also reiterated that the foreign Court order was a factor to be considered but that with the greater amount of time that passes, the more suitable it is for the Court to conduct an elaborate inquiry rather than a summary inquiry regarding whether return is appropriate.[69] Essentially the Court dictates that if the abducting parent manages to draw out the litigation process and keeps the child in India for a longer period of time, because of the length of time itself, it becomes imperative for the Court to conduct an elaborate inquiry rather than a summary one.[70] This is problematic as it rewards the parent who wrongfully removes if they manage to draw out and delay the process as much as possible so that the children are India for a lengthier amount of time, thereby triggering an elaborate inquiry. It is no secret, that litigation in India (or most places in the world) itself is a very long and arduous process thereby further causing delay in the prompt return of the child to her habitual residence. The Court then *sua sponte* it appears places several conditions on the return of the children making the aggrieved party, in this case Surya was ordered by the Supreme Court to be,

---

[68]Ibid., para 60.

[69]Ibid.

[70]Ibid., para 49.

a. Responsible for the costs of Mayura's litigation even though she is the one who wrongfully removed the children.
b. Responsible for the costs of airline tickets for Mayura and the children.
c. Reasonable maintenance.
d. "Comfortable" stay in the matrimonial residence.
e. 1000 pounds to Mayura prior to departure.
f. Ensure that any criminal or penal action is not brought against Mayura or certainly not participate in bringing one himself.[71]

Even if Surya petitioned the U.K. Court to set aside the requirements of the Indian Supreme Court as enlisted above, Surya would certainly be responsible for fulfilling conditions such as the pay for travel and delivery of the 1000 pounds to Mayura. Further, the U.K. Court of course would be presented with the Indian Supreme Court order and again it would be in part persuasive evidence regarding Mayura's economic needs etc.

Therefore, while there is clearly a recognition and the Court is leaning in the direction of respecting a comity of Courts, via a habitual residence type analysis, thereby incorporating some basic principles of the Convention, it has remained loyal to the concept that the Indian court may choose to exercise jurisdiction over custody of children even when they are foreign citizens, having resided in a foreign country for the majority of their lives. The Court clings to the concept that because the paramount consideration is that of the welfare of the child and that the Indian Court can adjudicate substantive custody matters even if the child has never lived in India. In fact, even when the child has been taken in violation of foreign Court orders and the bulk of the evidence regarding the child's education, health and social acclimatization is not in India, the Indian Court does not refuse jurisdiction.

Further, there is as noted above, a lack of any clear progression or precedence and the Court at times presumes it is better situated to do justice to the welfare of a child. This is the case even, when the child has few if any connections to India, has never lived there, and who is a resident of a completely foreign place rather than the Court where the child has resided for the majority of their life. While, the spirit of the "best evidence" doctrine etc. stands for the concept that the Court should have access to the best possible evidence, the Court in India, makes substantive custody rulings even when the bulk of evidence of regarding the child's adjustment, relationship historically to the parents, involvement of the parents with the child's education and participation in rearing of the child, ties to the community and the like. It is interesting to note that where the Court has returned the child(ren) to the habitual residence, the Court has been able to conduct a full best interest analysis without prejudice to the removing parent. In the Vadanan case, the U.K. Court ultimately granted the mother custody of the children without prejudice to her having removed them to India. In fact, the Court was equipped with the evidence it needed to rely on to be able to determine which parent was better able to act as the primary custodian.

[71]Ibid., para 73.

As stated in the 2009 Indian Law Commission Report it can be observed that, the Indian Courts while deciding cases pertaining to minor children have not followed a uniform pattern.[72] There also is an absence of progressive development in the subject. If some matters are decided with prime importance placed on the welfare of the child, some are based on the technicalities of various provisions of law and jurisdictional concerns. This could adversely affect the condition both physical and emotional of the child, who is caught in the fire/midst of shattered relationships. The fact of India not being a signatory to the Convention on the Civil Aspects of International Child Abduction may have a negative influence on a foreign judge who is deciding on the custody of a child."[73]

Interestingly, the High Court of Punjab and Haryana have recently asked the Indian Law Commission to recommend steps towards India becoming a signatory of the treaty.[74] The request arose from a case of a child wrongfully abducted from India to the UK under a false passport. As India is not a signatory to the Convention, there is no clear procedure nor process of return. Specifically Justice Rajiv Bhalla states "the removal or retention of a child in breach of custody rights is a wrong under the Convention but for want of the Union of India acceding to the Convention and or enacting a domestic law children will continue to be spirited away from India with Courts or authorities standing by in despair.[75] Reference is therefore made to the Law Commission of India to examine multiple issue in inter country inter parental child removal amongst families and thereafter whether recommendations should be made in enacting a suitable law and for the signing the Convention on Child Abduction."[76]

## 3 India's Objections to the Convention

The question remains as to why India refuses to sign the Convention. There are several reasons given, such as prevention of domestic abuse and welfare of the child. In the majority of cases it is mothers who bring the children to India without consent or knowledge of the father. Most women argue that they have been victims of domestic violence and are returning to India to be with family. However, there is no statistical evidence of how many women in fact are leaving for reasons for domestic violence. Interestingly most of them do not make the same argument in the foreign Court where the husband is present to refute the allegations or an

---

[72]Law Commission of India Report 218 (n 31) para 2.16.

[73]Ibid.

[74]*Seema Kapoor v Deepak Kapoor* (2016) SCC online P&H 1225.

[75]Ibid., para 10.

[76]Ajay Sura, "High Court urges law commission to recommend signing of the Hague Convention", The Times of India, (Chandigarh, 5 March 2016). http://timesofindia.indiatimes.com/city/chandigarh/High-court-urges-law-commission-to-recommend-signing-of-Hague-Convention/articleshow/51267040.cms, accessed 20 July 2016.

evidentiary hearing on the issue is possible with both parties' present. The women also claim lack of access to the legal system in foreign courts, however, this is also problematic given that many of them are in violation of foreign court order in proceedings in which they have fully participated. The issue of abuse is a crucial one, and the foreign court is equipped with powers such as issuing restraining orders, restricting visitation and even denying custody to the abuser spouse when appropriate. In fact any evidence of abuse would be in the foreign country so again the Court there would be best situated to make a substantive custody decision after considering all the evidence of abuse and the like.

## 4 Indian Legislative Response

A bill has been introduced in the Indian Parliament in 2007 known as the Indian Civil Aspects of International Child Abduction Bill, 2007.[77] This bill has incorporated many aspects of the Convention even though it continued to give Judges wide discretion in choosing to exercise jurisdiction on substantive custody matters when a child was removed from a foreign country.

### *4.1 The Salient Features of the Bill Include*

A Central Authority for performance of duties under the Convention for securing the return of removed children by instituting judicial proceedings in the High Court.

- The appropriate authority or a person of a contracting country may apply to the Central Authority for return of a removed child to the country of habitual residence.
- The High Court may order return of a removed child to the country of habitual residence but may refuse to make such an order if there is grave risk of harm or if it would put the child in an intolerable situation. Consent or acquiescence may also lead to refusal for return of a child by the court.
- The HC may refuse to return a child if the child objects to being returned upon it being satisfied that the child has attained an age and maturity to take into account his views.[78]

However, this bill is now for all practical purposes dead and must be reintroduced. Indeed given the magnitude of the problem and the lack of judicial consistency in response to the issue, the only coherent and predictable solution is

[77]Anil Malhotra, Ranjit Malhotra, 'India, A Perspective, in Elaine E. Sutherland, (ed), *The Future of Child and Family Law-International Predictions* (Cambridge University Press, 2012), 158.
[78]Ibid.

legislative. It should be stated that the Indian Law Commission report does not make specific recommendations on the 2007 bill.... It describes the Convention, then the Indian case law and then recommends signature to the Convention.

In 2016, a second attempt has been made in the form of a bill proposed by the Ministry of Women and Child Development. The "The Civil Aspects of International Child Abduction Bill, 2016"[79] has been placed on the ministry's website for comments and it recommends ascension to the Convention given the number of cases that have inundated Indian Courts on the issue. The salient and salutary features of this proposed law are as follows.

The draft Bill proposes to establish a Central Authority[80].

The basic functions of the authority include:

- Discovering the where about of the child who has been wrong fully removed and retained. In appropriate cases the assistance of the police can be sought to locate the child.[81]
- Take all preventive steps and measures to prevent harm to the child.[82]
- Secure the voluntary return of the abducted child to his or her habitual residence or reaching an amicable solution to resolve the difference between the parties to the dispute.[83]

The draft prescribes the procedure needed to follow in case of an application made to the Central authority. Every application needs to be accompanied by

(a) A duly authenticated copy of any relevant decision or agreement-giving rise to the rights of custody claimed to have been breached;
(b) A certificate or affidavit from a Central Authority or other competent authority of the Contracting State in which that child has his or her habitual residence or from a qualified person setting out the law of that Contracting State relating to the rights of custody alleged to have been breached;
(c) Any other relevant document.

The Central Authority may refuse to accept an application made to it if it is manifest that the requirements of this Convention are not fulfilled.[84] The draft legislation provides an appeal mechanism to the Secretary, Ministry of Women and Child Development, Government of India. The appeal needs to be filed within

[79]Minstry of Women and Child Development, Government of India, 'The Civil Aspects of International Child Abduction Bill, 2016'. http://www.wcd.nic.in/sites/default/files/Draft_Implemnting_Legislation_Hague_Convention_0.pdf, accessed 25 August 2016.

[80]The Civil Aspects of International Child Abduction Bill, India, 2016, s 16(1)(b), (hereinafter Abduction Bill). http://www.wcd.nic.in/sites/default/files/Draft_Implemnting_Legislation_Hague_Convention_0.pdf, accessed 20 July 2016; (discussed later in this chapter).

[81]Ibid., s 5(a).

[82]Ibid., s 5(b).

[83]Ibid., s 5(c).

[84]Ibid., s 10.

fourteen days of the order of the Central Authority.[85] Central Authority is empowered to apply to the High Court within whose territorial jurisdiction the child is physically present.[86]

The High Court while making an order may request the Central Authority to obtain from the relevant authorities of the country of habitual residence, a decision with regard to the wrongfulness of the removal or retention of the child. On the basis of such a founding, court can make an order on the return of an abducted child to the country of habitual residence. However when there is well founded fear of grave risk of harm to the child the court may refuse to make an order returning the child.[87] High Court shall have regard to any information relating to the social background of the child provided by the appropriate authority of the Contracting State in which that child has his or her habitual residence.[88]

## 5 Consequences of India's Non Accession

India's refusal thus far to accede to the Convention has resulted in the consequence of children becoming disconnected with their ethnic origin nation. An absence of an established and settled precedent in India complicates the scenario inadvertently contributing to the incidence of the wrongful removal of the children to India and not returned to their habitual residence. Consequentially the foreign courts, seized with custody matters involving Indian children, have been circumspect about the scenario and this had adversely affected the visitation and travel rights of the parents. For example, in a recent case in Illinois, despite having joint legal custody of his child, a father of Indian origin (Sixteenth Judicial District, Kane County, Illinois)[89] was unable to take his son to India even for a vacation, to meet relatives or visit his grandparents because of the lack of any clear protocol of enrolling the foreign judgment, predictability of outcome if the child was not timely brought back to the United States and Indian remaining a non-signatory country.

India has a high number of cases of parental abduction. According to the U.S. Department of State, 2015 India figures prominently among the non-Abduction Convention signatory destination of International Parental Child Abduction (IPCA) from the United States.[90] To prevent and secure return of children abducted by a parent, the US enacted the Sean and David Goldman International Child Abduction

[85]Ibid., Chap. 4.

[86]Ibid., s 13.

[87]Ibid., s 16(1)(b).

[88]Ibid., s 16(4).

[89]*Vishal Malhotra v Laura Malhotra*, Case No. 11D1230 (2011).

[90]U.S. Department of State Bureau of Consular Affairs, "Annual Report on International Parental Child Abduction (IPCA)" (2016), online: https://travel.state.gov/content/dam/childabduction/complianceReports/2016%20IPCA%20Report%20-%20Final%20(July%2011).pdf, accessed 20 July 2016.

Prevention Act,[91] which requires US foreign missions to complete a number of tasks, such as:

a. Report on child abductions annually, identify the Central Authority in a country where a child has been wrongfully removed,
b. identify countries with a pattern of non compliance,
c. attempt to enter into treaties or bi-lateral agreements with countries unlikely to sign the treaty in the foreseeable future etc.
d. and a host of other mechanisms to promote the overall goal of the act which is to "To ensure compliance with the 1980 Convention on the Civil Aspects of International Child Abduction by countries with which the United States enjoys reciprocal obligations, to establish procedures for the prompt return of children abducted to other countries, and for other purposes."[92]

Under Sean and David Goldman Act, the US president could take action against India and other countries which either have not signed the 1980 Convention on the Civil Aspects of International Child Abduction or do not have any agreements with the US for the repatriation of children subjected to global "parental abductions". The steps the US president could take include limiting security assistance, withdrawal of development assistance and using diplomatic tools to block loans from the World Bank and the IMF, apart from imposing visa restrictions, sources said.[93] There have also been parent led organizations, compromising of left behind parents who push for the return of their and others wrongfully removed children.[94]

Recently there has been the case of Mr. Ravindar Parmar whose son Reyansh was taken to India by his wife Dimple and then simply not returned despite all the parties' being US citizens and the child Reyansh having lived his entire life in the United States. Despite it being clear that Reyansh had been born and raised in the United States and Dimply had not resided in India with the child until she took him without permission, the Court refused to return the child to US for a custody adjudication. In fact, the Mumbai High Court ruled that because Mr. Parmar owned some property in India (with his parents), he had indicated some intent to possibly return to the domicile of his origin namely India and also that this then resulted in the application of the Hindu Marriage Act. Further, that because the child was

[91]H.R. 3212 (113th): Sean and David Goldman International Child Abduction Prevention and Return Act, 2014.

[92]Ibid.

[93]US law plans penalties for refusing to return American children 'abducted' by parents. Dipanjan Roy Chaudhary, Economic Times Bureau, January 1, 2014. http://articles.economictimes.indiatimes.com/2014-01-01/news/45764585_1_civil-aspects-international-child-abduction-india-america, accessed 22 July 2016.

[94]Bring our Kids Home (A Parent Led Organization), 'Parent Child Abduction is a CRIME and Child Abuse!'. http://www.bringourkidshome.org/index.html, accessed 22 July 2016.

enrolled in school in Pune (despite the father's objection) it showed the mother's intention to change domicile.[95]

## 6 Conclusion

India's refusal to accede to Convention has legal and social consequences. Children with parents of Indian origin living in foreign nations are less likely to experience their Indian heritage first hand, as foreign Courts have become aware of the burgeoning cases where children are wrongfully removed to India and then not returned. Therefore, the somewhat ironic effect is that the child is hampered from developing emotional and physical ties to India as foreign Courts refuse to Order travel there for any period of time. As an example, in a trial case in Kane County Illinois, a father was ultimately unable to take his son to India even for a vacation. This was because of the lack of any clear protocol of enrolling the foreign judgment or predictability of outcome when a child is taken to India.[96] There is a pertinent need for India to accede to the Convention, especially owing to the fact that there is a lack of cohesiveness in its jurisprudence on the subject, and also that there is a recommendation by the Law Commission of India for such accession. Certainly, the issue is one of immediate relevance and must be resolved with expeditiousness. The welfare of the child is inextricably linked to that of his/her family unit and even when the unit of the family is modified, the benefit of a relationship with both parents is an essential right. The merits of a custody case are based on a fact intensive analysis, usually involving details of the child's upbringing, socialization in the community, education and response of peers and teachers, the parties' parenting skills and involvement all of which evidence resides in the country of the child's habitual residence.

Contrary to some perceived fears, acceding to the Convention shall not divest the judiciary of the ability to make rulings on the matter but simply arm the judiciary with a settled law, thereby enabling the ability to either accept or deny jurisdiction depending on the circumstance. Should there be concerns that the child shall be exposed to abuse that would shock the conscience the Convention continues to provide the Court with the ability to deny return to the habitual residence even of a child who has been wrongfully removed. As a result, the Convention in fact empowers and adds to the judiciaries' arsenal by interpreting and applying the articles of the Convention be it that of determining habitual residence or the merits of the defenses to removal.

---

[95]In the High Court of Judicature at Bombay, Civil Appellate Jurisdiction, Family Appeal No. 72 of 2014. Civil Application No. 77 of 2014.

[96]Vishal Malhotra (n 91).

However, without accession to the Convention, the wider and unintended consequences that the Indian Law Commission Report of 2009[97] warned seem to be coming true. There is neither settled progression nor real precedence on the issue, therefore it encourages either forum shopping or is at best a roll of the dice. India has been noted to have become in some ways a haven for parental abductors and the sheer number of cases reported support that assertion. Therefore, while India seeks to be a key player in the global economy, trade and to be viewed as a stable, peaceful fast developing nation with settled judicial principles and institutions, it's refusal to be part of the global community on certain civil aspects or treaties of private international law, compromise its progress. Indeed, while India wishes to portray herself as a leader in South Asia, it is notable that the only South Asian country to sign the Convention thus far and lead in that regard is Sri Lanka.

Further, as Indians live abroad, their children are intensely enriched by traveling to their parents' countries of origin as they imbibe their own heritage and develop ties that may be invaluable to their development and the larger development of the country. However, foreign Judges have become increasingly aware of the lack of predictability in response of India's judiciary to matters of custody jurisdiction and are reticent to allow the parents of these children to travel to India even for legitimate vacations and trips. Essentially, the path forward must be of some resolution to these issues either in the short term by entry of multiple bi-lateral treaties or more effectively so, becoming a signatory to the Convention on Civil Aspects of Child Custody and Abduction.

[97] Law Commission Report No. 218, (n 31).

# Inter-country Child Abduction—Pakistan's Legal Response

**Sarmad Ali**

**Abstract** The number of international child abduction in the territory of Pakistan has increased in the wake of a growing trend of cross-cultural marriages. However legal aspects of International child abduction has not received much attention and awareness from the government of Pakistan and relevant authorities. The international community through Hague Convention mechanism lays down procedure to bring back the abducted child to his/her place of habitual residence and attempt to prevent parental child abduction. Hague convention is a multilateral treaty, which addresses parental abduction by facilitating co-operation between central authorities of the signatory countries to expedite the return of the child to the country of their habitual residence. Pakistan is not a party to Hague Convention but cross border families disputes particularly child abduction has been treated with immense importance by the judiciary of Pakistan on the basis of the welfare of child as a guiding principle of family law in custody matters.

**Keywords** Inter country child abduction · Public policy · UK Pakistan judicial protocol · *Sharia* · *Hizanat*

## Introduction

Every year thousands of children are abducted and trafficked for illegal purposes of sexual exploitation, physical labour, torture etc. Such practices are against the right of every child to have a decent childhood filled with parental love and care guaranteed under the UN Convention on the Rights of the Child, 1989[1] ratified by 196

[1]The Convention on the Rights of the Child (adopted 20 November 1989, entered into force 2 September 1990) 1577 UNTS 3 (hereinafter CRC Convention).

S. Ali (✉)
Lahore High Court, Lahore, Pakistan
e-mail: greenlaw123@hotmail.com

© Springer Nature Singapore Pte Ltd. 2017

S.R. Garimella and S. Jolly (eds.), *Private International Law*,
DOI 10.1007/978-981-10-3458-9_11

countries of the world.[2] The problem becomes exacerbated when a parent becomes the abductor. Statistics from Foreign and Commonwealth Office of United Kingdom reveal that the parental child abduction complaints received at the office increased by a massive 88% by 2012.[3] The U.S. State Department Report on child abduction revealed that the number of new international parental child abduction cases in the United States had nearly doubled since 2006, from 642 to 1135—most abductions involved children withdrawn the non-convention member countries.[4] In a typical scenario of parental abduction, a Pakistani national married to a non-Pakistani would withdraw the couple's child born abroad to Pakistan, thus removing the child from the custodial parent.[5] International community has attempted to remedy the situation through Hague convention that addresses parental abduction by facilitating co-operation between central authorities of the signatory countries to expedite the return of the child to the country of their habitual residence.

**Structure of the Chapter**

The present chapter addressing the issue of inter-country parental child abduction with reference to Pakistan is arranged in three sections. Section 2 presents the scenario of international child abduction. Section 3 attempts to discuss the statutory provisions dealing with custody of a child and maintenance focusing on Guardians and Wards Act, 1890 and the other provisions of the regulatory structure including the judicial opinion. Section 3.1 discusses the Hague Convention on the Civil Aspects of International Children Abduction, 1980. Pakistan is not, yet, a signatory, however it does have a bilateral judicial protocol with the UK to address the parental abduction issues between the two countries. The chapter contextualizes the lacunae in the Pakistan law on the issue of international parental child abduction with the need to address the increasing incidence of cross-border child abduction.

[2]192 countries are parties to the convention as of November 2005. For details see, the Convention on the Rights of the Child, 1989. https://treaties.un.org/doc/Publication/MTDSG/Volume%20I/Chapter%20IV/IV-11.en.pdf, accessed on 25th July, 2016.

[3]Foreign and Commonwealth Office, United Kingdom, 'Parental Child Abduction is a worldwide problem', (12 December 2012). https://www.gov.uk/government/news/parental-child-abduction-is-a-worldwide-problem, accessed on 3 April 2016.

[4]Convention on the Civil Aspects of International Abduction, Oct 25 1980. T.I.A.S No. 11,670 (entered into force December 1, 1983 (hereinafter Convention) Annette Schmit, 'The Hague Convention: The Problems with Accession and Implementation' (2008) 15(1) I J GLS 378.

[5]Sarmad Ali, 'International Child Abduction' (Daily Times 07 January 2013).
http://www.dailytimes.com.pk/opinion/07-Jan-2016/international-child-abduction, accessed 24 April 2016.

## 1 Child Abduction—An Overview

Based on the person who abducts the child, child abduction is divided into two broad categories:

(a) **Abduction by a Stranger**: An abduction of a child by a stranger, such abduction given effect for ransom, sexual abuse, trafficking, torture, brawl or in minor cases for want of a child, i.e., to raise the child as one's own.[6]

(b) **Parental Child Abduction**: Abduction of a child by a parent to prevent access to the child for the other parent leads to the situation of parental child abduction. According to Finkelhor, Hotaling, and Sedlak,[7] parental abductions occur in any of the three scenarios, "(a) an attempt is made by one parent to conceal the taking or the whereabouts of the child and to prevent contact with the child; or (b) the child was transported out of state; or (c) there was evidence that the abductor had intended to keep the child indefinitely or permanently affect custodial privileges."[8] This kind of child abduction mostly occurs where there is a separation and/or divorce battle is going between the parents of that child. Generally, the abductor takes the child to a different place within the same country.[9] On the other hand, International child abduction is when the parent takes the child out of his ordinary habitual residence to prevent the other parent from an access to visit the child.[10]

A total of 512 cases involving 84 different countries were reported to British authorities in 2011/2012—a definite increase from 272 in 51 countries in 2003/2004.[11] There is no formal statistical source of data available on international child abduction with reference to Pakistan.[12] But, unofficial sources, which the author is associated with, observe that there were 11 cases of international child abduction reported between Pakistan and the UK in 2008, 24 cases from April 2009

[6]HG.org Legal Resources, 'Child Abduction Law-Child Kidnapping Law'. https://www.hg.org/child-abduction.html, accessed 16 April 2016.

[7]David Finkelhor, Gerald Hotaling and Andrea Sedlak, 'Children Abducted by Family Members: A National Household Survey of Incidence and Episode Characteristics', (1991) 53, *Journal of Marriage and Family* 805–817.

[8]Taryn Lindhorst and Jeffrey L. Edleson 'Battered Women, Their Children, and International Law: The Unintended Consequences of the Hague Child Abduction Convention' (1st Edn Northeastern University Press 2012) 58, Ericka A. Schnitzer-Reese, "International Child Abduction to non-Hague Convention Countries: The need for an International Family Court', (2004) 2 Nw. J. Int'l Hum. Rts. 1,7.

[9]Maureen Dabbagh, 'Parental Kidnapping in America: An Historical and Cultural Analysis' (Mc Farland 2011)56.

[10]Convention, (n) 4.

[11]'Parental Child Abduction Cases Almost Double' (Sky News, 12 December 2012). http://news.sky.com/story/1023950/parental-child-abduction-cases-almost-double, accessed on 20 December 2015.

[12]Ibid.

to March 2010, and 55 cases in 2011.[13] Some individual cases of international child abduction were also reported between France and Pakistan and also between Canada and Pakistan.[14] The research conducted by Reunite International Child Abduction Centre revealed that the Middle Eastern countries, India and Pakistan figure prominently as destination of international parental child abduction. Interestingly these countries are not party to the Hague Convention on the Civil Aspects of International Child Abduction, 1980.[15] International parental child abduction is a condemnable act because of its serious repercussions on child, parents, family and finally on society at large.[16]

## 2 Impact of International Child Abduction

Through different studies it has been found that the impact of abduction varies from child to child.[17] The emotional bonding between the child and the abducting parent, behavioral patterns of the child, the nature and manner of abduction including the duration and place of the abduction, the age of the abducted child and the awareness of the abducted child of the reasons for his/her abduction etc. are some of the major factors that explain the impact caused due to parental child abduction.[18] As Geoffrey Greif observes, "the reactions of children who have been a victim of parental child abduction vary significantly. Such reactions include: nightmares, fears of doors and windows, bedwetting (depending on age), fear of authority and strangers, anger at abductor and/or left-behind parent, depression, anxiety, and school and peer problems".[19] It is also a possibility that continued habitation in the care of known people might result in the abducted children not realizing that they have been abducted for significant number of years or may be even for their whole

[13]https://abpworldgroup.com/author/abpworld/page/14/, accessed on 27th May, 2016.

[14]The Institute of Social Justice, 'Pakistan and the Hague Convention 1980'. http://www.isj.org.pk/policy-research/pakistan-and-the-hague-convention1980/#sthash.btp0t4vZ.dpuf, accessed on 22nd December, 2015.

[15]'Parental Child Abduction Cases Almost Double' (Sky News, 12 December 2012). http://news.sky.com/story/1023950/parental-child-abduction-cases-almost-double, accessed 20 December, 2015.

[16]Anis Shuhaiza Bt Md Salleh, 'Parental Child Abduction in Malaysia: Is Everything Right With Our Domestic Laws?' (2015) 23 (2) IIUMLJ, 247; Rhona Schuz, *The Hague Child Abduction Convention: A Critical Analysis (Studies in Private International law)*, (Hart Publishers, 2013) 24.

[17]Georgia K. Hilgeman, 'Impact of Family Child Abduction'. http://www.childabductions.org/impact2.html, accessed 16 April 2016.

[18]Geoffrey L. Greif, The long-term aftermath of child abduction: Two case studies and implications for family therapy (2009) 37 American Journal of Family Therapy, 273 See Trevor Buck, *International Child Law* (Routledge, 2014) 275.

[19]Geoffrey L. Greif, 'Parental child abduction and its impact' (Psychology Today, 13 November 2010). https://www.psychologytoday.com/blog/buddy-system/201011/parental-child-abduction-and-its-impact, accessed on 22 December, 2015.

lives. Given the kind of impact that parental abduction has on the child so abducted, various scholars have even gone to the extent of equating it with child abuse.[20] Janvier, McCormick, and Donaldson reported that the mean cost for search of an abducted child was upwards of $8000 in domestic cases and $27,000 in international cases, often more than the annual earnings of the left-behind parent.[21]

## 2.1 *Conflict of Laws Issues Arising Out of International Parental Child Abduction*

Parental child abduction—removal of a child from a place of his/her habitual residence from the custody of the left-behind parent to another jurisdiction probably to the nationality of the parent presents a few conflict of laws issues.

(a) Jurisdictional issues: As the abducted child is taken form one territory to another territory, there are several connecting factors like habitual residence or nationality of the child, nationality of the parent who abducts the child etc., which play significant role in deciding onto the question of jurisdiction.
(b) Issue of choice of applicable law: Identification of the applicable substantive law and procedural law to decide the issues in relation to custody of the child on merits. This too shall depend on the conflict of law rules of the country having jurisdiction to decide such case, which has been bought before it.
(c) Issue of recognition: Recognition of a foreign court's custody-related order by the forum courts is another concern in cross-border parental child abduction disputes. The criteria provided under the domestic law/conflict of law rules of a country must be satisfied in order for a foreign judgment to get enforced within the jurisdiction of that country. In majority of cases, inconsistency of the foreign judgment with the domestic legal provisions or public policy of the country leads to refusal of that foreign judgment within the territory of such jurisdiction. For example, courts is Pakistan have been circumspect about deciding custody of the child in favour of a parent not professing Islam. Although there have been occasions when they held that religion is not a ground to refuse custody of a minor to a non Muslim mother living in another country such judicial opinion has been only persuasive—judges deciding custody matters tend to hold in favour of father where the mother of the child is a non Muslim. Courts address two issues in custody-related disputes—the best interest of a minor and parent right.

---

[20]Nigel Lowe, Gillian Douglas, *Bromleys Family Law* (Oxford University Press, 2015) 579.

[21]RF Janvier, K. McCormick, & R. Donaldson, 'Parental kidnapping: A survey of left-behind parents' (1990) 41 Juvenile & Fam. Court J 1.

In international parental child abduction, the time involved in the court's decisional process could impact and alter the factual matrix surrounding such cases and the significant gap from filing of custody case till pronunciation of judgments come at the cost of childhood.

## 2.2 Parental Child Abduction—Pakistan

United Nations International Children Emergency Fund's (UNICEF) situation analysis report brings forth the alarming fact that Pakistan is an important destination for parent child abduction.[22] This could be ascribed to the increasing inter-cultural personal relationships between Pakistani men and foreign origin women—Pakistani men, faced with custody-related disputes in divorce and/or separation proceedings, could bring children to Pakistan, prior to any final decision on custody of the child.

## 2.3 Parental Child Abduction—Statutory Provisions in Pakistan

The 1973 Constitution is the governing document in the Islamic Republic of Pakistan, but a rider is there that it should be based on the tenets of Islam and it must be construed considering the Islamic injunctions avoiding contradictions between Sharia Law and interpretation of Constitution.[23] *Sharia* is believed to be the divine law, and is comprised of four sources, including the word of *Allah*, as spoken through his Prophet and preserved in the Qur'an and *Hadith*; collections of *Muhammad*'s sayings.[24] *Sharia* is a personal code and also an intrinsic part of Islam and obedience to it by a Muslim is expected regardless of his nationality or regular domicile. Sharia thus "draws no distinction between the religious and the secular, between legal, ethical, and moral questions, or between the public and private aspects of a Muslim's life."[25]

---

[22]Situation Analysis of Women and Children in Pakistan, National Report, Pakistan (2012) UNICEF.

[23]Preamble, Pakistan Constitution 1973.

[24]John L. Esposito and Natana J. Delong Bas, *Women in Muslim Family Law* (2nd Edition Syracuse University Press, 2001) 10.

[25]Bharati Anandhi Venkatraman, 'Islamic States and the United Nations Convention on the Elimination of All Forms of Discrimination Against Women: Are the Shari'a and the Convention Compatible' (1995) 44(5) Am.U. L. Rev 1949.

## 2.4 *Child Abduction Under Pakistan Penal Code*

The Pakistan Penal Code, 1860 (hereinafter, PPC) recognizes kidnapping (whether from Pakistan or from lawful guardianship) and abduction as crimes. The PPC extensively defined and explained abduction/kidnapping in general; sections starting from 359 to 374 of the PPC deal with the crime of kidnaping and abduction.

Section 362 of the PPC specified, "Whoever by force compels, or by any deceitful means induces, any person to go from any place, is said to abduct that person". If a Pakistani parent disobeys the court's orders issued under Section 491 of the Code of Criminal Procedure or under Sections 7 and 25 of the GWA, the court may order the arrest and detention of that parent. However, there are no reported cases of courts handing out such orders.

Under the Pakistan legal system, removal of a child by a parent is not criminal and is dealt with by the family or civil court. Consequently, trans-national movement of a child without the consent of the foreign parent would not lead to the detention of the alleged abductor, nor would that parent be punished under any section of the PPC for bringing the child to Pakistan.

The judiciary, in various cases, opined that parents could not be held responsible for the offence of abduction of their children. The leading case on this point is *Muhammad Ashraf v SHO and others*[26] in which the court held that a parent couldn't be punished for abducting his own child. However, there was an instance where the Federal Shariat Court of Pakistan in *Mst Asia Bibi v Alam Khan*[27] maintained a view that a father was held liable for abduction his daughter from lawful custody of her maternal uncle and maternal grandfather. It could thus be stated that the law relating to child custody is uneven, and courts have demonstrated favour for the opinion that a parent couldn't be viewed an abductor of his child.

Parental child abduction in Pakistan being a civil issue of child custody rather than a crime of abduction is dealt under the Guardians and Wards Act, 1890 (hereinafter, GWA).[28] Cassandra Balchin observed that courts have, while deciding the GWA petitions, embarked upon a factual analysis of each case, rather than favouring a rigid application of the principles of established Muslim Jurisprudence.[29] The analysis of judicial opinion in the later sections of this chapter demonstrates that courts often accorded primordial consideration to the welfare of the minor.

---

[26]2001 P Cr. L J 31.

[27]2009 PCrLJ 322.

[28]Aayesha Rafiq, 'Child Custody in Classical Islamic Law and Laws of Contemporary Muslim World—An Analysis' (2015) 4 IJHSS 271.

[29]Cassandra Balchin, *A Handbook on Family Laws in Pakistan* (1994) (Lahore: Shirkatgah) 164.

## 2.5 Child Custody under the GWA

Custody is described as the legal right to take care of a child.[30] Child custody also involves issues other than physical custody and control of child like parental rights, privileges, duties and powers connected to child rearing.[31]In Pakistan GWA[32] regulates the issues of custody and maintenance of a minor. Like many other legislations, GWA is of colonial inheritance. It continues to exist in its original version.

GWA uses the terminology of guardianship and custody interchangeably. It aims to,

- promote the interests of child,
- make sure that he/she may not suffer discrimination or disadvantage as a result of the marital status of his/her parents,
- addresses both facets of guardianship i.e. of the person and property[33] and
- ensure that the provisions of the Act take into account the personal law to which the minor is subject to.

The term guardianship is defined in the Section 4(2) as 'A person having the care of person of minor or of his property or of both his person and property'.

GWA prescribed the method of obtaining the lawful custody of the minor. The three parties involved in a case of custody before a guardian/family court in Pakistan:

- the custodial parent,
- the non-custodial parent and
- the minor.

---

[30]Shahzadi Pakeeza and Ali Asghar Chishti, 'Custody and Guardianship of Children According to Muslim Jurisprudence in Pakistan' (2012) 3 Academic Research International 461.

[31]Ibid.

[32]The Guardians and Wards Act 1890 was enacted to consolidate and amend the laws relating to guardian and wards. It was made applicable to all of India by the British rulers except the state of Jammu and Kashmir. This law was particularly outlined for Muslims, Christians, Parsis and Jews as their personal laws did not allow for full adoption only guardianship. It was made applicable to all children regardless of race or creed. For details see, The Guardian and Wards Act 1890, 'Preamble'. http://bdlaws.minlaw.gov.bd/print_sections_all.php?id=>64, accessed on 20 April 2016.

[33]Ibid., s 12.

Power to make interlocutory order for production of minor and interim protection of person and property.

(1) The Court may direct that the person if any, having the custody of the minor, shall produce him or cause him to be produced at such place and time and before such person as it appoints, and may make such order for the temporary custody and protection of the person or property of the minor as it thinks proper.

If the minor is a female who ought not to be compelled to appear in public, the claiming to be her guardian on the ground of his being her husband, unless she is already in his custody with the consent of her parents, if any, or

Any person to whom the temporary custody and protection of the property if a minor is entrusted to dispossess otherwise than by due course of law any person in possession of any of the property. See Merajuddin Farani, *Family Laws in Pakistan*, (Nadeem Law Book House 2006) 748.

Various provisions of GWA come into play when seeking child custody; for instance, in a case where a Pakistani man marries an American woman and he brings his child to Pakistan without the consent of child's mother, she can come to Pakistan to file a suit under Section 25 of GWA in order to get relief.[34]

Section 25 of GWA confers discretion upon the court to decide the matter after looking into various factors like the financial position of father and/or mother; gender of the minor, the character of custody seeking parent; welfare of a child, etc. The court in *Syed Zia Ul Hassan Gilani v Mian Khadim Hussain and Ors*[35] observed that the father is not under any legal duty to tender maintenance to male child but in case of female child the father is under legal duty to extend maintenance despite attaining of age of majority of female child till she is not married. The welfare of the child is the paramount consideration in all custody disputes under the Act. Though it does not precisely define the concept of welfare of the child, but it provides a check-list of factors that constitute the welfare and best interests of the child. Including future life, education, fulfillment of basic needs of a child, etc.

An important concept of the Pakistan legal system on child custody is the right of *Hizanat*.

## 2.6 *Hizanat*

Custody of children under Islamic law exists within two spheres referred to as *hadanah/Hizanat* and *Wilayah*. *Hadanah/Hizanat* relates to the right to physical custody of the child whereas *wilayah* is guardianship of the person and property of the child.[36] Different sects and schools of Islamic jurisprudence agree that, unless disqualified, a mother has the first claim to *hadanah* and is considered the natural custodian of the child.[37]

The word *Hizanat* is derived from a word "*Hizan*" which means 'lap of a mother'.[38] It is generally viewed in Pakistan that the right of *Hizanat* under Muslim

---

[34]Ibid., s 25; See, Alhaji Ajijol, *Introduction to Islamic Law* (Adam Publishers, 2006) 196.

Title of guardian to custody of ward (1) If a ward leaves or is removed from the custody of a guardian of his person, the Court, if it is of opinion that it will be for the welfare of the ward to return to the custody of his guardian, may make an order for his return and for the purpose of enforcing the order may cause the ward to be arrested and to be delivered into the custody of the guardian.

(2) For the purpose of arresting the ward, the Court may exercise the power conferred on a Magistrate of the first class by section 100 of the Code of Criminal Procedure, 1882 (10 of 1882)1.

(3) The residence of a ward against the will of his guardian with a person who is not his guardian does not of itself terminate the guardianship.

[35]PLD 2001 Lahore 188.

[36]Asma Jahangir, S. A. Abid, *Comprehensive and Exhaustive Commentary on Manual of Family Laws in Pakistan* (Civil & Criminal Law Publication, 2004) 419, 421.

[37]Alhaji, (n 34) 90.

[38]See S.N Ebrahimi, 'Child Custody (Hizanat) Under Iranian law: An Analytical Discussion' (2005) 39 Fam.L.Q 459.

Personal Law is primarily and substantially vested in the mother to have the custody of a minor child though this right is not absolute.[39] The "*Hanafi Fiqh*" of Muslims, the mother has the right to get the custody of a child till seven years in case of a boy and in case of a girl until she attains the age of puberty.[40] However, age limit varies according to different schools and there is nothing significant that can be traced from the Holy Quran regarding the age limit of male or female child in the above context.[41]

The father is vested with the right of *Hizanat* upon the male child attaining seven years of age and the female child after the age of puberty as he is the natural guardian of children.[42] The right continues even though the parents may be divorced. Statistics proves that around 75% of all child custody is awarded to the mothers.[43]

The Supreme Court in *Feroze Begum v Muhammad Hussain*[44] laid down the principle that the paramount and overriding consideration in the custody cases is the welfare of the minor. The father being legal guardian cannot compel the court to order in his favour unless it is in the welfare of the child.[45] It appears that the courts of Pakistan follow the principle of welfare of minor in every case of custody while passing orders, whether it is an interim or final judgment.[46]

While appointing the guardian the courts take into account Section 17 of GWA[47]and several factors, which are discussed below.

---

[39]*Razia Bibi v Riaz Ahmed* 2004 SCMR 821; *Nasreen Akhtar v Javed Ahmed* 2004 CLC 228.

[40]Safia Iqbal. *Woman and Islamic Law* (Adam Publishers, 2004) 207, 208.

[41]Kashi Prasad Saksena, *Muslim Law as Administered in India and Pakistan*, (Eastern Book Company, 1963) 332.

[42]GWA (n 32) s 25.

[43]Murtaza Haider, Children giving birth to children in Pakistan, 08 December 2014. http://www.dawn.com/news/1149176, accessed on 1 may 2016. See Merajuddin Farani, (n 33) 755.

[44]1978 SCMR 299.

[45]Ibid. 300.

[46]Dr. Ijaz Ali Chishti and Ataullah Khan Mahmood 'Adjective Law Undermining the Substantive Law (The Hague Convention on the Child Abduction)' (2012). http://ssrn.com/abstract=2083081, accessed 3 April 2016.

[47]GWA (n 32) s 17; See, Asma Jahangir (n 36) 423.

(1) In appointing or declaring the guardian of a minor, the Court shall, subject to the provisions of this section, be guided by what, consistently with the law to which the minor is subject, appears in the circumstances to be for the welfare of the minor.
(2) In considering what will be for the welfare of the minor, the Court shall have regard to the age, sex and religion of the minor, the character and capacity of the proposed guardian and his nearness of kin to the minor, the wishes, if any, of a de-ceased parent, and any existing or previous relations of the proposed guardian with the minor or his property.
(3) If minor is old enough to form an intelligent preference, the Court may consider that preference.
(4) The Court shall not appoint or declare any person to be a guardian against his will.

### 2.6.1 Welfare of the Minor

The courts in Pakistan consider the "welfare of the minor" or "the best interest of the minor" as the prime factor while deciding the matters of custody of child. The test of welfare of the minor is similar to that of English Family Law.[48] Moreover, it is the duty of the father to provide for the maintenance of the children even if the custody is granted to the mother.[49] The Pakistani courts in various judgments have opined that while deciding the matters of child custody the courts are not supposed to go into the technicalities of law and should decide the matter of custody with the sole aim of child welfare.[50] "The legal technique used by the Pakistani courts to incorporate the "best interests" test into the Pakistani law is the ancient concept of *ijtihad* or the exercise of human reason to ascertain a rule of Muslim law."[51]

The Court in *Mst. Firdous Iqbal v Shifaat Ali and others*[52] held that the welfare of the child was to be given paramount consideration in the determination of custody of a minor notwithstanding the fact that the father initiated the custody petition after the minor was of seven years of age. The rights of the parents, either of them, are not the determinant principles in a child custody case. The court observed that right of the father to claim the custody of a minor son is not an absolute right and it shall depend on the facts and circumstances of every case as to which of the either parents shall be given the custody of the child keeping in mind the supreme consideration of child welfare.[53] In *Attique Ahmed v Adla Noreen*[54] the father of a three-year old child appealed in The Supreme Court of Azad Jammu and Kashmir (AJK) against an order of the family court and the federal shariat court awarding the custody of the minor boy to the mother. The Supreme Court of AJK upheld earlier judgments stating that in any custodial dispute the welfare of the minor remains the paramount consideration. Islamic law as applied under the Guardian and Wards Act 1890 gave the right of custody of a child of tender years to the mother. The child of such an age was believed to be in need of full time attention, care, and love, which a mother was more able to provide as compared to a father.[55]

---

[48]S (BD) v. S(ID) (1977) 1 All E.R. 656; J v. C 1970 A.C. 668; See generally, Joseph Goldstein, Anna Freud, & Albert J. Solnit, *Beyond the Best Interests of the Child* (New York: The Free Press 1973).

[49]*Ayesha Tahir Shafiq v Saad Amanullah Khan* PLD 2001 Kar.371.

[50]*Rukhsana Malik v Abdul Aziz*: PLD 2004 Lah. 801.

[51]Martha F. Davis, 'Child Custody in Pakistan: The Role of Ijtihad' (1985) 5 *B.C. Third World L. J.*119.

[52]*Mst. FirdousIqbal v Shifaat Ali and others* (2000 SCMR 838).

[53]Ibid.; see, Syed Mohammed Ali, *Position of Women in Islam, The: A Progressive View* (SUNY Press, 2004) 81.

[54](2013) CLC 568 Supreme Court (AJ&K).

[55]Shabnam Ishaque and Muhammad Mustafa Khan, 'The Best Interests of the Child: A Prevailing Consideration within Islamic Principles and a Governing Principle in Child Custody Cases in Pakistan' (2015) IJLPF 29.

In *Abida Bibi v Abdul Latif*,[56] it was held that the basic criterion for appointment of guardian and restoration of custody was the welfare of the minor, mother being preferred in comparison with any other relatives for fulfillment of the above criterion. In *B. Peggy Collins v Muhammad Ishfaque Malik*[57] a French mother, applied to the court in Pakistan against her ex-husband who had brought her minor son to Pakistan forcibly. The court handed over the custody of that child to the French mother dismissing the claims of the father that the child's Muslim faith and his identity as a Pakistani citizen would be compromised if custody were granted to the Christian mother.[58] The Supreme Court of Pakistan later on held that the judgment referred above will have no effect and cannot be cited a precedent in future cases relating to child custody matters. It is arguable that the judgment of court in *Peggy Collins* seemed to be correct in letter and spirit and was based on logical reasoning while handing over the custody to the French mother.

Sections 12 and 17 in the GWA symbolize the spirit of the Act, ensuring the welfare of the minor as the primary concern of a decision on custody.[59] The factors of age, sex, religion, capacity and character of the proposed custodian, the nearness of kin to the minor, the property rights of the minor are some of the important factors which are for deciding the moral, spiritual and material wellbeing of a child.

---

[56] 2002 CLC 1416.

[57] 2009 PLD 48 Lahore High Court.

[58] Ibid.

[59] GWA (n 32) s 12.

Power to make interlocutory order for production of minor and interim protection of person and property.

(1) The Court may direct that the person if any, having the custody of the minor, shall produce him or cause him to be produced at such place and time and before such person as it appoints, and may make such order for the temporary custody and protection of the person or property of the minor as it thinks proper.

If the minor is a female who ought not to be compelled to appear in public, the claiming to be her guardian on the ground of his being her husband, unless she is already in his custody with the consent of her parents, if any, or

Any person to whom the temporary custody and protection of the property if a minor is entrusted to dispossess otherwise than by due course of law any person in possession of any of the property.

Section 17

Matter to be considered by the Court in appointing guardian.

(1) In appointing or declaring the guardian of a minor, the Court shall, subject to the provisions of this section, be guided by what, consistently with the law to which the minor is subject, appears in the circumstances to be for the welfare of the minor.

In considering what will be for the welfare of the minor, the Courts shall have regard to the age, sex and religion of the minor, the character and capacity of the proposed guardian and his nearness of kin to the minor, the wishes,

if any, of a deceased parent, and any existing or previous relations of the proposed guardian with the minor or his property. If the minor is old enough to form an intelligent preference, the Court may consider that preference.

The Court shall not appoint or declare any person to be a guardian against his will. See Asma Jahangir, (n 38) 412.

### 2.6.2 Character of the Guardian

Character of the proposed guardian could be a significant factor in custody-related decisions.[60] But it is important to note here that the courts of Pakistan also maintain a view that a mere ground of poverty is not a ground for depriving the mother of her child's custody. The court years ago held that the mother's poverty would be no hindrance for the award of the child's custody to her, as it is for the father to provide for the maintenance.[61]

### 2.6.3 Capacity of the Proposed Guardian

In custody-related orders the custody of a child is to given to either parent capable of and could satisfy the court that he/she would look after the child with due diligence, providing him/her with all necessities of life.[62] It is a requirement of Islamic law that the custodian is physically able and fit to perform his/her duties and responsibilities towards that child.

### 2.6.4 Religion

In Pakistan law the religion of the parent has a role in the custody-related applications. *Hanbali*s and *Shafi'i*s opine that a non-Muslim mother cannot be a custodian of the child since there is high likelihood that she may influence the child towards a non-Islamic faith and a way of life inconsistent with Islamic faith. They base their beliefs on *Quranic* verses and Prophet's traditions. However, according to *Hanafi*s and *Maliki*s, non-Muslim mothers who are *kitabiyah* or *majousiyah* can be custodians of a child provided that no harm is caused to the child either physically or religiously. The case of *Amina Tarar*[63] was a landmark judgment decided by the Lahore High Court in 2012. The case involved a custody restoration application made by the mother of the minor (female) against the father who withdrew the child from France. The father took that child to Pakistan despite restraining orders and forced the child to stay with him in Pakistan. The mother filed a petition in the Lahore High Court and the court asked the father to hand over the custody of the child to the French mother. The court opined that the child was

[60]Shabnam Ishaque (n 55) 79.

[61]*Harbai v Usman* PLD 1963 (WP) Karachi 888.

[62]*Imran Ali v Mst. Iffat Siddiqui and two Others*, PLD 2008 Karachi 198.

[63]Nicole, 'Gender, Religion, Custody: The Case of Amina Tarar' (Muslimah Media Watch, 8 March 2012). http://www.patheos.com/blogs/mmw/2012/03/gender-religion-custody-the-case-of-amina-tarar/, accessed on 3 April 2016.

an eleven years old girl and under GWA the mother could have the custody of a girl child until that child has attained the age of puberty.[64]

The Lahore High Court in *Roshni Desai v Jahanzeb Niazi*[65] handed the custody of the minor child born of a common law marriage, to the mother. The father withdrew the child to Pakistan. Handing over the custody the Court also held that the mother should move a Canadian court for getting compensation, if any, from the Canadian national father of Pakistani origin who unlawfully brought the child to Pakistan.[66] The child was born out of common law marriage, seen illegitimate under Islamic Law; hence the father has no legal ties to the child despite being the biological father. The mother of an illegitimate child is not only entitled to the custody of the child, but is also regarded as the guardian of the child to the total exclusion of the father.[67] Non-Muslin mother suffers no disability as Islamic Law allows a non-Muslim mother to exercise the same rights of custody as are enjoyed by a Muslim mother.[68]

Pakistani Superior Courts have generally purported to exclude religious considerations by granting equal rights to non-Muslim (*Kitabiyah*) as that of Muslim mothers. It is in the nature of the inquiry underpinning a child's best interests that factors such as a child's wishes, educational, emotional and other needs, stable environment, trustworthiness, and character of the proposed custodian/guardian are considered by the courts.

## 3 The Hague Convention on Civil Aspects of International Child Abduction

As a response to the growing incidence of international child abduction, the Hague Convention on the Civil Aspects of Child Abduction, 1980 was opened for accession and it entered into force between the signatories on 1st December 1983. The Hague Convention is a multilateral treaty that provides an expeditious method for return of an internationally abducted child from one member-State to another.

[64]'Custody row: French mother handed Pakistani daughter', (The Express Tribune, 18 February 2012). http://tribune.com.pk/story/338037/custody-row-french-mother-handed-pakistani-daughter/ , accessed 8 January 2016.

[65]*Roshni Desai v Jahanzeb Niazi* 2011 PLD 423 Lahore High Court.

[66]Ibid.

[67]Ibid., 423.

[68]Salman Khan Golra, 'Father is not entitled for child custody in case of common law marriage', (International Lawyer, 10 August 2012). http://www.internationallawyer.info/2012/08/father-is-not-entitled-for-child.html, accessed 3 April 2016.

It provides to seek help of authorities of a member country where the child is being taken in order to bring him back to the country of his habitual residence.[69]

The objective was to enhance uniformity throughout the world over laws on international child abduction and it intended to provide remedies in case of international child abduction along with appropriate legal procedure for prompt return of the children to their State of habitual residence.[70] Removal or retention of a child is "wrongful" whenever,

> "a. It is in breach of rights of custody attributed to a person, an institution or any other body, either jointly or alone, under the law of the State in which the child was habitually resident immediately before the removal or retention; and
> b. At the time of removal or retention those rights were actually exercised, either jointly or alone, or would have been so exercised but for the removal or retention." These rights of custody may arise by operation of law or by reason of a judicial or administrative decision, or by reason of an agreement having legal effect under the law of the country of habitual residence."[71]

The Convention specifies provisions for cooperation amongst member countries to address the issue of international child abduction and to provide a prompt redressal mechanism for bringing the child back to his country of habitual residence. The fundamental notion of cooperation was embedded in the fact that it was required that the countries party to the Convention must adhere to decrees of another country in order to strengthen the purpose of the convention and currently 94 countries are party to the Convention.[72] Furthermore, the Convention does not provide procedural rules to adjudicate issues of custody of children.[73]As per the Convention, the court where the complaint of wrongful removal is lodged must determine the wrongful removal and/or retention, not the custody issue. The court upon determination of the same, orders the return of the child to his/her habitual

[69]Convention (n 4) Art 1.

The objects of the present Convention are—

(a) to secure the prompt return of children wrongfully removed to or retained in any Contracting State; and
(b) to ensure that rights of custody and of access under the law of one Contracting State are effectively respected in the other Contracting States.

[70]Ibid.; see also Rebecca K. McKelvey, 'An Overview of the International Parental Child Abduction Provisions of The Hague Convention' (2010) 7(1) Ankara L Rev. 67.

[71]Convention (n 4) art 3.

The rights of custody mentioned in sub-paragraph a) above, may arise in particular by operation of law or by reason of a judicial or administrative decision, or by reason of an agreement having legal effect under the law of that State.

[72]Status table: Convention of 25 October 1980 on the Civil Aspects of International Child Abduction. Hague Conference on Private International Law. See Katherine Sohr, "Difficulties Implementing the Hague Convention on the Protection of Children and Co operation in Respect of Inter-country Adoption: A Criticism of the Proposed Ortega's Law and an Advocacy for Moderate Adoption Reform in Guatemala," (2006) 18 Pace Int'l L. Rev. 559–593.

[73]Tom Harper, 'The Limitations of the Hague Convention and Alternate Remedies for a Parent Including Re-Abduction' (1995) 9 Emory Int'l L Rev. 257.

residence promptly unless covered under any of the exceptions provided under the Convention.[74] Once the child has been sent back to his/her country of habitual residence the local authorities/family courts will determine the custody issue in accordance with the local family laws and regulations of that country.[75] The Convention is applicable to a child below the age of 16 years[76] and ensures prompt return of the child to its habitual residence.

## 3.1 *The Hague Convention on Civil Aspects of International Child Abduction and Pakistan*

Although a significant increase is noticed in the number of parental child abduction cases where a parent abducts the child from a foreign land and brings him/her to Pakistan, the Pakistani government is yet to respond and ratify the Hague Convention. In view of the above fact, the left-behind parent belonging to a Hague Convention country is unable to invoke the application of the Convention to ensure prompt return of the child. Such parent may need to apply to the Pakistan courts under local laws of Pakistan dealing with custody of the child. Such application

---

[74]Convention (n 4) Art 7 lays down the duties and cooperation to be followed by authorities.

Central Authorities shall co-operate with each other and promote co-operation amongst the competent authorities in their respective States to secure the prompt return of children and to achieve the other objects of this Convention. In particular, either directly or through any intermediary, they shall take all appropriate measures—

(a) to discover the whereabouts of a child who has been wrongfully removed or retained;
(b) to prevent further harm to the child or prejudice to interested parties by taking or causing to be taken provisional measures;
(c) to secure the voluntary return of the child or to bring about an amicable resolution of the issues;
(d) (d) to exchange, where desirable, information relating to the social background of the child;
(e) to provide information of a general character as to the law of their State in connection with the application of the Convention;
(f) to initiate or facilitate the institution of judicial or administrative proceedings with a view to obtaining the return of the child and, in a proper case, to make arrangements for organising or securing the effective exercise of rights of access;
(g) where the circumstances so require, to provide or facilitate the provision of legal aid and advice, including the participation of legal counsel and advisers;
(h) to provide such administrative arrangements as may be necessary and appropriate to secure the safe return of the child;
(i) to keep each other informed with respect to the operation of this Convention and, as far as possible, to eliminate any obstacles to its application.

[75]Tai Vivatvaraphol, 'Back to Basics: Determining a Child's Habitual Residence in International Child Abduction Cases Under the Hague Convention' (2009) 77 Fordham L Rev. 3325.

[76]Convention (n 4) Art 4.

The Convention shall apply to any child who was habitually resident in a Contracting State immediately before any breach of custody or access rights. The Convention shall cease to apply when the child attains the age of 16 years.

would be of a civil nature suit with an option to apply to the criminal court complaining of abduction of the child by the other parent who is a citizen of Pakistan. However, with regard to the abductions from United Kingdom, Pakistan has signed a judicial cooperation protocol dealing with child abduction.[77] Pakistan's interim law minister has reportedly said that the Pakistan government would ratify the 1980 Hague Convention on the Civil Aspects of Child Abduction.[78]

## 3.2 *Pakistan's Opposition to the Hague Convention*

The reason for the reluctance of Pakistan to accede to the Hague Convention is the inconsistency of the said Convention with the *Sharia* law. It is perceived that the fundamental principles of the Hague Convention are divergent to the Sharia, and hence the legal fraternity is opposed to accession to it.[79] Article 227 (1) of the constitution of Pakistan stipulates that all existing laws shall be brought in conformity with the injunctions of Islam as laid down in Holy Quran and Sunnah.[80] Even though the Pakistan Penal Code recognizes kidnapping and abduction as crimes, rarely have the parents been held accused of an offence of kidnapping of their own children.

## 3.3 *UK-Pakistan Protocol on Child Abduction*

There has been an increased incidence of parental child abduction between UK and Pakistan, especially in instances of inter-cultural marriages.[81]To address this problem, the judiciary in Pakistan and UK formulated a mechanism for handling child abduction cases between the two countries. In 2002 Dame Elizabeth Butler-Sloss, President of the Family Division in England and Wales, together with

[77]UK-Pakistan Judicial Protocol on Child Matters. https://www.gov.uk/government/uploads/system/uploads/attachment_data/file/210147/FCO_PCAPakistanProt_AW_0613.pdf, accessed 16 April 2016.

[78]Abigail Lowther, 'Child Abduction-Pakistan's plans to sign up to the Hague Convention'. http://www.pannone.com/media-centre/blog/family-blog/child-abduction-%E2%80%93-pakistan%E2%80%99s-plans-sign-hague-convention#sthash.VfhtXg6z.dpuf, accessed 16 April 2016.

[79]Yearbook of Islamic and Middle Eastern Law, (2002) 8 Kluwer Law International, 99.

[80]The Constitution of Pakistan Part IX Islamic Provisions, Provisions relating to the Holy Quran and Sunnah, Art 227(1) All existing laws shall be bought in conformity with the injunctions of Islam as laid down in the Holy Quran and Sunnah, in this part referred to as the injunctions of Islam, and no law shall be enacted which is repugnant to such injunctions.*Explanation*-In the application of this clause to the personal law of any Muslim sect, the Expression 'Quran' and 'Sunnah' shall mean the Quran and the Sunnah as interpreted by the sect.

[81]Amber Darr, 'Child Abuctions', (Dawn, 29 March 2010). http://www.dawn.com/news/844927/child-abductions, accessed 3 April 2016.

officials from the Foreign and Commonwealth Office, visited Pakistan and met members of the Pakistan judiciary. Following the visit, Chief Justice of Pakistan, Choudhary Iftikhar Mohammad led a delegation for a meeting with Lord Thorpe, Head of International Family Law, and other senior members of UK judiciary in January 2003. A consensus was reached and shaped into the Protocol on Parental Child Abduction between UK and Pakistan.[82] It was laid down that the Protocol is a judicial understanding with an objective to secure the return of the abducted child to the country where they normally live without regard to the nationality; religion or culture of the parent i.e. the welfare of the child was to be given prime importance.[83]

The judges of both countries agreed that the welfare of the children should be given the highest priority in normal circumstances and the courts of country from where he has been taken must decide the matter of custody as they are in best position to decide and determine what is best for the child including the issue of where he/she should live.[84] The protocol ensured that the courts of UK and Pakistan honour the decrees of each other concerning child custody.[85] It was also agreed that both countries notify the administrative procedure for the smooth and effective functioning of UK-Pakistan protocol in child-custody disputes.[86]

The protocol is yet to be ratified into law, hence it is not legally binding on the Pakistan judiciary. The legal status (binding character) of the Protocol is doubtful as whilst the Protocol has not yet been ratified, its provisions are in line with the usual practices of the courts, so judges could, and, do make orders referring to the Protocol. The protocol also provides that the court has to initially determine the habitual residence/residence habitual residence that court should determine the issue of removal of a child from the habitual residence.[87] Court proceedings in

---

[82]Afshan Ghazanfar, 'Child Abduction and Transnational Jurisdiction'. http://www.supremecourt.gov.pk/ijc/Articles/12/3.pdf; See also James Young, 'The Constitutional Limits of Judicial Activism: Judicial Conduct of International Relations and Child Abduction' (2003) 66 MLR 828.

[83]The UK-Pakistan Judicial Protocol on Children Matters, 2003 (n 77).

[84]Ibid., art 3.

If a child is taken from the UK to Pakistan, or from Pakistan to the UK, by a parent with visitation/access/contact rights with the consent of the parent with a custody/residence order or a restraint/interdict order from the court of the child's habitual/ordinary residence or in consequence of an order from that court permitting the visit, and the child is retained in that country after the end of the visit without the consent or in breach of the court order, the judge of the court of the country in which the child has been retained shall not ordinarily exercise jurisdiction over the child, save in so far as it is necessary for the court to order the return of the child to the country of the child's habitual/ordinary residence.

[85]Ibid. Article 8 it is further recommended that the judiciaries, the legal practitioners and the nongovernmental organisations in the UK and Pakistan use their best endeavours to advance the objects of this protocol.

[86]Ibid. Article 7 It is recommended that the respective governments of the UK and Pakistan give urgent consideration to identifying or establishing an administrative service to facilitate or oversee the resolution of child abduction cases (not covered by the 1980 Hague Convention on the Civil Aspects of International Child Abduction).

[87]Ghazanfar (n 82).

Pakistan in such custody cases could extend to years to reach a conclusion.[88] With these constraints, the Protocol is only an option for inter-country couples of UK and Pakistan to discuss with their lawyers. If parents decide not to use the Protocol to seek the return of children, they shall still need to make a decision on initiation of legal proceedings in Pakistan in case they cannot come to an agreement with each other on the custody issue.

*Louise Ann Fairely v Sajjad Ahmed Rana*[89] is an important judgment with regard to the application of the above-mentioned Protocol. In this case, Sajjad Ahmed Rana (Respondent) a citizen of Pakistan married the petitioner, a British citizen on 22nd January in 1986 in UK. A child named Misbah Irum Rana was born, before the couple divorced in 2001. The child lived with her father in Scotland; in 2005 the petitioner took her and his other children to Pakistan on vacation despite a 2005 restraining order of the Session Courts of Scotland. During the proceedings in the Scottish court the father promised not to remove the child from care and control of mother and Court, was debarred to bring the child to Pakistan. The mother contended forcible removal of the child to Pakistan in violation of Court's orders. She petitioned the Lahore High Court under Article 199 of the Constitution of Pakistan read with Section 491 of Criminal Code of Procedure 1890 for a writ of habeas corpus. The petitioner pleaded that the exercise of custody of the child by her father in Pakistan is "illegal and improper", in view of the foreign court's order. The respondent pleaded being the natural guardian and hence to be awarded custody of the child. The Lahore High Court allowed petition and held that the custody of the child be handed over to her mother through British High Commission in Pakistan within seven days. The Lahore High Court endeavoured to follow the UK-Pakistan protocol in order to promote sense of confidence between the two countries' judiciary.

The respondent appealed to the Supreme Court of Pakistan challenging the impugned order of the Lahore High Court. The counsel of the appellant (father) observed that the child reached the age of puberty therefore her statement in the court seemed relevant and important. He further submitted that father being the natural guardian shall be granted the custody of the child not the mother under the law of Pakistan. The counsel for the respondent (mother) contended that the child should be returned to Scotland, which is her habitual residence and let the local court of Scotland decide the custody matter. Therefore, the Supreme Court of Pakistan may not interfere into controversy of custody issue. The Court, after prolonged hearings noted the fact that the disputant parties reached a compromise, hence the disposed the petition.

*Razia Rehman v Station House Officer*[90] is an illustration of the positive effect that have flown from the UK-Pakistan Judicial Protocol. The case concerned a mother, and her three children, all British citizens, living in Multan. Pakistan.

---

[88]Ibid.

[89]*Sajjad Ahmed Rana v Louise Ann Fairely* PLD 2007 Lahore 300.

[90]2006 PLD SC 533.

Following the collapse of the marriage and allegations of false imprisonment there writ petitions filed to ensure release of the mother and reuniting with the children. On custody dispute the Supreme Court, hearing a habeas corpus petition and an appeal from the Lahore High Court decision, declared, "according to the law of the land, any agreement reached between the two parents, inter alia, regarding the custody of the minor children is neither valid in law nor even enforceable."[91] There would, therefore be no waiver of custody-related rights. Applying the Islamic law on *hizanat,* the mother was awarded the custody of her children, who were below the age of seven. The judicial Protocol was referred to for deciding upon the rights of the father. The Supreme Court observed that the father should be allowed to visit his children in the UK, stating that faced with this situation and also in view of the UK-Pakistan Protocol the UK consular offices in Pakistan were suggested to facilitate the respondent father to visit his children in the United Kingdom.[92]

Although the said Protocol has bought some relief to parental child abduction matters in context of UK and Pakistan, problems persist for similar matters between Pakistan and other nations. In addition to this, parents do encounter procedural hurdles during the pendency of child-custody matters in Pakistani courts. Custody-related disputes in courts involve long and protracted deliberations, the minor whose custody matter is pending before the court for adjudication could be deprived of the love and affection for the non-custodial parent who is seeking court indulgence for the custody. Furthermore, it has also been noticed in Pakistan that the guardian/family courts during the pendency of the custody-related matter, do not order on the visitation schedule of the non-custodial parent. It is pertinent that such orders need to be made so that the minor benefits from the visit of the non-custodial parent. It would help enhance the trust and faith in the legal system with regard to child custody in Pakistan.

Recently, it was announced in the media that Pakistan is contemplating ratification of the Hague Convention soon.[93] This decision has generated debate in the public space—the legal and intellectual community prefers ratification of the Convention as an immediate priority activity. However, there is also a jarring opposition from the Islamic Ideology Council led by Maulana Aftab Sherani. It has labeled the Government's opinion favouring ratification as a mistake, because the Convention contained few provisions that are un-Islamic and hence, opposed to the Constitution of Pakistan, 1973. The Council's opposition may affect the progression towards ratification of the Convention and may foster some opposition from the civil society in Pakistan. The author suggests that along with the ratification of the Convention there should also be a discussion on considering international child abduction as heinous as other criminal offences listed in Pakistan Penal Code.

---

[91]Ibid., para 8.

[92]Id, para 12.

[93]'Pakistan on Track to sign the Child Abduction Convention', The Nation August 24, 2016. http://nation.com.pk/national/24-Aug-2016/pakistan-on-track-to-sign-hague-child-abduction-convention.

## 4 Conclusion

The Hague Convention attempts to provide an important deterrent against wrongful removal of the child. Pakistan, owing to the perception that the Convention's provisions are un-Islamic did not attempt to address the problem of international parental child abduction, either through a national legislation or by ratifying the Hague Convention. Accession to the Convention could help Pakistan address the problem and help ensure primacy of the welfare of the minor, a major objective as reflected in the GWA. To address the issue of expedited redressal of custody-related disputes, the UK-Pakistan protocol, needs to be operationalized through legislation so that the forum that is best positioned to ensure the welfare of the minor could address custody-related disputes. Further, as is evidenced in the Misbah Rana decision, mediation could be a method to address disputes related to international parental child abduction. It is necessary that standard criteria for such mediated settlements need be legislated upon. The Supreme Court has emphasized on the appointment of liaison judges to ensure cooperation in child-custody related disputes. There is little information available on this front. It is important that these liaison judges' appointments is expedited so that there would be prompt address of the problems concerning international parental child abduction.

# Inter-country Child Abduction—Sri Lankan Legal Response

**Rose Wijeyeskera**

**Abstract** Despite being a signatory to some key Hague Conventions on private international law related aspects, Sri Lanka is skeptical as far as the private international law is concerned. A first glance at the situation gives the definite imprint of legal uncertainty, caused by diverse reasons ranging from religious to political. Judicial determinations oscillate between tradition and novelty based on positivism and modernism affecting various aspects of human life. Amidst this background, the chapter attempts to analyze the legal statement affecting the lives and rights of citizens who choose to make bonds beyond horizons, and the approaches adopted to resolving the legal issues arising from and related to such bonds, specifically in respect of inter-country child abduction. In the context of the broad objectives of the Civil Aspects of International Child Abduction Act of 2001, which Sri Lanka enacted in honoring its international obligations and to give effect to the Hague Convention on the Civil Aspects of International Child Abduction of 1980, the chapter analyses the Sri Lankan pre-legislation and post-legislation legal position in respect of parental obligations, duties and responsibilities of the Central Authority, and procedural aspects including jurisdiction. A selection of Sri Lankan judgments are analyzed to examine judicial conceptualization of inter-country child abductions in the context of its international obligations and local law, and the relevance and applicability of foreign judgments in local courts. The impact of the 2001 legislation is assessed on its own provisions as well as compared to the Reciprocal Enforcement of Judgments Ordinance of 1921 and of 1935.

**Keywords** Inter country child abduction · Welfare of the child · Civil aspects of international child abduction act Sri Lanka · Constitutional rights

R. Wijeyeskera (✉)
Department of Private and Comparative Law, Faculty of Law, University of Colombo, Colombo, Sri Lanka
e-mail: rosewijeyesekera@gmail.com; rose@law.cmb.ac.lk

© Springer Nature Singapore Pte Ltd. 2017

S.R. Garimella and S. Jolly (eds.), *Private International Law*,
DOI 10.1007/978-981-10-3458-9_12

**Introduction**

The Constitution of Sri Lanka recognizes and protects the family as the basic unit of society, it entrusts this responsibility on the State.[1] Citizenship in Sri Lanka is by descent, in case of a child born to Sri Lankan overseas citizens (Sri Lanka recognizes dual citizenship) he could be registered as a citizen if one of the parents is Sri Lankan. Where both parents are domiciled in the country, children are governed by the personal law applicability to their parents irrespective of where they live. However, if one parent, without the consent of the other, took the child out of the country or a parent upon arrival in Sri Lanka with the child, changed the domicile of the parent and the child, the applicability of personal law in respect of rights and duties relating to the custody of the child presents a concern with regard to the determination of the applicable law to the dispute. The concern is further complicated if one parent is a non-Sri Lankan citizen or a Sri Lankan holding dual citizenship. In such situations jurisdictional issues constrain courts from following normal procedures, and applying personal law would be unjust and impracticable. Since uncertainty and inconsistency of law create a gap preventing the parties concerned of realizing their rights and responsibilities, a need arises for a common ground. The Hague Convention on International Child Abduction attempts to fill this gap. Sri Lanka has acceded to the application of the principles and procedures in the Convention by adopting an enabling legislation.

**Structure of the Chapter**

This chapter discusses the legal situation in Sri Lanka in respect of international child abduction, with particular emphasis on judicial responses. The chapter begins with an introduction of the Sri Lankan legal framework on custody, guardianship and maintenance of children. A discussion on the recognition of foreign judgments in Sri Lanka, before and after its independence, is followed by the country's response to the Hague Convention on Inter-Country Child Abduction. It concludes with a discussion on the challenges faced by the Sri Lankan judiciary in achieving the objectives of the Convention in the absence of child-friendly judicial and administrative procedures.

## 1 Sri Lankan Family Law on Custody of Children

The Sri Lankan family law regime is a mixed legal system consisting of legislation and a wealth of jurisprudence, which derives from indigenous custom as well as laws of the colonial rulers, i.e. Dutch and the British. As such, the present family

[1]Constitution of Sri Lanka (1978), Art 27 (12)—Directive Principles of State Policy and Fundamental Duties. It states that the State shall recognize and protect the family as the basic unit of society.

law of Sri Lanka is a combination of laws featuring a wide variety of principles derived from Roman-Dutch law, English law and indigenous customs mainly of the Sinhalese, Tamils and Muslims. The merging of the customary laws with Western principles and concepts, some of which were contrary to local norms particularly those relating to family relations and children, took place mainly during the British rule, and have been retained to date.[2]

Two legal concepts take prominence among several legal norms introduced through the jurisprudence of the colonial period and immediately prior to independence,

- the recognition of 'Courts of Law as the upper guardian of children' with the objective of protecting the interests of minors, and
- preferential right of the father relating to custody and guardianship of children.

In keeping with international standards, the court remains the upper guardian of all minors. The notion of 'preferential right of the father' based on the concept of 'male breadwinner' prevailed long after independence, giving preference to the father despite equality between men and women being recognized in the national Constitution as a fundamental human right. The validity of the application of Roman-Dutch law policy of the father's preferential right in respect of children was changed through judicial interpretation after the country ratified the Convention on the Rights of the Child, without any reservation, in 1991. The Constitution of Sri Lanka encourages special provisions enacted for the advancement of children[3] and this has paved the way for the enactment of two important legislative measures for the advancement of children, i.e.

(1) recognition of the Children's Charter, which is the main national policy document in respect of children; and
(2) International Covenant on Civil and Political Rights Act (hereinafter, the ICCPR Act)[4] which accords legislative recognition for the rights of children.

The ICCPR Act specified that every child has the right to

(a) registration of the birth and an identity;
(b) nationality;
(c) protection from maltreatment, neglect, abuse or degradation; and
(d) claim for legal assistance from the State in criminal proceedings affecting the child, if substantial injustice would otherwise result.[5]

---

[2]Savitri Goonesekere, *The Sri Lanka Law on Parent and Child*, (Gunasena, Colombo 1987) 1–2.

[3]Constitution of Sri Lanka 1978, Art. 12(4)—Nothing in this Article shall prevent special provision being made, by law, subordinate legislation or executive action, for the advancement of women, children or disabled persons.

[4]International Covenant on Civil and Political Rights (ICCPR) Act No. 56 of 2007, Republic of Sri Lanka.

[5]Ibid., s 5(1).

It further specifies that in all matters concerning children, whether undertaken by public or private social welfare institutions, courts, administrative authorities or legislative bodies, the best interest of the child shall be of paramount importance.[6]

## *1.1 Definition of Child*

The age threshold for the determination of childhood in Sri Lanka has been amended by the Age of majority (amendment) Act No. 17 of 1989,[7] and every person below the age of 18 years, except for those who are governed by Muslim law,[8] has since been accorded the legal status of a child. The Charter on the Rights of the Child of Sri Lanka defined a child as a person aged less than 18 years.[9]

The Hague Conference on Private International Law took notice of the principles of the United Nations Convention on the Rights of the Child (hereinafter, the UNCRC).[10] However, the Hague Convention on the Civil Aspects of International Child Abduction, 1980 (hereinafter, the Convention)[11] specified that the application of the Convention ceases when the child turned sixteen. The relevant age is considered at the time of the hearing of the case, and where more than one child is involved such of them sixteen and older would be dropped from the return application before the authority.[12] The Civil Aspects of International Child Abduction Act no. 10 of 2001 of Sri Lanka defined a child as 'a person who has not attained sixteen years of age'.[13] Even though there appears to be a contrast in the age

---

[6]Id, s 5(2).

[7]Id, s 2.

[8]Age of Majority Ordinance No. 7 of 1865, s 3, provides for earlier age for attainment of majority by operation of law; *Marikkar v. Marikkar* [1915] 18 NLR 481; *Abdul Cader v. Razik* [1977] PC 54 NLR 201 where the court held that a Muslim in Ceylon attains majority on reaching the age of puberty.

[9]Charter on the Rights of the Child, Art 1. For the purposes of this Charter a child means every human being below the age of 18 years, http://www.hrcsl.lk/PFF/The%20Charter%20on%20the%20Rights%20of%20the%20Child.pdf, accessed on 3 June 2016.

[10]See Preamble of the Convention on Jurisdiction, applicable law, recognition, enforcement and co-operation in respect of parental responsibility and measures for the protection of children (1996). https://www.hcch.net/en/instruments/conventions/full-text; Convention on the Protection of Children and Co-operation in respect of Inter-country adoption (1993). https://www.hcch.net/en/instruments/conventions/full-text, accessed 20 March 2016.

[11]https://assets.hcch.net/docs/e86d9f72-dc8d-46f3-b3bf-e102911c8532.pdf, accessed 20 March 2016.

[12]James D. Garbolino, The 1980 Hague Convention on the Civil Aspects of International Child Abduction: A Guide for Judges, Federal Judicial Centre (USA 2012) (hereinafter, The Judges Guide) 62, 244, 245.

[13]Civil Aspects of International Child Abduction Act (No. 10 of 2001).

Section 25 states that In this Act unless the context otherwise requires—"child" means a person who has not attained sixteen years of age; "rights of access" in relation to a child includes the right to lake a child for a limited period to a place other than the child's habitual residence;

threshold of a child, the Convention gives practical meaning to 'child' as embodied in the UNCRC[14] and other international standard setting documents. The preamble of the Convention explained that the interests of children are of paramount importance in matters relating to their custody. Article 13 states that when a child who has attained an age and degree of maturity at which it is appropriate to account of its views, the judicial or administrative authority may refuse to order the return of the child if it finds that the child objects to being returned. This means that the authority is required to take into consideration the wishes of a child who has attained an age and a degree of maturity, though the final decision is to be taken by such authority where the child is below sixteen years of age. However, the Convention ceases to apply as 'a legal vehicle for securing return of a child'[15] when the child turned sixteen and according to general international standards, both parents and the court must address the child's wishes in decisions regarding his or her custody.[16] This accords with the requirements of Article 12, UNCRC.[17]

## 1.2 Sri Lankan Law Relating to Custody and Maintenance

The modern Sri Lankan law relating to parent and child reflects a balance between parental authority and the best interest of the child. Child's interests, including his or her sense of security, the capability of the custodian to provide for the educational (both religious and secular) wellbeing and security of the child, dangers of removing the child from the circumstances that he is used to, are the relevant factors considered by the court in respect of custody and guardianship of children. Joint custody of the child is recognized in Sri Lanka and is awarded if the Court is of the opinion that it is in the best interest of the child. Even where sole custody is awarded for one parent, the other could be granted visitation rights and is not free from support obligations, which may vary on the non-custodian parent's financial

(Footnote 13 continued)

"rights of custody" in relation to a child include the rights relating to the care of the person of the child and in particular the right to determine the child's place of residence.

[14]UN General Assembly, *Convention on the Rights of the Child*, 20 November 1989, United Nations, Treaty Series, vol. 1577, p. 3. http://www.refworld.org/docid/3ae6b38f0.html, accessed 3 August 2016. Adopted by the General Assembly of the United Nations on 20 November 1989.

[15]Elisa Pérez-Vera, Explanatory Report on the Convention, (commonly known as "Pérez-Vera Report") Translation of the Permanent Bureau (herein after Pérez-Vera Report), (1982).

[16]The Judges Guide (n 12) 61.

[17]UNCRC (n14) Art 12. It states that States Parties shall assure to the child who is capable of forming his or her own views the right to express those views freely in all matters affecting the child, the views of the child being given due weight in accordance with the age and maturity of the child.

2. For this purpose, the child shall in particular be provided the opportunity to be heard in any judicial and administrative proceedings affecting the child, either directly, or through a representative or an appropriate body, in a manner consistent with the procedural rules of national law.

capabilities. The Sri Lankan law on support obligations is embodied in the Maintenance Act No. 37 of 1999 and applies to all citizens, except Muslims. According to the section 2 there is a primary obligation of maintenance of children until they reach majority at the age of 18 years. However, the Section also specified that the support obligation in respect of one's offspring does not automatically cease once the child reaches 18 years.

## 2 Jurisdiction

The Family Court (established through the Judicature Act, 1978)[18] exercised the exclusive original jurisdiction in respect of custody, guardianship and maintenance of minor children. In 1981 through an amendment to the Judicature Act[19] the District court was vested with the jurisdiction in respect of custody and guardianship and the Magistrate Court with the jurisdiction relating to support obligations that was earlier exercised by the Family court. The District Court exercises the primary jurisdiction relating to custody issues between parents and between parents and third parties, while the Court of Appeal[20] and the Provincial High Court[21] exercise the jurisdiction to issue writ of habeas corpus. Magistrate Court exercises the jurisdiction in matters relating to maintenance of children.

For children born of Muslim parentage, the Muslim law founded upon Islamic principles as specified in the Muslim Marriages and Divorces Act, 1951 (Cap. 134)

[18]Judicature Act No. 2 of 1978 section 24(1).

[19]Judicature (Amendment) Act No. 71 of 1981 section 2.

[20]Constitution of the Democratic Socialist Republic of Sri Lanka 1978, Art 141 **Power to issue writs of *habeas corpus*** The Court of Appeal may grant and issue orders in the nature of writs of habeas corpus to bring up before such Court—(a) the body of any person to be dealt with according to law; or (b) the body of any person illegally or improperly detained in public or private custody, and to discharge or remand any person so brought up or otherwise deal with such person according to law.

[21]Thirteenth amendment to the Constitution of Sri Lanka 1978, Art 154 (4)(a). It states 154A.

(1) Subject to the provisions of the Constitution, a Provincial Council shall be established for every Province specified in the Eighth Schedule with effect from such date or dates as the President may appoint by Order published in the *Gazette*. Different dates may be appointed in respect of different Provinces.

(2) Every Provincial Council established under paragraph (1) shall be constituted upon the election of the members of such Council in accordance with the law relating to Provincial Council elections.

(3) Notwithstanding anything in the preceding provisions of this Article, Parliament may by, or under, any law provide for two or three adjoining Provinces to form one administrative unit with one elected Provincial Council, one Governor, one Chief Minister and one Board of Ministers and for the manner of determining whether such Provinces should continue to be administered as one administrative unit or whether each such Province should constitute a separate administrative unit with its own Provincial Council, and a separate Governor, Chief Minister and Board of Ministers.

is applicable. If the statute law is silent in respect of a specific aspect issue, it is determined according to *Shariat* law as interpreted and applied by the sect to which a person belongs. The age criterion for a Muslim child was therefore the age of puberty interpreted by Sri Lankan courts as fifteen years old for girls and boys.[22] Muslim law retained the notion of parental authority over children (*wilaya*) particularly in respect of girl children until their marriage[23] and in the case of boys until they reach the age of seven years.[24] The father's rights with regard to guardianship of minor children are recognized, though custody of very young children is usually granted to the mother.[25] The Supreme Court in *Ummul Marzoona v Samad*[26] held that a Muslim father is obliged to maintain his son until he reaches puberty or 15 years of age. The court held further that the father's liability continues even afterwards where the son is disabled by disease or infirmity, such as engaged in education. The *Quazi* court exercises the primary jurisdiction in these matters, and parties can appeal to Board of *Quazi*s against such decision.

## 3 Recognition of Foreign Judgments in Sri Lanka

Certainty in respect of both the substantive law and procedural law is fundamental to an acceptable legal system. Conflict of laws raises concerns relating to certainty, and the non-recognition of a foreign court's judgment could create difficulty for the party(s). The risk of such refusal could remain, *inter alia*, due to a lack of jurisdiction. Hence clarity of jurisdiction and certainty of applicable law to the situation at hand reduce the risk as well as ensuing hardship.[27] Such clarity is expected from the legislature and/or the courts, and this is usually done using two principles, namely, the principle of 'nationality' or 'domicile'.

During its colonial history, Sri Lankan legal system has had to encounter jurisdictional issues related to personal and family relations; uncertainty in the interpretation of jurisdiction has been a feature, not frequent though. One such incident was *Le Mesurier v Le Mesurier*[28] where the Privy Council decision created legal history. The appellant, an Englishman, and the first respondent, a French woman, were husband and wife respectively. The marriage was solemnized in England. The

[22] *Marikkar* v. *Marikkar* (1915) 18 NLR 481; *Narayanan* v. *Saree Umma* (1920) 21 N.L.R. 439; *Abdul Cader* v. *Razik* (1952) 54 NLR 201.

[23] Statute law permits a father to give her daughter in marriage when she is as young as 12 years of age. See Muslim Marriage and Divorce Act No. 31 of 1951, s 23.

[24] Saleem Marsoof, Muslim Law Relating To the Custody of Children. www.academia.edu/.../Muslim_Law_Relating_to_Custody_of_Children, accessed 20.03.2016.

[25] Rose Wijeyesekera, Protection Rights of Children, in *Guidebook on the Rights of the Child in Sri Lanka* (International Development Law Organization, Colombo, 2007), 31.

[26] (1977) 79 NLR 209.

[27] JC Hall, Conflict of Laws—Recognition of Foreign divorce (1958) 16 (01) The Camb. L J 15.

[28] *(1895) A.C. 517.*

appellant resided within the jurisdiction of the Matara (a town in the Southern coastal area of the island) District Court. The appellant sued for a divorce a *vinculo matrimonii* on the ground of adultery on the part of his wife. None of the co-respondents, with whom she was alleged to have committed adultery, were domiciled in Ceylon. Though his official duty as an Assistant Government Agent required him to reside in Ceylon, the Appellant retained his English domicile of origin. There was uncertainty as to the jurisdiction of the Matara District Court to determine the case. The District Judge exercising jurisdiction under Civil Procedure Code, 1889 (hereinafter, the CPC) granted a decree of divorce.[29] On appeal, the Supreme Court of Ceylon held that the courts of Ceylon had no jurisdiction to dissolve a marriage between British or European spouses resident in the island. The Privy council's position was that 'the domicile of the couple affords the true jurisdiction'[30] and that the Matara Court can be held to have had the necessary jurisdiction only if the Appellant proved that the Court derived jurisdiction from some recognized principle of international law. In absence of such an international law principle, the Privy Council held that the District Court in Ceylon had no jurisdiction to grant divorce in the case of a married person who had domicile out of Ceylon. Though the judgment remedied the then prevalent legal uncertainty it unfortunately resulted in a lot of hardship to many who were similarly situated. The Indian and Colonial Jurisdiction Act of 1926 remedied the hardship caused by the *Le Mesurier* decision. In *Morris v Morris*[31] the Court held that the Indian and Colonial Divorce Jurisdiction Act of 1926 applied to Ceylon by order of the Ceylon Divorce Jurisdiction Order of Council of 1936, as both countries were British colonies then. Section 1 of the 1926 Act read together with the Order of Council of 1936, the Supreme Court of Ceylon had the jurisdiction to determine a divorce application where the parties to the marriage are British subjects domiciled in England or Scotland, provided the petitioner resided in Ceylon at the time of presenting the petition or the place where the parties last resided together was in Ceylon and that either the marriage was solemnized in Ceylon or the matrimonial offence was alleged to have committed in Ceylon. The respondent (husband) was a British citizen, domiciled in England at the time of the trial; the petitioner (wife) was an inhabitant of Ceylon, and their marriage had taken place in Ceylon. The main issue in question was the petitioner's domicile. The court held that a married woman acquired the domicile of her husband upon marriage and retains such domicile until the marriage subsists and it lasts even after the death of her husband until she makes a choice to change her domicile.[32] The court held that even though the petitioner wife acquired her husband's domicile, which was England, the Supreme Court of Ceylon had the jurisdiction to determine the application for divorce by virtue of Ceylon Divorce Jurisdiction Order in Council, 1936, and provisions of section 1 of the Indian and Colonial Divorce Jurisdiction Act, 1926.

---

[29]Sri Lankan Civil Procedure Code No. 2 of 1889, s 597.

[30](n 28) 540 (Watson LJ).

[31]*Morris v Morris* (1938) 40 NLR 246.

[32]Ibid., 248 (Koch J).

In *Morris*[33] the Supreme Court did not address the issue whether the British court could have determined the issue, had the husband applied for dissolution of marriage. However, it may well be assumed that, given the fact that this was a time when the courts of Ceylon, as subjects of the British crown, were bound by judgments given by the Privy Council, and one party to the marriage was domiciled and actually lived in England, the British court also had the jurisdiction. In other words, arguably, the jurisdiction of the British court has only been extended to the Indian Supreme Court[34] by Indian Colonial Divorce Jurisdiction Act of 1926, which was later extended to Ceylon by order of the Ceylon Divorce Jurisdiction Order of Council of 1936. Clearly, the expansion of the jurisdiction was by statute and/or orders of Council, and even that prior to independence.

*Blanche Anley v. Herbert Bois*[35] considered an application for modification of order for the custody of children, particularly in relation to secure access to children. The children were taken overseas by the custodian parent, a British citizen. In a plea before the Supreme Court of Ceylon the respondent raised a preliminary objection to jurisdiction as the respondent was domiciled outside its jurisdiction. By Rule 21 of the Statutory Rules and Orders 1936 proceedings of alimony, maintenance, custody of children, and to the payment, application or settlement of damages assessed by the Court shall be conducted in accordance with the provisions of the CPC. The CPC specified that the Supreme Court of Ceylon shall not decree/modify any order related to matrimonial causes where the parties were domiciled in Scotland, except when the person on whose petition the decree for the dissolution of the marriage was pronounced was a resident of Ceylon at the time of application. The Court rejected the respondent' objection and held that since the applicant's residence is in Ceylon it had jurisdiction notwithstanding the applicant being a Scottish or British citizen. (Soertsz A.C.J) The Court also relied upon the Ceylon (Non-Domiciled Parties) Divorce Rules, 1936 that conferred jurisdiction to the Supreme Court of Ceylon.

In *Robinson Scott v Robinson Scott*[36] the Court emphasized upon the grounds of divorce rather than the parties' domicile. The Court reasoned that it would have jurisdiction to determine the case if the law relating to the matter in dispute is similar irrespective of the domicile. This appears to be a realistic approach and reduces the risk of rejection of the application and subsequent difficulties faced by the parties.

In *Varuna Jayasuriya v Krishanjini Jayasuriya*[37] the Sri Lankan Court of Appeal was faced with the issue of according recognition to an order of a Canadian court, while deciding upon the jurisdiction issue.[38] The disputants were married in

[33]Morris (n 31) 247.

[34]India also was under British rule at that time.

[35](1945) 46 NLR 464.

[36](1957) 3 WLR 842.

[37][2005] (2) Sri LR 382, CA 1201/2004 (REV).

[38]Case No. 500/12/2514/91/001 (Montreal, Quebec).

Sri Lanka and lived there until 1998 when the defendant (wife) left for Canada. In the divorce application filed by the plaintiff in the Colombo District Court the defendant, within the same suit, counter applied for a decree of divorce on the ground that a divorce action filed in Canada against her husband (the plaintiff in the present case) was pending. The Court of Appeal, hearing a revision application on the dismissal order of the District Court held that the District Judge had erred in dismissing the plaintiff's action. The Court reasoned that the jurisdiction in matrimonial matters ought to be premised on domicile; the domicile of a married woman being the same as, and changes with, the domicile of the husband[39]; and the wife acquired the domicile of the husband until the marriage is dissolved absolutely.[40] Accordingly the Court of Appeal held that only the District Court in Colombo had jurisdiction over the matter, hence an order of the foreign court need not be accorded recognition for lacking in jurisdiction. This judgment is a clear indication on the Sri Lankan position on jurisdiction in matrimonial matters—jurisdiction rests with the courts at the place of the parties' domicile—the wife's domicile being that of the husband till the subsistence of the marriage.

In *T.V.P.S. Perera v. C. Bandarage*[41] upon a foreign divorce in Australia, being the domicile of the defendant, a case had been filed in the Magistrate Court for an increase in the quantum of maintenance as ordered by the Australian court. The Magistrate has rejected the applicant's plea on the basis that at the time of the application there was no marriage between the parties. In other words, the Magistrate court has recognized the validity of the divorce decree given by the Australian court. The applicant then appealed to the High Court of Colombo mainly on the basis that the decree given by the Australian Court was not valid in Sri Lanka, as the decree had not been registered as per the Reciprocal Enforcement of Judgments Ordinance.[42] According to the interpretation clause of this Ordinance, "judgment" means a judgment or order given or made by a court in any civil proceedings, or a judgment or order given or made by a court in any criminal proceedings for the payment of a sum of money in respect of compensation or damages to an injured party.'[43] section 12 (2) specifically says that "action in personam" shall not be deemed to include any matrimonial matters or any proceedings in connexion with any of the following matters, that is to say, matrimonial matters, administration of the estates of deceased persons, insolvency, winding up of companies, lunacy, guardianship of a minor or curatorship of the estate of a

[39](n 37) 385, Wimalachandra J. citing Shirani Ponnambalam, The Law and the Marriage Relationship in Sri Lanka, 2nd ed. p. 370, (1987).

[40]Atp.386 citing *Annakedde* v. *Myappen* (1932) 33 NLR 198.

[41]HCMCA 13/2012.

[42]Reciprocal Enforcement of Judgments Ordinance No 4 of 1937. This Ordinance provided for the enforcement in Ceylon of judgments given in countries which accord reciprocal treatment to judgments given in Ceylon, for facilitating the enforcement in other countries of judgments given in Ceylon and for other purposes in connection of related matters.

[43]Ibid., section 12(1).

minor. Despite these statutory provisions, the High Court of Colombo relied on the Court of Appeal judgment in *Varuna Jayasooriya v. Krishangani Jayasooriya*[44] and allowed the appeal rejecting the Magistrate's order.

## 4 Inter-country Child Abduction

As the world moves towards revealing itself as a global village, becoming smaller with advanced inter-country relations, economic and otherwise, trans-cultural matrimonial unions have been on the increase especially because of ease of cross-border travel and activity, global communication, increase in migration and marriages between citizens of different countries. The government statistics reveal that in 2014 departures for foreign employment alone stand at 300,413.[45] While legal travel remains high, Sri Lanka records of considerably high rates at the international status of human trafficking, as primarily a source country and as a destination as well.[46]

These high numbers obviously increase inter-country marriages and children with cross-cultural parentage and multi-citizenship, enriching relationships across geographical borders. On the other hand, internal and international conflicts also have contributed to this situation as a result of the increase in numbers of refugees. Cross-border trafficking and human smuggling also have their implications on this issue.

In Sri Lanka kidnapping and abduction of children from Sri Lanka and/or from lawful guardianship is an offence under the Penal Code[47] and from civil law consequences relating to violation of custody rights. The Hague Convention is an attempt to resolve matters arising as a result of the increasing number of cross border child abductions. Sri Lanka's commitment in this regard is reflected in its ratification of the Convention and the enactment of specific domestic legislation thereafter.

### *4.1 Hague Convention on Inter-country Child Abduction*

The Hague Convention on the Civil Aspects of International Child Abduction (hereinafter, the Convention) compels the return of the wrongfully abducted/retained child to the country where she or he had her/his habitual residence prior to the abduction within the shortest possible time, and intends to ensure the interests of

---

[44](n 37).

[45]Statistical Data Sheet-2015, Department of Census and Statistics. www.statistics.gov.lk, accessed 03 March 2016.

[46]www.refworld.org/docid/55b73b9c11.html. In most cases Sri Lankans migrate to the Middle East, Southeast Asia, and Afghanistan to work in the construction, garment, and domestic service sectors.

[47]Sri Lanka Penal Code No. 2 of 1883, sections 350–354.

the child in the process. It neither imposes criminal sanction on the abductor nor acts as an extradition agreement. This Convention does not determine the merits of parents or third parties as custodians and/or guardians, but leaves that to domestic legal system to deal with. It attempts to enable the domestic legal system to resolve the issue of custody by clearing the complications created by jurisdictional issues, so as to remedy a most distressing situation caused to parents as well as children as a result of the disturbance of status quo. The main objectives of this convention are twofold:

(1) the restoration of the status quo ante of a child's custody, which one parent claims to have been disturbed by the other's wrongful removal and/or retention; and
(2) to provide a prompt and efficient process for the return of the child to the status quo ante that existed prior to such abduction.

In order to achieve these objectives the Convention creates artificial jurisdictional links in order to remove legal obstacles to restore custody of children across international borders.[48]

The Convention is unique in four aspects:

- it requires expeditious handling of international child abduction cases—cases are to be determined within a period of six weeks;
- executive intervention in appointing a central authority to act as a conduit between the two countries;
- administrative intervention via the central authority as both an alternative to court procedures and an avenue for summary proceedings in court; and
- local courts are encouraged to refer and follow foreign judgments where applicable.[49]

Thus the ratification of the Convention does not preclude the local courts from determining custody according to applicable local laws. The Convention becomes applicable only where the two countries involved in the abduction have signed it.

The Convention does not address the de jure custody rights of a parent,[50] it recognizes the existence of de facto situation of custody; a child dislocated across an international border without the consent of the party who held custody of the child and/or without a court order permitting that relocation[51]; and the need to reinstate the status quo ante by returning the child to his/her habitual residence. The call for return is based on the artificial presumption that the status quo ante was

[48]Pérez-Vera Report, (n 15) para 11–15.

[49]The Judges Guide, (n 12) pp x–xii.

[50]Hague Convention on the Civil Aspects of International Child Abduction is the first concerted attempt by the international community to prevent inter-country child abduction, Convention on the Civil Aspects of International Child Abduction, Oct. 25, 1980, 1343 U.N.T.S. 89 (entered into force 1 December 1983). The Hague Convention on the Civil Aspects of International Child Abduction, Article 19.

[51]The Judges Guide, (n 12) 18.

legal and is the best for the child. Even though the Convention does not refer to the 'best interests standard' as a direct point of reference in ordering the return of the child to his/her status quo ante, the signatory States declare themselves to be 'firmly convinced that the interests of children are of paramount importance in matters relating to their custody' and it is their desire 'to protect children internationally from the harmful effects of their wrongful removal or retention'[52] that drove them to commit themselves to agree on the terms of the Convention. On this conviction the Convention supports a non-return of a child to his/her status quo where return is not for the best interest of the particular child, who is the victim of his/her abduction. While the best interest is to be considered in the socio-cultural context of a given situation rather than as a purely legal matter, the Convention provides guidelines for the determination of what is best for child, viz, the age limit, i.e. the Convention ceases to apply 'when the child attains the age of 16 years'[53]; compelling the court to consider the wishes of the child[54]; judicial discretion in respect of return of the child in certain instances specified in Article 13, particularly where there are convincing evidence of grave risk of 'physical or psychological harm or otherwise place the child in an intolerable situation' the return of the child would expose him/her to; a mature child's objection for return[55]; "custody and access",[56] which aims at providing a child 'family relationships which are as comprehensive as possible, so as to encourage the development of a stable personality'[57]; and the delay of more than one year in submitting the application[58] that presumes the child's settled status, which as the Convention believes, ought not be disturbed.

## 4.2 Civil Aspects of International Child Abduction in Sri Lanka Prior to 2001

Beyond penal provisions afore-mentioned, Sri Lankan legal regime on a situation leading to conflict of laws including wrongful removal of children across international borders, was minimal. The first statutory effort following the judgment in *Le Mesurier*[59] was the Reciprocal Enforcement of Judgments Ordinance No. 41 of 1921 to provide for the enforcement in Ceylon of judgments obtained in the

[52]Hague Convention on the Civil Aspects of International Child Abduction (n 50).

[53]Ibid., Art 4.

[54]The age however, is not an absolute prohibition on courts; Article 29 of the Convention provides for judicial discretion under any other law to grant custody and access rights even where the child is above 16 years of age.

[55]The Hague Convention on the Civil Aspects of International Child Abduction, (n 50) Art 13.

[56]Ibid., Art 5.

[57]Pérez-Vera Report, (n 15) para 26.

[58]The Hague Convention on the Civil Aspects of International Child Abduction (n 50) Art 12.

[59](n 28).

superior courts of the United Kingdom and its territories. This however, was specifically to apply in civil matters involving money. This was followed by the Reciprocal Enforcement of judgments Ordinance No. 4 of 1937 intended for reciprocal application of judgments or orders given or made by a court in any civil or criminal proceedings, for the payment of a sum of money in respect of compensation or damages to an injured party.[60] Later the Ceylon Divorce Jurisdiction Order of Council was enacted in 1936 to determine jurisdiction in divorce cases.

In the absence of clear statutory provision in respect of custody and guardianship of children governed by general law, Kandyan law and Thesawalamai, the principles of Roman-Dutch law applied while the District Court exercised the original jurisdiction in determining such matters. As far as Muslims were concerned the *Qazi* court exercised the jurisdiction in this regard. The Judicature Act No. 2 of 1978 made things clearer and the Family court has been conferred the sole original jurisdiction in matters relating to custody, guardianship and curatorship of children, except in the case of Muslims.[61] The jurisdiction of the Family Court was later conferred to the District Court,[62] which now functions as the upper guardian of children and the court with sole original jurisdiction in matters concerning custody, guardianship and curatorship of non-Muslim children.

Custody and access rights relating to children whose parents belonged to different jurisdictions arose in a recent case of *Asokan nee Kandasamy v. Asokan.*[63] The plaintiff and the defendant were married and lived in India and the parties raised the children there. The plaintiff on a visit to her parental home in Sri Lanka with the children initiated action for divorce *vincula matrimonii* and for custody of the children in the District court in Colombo. Failing submission of defence by the defendant, the Court decided ex parte, and applied the *Le Mesurrier* ratio. The plaint was dismissed for lack of jurisdiction on the following grounds:

- That the constructive malicious desertion took place in Madras, and the cause of action did not arise in Sri Lanka;
- The matrimonial home was outside Sri Lanka;
- That section 597 of the CPC[64] is not applicable, as the marriage was contracted in Madras;
- It is the Court of the husband's domicile that has the jurisdiction to grant a divorce; and

[60]Reciprocal Enforcement of Judgments Ordinance No. 4 of 1937(n 42) S.12.

[61]The Judicature (Amendment) Act No. 2 of 1981, (n19) S 24 (1).

[62]Ibid.

[63][1994] (1) Sri LR 413.

[64]Civil procedure Code (n 29) section 597 of the Civil Procedure Code, No. 12 of 1895, states: "Any husband or wife may present a plaint to District Court within the local limits of the jurisdiction of which he or she, as the case may be resides, praying that his or her marriage be dissolved on any ground for which marriage may, by the law applicable in Sri Lanka to his or her case, be dissolved".

- Plaintiff-petitioner has failed to prove that she is not subject to the law applicable to her husband.

On appeal the Court of Appeal, distinguishing from *Le Mesurrier*, held that the District Court in Sri Lanka possessed the jurisdiction in the matter before the court; section 597 CPC applied notwithstanding that the marriage had been contracted in India, similar rationale applied regarding the custody of children brought to Sri Lanka by their mother without the consent of their father residing in India. Undoubtedly the Sri Lankan appellate court's approach was progressive in terms of equality before the law and non-discrimination based on sex against a wife. The court may also have considered the best interests of the children before awarding their custody to the mother. Yet, a question arises as to whether the court had any institutionalized mechanism and method of compelling the children to be given back to their father, had the court decided that awarding custody to the mother is against the best interests of the children. Incidentally, at the time when *Asokan* case was decided, the general approach of the Sri Lankan courts in respect of custody of children had been on the basis of the Roman-Dutch law principle of 'preferential right of the father' rather than the contemporary approach of the 'best interest of the child', which was emphasized as the criterion later in the case of *Muthiah Jeyarajan v. Thushiyanthi Jeyarajan and Others.*[65] In *Asokan* there was a greater chance for the father to get the children back, had he defended his interests. Such a situation would have given rise to the issue as to the procedures to be followed in Sri Lanka where a child had been removed from another jurisdiction and retained in Sri Lanka by one parent without the consent of the other. Not only Sri Lanka did not have a specific institutional mechanism to deal with international child abduction cases, the available child custody procedure has been expensive and time-consuming. It was in this context that Sri Lanka signed the Hague Convention on the Civil Aspects of International Child Abduction.

## 4.3 Sri Lankan Legislative Response

Sri Lanka became a member of the Hague Conference on 27.09.2001. Honoring the States Parties' obligations under Hague Convention on the Civil Aspects of International Child Abduction, Sri Lanka enacted the Civil Aspects of International Child Abduction Act no. 10 of 2001[66] (hereinafter, the International Child Abduction Act) specifying the mechanism for the return of children abducted from or wrongfully retained in Sri Lanka. The main objectives of the statute are to 'make provision for the return of children wrongfully removed from Sri Lanka or other country of habitual residence and retained in any specified country or Sri Lanka and

[65](1999) 1 Sri LR 113.

[66]Enforced on 1st March 2002.

to extend the jurisdiction of the High Court of a province to hear applications for the return of children wrongfully removed or retained.'[67]

Removal or retention of a child is deemed wrongful where such removal or retention is in breach of rights of custody attributed to any person or institution or other body; either jointly or alone, under the law of the specified country in which that child had his or her habitual residence, immediately prior to such removal or retention.[68] Rights of custody as referred to in the Act, generally include the rights relating to the care of the person, of the child and in particular the right to determine the child's place of residence[69] which could have been arisen by operation of law or by reason of a judicial or administrative decision or by reason of any agreement having legal effect under the law of any specified country.[70] The Secretary to the Ministry of Justice has been identified as the central authority,[71] who would act upon[72] an application in respect of a child alleged to have been wrongfully removed to/retained in Sri Lanka in breach of rights of custody.[73] In an application made in respect of a child wrongfully retained in another country the central authority shall immediately transmit the application to the appropriate authority in that country, and inform the applicant of the action taken by the Central Authority.[74] The designated Court under the statute for presenting such application, without prejudice to any other means by which the return of the child could be secured, is the High Court of the Western Province.[75] The High Court, upon being satisfied after summary procedure that the child has been wrongfully removed or retained in Sri Lanka and where the application has been made within one year of the date of such removal or retention, shall order the return of such child to his or her habitual country of residence.[76]

The Act attempts to ensure the return of a child to his or her habitual residence and restore status quo ante on the custody. In an application made within one year of such alleged wrongful removal the Court shall order restoration of the child to its habitual residence before such removal. If such removal occurred beyond an year on the date of the application the Court could still order return of the child to its habitual residence upon being satisfied that the child has not yet settled into its 'new' environment. The Act thus aims to serve the best interest of the child. The

[67]Civil Aspects of International Child Abduction Act no. 10 of 2001 (n 13).

[68]Ibid., s 3 (1)(a).

[69]Id, s 25.

[70]Id, s 3 (2).

[71]Id, s 4.

[72](n 13 s 7) such an application can be refused by the 'central authority' only where there are no grounds for accepting the particular application, and the reasons for such refusal have to be informed to such an applicant.

[73]Ibid., s 6(1).

[74]Id, s 8.

[75]Id, s 9(1).

[76]Id s 10.

requirement of the one year period has been considered as a 'criterion' to ensure that reinstating the status quo ante would not have an adverse effect on the 'settled status' of the child. The proviso to section 10 makes it clear that even where a period of one year has been lapsed, the High Court can still make an order for reinstatement of the status quo ante where the court is satisfied that such a move will not affect the child's settled status.

The ICCPR Act did not include the terminology of the 'best interest of the child', neither did it discuss international parental child abduction, yet its provisions reinforce the belief that the Statute is premised upon such intention.[77] Adopting such vision-founded reasoning of the ICCPR Act, the High Court has attempted to contextualize the focal goals of the legislation into the disputes on alleged wrongful removal of the child under the International Child Abduction Act, especially in applications made beyond the period of one year. In such applications, the Court has adopted a wide meaning to the terminology, drawing inspiration from the ICCPR Act. The media reports of the first dispute[78] decided under the International Child Abduction Act exemplified the above-mentioned analysis. Two children, born in Germany to German-domiciled parents of Sri Lankan nationality, were, during a vacation in Sri Lanka, separated from each other, owing to the marital discord of the parents. The father returned to Germany with one child and the mother, it was alleged, forcefully retained the other in Sri Lanka. This was a case of a refusal to restore a child to its own environment after a stay abroad, similar to the scenario discussed in the Pérez-Vera Report,[79] a situation that the Convention attempts to remedy. In the instant case, however, since the alleged wrongful retention of child occurred in 2001 prior to the decided under the International Child Abduction Act the Court of Appeal refused to apply the Act, citing the general rule against retrospectivity. Yet, the court highlighted the statutory recognition of judicial discretion to be used to preserve the best interest of the child.[80]

The 'best interest of the child' guided the decision of the Court of Appeal in *Suhada Gamlath, Secretary to the Ministry of Justice and Law Reform* v. *Kristina Ivasauskaite-Rosairo.*[81] A child born to parents who were foreigners was brought to Sri Lanka by his father removing him from the custody of the mother in France. The mother had sought legal redress from the Colombo High Court to get the child back. The High Court refused to grant her application stating that the application

[77](n 4) s 5(2).

[78]High Court of Negombo application No. 249/2002 (Court of Appeal). http://archives.dailynews.lk/2003/07/04/new06.html, accessed 21 July 2016.

[79](n 15) 3.

[80]Nalin Jayawardena (petitioner) and Kalhari Jayawardena (Respondent) (n 78).

[81]No. (PHC) APN 3/2010 [Court of Appeal Revision 01.06.2011]. courtofappeal.lk/index.php?…suhada…vskristina-ivasauskaite-rosario…, accessed 21st July 2016.

was not accompanied by the translation in Sinhala, Tamil or English, of the application and the annexed documents as per section 6 of the Act.[82] The other reason for rejection of the application was that the application was filed after a year, which is not in accordance with the provisions of section 12 of the Act. Quoting extensively from judicial opinion as well as scholarly opinion from other jurisdictions[83] the Court concluded that the requirements of section 6(3) were of procedural nature and should be read along with the intention of the statute, hence rejection of the application by the lower court was not valid.[84] On the second reason for the lower court's decision, the Court of Appeal referred to a variety of evidence, supplemented with references to opinion from other jurisdictions, concluded that literal interpretation of section 12 requirement of application being made within one year should be read along with judicial discretion founded upon an understanding of the best interest of the child. Disposing the revision application, the Court of Appeal ordered the claimed relief of allowing the petition[85] for an order on the return of the child to its habitual residence before such wrongful removal.

## 5 Conclusion

The Sri Lankan position on conflictof laws is facultative; courts generally apply the domestic law (*lex fori*) unless a party raises the issue of conflict-of-laws.[86] The application of foreign law accordingly is a question of fact, and the higher courts, i.e. High Court, Court of Appeal and the Supreme Court, are mandated to review the errors in respect of the application of foreign laws.

Taken together the situation has been complicated, to say the least. The legal arena relating to cross border child abduction also was not an exception, the experience being a legal dilemma for both parents and children. However, with the intervention of the Hague Convention based on principles of private international law, followed by the enactment of the Civil Aspects of International Child Abduction Act of Sri Lanka, the matter has now been made less cumbersome. The judicial opinion especially in the *Kristina*[87] has been encouraging and leads to a

---

[82](n 13).

[83](n 81) 5–7.

[84](n 81) 4–5.

[85]Ibid., 8.

[86]Shaheeza Lalani, Establishing the Content of Foreign law: A Comparative Study, (2013) 20 MJ I78. www.maastrichtjournal.eu/pdf_file/its/mj_20_01_0075.pdf, accessed 2 April 2016.

[87](n 81).

belief that Courts would read the statute in its entirety with an eye on the purpose and the objectives; further while deciding upon applications for return of the child they would exercise discretion taking note of the best interest of the child in cases of wrongful removal and while ordering return.

# Part III
# Private International Law in South Asia—States' Practice in Commercial Law

# Conflict of Laws—State Practice of Bangladesh

**Mohammed Abdur Razzak**

**Abstract** During a negotiation for a transaction between individuals/businesses of two different nations, selection of proper law and forum for settlement of disputes arising out of the transaction is not an easy task to accomplish. Further, it always haunts the legal practitioners when they are asked to bring a proceeding in a local court against a foreign party. The haunting aspect is that the court of foreign jurisdiction, where the judgment may be enforced against the foreign defendant, may refuse to recognize the judgment. The legal principles are not so solidified in this area of law. This study of conflict of laws tends to explain the unsettled aspect of it in the context of the State of Bangladesh. Bangladesh (formerly East Pakistan, prior to its independence) has been experiencing the dilemma of conflict of laws. A number of statutes address the issue of choice of forum, proper law and enforcement of foreign judgment. Disputes have generated several legal decisions focusing on these issues. Still the jurisprudence is not settled with regard to the interpretation of foreign jurisdiction and proper law clauses in a contract. A formidable challenge is thrown by the rules on civil procedure of Bangladesh. The law requires that a foreign judgment, to be enforced in Bangladesh, ought to be issued by a legal system the subject law of which is not in conflict with the laws of Bangladesh. This single criterion may allow the courts of Bangladesh not to recognize the judgments of many foreign courts regarding matrimonial, adoption, corporate, property disputes etc. This study attempts to revisit the present jurisprudence of Bangladesh in respect of foreign jurisdiction and proper law clauses in a contract and the enforcement of foreign judgment in Bangladesh, especially in the light of this clause in the Civil Procedure law of Bangladesh.

**Keywords** Foreign jurisdiction clause · Transnational contract · Bill of lading · Conflict of laws

M.A. Razzak (✉)
Law Society of Upper Canada, Toronto, ON, Canada
e-mail: mrazzak@emeraldlpc.ca

M.A. Razzak
Bangladesh Bar Council, Dhaka, Bangladesh

© Springer Nature Singapore Pte Ltd. 2017

S.R. Garimella and S. Jolly (eds.), *Private International Law*,
DOI 10.1007/978-981-10-3458-9_13

## Introduction

In the era of globalization, "no country lives in an island these days".[1] Nations are intertwined with one another: the interaction occurs through State machineries as well as movement of people, goods and services: a Bangladeshi may enter India for marriage purposes. An Indian trader may contract with a European counter-part to supply goods manufactured in Bangladesh. A national of Pakistan may enter into an employment contract with an employer located in Bangladesh. In all these situations, one factor is common: they contain foreign elements. It is a foreign element because the factor relates to a geographical area other than Bangladesh. If, in any other said situations, disputes arise between the parties, it is probable that the legal proceeding may be initiated either in Bangladesh or in a designated foreign country. The commencement of litigation in one territorial jurisdiction may invite the other party to the litigation to challenge the legality of the proceeding on the plea of lack of jurisdiction. Rules and principles applied to disputes with a foreign element is categorized as private international law.[2] They enable the courts to determine what effect they should give to the fact that a matter is substantially connected to two territorial jurisdictions foreign to one another.

Issues falling under the domain of private international law are peculiar and unknown in domestic proceedings. The scope of the subject concerns itself with a determination of the court, amongst competing ones, that could assume jurisdiction. Further they might need to determine the law applicable to the dispute and further the conditions of recognition and enforcement of the foreign judgment.[3]

The domain of private international law addresses issues with foreign element, nevertheless, is characterized and sourced within national law. In Bangladesh, the first source about the domain area of conflict of laws is the Constitution. Further, the functional principles and rules emanate from statutes and judicial opinion.

## Structure of the Chapter

The first section of the chapter introduces the statutory regime related to private international law in Bangladesh. In the second section, it maps the role of the judiciary in formulating the basic rules of private international law in Bangladesh. Finally, the chapter addresses three major strands of the subject—proper law, appropriate forum of adjudication and conditions for recognition and enforcement of foreign judgment.

---

[1] *Bangladesh Air Service (Pvt.) Ltd. v British Airways Plc* (1997) 49 DLR (AD) 187 [26] [Mustafa Kamal J.] (hereinafter, the *Bangladesh Air Service (Pvt.) Ltd.*).

[2] Private international law is separate from public international law. Whereas private international law deals with the disputes between private individuals or organizations which are foreign to each other; the public international law regulates matters between sovereign states and international organizations. Jet Walker and Jean-Gabriel Castel: *Canadian Conflict of Law*, vol 1 (6th edn, LexisNexis 2005) ch 1.

[3] Ibid.

## 1 Evolution and Framework of Private International Law

Bangladesh, independent in 1971, inherited the legal system that existed in the region for nearly two centuries. A derivation of the colonial rule, the legal system of the country received procedural as well as substantive laws and certain provisions that concerned with the conflict of laws. These colonial laws were adopted by the legislature of independent Bangladesh without much substantive change. However, they were augmented by legislations encouraging resolution of trans-national disputes through alternative dispute resolution methods.

The Constitution of Bangladesh embodies in Part II certain fundamental principles for guiding the policy-making for the nation. Article 25 of the Constitution underscores the need for peaceful settlement of international disputes. The principles enunciated in this Article envision a system for the nation that respects international law without compromising national sovereignty and dignity as opined in the judgement of the Appellate Division of the Supreme Court in *Bangladesh Air Service (Pvt.) Ltd. v British Airways PLC.*[4] Apart from the Constitution, the Code of Civil Procedure, 1908, the Arbitration Act, 2001 and the Contract Act, 1972, contain provisions related to private international law.

The civil courts, through the law during the colonial rule - Civil Courts Act 1887, have statutory authority to deal with suits of civil nature, including the enforcement of the judgement as the judgement-debtor commences execution proceedings. The Code of Civil Procedure, 1908 lays down the general rules relating to procedure of the civil courts. One of the cardinal principles regarding jurisdiction of civil courts as encapsulated in section 9 of the Code of Civil Procedure, is that courts shall have jurisdiction to try all suits of a civil nature except suits of which their cognizance is either expressly or impliedly barred under the provisions of laws. The implication of this rule is that a civil court shall entertain all suits of civil nature, the cause of action of which has arisen within the territorial limit of the Court; provided that the suit value falls within the pecuniary limit of the Court and the assumption of jurisdiction over the suit by a civil court is not barred by any statute.[5] This fundamental rule of procedure has a counterpart. Section 28 of the Contract Act of 1872 puts a restriction of freedom of contract. This section, subject to some exceptions, makes all agreements void in which parties agree to restrict absolutely from enforcing their rights under or in respect of any contract by the usual legal proceedings in the ordinary tribunals. The regime of conflict of laws prevailing in Bangladesh by the activism of the judiciary has evolved based upon the functionality of this fundamental rules enunciated by section 9 of the Code of Civil Procedure and section 28 of the Contract Act.

---

[4](n 1).

[5]Mohammad Abdur Razzak, 'Judicial Interpretation of Foreign Jurisdiction Clause in a Contract—Calls for Review' [2008] 28 BLD 01.

International contracts[6] for sale/purchase of commodities often contain clauses that stipulate competent court/tribunal and applicable law for settlement of disputes arising out, or in relation to, the international sales contract between the parties thereto. Such dispute resolution clauses appear to oust the jurisdiction of the local courts in whose territorial limit the alleged dispute has arisen, in a deviation from the rules specified in CPC and the Contract Act.

Further, private international law rules related to enforcement of foreign judgments/orders have been specified within section 13, CPC. Another leading area in which conflict of laws is relevant is the enforcement of foreign judgement or orders. Similar rules are embodied in the Arbitration Act of 2001. Section 46 of this Act empowers a competent court to refuse to recognize and execute a foreign arbitral award if the enforcement of the same offends the laws and public policy.

The judiciary has significantly contributed to the development of the content of private international law in Bangladesh.

The first reported case came up for consideration before the Dhaka High Court[7] that called for judicial determination of the foreign jurisdiction clause was *Abdur Razzak v East Asiatic Co.* (hereinafter, *Abdur Razzak*).[8] The Dhaka High Court upheld the lower court's order holding the foreign jurisdiction clause as not being void under section 28 of the Contract Act. For about a decade, the precedent was followed in a number of subsequent judgements. However, in 1965, the opportunity came for the Pakistan Supreme Court to review the correctness of this judgement. Hearing a joinder of applications[9] Hamoodur Rahman, C.J., overruled the ratio established in *Abdur Razzak* and a series of judgements of the Dhaka High Court that followed the ratio of *Abdur Razzak*. However, in 1997, the Appellate Division of the Supreme Court of Bangladesh[10] in *Bangladesh Air Service (Pvt) v British Airways Plc*[11] revisited the decision of Hamoodur Rahman, C.J. while deciding upon an arbitration clause referring the dispute to a foreign arbitral tribunal. The above three decisions have laid down the perimeter of current regime related to private international law related to applicable law, forum and recognition and enforcement of foreign judgment in Bangladesh.

---

[6]Michael Bridge, *The International Sale of Goods—Law and Practice*, (OUP 1999) Ch 1.

[7]Dhaka High Court was the highest court of East Pakistan, now Bangladesh, which had the status of a province of Pakistan before becoming an independent state in 1971.

[8](1953) 5 DLR 394.

[9]Reported in 22 DLR (SC) (1965) 334.

[10]The Supreme Court is the highest court in Bangladesh with two divisions: Appellate Division and the High Court Division. The Appellate Division is the apex court. See Part VI of the Constitution of People's Republic of Bangladesh.

[11](n 1).

## 2 Applicable Law

The legal system of Bangladesh is based on the common law. It is a standard practice of the judges, especially in the higher judiciary, to make reference, apart from the decisions of the apex court of the country, to the decided cases from the English legal system as well as decisions of neighbouring countries like India and Pakistan.

In *Bangladesh Air Service (Pvt) v British Airways Plc.*[12] Mustafa Kamal J. defines the meaning of the term "proper law of contract",

> "The proper law of the contract", observed Lord Wright in *Mount Albert Borough Council v. Australasian Temperance etc. Society,*[13] "means that law which the English Court is to apply in determining the obligations under the contract". In *Channel Tunnel Group Ltd. v. Balfour Beatty Ltd.,*[14] Lord Mustill defines proper law of contract as that "which regulates the substantive rights and duties of the parties to the contract from which the dispute has arisen". Lord Denning observed in *Tzortzis v Monark*[15] "… if there is an express clause in a contract providing what the proper law is to be, that is conclusive in the absence of some public policy to the contrary. But where there is no express clause, it is a matter of inference from the circumstances of the case". There is a third and final way, failing either of these, ie, by judicial determination of the system of law with which the transaction has the closest and most real connection.

On this basis, Mustafa Kamal J arrived at a conclusion that the proper law of contract in a given situation refers to a regime of law or a particular legislation emanating from an identified regime of law, expressly or by implication, stipulated in the contract and which determines the rights and obligations of the parties in dispute.[16]

Mustafa Kamal J then discussed the possibility of the procedural law governing dispute resolution may be different from the proper law of the contract.[17] To substantiate his conclusion, Mustafa Kamal J made reference to a number of English decisions embodied in Halsbury's Laws of England. He observed,[18]

> Now, a contract may contain more than one selection of law in respect of various contractual components, say, one for mutual rights and obligations, another for arbitration and its procedure, the 'curial law' of the arbitration as it is often called. The position is summarised in Halsbury's Laws of England[19] under the heading "Scope of the proper law", as follows: "Splitting of the contract. Whilst most contractual issues are governed by the

---

[12]Ibid., para 15.

[13](1938) AC 224 [240].

[14](1993) 1 All ER 664 [682].

[15](1968) 1 W LR 406 [409].

[16](n 1) para 18.

[17](1997) 49 DLR (AD) 187, para 17.

[18](n 1), para 16.

[19]4th Edn. Vol. 8, para 592, p. 414; (See *Hamlyn and Co. v Talisker Distillery* (1894) AC. 202, HL and *CompagNie d' Armement Maritime SA v Compagnie Tunisienne de Navigation SA* (1970) 3 All ER 71 HL.

proper law, the parties can agree that different contractual issues may be governed by different laws."

Justice Mustafa Kamal referred to some decisions of the Indian Courts.[20] When an international contract is silent regarding the proper law of contract or procedure, it is for the tribunal or court of competent jurisdiction to answer that question of law. A court or tribunal identified within the contract could determine the question of law - proper law of contract and procedure - even if such assumption of jurisdiction has been challenged by the foreign defendant.[21] In arriving to this conclusion, Mustafa Kamal J quoted principles laid down in English cases[22] as well as cases decided by the Indian courts.[23]

The Judge, however, declined to authoritatively identify the proper law of contract.[24] He observed that Clause 14 of the contract referred to arbitration "in accordance with, and subject to, the provisions of the (English) Arbitration Act, 1950".[25] So there was a chosen arbitration law within the contract. Further, having discussed the meaning assigned to the words "in accordance with" and "subject to", by making reference to leading English texts and case laws of different jurisdiction, the Judge observed that the Court had no doubt that the parties to the contract consciously made the arbitration to be in consonance with and conditional upon the

---

[20](1997) 49 DLR (AD) 187, para 17—In *Michael Golodetz v Serajuddin and Co.* AIR 1963 1044, an Indian Firm and an American Company entered into an agreement for supply of manganese providing for arbitration of their disputes in New York according to American Arbitration Association Rules. In the case of *Oil and Natural Gas Commission v Western Company of North America*, AIR 1987 (SC) 674, the appellant ONGC of India and the respondent American Company entered into a drilling contract. The arbitration proceedings to resolve disputes between the parties were to be governed by the Indian Arbitration Act, 1940. London was the agreed venue for hearing of arbitration matter as per the arbitration clause.

[21]Ibid., para 18.

[22]Ibid.: "Thus in *Compagnie d`` Armement Maritime SA v. Compagnie Tunisiennc d' Navigation SA* (1970) 3 All ER 71(HL), a dispute arose and proceeded to arbitration which according to the contract was to take place in England. The arbitrators stated a case in the form of a question of law whether the law applicable was French or English law. The House of Lords finally decided that French law was the proper law of contract. The proper law of contract was thus decided on a case stated by the arbitrators. Again, in *James Miller and Partners Ltd. v. Whitworth Street Estates (Manchester) Ltd.* (1970) 1 All ER 96, the House of Lords decided that the arbitration was subject to arbitrator who issued the final award refusing to state a case for the decision of the English High Court. In *Tzortzis v. Monark Line A/B*, (1968) 1 WLR 406, the arbitrators stated an interim award in the form of a special case for the decision of the English High Court and the Court of Appeal upheld the decision of the High Court that the proper law of the contract was English law ...".

[23]Ibid.: "In the case of *Rabindra N Maitra v Life Insurance Corporation of India*, AIR 1964 (Cal) 141, a suit was filed by the assignee of the insured to realize insurance claim in Calcutta High Court and the proper law of contract was decided in the suit itself."

[24]Ibid.

[25]Id.

observance of the provisions of the (English) Arbitration Act, 1950, which was held to be the law of procedure.[26] Furthermore,

> There is nothing in Exception 1 to section 28 of the Contract Act prohibiting the parties to a contract from choosing a foreign forum under the supervision of a foreign court for arbitrating its disputes. Such contract does not offend the main provision of section 28, because the local Courts still retain the jurisdiction to decide the case between the parties. The appellant is free to file a suit for damages against the respondent in the local court. The respondent is also free to ask for a stay of the suit, pending arbitration, and it is for the local court having regard to all circumstances, to arrive at a conclusion whether sufficient reasons are made out (by the plaintiff) for refusing to grant a stay.[27]

## 3 Proper Forum for Adjudication

It is now a common practice in international commercial contracts to include clauses requiring the traders to agree to submit their dispute arising out of the trade transaction to a pre-determined forum or forums of a pre-determined country. The primordial principle of party autonomy has been applied to explain the presence of such clauses.[28]The legal regime of Bangladesh has also experienced the dynamics of the controversy relating to the foreign jurisdiction clauses in an international contract.

It appears that the prevailing jurisprudence of Bangladesh on foreign jurisdiction clauses evolved in three stages—Liberal Regime, Nationalistic Regime and Pro-Trade Regime. The exponent of Liberal Regime was the Dhaka High Court.[29] This Regime supported the principles with regard to the determination of forum that based upon "business convenience" and upon "the comity of nations". Subject to public policy consideration, Dhaka High Court emphasized on the intention of the parties fairly derived from the contract itself. The Nationalistic Regime, as adhered to by the Pakistan Supreme Court, emphasized the national sovereignty and laid down principles to limit the aggressiveness of the foreign jurisdiction clauses. The Pro-Trade Regime attempted to strike an appropriate balance between economic and political interest. The Appellate Division of the Supreme Court of Bangladesh[30] adopted this rational approach to promote trading ventures of Bangladesh with other trading nations keeping in constant view the national dignity and interest.

---

[26](n 1) para 18.

[27]Ibid., para 24.

[28]See, generally, MENG Zhaohua, 'Party Autonomy, Private Autonomy, and Freedom of Contract' (2014) 10(6) Can. Soc. Sci 212; Felix Maultzsch, 'Party Autonomy in European Private International Law: Uniform Principle or Context-Dependent Instrument?' http://www.law.cam.ac.uk/repo-documents/pdf/events/PILConf/Party_Autonomy_in_European_Private_International_Law.pdf.

[29]Ref. " Evolution and Framework of Conflict of Laws" in Sect. 2.

[30]Ibid.

## 3.1 The Liberal Regime

One of the early decisions on the status of clauses regarding "foreign jurisdiction" clause pronounced by a Court in Bangladesh was the *Abdul Razzak* case.[31] Guha J delivering the judgement for the Full Bench of the Dhaka High Court dismissed an appeal preferred against the decision of the Learned Munsiff Court of Chittagong that, upon the application of the foreign defendant, upheld the validity of the foreign jurisdiction clause in an international contract and ordered the plaint[32] to be returned for presentation in the proper court in Denmark.

In this case, goods were sent to Pakistan under a bill of lading.[33] Paragraph 2 of the bill of lading governed the right of the parties as regards the forum of the suit and it was to the following effect:

"2. Jurisdiction. Any dispute arising under this Bill of Lading to be decided in Denmark according to Danish Law".

Dispute arose between the consignee[34] and the carrier[35] over the non-delivery of goods represented by the bill of lading and consequently a suit was instituted by the consignee in Court of Munsiff, Chittagong. The carrier (defendant) appeared before the Court and filed an interlocutory application seeking an order for returning of the plaint for being filed in the proper court in Denmark. Learned Munsiff allowed the defendant's application against which an appeal was preferred before the then Dhaka High Court. The Dhaka High Court was appealed to decide whether under the contract the Danish Court, a foreign court, would be the proper forum for the decision of the present dispute regarding non-delivery of the goods or whether the Chittagong Court would have jurisdiction to try the dispute in spite of the covenant in Paragraph 2 of the bill of lading. The Dhaka High Court held that in the presence of an express clause in the bill of lading, the validity of which was not challenged by the Appellant, whereby the contracting parties agreed to submit all disputes arising out of, or in relation to, the contract to the Danish Court, the Munsiff Court shall have no jurisdiction to try the matter and accordingly the Court ordered the plaint to be returned for filing in the appropriate Danish Court. The Court, in support of its decision, referred to the jurisprudence related to section 28 of the Contract Act as well as the English courts' decisions on the choice of forum clauses.

Distinguishing between trade intra-country and trade inter-countries the Court observed that while judicial opinion is not uniform as regard a covenant to submit a dispute to the decision of one of our several courts within this country, however, the

---

[31](n 8).

[32]CPC, 1908s 26.

[33]John F. Wilson: *Carriage of Goods by Sea* (Fourth Ed., Longman, 2001) Ch 5; Also see, Mohammad Abdur Razzak, Bill of Lading: A Pivotal Document in International Sale Transactions' [2005] 25 BLD 29.

[34]Ibid. See also Article I (a) of the International Convention for the Unification of Certain Rules of Law Relating to Bills of Lading, Brussels, August 25, 1924, (The Hague Rules).

[35]Ibid.

principle that governed a covenant to submit a dispute arising out of a contract between parties resident and domiciled in two foreign countries to a foreign tribunal was well settled.[36] The Court first engaged in analyzing section 28 of the Contract Act.

> 28. Agreement in restraint of legal proceedings void. Every agreement, by which any party thereto is restricted absolutely from enforcing his rights under or in respect of any contract, by the usual legal proceedings in the ordinary tribunals, or which limits the time within which he may thus enforce his rights, is void to that extent.
>
> Exception 1. - This section shall not render illegal a contract by which two or more persons agree that any dispute which may arise between them in respect of any subject or class of subjects shall be referred to arbitration, and that only the amount awarded in such arbitration shall be recoverable in respect of the disputed so referred.
>
> When such a contract has been made, a suit may be brought for its specific performance, and if a suit, other than for such specific performance, or for the recovery of the amount so awarded, is brought by one party to such contract against any other such party in respect of any subject which they have so agreed to refer, the existence of such contract shall be a bar to the suit.
>
> Exception 2. - Nor shall this section render illegal any contract in writing, by which two or more persons agree to refer to arbitration any question between them which has already arisen, or affect any provision of any law in force for the time being as to references to arbitration.

The reasoning of the Court in support the decision is as follows:

(a) When two parties domiciled in two different countries contractually stipulated, inter alia, the forum of settling dispute by a particular court, unless anything is shown in contrary, the intention of the parties gathered from the contract as a whole would be decisive.[37]
(b) An agreement is void when it absolutely restricts a party to a contract from enforcing his right under the contract in ordinary tribunals.[38]
(c) Section 28 of the Contract Act prevents parties to a contract from divesting courts inherent jurisdiction, but does not in any way nullify and vitiate an agreement between them by which one of the contracting parties, who has the choice of the forum, agrees to a limitation of that choice.[39]

---

[36](n 8) para 9.

[37]Ibid., para 15 The Court referred to the decision in *Feyerick v Hubbard* (1902) 71 L.J.KB 509 cited in Dicey's Conflict of Laws, 6th Edition, at page 360. There A, a Belgian firm carrying on business in Belgium enters into a contract with X, a British subject domiciled and resident in London and X contracts to assign certain patent rights to A in Belgium and the contract provides that all disputes as to the present agreement and its fulfillment shall be submitted to the Belgium Jurisdiction. In an action by A against X brought in the Belgian Court for alleged breach of the contract and in which, in accordance with the provisions of Belgian Law, citation is only served upon in London, judgement was obtained for £1000. It was held that Belgian Court had jurisdiction.'

[38]Ibid.

[39]Id.

(d) There is nothing against public policy in an agreement reached between the parties to a contract with the provision that, where several courts have territorial jurisdiction to hear a case, they may limit their choice to one of those courts.[40]

(e) The restriction found in the bill of lading as to the place of suing is only partial and not absolute. The position would have been different if the parties covenanted not to institute a suit in any of the courts having jurisdiction to entertain the same but in a court which possessed no jurisdiction at all and that would have been a case of absolute restriction and of conferring jurisdiction on a court, where none existed.[41]

(f) The Court observed that the expression "ordinary tribunal" included any tribunal.[42]

(g) The Court cited with approval[43] the following principles as laid down in *Jacobs, Marcus & Co. v The Credit Lyonnais*.[44]

  (1) The law by which contract or any part of it, is to be governed or applied, must always be a matter of construction of the contract itself as read by the light of the subject-matter and or surrounding circumstances.
  (2) Certain presumptions/rules in this respect have been developed in different countries and accepted by the courts, based upon business convenience, and upon the comity of nations, but these are only presumptions or prima facie rule that are capable or being displaced, wherever the clear intention of the parties can be gathered from the document itself and from the nature of the transaction.
  (3) The law of a country where a contract is made presumably governs the nature, the obligation and the interpretation of it, unless the contrary appears to be the intention of the parties.

The Court opined that in an international contract, if the parties expressly stipulated their intention as to the proper law and forum, the intention of the parties shall be decisive and Courts ought to give effect to such covenant. Where this intention of the parties cannot be gathered from the document, Court should decide the question as to jurisdiction by making reference to the principles based upon "… common senses, upon business convenience, and upon the comity of nations…".[45]

The principle established by the Court in *Abdur Razzak* as to the status of clause in contracts stipulating the forum for settling dispute arising out, or, in relation to

[40](n 8) para 15.
[41]Ibid.
[42]Id.
[43](n 8) para 25.
[44][1884] L.R.12 Q.B.D. 589 [Bowen LJ].
[45]Razzak (n 5).

the contract, had been followed in a series of subsequent legal decisions[46] pronounced by Dhaka High Court and a liberal and commercially responsive regime of rules relating to foreign jurisdiction clauses started to be formed. However, this liberal regime came under severe criticism and in fact, was overruled by the Pakistan Supreme Court in 1965. It ends the evolution of the Liberal Regime as initiated by the decision in *Abdur Razzak.*

## 3.2 *The Nationalistic Regime*

In 1965, the Pakistan Supreme Court disposed of a few civil appeals by a single judgment.[47] The question that was presented in all the appeals was related to the status of a clause in a bill of lading conferring jurisdiction to a foreign court to try any matter arising out of the contract as evidenced by the bill of lading. Chief Justice Hamoodur Rahman, speaking for the Supreme Court of Pakistan, observed,

> My examination of the treatment given to such foreign jurisdiction clauses by Courts in different countries leads me to the irresistible conclusion that nowhere have the courts gone to the same extent as the courts in East Pakistan. In no country has any court accepted that such a foreign jurisdiction clause in a contract can legally oust the jurisdiction of the municipal courts of the country…[48]

The Chief Justice continued,

> In this view of the matter, in spite of the consistent decisions of the High Court of East Pakistan, I have, with utmost respect, to hold that these decisions have diverted the law of the country into a wrong channel and must, therefore, be over-ruled.[49]

The principles as enunciated by the Pakistan Supreme Court in *M.A. Chowdhury v Messrs. Mitsui O.S.K. Lines Ltd. and others* (hereinafter, *M.A. Chowdhry*)[50] regarding foreign jurisdiction clause in an international contract may be paraphrased as under:

(a) Exclusive jurisdiction clause in a contract like a bill of lading, whereby the jurisdiction of local court in the country is completely ousted in respect of any

---

[46]Some of such leading decisions are as follows: *Tar Md. & Co. v Federation of Pakistan* (1957) 9 DLR 197; *Narayanganj Iron Works Ltd. v. Pakistan* (1963) 15 DLR 434; *Osaka Shosen Kaisha v. Prov. of E. Pakistan* (1965) 17 DLR 659; *British India Steam Navigation Co. Ltd. v A.R. Choudhury* (1967) 19 DLR 54.

[47]*Eastern Federal Union Insurance Co. Ltd. v Messrs Holland Bengal Burmah Line and others* [1965] 22 DLR (SC) 334; see, also appeal in *M.A. Chowdhury v Messrs Mitsui O.S.K. Lines Ltd. and others.*

[48]Ibid., para 54.

[49]Id, para 56.

[50]PLD 1970 SC 373.

dispute referred to in the contract as being opposed to public policy and derogatory to a country's sovereignty is null and void.[51]

(b) Where there is an express provision in a local law forbidding the making of such a contract then it would, as well, be void on the same principle. Whatever a law prohibits is also opposed to public and hence be opposed to public policy.[52]

(c) A contractual stipulation cannot take away the statutory authority of the courts; nor such authority be conferred upon the courts by private agreement.[53]

(d) If a jurisdiction clause has indirectly the effect of relieving the carrier from the liability he would normally have incurred under the legislation of the country, then the Courts wouldn't honour such a jurisdiction clause. In the same vein, if the result of the enforcement of the jurisdiction clause, in effect, deprives one of the parties to a contract of his right to seek any remedy at all, then to the clause will not be given effect to.[54]

(e) Section 28 of the Contract Act specified that a contract that restricts any party to it from enforcing his rights under or in respect of such a contract by the "usual legal proceedings" in the "ordinary tribunals" of the country, will, to that extent, be void unless protected by the exceptions to the section.[55]

(f) While the Court was not finding a problem with a contractual clause leading to competing jurisdiction within the country, but it cannot be said that where the jurisdiction of all courts within the country is taken away and exclusive jurisdiction is given to a foreign court by a contract, it will not come within the mischief of Section 28.[56]

(g) The "legal proceedings" and "tribunals" referred to in Section 28 of the Contract Act can only mean legal proceedings and tribunals known to the legislature as ordinary tribunals in the country and the usual proceedings available in these Courts. These expressions shall not include any foreign tribunal or legal system.[57]

(h) Exclusive jurisdiction clauses, even when they purport to give jurisdiction to a Court in a foreign country, are really in the nature of arbitration clauses, an exception to Section 28 Contract Act and should be dealt with in the same manner as other arbitration clauses.[58]

---

[51](n 47), para 56.

[52]Ibid., para 57.

[53]Id.

[54]Id, para 59.

[55]Ibid., para 46.

[56]Id.

[57]The Court observed, the argument that because a foreign judgement can be enforced under the provisions of the Code of Civil Procedure, and, therefore, a foreign tribunal making an order is also an "ordinary tribunal" within the meaning of section 28 of the Contract Act, is clearly untenable.

[58](n 47) para 57.

(i) Arbitration clauses do not altogether oust the jurisdiction of the courts. The local courts allow the parties to resort to the chose form of dispute resolution. Courts still retain the jurisdiction to resume the case if the arbitration failed.[59]

The judgement of Pakistan Supreme Court in *M.A. Chowdhury*[60] is taken as authority regarding the rules on conflict of laws in force in Bangladesh. The Court held that in order to preserve the sanctity of contracts it ought also be held that such foreign jurisdiction clauses, even when they purport to give jurisdiction to a Court in a foreign country, are really in the nature of arbitration clauses which come within the exceptions to Section 28 and therefore should be dealt with in the same manner as other arbitration clauses.

## 3.3 Pro-trade Regime

In 1997, the Appellate Division of the Supreme Court of Bangladesh in *Bangladesh Air Service (Pvt.) Ltd.*[61] revisited the law relating to foreign jurisdiction and proper law clauses in a contract, while exercising its appellate jurisdiction. The Court referred with approval to the reasoning in *Eastern Federal Union Insurance Co. Ltd.*[62] although the notion of "national sovereignty" could not escape criticism.[63]

The facts of the case are summarized thus: the respondent, British Airways Plc, London contracted a General Sales Agreement (GSA Agreement) with the appellant, Bangladesh Air Services (Pvt.) Ltd., a company incorporated in Bangladesh on April 18th, 1980 at Dhaka, wherein the appellant was appointed as General Sales Agent (GSA) of the respondent.

Two clauses of the GSA Agreement came up for dispute resolution. The first one, Clause 14,

> Arbitration - Any difference or dispute concerning the scope, meaning, construction or effect of this Agreement, or any matter or thing contained therein or related hereto, shall be referred to Arbitration in accordance with, and subject to, the provisions of the Arbitration Act, 1950. The arbitral award shall be final and conclusively binding upon the parties.

The second clause, Clause 23,

> Jurisdiction - This Agreement shall be interpreted in all respects in accordance with the Law of England.

---

[59]Ibid.

[60](n 50); also, the decision in *Swedish East Asia Company Ltd. v B.P. Herman and Mohatta (India)* AIR 1962 Cal 601, In a decision that is a persuasive precedent, the Calcutta High Court stayed a suit in India where Swedish law was designated as the governing law and Swedish courts were designated as the chosen forum for dispute resolution.

[61](n 1).

[62]*Eastern Federal Union Insurance Co. Ltd. v Messrs Holland Bengal Burmah Line and others* (n 47).

[63](n 1) para 26.

In 1994, a dispute arose out of the GSA Agreement between the appellant and the respondent. The dispute was referred to arbitration. No agreement was reached as to the appointment of the arbitrator. In this context, on May 2nd, 1994, the appellant filed an application in the 3rd Court of Subordinate Judge, Dhaka for the appointment of an arbitrator. The respondent filed a written objection contending that since Clause 14 of the Agreement provided that arbitration shall be in accordance with and subject to the provisions of the Arbitration Act, 1950 (of England) and since, further, Clause 23 provided that the Agreement shall in all respects be interpreted in accordance with the Law of England. Hearing the parties, the trial Court held that the jurisdiction of the local Court was not ousted and appointed Mr. Justice Ruhul Islam as the Arbitrator. The respondent preferred civil revision challenging the legality of the order of the trial Court. The High Court Division held, inter alia, that the Courts in Bangladesh have no jurisdiction over the arbitration in view of the stipulations contained in Clauses 14 and 23 of the GSA Agreement. The appellant preferred an appeal before the Appellate Division of the Supreme Court of Bangladesh and the leave was granted.[64]

The full Bench of the Appellate Division, having heard the submissions for the Appellant and the Respondent, dismissed the appeal. The Court observed that the High Court made no error in interpreting the provisions contained in Exception 1 to Section 28 of the Contract Act and the parties having agreed to be bound by the English Law of Arbitration cannot be allowed to resile from the same.[65]

Discussing the submission clause related to arbitration, the Appellate Division revisited the jurisprudence on foreign arbitration clause in a contract. The judgment discussed many issues related to foreign jurisdiction clause, but determined those issues that were relevant to be disposed of the Appeal. The salient features of the judgment related to foreign arbitration clause in an international contract are,

---

[64]The leave was granted on the following terms: first, that the High Court Division failed to consider the true import of Exception 1 to Section 28 of the Contract Act by holding erroneously that the said exception validated conferment of exclusive jurisdiction by the parties on English Courts ousting the jurisdiction of local Courts. Secondly, Section 8(2) of the Arbitration Act, 1940 of Bangladesh and Section 10(d) of the Arbitration Act, 1950 of England about the appointment of an Arbitrator being in *pari materia* and in view of the principle of law enunciated in the case of *MA Chowdhury v Mitsui OSK Lines Lid* the High Court Division wrongly held that only the English Court had jurisdiction over the arbitration or the appointment of an Arbitrator. Thirdly, the law of contract being similar in England and Bangladesh and the relevant provisions of the Arbitration laws of these countries being in *pari materia*, Clauses 14 and 23 of the Agreement were wrongly interpreted conferring exclusive jurisdiction to the Courts in England. Fourthly, the Agreement dated April 18th, 1980 having been executed in Bangladesh and other factors relevant to arbitration, namely, availability of evidence, convenience of parties and expense being also favourable for holding arbitration in Bangladesh, the High Court Division has erred in deciding otherwise. Finally, the High Court Division did not properly consider the submission that a foreign arbitral award is not enforceable in Bangladesh. See, (n 1) para 5.

[65](n 1) paras 44, 71.

(a) A clause in a contract providing for determination of all disputes arising between the parties to the contract by a foreign tribunal must be construed as a submission clause for arbitration purposes.[66]
(b) Section 28 of the Contract Act makes void to that extent every agreement by which any party thereto is restricted absolutely from enforcing his rights under or in respect of any contract by the usual legal proceedings in ordinary tribunals, but Exception 1 to Section 28 provides that Section 28 shall not render illegal a contract if disputes are referred to arbitration.[67]
(c) When parties to an international contract agree, in relation to a submission clause for arbitration, with the expressions like "in accordance with" and "subject to" a particular legislation, the court shall, as far as the arbitral procedure is concerned, hold that the parties have consciously made the arbitration to be in consonance with and conditional upon the observance of the provisions of the referred legislation.[68]
(d) There is nothing in Exception 1 to Section 28 of the Contract Act prohibiting the parties to a contract from choosing a foreign forum under the supervision of a foreign court for arbitrating its disputes. Further, such a contract does not offend the main provision of Section 28 since there is no absolute bar of any legal proceeding and the local Courts still retain the jurisdiction to decide the case between the parties.[69]
(e) The appearance of the foreign defendant before the local court in order to challenge the assumption of jurisdiction shall not be held to be the waiver of compliance with the agreed governing law of the foreign arbitration clause in the contract.[70]
(f) If an international contract with a submission clause for arbitration purpose referred to a particular legislation, the inquiry of the court for the proper venue of arbitration ought primarily be focused on such clause alone.[71]
(g) Courts ought to insist that they should have recourse to arbitration that was agreed to, before pursuing any other remedy.[72]
(h) An arbitration agreement between the parties to a commercial contract shall act as an estoppel and the party attempting to prevent the enforcement of the

[66]Id, paras 58 and 59.

[67]Id, para 26.

[68]Id, para 24.

[69]As a result, the plaintiff is free to file a suit for damages against the defendant in the local court. The defendant is also free to ask for a stay of the suit, pending arbitration, and it is for the local court having regard to all circumstances, to arrive at a conclusion whether sufficient reasons are made out by the plaintiff for refusing to grant a stay. (n 1) paras 24, 29, 61.

[70]Ibid., para 28.

[71]Id, para 25.

[72]Id, para 56.

bargain shall be estopped, for fairness and maintaining integrity of the bargain, from denying the enforcement of the arbitration clause.[73]

(i) Questions of appropriate venue are legal questions and have to be decided without reference to extraneous considerations like hardship, availability of the witnesses, expense and the like. These are not sufficient consideration to allow the parties to a contract to resile from lawfully contracted obligations.[74]

While the appellant relied upon the ratio of *M.A. Chowdhury* and argued that foreign arbitration clauses are not to be upheld because they were derogatory to the national sovereignty of the country and hence oppose to public policy, Mustafa Kamal J. while speaking for the Appellate Division observed in forthright terms:

> … The plea of sovereignty and interest of the country and its citizens, if accepted, will render foreign arbitral jurisdiction absolutely nugatory, we venture to say that such a consequence will itself be opposed to public policy, for no country lives in an island these days. Foreign arbitration clause is an integral part of international trade and commerce today.[75]

Further, the view put forward by Mustafa Kamal J was also endorsed by Latifur Rahman J. While addressing the question as to the validity of foreign jurisdiction clauses he observed,

> In this regard, I may also refer to a passage from Cheshire and North's Private International Law (11th Edition, 495), while discussing about the interpretation of contracts the authors say: "There is, speaking generally, no reason in principle why the parties should not be free to select the governing law. The express choice of law made by parties alleviates need for interpretation. In the absence of an express choice, the question of the proper law of contract would arise; the parties to a contract should be bound by the jurisdiction clause to which they were agreed unless there is some strong reason to the contrary". The parties having chosen the law, the question of deciding the proper law of contract does not arise. The parties to a contract should be bound by the jurisdiction clause to which they have agreed unless there is some strong reason to the contrary.[76]

It can be safely vouched that the decision in *Eastern Federal Union Insurance* and its reliance on nationalistic approach—national sovereignty and supremacy of national law—was rejected by the Appellate Division. The Court emphasised on the sanctity of contract with a view to paving a way for rule-making conducive for trade and commerce.

Application of foreign law by forum courts has been explained through three theoretical constructs,[77] the international, the neo-statutory, and the territorial. The internationalists hold the view that the forum administering private international

[73] Id, Latifur Rahman J. made reference to Cheshire and North's Private International Law (12th Edition) 205 to substantiate his argument.

[74] (n 1) para 71.

[75] Ibid., para 26.

[76] Id, para 56.

[77] Jet Walker and Jean-Gabriel Castel, *Canadian Conflict of Laws vol. 1* (6th edn, LexisNexis 2005) ch 1.

law applies foreign laws because it is based on principles of customary international law. The Neo-Statutist construct rejected the idea of deriving the obligation from any international law; the explanation for applying the foreign law is the view that the personal law governs their capacity to act, and extends beyond the territorial jurisdiction. The Territorialist construct explains that the principles and rules of private international law are part of domestic law. The citizens and the aliens are equally subject to the laws.[78] It appears that the current jurisprudence as prevail in Bangladesh on conflict of law, as specified in *Eastern Federal Union Insurance*,[79] favoured the territorial theory.

## 4 Enforcement of Judgment and Awards

The Code of Civil Procedure, 1908 contains provisions relevant for the enforcement of foreign judgements and orders while the Arbitration Act, 2001 deals with foreign arbitral awards.

### *4.1 Enforcement of Judgment/Decree*[80]

The Code of Civil Procedure specified a uniform procedure for the enforcement of decrees and judgments originating from any civil court established by the Civil Courts Act. A court is defined as "foreign court" which situates beyond Bangladesh, does not exercise any authority in the territory of Bangladesh and is not set up and administered by the Government of Bangladesh.[81]

A foreign decree to be enforced under the provisions of the Code of Civil Procedure has to meet a two-stage test specified in section 44A of the Code of Civil Procedure.

1. the foreign court passing the decree shall be a "superior court" located either in United Kingdom or in any reciprocating territory. A certified copy of the foreign decree has to be filed with the relevant District Court in whose jurisdiction the decree's enforcement is sought.[82] "Reciprocating territory" means the United

---

[78]Id.

[79](n 47).

[80]"Decree" is the operative portion of the judgement. This operative portion is enforced. Section 2 (2) of the Code of Civil Procedure defines a "decree" as the formal expression of an adjudication which, so far as regards the Court expressing it, conclusively determines the rights of the parties with regard to all or any of the matters in controversy in the suit and may be either preliminary or final.

[81](n 32) s 2(5).

[82]Ibid., s 44A.

Kingdom and such other country or territory as the Government may, from time to time, by notification in the official Gazette, declare[83] to be reciprocating territory for the purposes of section 44A of the Code of Civil Procedure.[84] Further, the Government, from time to time, by gazette notification, declare the courts of a particular country/territory to be the "superior court".[85]
2. the foreign decree sought to be enforced shall satisfy that it does not fall under any exceptions as specified in Section 13 of the CPC.[86]

As specified in Section 13, a foreign judgement shall be conclusive as to any matter thereby directly adjudicated upon between the same parties or between parties under whom they or any of them claim litigating under the same title, subject to a few exceptions.

(1) it has not been pronounced by a Court of competent jurisdiction;
(2) it has not been given on the merits of the case;
(3) it appears on the face of the proceedings to be founded on an incorrect view of international law or a refusal to recognize the law of Bangladesh where such law is applicable;
(4) the proceedings leading to the judgment vitiated natural justice;
(5) it has been obtained by fraud;
(6) it sustains a claim founded on a breach of any law in force in Bangladesh.

Upon fulfillment of the above-mentioned criteria such foreign decree shall be enforced by the District Court as if the decree had been passed by the District Court.[87] The Court shall presume, subject to rebuttal,[88] upon the production of any document purporting to be a certified copy of a foreign judgment, that a Court of competent jurisdiction pronounced such judgment.

---

[83]Following are the major countries/territories that have been declared to be the reciprocating territories: United Kingdom (Explanation to section 44A of the Code of Civil Procedure), Pakistan (Gazette of Pakistan, 1953 Pt. I, pp 143–44), Fiji (Gazette of Pakistan, 1949, Pt. I, p 275), Singapore (Gazette of Pakistan. 1954, Pt. I, p 106), the Australian Capital Territory (Gazette of Pakistan, 1957, Pt. I, p 174), the Northern Territory of Australia (Gazette of Pakistan, 1959, Pt. I, p 425), New Zealand including the Cook Islands (including Nive) and the Trust Territory of Western Samao, (Gazette of Pakistan, 1958 P. I. p 455) etc.

[84](n 32) s 44A, Explanation 2.

[85]Following are some of the courts that have been declared to be the "superior court" for the purpose of section 44A of the Code of Civil Procedure: High Court in England, the Court of Session in Scotland, the High Court in Northern Ireland, the Court of Chancery of the Country palatine of Lancaster, the Court of Chancery of the Country Palatine of Durham (Explanation 1 to section 44A of the Code of Civil Procedure), Supreme Court of Fiji (Gazette of Pakistan, 1949, Pt. I, p 275), the Supreme Court of Singapore (Gazette of Pakistan. 1954, Pt. I, p 106), the Supreme Court of Australian Capital territory (Gazette of Pakistan, 1957, Pt. I, p 174), Supreme Court of the Northern Territory of Australia, (Gazette of Pakistan, 1959, Pt. I, p 425), the Supreme Court of New Zealand (Gazette of Pakistan 1958, P. I. p 455) etc.

[86](n 32) s 44A (3).

[87]Ibid., s 44A (1).

[88]Id, s 14.

## 4.2 *Enforcement of Arbitral Award*

The Arbitration Act, 2001 was enacted to make rules relating to, amongst others, international commercial arbitration and recognition and enforcement of foreign arbitral awards. A foreign arbitral award is defined as "an award made in pursuance of an arbitration agreement in the territory of any state other than Bangladesh but it does not include an award made in the territory of a specified state;"[89] An arbitration is 'international' if it arises out of a contractual relationship or otherwise where, at least, one of the parties is (i) an individual who is a national of, or habitually resident in, any country other than Bangladesh; or (ii) a body corporate which is incorporated in any country other than Bangladesh; or (iii) a company or an association or a body of individuals whose central management and control is exercised in any country other than Bangladesh; or (iv) the Government of a foreign country.[90]

The Arbitration Act, 2001 provides for the enforcement of foreign arbitral award through the procedure specified in the CPC.[91] The party seeking the enforcement of the foreign award is required to institute an execution proceeding in the Court of District Judge. The application for enforcement should include the (a) the original arbitral award or a copy thereof, duly authenticated in the manner required by the law of the country in which it was made; (b) the original agreement for arbitration or a duly certified copy thereof; and (c) such evidence as may be necessary to prove that the award is a foreign award as defined in Section 2 of the Arbitration Act, 2001.[92] The Court of District Judge in which the execution proceeding is filed may refuse the recognition or execution of the foreign arbitral award on the proof that (i) the foreign arbitral tribunal in passing the award failed to give effect to the substantive and procedural laws agreed in the foreign arbitration agreement; or (ii) the recognition or enforcement of the foreign arbitration award is opposed to laws of Bangladesh.[93] A foreign arbitral award enforceable shall be treated as

---

[89]AA, 2001 s 2 (k).

[90]Ibid., s 2 (c).

[91]Id, s 45.

[92]Id, s 45 (2).

[93]Section 46 (1) of the Arbitration Act, 2001: Grounds for refusing recognition or execution of foreign arbitral awards—(1) Recognition or execution of foreign arbitral award may be refused only on the following grounds, namely—(a) if the party against whom it is invoked furnishes proof to the Court that—(i) a party to the arbitration agreement was under some incapacity, (ii) the arbitration agreement is not valid under the law to which the parties have subjected it; (iii) the party against whom the award is invoked was not given proper notice of the appointment of the arbitrator or of the arbitral proceedings or was otherwise unable due to some reasonable causes to present his case; or (iv) the concerned foreign arbitral award contains decisions on matters beyond the scope of the submission to arbitration: Provided that, if the decisions on matters submitted to arbitration can be separated from those not so submitted, that part of the award which contains decisions on matters submitted to arbitration may be recognized and enforced. (v) the composition of the arbitral tribunal or the arbitral procedure was not in accordance with the agreement of the parties or, failing such agreement, was not in accordance with the law of the country where the

binding for all purposes on the persons as between whom it was made, and may accordingly be relied on by any of those persons by way of defense, set of or otherwise in any legal proceedings in Bangladesh.[94]

The Arbitration Act, 2001 is a much-needed legislation to harmonize the law relating to enforcement of foreign arbitral awards. In *Bangladesh Air Service (Pvt.) Ltd.* the members of the bar and the bench of Bangladesh expressed concern about the uncertainty associated with the rules related to enforcement foreign arbitral awards. The Attorney General, in his *amicus curiae* submission, observed that there was not legislative framework other than the common law.[95] Averring to the absence of a law, the government not issuing a notification renewing the 1937 Arbitration (Protocol and Convention) Act, 1937, he suggested for the enactment of specific rules for the enforcement of foreign arbitral award.[96] The Arbitration Act, 2001 was promulgated by the Parliament within four years of the pronouncement of the judgement in *Bangladesh Air Service (Pvt.) Ltd.*

## 5 Conclusion

Bangladesh has a comprehensive legislation relating to international arbitration. However Bangladesh also needs to address specific issues concerning proper law of the contract, and the enforcement of foreign court's interim orders in a dispute related to an international commercial contract. The need of the hour is to recognize the winds of change in transnational commercial law and move towards increased regulation in harmony with the needs of international commerce. To begin with, Bangladesh must consider membership of the Hague Conference on Private International Law and accede to their conventions in the commercial law domain. Further it could also consider membership of the UNCITRAL Convention on International Sale of Goods, 1980, as it could be of significant help in international commerce to have harmonized legal platforms.

---

(Footnote 93 continued)

arbitration took place. (vi) the award has not yet become binding on the parties, or has been set aside or suspended by a competent authority of the country in which, under the law of which, that award was made; (b) the court in which recognition or execution of the foreign arbitral award is sought, finds that—(i) the subject matter of the dispute is not capable of settlement by arbitration under the law for the time being in force in Bangladesh; or (ii) the recognition and execution of the foreign arbitral award is in conflict with the public policy of Bangladesh.

[94]AA, 2001 s 45 (1) (a).

[95]*27 DLR 583; 30 DLR (94); 32 DLR (AD) 107.*

[96](1997) 49 DLR (AD) 187, para 43.

# Issues of Jurisdiction, Choice of Law and Enforcement in International Commercial Arbitration: A Bangladesh Perspective

**Maimul Ahsan Khan**

**Abstract** In the era of globalization in the field of international trade and commerce, international commercial arbitration has emerged as the prominent dispute settlement mechanism. It has successfully helped business traverse dispute resolution through avoiding the complexities in traditional cross-border commercial dispute litigation system. Parties have greater autonomy and control over dispute resolution process in terms of choice of law, lex arbitri and seat of arbitration among others. The New York Convention on enforcement of foreign arbitral awards has contributed significantly to international arbitration by ensuring that signatory countries would recognize and enforce arbitral awards given in the Convention countries. The UNCITRAL Model Law further offered guidance for States to help harmonize their laws related to international arbitration. Bangladesh's arbitration law premised upon the NYC and the UNCITRAL ML embodies inter-alia the provisions of choice of law, party autonomy, the scope of applicability of lex arbitri, lex mercatoria and enforceability of foreign arbitral award in Bangladesh. Another notable development is the courts' role has been capped to a minimal level. This chapter discusses the features of Bangladesh arbitration law related to international arbitration and suggests a few areas that require a statutory revisit.

**Keywords** Bangladesh Arbitraton Act · Arbitrability · Arbitral tribunal · UNCITRAL model law · Enforcement of foreign awards

## Introduction

Arbitration as a formal mechanism for dispute resolution is rather a new addition to the dispute resolution methods in South Asia, especially Bangladesh. It was about thirty years after independence from Pakistan that Bangladesh (formerly, East Pakistan) attempted to modernize its arbitration law. This modernization attempt

M.A. Khan (✉)
Law, University of Dhaka, Dhaka, Bangladesh
e-mail: khanmaimul@gmail.com

© Springer Nature Singapore Pte Ltd. 2017

S.R. Garimella and S. Jolly (eds.), *Private International Law*,
DOI 10.1007/978-981-10-3458-9_14

was largely necessitated by an increased interaction with global economy and institutions through trade, commerce and investment. Bangladesh acceded to the New York Convention on the Recognition and Enforcement of Foreign Arbitral Awards, 1958 (hereinafter, the NYC) on 6th May 1992. However, it was only in 2001 that the State attempted to revisit its arbitration law; it drafted a new law based upon the UNCITRAL Model Law (hereinafter, the UNCITRAL ML). This chapter attempts to critique the 2001 Arbitration Act on its strengths and the challenges faced in the enforcement of foreign arbitral agreements and awards in Bangladesh.

**Structure of the Chapter**

This chapter is arranged in four parts. The first part traces the evolution of the arbitration law in Bangladesh, and also attempts to state the law on such aspects as arbitrability of disputes in Bangladesh, the crystallization of the principle of separability in the law, the provisions relating to arbitral agreements and their validity.

The second part deals with jurisdiction of the tribunal, and the role of the Bangladeshi courts with regard to matters pending before a foreign-seated tribunal. The third part discusses the choice of law related provisions in the Arbitration Act. The fourth part discusses the provisions related to recognition and enforcement of foreign arbitral awards.

## 1 International Commercial Arbitration in Bangladesh

Like its neighbours in the Indian peninsula, Bangladesh inherited the colonial legacy in the space of arbitration law. Geographically situated in the eastern part of the Peninsula, also known as the Bengal Presidency during the British rule, the earliest recorded law on arbitration was the Bengal Regulation, 1772.[1] Further references to arbitration, applicable to the Bengal Presidency were seen in the Civil Procedure Code, 1908.[2] At the time of the partition of British-ruled India in 1947, there were two laws on the subject—the Arbitration (Protocol and Convention) Act, 1937 (hereinafter, the APC Act) enacted by the British India in furtherance of the commitments under the Geneva Protocol on Arbitration Clauses, 1923 and the Geneva Convention on the Execution of Foreign Arbitral Awards, 1927; and The Arbitration Act, 1940. Post-partition of the Indian State, the new countries, India and Pakistan inherited these legislations, which remained the law in India till 1996 (when a legislation modelled on UNCITRAL ML was enacted); in Pakistan the AA, 1940 continues to govern the domestic arbitration. Bangladesh post-independence inherited the AA, 1940 and the APC Act, 1937 for domestic and international arbitrations, respectively. However, as was commented in all the three countries, the AA Act, 1940 was not able to keep pace with the requirements of a strong and

[1]Stephan Balthasar (ed.), *International Commercial Arbitration—A Handbook* (Munich: Beck, Hart, Nomos, 2015) 448.

[2]Ibid.

effective dispute resolution system catering to the needs of an increasingly globalized economy. Commentators have identified a few lacunae in the AA, 1940—the conduct of the proceedings by the tribunal resembled litigation proceedings, resultant award subjected to inevitable challenge in the courts,[3] 'proceedings under the Act have become highly technical accompanied by unending prolixity, at every step providing a legal trap to the unwary.'[4]

In fulfilment of its international commitment with the NYC, Bangladesh enacted the Arbitration Act, 2001 (hereinafter, the AA, 2001). The Act was enforced on April 10, 2001.[5] Modelled upon the UNCITRAL ML, Bangladesh, through this legislation, attempted to consolidate the arbitration law applicable to domestic and international arbitrations. The new legislation has repealed the APC Act, 1937 and the AA, 1940. The new Act thus created a single and unified legal regime for arbitration in Bangladesh which has also been the trend in recent years elsewhere.[6] However, in the context of international commercial arbitration, the Act has specific prescriptions that are not applicable to domestic arbitration.[7] With this new enactment Bangladesh has kept pace with the recent trends in the field of international commercial arbitration in the rest of the world.[8]

It may also be mentioned here that Bangladesh ratified the 1965 Convention on the Settlement of Investment Dispute between States and Nationals of other States (ICSID Convention), (hereinafter, Washington Convention) The ICSID Convention entered into force for Bangladesh on April 26, 1980.[9]

The chapter attempts to discuss the provisions of the AA, 2001 in the context of the UNCITRAL ML, its inspiration; and also compare it with the Indian Arbitration and Conciliation Act, 1996, which also drew inspiration from the same source.

Inspired though by the UNCITRAL ML, the AA, 2001 deviated from it in defining international commercial arbitration. The meaning attributed to the word 'international' drew inspiration from the Indian Arbitration and Conciliation Act,

---

[3]A.F.M. Maniruzzaman, 'The New Law of International Commercial Arbitration in Bangladesh: A Comparative Perspective' (2003) 14 The Am. Rev. of Int. Arbtn. 139, 140.

[4]See, for example, *Gurunanak Foundation v Rattan Singh & Sons* AIR 1981 SC 2075 [Desai J].

[5]Vide Notification No. SRO 87-Law/2001 dated 9-04-2001, published in BANGLADESH GAZETTE EXTRAORDINARY, dated 10-04-2001. Section 56 of The Arbitration Act, 2001 [hereinafter the Act] states: "After the commencement of this Act [the Bangla text], the Government shall, by notification in the official Gazette, publish an Authentic text in English which shall be known as the Authentic English Text, of this Act: Provided that in the event of any conflict between this Act and the English text, this Act shall prevail." It should be noted that the official Authentic English Text of the Act has not been published yet by the Government of the People's Republic of Bangladesh.

[6]Within the Indian subcontinent, India's Arbitration and Conciliation Act, 1996 is also modeled on UNCITRAL ML; more than 70 countries have revisited their arbitration law inspired by the UNCITRAL ML.

[7]Maniruzzaman (n 3) 140.

[8]Ibid.

[9]K.U Bhuiyan and J Alam, Niko Case and the prospect of foreign investment in Bangladesh, *The Daily Star*, 08 March 2015, 15.

1996. While the ML defined 'internationality' in terms of place of business of the disputing parties or of the subject matter of the dispute, the Bangladesh arbitration law defined it in terms of natural or juridical personality, i.e., nationality, or status of the parties.[10] The AA, 2001 states that an arbitration is international if

(a) an individual who is a national of, or habitually resident in, any country other than Bangladesh, or
(b) a body corporate which is incorporated in any country other than in Bangladesh, or
(c) a company or an association or a body of individuals who central management and control is exercised in any country other than Bangladesh, or
(d) the government of a foreign country.[11]

It could therefore be inferred from the above definition of 'international' that a commercial dispute between two Bangladeshi nationals, having business in different States would not be an international commercial arbitration, though it would be under the Model Law. It is pertinent to mention here that the Arbitration and Conciliation Act, 1996 in India also adopted similar rationale—Section 2(1)(f) defined an international commercial arbitration as an arbitration where at least one of the parties is a national or habitually resident or is incorporated in a country other than India.

## 2 Jurisdiction of the Arbitral Tribunal

### *2.1 Arbitration Agreement*

The Act of 2001 defined an arbitration agreement as an agreement, either as a clause or a separate agreement, to submit all disputes, present and future, to arbitration.[12] An arbitration agreement has to be in writing, either in the form of an arbitration clause in a contract or in the form of a separate agreement, and may be concerned with future and existing disputes respectively.[13] In this regard, the AA, 2001 has followed the UNCITRAL ML, verbatim. Further the legislation also specified that an electronic communication related to an intention to arbitrate would be considered an arbitration agreement.[14] Existence of a valid arbitration agreement prevents access to the courts. In *Governor, Bangladesh Bank and Ors. v M/s. Shah Islam Construction Ltd.*[15] The Court held that presence of an valid arbitration

[10]Maniruzzaman (n 3) 141.

[11]AA, 2001, s 2(c). It is similar to s 2(1) (f) of the Indian Arbitration and Conciliation Act, 1996.

[12](n 11) s 2(n).

[13](n 11) s 9(2).

[14](n 11) s 9(2)(b) an exchange of letters, telex, telegrams, Fax, e-mail or other means of telecommunication which provide a record of the agreement.

[15]6 MLR (AD) 245.

clause contained in the contract providing for arbitration within Bangladesh, entails the disputes to be resolved through arbitration. Writ Jurisdiction cannot be invoked against breach of contract without resort to arbitration. The court shall refer the matter to arbitration and stay the legal proceedings.[16]

In arbitrations seated outside Bangladesh, there remains a doubt whether the provisions of the AA, 2001 are applicable in the context of arbitration agreements and the powers of the court to stay pending proceedings or issue anti-suit injunctions to facilitate arbitration. In *Union Traders Limited v Motorola Technology*[17] it was held that the provisions of the Act may not be applicable to stay local court proceedings where there is an arbitration agreement to arbitrate a dispute outside Bangladesh. However, the parties' agreement to choose a particular forum for the resolution of their disputes will be considered and upheld by the courts and proceedings that are in breach of the parties' agreement to resolve the dispute by arbitration will be stayed permanently or dismissed by the courts.

## 2.2 *Arbitrability*

Section 54 of the AA, 2001 specified that the Act is not applicable to the Industrial Relations Ordinance, 1968 or to any other law making special provisions for arbitration.[18] Section 10(2) of the Act specified that the Court, if it is satisfied that an arbitration agreement exists, refers the parties to arbitration and stays the proceedings, unless it finds established that the arbitration agreement is void, inoperative or incapable of determination by arbitration. Decisions under the old Arbitration Act, 1940 would have a bearing on this issue. Under the old Act a court decided on the facts of each case whether sufficient cause had been made out or not for the dispute to be referred to arbitration and in doing so, the Court was not limited to the kind of causes referred to in the Arbitration Act. When the dispute required investigation into the charge of fraud the court could have refused to refer the matter to arbitration. When the dispute between the parties raised difficult and complicated questions of law that required a decision by the court, it could have refused to refer the dispute to arbitration. The Court also considered the conduct of the applicant and considered whether such conduct was sufficient cause for not making the reference. Moreover, undue delay could be sufficient cause for not ordering the reference.[19]

[16](n 11) Ss. 7 and 10.

[17]19 BLT (HCD) 396.

[18](n 11) s. 54 Application of this Act to other laws providing for arbitration—Nothing of this Act shall apply to the Industrial Relations Ordinance, 1969 (XXXIII of 1969) or to any other law making special provisions for arbitration.

[19]http://sarco.org.pk/bangladesh.html, accessed 21 July 2016.

## 2.3 Separability

The doctrine of separability, also known as severability in some jurisdictions, ensures that the arbitration clause/agreement be considered as a distinct agreement disjointed from the main contract. This distinction allows that arbitral tribunal to decide upon the agreement that is the source of its existence. Autonomy of the arbitration clause is an important feature of international arbitration, and as Schwebel observed,[20] has to be viewed together with the principle of *competence-competence* (discussed in the following section). Schwebel further noted. If it is inherent in the arbitral (and judicial) process that a tribunal is the judge of its own jurisdiction, that it has *compétence de la compétence*, it is no less inherent in that process that an arbitral tribunal shall have the competence to pass upon disputes arising out of the agreement which is the immediate source of the tribunal's creation even where those disputes engage the initial or continuing validity of that agreement.[21]

Further practical necessity explains the international arbitral practice of loyalty to the separability principle. The presence of the clause provides the disputant parties with a mechanism for dispute resolution. If the clause were considered to die with the presumed death of the principal agreement, it would leave parties with no option for dispute resolution.

The AA, 2001 legislated this principle of separability into the law under the nomenclature of severability.[22] Maniruzzaman commented that as compared to the UNCITRAL ML and The Arbitration and Conciliation Act, 1996 of India the Bangladesh legislation understands that the validity of the arbitration agreement has to be determined on its own and has nothing to do with the principal agreement of which it is part.[23] In other words, the invalidity of the principal agreement would not affect the arbitration clause in which it is contained. He further explained that unlike the UNCITRAL ML, which does not clearly answer the question of survival of the arbitration clause when the agreement of which it forms of was declared nullity ab initio, the Bangladesh law appears more straightforward. Inspired by the English Arbitration Act, 1996[24] the AA, 2001 authorizes the arbitral tribunal in broad terms to have jurisdiction on such issues.[25]

---

[20]See, generally, the section on the Severability of the Arbitration clause in Stephen Schwebel, [Cambridge: Grotius Publications Ltd. 1987] *International Arbitration: Three Salient Problems*.

[21]Ibid., at 3.

[22](n 11)s 18—Severability of agreement—An arbitration agreement which forms part of another agreement shall be deemed to constitute a separate agreement while giving decision for the purpose of determining the jurisdiction of the arbitral tribunal.

[23](n 3) 150.

[24]AA, 1996—s 7 an arbitration agreement which forms or was intended to form part of another agreement … shall not be regarded as invalid, non-existent or ineffective because that other agreement is invalid or did not come into existence or has become ineffective, and it shall for that purpose be treated as a distinct agreement.

[25](n 11) Ss 17–18.

## 2.4 Competence-Competence

The principle of competence-competence (*competence-competence, Kompetenz-prilfung durch dos Schiedsgericht*) empowers the arbitral tribunal to determine its jurisdiction and related objections over the disputed claims. Derived from the German concept of *Kompetenz-Kompetenz* the principle though has moved away from the understanding that was attributed to it in the German law.[26] There however seems to be a preference for competence-competence principle, many jurisdictions have adopted what seems to be a chronological priority of the tribunal on the gateway question (George Bermann termed the issues related to jurisdiction as the gateway questions).[27] The UNCITRAL ML offers guidance on the power of the tribunal to make jurisdictional rulings. Article 16 paragraph 3 states,

> (3) The arbitral tribunal may rule on a plea referred to in paragraph (2) of this article either as a preliminary question or in an award on the merits. If the arbitral tribunal rules as a preliminary question that it has jurisdiction, any party may request, within thirty days after having received notice of that ruling, the court specified in article 6 to decide the matter, which decision shall be subject to no appeal; while such a request is pending, the arbitral tribunal may continue the arbitral proceedings and make an award.

The English Arbitration Act, 1996 required that a court stay legal proceedings "unless satisfied that the arbitration agreement is null and void, inoperative, or incapable of being performed." The negative competence-competence[28] issue here concerns whether "unless satisfied" entails only a prima facie review. Indeed, it seems arguable that "unless satisfied" is closer to "unless it is manifest" as compared to the UNCITRAL ML terminology in Article 8(1) "unless it finds."[29] Further to prevent and address any concerns of abuse of discretion while ruling an award on jurisdiction, the Act provides that parties may agree to force the arbitrators to decide jurisdiction preliminarily; further provides that a Court on an application by the

---

[26] In Germany this doctrine meant that arbitrators could make a final ruling on their jurisdiction, there being no subsequent review of the decision by any court. The German Law has, since, aligned much with the UNCITRAL ML thus moving away from the strict no-review standard. See, Klaus Peter Berger, 'Germany Adopts the UNCITRAL Model Law' (1998) 1(3) Int'l Arbtn. L Rev. 121, 122; Also see, Philippe Fouchard, Emmanuel Gaillard, Berthold Goldman, John Savage, *Fouchard, Gaillard, Goldman on International Commercial Arbitration* (Kluwer Law International, 1999) 396.

[27] See, George A. Bermann, 'The "Gateway" Problem in International Commercial Arbitration' (2012) 37(1) Yale Jour. Of Int'l L 1.

[28] Negative effect of the principle of competence-competence refers to the principle that the courts should refrain from engaging into the examination of the arbitrators' jurisdiction before the arbitrators themselves have had an opportunity to do so. This rule of priority in favour of the arbitrators, increasingly recognised in practice, exemplifies the specific nature and autonomy of international arbitration, in full harmony with the New York Convention's philosophy of recognition of the validity of the arbitration agreement and of the award resulting from the arbitral process. For a detailed discussion, see, generally, George A. Bermann, ibid.

[29] John J. Barceló III, 'Who Decides the Arbitrators' Jurisdiction? Separability and Competence-Competence in Transnational Perspective' (2003) Vand. Jour. of Transnational L 1115.

party(s) either along with the arbitrators or otherwise, decide upon the jurisdiction if it is satisfied that there are circumstances to intervene on the jurisdiction question and the parties were not otherwise indulging in dilatory tactics.[30]

The AA, 2001, unlike the UNCITRAL ML, while providing for the competence-competence principle also places restrictions upon the tribunal in deciding upon its competence. Section 17 restricts the unbridled freedom of the arbitral tribunal[31] with the words "unless otherwise agreed by the parties."[32] It enumerated five jurisdictional questions, not an exhaustive list,[33] on which the arbitral tribunal may exercise its power of competence-competence,

(a) whether there is in existence a valid arbitration agreement;
(b) whether the arbitral tribunal is properly constituted;
(c) whether the arbitration agreement is against public policy;
(d) whether the arbitration agreement is incapable of being performed, and
(e) what matters have been submitted to arbitration in accordance with the arbitration agreement.

The arbitral tribunal addresses the competence question upon the application of either of the parties, or *suo moto*, for examples in instances of public policy concerns.[34]

## 2.5 Co-relation Between Court and Arbitration Tribunal

The great paradox of arbitration is that it seeks the co-operation of the very public authorities from which it wants to free itself.[35] S.19, AA, 2001 specifies that jurisdictional objections before the court shall be raised not later than the submission of the statement of defense. This is in alignment with the UNCITRAL ML as well as the Rules of arbitral institutions like ICC, LCIA and such.

[30]AA, 1996, Ss 30–32; John J. Barceló III, ibid., 1130.

[31]Maniruzzaman (n 3) 147–48.

[32](n 11) Section 17: Competence of arbitration tribunal to rule on its own jurisdiction—Unless otherwise agreed by the parties, the arbitral tribunal may rule on its own jurisdiction on any questions including the following issues, namely—(a) whether there is existence of a valid arbitration agreement. (b) whether the Arbitral Tribunal is properly constituted; (c) whether the arbitration agreement is against the public policy; (d) whether the arbitration agreement is incapable of being performed; and e) whether the matters have been submitted to arbitration in accordance with the arbitration agreement.

[33]Maniruzzaman (n 3) 148.

[34]Ibid.

[35]Williams, David AR., 'Defining the Role of the Court in Modern International Commercial Arbitration' (2014) 10(2) Asian Int'l Arbtn Jour. 137.

Further Section 25(1), following Article 19(1) of the Model Law, prescribes,

> Subject to this Act the arbitral tribunal shall follow the procedure to be agreed on all or any by the parties in conducting its proceedings.

It is, however, unclear about the extent to which the parties' choice of arbitral procedural law would prevail in situations of inconsistency with the Act.

On jurisdictional objections, the AA, 2001 prescribes that such objections shall be raised during the course of arbitral proceedings as soon as such matters arise, with delayed pleas being allowed at discretion.

Further, regarding objections to jurisdictional determinations of the tribunal, the AA, 2001 allows the parties to apply to the High Court Division (HCD) of the Bangladesh Supreme Court.[36] The High Court Division, only on a reasoned application by the parties, allow and make its determinations on jurisdictions if it is satisfied that (a) the determination of the question is likely to produce substantial savings in costs; (b) the application was submitted without any delay; and (c) there is good reason why the matter should be decided by the Court.[37]

On the role of the courts in international arbitration, Professor David Williams observed that a harmonious relationship between the courts and the arbitral process is vital.[38] Courts should abstain from finding reasons to assume jurisdiction over a matter that the parties have agreed to refer to arbitration. The Singapore Court of Appeal similarly opined that courts ought to remember that the stated intention of the International Arbitration Act was geared to minimising court involvement in matters that the parties have agreed to submit to arbitration.[39]

Bangladesh's arbitration law seems to be attempting at this harmonious relationship while preserving the inherent space of each mechanism as delimited within the arbitration clause by the parties. The AA, 2001 illustrates the above-mentioned harmonious relationship especially in provisions related to jurisdiction when it specifies that the arbitral tribunal could continue with the arbitration, despite a pending application on jurisdiction before the HCD.[40] Maniruzzaman commented that this provision would help minimize the delay by judicial intervention and help in expediting the dispute resolution process.[41]

---

[36](n 11) s 20—Powers of the High Court Division in deciding jurisdiction—(1) The High Court Division, may on the application of any of the parties to the arbitration agreement, after serving notice upon all other parties, determine any question as to the jurisdiction of the arbitral tribunal.

[37]Ibid., s 20(2).

[38]Professor David A R Williams QC, Herbert Smith Freehills, "Defining the Role of the Court in Modern International Commercial Arbitration,"—SMU Asian Arbitration Lecture, Singapore—2012.

[39]*Tjong Very Sumito v Antig Investments* [2009] 4 SLR(R) at [28].

[40](n 11), s 20 (4) Unless otherwise agreed by the parties, where any application is pending before the High Court Division under this section the arbitral tribunal shall continue arbitration proceedings and make an arbitral award.

[41]Maniruzzaman (n 3) 153.

Bangladesh's Arbitration law makes a detailed statement on the interim measures, from the arbitral tribunal and the court, as compared to the UNCITRAL ML. Party autonomy remains paramount in the matter of interim measures in that the parties can bypass the arbitral tribunal and have recourse directly to the court for interim measures. The legislation allows the arbitral tribunal, unless otherwise agreed by the parties, to order a party to take any interim measure as it may consider necessary in respect of the subject matter of the dispute and at the same time allows no appeal to be taken against such order.[42] It has features such as the requirement of notification to the other parties involved and application to a court for enforcement of an arbitral tribunal's order of interim measures,[43] especially because interim measures from the tribunal are not enforceable per se as a decree or order of the court, and require court assistance.

With regard to interim measures from an arbitral tribunal seated outside Bangladesh if the interim measure is merely in the form of an order and not an award, section 3(1), AA, 2001 renders it non-enforceable, as it states that the legislation is applicable to arbitrations seated in Bangladesh. So the application of section 21 for enforcement of interim measures from a foreign-seated arbitral tribunal is not possible. However, enforcement of an interim measure in the form of an award from a foreign-seated tribunal may not be a difficulty, as such measure being treated as a foreign award will invite the application of sections 45–47 of the AA, 2001 related to enforcement of foreign awards.

Surprisingly, the AA, 2001, unlike the UNCITRAL ML, does not contain any provision with regard to interim measures by the court. This is a marked weakness of the new Act as far as it relates to the protection of parties who intend to arbitrate in Bangladesh. Even before the constitution of the arbitral tribunal or the commencement of arbitral proceedings, situations or circumstances might warrant interim measures to be taken by the court to protect the interest of a party.[44]

The AA, 2001 is also silent on the power of the arbitral tribunals to order interim measures in the nature of freezing injunctions and measures against third parties. Since such orders are a feature of international arbitral jurisprudence, it is necessary that the Bangladesh law take notice of the same in its future legislation work.

Arbitral Jurisprudence on the issue of interim measures from courts in Bangladesh is incomplete without a discussion of two important decisions—the HRC Shipping *Ltd. v M.V. X press Manaslu and Others*[45] (hereinafter, the *HRC*) and the STX *Corporation Ltd. v Meghna Group of Industries Ltd. and Ors.*[46] (hereinafter, the *STX Corporation*). In the *HRC* the HCD held that in the absence of the word 'only' within Section 3(1) of the AA, 2001, it cannot be assumed that the section is inapplicable when the place of arbitration is not in Bangladesh. Hence the

---

[42](n 11) s 21(1).

[43]Ibid., s 21(3) and (4).

[44]Maniruzzaman (n 3) 157.

[45][2007] 12 MLR 265.

[46]*STX Corporation Ltd. v Meghna Group of Industries Ltd. and Ors.* [2012] 32BLD 400.

Court could order interim relief even in arbitrations that are placed outside Bangladesh.

However another bench of the HCD in the *STX Corporation* held a contrarian position by wording a literal construction of the AA, 2001 and holding that interim relief from the courts in Bangladesh cannot be applied where the arbitration is not seated in Bangladesh. STX Corporation is based on a judgment of the AD in *Unicol Bangladesh v Maxwell*[47] where the AD held,

> the law as in Sections 3(1) and 3(4) of the Act … is limited in application as to the arbitration being held in Bangladesh, but not as to matter restraining a particular party from proceeding with arbitration in foreign country in respect of a contract signed in Bangladesh.[48]

The ratio of *STX Corporation* was adopted in the recent case of *Egyptian Fertilizer Trading Limited (Egyptian Fertilizer) v East West Property Development (Private) Ltd.*[49] where the court did not grant interim relief to in an application related to an arbitration seated outside of Bangladesh.

Section 7 restricts the role of the courts to instances where one of the parties involved in the arbitration proceedings triggers the court proceedings. In the case of *Bangladesh Jute Mills Corporation v Maico Jute and Bag Corporation and Others*[50] it was held that the court cannot admit a dispute that was pending before the arbitral tribunal. A proviso to section 7, termed as section 7A within the Act, empowered the HCD to make interim orders in respect of certain matters, such as, *inter alia,* interim injunctions to restrain the transfer of property which is likely to create an impediment to the enforcement of the arbitral award.

Upon the plea of the presence of an arbitration agreement, the Bangladesh court shall, unless convinced that the agreement is void, inoperative or incapable of determination *by arbitration*, stay the proceedings and refer the parties to arbitration. This section affirms the widely accepted principle that the right to seek arbitration is a contractual right and a contract cannot be unilaterally abrogated in order to bypass the arbitration clause. It is important to note here that the use of the term 'shall' implies that the local court is under a positive obligation to refer the parties to arbitration and not merely *on exercise of its* discretion, albeit to be exercised sparingly and for the reasons mentioned in the legislation. This positive obligation under section 10 of the Act reinforces the spirit of the New York Convention.

Few decisions of the Bangladeshi courts vouch for the local court's intention to apply such principles strictly. For example, in the case of *Civil Engineering Company v Mahkuta Technology and Others*[51] it has been held that the court shall not interfere with a matter covered by an arbitration agreement.

---

[47] 56 DLR (AD) (2004).

[48] Ibid., para 15.

[49] (Arbitration Application No. 11 of 2010, 10 June 2014).

[50] 22 BLD (HCD) (2002) 320.

[51] 14 BLT (HCD) (2006) 103.

In a recent judgment in *Mosharaf Com. Tex. Mills Ltd. and ors v ECOM Agro. Corp. Ltd. and ors*[52] the AD of the Supreme Court of Bangladesh hearing a revision application from the order staying further proceeding in a suit in a pending arbitration seated outside Bangladesh, held that the HCD was in the right in for staying further proceeding of the suit with a direction to settle the dispute in the arbitration proceeding. The AD noted that the HCD found that there was a valid agreement between the plaintiff and defendant wherein an arbitration clause has been stipulated and pursuant to the said agreement the arbitration proceeding has already been commenced before the Arbitration Tribunal at Liverpool. The suit has been instituted subsequent to the arbitration proceeding. The High Court Division held that though written statement has been filed but, in fact, the same can be treated as information to the court regarding pendency of arbitration proceeding before Arbitration Tribunal at Liverpool.[53]

However, a significant development in this respect is the amendment and the introduction of section 89B within the Code of Civil Procedure 1908.[54] According to this section, if the parties to a suit, at any stage of the proceeding, apply to the court for withdrawal of the suit on the ground that they will refer the dispute to arbitration, then the local court shall allow the suit to be withdrawn and thereafter the dispute shall be settled in accordance with the Act.[55] Further sub-section (2) of section 89B specified that an application under sub-section (1) shall be deemed to be an arbitration agreement under section 9 of the AA, 2001.

## 3 Choice of Law

The ability to choose a totally neutral seat—with no connection to the parties or the underlying dispute—is one of the many advantages of international arbitration over litigation. Preference for international arbitration over litigation is founded upon presence of laws and courts that are favorable to international arbitration.[56] The

[52]4 SCOB [2015] AD 28.

[53]Ibid., para 7.

[54]By an amendment to the Code of Civil Procedure, 1908 in 2003 Sections 89A and B specifying that court may refer the parties to mediation and arbitration, respectively. In 2006 the next amendment to the Code provided for an option for mediation during appeal. In 2012 the Code was further amended to replace the word 'may' with 'shall' in section 89A (mediation) and 89C (mediation at the stage of appeal) to make mediation mandatory in both pre-trial and appellate stage in every civil litigation.

[55]Unpublished work of Md Mamonor Rashid, Arbitration and Mediation As A Mechanism to Settle Corporate Dispute in Bangladesh, School of Law, University Utara Malaysia, (2015) 28.

[56]John B. Tieder, 'Factors to Consider in the Choice of Procedural and Substantive Law in International Arbitration' (2003) 20(4) Jour. of Int'l Arbtn. 393.

trend in the modern international arbitration laws such as Model Law jurisdictions is for a very limited degree of judicial control, or highly delocalized arbitration proceedings.

The AA, 2001 upholds the principle of party autonomy; it allows the parties to choose any rules of law to govern the arbitration agreement,[57] not necessarily the law or the legal system of the country whose law is applicable to the substance of the dispute.[58] Parties could also prefer the *lex mercatoria* or the rules of transnational commercial law, rules or usages related to a specific international trade. Or usages. It further provides that if the law or the legal system of such designated law is meant to refer directly to the substantive law of that country and not to its conflict of laws rules.[59] AA, 2001 thus expressly avoids the *renvoi* situation.

In the absence of a parties' choice of law to determine the substance of their dispute, the AA, 2001 section 36(2) provides that the tribunal may apply the law appropriate to the circumstances of the case. This is a legislative expression of the *voie directe* method followed to determine the substantive rights of the parties. The power vests in the tribunal to select the law or the rules of law applicable to the merits of the dispute directly. The tribunal considers the contract, the circumstances leading to the dispute and the submissions of the parties. Applying this method the tribunal has to determine the law most relevant to the contractual circumstances of the case, the rules that best suit the international transaction, accounting for the circumstances of each case.[60]

Surprisingly, the AA, 2001 makes no provision for the decision of the tribunal based on *ex aequo et bono* or as *amiable compositeur*, however it does not expressly prohibit such authority.[61] The reason to deny the presence of an express prohibition is in the language of Section 36(3) of the Act. The tribunal is also mandatorily required to decide in accordance with the terms of the contract and to take into account the usages of the trade applicable to the transaction. However, unlike the Model Law, the Act expressly states the purpose of this specific requirement to be the "ends of justice."

---

[57](n 11) s 36(1).

[58]Maniruzzaman (n 3).

[59](n 11) s 36(1) Provided that any designation by the parties of the law or legal system of a given country shall be construed, unless otherwise expressed, as directly referring to the substantive law of that country.

[60]Doug Jones, 'Choosing the Law or Rules of Law to Govern the Substantive Rights of the Parties: A discussion on Voie Directe and Voie Indirecte' (2014) 26 SAc.L J 911, 914.

[61]Maniruzzaman (n 3).

# 4 Recourse Against Arbitral Awards

## *4.1 Set Aside Proceedings*

Chapter VIII, AA, 2001 discusses recourse against an arbitral award, domestic and international. An application for recourse against an arbitral award shall be applied for by a party to arbitration within three months of the receipt of the award.[62] S.43 enumerates a few grounds for setting aside an arbitral award, almost similar to Article 36, UNCITRAL ML regarding refusal of recognition and enforcement of foreign awards. While Model Law indicates the exclusive nature of the grounds as evidenced by the use of the word "only" in its Article 34 (2), the Bangladesh Act omits the word. Nevertheless, since the Act models its relevant provision on that of the Model Law, despite such an omission the spirit of the latter should prevail. This means that Section 43 (1) of the new Bangladesh Act contains an exclusive list of limited grounds on which an award may be set aside and no other ground should be entertained for such a purpose. Recently, the AD of the Supreme Court of Bangladesh made an effective statement about the set aside application in *Md. Nurul Abser v Alhaj Golam Rabbani and others.*[63] It held that a concerted reading of the provisions of sections 42, 43 and 39 of the Act, 2001 clearly shows that the only remedy open to a person who wants to set aside an arbitral award is to file an application under section 42 of the Act, 2001 within sixty days from the date of receipt of the award and after the expiry of the period of sixty days as envisaged in the section, the award becomes enforceable within the meaning of section 44 thereof and thus, jurisdiction of the civil Court has been barred.

AA, 2001 introduces a safeguard against the move to set aside either domestic or international awards. The Act authorizes the court, where the application for setting aside an award is made, to order that any money payable by the award be deposited with that court, or otherwise secured, pending the determination of the application.[64] This safeguard will be a deterrent to the losing party's playing prank with the arbitral award and it also will save the court's valuable time.

An award may be set aside if a party to the arbitration agreement was under some legal incapacity; established that the arbitration agreement was not valid under the law to which parties have subjected it; proved that the applicant was not given any notice of the appointment of an arbitrator or of the arbitral proceedings; or that a party was prevented by sufficient reason from presenting his case before tribunal; or that the award is made on matters not submitted to the tribunal; or that the composition of the tribunal was not in accordance with the provisions of the Act.[65]

---

[62](n 11) Ss 42(1) and (2).

[63]6 SCOB [2016] AD 54.

[64](n 11) s 43(2).

[65]See, for example, *Bangladesh Railway v Pamkaya (M) SDN. BHD. (Arbitration Application No. 07 of 2010[HCD]); Joinal Abedin Jamal and others v Noor Afza* 63 DLR 432: party waived right to object to tribunal.

## 4.2 Enforcement of Foreign Arbitral Awards

Chapter X of the AA, 2001 specifies the provisions related to enforcement of foreign arbitral awards. Under the law, an award is enforceable per se; it does not require leave of the court for enforcement, an exequatur or a double exequatur. It possesses the status of a decree or the court, they shall be enforceable according to the provisions of the Code of Civil Procedure as if were a decree of the Court. This principle has been reiterated in *Canada Shipping and Trading SA v TT Katikaayu and another* (*Admiralty Jurisdiction*)[66] where it was held, 'Once an arbitration proceeding in a foreign country is completed, the Arbitral Award, on an application by any party, will be enforced by a court of this country under the Code of Civil Procedure in the same manner as if it were a decree of the court.'[67] Thus, there is no requirement to obtain a separate permission from the local court for enforcement.

In *Goenka Impex S.A. v Tallu Spinning Mills Ltd.*,[68] the HCD reasoned that the district court faulted in the reading of the law on enforcement of foreign awards. Hearing a revision application from the award-holder contesting the district court's rejection of an attachment application, the HCD held that Section 45(b) intended that the court where enforcement application is made to treat the foreign award as if its own decree, subject to the grounds enumerated in section 46 of the AA, 2001. Such court shall not function as a transferee court. in the instant case it was held that the District Court had committed an error of law by not allowing the application for attachment under the execution proceedings.[69]

The Act defined a foreign award as an award made in pursuance of an arbitration agreement in the territory of any state other than Bangladesh,[70] but it does not include an award made in the territory of a specified state.[71] The 'specified state' feature of the legislation makes the scope of the rules concerning the recognition and enforcement of foreign arbitral awards in the new Bangladesh Act is narrower than that in the Model Law and in the New York Convention.

While Bangladesh acceded to the NYC in 1992, absence of an enabling statute lead to a reluctance of the courts to apply the NYC in matters of recognition and enforcement of foreign arbitral awards.[72] AA, 2001 ensured that the NYC's objective and content find endorsement in the Bangladesh law. Section 45 (1) (a)

---

[66]54 DLR [2002] 93.

[67]Ibid., 94.

[68][2013] 33 BLD 340.

[69]Ibid., paras 15, 16.

[70](n 11)s 2(k); see, Maniruzzaman, M, 'Bangladesh embraces the UNCITRAL model law on international commercial arbitration—but not quite!' (2004) 19(3) Mealey's Int'l Arbtn. Rep. 1, 3.

[71]Ibid., s 47—Power of Government to declare specified state—For the purposes of this chapter, the Government may, by notification in the official Gazette, declare a state as a specified state.

[72]See, *Bangladesh Air Service (PVT) v British Airways PLC* 49 DLR 187(AD) (1997); also see, YB Comm Arb XXIII (1998) 624, 625.

states that subject to section 46 all foreign awards are binding and enforceable on the persons as between whom it was made, any award may accordingly be relied upon by any of those persons by way of defense, set off or otherwise in any legal proceedings in Bangladesh. Section 46 replicated the grounds for refusal to recognition and enforcement of foreign arbitral awards[73] enumerated in Article V, NYC.

An important judicial statement on refusal to enforce a foreign arbitral award on grounds of public policy exception to enforcement has been the decision in *Tata Power Company Ltd. v M/S Dynamic Const.*[74] The Appellate Division held that unless the contract by the parties or the award made by the arbitrator had a negative or uncalled for impact on the State and the society, it would not be considered as contrary to public policy. While the Court did not define the parameters of such

---

[73](n 11) s 46. Grounds for refusing recognition or execution of foreign arbitral awards—(1) Recognition or execution of foreign arbitral award may be refused only on the following grounds, namely:

(a) if the party against whom it is invoked furnishes proof to the Court that

(i) a party to the arbitration agreement was under some incapacity;
(ii) the arbitration agreement is not valid under the law to which the parties have subjected it;
(iii) the party against whom the award is invoked was not given proper notice of the appointment of the arbitrator or of the arbitral proceedings or was otherwise unable due to some reasonable causes to present his case; or
(vi) the concerned foreign arbitral award contains decisions on matters beyond the scope of the submission to arbitration; Provided that, f the decisions on matters submitted to arbitration can be separated from those not so submitted, that part of the award which contains decisions on matters submitted to arbitration may be recognised and enforced;
(v) the composition of the arbitral tribunal or the arbitral procedure was not in accordance with the agreement of the parties or, in absence of such agreement was not in accordance with the law of the country where the arbitration took place;
(vi) the award has not yet become binding on the parties, or has been set aside or suspended by a competent authority of the country in which, or under the law of which, that award was made; or

(b) the court in which recognition or execution of the foreign arbitral award is sought, finds that

(i) the subject matter of the dispute is not capable of settlement by arbitration under the law for the time being in force in Bangladesh; or
(ii) the recognition and execution of the foreign arbitral award is in conflict with the public policy of Bangladesh.

(2) If an application for setting aside or suspension of the enforcement of the foreign arbitral award has been made to a competent authority referred to in sub-clause (v) of clause (a) of sub-section (1) the Court may, f it considers it proper, adjourn the decision on the enforcement of the foreign arbitral award and may also, on the application of the party claiming enforcement of the foreign award, order the other party to give suitable security.

[74][2015] 2 SCOB 15 (AD).

impact, nevertheless, it made a distinction between matters relating to propriety and matters relating to public policy, thus leading to a derivation that public policy exception would receive a narrow or restricted construction in Bangladesh law on international arbitration.

## 5 Conclusion

A decade and a half into its existence, while the existence of a modern arbitration law aligned with the NYC and the UNCITRAL ML is a cause for optimism, the working of the legislation has thrown a few challenges. Further there are other non-statutory reasons that cause a revisit to the legislation to ensure the arbitral legislation strengthened against non-statutory challenges. Few of the areas that merit attention in a revisit of the AA, 2001 include

1. A statutory address on the interim relief in international arbitration—interim relief ordered by the foreign-seated tribunal as well as the courts at the seat. The difficulty in enforcing only such interim orders of the tribunal that are in the form of interim awards, ought to be removed, and all orders of the tribunal ought to be enforced. Further to prevent dissipation of assets by the party against whom an award is likely, courts in Bangladesh ought to possess the power to make interim orders. Taking cue from the Arbitration and Conciliation (Amendment) Act, 2015 in India that allowed Indian courts to order interim relief in foreign-seated arbitrations, when the tribunal is not yet functional, Bangladesh should also amend its law suitably to allow a detailed structure for interim relief orders from foreign-seated tribunals and courts to be enforceable in Bangladesh.
2. A clear legislative statement with regard to application of the AA, 2001 with regard to arbitrations seated outside Bangladesh when applications are presented to Bangladesh courts.
3. Despite the statutory provisions related to law applicable to the dispute and the primacy to the principle of party autonomy, there are a few statutory gaps with regard to the identification of the applicable law and governing law for the arbitration agreement, especially in the absence of a choice by the parties. Further the arbitration legislation could also consider making a statutory space for *ex aequo et bono* and *amiable compositeur*.
4. It is of utmost necessity that there is a statutory statement delimiting the public policy exception.
5. The statutory provisions within the AA, 2001 related to set-aside of arbitral awards create a concern that an award given by a foreign-seated tribunal could be set aside in Bangladesh, a possibility not in line with the general international arbitration where only the courts at the seat of arbitration could set aside an arbitral award. An amendment process should also consider the set aside feature within the legislation.

6. There are a few non-statutory features that negatively impact the international arbitration system in Bangladesh. Foremost among them is the institutional support from all stakeholders—courts, arbitral institutions and user councils of the chambers of commerce. Prioritized among them is the urgent need to set up an exclusive arbitration division in the HCD, with judges trained in arbitration process to ensure speedy disposal of enforcement application. Further efforts could be directed at sensitizing the judicial personnel in handling arbitration-related applications on the effective and expeditious disposal of such applications.

# Enforcement of Foreign Arbitral Awards in Bangladesh: The Law, Its Implementation and Challenges

**Sameer Sattar**

**Abstract** In this age, no one lives in an island. All are connected across the globe. This world is greatly premised on the free flow of trade, investment, knowledge, information and technology. Arbitration has been an important tool to expedite the process of international trade and investment by providing a speedy and, in some cases, a cost friendly method for dispute settlement. Arbitration has been successful in batting cross border jurisdictional and legal issues. However, the law and practice in some countries have shown that arbitration is again tied to the general mechanism of civil justice. This procedural intricacy makes arbitration a victim of delay, one of the evils of civil justice today. Recently, the World Bank has declared Bangladesh as a middle income country recognizing its sustained growth and resilient economy. In the context of current wave of economic transformation, international commercial arbitration has become a more relevant issue for Bangladesh. To progress and meet the demands of the international community, the Arbitration Act 2001 (the AA 2001) had been enacted in 2001 in line with the UNCITRAL Model Law on the International Commercial Arbitration. This includes provisions relating to the recognition and enforcement of foreign arbitral awards. This chapter shall focus on the provisions of AA 2001 in respect of the enforcement of foreign arbitral awards in Bangladesh, the requirements to be addressed for enforcement and the challenges the parties may face in enforcement of foreign arbitral awards in Bangladesh. The Author analyzes the provisions of AA 2001 regarding enforcement of foreign arbitral awards and identifies some definitional, jurisdictional, territorial and interpretational challenges that the AA 2001 may face.

---

The Author would like to thank Morshed Mannan along with Advocate Ali Azgar Faisal for their invaluable assistance with this chapter

---

S. Sattar (✉)
Lincoln's Inn, London, UK
e-mail: ssattar@sattarandco.com

S. Sattar
Head of Chambers, Sattar&Co, Dhaka, Bangladesh

© Springer Nature Singapore Pte Ltd. 2017

S.R. Garimella and S. Jolly (eds.), *Private International Law*,
DOI 10.1007/978-981-10-3458-9_15

**Keywords** International arbitration · New York Convention · Enforcement of foreign awards · Exceptions · Public policy

## Introduction

Cross-border trade and investment disputes have been a common phenomenon in today's integrated global economy. As a result, arbitration has increasingly been used as an effective tool to amicably resolve these disputes. The International Chamber of Commerce (ICC) has reported that, in 2015, 801 Requests for Arbitration were filed with the ICC Court from 133 different countries with the seat of arbitration being in 56 different countries.[1] Concomitantly, courts around the world have shown a positive attitude in recognising and enforcing these awards so as to give meaningful effect to arbitration proceedings.

The United Nations Convention on Recognition and Enforcement of Foreign Arbitral Awards 1958 (hereinafter, the NYC) ushered a unified regime for recognition and enforcement of foreign arbitral awards and has been adopted in 156 states.[2] It is an important derivation of the NYC that countries ought to restrict the scope for refusing recognition and enforcement of arbitral awards.[3] A pro-arbitration regime ensuring enforcement of foreign awards could be of significant help to international commerce, else the scenario would not be different from disputes in national courts characterized by complex procedural formalities.[4] International commercial arbitration's effectiveness is premised upon national courts furthering the realization of the intention of the parties to arbitrate their dispute. This chapter attempts to critique the recognition and enforcement regime in Bangladesh.

## Structure of the Chapter

The chapter begins with a discussion on the role of national courts in international arbitration to contextualize the jurisprudence related to enforcing and refusing to enforce foreign arbitral awards, the next section discusses the enforcement scenario in Bangladesh and emerging trends. The chapter will conclude with recommendations as to how the current scenario may be improved.

---

[1]ICC, "Statistics: ICC - International Chamber Of Commerce" (2015). http://www.iccwbo.org/Products-and-Services/Arbitration-and-ADR/Arbitration/Introduction-to-ICC-Arbitration/Statistics/, accessed 10 January 2016.

[2]New York Arbitration Convention, "Contacting States: New York Convention" (2016). http://www.newyorkconvention.org/countries, accessed 08 January 2016.

[3]For example, Chinese law prescribed an onerous procedure for refusing to recognize and enforce a foreign award. An 'automatic appeal' system that requires national courts to submit an arbitration matter to the High People's Court for consideration if the former is of the view that the award should not be recognised and enforced. Even if the High People's Court concurs with the lower court, it has to seek an opinion from the Supreme People's Court—the highest court in China—before confirming the refusal of recognition and enforcement. *See* Xiahong Xia, 'Implementation Of The New York Convention In China' (2011) 1 Int'l Comm. Arbtn Brief 20, 21.

[4]Choi Y Jin, Vishnu K Konoorayar and Jaya V Suseela, 'International Commercial Arbitration in South Asia: A Comparative Study' (2012) Korea Legislation Research Institute 35. http://ssrn.com/abstract=2359220, accessed 09 January 2016.

## 1 National Courts and International Arbitration

The presence of arbitration in South Asia dates back to the colonial period. Through the passage of the Bengal Regulation Act 1772, the Code of Civil Procedure 1859, the Indian Arbitration Act 1899 and the Code of Civil Procedure 1908,[5] the practice of arbitration was gradually introduced to the region. However, till the first half of the twentieth century, the existing arbitration legislation was silent on the issue of recognising and enforcing foreign arbitral awards.

While this lacuna in the law was filled through the enactment of the Arbitration (Protocol and Convention) Act 1937, to give effect to the Geneva Protocol on Arbitration Clauses, 1923 and the Geneva Convention on the Execution of Foreign Arbitral Awards, 1927, the recognition and enforcement of awards delivered from tribunals seated outside of India (and subsequently Pakistan and Bangladesh) continued to be marred with difficulties—parallel civil suits, the broad interpretation of exceptions to recognition, the unavailability of interim relief and long procedural delays. Though the sovereign states of modern South Asia have each tried to address these issues in their own way in recent years, the concerns have not beeneffectively addressed, as yet.

Parties generally submit disputes to arbitration to avoid the encumbrances of litigation, such as protracted and convoluted court procedures, unfamiliar laws and language and the potential for judicial bias in certain jurisdictions; however, national courts are required for the support mechanism for dispute resolution. The role of the national courts manifests at several stages of an arbitral process, because arbitration is regulated within the national laws. Professor Mann observed,

> No private person has the right or power to act on any other level other than that of a municipal law. Every right or power a private person enjoys is inexorably conferred by or derived from a system of municipal law.[6]

National courts at the seat of arbitration and in the State where the enforcement of the award is sought may have to deal with questions regarding the validity of an arbitration agreement, the establishment of an arbitral tribunal, challenges to jurisdiction, granting interim measures in support of foreign seated arbitration and the setting aside of awards.[7] Due consideration to party autonomy apart, arbitration laws of States allow national courts, on application, to ascertain that arbitrations

[5]*See*, e.g. Mustafa Motiwala, Anupam Prakash, Ranjit Shetty, 'India' (2015) The Asia Pacific Arbitration Review. http://globalarbitrationreview.com/reviews/64/sections/224/chapters/2568/india/, accessed 10 January 2016.

[6]Francis A. Mann, 'Lex Facit Arbitrum' in Martin Domke and Pieter Sanders (eds), *International Arbitration: Liber Amicorum for Martin Domke* (Martinus Nijhoff 1967) 159; Roy Goode, 'The Role of Lex Loci Arbitri in International Commercial Arbitration' (2001) 17 Arbtn. Int'l 19.

[7]See, generally, Vera Korzun and Thomas H. Lee, 'An Empirical Survey of International Commercial Arbitration Cases in the US District Court for the Southern District of New York, 1970–2014' (2015) 39 Fordham Int'l L. Jour. 2, 5.

meet a general standard of fairness[8] and prevent parties from taking steps to avoid or subvert arbitration. Courts assist in constitution of arbitral tribunals, order anti-suit injunctions when a party seeks legal proceedings in breach of an arbitration agreement[9] and help prevent the destruction of evidence.[10] The decision in *Coppeé Levalin N.V. v Ken-Ren Fertilisers & Chemicals*[11] effectively summarized the role of the courts,

> palatable or not…it is only a court possessing coercive powers which could rescue the arbitration if it is in the danger of foundering.[12]

However, in spite of being essential for the arbitral process, there has been aggravated concern regarding the national courts' intervention in arbitral proceedings. Taking note of this encroachment the UNCITRAL Model Law on International Commercial Arbitration, 1985 [as amended] (hereinafter, the UNCITRAL ML) sought to delimit the scope of judicial involvement in the arbitral process. Article 5 restricted the role of national courts by stating that in matters governed by this law, no court shall intervene except so provided in this law.[13] The commentary to the Model Law elaborates that the intention of the provision is 'to exclude any general or residual powers given to the courts in a domestic system which are not listed in the Model Law'.[14]

## 2 National Courts and Enforcement of Arbitral Awards

Enforcement of foreign arbitral awards requires the assistance of national courts.[15] In *Mitsubishi Motors Corp v Soler Chrysler-Plymouth*[16] the Supreme Court in the USA held that the successful end of arbitration depends on the minimum

---

[8]Margaret L. Moses, *The Principles and Practice of International Commercial Arbitration* (1st edn, CUP 2008) 85.

[9]See, e.g., *Noble Assurance Co. v Gerling-Konzen Generla Insurance Co., U.K. Branch* [2007] EWHC 253.

[10]Sameer Sattar, 'National Courts and International Arbitration: A Double-edged Sword?' (2010) 27 J of Int'l Arbtn 53, 54.

[11][1994] 2 Lloyd's Rep. 109 (HL).

[12]Ibid., 116.

[13]Article 5.

[14]Analytical Commentary on the Draft Text of a Model Law on International Commercial Arbitration, UNCITRAL Yearbook, Vol. XVI (1988) 112.

[15]"The courts, as we have emphasized in our decisions, have a limited role to play, in that they essentially assist rather than subvert the arbitral process. No international arbitration award has been set aside in Singapore in the course of the last decade and we hope this trend will continue" Justice VK Rajah, 'Key Note Speech' (Singapore Arbitration Forum, Singapore, 23 January 2010) (on file with author); See, for example *Tjong Very Sumito v Antig Investments* [2009] 4 SLR(R), 28.

[16]*Mitsubishi Motors Corp. v Soler Chrysler-Plymouth* [1985] 473 US 614, 638.

interference of the court at the award enforcement stage. The English courts adopted a similar approach. In *Zermalt Holdings v Nu-Life Upholstery Repairs*[17] Lord Bingham opined,

> … [A]s a matter of general approach, the courts strive to uphold arbitration awards. They do not approach them with a meticulous legal eye, endeavouring to pick holes, inconsistencies and faults in awards and with the objective of upsetting or frustrating the process of arbitration. Far from it. The approach is to read an arbitration award in a reasonable and commercial way, expecting, as is usually the case, that there will be no substantial fault that can be found with it.[18]

Further, unlike national courts, an arbitral tribunal cannot, by itself, exercise the power to enforce an arbitral award against a reluctant party by attaching bank accounts or sequestrating assets or by any other means.[19]

As the majority of states have adopted the NYC—including Bangladesh—and many have reformed their arbitration legislation in line with the UNCITRAL ML it is generally expected that foreign arbitral awards will be recognised and enforced by states with limited exceptions. While there would be sound justifications for some awards to be set aside, such action ought to be premised on narrowly defined grounds. For most countries, the ambit of court intervention is determined in the light of the UNCITRAL ML and the NYC.[20] Article V, NYC and Article 36, UNCITRAL ML enlist the limited grounds on which such awards can be refused recognition and enforcement. Several arbitral decisions have held that courts do not have the power to refuse enforcement on any other ground(s) other than those enumerated in the NYC, Article V.[21] Article V(1) reads "Recognition and enforcement of the award may be refused … only if that party furnishes proof" meant that on of the enlisted grounds is satisfied and no residual discretion exists not to enforce an award. Academic writings observed that no such residual discretion exists and it was the clear intention of the drafters of Article V that the defences to enforcement in that Article were to be exhaustive and not capable of supplementation by grounds existing under the law of

---

[17] [1985] 2 EGLR 14.

[18] Ibid., 15; The court's role in assisting arbitration was also affirmed in *Lesotho Highlands v Impreglio SpA* [2005] UKHL 43, para 26–28 [Steyn LJ].

[19] Nigel Blackaby and Constantine Partasides with Alan Redfern and Martin Hunter, *Redfern and Hunter on International Arbitration* (5th ed., Oxford 2009) 632.

[20] This view was maintained by Singaporean courts in *Mitsui Engineering & Shipbuilding Co. Ltd. v Easton Graham Rush* (2004) 2 SLR 14, [2004] SGHC 26.

[21] *M. A. Industries Inc. v Maritime Battery Ltd.*, (1991), 118 N.B.R. (2d) 127 (Q.B.), Aaff'dreflix (1991), 123 N.B.R. (2d) 305 (C.A.). Also see, e.g. *Chromally Aeroservices Inc. (U.S.) v Arab Republic of Egypt* (1997) 22 Yearbook Commercial Arbitration (US No. 230), 1001, *Polytek Engg. Co. Ltd. (Hong Kong) v Hebei Import & Export Corp.* (PR China, (1998) 23 Yearbook Commercial Arbitration (Hong Kong No. 12) 666; referred in RS Bachawat, *Law of Arbitration & Conciliation*, vol 2 (5th ed., LexisNexis Butterworths Wadhwa Nagpur 2012) 2350.

the place of enforcement.[22] The exhaustive nature of the defences is a reflection of the Convention's objective of decreasing the scope for obstruction by national courts and laws. The intrusion of peculiarly domestic law principles into enforcement of awards would defeat the goals of uniform interpretation and liberal enforcement.[23]

The grounds for refusing the enforcement of foreign arbitral awards as specified within the NYC are discussed under the following general headings.

## *2.1 Invalidity of Arbitral Agreement and Lack of Capacity*

Enforcement of a foreign arbitral award may be refused at the request of the party against whom it is invoked if such party proved that the parties to the agreement were, under the law applicable to them, under some incapacity or the said agreement is not valid under the law to which the parties have subjected to.[24] The Cour de Appel, Paris in *Arab Republic of Egypt v Southern Pacific Properties Limited and Southern Pacific Properties (Middle East) Limited*[25] set aside an arbitral award for absence of a valid arbitration agreement, it followed that there could be no valid arbitration. Similarly, in *Dallah Real Estate and Tourism Holding Company v The Ministry of Religious Affairs, Government of Pakistan*[26] the UK Supreme Court held that as the arbitration agreement was between Dallah and a specially constituted Trust that was no longer in existence—rather than the Government of Pakistan—the agreement was not valid under the applicable law and the award could not be enforced against the Government. The Court, assessing the parties to the arbitration agreement, held that an independent determination of that issue was required and "the findings of fact made by the arbitrators and their view of the law can in no sense bind the court."[27] In the absence of a law governing the arbitration agreement, it held that French law applied to the question whether the Government was a party, since this was the law of the country where the award was made. The existence of a common intention to submit to the arbitration agreement, a requirement under the French law, would be determined by the parties' actions during the negotiation, performance and termination of the Agreement. On an extensive examination of the process of the agreement, the Court found that the Government was only a guarantor of the loans to the trust; hence, there was no common intention between the parties

[22]Richard Garnett and Michael Pryles, 'Recognition and Enforcement of Foreign Awards under the New York Convention in Australia and New Zealand' (2008) 25(6) Jour. of Int'l Arbtn 899, 904; Albert J van den Berg, *The New York Arbitration Convention of 1958: Towards a Uniform Judicial Interpretation*, (Kluwer 1981) 265.

[23]Ibid., 905.

[24]NYC, Article V(1)(a).

[25]Court of Appeal of Paris, Decision of July 12, 1984 referred in R S Bachawat (n 21) 2363.

[26]*Dallah Real Estate and Tourism Holding Company v The Ministry of Religious Affairs, Government of Pakistan* [2010] UKSC 46.

[27]Ibid., 160 [Saville, LJ].

for the Government to be a party to the arbitration agreement. The Court further held that applications resisting enforcement under Article V(1)(a) lead to a revisit of the tribunal's decision on jurisdiction.[28] The *Dallah* decision, opining that the NYC did not discuss the preliminary awards related to jurisdiction,[29] opened the floodgates for jurisdictional issues to be litigated after the arbitral tribunal had made its award on them, on grounds of serious defects in the arbitration and/or the award.

Interestingly, a Spanish court in *Shaanxi Provincial Medical Health Products I/E Corporation v Olpesa S.A.*[30] held that if a party extensively participated in the arbitration, it couldn't plead an absence of arbitration agreement for refusal of enforcement.

## 2.2 *Notice of the Arbitral Proceedings*

Courts may refuse the enforcement of arbitral awards if the party against whom the award's enforcement is sought could prove absence of notice of the appointment of an arbitrator or was otherwise unable to present his case.[31] In *Kanoria and others v Guinness and another*[32] the English Court of Appeal refused to enforce an arbitral award on the ground that the party contesting enforcement had been unable to defend his case and had never been given notice about the proceedings. However, if a party fails to appear in the case due to his own negligence, he cannot challenge the enforcement of an arbitral award on the ground of inability to present his case.

## 2.3 *Arbitral Award Decided Ultra Petita*

Enforcement of an arbitral award may be refused on the ground that the award dealt with a dispute that was not contemplated by or does not fall within the terms of the submissions.[33] However, this ground should not restrict the arbitrators' power and an arbitrator should be allowed to look into the intention of the parties for rendering a better arbitral award. An arbitral award, based on the above-mentioned reasoning, cannot be set-aside merely on the ground that the arbitrator had exceeded his authority.[34] Instead, the court may order the enforcement of the part of award that falls within the terms of the arbitration agreement. In *Hatton National Bank Limited*

---

[28]Ibid., para 104.

[29]Ibid., para 22.

[30]*Shaanxi Provincial Medical Health Products I/E Corporation v Olpesa, S.A.*, (2005) YBCA, XXX, Spain No. 40, 617 referred in R S Bachawat (n 21) 2364.

[31]NYC, Article V(1)(b).

[32][2006] All ER 290, paras 15, 32, 34.

[33]NYC, Article V(1)(c).

[34]R S Bachawat, (n 21) 2377.

*v Casmir Kiran Atapattu and another*[35] the arbitration tribunal overstepped the limits of its mandate and sought to deal with a dispute not contemplated by the arbitration agreement but the Supreme Court of Sri Lanka enforced the part of the award that fell within the scope of the arbitration. It is generally assumed that arbitrators act within their powers until and unless the contrary is proved. As such, the burden of proof always lies on the award-debtor who wishes to oppose the enforcement of the award under this ground. However, there are few examples of such partial enforcement of the award in other jurisdictions in the region.[36]

## 2.4 *Irregularity in the Composition of the Tribunal or Procedure of the Arbitration*

Enforcement of an arbitral award may be refused on the ground that the composition of the arbitral tribunal or the arbitral procedure was not in accordance with the agreement of the parties, or failing such agreement, was not in accordance with the law of the country where the arbitration took place.[37] The case *E20, Supplier (US) v State Enterprise (Belarus)*[38] is an important illustration. The contract contained an arbitration clause referring disputes to the International Arbitration Court (IAC) at the Belarusian Chamber of Commerce and Industry in Minsk. A dispute arose between the parties in respect of the payment of a delivery; the US supplier commenced IAC arbitration. An IAC arbitral tribunal found in favor of the US supplier. The tribunal president and the US-supplier appointed arbitrator signed the award; a statement of the president that the third arbitrator was on vacation replaced the signature of the third arbitrator, who had been appointed by the Belarusian defendant. The Belarusian Supreme Commercial Court set aside the award holding, *inter alia*, that the tribunal violated the rules of the IAC that prescribe that the tribunal hearing the proceedings had to render the award. In the instant case the third arbitrator, it was found, did not sign the award owing to a disagreement with the other arbitrators and the eventual non-participation in the decision-making. The President, under the IAC rules, ought to have requested for a substitute arbitrator. The Dresden Court of Appeal hearing the enforcement application noted the fact of set aside order of the Belarusian Court and denied enforcement, citing Article V(1)(d).

---

[35]SC Appeal No. 38-39/2006, 25 June 2013.

[36]See, for example *ONGC Ltd. v Western Geco International Ltd.* (2014) 9 SCC 263, an Indian decision discussed elsewhere in the chapter.

[37]NYC, Article V(1)(d).

[38]*E20, Supplier v State Enterprise (Belarus)* [2008] XXXIII YBCA 510.

## 2.5 *Award Not Yet Binding, Set Aside or Suspended*

Enforcement of an arbitral award can also be refused on the ground that the award has not yet become binding on the parties, or has been set aside or suspended by a competent authority of the country in which, or under the law of which, that award was made.[39] Two approaches explain the binding nature of the award, especially the time when the award is considered binding. Some courts have assessed the binding nature of the award by reference to the law of the country of origin of the award.[40] The other approach is referred to as the autonomous approach, courts have interpreted the 'binding nature of the award' autonomous of the law at the country of the origin of the award.[41] However, two principles could be derived from the jurisprudence and the commentaries on assessing the binding nature of the award,

- binding nature of the award is not dependent upon the award's enforceability in the country where it was issued, as any such condition would lead to a possible reinstatement of the mechanism of *double exequatur*, a mechanism that was rejected in many jurisdictions,[42]
- existence, or the possibility set aside application in the courts of the country where the award was issued, does not lead to an understanding that the award is unenforceable under the NYC.[43]

Judicial opinion on the 'binding nature of an award' has particularly favoured the implementation of parties' intention as derived from the arbitration agreement or the arbitration rules. In *Inter-Arab Investment Guarantee Corp. (Kuwait) v Banque Arab et Internationale d' Investissements (France)*[44] the Belgian Cour de Appel considered an enforcement challenge to an award issued under the Jordanian law. The arbitration agreement stated that the award of the tribunal shall be final and binding upon the parties and shall be enforced immediately after it has been rendered, unless the tribunal has fixed an interval for its enforcement or the enforcement of any part thereof. The appellant raised a challenge under Article V(1)(e) pleading that while the NYC prohibited the double exequatur, an exequatur under the Jordanian law was still possible. The Court referred to the Jordanian Arbitration law in the chapter on Enforcement of Judgments, which specified that after the

[39]NYC, Article V(1)(e).

[40]The Guide to the New York Convention, 4. http://newyorkconvention1958.org/pdf/NYC1958-GuideV1e-20151015.pdf, accessed 05 September, 2016.

[41]Ibid., 5, 6: See, Linda Silberman, 'The New York Convention After Fifty Years: Some Reflections on the Role of National Law' (2009) 38 Ga. J. Int'l & Comp. L. 25, 27.

[42]See, for example, *AB Götaverken v. General National Maritime Transport Company (GMTC), Libya and others*, Supreme Court, Sweden, 13 August 1979, SO 1462.

[43]*Joseph Müller AG v. Bergesen und Obergericht (II. Zivilkammer) des Kantons Zürich*, Court of First Instance, Switzerland, 26 February 1982 stating that "[t]he requirement of a declaration of enforcement in the country of the arbitral award's origin would go squarely against the New York Convention's aim of avoiding the double exequatur".

[44][1997] 22 YBCA 643.

arbitral award has been granted *exequatur* by the court, it shall be enforced as any other judgment or court decision. The Belgian law (the law applicable to the enforcement application) specifies that the arbitral award, similar to a judgment, could be enforced after the enforcement formula has been apposed, such formula being a copy or the minute thereof be supplied. Referring to NYC, Article III that specified that more onerous conditions on the recognition or enforcement of NYC-arbitral awards as compared to the recognition or enforcement of domestic arbitral awards, shall not be imposed, the Court found that appellant's request for a Jordanian law preliminary exequatur appeared onerous, the challenge of exequatur requirement under Article V(1)(e) was rejected.[45]

The Cour de Cassation, hearing a further appeal, held that the binding nature of the award should be determined "by referring, successively and one in the absence of the other, to the arbitration agreement, the law that it designates for such purpose, and last, the law of the country in which the award was rendered."[46]

## 2.6 *Non-arbitrability of the Subject—Matter of the Dispute*

National courts may also be able to refuse enforcement of an arbitral award if the subject matter of the dispute cannot be settled by arbitration under the law of the country where it's enforcement.[47] For instance, a corporate dispute on title to shares is not arbitrable in Russia[48] and non-contractual obligations, such as those under tort law, are sometimes beyond the scope of arbitration agreements. However, challenging the enforcement of arbitral award under the ground of arbitrability does not come up often due to the broad international policy to encourage arbitration. There are very few express declarations of disputes that cannot be resolved by arbitration.[49]

## 2.7 *Public Policy*

Public policy is an important ground to refuse enforcement of foreign arbitral awards. National courts may refuse to enforce an arbitral award if the award is contrary to the public policy of that country.[50] The term public policy is not

---

[45]Ibid., 660, 661.

[46]*Inter-Arab Investment Guarantee Corporation v. Banque Arabe et Internationale d'Investissements*, Cour de Cassation, Belgium, 5 June 1998, (1998) XXIV YBCA 603–614.

[47]NYC, Article V(2)(a).

[48]Ilya Kokorin, 'Arbitrability of Corporate Disputes in Russia: Current and Future Regulation' (CIS Arbitration Forum, 18 January 2016). http://www.cisarbitration.com/2016/01/18/arbitrability-of-corporate-disputes-in-russia-current-and-future-regulation/, accessed 20 January 2016.

[49]R S Bachawat (n 21) 2398.

[50]NYC, Article V(2)(b).

explicitly defined in the UNCITRAL ML and the NYC. Courts may interpret the provision entirely at their discretion or on their interpretation of local law. Despite the definition of public policy remaining in flux, arbitral tribunals in some jurisdictions construe the term narrowly, on the basis that a pro-enforcement attitude is, in itself, a public policy.[51]

Interpretation on public policy exception in South Asian jurisdictions is still in its evolutionary stages. In India, for example, in the *Renusagar v General Electric*[52] the Supreme Court of India held that the enforcement of foreign arbitral award can be refused on the ground of 'public policy' if the enforcement is contrary to (i) fundamental policy of Indian law, or (ii) the interests of India, or (iii) justice or morality. However, in *ONGC v Saw Pipes*[53] the Supreme Court held that the ground of 'public policy' presaged a wider meaning than the *Renusagar ratio* because the concept of public policy suggested matters concerning public good and public interest.[54] The Supreme Court thus added a ground of 'patent illegality', as being contrary to 'public policy'. However, such an interpretation allowed the national courts to review the substantial merits of the award, under the guise of public policy. It has been correctly pointed out that mistakes in fact or law by the arbitrator were deliberately not included as one of the exceptions to enforcement under the NYC and that this limitation must be seen in the light of the principle of international commercial arbitration that a national court should not interfere with the substance of arbitration.[55]

The decisions in *Venture Global Engineering v Satyam Computer Services*[56] and *Phulchand Exports v OOO Patriot*[57] (hereinafter, the *Phulchand Exports*) following the precedent in *Bhatia International v Bulk Trading SA & Anr*[58] on the linkages between Parts I and II of the ACA, 1996, held that the extended meaning of public policy as specified in *ONGC v Saw Pipes* applied to international arbitration also, the result being an extended review of the foreign award by the enforcement courts in India. However, fortunately, in the case *Bharat Aluminium Co. v Kaiser Aluminium Technical Service Inc.* (hereinafter, the *BALCO*)[59]

[51]O. Ozumba, 'Enforcement of Arbitral Awards: Does the Public Policy Exception Create Inconsistency?'. http://www.dundee.ac.uk/cepmlp/gateway/files.php?file=cepmlp_car13_8_127246631.pdf, accessed 07 January 2016.

[52]*Renusagar v General Electric* [1994] AIR 860 (SC).

[53][2003] 5 SCC 705.

[54]Sameer Sattar, 'Enforcement of Arbitral Awards and Public Policy: Same Concept, Different Approach?' (2011) 8 Transnational Dispute Management Journal 1, 10.

[55]Albert J van den Berg, *The New York Arbitration Convention of 1958: Towards a Uniform Judicial Interpretation*, (Kluwer 1981) 269.

[56]AIR 2008 SC 1061.

[57](2011) 10 SCC 300 In *Phulchand Exports Limited v OOO Patriot* it was clarified that this broader interpretation of public policy applied to both domestic and foreign arbitration.

[58][2002] 4 SCC 105.

[59][2012] 9 SCC 552.

a constitutional bench of the Supreme Court conclusively reversed the ratio of the *Bhatia* and held that Part I of India's Arbitration Act would only apply to domestic arbitrations. As a result, foreign arbitral awards can no longer be set aside for being contrary to the substantive provisions of Indian law. Subsequently, *Shri Lal Mahal Ltd. v ProgettoGranoSpA*[60] (hereinafter, the *Shri Lal Mahal*) overruled the *Phulchand Exports* decision, thereby restoring the original understanding of public policy as specified in the ratio of the *Renusagar* decision. Indian courts, post-*Shri Lal Mahal*, can no longer review foreign awards on grounds of patent illegality. However, there has been a different opinion with regard to India-seated arbitration. In *ONGC v Western Geco*[61] the Supreme Court, reversing the decision of the lower courts and upholding partially the ONGC's challenge against the award, restated the *ONGC v Saw Pipes* approach to public policy. It said this includes "all such fundamental principles as providing a basis for administration of justice and enforcement of law in this country."[62] In particular, a court could assess whether a tribunal: (i) has applied a judicial approach, i.e. has not acted in an arbitrary manner; (ii) has acted in accordance with the principles of natural justice, including applying its mind to the relevant facts; and (iii) has avoided reaching a decision which is so perverse or irrational that no reasonable person would have arrived at it.

It seems that Sri Lankan courts have demonstrated restraint in their interpretation of the 'public policy' exception.[63] The Supreme Court of Sri Lanka, in *Light Weight Body Armour Ltd. v Sri Lanka Army*[64] defined public policy as being the fundamental principles of law and justice in substantive as well as procedural aspects and further clarified in *Kiran Atapattu v Janashakthi General Insurance Co. Ltd.* that 'while the dynamism of the concept of public policy cannot be denied, it is important to exercise extreme caution in applying the concept'.[65]

Despite instances of interference with the arbitral process in the past, Pakistan has presented few encouraging indications from the country's High Courts on willingness to recognise and enforce foreign arbitral awards. For instance, in *Islamic Republic of Iran Shipping Lines v Hassan Ali & Co. Cotton (Pvt.) Limited*[66] the Sindh High Court held that it does not sit as an appellate court when considering the enforcement of foreign arbitral awards but merely acts as an executing court.

---

[60] [2013] 8 SCALE 489.

[61] 2014 (9) SCC 263. http://judis.nic.in/supremecourt/imgs1.aspx?filename=41878.

[62] Ibid., 28.

[63] *Kristley (Pty.) Ltd. v State Timber Corporation* [2002] 1 Sri L.R. 225.

[64] [2007] BALR 10 (SC).

[65] (SC Appeal 30-31/2005, 22 February 2013) 1, 6.

[66] [2006] CLD 153.

## 3 Enforcement of Arbitral Awards: The Bangladesh Perspective

In 1971, when Bangladesh gained its independence, the Arbitration (Protocol and Convention) Act 1937 (the APC Act, 1937) and the Arbitration Act 1940 (the AA, 1940) were the governing laws for arbitration in Bangladesh. The 1937 Act dealt with the filing of foreign awards, their effects, and the procedure and conditions for the enforcement of foreign awards while the 1940 Act dealt with domestic arbitrations and gave national courts the scope to interfere, even at the enforcement stage.[67] As a result, a nebulous arbitration culture arose under these laws. Such problems were addressed through the adoption of the Arbitration Act 2001 (the AA 2001) based on the Model Law and supplemented with some unique features from the Arbitration and Conciliation Act 1996 (India) and the Arbitration Act 1996 (UK). After Bangladesh became a signatory to the New York Convention in 1992, the AA 2001 gave force to its provisions through Chapter X of the AA 2001. The Bangladesh courts had, earlier, held that since the arbitration law in the country was the APC Act, 1937, the NYC did not apply.[68] It is pertinent here to state the structure of the judicial system in Bangladesh and also identify the designated court for arbitration-related issues. The Supreme Court of Bangladesh has two divisions —the Appellate Division (AD) and the High Court Division (HCD). While the AD has no original jurisdiction and could hear appeals from the HCD, the HCD exercises both ordinary and constitutional jurisdiction. The HCD is vested with a variety of jurisdictions—within its ordinary jurisdiction, it exercises original, appellate, revisionary and reference jurisdiction; within its constitutional jurisdiction, it exercises writ jurisdiction as well as jurisdiction to transfer cases. Next in the hierarchy of courts are the District Courts, civil and criminal. The jurisdiction in respect of international commercial arbitrations is with the HCD.

The AA, 2001 was enacted to expedite arbitration proceedings, particularly the enforcement of foreign arbitral awards in Bangladesh. It makes it obligatory for the national courts of Bangladesh to enforce foreign arbitral awards, as if they were a decree of the court,[69] subject to the exceptions provided in Section 46. As in India, Pakistan and Sri Lanka, a court shall enforce a foreign arbitral award upon an application being made to it by any party under the Code of Civil Procedure 1908 (the CPC), in the same manner as if it were a decree of the court.[70]

---

[67]See, for example, Sections 15 and 16 of the 1940 Act.

[68]See, for example, *M/s. HajiAzam v Singleton Binda & Co. Ltd.* [1975] 27 DLR 583.

[69]AA 2001, s 45.

[70]AA 2001, s 45(1)(b). This was strictly interpreted in the cases of *Canada Shipping and Trading SAv TT Katikaayu and another* (2002) 54 DLR (HCD) 93, 7.

Inspired by the NYC and the UNCITRAL ML, the legislature restricted the grounds on which a foreign arbitral award can be denied enforcement.[71] While these grounds are provided to check improper arbitral awards, it also provides ample scope for the national courts to frustrate the execution of foreign arbitral awards in Bangladesh by interpreting them too broadly.

However, the necessity of court intervention becomes crucial if a party declines compliance with the award of the tribunal.

In *Uzbekistan Airways and another v Air Spain Ltd.*,[72] the HCD re-iterated the general rule that a foreign arbitral award can be enforced in Bangladesh pursuant to Section 3(2) read with Sections 45–47 of the AA 2001. A similar position was taken by the HCD in the case of *Smith Co-Generation (BD) Pvt. Ltd. v Bangladesh Power Development Board*[73] where it was held that Sections 45 and 46 of the AA 2001 provide the appropriate forum for seeking remedy against the execution of an arbitral award. The HCD reiterating the statutory jurisdiction vested in Courts upheld the spirit and ethos of NYC, Article V regarding challenges for enforcement of foreign arbitral awards. These cases reflect the principle of minimal court intervention and the positive attitude shown by Bangladeshi courts towards the concept of arbitration.

Recently, in *Goenka Impex S.A. v Tallu Spinning Mills Ltd.*,[74] the positive approach of the HCD towards international arbitration was further evident. In this case, pending execution application, the award-holder filed an application for attachment of the award-debtor's properties, situated outside Dhaka. The award-debtor appeared and contested the application. The District Judge of Dhaka, after hearing the parties, rejected the award-holder's application for attachment on the ground that the Court was a mere Transferee court and is not competent to issue a precept (under Section 46 of the CPC) for attachment of properties outside Dhaka. Hearing the award-holder's Revision Application the HCD analysed the intent of Section 45(b) of the AA 2001 and held that the legislative intention was to extend the jurisdiction of the District Court for execution of foreign awards in Bangladesh. The HCD held that, a reading of Section 45(b) of the AA 2001, clarified that when executing foreign awards, the District Court, before which the enforcement application is made, should treat the foreign award as its own decree. The HCD held that the Court where the enforcement proceedings were initiated is not a Transferee Court; in the instant case it was held that the District Court had committed an error of law by not allowing the application for attachment under the execution proceedings.[75]

---

[71]AA 2001, s 46 The grounds stated in Sect. 46 are materially the same as enumerated in Article 36 of UNCITRAL ML and in NYC, Article V.

[72]*Uzbekistan Airways and another v Air Spain Ltd.* [2005] 10 BLC 614, para 5.

[73](2010)15 BLC (HCD) 704, para 24.

[74][2013] 33 BLD 340.

[75]Ibid., paras 15, 16.

Recently the binding nature of arbitral awards was re-affirmed in *Tata Power Company Ltd. v M/S Dynamic Const.* (*Tata case*).[76] The Appellate Division held that an arbitral award is generally not open to review by the courts for any error in finding facts and/or applying law, for the simple reason that it would defeat the very purpose of the arbitration proceedings. The AD clarified that the AA, 2001 is a special law enacted with the aim of giving expeditious relief to parties who accede to the system of arbitration as agreed upon in a contract. The scope of interference is very limited. The AD further confirmed that the factual and contractual positions are matters to be decided by the arbitrator and, as such, unless there appears to be gross illegality, the court should not entertain such arguments.[77] By gross illegality, the AD referred to the inconsistency with the law of the land in the context of Section 43(1)(b)(ii) of the AA, 2001 [which states that award may be set aside if it violates the laws of Bangladesh]. The AD did not discuss gross illegality separately. Further the court attempted at outlining the contours of public policy under AA 2001 drawing resources from the definition of public policy as stated in *Black's Law Dictionary*:

Broadly, principles and standards regarded by the legislature or by the courts as being of fundamental concern to the state and the whole of society.[78]

The Appellate Division also observed that a decision contrary to the law of the country is not necessarily in conflict with public policy as envisaged by the AA 2001. That would be a mere illegality. It further observed that it would be giving too broad a meaning to the phrase 'in conflict with public policy' to include decisions which are contrary to law, or where the learned arbitrator has traveled beyond the terms of his reference, or has misinterpreted a principle of law or precedent, or for misreading or non-consideration of evidence. These matters could be considered as matters relating to propriety, but were not, in the Appellate Division's view, matters relating to public policy.[79] The *Tata* decision is the only instance where the court had an opportunity to discuss public policy.

To prevent parties from taking advantage of the absence of judicial avenue and alienate the property that is the subject matter of the award, domestic courts may need to exercise statutory powers and provide interim relief. While Section 7A of the AA, 2001 has empowered the HCD to make interim orders, there is considerable debate as to whether the HCD has the necessary powers to provide interim orders in respect of arbitrations seated outside Bangladesh. Section 3, AA 2001 states that, except for Sections 45–47, which concern recognition and enforcement of foreign arbitral awards, the legislative provisions are only applicable

---

[76] [2015] 2 SCOB 15 (AD).

[77] Ibid., para 24.

[78] Ibid., para 27.

[79] Ibid.

when the place of arbitration is in Bangladesh. As a result, Bangladesh is now faced with 2 (two) conflicting decisions from the HCD.[80]

On the one hand, in *HRC Shipping Ltd. v M.V. X press Manaslu & Others*[81] (hereinafter, the HRC), the court held that the legislature has prepared the AA 2001 based on the Model Law, so the harmonization and flexibility fostered by the Model Law were also enshrined in the AA 2001. Accordingly, the court held,

> It is evident that Section 3(1) provides that the 2001 Act would apply where the place of arbitration is in Bangladesh. It does not state that it would not apply where the place of arbitration is not in Bangladesh. Neither does it state that the 2001 Act would 'only' apply if the place of arbitration is Bangladesh.[82]

The decision of the bench of the HCD in this case helps disputant parties to an international arbitration to approach Bangladesh courts for interim relief against assets located in Bangladesh. While this may help prevent a party from dissipating the assets and also noting the difficulty in enforcing a foreign tribunal/foreign court's interim relief order, such opinion of the HCD could, when not statutorily delimited, lead to the increased role of the Bangladesh courts in foreign-seated arbitration.

Taking a contrarian position, in *STX Corporation Ltd. v Meghna Group of Industries Ltd. & Ors.*[83] (hereinafter, the *STX*), another bench of the HCD adopted a literal construction of the statute and held that there is no doubt that the provisions of AA 2001 shall apply only if the seat of arbitration is in Bangladesh.[84] The Court held that it could not grant stay or interim relief in support of arbitrations seated outside of Bangladesh. It further opined that, as the wording of Section 3(1) is clear and unambiguous, unless the Parliament enacted a provision explicitly providing interim measures for foreign arbitration, such measures could not be granted by a Bangladeshi court. The bench of the HCD arrived at this decision citing the AD judgment in *Unicol Bangladesh v Maxwell*[85] where the AD held,

> the law as in Sections 3(1) and 3(4) of the Act … is limited in application as to the arbitration being held in Bangladesh, but not as to matter restraining a particular party from proceeding with arbitration in foreign country in respect of a contract signed in Bangladesh.[86]

In *STX* the Court held that since the AD had categorically ruled on this issue, there was no further scope for the HCD to depart from their findings in the light of the

---

[80]Sameer Sattar, 'Bangladeshi courts at odds in respect of its powers in relation to arbitrations seated outside of Bangladesh' [2013] 1 International Arbitration Law Review 20.

[81][2007] 12 MLR 265.

[82]Ibid., para 32.

[83]*STX Corporation Ltd. v Meghna Group of Industries Ltd. & Ors.* [2012] 32BLD 400.

[84]Ibid., para 28.

[85]56 DLR (AD) (2004).

[86]Ibid., para 15.

binding precedent rule enshrined in Article 111 of the Constitution of the People's Republic of Bangladesh.

The HCD followed the approach of the *STX* case in the recent case of *Egyptian Fertilizer Trading Limited* (hereinafter, the *Egyptian Fertilizer*)[87] and did not grant interim relief to arbitration seated outside of Bangladesh.

## 3.1 Judicial Opinion on Public Policy Challenges to Foreign Awards

Public Policy is another ground for challenging an enforcement of a foreign award, where in deciding that an award is contrary to public policy, national courts should ensure that the basic elements of fairness and impartiality are met. In this regard, it is safe to say that the courts in Bangladesh have followed a restrictive approach in line with the spirit of the New York Convention and the Model Law. In the *Tata Power Company Ltd.*[88] the Appellate Division in Bangladesh held that, unless the contract or the award made by the arbitrator had a negative or uncalled for impact on the State and the society, it would not be considered as contrary to public policy. The Court preferred an inclusive meaning to the phrase 'in conflict with public policy' to include decisions which are contrary to law, or where the learned arbitrator has travelled beyond the terms of his reference, or has misinterpreted a principle of law or precedent, or for misreading or for not considering certain evidence. It held those could be considered as matters relating to propriety, but not matters relating to public policy.[89] The above decision leads to a derivation that the courts in Bangladesh are not construing public policy broadly; rather it has limited the scope of application of public policy.

## 3.2 Delay in Decisions on Enforcement Applications

Bangladesh's tryst with arbitration is also affected by extended delays in decisions on enforcement applications. Although the AA 2001 was enacted to expedite arbitration, the reality is that the enforcement of foreign award in Bangladesh is inordinately time-consuming, which ultimately vitiates the very purpose of choosing arbitration as the preferred method for resolving international commercial disputes. A willingness to enforce foreign arbitral awards notwithstanding, such enforcement could be compromised upon owing to extended delay in the process at

[87] *Egyptian Fertilizer Trading Limited (Egyptian Fertilizer) v East West Property Development (Private) Ltd.* (Arbitration Application No. 11 of 2010, 10 June 2014).

[88] Tata Power Company (n 76).

[89] Ibid., para 27.

the lower courts. In *Smith Co-Generation (BD) Pvt. Ltd. v PDB*,[90] the petitioner received three ICC awards in their favour against the Bangladesh Power Development Board for breaches of contract but as the PDB filed an application against the petitioner's execution suit in the District Court and challenged the legality of the arbitral proceedings, it took them 10 (ten) years before the petitioner's award was upheld.

## 4 Enforcement in Practice—Causes for Concern

Enforcement of foreign arbitral awards is dependent upon a State's legal infrastructure, legal culture, exposure to arbitration and proper understanding of the judges and advocates regarding the applicable laws, rules and regulations of international arbitration and its practice. In addition to that, the government's approach to arbitration may also influence the enforcement of foreign arbitral awards. In practice, the procedural difficulties in enforcing foreign arbitral awards can be discussed under two broad headings: statutory claptrap and non-statutory claptrap.

### *4.1 Statutory Claptrap*

The current arbitration regime of Bangladesh does not lay down any special rules to be followed by national courts while disposing of the execution of foreign award, which means that there is no time limit for disposing an execution case. Instead, it requires that the antiquated general provisions of the CPC be applied at the time of enforcement. While India's Arbitration and Conciliation Act 1996 has been amended to include a fast-track procedural regime,[91] the AA 2001 has not undergone a similar revision, long overdue. Moreover, the present legal regime of Bangladesh cannot prevent a party opposing the execution of an award from tactically delaying enforcement by filing parallel civil proceedings. One of the judges reflect upon this in an article on the Administration of Civil Justice (which is equally applicable to arbitration cases in Bangladesh):

---

[90]*Smith Corporation* (n 73).

[91]See *Arbitration and Conciliation (Amendment) Act 2015* generally. (Sections 29A and 29B). These provisions prescribe a time-bound structure for domestic arbitration. Further the provisions also suggest that parties could agree upon a fast-track arbitration of their dispute. These provisions are, however, limited to the process of arbitration till the making of an award. There are no timelines that are attached to enforcement, the provisions suggested that the award would be deemed to be decree of the court and enforced accordingly.

> In the execution stage, judgment-debtors take advantage of technicalities and adopt dilatory tactics and make application of tricks with intent to delay the execution. The entire judicial process in civil suit has been brought to disrepute by the manner and method of executing proceedings that protract over decades.[92]

The practice of such dilatory tactics is a cause of great concern to the international business community undertaking business in Bangladesh. In addition to this, it is a matter of fact that the national courts of Bangladesh are already overburdened with cases and hence will not be able to give full concentration to arbitration cases exclusively. Although the AA, 2001 enabled the creation of a separate Bench of the HCD to deal with certain arbitration matters, such as the appointment of arbitrators, it is yet to be constituted. As a result, it is obvious that if a court has to address the enforcement of foreign arbitral awards along with other civil matters, it cannot dispose the same expeditiously.

The AA, 2001 ought to be revised to deal with and incorporate or clarify developments that have taken place in the arbitration world—with regard to interim relief, public policy and such.

### *4.2 Non-statutory Claptrap*

Few non-statutory factors could also bear hindrance to the enforcement of foreign arbitral awards. With regard to the courts, a lack of specific knowledge or training about the rules, regulations and norms of international arbitration may lead judges to incorrectly interpret the law and misunderstand the court's role in the arbitral process. A study reported by the Bangladesh International Arbitration Centre discussed the docket details of Bangladesh courts as of 2013, a little over a decade after the AA, 2001 has been enacted.[93] A total pending litigation with 2,454,360 cases, out of which 963,081 cases were of civil nature—869,614 cases were pending before the District Courts and Tribunals, 80,588 cases before the HCD, and 12,879 cases before the AD. The BIAC also reported that many of these cases could be disposed of using ADR methods, without taking recourse to courts.[94] The UNDP project on Judicial Strengthening[95] reported that, as compared to the volume of pending cases, only 1340 cases were disposed off through the utilization of ADR

[92]Muhammad S Hossain and Mohammad I Hossain, 'Causes of Delay in Administration of Civil Justice: A Look for Way Out in Bangladesh Perspective' (2012) 6 ASA University Review 103, 107.

[93]Bangladesh International Arbitration Centre. http://biac.org.bd/court-statistics/#, accessed 01 September, 2016.

[94]Ibid.

[95]Supreme Court of Bangladesh, Summary Report on Court Services Situation Analysis (2013). http://www.undp.org/content/dam/bangladesh/docs/Projects/JUST/Summary_Report_on%20Court%20Services%20Situation%20Analysis.pdf, accessed 03 September, 2016.

methods by 2013 in the three districts of Dhaka, Kishoreganj and Rangmati.[96] While the study reported that all these cases were civil disputes, there is no information on the number of arbitration-related matters in this data.

A failure to embrace the spirit of such a process encumbers the development of an arbitration-friendly regime and, in turn, impedes a country's prospects as an investment destination.

## 5 Conclusion

To address the challenges of resolving international commercial disputes expeditiously, there is no alternative to an arbitration friendly legal regime. To that end, laws favourable to arbitration, skilled and knowledgeable advocates and judges and a pro-arbitration attitude of the government are necessary preconditions. In order to make a country reputed for being arbitration-friendly, national courts should act neutrally in enforcing foreign arbitral awards and advocates and judges should avoid a tendency towards protectionism. Moreover, national courts should encourage the enforcement of foreign arbitral awards, by narrowly interpreting the exceptions to the general rule of enforcement and promptly deciding such matters. The cases in Bangladesh reflect a mixed experience in this regard. While the Supreme Court of Bangladesh has, for the most part, demonstrated a positive intent in interpreting the 'public policy' exception restrictively and a willingness to enforce foreign arbitral awards, the lower courts have muddied the waters by allowing parallel civil proceedings and causing unconscionable delays. In terms of a coherent, pro-arbitration approach, countries like Bangladesh in South Asia can follow the salutary examples of Singapore and, more recently, India.

A few amendments are in order to the AA 2001 in line with the amendments to the revised UNCITRAL Model Law. The amendments should, *inter alia*, include a clarification regarding the availability of interim relief in support of arbitration proceedings seated outside of Bangladesh, the inclusion of a more restrictive definition of public policy, a timeline for the disposal of an enforcement application and the establishment of a separate Arbitration bench/Court exclusively for disposal of arbitration-related matters. Legislative revision effort could also attempt to define procedural rules for courts in arbitration-related applications, in the place of the general rules of the Code of Civil Procedure.

Legislative reform should be supplemented with the training of judges and advocates in how to resolve cross-border disputes efficiently and gaining in depth knowledge about the laws of arbitration (including having a deep understanding of the ethos of arbitration). Further, advocates could also be trained in drafting arbitration clauses and such. The lower court judges ought to be trained on expeditious disposal of arbitration-related applications. Such small steps would significantly impact Bangladesh's image in being recognised as a pro-arbitration jurisdiction.

---

[96] Ibid., 27.

# Issues of Jurisdiction, Choice of Law and Enforcement in International Commercial Arbitration: An Indian Perspective

**Sai Ramani Garimella**

**Abstract** International arbitration, characterized by increasing regulatory activity and escalating institutionalization of the mechanism across jurisdictions, presents an interesting yet complex structure. Flexibility within the process, primacy to the party autonomy principle and enforcement across jurisdictions are the factors that explain its increased utility. Nevertheless while most arbitration laws drew inspiration from the UNCITRAL Model Law, there have been marked shift from the guidance given in that document, within the national laws. This chapter aims to present the Indian law on international commercial arbitration, discussing the issues related to jurisdiction, choice of law and the enforcement of foreign arbitral awards and the role of the courts at the enforcement forum in deciding upon challenges to such enforcement.

**Keywords** Indian arbitration act · UNCITRAL model law · Jurisdiction of the arbitral tribunal · Governing law · Foreign arbitral awards · Public policy

## Introduction

Moving much ahead from its moorings within the conflict of laws realm, international arbitration reflects flexibility even while requiring increased clarity from regulatory space. An alternative to litigation before domestic courts, International arbitration combines effectively the elements of neutrality, flexibility and the necessity to look for resolution beyond parochial positions, which are often the problem areas in litigation. Gilles Cuniberti commented that arbitration, for the reasons mentioned above, could be considered as the default mechanism for

- The author thanks the reviewers whose comments have enriched the content of this chapter.

S.R. Garimella (✉)
Faculty of Legal Studies, South Asian University, New Delhi, India
e-mail: ramani@sau.ac.in; saisavi@gmail.com

© Springer Nature Singapore Pte Ltd. 2017

S.R. Garimella and S. Jolly (eds.), *Private International Law*,
DOI 10.1007/978-981-10-3458-9_16

international commercial transactions.[1] International arbitration has gained immensely from the near universal acceptance of the New York Convention on Enforcement of Foreign Arbitral Awards, 1958 (hereinafter, NYC).[2] The UNCITRAL Model Law, 1985 (hereinafter, UNCITRAL ML)[3] has significantly contributed to help harmonize national laws on arbitration in many countries, post accession to the NYC, thereby impacting party autonomy, the feature that enables the parties to the arbitration to derogate from national law in significant measure, save the mandatory rules of the laws touching the contract, and the content of public policy at the seat and in the enforcement jurisdictions.[4]

Flexibility has been the hallmark of arbitration, nevertheless, few concerns remain—*lex fori* offers significant interpretational strength in international litigation; its absence in international arbitration meant that there is no fallback forum to address typical jurisdictional issues that come up in a dispute with a foreign element in it; *Lex arbitri* being no effective substitute to *lex fori* the arbitral tribunal does not have readily available methodology to decide questions of applicable law.

International Conventions have significantly helped harmonize many aspects related to transnational commercial contracts; nevertheless, the relevance of private international law rules cannot be gainsaid.[5] The knowledge domain is increasingly becoming relevant because of the increased scope of party autonomy, the diversity amongst the rules applicable to international arbitration in any country and also the increasing acceptance of trade usages and practices, and *lex mercatoria* to explain the rules applicable to the merits of the dispute.[6]

Party autonomy is the fundamental choice of law rule in international contracts nevertheless restrictions apply on the express choice of law by the parties. These restrictions, mandatory rules and *lois de police*, sourced within national laws that

[1]Gilles Cuniberti, 'Beyond Contract—The Case of Default Arbitration in International Commercial Disputes' (2009) 32(2) Fordham Int'l LJ 417.

[2]The Convention has a current membership of 156 countries. http://www.newyorkconvention.org/list+of+contracting+states, accessed 12 March 2016.

[3]https://www.uncitral.org/pdf/english/texts/arbitration/ml-arb/07-86998_Ebook.pdf, accessed 10 February 2016.

[4]H. Carlquist, 'Party autonomy and the Choice of Substantive Law in International Commercial Arbitration'. https://gupea.ub.gu.se/bitstream/2077/3079/1/200656.pdf, accessed 10 February 2016.

[5]See Filip De Ly, 'The Place of Arbitration in the Conflict of Laws of International Commercial Arbitration: An Exercise in Arbitration Planning' (1991) 12(1) Nw. J. Int'l L. & Bus. 48.

[6]Guidetta Cordero Moss, 'International Arbitration and the Quest for the Applicable Law' (2008) 8 (3) Global Jurist 1. http://folk.uio.no/giudittm/Quest%20for%20applicable%20law.pdf, accessed 6 January 2016.

govern the contract, make the argument for relevance of private international law in international arbitration.[7]

While all conflicts issues may not arise in an international commercial arbitration, the applicable conflicts system remains relevant for many issues related to arbitral process—for example, the arbitration agreement and its validity and its extension to non-signatories, the subjective and objective arbitrability, arbitral procedure, recognition of prior or intervening court judgments and arbitral awards that may raise *res judicata*, ascertaining the contents of applicable law(*jura novit curia*), amongst others.[8]

An international arbitral tribunal would also have to make a determination on applying either the conflict of laws rules of the seat or rely upon a conflict rule different from that prevailing at the seat.[9]

This chapter attempts to discuss the basic strands of the domain of private international law—jurisdictional issues, choice of law and enforcement of foreign awards—within the space of international arbitration in Indian law.

**Structure of the Chapter**

The chapter traces the historical progression of arbitration legislation in India, its accession to the NYC and the adoption of the UNCITRAL ML into the 1996 Arbitration and Conciliation Act and the 2015 Arbitration Amendment.

This section discusses the scope of the arbitration agreement, principle of separability and the arbitrability of disputes.

The second section of the chapter addresses the jurisdiction-related issues.

- the nature of the competence principle as stated within the legislation and judicial opinion
- anti-suit injunctions
- jurisdiction of the Indian courts to order interim measures in foreign-seated arbitrations—the principle of territoriality, and the changes brought about by the 2015 amendment.

The third section of the chapter presents a discussion on choice of law

- maps the judicial opinion on law governing the arbitration agreement—from *NTPC v. Singer* to the *Enercon Gmbh* case
- the law governing arbitral procedure

---

[7]Guidetta Cordero Moss, 'International Arbitration is not only International' in Guidetta Cordero Moss(ed) *International Commercial Arbitration—Different Forms and their Features* (Cambridge University Press, 2013) 1–39; see, generally, Guidetta Cordero Moss, *International Commercial Arbitration: Party Autonomy and Mandatory Rules*, (Oslo: Tano Ashehoug 1999); Doug Jones, 'Choosing the Law or Rules of Law to Govern the Substantive Rights of the Parties: A discussion on Voie Directe and Voie Indirecte' (2014) 26 SAc.L J 911.

[8]Filip De Ly, 'Conflict of Laws in International Arbitration—an overview' in Franco Ferrari and Stefan Kroll (eds.) *Conflict of Law in International Arbitration* (Munich: Sellier 2011) 3, 4.

[9]Ibid., 5.

- the role of the arbitral tribunal in identifying the law applicable to the dispute in the absence of an express or implied choice of law

The fourth section discusses the law on the recognition and enforcement of foreign arbitral awards. The narrative discusses the grounds for challenging enforcement, scope of mandatory rules and public policy and makes an evidently required comparison with the scope of public policy in a few other jurisdictions.

The chapter concludes with suggestions to re-visit the arbitration law on a few specific issues.

## 1 History of Arbitration Legislation in India

The earliest known law on regulation of arbitration in colonial India was the Bengal Regulation of 1772.[10] Later in 1899 the Indian Arbitration Act modeled on the English Arbitration law was enacted but applied only to the Presidency towns of Bombay, Madras and Calcutta.[11] In 1908, the Civil Procedure Code was revised to include provisions related to arbitration.[12] Consolidating both these regimes a new arbitration law was enacted in 1940, it allowed for and created space for substantial court intervention in arbitral process. In 1937 the Arbitration (Protocol and Convention) Act 1937 was enacted to give effect to the Geneva Protocol on Arbitration Clauses of 1923 and the Geneva Convention on the Execution of Foreign Awards of 1927. The Foreign Awards (Recognition and Enforcement) Act, 1961 implemented India's commitment to New York Convention on Recognition and Enforcement of Foreign Arbitral Awards, 1958. Further while India is not a party to the ICSID Convention, it has entered into many bilateral investment treaties, which provide for arbitration.

The Arbitration Act 1940 allowed multiple opportunities to litigants to approach the court for intervention, thus compounding delays and thereby rendering arbitrations inefficient and unattractive. Important lacunae of this legislation related to the reasons for setting aside an award[13]—an award improperly procured or is otherwise invalid; and the jurisdiction of the courts.[14] In 1996, Parliament enacted

[10]Ben Steinbruck, 'India' in Stephan Balthasar (ed.), *International Commercial Arbitration—A Handbook* (Munich: Beck, Hart, Nomos, 2015) 448.

[11]Ibid., 449.

[12]Id.

[13]Section 30. Grounds for setting aside award:- An award shall not be set aside except on one or more of the following grounds, namely:- (a) that an arbitrator or umpire has misconducted himself or the proceedings; (b) that an award has been made after the issue of an order by the Court superseding the arbitration or after arbitration proceedings have become invalid under Section 35; (c) that an award has been improperly procured or is otherwise invalid.

[14]31. Jurisdiction:- (1) Subject to the provisions of this Act, an award may be filed in any Court having jurisdiction in the matter to which the reference relates. (2) Notwithstanding anything

The Arbitration and Conciliation Act[15] (hereinafter, ACA), modeled upon the UNCITRAL ML. Further there is much reference to the English law and practice of arbitration, owing to the historical ties with English legal system.

## 1.1 Few Features of the ACA

The ACA arranged the law regulating arbitration into Parts I and II for domestic arbitrations and enforcement of foreign arbitral awards, respectively.

International arbitration in India, unlike in other countries and as explained by the approach of the UNCITRAL ML in Article 1(3), is categorized upon the principle of nationality of the disputing parties. Section 2(1)(f) of the ACA states that an arbitration is international where at least one of the parties is either a national, or habitually in any country other than India, or is a body corporate incorporated outside India, or its central management and control is exercised in any country outside India, or is the government of a foreign country. The characterization of an international arbitration thus is understood as being founded in the status of the parties, rather than on the place of performance of the contract. The emphasis, in the Indian law, is on the form rather than the substance.[16]

Interestingly while Part I of the Act, which contains the definition of International Commercial Arbitration, governs commercial as well as non-commercial arbitrations, Part II of the Act applies only to foreign arbitral awards relating to disputes arising out of relationships considered as constituting commercial law under Indian Law. This restriction flows from India's accession to the NYC with the declaration under Article 1(3) of the NYC[17] that it would apply the NYC only to 'commercial'

(Footnote 14 continued)

contained in any other law for the time being in force and save as otherwise provided in this Act, all questions regarding the validity, effect or existence of an award or an arbitration agreement between the parties to the agreement or persons claiming under them shall be decided by the Court in which the awarded under the agreement has been, or may be, filed, and by no other Court. (3) All applications regarding the conduct of arbitration proceedings or otherwise arising out of such proceedings shall be made to the Court where the award has been, or may be, filed, and to no other Court. (4) Notwithstanding anything contained elsewhere in this Act or in any other law for the time being in force, where in any reference any application under this Act has been made in a Court competent to entertain it, that Court alone shall have jurisdiction over the arbitration proceedings and all subsequent applications arising out of that Court and in no other Court.

[15]Arbitration and Conciliation Act, 1996 [16th August, 1996].

[16]V Reddy and V Nagaraj, 'Arbitrability: The Indian Perspective', (2002) 19(2) J Int'l Arb 117, 135.

[17]Article 1(3). When signing, ratifying or acceding to this Convention, or notifying extension under Article X hereof, any State may on the basis of reciprocity declare that it will apply the Convention to the recognition and enforcement of awards made only in the territory of another Contracting State. It may also declare that it will apply the Convention only to differences arising out of legal relationships, whether contractual or not, which are considered as commercial under the national law of the State making such declaration.

arbitrations. The word "commercial" has however been attributed with an expansive meaning, and the judiciary has been convinced about its inclusive nature.[18]

### 1.1.1 Scope of the Arbitration Agreement

The ACA ensures that the arbitration agreement binds only the parties[19] and not third persons.[20] An exception to this principle could be found within Section 45 of the ACA,[21] a *non-obstante* clause, that states that in an international commercial arbitration, arbitration agreements could also be enforced by "any person claiming through or under one of the parties"—the rights and obligations arising from the agreement to arbitrate could be vested in such a person. The Supreme Court in *Chloro Controls (I) Pvt. Ltd. v Severn Trent Water Purification Inc*,[22] explained that the legislative intent of enlarging the scope of application of the arbitration agreement beyond the signatories to the agreement, is evident from the usage of the phrase 'any person'. Therefore non-signatories such as third-party beneficiaries, guarantors, or assignees could also be bound to an arbitration agreement.[23] However, trust beneficiaries are not bound by the arbitration agreement.[24]

Indian courts have construed the substantive scope of the arbitration agreements expansively. In *Enercon (India) Limited & Ors. v Enercon GmbH & Anr.*[25] the Supreme Court interpreting 'disputes arising under or in connection with that agreement'[26] opined that a widely worded arbitration agreement could include all disputes arising in respect of the main contract, including its validity, interpretation, construction, performance, enforcement, or its alleged breach.[27]

---

[18]*RM Investment and Trading Co. v Boeing Co.* AIR 1994 SC 1136 Opining that an agreement for consultancy services was a commercial contract, the court held that the word 'commercial' must be given a wide interpretation consistent with the purpose of the NYC. Also see *Union of India v Leif Hoegb & Co.* (1982) IX YB Comm Arbtn 405.

[19]ACA s 2(1), s 7.

[20]*Deustche Post Bank Home Finance Ltd. v Taduri Sridhar & Anr* (2011) 11 SCC 375, 13.

[21]s 45. Power of judicial authority to refer parties to arbitration:- Notwithstanding anything contained in Part I or in the Code of Civil Procedure, 1908, a judicial authority, when seized of an action in a matter in respect of which the parties have made an agreement referred to in Section 44, shall, at the request of one of the parties or any person claiming through or under him, refer the parties to arbitration, unless it finds that the said agreement is null and void, inoperative or incapable of being performed.

[22](2013) 1 SCC 641, 64.

[23]Ibid., 100.

[24]Shradha Rakhecha, 'The Curious Case of Arbitration of Trust Disputes' (2013) 2(2) Ind J Arbtn L 59, 82. http://www.ijal.in/sites/default/files/IJAL%20Volume%20II%2C%20Issue%202%20%28Part%20B%29.pdf, accessed 14 March 2016.

[25]Civil Appeal No. 2806 of 2014.

[26]ACA, s 7.

[27]*Enercon* (n 25) 79.

### 1.1.2 Pathological Arbitration Clauses

The Indian courts have adopted the principle of harmonious interpretation to give effect to parties' intention in deciding upon pathological arbitration clauses. A recent example has been the *Pricol Limited v Johnson Controls Enterprise Ltd. & Ors*[28] decision related to an incomplete arbitration clause in a joint venture agreement with the following features

(a) the arbitration proceedings would be held at Singapore; and
(b) it would be governed and construed in accordance with the laws of India.

The Supreme Court adduced the real intention of parties to arbitrate, notwithstanding the fact that it was under a non-existent institution, thereby, ensuring that the arbitral process was not derailed by further litigation.

### 1.1.3 Separability Principle

The ACA, Section 16(1)(a) crystallized the principle of separability. It stated that an arbitration clause that forms part of a contract shall be treated as an agreement independent of the other terms of the contract. The tribunal is, therefore, empowered to declare the main contract a nullity, without invalidating the arbitration clause that was the basis of the jurisdiction[29]; this principle was widely accepted in the arbitration jurisprudence in India.[30] In *Enercon*[31] the Supreme Court emphasized upon the separability principle as an intrinsic feature of arbitration, and the "necessity to ensure that the intention of the parties to resolve the disputes by arbitration does not evaporate into thin air with every challenge to the legality, validity, finality or breach of the underlying contract."[32]

### 1.1.4 Arbitrability

Section 2(3) ACA states that Part I does not affect any other law that prohibits certain disputes from arbitration. For example, in India anti-trust disputes cannot be submitted for arbitration.[33] Matters covered by statutory reliefs through statutory tribunals would be non-arbitrable. However, the ACA does not contain an

---

[28]Arbitration case (civil) No. 30 of 2014 (SC original jurisdiction).

[29]ACA s 16 (1)(b).

[30]For example, *Reliance Industries Limited & Anr. v Union of India*, Civil Appeal No. 5765 of 2014.

[31]*Enercon* (n 25).

[32]Ibid., 80.

[33]*Union of India v Competition Commission of India* W.P. (C) 993/2012 & C.M. Nos. 2178-79/2012 (Delhi High Court).

inventory of disputes that are arbitrable. The only available guidance is that any commercial matter could be referred to arbitration, thus leading to an understanding any dispute arising out of a commercial matter, including an action in tort if it arises out of a contract could be referred to arbitration. Disputes about property, money or damages payable for breach of contract could be referred to arbitration[34] while matters involving status and public policy such as matrimonial, guardianship, criminal law issues, insolvency matters as well as employment contracts or matters related to disputes involving rights in rem cannot be submitted to arbitration[35]; disputes that involve rights in rem are, therefore, not arbitrable. [36] Director—company disputes are arbitrable[37] as no master servant relationship exists.[38]

On the arbitrability of claims of fraud, the Supreme Court made a distinction between domestic and international arbitrations. In *World Sport Group (Mauritius) Ltd. v MSM Satellite (Singapore) Pte. Ltd.*[39] (hereinafter, *WSG*) the Court explained that in a foreign-seated arbitration, referring to Section 45 ACA, allegation of fraud, even if proven, did not render the arbitration agreement invalid; the agreement being separable from the main contract unless it is found that the agreement is a nullity, inoperative or incapable of being performed, the parties are to be referred to arbitration. The Court opined that the words "inoperative or incapable of being performed" in Section 45 of the Act are a purposeful incorporation of the language in Article II (3) of the New York Convention, and ought to be construed in the context thereof.[40]

## 1.2 Jurisdiction of the Arbitral Tribunal—Competence-Competence Rule

The doctrine of Competence-Competence refers to the power of the arbitral tribunal to determine its own jurisdiction. Derived from the German concept of *Kompetenz-Kompetenz* the principle though has moved away from the understanding that was attributed to it in the German law.[41] There however seems to be a preference for

---

[34] *Booz Allen and Hamilton Inc. v SBI Home Finance Ltd. And Ors.* (2011) 3 SCC532.

[35] Ibid., 22.

[36] Ibid., 23.

[37] *Comed Chemicals Ltd. v C.N. Ramchand* AIR 2009 SC 494.

[38] S.Kachwaha, Arbitration in India: An Overview. https://ipba.org/media/fck/files/Arbitration%20in%20India.pdf, accessed 02 May 2016.

[39] AIR 2014 SC 968.

[40] Ibid., 29.

[41] In Germany this doctrine meant that arbitrators could make a final ruling on their jurisdiction, there being no subsequent review of the decision by any court. The German Law has, since, aligned much with the UNCITRAL ML thus moving away from the strict no-review standard. See, Klaus Peter Berger, 'Germany Adopts the UNCITRAL Model Law' (1998) 1(3) Int'l Arbtn. L Rev. 121, 122; Also see, Philippe Fouchard, Emmanuel Gaillard, Berthold Goldman, John Savage, *Fouchard, Gaillard, Goldman on International Commercial Arbitration* (Kluwer Law International, 1999) 396.

competence-competence principle[42] many jurisdictions have adopted what seems to be a chronological priority of the tribunal on the gateway question (George Bermann termed the issues related to jurisdiction as the gateway questions).[43] S 16 ACA crystallized this doctrine into Indian law.[44] Redfern and Hunter comment[45] that Indian courts have, unlike earlier, shown faith in this principle.[46] However, a few exceptions highlighting the instances when courts could address the issues of jurisdiction of the arbitral tribunal have been included in Section 16(2). They are

- A request for appointment of arbitrator in case of default by the party(s),
- A request to the court to refer a pending dispute to arbitration,
- Jurisdictional challenges to the award.

In *Wellington Associates v Kirit Mehta*[47] the Supreme Court held that Section 16 allowed the tribunal to decide a question relating to the "existence" of the arbitration clause, but it does not take away the jurisdiction of the Chief Justice of India or his designate to decide the question of the "existence" of the arbitration agreement, since it does not declare that except the Arbitral Tribunal none else can determine such a question. Ben Steinbruck commented that Indian courts, similar to courts in Germany, Canada and Hong Kong, engaged in a full review of the arbitration agreement in deciding upon applications for reference to arbitration.[48]

An application on preclusion of jurisdiction should be submitted to the tribunal not later than the submission of the statement of defence.[49] The decision in *Booz Allen and Hamilton Inc*[50] specified that filing of a detailed affidavit opposing an interim relief application could not be considered to be a statement of defence 'on the substance of the dispute'.[51]

---

[42]Nigel Blackaby and Constantine Partasides with Alan Redfern and Martin Hunter, *Redfern and Hunter on International Arbitration* (6th edn, Oxford University Press 2015) 340.

[43]See, George A. Bermann, 'The "Gateway" Problem in International Commercial Arbitration' (2012) 37(1) Yale Jour. of Int'l L 1.

[44]16. Competence of arbitral tribunal to rule on its jurisdiction:- (1) The arbitral tribunal may rule on its own jurisdiction, including ruling on any objections with respect to the existence or validity of the arbitration agreement, and for that purpose,———

(a) an arbitration clause which forms part of a contract shall be treated as an agreement independent of the other terms of the contract; and
(b) a decision by the arbitral tribunal that the contract is null and void shall not entail ipso jure the invalidity of the arbitration clause.

[45]Nigel Blackaby et al. (n 42) 341.

[46]*Kvaerner Cementation India Ltd v Bajranglal Agarwal*, (2012) 5 SCC 214.

[47](2000) 4 SCC 272.

[48]Steinbruck (n 10) 460.

[49]ACA s16.

[50](n 34).

[51]ACA s 17.

## 1.3 Designated Court in Matters Related to Foreign-Seated Arbitrations

The AC (Amendment) Act, 2015[52] amended the definition of the term 'Court' to provide that certain provisions of Part I of the Act such as interim relief (Section 9), court assistance in taking evidence (Section 27) shall also apply to International Commercial Arbitration, even if the place of arbitration is outside India, subject to an agreement to the contrary between the parties to the dispute. In case of International Commercial Arbitration, the High Court shall be the 'court' for reliefs under the Act.[53]

## 1.4 Anti-suit Injunctions

Anti-suit injunctions, conflict with the principle of comity as granting such an injunction de facto affects the capability of the other forum to hear the dispute, hence used with caution.[54] On enjoining international arbitrations, the Supreme Court opined that they should not ordinarily be enjoined, and in exceptional circumstances when the matter is enjoined, it should be disposed of with utmost dispatch.[55] Anti-arbitration injunctions are maintainable under S 45 ACA[56] where the arbitral proceedings seem vexatious and oppressive and hence, constitute an abuse of due process of law.[57] However in *WSG*[58] the Supreme Court held that such injunctions may be granted only if it is established that the arbitration agreement is null and void, inoperative, or incapable of being performed. The plea of parallel and vexatious proceedings was explicitly found to be insufficient to merit the grant of an anti-arbitration injunction.[59]

---

[52]http://www.prsindia.org/uploads/media/Arbitration/Arbitration%20and%20Conciliation%20Act,%202015.pdf, 12 February 2016.

[53]Ibid. sub-Section (1) clause (e) rewritten with detailed identification of court for ICA as (ii) in the case of international commercial arbitration, the High Court in exercise of its ordinary original civil jurisdiction, having jurisdiction to decide the questions forming the subject-matter of the arbitration if the same had been the subject-matter of a suit, and in other cases, a High Court having jurisdiction to hear appeals from decrees of courts subordinate to that High Court'.

[54]Marco Stacher, 'International Antisuit Injunctions: Enjoining Foreign Litigations and Arbitrations—Beholding the System from Outside' (2005). 8 Cornell Law School Graduate Student Papers 12.

[55]*Dresser Rand SA v KG Khosla Compressors Ltd.* [1993] Supp. (3) SCC 181, 2.

[56]Sharad Bansal, Divyanshu Agrawal, 'Are anti-arbitration injunctions a malaise? An analysis in the context of Indian law', (2015) 31(4) Arbtn Int'l 613.

[57]*Union of India v Dabhol Power Co*, IA No 6663/2003 Suit No 1268/2003 (Delhi High Court 2004).

[58](n 39).

[59](n 53) 627.

## 1.5 *Indian Courts and Jurisdiction in Foreign-Seated Arbitrations*

In a foreign-seated arbitration, the Indian courts could be applied for with regard to refer parties to arbitration.[60] In *Shin-Etsu Chemical Co Ltd v Aksh Optifibre Ltd.*[61] it was held that held that following a *prima facie* showing of validity and existence of the arbitration agreement, it was for the arbitral tribunal to rule on its own jurisdiction.

The AC (Amendment) Act, 2015 states that such applications would now be addressed to the Supreme Court or the High Courts[62] they shall be disposed off expeditiously and not later than sixty days from the date of service of notice on the opposite party.[63]

The law and the courts at the seat of arbitration have a significant role with regard to international arbitration.[64] Emphasizing the significance of the seat, F.A. Mann opined that the validity of arbitration agreements and arbitration procedures needed to be regulated by national laws.[65] Yu commented that the territoriality principle derives its existence from the fact that international arbitration is anchored to the seat and the laws of the seat decide the validity of an arbitral award.[66] However, India has had binaries-based engagement with the territoriality principle. The disengagement and engagement with the territoriality principle could be summarized through the position held in two Supreme Court decisions that span a decade on the timeline - *Bhatia International v Bulk Trading*[67] (hereinafter, *Bhatia*) decision holding that Indian courts could receive applications for interim relief in foreign-seated arbitrations forming the first binary, while commitment to the territoriality principle reiterated in the *Bharat Aluminium v Kaiser Aluminium*[68] (hereinafter, *BALCO*) decision being the other binary.

In *Bhatia*, the Supreme Court held that it could order an interim relief under Part I, ACA in a foreign-seated arbitration, unless the parties had expressly or

---

[60]ACA, s 45.

[61](2005) 7 SCC 234.

[62]In Section 11 of the principal Act,—(i) in sub-Sections (4), (5) and (6), for the words “the Chief Justice or any person or institution designated by him” wherever they occur, the words “the Supreme Court or, as the case may be, the High Court or any person or institution designated by such Court” shall be substituted.

[63]Sub-Section 13, added to Section 11 ACA, by the 2015 Amendment.

[64]Sai Ramani Garimella, Territoriality Principle in International Commercial Arbitration—The Emerging Asian Practice, (Annual Conference of the Asian Law Institute (ASLI), 2014). http://dx.doi.org/10.2139/ssrn.2584332.

[65]Francis A. Mann, ‘Lex Facit Arbitrum’ (1983) 2(3) Arbtn. Int’l 241, 245.

[66]Yu, Hong-Lin, ‘A Theoretical Overview of the Foundations of International Commercial Arbitration’ (2008) 1(2) Contemp Asia Arbtn J 255.

[67](2002) 4 SCC 105.

[68](2012) 9 SCC 552.

impliedly excluded the application of Part I, reasoning that Section 2(2) ACA did not imply that Part I would "only" apply when the place of arbitration was in India. The provision enabling the courts to grant interim relief—contained in Part I of the Act, which concerned with domestic arbitrations—could equally be applied to foreign-seated arbitrations, unless otherwise agreed by the parties.[69]

The Constitution Bench in *BALCO* specifically addressed the territoriality principle and the primordial importance of the seat of the arbitration in explaining the nature of judicial intervention in arbitration. Through a concerted readings of Sections 2(1)(e), 20 and 26 read with Sections 45 and 48 (1)(e) it was pleaded that Indian arbitration law on foreign-seated arbitration preferred a subject-matter centric arbitration rather than a seat-centric arbitration. Rejecting this argument, the Court held that these points should be read with the "territoriality" as the focal point in view of Section 2(2). The Court held that the omission of the word "only" in Section 2(2) of the Act, which was subjected to much discussion in *Bhatia*, was not an indication of deviation from the territorial principle. *BALCO* thus presented the other binary viewpoint of the role of the local courts in foreign-seated arbitration.

While *BALCO* reaffirmed commitment to the territoriality principle and seat-centric arbitration, the decision did present a difficulty—remedies available against a party with assets located in India and likely to dissipate them pending arbitral proceedings and award. The Law Commission of India in its 246th Report on the ACA[70] (hereinafter the Report), illustrated two possibilities, neither, as it opined, being efficacious

- the latter party could obtain an interim order from a foreign Court or the arbitral tribunal itself and file a civil suit to enforce the right created by the interim order. Such order would not be enforceable directly by filing an execution petition, as it would not qualify as a "judgment" or "decree" for the purposes of Sections 13 and 44A of the Code of Civil Procedure (which provides a mechanism for enforcing foreign judgments).
- in the event that the former party does not adhere to the terms of the foreign Order, the latter party can initiate proceedings for contempt in the foreign Court and enforce the judgment of the foreign Court under Sections 13 and 44A of the Code of Civil Procedure.

The AC (Amendment) Act 2015 enabled the Indian Courts to grant interim relief in support of foreign-seated arbitrations. The reinforced Section 9 ACA with additional sub-Sections (2) and (3) permits interim relief in two circumstances

- where an Indian court orders interim relief before the commencement of the arbitral proceedings, such arbitral proceedings shall commence within 90 days

[69]Simon Greenberg, Christopher Kee, J. Romesh Weeramantry, *International Commercial Arbitration—An Asia-Pacific Perspective* (Cambridge, 2011) 366.

[70]Law Commission of India, *Amendments to the ACA, 1996* (Report 246, 2014). http://lawcommissionofindia.nic.in/reports/Report246.pdf, accessed 01 March 2016.

of such grant of interim relief by the court (or such further time as the court orders)[71];
- the jurisdiction of the courts to grant interim measures after the tribunal has been appointed is limited only to circumstances where tribunal-ordered interim measures would not be "efficacious"[72]

The amendment ensured that the Indian law related to interim relief is similar to the law existing in countries like Germany, Austria and the United States—national courts in these countries are empowered to assist foreign arbitrations.[73]

## 2 Choice of Law

Flowing from the rule of party autonomy, as expressed in parties' choice of law, international arbitration generates the possibility of at least a few legal regimes touching the dispute. Important amongst them are

- law governing the arbitration agreement (also referred to as governing law)
- law governing the arbitration procedure (curial law at the seat of arbitration), and
- law governing the underlying contract (substantive law)

While the rules of private international law relating to characterization are important for determining the law in each of these categories, the jurisprudence on international arbitration has guardedly approached this knowledge domain.[74] Nevertheless, the methods of determination developed within that knowledge domain hold significant utility in the resolution of issues connected with the applicable laws in an international arbitration.

### 2.1 *Law Governing the Arbitration Agreement*

An arbitration agreement, similar to other agreements, creates certain substantive rights for its signatories. Its governing law could be determined either according to the intention of the parties to such agreement, or in any of the following ways

- by the law where such agreement is entered into, or
- by the law where the arbitration is to take place, or

[71]ACA s 9(2).

[72]ACA s 9(3).

[73]Steinbruck (n 10) 452.

[74]Harisankar K.S., 'International Commercial Arbitration in Asia and the Choice of Law Determination' (2013) 30(6) J of Int'l Arbtn 621.

- by the law of the common nationality of the parties, or
- by any other law[75]

In the absence of the parties' choice of law, express or implied, the determination of the governing law for the arbitration agreement would be by applying the 'closest and the most real connection test'.

Two strands of judicial opinion could be derived at this point on the nature of the law governing the arbitration agreement—firstly, if there is an express choice of law to govern the whole contract, it could be presumed that the arbitration agreement would normally be governed by the same law[76] irrespective of the seat of arbitration. In *Sonatrach Petroleum Corp. v Ferrel International Ltd.*[77] the Court adopted a similar approach.

> Where the substantive contract contains an express choice of law, but the agreement to arbitrate contains no express choice of law, the latter agreement will normally be governed by the body of law expressly chosen to govern the substantive contract.[78]

The obiter in the *Sulamerica Cia Nacional De Seguros SA & Others v Enesa Engenharia SA & Others*[79] restated the above-mentioned proposition - 'an express choice of law governing the substantive contract' operates as a strong indication of the parties' intention in relation to the agreement to arbitrate.[80] Gary Born commented that the English courts while holding that the arbitration agreement's governing law could be the law of the substantive contract, adopted the rubric of the closest and most real connection test in the conflict of law analysis.[81]

In India, in *NTPC v Singer*[82] the Supreme Court held that where the parties made an express choice of the law governing the contract, such law must, in the unmistakable intention to the contrary, govern the arbitration agreement, which though collateral or ancillary to the main contract, is nevertheless, a part of such contract. Few other Indian courts' decisions[83] adopted similar ratio.

The second strand of the judicial opinion derived its content from the proposition that arbitration agreement being separate and independent from the underlying contract ought to be governed by a law other than the law applicable to such

---

[75]Ibid., 630.

[76]*Union of India v Mcdonnell Douglas Corp.*, [1993] 2 Lloyd's Rep 48.

[77][2002] 1 All E.R. 627.

[78]Ibid., [32].

[79][2012] EWCA Civ 638.

[80]Gary Born, 'The Law Governing International Arbitration Agreements: An International Perspective' (2014) 26 SAcLJ 815, 828. http://www.sal.org.sg/digitallibrary/Lists/SAL%20Journal/Attachments/699/(2014)%2026%20SAcLJ%20814-848%20(Intl%20Arb%20Agreements%20-%20Gary%20Born).pdf, accessed 02 March 2016.

[81]Ibid., 828.

[82](1992) 3 SCC 51.

[83]*Sumitomo v ONGC Ltd.*, (1998) 1 SCC 305; *Eitzen Bulk A.S. v Ashapura Minechem Ltd.* AIR 2011 Guj 13; *Aastha Broadcasting Network Ltd. v Thaicom Public Co. Ltd.* MANU/DE/4410/2011.

contract. Holding this view, English courts have held that the law with which the arbitration agreement has the closest connection is the law of the place of arbitration (seat of arbitration), irrespective of the governing law of the underlying contract.[84] The closest connection test borrowed from the conflict of laws domain was used to achieve a different result—in the absence of an express or implied choice of governing law for the arbitration agreement, the objective analysis of an arbitration agreement would lead to an understanding of its purpose being to arbitrate disputes; such obligation has its closest connection to the place where it is scheduled to happen, as in the seat of arbitration. Therefore the Court concluded that the arbitration agreement has its closest connection with the law at the place of arbitration.

## 2.2 *Law Governing Arbitral Procedure*

International Arbitrations, characterized as instances of procedure are subject to the laws of the chosen State. Mann commented that all dispute resolution procedures are connected to national laws and, therefore, any such procedure could not be floating in international firmament.[85] Thus *lex arbitri* governs all procedural issues. While there is an alternative view on disconnecting/delocalizing international arbitration from the seat laws and seat courts, the commonly accepted view[86] borrowed from the seat theory (territoriality principle and the jurisdiction theory) is that the *lex arbitri* is the law at the place where the tribunal is seated. A change in the geographical location of the arbitration bears no effect on the seat of the arbitration.[87] Indian courts' decisions[88] subscribe to the opinion that the seat is a juridical concept, and not a mere geographical location. It is pertinent to identify the distinction between the seat that connects the arbitration to a legal system, and the location (also known as venue) of the arbitral process, as in the place where some hearings of the arbitration may be held. In *PT Garuda Indonesia v Bergein Air*[89] averring to the difference between an agreed seat of the arbitration and a venue of convenience to the parties, the Court opined that where the parties have agreed upon the seat of arbitration, it does not affect the fact that the tribunal could have held its proceedings at a convenient location. The distinction between the seat of arbitration and the location of the proceedings has

---

[84] *Sulamérica CIA Nacional De Seguros S.A. v Enesa Engenharia S.A.*, [2012] EWHC 42; *Abuja Int'l Hotels Ltd. v Meridien SAS*, [2012] EWHC 87.

[85] Editors' Note, 'The UNCITRAL Model Law: Lex Facit Arbitrum' (1986) 2(3) Arbtn Int'l 241.

[86] (n 74) 632.

[87] (n 76).

[88] See for example *Dozco India P. Ltd. v Doosan Infracore Co. Ltd.* (2011) 6 SCC 179; *Videocon Industries v Union of India* (2011) 6 SCC 161.

[89] *PT Garuda Indonesia v Bergein Air* (2002) S.G.C.A. 12.

been clarified by the Indian Supreme Court in the *BALCO*[90] decision and the primacy of the seat of arbitration reinforced.

## 2.3 Substantive Law Applicable to the Merits of the Dispute

International arbitral tribunals could also be called to determine the substantive law applicable to the dispute. Unlike the other two aspects of arbitration agreement and the arbitral procedure, the UNCITRAL ML has provided guidance for such determination. Article 28 states that the tribunal shall decide the dispute in accordance with such rules of law as chosen by the parties, such choice only referring to the substantive law of that state and not inclusive of its conflict of laws rules. Failing such party choice, the tribunal shall apply the law determined by the conflict of laws rules that it may consider applicable. The arbitral tribunal, upon parties' authorization, could also decide the dispute *ex aequo et bono*. The tribunal shall consider the trade usages applicable to the transaction.

Party autonomy in international contracts extends to the choice of governing law of the contract, such choice being appropriate and bona fide and legal.[91] While there is not much case law to explain 'bona fide' and 'legal', there have been commentaries alluding to States setting a connection requirement for the chosen law.[92]

Indian Arbitration Law, in a deviation from the UNCITAL ML, specified a direct approach in selecting the substantive law.[93] Section 28(1)(b) specified that in the absence of parties' express or implied choice of law the tribunal shall apply the rules of law that it considers appropriate, the reference being to 'rules of law' and not 'conflict of laws' rules.[94] While this approach could be with an intention to eliminate complexities that might arise in the application of private international law rules, there does exist a space for uncertainty, as it leaves little guidance to the tribunal in the choice of appropriate law, given the fact that there is no *lex fori* in

---

[90](n 68).

[91]*Vita Food Products Inc. v Unus Shipping Co. Ltd.* [1939] A.C.277 (PC).

[92]Gokhan Aytar, 'Party Autonomy, Choice of Law and Wrap Contracts' (Thesis, University of Oslo 2012). https://www.duo.uio.no/bitstream/handle/10852/34430/1/8014.pdf, accessed10 March 2016.

[93]See, generally, on the direct approach, Doug Jones, (n 7) 914.

[94]Rules applicable to substance of dispute:- (1) (b) in international commercial arbitration,——

(i) the arbitral tribunal shall decided the dispute in accordance with the rules of law designated by the parties as applicable to the substance of the dispute;
(ii) any designation by the parties of the law or legal system of a given country shall be construed, unless otherwise expressed, as directly referring to the substantive law of that country and not to its conflict of laws rules;
(iii) failing any designation of the law under clause (a) by the parties, the arbitral tribunal shall apply the rules of law it considers to be appropriate given all the circumstances surrounding the dispute.

international arbitration. Further, according to Section 28(2) the tribunal would decide '*ex aequo et bono*' only with the express authorization of the parties.

The AC (Amendment) Act, 2015 reworded the Section 28(3) to specify that the tribunal while deciding and making an award shall take into account terms and usages of trade applicable to the transaction.[95]

## 3 Recognition and Enforcement of Foreign Arbitral Awards

India is a founding member of the NYC, having signed and ratified it, with reservations—commercial and reciprocity. Part II of the ACA specified the process for enforcement of foreign arbitral awards.

Section 44 defines a foreign award as an award from a country that is a signatory to the NYC and that has been 'notified' by the Government of India.[96] A little over a third NYC-signatory countries have been notified by the Government in the Official Gazette—China, Hong Kong and Macao have been added in 2012. In 1998 the Supreme Court decided[97] the question of enforceability of an award given in a non-notified country, Ukraine. The Court held that the creation of a new political entity would not make any difference to the enforceability of the award rendered in a territory that was initially part of a notified territory. The judgment exemplified the willingness of Indian courts to overcome technicalities and support enforcement of the foreign awards.[98]

The designated court shall decide upon an application of the party seeking enforcement of a foreign award; upon an order of the court such award becomes enforceable as a decree of the court and executable as such.[99] Further, the foreign

[95] s 28(3) While deciding and making an award, the arbitral tribunal shall, in all cases, take into account the terms of the contract and trade usages applicable to the transaction.

[96] ACA, Section 44. foreign award means an arbitral award on differences between persons arising out of legal relationships, whether contractual or not, considered as commercial under the law in force in India, made on or after the 11th day of October, 1960–

(a) in pursuance of an agreement in writing for arbitration to which the Convention set forth in the First Schedule applies, and
(b) in one of such territories as the Central Government, being satisfied that reciprocal provisions have been made may, by notification in the Official Gazette, declare to be territories to which the said Convention applies.

[97] *Transocean Shipping Agency Pvt Ltd v Black Sea Shipping & Ors.* 1998 (2) SCC 281.

[98] Sumeet Kachwaha, 'Enforcement of Arbitration Awards in India' (2008) 4(1) Asian Int'l Arbtn J 64, 76.

[99] *Fuerst Day Lawson Ltd. v Jindal Exports Ltd.*, (2001) 6 SCC 356 (370).

awards, enforceable under Part II of the ACA, are deemed to be a decree of the courts and hence, enforced as such pursuant to the Code of Civil Procedure, 1908.[100]

## *3.1 Designated Court for Filing Enforcement Application*

Section 47 of the Act, whilst dealing with enforcement of certain foreign awards has defined the term "court" as a court having jurisdiction over the subject-matter of the award. This has a clear reference to a court within whose jurisdiction the asset/person is located, against which/whom the enforcement of the international arbitral award is sought.[101] Where the subject matter of the award is money, the enforcement application can be filed in the court within whose jurisdiction the bank account of the respondent is located. Therefore, a party seeking to enforce a foreign award can file the application in any court in India as long as the money asset is located within the jurisdiction of the court in which he intends to file the application. If the applicant does not find money in the account maintained by the Respondent within the court's jurisdiction, he may file another application for enforcement of the award in the court within whose jurisdiction respondent's assets are located.[102] The expression 'subject matter' of the award to the explanation under Section 47 is different from the expression subject matter of the arbitration under Section 2(e) of Part I of the Act.[103] If the subject matter of the award is not money then the party seeking to enforce is seeking to ensure that the award is implemented by the respondent and enforcing party's rights and interest are given effect to. Therefore, a successful party in order to enforce and execute an award has to initiate legal proceeding as envisaged under Section 47 of the Act.

## *3.2 Evidence Required for Enforcement*

Section 47 specifies that a party applying for the enforcement of a foreign award in India must at the time of filing of the application submit to the Court the following evidence

(a) the original award or a copy thereof, duly authenticated in the manner required by the law of the country in which it was made;
(b) the original agreement for arbitration or a duly certified thereof; and
(c) such evidence as may be necessary to prove that the award is a foreign award.

---

[100]ACA, Ss 49, 58.

[101](n 57).

[102]*Wireless Developers Inc v India Games Ltd.*, 2012 (2) ARBLR 397 (Bom).

[103]*Tata International v Trisuns Chemical*, 2002 (2) Bom CR 88.

Sub Section (2) clarifies that where such an award is in a foreign language, the party applying for enforcement shall produce an English translation of the same certified as correct by a diplomatic or consular agent of the country to which that party belongs or certified as correct in such other manner as may be sufficient according to the law in force in India. The burden of proving that the award sought to be enforced is a genuine 'foreign award' and based on a foreign agreement for arbitration, is on the party seeking to enforce it by moving an application for enforcement. The aforesaid documents shall form prima facie evidence to prove that the award is a genuine foreign award. The applicant, i.e. party applying for the enforcement of a foreign award is not required to produce any further evidence.[104]

## 3.3 *Absence of Appeal Against Order on Enforcement of Award*

The ACA does not allow an appeal against an order of the court for the enforcement of a foreign award. If the court were satisfied that the foreign award is enforceable, the award itself would be deemed to be a decree of the court.[105] The procedural formality for the court to pronounce judgment and a decree to follow on that basis is omitted. Further, the possibility of the decree being in excess of, or not in accordance with the award is also removed. It is for this reason that Section 50(1)(b)[106] of the Act provides for an appeal only against an order refusing to enforce a foreign award under Section 48.

## 3.4 *Challenge Against Enforcement*

Section 48 specifies the grounds that could be invoked to resist an enforcement application. A foreign award will not be enforced in India if,

- it is proved by the party against whom it is sought to be enforced that the parties to the agreement were, under the law applicable to them, under some incapacity, or,
- the agreement was not valid under the law to which the parties have subjected it, or, in the absence of any indication thereon, under the law of the place of arbitration; or there was no due compliance with the rules of fair hearing; or

---

[104] *Glencore Grain Rotterdam B.V. v Shivnath Rai Harnarain (India) Co.*, 2008 (4) ARBLR 497 (Delhi).

[105] ACA, s 49—Enforcement of foreign awards. Where the Court is satisfied that the foreign award is enforceable under this Chapter, the award shall be deemed to be a decree of that Court.

[106] ACA, s 50—Appealable orders—(1) An appeal shall lie from the order refusing to- (a) refer the parties to arbitration under Section 45; (b) enforce a foreign award under Section 48, to the court authorised by law to hear appeals from such order. (2) No second appeal shall lie from an order passed in appeal under this section, but nothing in this section shall affect or take away any right to appeal to the Supreme Court.

- the award exceeded the scope of the submission to arbitration; or
- the composition of the arbitral authority or its procedure was not in accordance with the agreement of the parties, or, failing such agreement, was not in accordance with the law of the place of arbitration; or
- the award has not yet become binding on the parties, or has been set aside or suspended by a competent authority of the country in which, or under the law of which, that award was made.[107]

The court could refuse enforcement of a foreign award if it dealt with a subject matter incapable of settlement by arbitration under Indian law or the enforcement of the award is contrary to the public policy.[108] The burden of proof is on the party against whom a foreign award is sought to be enforced to prove that the arbitral procedure was not in accordance with the *lex arbitri*. If the respondent's reply to the application for enforcement contains ground(s) mentioned in sub-Section (1) of Section 48, the respondent would be called upon to furnish to the court proof of the existence of any one or more such grounds as mentioned in clauses (a) to (e) of sub-Section (1) of Section 48 of the Act. The word 'proof' would necessarily imply the establishment of the alleged fact through oral and documentary evidence as well as depositions of witnesses in relation to matters of fact under inquiry. The proceedings under Part II of the Act would not be treated as a suit. However, a party requesting the court to refuse the enforcement of foreign award will be entitled to lead evidence in support of the grounds.[109]

### 3.4.1 Public Policy—Refusal of Enforcement of Foreign Arbitral Award

Public policy as a ground for refusing enforcement of a foreign arbitral award has had universal acceptance, tempered upon each country's national needs. Some common features found within the conceptual understanding in many national jurisdictions are public good and public interest.[110]

The NYC specified that recognition and enforcement of the award may be refused, at the request of the party against whom it is invoked only if that party furnishes to the competent authority where the enforcement is sought, sufficient proof that, amongst other grounds, the recognition or enforcement of the award would be contrary to the public policy of that country.

The UNCITRAL ML stated that an arbitral award, irrespective of the country in which it is made shall be recognized as binding and upon an application to the

[107]ACA, s 48.

[108]Ibid., s 48(b)(1) & (2).

[109]*Ittgrani Spa v Shivnath Rai*, MANU/DE/1130/2005.

[110]Sai Ramani Garimella, 'Emerging Public Policy Contours: Is Indian arbitration moving closer to the Asian Scenario?' (2013) 2(1) AALCO J of Int'l L 55.

competent court shall be enforced.[111] Such recognition may be refused, amongst other grounds, on the ground that the recognition or enforcement of the award would be contrary to the public policy of this State.[112]

The UNCITRAL Report stated–

> It was understood that the term 'public policy', which was used in the 1958 New York Convention and many other treaties, covered fundamental principles of law and justice in substantive as well as procedural respects. Thus instances such as corruption, bribery and fraud and similar serious cases would constitute a ground for setting aside an award.[113]

In *Renusagar Power Plant Co. v General Electric Corporation*[114] the Court, drawing inspiration from English Private International Law explanation of public policy[115] interpreted the contours of public policy—the enforcement of a foreign award would be refused on the ground that it is contrary to public policy if such enforcement would be contrary to

(a) fundamental policy of Indian law; or
(b) the interests of India; or
(c) justice and morality.[116]

In the *ONGC v Saw Pipes*[117] the Supreme Court held, in a setting aside application, that public policy ought to be interpreted 'with a wider meaning'.[118] An award would be contrary to public policy, if it was 'patently illegal' meaning thereby if the award is contrary to the substantive provisions of law or the provisions of the Act or against the terms of the contract, it would be patently illegal, and hence it is likely that a set aside proceedings under Section 34 ACA would turn into an appeal proceedings.[119]

In *Venture Global Engineering v Satyam Computer Services*,[120] following the decision in *Bhatia*[121] on the linkages between Parts I and II ACA, the Court held

---

[111] Article 35(1).

[112] Article 36(1)(b)(i) and (ii).

[113] UNCITRAL Report on the work of its 18th session, UN Doc: A/40/17, June 3–21, 1985.

[114] AIR 1994 SC 860.

[115] (i) Where the fundamental conceptions of English justice are disregarded;
(ii) Where the English conceptions of morality are infringed;
(iii) Where a transaction prejudices the interests of the United Kingdom or its good relations with foreign powers;
(iv) Where a foreign law or status offends the English conceptions of human liberty and freedom of action; Cheshire and North, *Private International Law* (12th edn, Oxford 1992) 131.

[116] Ibid., para 66.

[117] (2003) 5 SCC 705. http://judis.nic.in/supremecourt/imgs1.aspx?filename=19058.

[118] Ibid., 15.

[119] Promod Nair, 'Surveying a Decade of the 'New' Law of Arbitration In India' (2007) 23(4) Arbtrn Intl 699, 731.

[120] AIR 2008 SC 1061.

[121] (n 67).

that enforcement of foreign awards could be subjected to a challenge on the grounds of domestic public policy.

In *Phulchand Exports v OOO Patriot*,[122] the Court accepted the contention of the appellant to apply the ratio in *ONGC v Saw Pipes*[123] concerning domestic arbitrations to enforcement of foreign arbitral awards. It thus allowed parties to challenge enforcement of a foreign arbitral award on grounds of patent illegality, allowing the Indian Courts, in appropriate cases, to visit the merits of the case in enforcement proceedings.

In *Shri Lal Mahal v Progetto Grano Spa*[124] the Court overruled *Phulchand.*[125] It declined to consider the merits of a foreign arbitral award in an enforcement proceeding. Disallowing a challenge on the ground of 'patent illegality' in the enforcement proceedings, the Court stated that the scope of enquiry under Section 48(2)(b)(ii) of the ACA does not permit a review of the foreign award on merits, thus heralding a restrictive approach to public policy challenges against enforcement of foreign awards. The precedent of the *Shri Lal Mahal* has been followed in *Perma Container (UK) Line Limited v Perma Container Line (India) Pvt Ltd*[126] The Court while refusing to entertain the respondent's challenge to the foreign award contending that it is a nullity on the reasons of allegations of forgery, held that public policy ought to be construed only within the meaning attributed to it in Section 48 ACA, and opinions of the arbitrators ought not to be used to request examination of the merits of the award.

*Shri Lal Mahal* decision, of seminal importance to the jurisprudence on public policy, is however restricted to foreign-seated arbitration. The Supreme Court had an opportunity to equate Ss.34 and 48[127] but refrained from doing so, thereby retaining different thresholds for public policy in domestic and international arbitration. This differential approach of the Court gave space for a contrarian judgment in *ONGC v Western Geco.*[128]

> Even so, [fundamental policy] must, in our opinion, include all such fundamental principles as providing a basis for administration of justice and enforcement of law in this country.

The Court's dictum alluding to fundamental policy as inclusive of all fundamental principles that administration of justice is founded upon, equates it with

---

[122](2011) 10 SCC 300.

[123](n 117).

[124]Civil Appeal No. 5085 of 2013.

[125](n 120).

[126]Arbitration Petition Nos. 259 and 406 of 2013 (Bombay High Court).

[127]Arthad Kurlekar and Gauri Pillai, 'To be or not to be: the oscillating support of Indian courts to arbitration awards challenged under the public policy exception' (2016) 32(1) Arbtrn Int'l 179.

[128](2014) 9 SCC 263.

patent illegality. The Law Commission in its supplementary report[129] cautioned that the *ONGC v Western Geco* decision could shift away from the objective of minimal judicial interference on which the ACA is premised.

The 2015 Amendment revised Section 48 ACA. It specified that an award would be in conflict with public policy in India only if making of the award

- was induced or affected by fraud or corruption or
- was in violation of provisions of confidentiality or admissibility of evidence of conciliation proceedings in other proceedings; or
- is in contravention with the fundamental policy of Indian law;
- or it is in conflict with the most basic notions of morality or justice.

It further explained that such inquiry into any contravention of the fundamental policy of India did not entail an examination of the merits of the dispute.

## 3.5 *Can a Foreign Award Be Vacated in India?*

Extending the reasoning of the *Bhatia International*[130] the Supreme Court in *Venture Global*[131] extended the application of Section 34 ACA to the foreign arbitral awards. In *Venture Global* the criteria of public policy as explained in Section 34 was applied to set aside a foreign arbitral award that ordered transfer of shares, which the appellants contended as violation of public policy of India,—specifically, the criteria of patent illegality.[132] The result of this decision was that a foreign award could also be set aside on grounds included in Part I of the ACA, which was hitherto applicable only for domestic arbitration. Indian courts thus claimed jurisdiction to set aside foreign awards.

In *BALCO*[133] the Supreme Court held Part I inapplicable to foreign-seated arbitrations. The legislative intention behind Section 48 of the Arbitration Act and its demarcation from Section 34 prevented judiciary from delving into the merits of a foreign award. This reasoning given by the Court conformed to Article V, NYC. The Calcutta High Court in *Coal India Ltd v Canadian Commercial Corporation*[134] adopted the *BALCO* rationale refusing a petition that sought vacation of an ICC award on the ground that the governing law of contract was India and therefore could be set-aside under Section 34.

[129]http://lawcommissionofindia.nic.in/reports/Supplementary_to_Report_No._246.pdf, accessed 25 May 2016.

[130](n 67).

[131](n 120).

[132]Introduced into public policy by the *ONGC v Saw Pipes* (n 115).

[133](n 68).

[134](2013) 2 CHN 494.

## 4 Conclusion

With its inherent benefits like party autonomy, neutrality, expediency, expertise, confidentiality and finality, arbitration is, by far, the most promising method of dispute settlement especially in transnational commercial activities. The AC (Amendment) 2015 strengthened the legislation with some innovative features on timelines for arbitration, guidelines for fixing fees in domestic arbitration and resolving the problem of absence of interim orders jurisdiction for Indian courts in foreign-seated arbitrations, without moving from the seat-centric arbitration principle. Future efforts at arbitration law reform in India need to prioritize a few areas that require immediate address

- Ensure clarity to the methodology of determining governing law for the arbitration agreement, in the absence of an express or implied choice by the parties.
- Statutory clarity on the possibility of two or more Indian parties opting for a foreign-seated arbitration.
- Changes in the meaning and explanation of the public policy exception ought to be extended to domestic arbitration too.
- Explain the circumstances in which Indian courts would not entertain interim relief applications in foreign-seated arbitrations. This is an area that requires clarity especially because of the absence of Indian law on enforcement of foreign-seated tribunal/foreign court's interim orders.

# Issues of Jurisdiction, Choice of Law and Enforcement in International Commercial Arbitration: A Nepal Perspective

**Gandhi Pandit and Avdhesh Pant**

**Abstract** Arbitration, an accepted dispute resolution mechanism in Nepal, has been receiving increased interest in recent times, especially since the enactment of the new legislation on arbitration in 1999, attempting to harmonize the Nepalese law with the UNCITRAL Model Law as well as bring it on similarity with the other arbitration laws in the South Asian region. The Public Procurement Act and Regulations 2007 mandated ADR methods for dispute resolution in construction contracts. Interestingly, the legislation attempted to provide a structured methodology for the conduct of arbitration, and also specified timelines for the conduct and the completion of arbitration, a unique feature, especially because delayed arbitration has been a problem with many arbitral regimes within the region. This chapter attempts to showcase the Nepal Arbitration Act, 1999 and explain the jurisprudence developed in Nepal, especially related to the conduct of the arbitration and the enforcement of foreign arbitral awards.

**Keywords** Nepal Arbitration Act · Foreign investment order · Arbitrator immunity · Nepal law · Foreign arbitral awards · Enforcement

## Introduction

Enforcement mechanisms in arbitration are vital and essential so as to give pragmatic validity to arbitral awards. This is specifically true in cases wherein a party to the dispute does not comply with the arbitral award or in situations where the winning party needed to enforce arbitral award to avail the relief within it. A court or another competent body, in Nepal the district court, has the authority to enforce

G. Pandit (✉)
Faculty of Law, Nepal Law Campus, Tribhuvan University, Kathmandu, Nepal
e-mail: gandhi@lawgandhi.com

A. Pant
Gandhi and Associates, Kathmandu, Nepal

© Springer Nature Singapore Pte Ltd. 2017

S.R. Garimella and S. Jolly (eds.), *Private International Law*,
DOI 10.1007/978-981-10-3458-9_17

an award to ensure that the winning party could make a valid claim to the assets and properties of the losing party.

Arbitration, which is less formal than the court-based adjudication,[1] has been a popular choice for resolving commercial disputes. Party autonomy[2] in choosing the mode of arbitration and the applicable laws and procedure is one of its main benefits. Other reasons include privacy and confidentiality[3] flexibility of the process[4] and expertise in handling the dispute and the dispute resolution.[5]

Nepal, since the 1990s, is witnessing an increase in international commercial transactions and foreign investment. To ensure effective dispute resolution processes, Nepal amended its arbitration laws in 1999 in line with the UNCITRAL Model Law on Arbitration, 1985. Furthermore, Nepal ratified the Convention on the Recognition and Enforcement of Foreign arbitral Awards on 4th March 1998.[6]

In spite of these developments, there are no authoritative commentaries on the law of arbitration in Nepal. While there has been a reference to arbitration in many legislations, very little in the name of documentation has been pursued to chronicle the arbitrations effected under these laws. Institutional arbitration is a recent phenomenon; Nepal Council of Arbitration (NEPCA) has been established in 1991 and the Federation of Nepal Chambers of Commerce has become involved in dispute resolution through ADR mechanisms, especially arbitration. Further there have been few landmark decisions of the Supreme Court of Nepal highlighting the concerns related to the administration and development of arbitration in Nepal. It is pertinent that arbitration administration and the mechanisms related to enforcement of arbitral awards are prioritized for reform in the wake of increased foreign investment, direct as well as through transnational commercial contracts, especially in the field of construction. Furthermore, the dispute resolution process involving multi-tier dispute resolution clauses, a common feature of construction contracts in Nepal, would receive the much-needed stimulus with arbitration management. The Arbitration Act, 1999 (referred to as Arbitration Act, 2055 according to the official Nepali Calendar) has made important first steps in legislating upon the procedure of arbitration.

[1]William F. Fox, *International Commercial Agreements: A Primer On Drafting, Negotiating And Resolving Disputes* (4th ed. Kluwer, 2009), 182.

[2]R.U.S Prasad, *Resolving Disputes In Telecommunication: Global Practices And Challenges*, (Oxford, 2011).

[3](n 1) 187., Chris Carr & Michael R. Jencks, 'The Privatization of Business and Commercial Dispute Resolution: A Misguided Policy Decision' (2000) 88(2) *Kentucky Law Journal* 183, 187 (2000). Available at http://ssrn.com/abstract=308767, accessed on 3 June 2016.

[4]Ibid.

[5]Id.

[6]Available at http://www.newyorkconvention.org/list+of+contracting+states, accessed on 12 June 2016.

**Structure of the Chapter**

This chapter attempts to present the law related to arbitration in Nepal, with regard to the provisions related to jurisdiction, applicable law, and the recognition and enforcement of foreign arbitral awards. While presenting the statutory features this research chapter would attempt to critically evaluate the features for their contribution to facilitating enforcement of foreign arbitral awards, through judicial opinion. The chapter begins with mapping the history of arbitration legislation in Nepal. It will then attempt to discuss the provisions of the Arbitration Act, (AA) 1999, contextualizing them with the UNCITRAL Model Law, especially for the clarity that they provide with regard to the arbitration agreement, constitution and functioning of the tribunal and the timelines for arbitration. There is a discussion on the statutory provisions related to jurisdiction of the tribunal and the role of the courts with regard to jurisdictional issues related to the tribunal, followed by a discussion on the statutory provisions related to applicable law. The last section of the chapter discusses the statutory provisions related to recognition and enforcement of arbitral awards in Nepal.

## 1 History of Arbitration Legislation in Nepal

Arbitration in Nepal has had its traditional beginnings in the system of *Panchayat* (an informal tribunal of five gentlemen chosen from amongst the villagers) to render an impartial decision in the dispute settlement process.[7] The history of modern arbitration is brief and scattered, till 1981 when the first legislation related to arbitration was enacted. There were statutory provisions referring to arbitration as a dispute settlement mechanism for various kinds of disputes, including commercial and contractual. One such provision was section 9 of the Development Board Act, 1957 that provided for the resolution of a dispute under a contract to which the Board is a party. The objective behind such provisions introducing arbitral process for dispute resolution could be attributed to the need for inviting foreign capital and technology for economic enhancement and fostering development plans and industrialization in the country.[8]Furthermore, the Royal Nepal Airlines Corporation Act, 1962 contained a provision specifying that an arbitrator appointed by the Government of Nepal arbitrate any contractual dispute between the members or any official of the corporation. The Petroleum Act, 1983 stated that any dispute relating to a petroleum agreement that could not be amicably resolved be settled through arbitration.[9]

---

[7]Bharat B. Karki, 'UNCITRAL Model Law on International Commercial Arbitration (1985) and Nepalese Arbitration Law' (2005) 15 *NEPCA Half Yearly Bulletin* 8.

[8]Bed Prasad Uprety, 'Evolution of Commercial Arbitration in Nepal' (2008) 2(1) NJA L J 205, 208.

[9]Ibid., 211.

The judiciary has noted that arbitration has been a chosen method of dispute resolution - Nepalese government and statutory bodies were entering into contracts with various local companies[10] as well as international bodies (such as the World Bank) wherein arbitration was the mode of dispute resolution. This was despite the fact that Nepalese legal system did not have law relating to arbitration and enforcement mechanisms for arbitral awards.[11] Nepal promulgated its first statute specifically dealing with Arbitration, i.e. the Arbitration Act, 2038 (1981).

In 1981, Nepal enacted its first statute regulating foreign investment into Nepal, i.e. the Foreign Investment and Technology Transfer Act, 2038, FITTA 1981. Section 17 of the Act specified dispute resolution between the foreign investor and the local investor by way of arbitration.[12] Any dispute between the foreign investor, concerned industry and the Department of Industry[13] which cannot be settled mutually could be submitted to arbitration under the prevailing UNCITRAL rules.[14] Furthermore, the seat of arbitration had to be Kathmandu, Nepal and the law of arbitration had to be the Nepalese Law.[15] This provision was slightly modified in the Foreign Investment and Technology Transfer Act, 2047 (1992) ("FITTA 1992"). As per section 7 of FITTA, 1992 disputes that couldn't be resolved amicably must be settled through arbitration must be done as per the UNCTIRAL rules.[16] Furthermore, if the investment is less than Nepali Rupees 500 million, then the seat of arbitration must be Kathmandu, Nepal.[17] However, if the investment is Nepali Rupees 500 million or more, then the parties are free to choose a mode of dispute resolution.[18] While the monetary limit restriction is not in line with the contemporary practice worldwide[19] it was nevertheless a step forward for Nepal in terms of promoting the use of arbitration for the resolution of international commercial disputes.

FITTA 1981 was promulgated around two months before the Arbitration Act, 1981.[20] Considering that the FITTA 1981 contained a provision with regard to resolution of disputes through arbitration, it is but natural for Nepal to have finally adopted a statute that contained provisions for the recognition and enforcement of

---

[10] *Anang Man Sherchan v Chief Engineer of RTO*, Ne.Ka.Pa. 2020, issue 1, part 6, decision no. 220, 13/03/2064.

[11] The General Code (Muluki Ain), 1920(1963) governs the mechanism for enforcement of court judgments in Nepal. However, till date, the provision of the General Code, 1963 has not been updated in line with availability of different modes of dispute resolution.

[12] Foreign Investment and Technology Transfer Act, 2038 (1981), section 17(1).

[13] Foreign investment regulatory organization.

[14] (n 12) s 17(2).

[15] Ibid., s 17(3).

[16] Foreign Investment and Technology Transfer Act, 2047 (1992), section 17(2).

[17] Ibid., s 17(3).

[18] Id, s 7(4).

[19] Alan Redfern, et al., *Redfern And Hunter On International Arbitration* (Oxford University Press, 5th Ed., 2009).

[20] Arbitration Act, 2038 (1981).

arbitral awards and exclusively for arbitration. The Arbitration Act of 1981 specified that the parties to the agreement could choose the existing rules or make their own rules of dispute settlement, not contrary to the law.[21]

The 1981 Act was repealed in 1999 through the promulgation of the Arbitration Act, 2055 (1999) (hereinafter, the 1999 Act).[22] The causes for the repeal included, amongst others, it's ineffectiveness owing to unnecessary delay and interference by the courts in the arbitration process.[23] The 1999 Act is based upon the UNICTRAL Model Law on International Commercial Arbitration (hereinafter, the UNCITRAL ML) as well as the Convention on the Enforcement and Recognition of Foreign Arbitral Awards (hereinafter, the NYC). However, there are substantial differences in the 1999 Act in comparison to the UNCITRAL ML and the NYC with regard to enforcement of arbitral awards.

## 2 Arbitration Act, 2055, 2056 (1999)—Few Features

The 1999 Act comprises of 44 sections and 1 schedule arranged into six chapters. It discusses the process of arbitration, beginning with the arbitration agreement, the role of the courts in relation to arbitration, and finally the process of recognition and enforcement of a foreign arbitral award in Nepal. Surprisingly enough the legislation does not make a distinction between domestic and international arbitration. It restricts itself to discussing the law applicable to arbitration in disputes connected with the Nepal law and courts, or that would require enforcement-related activities in Nepal.

### *2.1 Arbitration Agreement*

The 1999 Act views the arbitration agreement as the foundation of arbitration. It specifies that a valid arbitration agreement has to address settlement of any dispute concerning any specific legal issue, contractual or otherwise.[24] While it clarifies on the form of the agreement or a submission clause in a contract, stating that any electronic transfer of an offer and acceptance to arbitration, the documentation of such exchange being available, would constitute an arbitration agreement,[25] it has stayed away from the language of the UNCITRAL ML by avoiding the usage of the

[21]Ibid., s 5(2); Also, Bindeshwar Yadav, 'Problems faced in Nepal in the Settlement of Disputes Through Arbitration' (2059) 11 NEPCA Half-yearly Bulletin 8 (2004).

[22]Arbitration Act, 2055 (1999), s 10(1).

[23]Karki (n 7) 09.

[24](n 22) s 2(a).

[25]Ibid., s 2(a)(2).

terminology 'defined legal relationship'.[26] Further the legislation also specified that absence of an objection to the other party's claim for reference to arbitration would also be considered within the meaning of an arbitration agreement.[27] The Act also provided for counter claim and rejoinder. A counter-claim is explained as a claim made by the respondent against the claimants.[28] A rejoinder refers to a claim to a counter-claim, made by the claimants.[29]

Courts in Nepal have insisted on compliance with a valid arbitration agreement. For example, in *Rakesh Kumar v Ram Krishna Rawal*[30] the Supreme Court clearly established the principle that no court will have primary jurisdiction over a dispute arising out of a contract in which parties have agreed upon arbitration as the form of dispute resolution.

## 2.2 Separability

This is a new provision of the arbitration law articulated in Section 16 of the 1999 Act. Section 16(3) specified the separability principle in the following words

> (3) For the purpose of taking a decision on the validity or effectiveness of a contract pursuant to Sub-Sect. (1), in case the contract contains provisions for the settlement of disputes through arbitration as its integral part, such provisions shall be taken as a separate agreement, and even if the arbitrator takes a decision holding the contract as null and void, such provisions shall not be held to be legally null and void for that reason alone.

According to section 16(3), the arbitration clause embedded in the contract can be separated ipso facto from the contract even if an arbitrator or court invalidated the main contract. This provision conforms to the generally accepted feature of international arbitration—the arbitration clause stands as a distinct agreement by itself and survives despite the invalidity of the main contract.

## 2.3 Subject-Matter Arbitrability

There isn't a specific legal provision in Nepal with regard to subject-matter arbitrability. Nevertheless inferences can be made from the 1999 Act and the civil code of Nepal, The General Code (*Muluki Ain*), 1920 and the jurisprudence under the 1981 Arbitration Act (now repealed).

---

[26]UNCITRAL ML, 1985 Article 7(1).

[27](n 22) s 2(a)(3).

[28]Ibid., s 2(g).

[29]Id, s 2(h).

[30]Nepal Law Digest/Ne Ka Pa, 2066 decision No. 8078, page 272, Division Bench.

As per section 34(2)(c) of the 1999 Act, subject to the provisions of the NYC and the declaration made by Nepal at the time of accession, a foreign award would be enforceable if it is "only to subject matters referred to the arbitrator."[31] Nepal acceded to the NYC with the commercial reservation.[32] Hence, reading this declaration along with section 34(2)(c) of the 1999 Act, the foreign arbitral award, to be enforceable in Nepal, must be confined to subject matters referred to the arbitrator and furthermore, these subject matters must have arisen out of commercial legal relationship.

Furthermore, a foreign arbitral award would be unenforceable in Nepal, if the award "is detrimental to public policy."[33] The law has left the import of the phrase "detrimental to public policy" to interpretation of the court. The 1999 Act provides that a foreign arbitral award should not be recognized if the dispute on which the foreign award has been made couldn't have been arbitrable under the Laws of Nepal.[34] Matters that are arbitrable have not been clearly defined under the 1999 Act. Section 2(e) of the 1999 Act contains the definition of dispute, *inter alia*, 'dispute which can be arbitrable under the laws of Nepal'.[35]While the 1999 Act did not identify the matters arbitrable, the matters capable of settlement through compromise could be inferred from the laws of Nepal. As per number 182 of court management section of the *Muluki Ain*, cases of corruption and criminal cases with state prosecution, cannot be dealt with through compromise.[36] It could therefore be inferred that any other civil or commercial matters can be arbitrable so long as the parties to the contract have agreed to do so as per the contract.

## 2.4 *Arbitrators' Immunity*

There has been no legislative provision assuring the arbitrator of immunity with regard to his role within the arbitral tribunal. In *M.D. Chandra Krishna Jha v Pro. Dinesh Bhakta* et al.[37] the Supreme Court ordered a counter affidavit to be submitted by the members (arbitrators) of the arbitral tribunal. The policy implication of such an order could flow much beyond the arbitration. It could also be that a person might be unwilling to function as an arbitrator in the future because he/she may face litigation even if he/she is acting in good faith. Some standards should be developed. As a general rule, an arbitrator enjoys testimonial immunity and may not be required to testify regarding the merits of an award. In this case, the Court held

[31](n 22) s 34(2)(c).

[32]Convention on Enforcement of Foreign Arbitral Awards, 1958, Article 1.

[33](n 22) s 34(3)(b).

[34]Ibid., s 34(3)(a).

[35]Id, s 2(e).

[36]The General Code (*Muluki Ain*), 1920, no. 182 of Court Management.

[37]NKP.285 (SC 2059).

that if there are no further avenues for appeal after trying all possible remedies in the Appellate Court, writ jurisdiction could be allowed in the Supreme Court. Following this precedent, every dispute falling within the purview of section 30[38] that discussed the power of the court to invalidate an award, would allow a writ application to the Supreme Court if the parties were interested to check the validity of award. This would open the floodgates for the supervisory and revisionary powers of the court, with the courts sitting as an appellate body for any party, including the recalcitrant one. It must be stated here that the Nepalese law is still in its evolutionary stages, and a statutory statement detailing the powers, role and immunity available to the arbitrator could be of significant help in establishing arbitration as an effective mechanism for resolution of transnational commercial disputes.

The legislation enacted a detailed structure with regard to the arbitrators and the process of functioning of the tribunal. Reposing faith in the principle of party autonomy, the legislation has prescribed a detailed procedure for appointing arbitrators, as a default procedure, activated when the parties did not decide upon it in their arbitration agreement. Section 5(1) specifies that subject to the parties' choice, the number of arbitrators shall be three. The importance of reaching a decision by majority seemed to be the legislative intention, the Act prescribed that in case the

---

[38]Circumstances in which decision may be invalidated: (1) Any party dissatisfied with the decision taken by the arbitrator may, if one wishes to invalidate the decision file a petition to the Appellate Court along-with the related documents and a copy of the decision within 35 days from the date the decision heard or notice received thereof under this Act. Petition shall also supply a copy of that petition to the arbitrator and the other party.

(2) In case a petition is filed pursuant Sub-section (1) the Appellate Court may, in case the petitioner proves that the arbitration decision contains any of the following matters, invalidate that decision or issue an order to have a fresh decision taken as per necessity: (a) In case any party to the agreement was incompetent for any reason to sign the agreement at the time of signing the agreement, or in case the agreement is not valid under the law of that the nation which governs jurisdiction over the parties, or in case such law is not clear and agreement is not valid under the laws of Nepal.

(b) In case the due petition was not given a notice to appoint an arbitrator or about the arbitration proceedings in time.

(c) In case the decision has been taken on a that disputed matter which had not been referred to the arbitrator, or

in a manner contrary to the conditions prescribed for the arbitrator, or by acting beyond the jurisdiction prescribed for the arbitrator.

(d) Except when an agreement has been signed contrary to the laws of Nepal, in case the procedure of designation of arbitrators or their functions and actions do not to the agreement signed between the parties, or in case there is no such agreement it has not been done as per this Act.

(3) Notwithstanding anything contained in Sub-section (2), the Appellate Court may invalidate the decision of the arbitrator in the following circumstances in case a petition is filed pursuant to Sub-section (1):

(a) In case the dispute settled by the arbitrator cannot be settled through arbitration under the laws of Nepal.

(b) In case the decision taken by the arbitrator is likely to be prove detrimental to the public interests or policies.

number of arbitrators appointed under the agreement is an even one, it shall be turned into an odd one by designating an additional arbitrator chosen by them.[39] Further, the legislation also provided for a timeline for initiating the arbitration. It specified that subject to arbitration agreement, the process of appointing arbitrators must be started within 30 days from the date when the dispute for arbitration arose.[40] While reposing faith in the principle of party autonomy, the Act suggested a default procedure with regard to appointment of arbitrators to the tribunal. The Act specified that if the parties could not reach an agreement on the choice for the third arbitrator, each party shall appoint one arbitrator and the arbitrators so appointed shall appoint a third arbitrator, who shall work as chief arbitrator.[41] It is not clear if the role of the chief arbitrator is the same as the presiding arbitrator. Parties could also apply to the Appellate Court for appointment of a tribunal of three arbitrators.

A unique feature of the 1999 Act (not usually found in Arbitration Acts) is the requirement of a written oath by the arbitrator, sworn to impartiality and honesty, in the format prescribed in the Schedule to the Act. A copy is to be sent to the Appellate Court. This provision presupposes that issues that present a reasonable doubt about the impartiality or independence of an arbitrator ought to be cleared by the arbitrator before signing the oath.[42]

Further, the legislation prescribed a few qualifications for the person appointed as an arbitrator. A person to be appointed as an arbitrator, must not be,

(a) disqualified for entering into contracts as per prevailing laws.
(b) punished by a court on criminal charges involving moral turpitude.
(c) an insolvent or been declared bankrupt.
(d) possess personal interest in the dispute which has to be settled through arbitration.
(e) does not possess the specific qualification as specified in the agreement for becoming eligible for appointment as an arbitrator.[43]

An interesting feature of the Arbitration Act of Nepal is the detailing with regarding to the claim and the subsequent pleadings of the parties, and annexures thereto.[44] The legislation also specified the timeline for the arbitral process as well as the limitation rules. Subject to the arbitration agreement or an agreement between the parties providing for a time schedule the following time-limits having being statutorily prescribed.

(1) claims are to be filed within three months from the date when the dispute arose or when the arbitrator is appointed (whichever is later);

---

[39](n 22) s 5(2).

[40]Ibid., s 6(1).

[41]Id, s 6(2)–(4).

[42]Id, s 9(1)–(2).

[43]Id, s 10.

[44]Id, s 14.

(2) objection and counter-claims to the claim is to be filed within thirty days from the date of receipt of the claim; counter-claims would be made within fifteen days of receipt of the claim.
(3) rejoinders/objection to counter-claims shall be filed within fifteen days of filing of the counter-claim. The arbitrator is empowered to extend the time limit for not more than seven days.

In *Rajendra Man Sherchan v Appellate Court, Patan*[45] the Supreme Court ruled that the process of appointing an arbitrator has to commence within three months from the date the dispute arises. Similar orders on limitation were issued by the Supreme Court in *Nepal Industrial and Commercial Bank Ltd v Arbitrators and ors.*[46]

## 2.5 Jurisdiction of the Arbitral Tribunal

Nepal's arbitration law conforms to the principle of competence-competence, which allows the arbitral tribunal to hear and decide upon challenges to jurisdiction.[47] It is pertinent here to quote the UNCITRAL ML's guidance on the power of the tribunal to make jurisdictional rulings. Article 16 paragraph 3 states,

> (3) The arbitral tribunal may rule on a plea referred to in paragraph (2) of this article either as a preliminary question or in an award on the merits. If the arbitral tribunal rules as a preliminary question that it has jurisdiction, any party may request, within thirty days after having received notice of that ruling, the court specified in article 6 to decide the matter, which decision shall be subject to no appeal; while such a request is pending, the arbitral tribunal may continue the arbitral proceedings and make an award.

However, the Arbitration Act, 1999 prescribed an elaborate procedure whereby challenges to the jurisdictional rulings by the tribunal could be presented to the courts. The first application of challenge to the jurisdiction shall be presented to the tribunal, on the following grounds,

- claims by a party that the arbitrator did not possess jurisdiction to hear the dispute
- the contract from which the dispute originated was a nullity and hence, void or is itself illegal

---

[45](Nepal Law Digest/Ne Ka Pa, 2064 Decision No. 7823, page 326, Division Bench).

[46](Writ No. 062-WO-2886, decision date BS 2069.6.1/17 September 2012).

[47]In Germany this doctrine, known as *Kompetenz-kompetenz* meant that arbitrators could make a final ruling on their jurisdiction, there being no subsequent review of the decision by any court. The German Law has, since, aligned much with the UNCITRAL ML thus moving away from the strict no-review standard. See, Klaus Peter Berger, 'Germany Adopts the UNCITRAL Model Law' (1998) 1(3) Int'l Arbtn. L Rev. 121, 122.

The tribunal, would first address and dispose the challenges to jurisdiction or the validity or effectiveness of the contract before starting the proceeding on the matter referred to it.[48]

The 1999 Act has allowed an appeal against such decision of the tribunal on jurisdiction. It specified that a party not satisfied with the tribunal's decision may file an appeal with the Appellate Court within 30 days from the date of decision, and the decision taken by that court on the matter shall be final.[49] The filling of a petition with the Appellate Court shall not be deemed to have prejudiced the power of the arbitrator to continue the proceedings and pronounce the decision before the petition is finally disposed of by the court.

Interestingly, Nepal's courts have been diffident with regard to hearing appeals on the appointment of arbitrators to the tribunal, holding that the tribunal's decision would prevail.[50]

Regarding the binding nature of the arbitration agreement towards the third parties, the Supreme Court held[51] that an arbitrator's ad hoc order to stop bank guarantees was *ultra vires* and illegal. The Court said that the arbitrator has no such legal power to enforce a bank guarantee because it is a matter related to a different contract between the plaintiff and the Nepal Bank Ltd. who was a third party.

## 3 Choice of Law

The primary advantage of international arbitration, flowing from the principle of party autonomy, is the right of the parties to choose the governing law, i.e. the applicable law for their arbitration agreement, and by logical extension to the arbitral procedure. In matters of applicable law, the position of Nepal is substantially different from the other countries. For instance, in *Sulamérica Cia Nacional De Seguros S.A. and others v Enesa Engenharia S.A*[52] the court propounded a three pronged test to enunciate the choice of law provisions,

(i) is there an express choice of law governing the arbitration agreement;
(ii) if not, can a choice be implied; and
(iii) in the absence of a choice, with which law does the arbitration agreement have the "closest and most real connection".

[48]Arbitration Act, 2056 (1999) s 16(1).

[49]Ibid., s 16(2).

[50]*G.M. Water Supply Corporation v Middle Regional Court*, NKP. 624 (SC 2044) (decided under the now repealed Arbitration Act, 1981; there has been no judicial precedent under the Arbitration Act, 1999).

[51]*On behalf of NEE, Kriti Chand v Appellate Court Patan* et al. (2055).

[52][2012] EWCA Civ 638.

This law is most likely to be the law of the seat of arbitration, rather than the governing law of the substantive contract. The last two stages of inquiry will often merge into each other. The dictum was reiterated in the case of *Habas Sinai.*[53] There is not much legislative statement with regard to the choice of law within the Arbitration Act, 1999. The Arbitration Act, 1999 specified default rules. The Act empowers the parties to choose explicitly the applicable law of their choice.[54] However, if the arbitration agreement is silent on this regard, the arbitrators will not inquire into the intention of the parties and the law of Nepal would be the substantive law applicable to the dispute. Significantly, keeping in line with the international practice, the tribunal would, if parties chose to, settle the dispute according to the principle of justice and conscience (*Ex aqua et bono*) or natural justice (*amiable compositeur*). Another interesting feature of the legislation is that it mandates the arbitrator to decide the dispute based on the agreed contract and while doing so take notice of the applicable commercial usages.[55]

Regarding the possible conflicts between the Arbitral Rules and the Laws of Nepal, in *Bikram Pandey v Ministry of Physical Planning and Construction*[56] the Supreme Court came up with a new interpretation to simplify the arbitration procedure. It ruled that internationally recognized rules like the UNCITRAL Arbitration Rules may govern arbitration, but when such rules come into conflict with domestic laws the provisions of domestic law will apply. The Supreme Court further ruled that, even if the parties agree to conduct arbitration under the UNCITRAL Arbitration Rules, their failure to name an appointing authority in the arbitration agreement will not give automatic authority under the UNCITRAL Rules to designate an appointing authority and that the Appellate Court will have jurisdiction to act as appointing authority.

## 4 Recognition and Enforcement of Foreign Arbitral Awards

At the time of acceding to the NYC Nepal in 1998 made the following declaration:

> [Nepal] will apply the Convention, on the basis of reciprocity, to the recognition and enforcement of awards made only in the territory of another contracting state. [The Government of Nepal] further declares that the Kingdom of Nepal will apply the Convention only to the differences arising out of legal relationship, whether contractual or not, which are considered as commercial under the law of the Kingdom of Nepal.[57]

---

[53] *Habas Sinai Ve Tibbi Gazlar Istihsal Endustrisi AS v VSC Steel Company Ltd* [2013] EWHC 4071.

[54] (n 22) s 18.

[55] Ibid., s 18(3).

[56] Nepal Law Digest/Ne Ka Pa, 2067 Decision No. 8437, p1346, Division Bench.

[57] http://www.newyorkconvention.org/list+of+contracting+states, accessed 15 September 2016.

This declaration specifies that Nepal has acceded to the Convention with the reciprocity and commercial reservations as specified in Article I of the Convention. The first part of the declaration is particularly relevant to enforcement of arbitral awards. Arbitral awards made in another country would be enforced in Nepal on the basis of reciprocity, only if the award has been made in another contracting state. The declaration therefore marks a deviation from the UNCITRAL ML, which required recognition of arbitral awards irrespective of the seat where they were made.[58] The UNCITRAL did not include reciprocity in the UNCITRAL ML, since it was recognized that the place of arbitration has "limited importance … in international cases"[59] and the UNCITRAL had "the desire to overcome territorial restrictions."[60] This was "significant policy decision"[61] made by the UNCITRAL. Furthermore, the UNCITRAL ML does not distinguish between foreign awards and domestic awards. The UNCITRAL ML contains provisions with regard to enforceability of arbitral awards "irrespective of the country in which it was made."[62] The UNCITRAL while recognizing the success of the NYC stated that the UNCITRAL Model Law "supplements, without conflicting with, the regime of recognition and enforcement created by that successful Convention."[63]

## 4.1 *Enforcement of Domestic Arbitral Awards in Nepal*

The 1999 Act substantially reduced the time period for making an enforcement application. Section 22 of the 1981 Act required the parties to "implement an award within 60 days of its making."[64] The 1999 Act further reduced this period to forty-five days.[65] The Act specified the reckoning date of the award as the date of its receipt. Section 31 of the 1999 Act specified "the concerned parties shall be under obligation to implement the award of the arbitrator within 45 days from the date when they receive a copy thereof."[66]

Where there was no voluntary compliance with the arbitral award by the parties within 45 days of receipt of a copy of the award, as per section 31 of the 1999 Act,

[58]Explanatory note by the UNCITRAL Secretariat on the Model law on International Commercial Arbitration, January 2008, United Nations Publication, 36. http://www.uncitral.org/pdf/english/texts/arbitration/ml-arb/07-86998_Ebook.pdf, accessed 31 August 2016.

[59]Ibid.

[60]Id.

[61]Id.

[62](n 26) Article 36(1).

[63](n 57) 36.

[64](n 20) s 22.

[65](n 22) 31.

[66]Ibid.

either of them could approach the District Court for its implementation. The District Court is the court of first instance in Nepal. As per section 32 of the 1999 Act, within thirty days of the time period stipulated in section 31 (i.e. 45 days), "the concerned party may file a petition to the District Court."[67] The District court, upon such application, may hear and decide the matter and implement the award "ordinarily within 30 days as if it was its own judgment".[68] There are three essential features in this section,

- court must be approached within 30 days of expiry of the time limit stipulated in section 31,
- the court must implement the award as a district court judgment, and
- court must ordinarily implement the award within 30 days.

An interesting provision in the 1999 Act with regard to arbitration taking place in Nepal is in relation to the power of arbitrator to require the foreign party to furnish either a bank guarantee or security in other forms.[69] The rationale explaining such power of the arbitrator is to ensure security for enforcement of the award.[70]

## 4.2 *Enforcement of Foreign Arbitral Awards in Nepal*

In Nepal foreign arbitral awards refers to "decision taken by arbitrators in foreign countries."[71] This implies that the Nepalese legal provision currently does not recognize delocalized arbitration. As per the 1999 Act, the Appellate court may be approached by a party for the purpose of enforcement of a foreign arbitral award.[72] The 1999 Act supplemented similar provisions of the 1981 Act[73] by specifying the documents required for such enforcement. As per section 34(1), the original (or certified copy) of the arbitral award[74] and the original (or certified copy) of the agreement[75] have to be submitted. If the award is not in Nepali Language, then an official translation in Nepali language must be submitted to the court.[76] The provision in the 1999 Act specifying the documents required for an enforcement

[67]Id, s 32.

[68]Id.

[69](n 22) s 21(1)(g).

[70]Id.

[71](n 22) s 34(2).

[72]Ibid., s 34(1).

[73](n 20) s 24(2).

[74](n 22) s 34(1)(a).

[75]Ibid., s 34(1)(b).

[76]Id s 34(1)(c).

application and the necessity to submit an official translation of the award in Nepali language has been drafted as per the UNCITRAL ML.[77]

It is pertinent to note that the 2006 amendment to the UNCITRAL ML only specified the submission of the original or a duly certified copy of the award, the requirement of submitting the original/certified copy of the arbitration agreement was omitted.[78] The Appellate court, upon satisfaction that the foreign award fulfilled the criteria set forth in section 34(2),[79] would direct the District Court for enforcement. The Appellate Court would also ensure that the award fulfills the twin requirements of section 34(4)[80]—the dispute that was the subject-matter of the foreign award should have been arbitrable under the laws of Nepal[81] and the foreign award cannot be recognized in Nepal if "is detrimental to public policy."[82] These two conditions are similar to the criteria provided under Article 36(1)(b) of the UNCITRAL ML.[83] Section 34 (2) prescribed certain criteria for enforcing foreign arbitral awards made in a NYC-contracting State. The award must also be such that "In case the laws of the country of the petitioner or the laws of country where the arbitration proceedings have been conducted, do not contain provision under which arbitration award made in Nepal cannot be implemented."[84] As mentioned above, this implies that the foreign arbitral award will only be implemented on the basis of comity in case the country where the award is made is signatory to NYC (or any other convention Nepal may be a signatory/accede to). The 1981 Act contained a similar provision. Section 24(4) specified "…no award made in any foreign country shall be [implemented] in the Kingdom of Nepal if, an award made in the Kingdom of Nepal in accordance with the prevailing law is not [implemented] by such foreign country."[85]

Unlike the UNCITRAL ML, the 1999 Act specified a timeline for presenting an enforcement application—"within 90 days from the date of the award".[86] The 1999 Act prescribed a few criteria for enforcement of foreign arbitral awards, which are similar to the guidance provided in the UNCITRAL ML.[87] The provisions of the legislation ensure that the foreign arbitral award sought to be enforced in Nepal, has been the result of arbitral proceedings that were founded upon the reference to

[77](n 26) Article 35(2).

[78](n 57) 21—Article 35(2) The party relying on an award or applying for its enforcement shall supply the original award or a copy thereof. If the award is not made in an official language of this State, the court may request the party to supply a translation thereof into such language.

[79](n 22) s 34(3).

[80](n 22) s 34(4).

[81]Ibid., s 34(4)(a).

[82]Id, s 34(4)(b).

[83]Id, s 36(1).

[84]Id, s 34(2)(e).

[85]Id, s 24(4).

[86]Id, s 34(2)(f).

[87](n 26) Article 36(1)(a) and (b).

arbitration based upon the party autonomy principle, and that the proceedings were fair and conformed to the highest standards of natural justice. The appointment of arbitrator and the award should have been "made according to the laws and the procedure mentioned in the agreement"[88]; the parties must have "been notified about the arbitration proceedings in time"[89]; the decision must be made as per the "conditions mentioned in the agreement or upon confining only to the subject matters referred to the arbitrator."[90] The 1999 Act also insists upon the decision of the arbitral tribunal (as in, the arbitral award) being "final and binding on the parties according to the laws of the country where the decision was made."[91] These criteria are similar to the 1981 Act.[92]

While these criteria, as stated above, are similar to the UNCITRAL ML's provisions on enforcement of arbitral awards[93] there is a substantial difference in the manner in which these criteria have been provided in the 1999 Act. Article 36(1)(a) of the UNCITRAL ML provides that recognition/enforcement of an award "[may be refused only] at the request of the party against whom it is invoked, if that party furnishes to the competent court where recognition or enforcement is sought proof that..."[94] On the other hand, as per the 1999 Act, prior to recognizing the award, the Appellate Court must be "satisfied that the conditions … have been fulfilled in the application."[95] This implies that the onus of proof lies on the appellant, which is in direct contrast to the UNCITRAL ML, to prove that the award is capable of enforcement in Nepal. The UNCITRAL ML suggested ease of the process of enforcement through a presumption of validity of the award[96] unless proven otherwise.[97]

## 4.3 Court Fee

The 1999 Act also specifies the applicable court fee to be paid for applying for the enforcement of a foreign arbitral award. As per section 41(1) 0.5% of the amount designated as the value of the award received after implementing the award should be paid as court fee for enforcing the award.[98] If the arbitral award is not with

---

88(n 22) s 34(2)(a).

89Ibid., 34(2)(b).

90Id, s 34(2)(c).

91Id, s 34(2)(d).

92(n 20) s 24(1).

93(n 26) Article 36(1)(a).

94Ibid.

95(n 22) s 34(3).

96(n 26) Article 34.

97Gary Born, *International Commercial Arbitration* ( Kluwer, 2001) 781.

98(n 22) s 41(1).

regard to receipt of an amount, then, if it is possible to be determined, 0.5% of the market value of the action to be taken or has to be taken according to the decision, is charged as court fee. In absence of such determination, a sum of five hundred rupees shall be paid as court fee.[99] On an application by the party seeking enforcement of the award, the District Court may order the other party to pay the court fee. The District court would order the amount from the other party "as court fees in accordance with the prevailing law."[100]

In international arbitration awards are pronounced inclusive of the quantum of damages, interest and the rate of interest. However, the law applicable in Nepal does not allow the award of interests in arbitration pending the statutory timeline for enforcement application. Section 33 specified against interest between the period of date of the award and the date of enforcement of award.[101]

It is of common understanding that an an appropriate court, generally confirms an arbitral award as final and binding.[102] The 1999 Act specifies the same. The Appellate Court has the jurisdiction to invalidate an arbitral award[103] whereas the District Court is where a party approaches so as to implement an arbitral award.[104] In light of these provisions, it becomes essential to look at the cases relating to enforcement of arbitral awards in Nepal.

The first recorded case in Nepal involving arbitration is the case of *Anang Man Sherchan v Chief Engineer of RTO*,[105] which was a 1964 full bench Supreme Court judgment. The dispute related to a contract between Regional Transportation Organization (RTO), a statutory body, and Sherchan Audhyogik Pvt. Ltd. It contained an arbitration clause for the resolution of disputes.[106] Further, the statute promulgated for the establishment of the RTO, i.e. the Development Committee Act, 2013 (1956) had recognized arbitration as a mode of dispute resolution with regard to any dispute that arises in contractual matters. The court in this case upheld the provision of the arbitration clause with regard to appointment of arbitrator. Although the *Anang Man Sherchan* decision is seen as an important precedent in the context of arbitration in Nepal, this case was decided at a time when there were no specific laws in Nepal with regard to arbitration. Therefore, this precedent does not hold out as a statement on enforcement of arbitral awards in Nepal.

After the promulgation of the 1999 Act, there have been important judgments related to the matter of challenging an arbitral award. For instance, in *Krishna*

---

[99]Id.

[100]Id, 41(2).

[101]Uprety (n 8) 219.

[102]Daniel Angualia 'The Role of Domestic Courts in International Commercial Arbitration,' (2010) 23. www.ssrn.com/abstract=1674760, accessed 31 August 2016.

[103](n 22) s 30.

[104]Ibid., s 32.

[105]NKP. 201 (SC 2020).

[106]Ibid.

*Chandra Jha v Dinesh Bhakta Shrestha*,[107] the Supreme Court held that the Appellate Court's authority is limited to correctional jurisdiction when an arbitral award is challenged.[108] The landmark case in Nepal regarding enforcement of arbitral awards is *Anil Kumar Pokhrel v District Court Kathmandu*[109] In this case the Supreme Court of Nepal held that the time limitation provided in the 1999 Act with regard to implementation of arbitral awards is calculated from the date the award is final. Furthermore, as per the judgment, in case an award has been challenged before the appellate court, the decision would be regarded to be final after the Appellate Court judgment.[110]

In this case, Larsen & Toubro Ltd. claimed compensation from the Morang Irrigation Board under the Ministry of Water Resources of the Government of Nepal for additional works done by them as per the construction contract agreed between them, which contained an arbitration clause. Upon denial by the other party, the aggrieved party approached the arbitral tribunal which gave its decision on August, 2000 in favor of Larsen and Toubro and directed the losing party to pay due compensation. The losing party approached the Appellate Court as per the 1981 Act for partial challenge to the arbitral award on the ground that it was in violation of sections 21(2)(a), (c), (d), (f) and (g) of the 1981 Act. Furthermore, the winning party also challenged the arbitral award partially under sections 21(2)(c), (d), (e), (f) and (g) of the 1981 Act.

The Appellate Court held the award valid on 21st November 2002.[111] An enforcement application to the District Court was made on the 13th of January 2003. It was pleaded against enforcement since there was a pending writ application for certiorari in the Supreme Court. The District Court rejected the plea and ordered enforcement of the arbitral award on 22nd August 2003.

The Supreme Court addressed two issues,

- whether the decision of the Appellate Court (with regard to challenging the award) or the arbitral award should be considered while implementing the arbitral award, and
- whether an arbitral award should be implemented by the District Court within 75 days from the date on which the Appellate Court makes a decision to validate the award when it is challenged.[112]

The provision related to challenging the arbitral award is specified in section 30 of the 1999 Act. The aggrieved party within 35 days from the date of hearing the

[107]Ne.Ka.Pa. 2059, Decision no. 7089, p. 285.

[108]Ibid.

[109]*Anil Kumar Pokharel v District Court Kathmandu and others*, Ne.Ka.Pa, Decision no. 7836 (2064/460).

[110]Ibid.

[111]Id.

[112]Id.

arbitral award[113] or receiving the award, the aggrieved party may file a petition so as to invalidate the arbitral award.[114] The grounds on which an arbitral award may be challenged under section 30(2) of the 1999 Act are procedural—arbitral award may only be evaluated on procedural grounds (or in case it is against public policy or a matter which is not arbitrable.[115] Section 32 of the 1999 Act specified that if a party has not complied with the award within 45 days of the receipt of the award,[116] then the winning party must approach the District Court within 30 days so as to enforce the award.[117]

The court in *Krishna Chandra Jha*[118] held that the provisions with regard to challenging an arbitral award and the provisions with regard to implementation of arbitral award are not "mutually exclusive" and they are "interconnected and interrelated".[119] Reading the two phrases together it held that in those circumstances wherein an arbitral award has been challenged before the Appellate Court, the arbitral award is final only after the decision of the Appellate court. Based upon this the Court upheld the decision of the District Court and held that the implementation of the arbitral award cannot be set aside since the winning party approached the district court within the time limit prescribed in the 1999 Act.[120]

In this judgment, the Supreme Court correctly interpreted the provisions of the 1999 Act and set a precedent for future cases. Another important aspect of the decision is with regard to the time it took to get a decision for the implementation of the arbitral award. The total time duration to enforce the arbitral award (including the time period in lieu of the challenge at the Appellate Court) was approximately three years. The arbitral award was made in August 2000[121] whereas the District Court's decided the matter of enforcement in August 2003.[122] Since the party approached the District Court for the implementation of the award in January 2003[123] a further seven months elapsed for the District Court to decide upon the implementation of the award. This is despite the fact that as per section 32 of the 1999 Act, the District Court must ordinarily execute the award within 30 days similar to a judgment.[124] The term 'ordinarily' has been placed deliberately in the provision since there may be circumstances wherein a decision may not be made

[113]There is a special provision under section 28 of the Arbitration Act, 1999 wherein the arbitral award is read out by the arbitrator in the presence of the parties.

[114](n 22) s 30.

[115]Ibid., s 30(3).

[116]Id, s 31.

[117]Id, s 32.

[118](n 105).

[119]Ibid.

[120](n 108).

[121]Ibid.

[122]Id.

[123]Id.

[124](n 22) s 32.

within 30 days. The Supreme Court followed the ratio of *Krishna Chandra Jha*[125] and stated that due to the onus on the district court to check the finality of the award, it is impossible to execute the award within 30 days.[126]

It is commendable that the District Court did not stay the implementation as per the request of the losing party who argued that there was a writ petition filed at the Supreme Court in relation to the implementation of the award.[127] This ensured that more time was not lost in realizing the relief granted in the arbitral award since the Supreme Court judgment came only in July 2007.[128] However, the fact that it took three years from the date of the arbitral award to get it implemented points out that there is still scope of improvement so as to efficiently reduce the time duration for implementation of an award.

Rarely was there an appeal against the arbitral award and the decision of the appellate court refusing to set aside the award challenged in the Supreme Court for gross violations of law. In *Ministry of Finance v Appellate Court Patan*[129] the Supreme Court issued a writ of certiorari to cancel the arbitral tribunal's award on the ground that the award failed to identify the precise provision of the contract under which the award was based. Upon cancellation of the award, the Supreme Court ordered both parties to re-initiate the arbitration proceeding.

There has been much misgiving with regard to the enforcement of arbitral awards in Nepal and it has been suggested that the judiciary has to demonstrate more favour for arbitration when the parties have preferred that mechanism and order strict action against defaulters of court orders.[130] Furthermore, the civil laws in Nepal with regard to implementation of judgments must be updated for increased efficiency.

## 4.4 Public Interest Clause

Section 30(3)(b) of the 1999 Act specified that an award can be set aside by the court if it is against the public interest. The term public interest has never been subjected to judicial delineation. Such terminology, without legislative clarity or judicial explanation could become an easy methodology for circumventing the entire arbitral process. It should be aligned with common international practice and reworded in the known terminology of public policy. The only known example of the usage of the term public interest along with the term public policy was in the Arbitration Act,

---

[125](n 105).

[126]Ibid.

[127](n 105).

[128]Ibid.

[129]Writ No. 2898 of 2059, year of order 2069 (2013).

[130]Anil Kumar Sinha, Chapter on Nepal, Global Arbitration Review, http://globalarbitrationreview.com/chapter/1036913/nepal, accessed 01 September 2016.

1996 of UK 1996. In the arbitration law, both the terms were adopted in section 1(b) and 33 of Arbitration Act, 1996, but the law acknowledged that they are different and yet, they may overlap.[131]

## 5 Conclusion

Based upon the above analysis, it can be concluded that the legal provisions in Nepal with regard to enforcement and recognition of arbitration award requires an update. The 1999 Act is insufficient in handling the complexities of modern arbitral awards. There are a few problem areas within the law. The separation of provisions for recognition and enforcement of awards based upon the country in which it is made is problematic. Furthermore, Nepal still recognizes arbitral awards only on the basis of comity, which may create issues.

In recognizing foreign awards as awards made in a foreign country the laws have ignored the contemporary developments. International arbitration is shifting towards delocalization wherein arbitration need not take place or an award need not be made in a specific location.[132] Awards no longer need to be linked to a country or even a specific place. It is theoretically possible to have awards anywhere in a manner that it is not linked to any particular nation. Paper based arbitration and online arbitration are stark examples of this. However, as per the current legal provisions applicable in Nepal with regard to enforcement of arbitral awards, the parties have to ensure that the decision of the award is linked to a particular country, specifically a NYC-contracting State on the reciprocity basis.

Apart from restructuring the enforcement mechanisms, Nepal's arbitration law also needs to revisit the definitional issues related to arbitration—the semantics of the arbitration agreement need to be more similar to international practice; there ought to be a clear delimitation of domestic and international arbitration; further delimitation with more clarity on the role of the courts on jurisdiction. Importantly, the 1999 Act has to be revisited for possible amendments in the area of applicable law—the insistence on the Law of Nepal for substantive law needs to be subjected to revision. Finally, the public interest clause needs more legislative clarity. It is interesting to see how the unique features of the 1999 Act, with regard to timelines for arbitration and enforcement, work. This is of much importance, especially in the context of increased foreign investment in Nepal. As pointed out above, drastic change in the system is not

[131]David St. John Sutton et al., *Russell On Arbitration*, 3 (Sweet & Maxwell, London, 1997) 17.

[132]See, Jan Paulsson, 'Delocalisation of International Commercial Arbitration: When and Why It Matters' (1983) 32(1) ICLQ 53 see generally Margret L.Moses, 'The Principles and Practice of International Commercial Arbitration' (Cambridge University Press 2012).

possible unless the judiciary appreciate arbitration as a dispute resolution mechanism and ensure strict action against defaulters of court orders.[133]

In the current scenario, the best way forward for Nepal is to review its laws on arbitration so as to ensure a robust procedure for conduct of arbitration and the recognition of arbitral awards. A revisit of the law to make it increasingly aligned with the UNCITRAL ML seems to be an option in favour.

[133](n 130).

# Issues of Jurisdiction, Choice of Law and Enforcement in International Commercial Arbitration: A Pakistan Perspective

**Ijaz Ali Chishti**

**Abstract** Pakistan enacted the Act of 2011 to implement the New York Convention, 1958. Section 2 of the Act, 2011 defines that foreign arbitral award is that award which is made in any of the New York Convention Contracting Sates or in such other States as may be notified by the Federal Government of Pakistan. This definition or determination of the scope of foreign arbitral award is, in fact, adaptation of principle of reciprocity provided for in the New York Convention. The New York Convention gives option to States that it can reserve application of the Convention to only those awards, which are made in the territory of another Contracting States. Pakistan availed this option and Section 2 of the Act, 2011 is not a definition of foreign arbitral award but the manifestation of that option. Admittedly, it is left with the law of the State where recognition of the award is sought to determine what constitutes an award enforceable under the New York Convention. There is no uniform approach amongst different countries on the definition of foreign arbitral award. Further, the New York Convention stipulates it application on the awards, which are non-domestic, and again there are divergent approaches on this terminology (non-domestic) as well. The chapter critically looks at the issue of enforcement of International Commercial Arbitration in Pakistan.

**Keywords** International arbitration · Pakistan arbitration law · Public policy · Arbitrability · *Shariat* · *Riba* · Enforcement of foreign awards

## Introduction

International Arbitration regime in Pakistan is still going through its rudimentary phases. The United Nations Convention on the Recognition and Enforcement of Foreign Arbitral Awards, 1958 (hereinafter, the NYC) was made applicable for the

I.A. Chishti (✉)
Court Associate, Supreme Court of Pakistan, FUUAST, Islamabad, Pakistan
e-mail: advocateijaz@gmail.com

© Springer Nature Singapore Pte Ltd. 2017

S.R. Garimella and S. Jolly (eds.), *Private International Law*,
DOI 10.1007/978-981-10-3458-9_18

first time in 2005 through an ordinance[1]—the Recognition and Enforcement (Arbitration Agreements and Foreign Arbitral Awards) Ordinance, 2005 (hereinafter, the REAO).[2] The REAO replaces the Arbitration (Protocol and Convention) Act 1937 (hereinafter, the APC Act, 1937) which previously applied the Geneva Protocol on Arbitration Clauses of 1923 and the Geneva Convention on the Execution of Foreign Arbitral Awards of 1927 (the Geneva Convention) to the enforcement of foreign arbitral awards in Pakistan. The application of the New York Convention brought a paradigm shift in Pakistan's approach towards the issues of jurisdiction, choice of law and enforcement of foreign arbitral awards. However, the international arbitration regime of Pakistan could be better appreciated through its contextualization with the law developed under its predecessor regime i.e. the Arbitration (Protocol and Convention) Act, 1937. In Pakistan Arbitration Act, 1940 deals with domestic arbitration, whereas Recognition and Enforcement (Arbitration Agreements and Foreign Arbitral Awards) Act of 2011 (hereinafter, the REA Act, 2011)[3] deals with foreign arbitration agreements and awards.

This chapter attempts to provide an overview of the law on international arbitration in Pakistan discussing the issues related to the arbitration agreement, arbitrability and such, before attempting to state the legal regime the issues of jurisdiction, choice of law and enforcement of foreign arbitral awards.

**Structure of the Chapter**

The chapter begins with a brief mapping of the history of the arbitration legislation in Pakistan from pre-independence era to present times.

The next section attempts to state the Pakistan law on a few fundamental concepts of international arbitration—arbitration agreement, separability, arbitrability and such.

The following section attempts to analyse the judicial opinion in Pakistan, minimal though, on the choice of law related issues affecting international arbitration.

The last section discusses the Pakistan arbitration law regarding the recognition and enforcement of foreign arbitral awards. There is a discussion on the criteria of public policy as a ground for refusal the enforcement of arbitral awards. This sub-section has brief discussions on the principles of *Sharia*, awards containing interests (*Riba*) and the precedents of the courts on issues concerning public policy.

---

[1]Under Article 89 of the Constitution of Pakistan, 1973 an Ordinance stands repealed at the expiration of one hundred and twenty days from the date of its promulgation. Therefore, after the lapse of the first Ordinance successive Ordinances for the purpose of applying New York Convention continued to be promulgated. It is of interest to note that Pakistan signed the NYC on 30th December 1958, but ratified it on 14th July 2005. http://www.newyorkconvention.org/countries, accessed 01 March, 2016.

[2]Ordinance No. VIII of 2005; This Ordinance ratified and implemented the New York Convention in Pakistan.

[3]No. F.9(3)/2011-Legis. Dated 19.7.2011 [Gazette of Pakistan, Extraordinary, Part-I, 19th July, 2011]. This is the enabling Act for the enforcement of New York Convention.

## 1 History of Arbitration Legislation in Pakistan

Pakistan inherited its arbitration regime dealing with domestic as well as international arbitration from the British India. British India was signatory to the Geneva Protocol on Arbitration Clauses of 1923 and the Geneva Convention on the Execution of Foreign Awards of 1927, both concluded under the aegis of the League of Nations. In order to give effect to these two legal instruments, the Arbitration (Protocol and Convention) Act, 1937 (hereinafter, the APC Act, 1937) was enacted. After the independence in the year 1947 and Partition of British India, Pakistan adopted this Act which continued to be the law of Pakistan for the enforcement of foreign arbitral awards till 2005.

In the year 2005, Pakistan enforced Recognition and Enforcement (Arbitration Agreements and Foreign Arbitral Awards) Ordinance which was promulgated in pursuant to the ratification of the New York Convention to which it was signatory since 1958. Thus it applied New York Convention for the first time in 2005 and till then the APC Act, 1937 remained the law on the subject. As the Ordinance could not take shape of the Act of Parliament therefore after its lapse,[4] in order to fulfill international obligations, another ordinance was promulgated in 2006.[5] This Ordinance was repeated by successive ordinances, viz., Recognition and Enforcement (Arbitration Agreements and Foreign Arbitral Awards) Ordinance 2007[6]; Recognition and Enforcement (Arbitration Agreements and Foreign Arbitral Awards) Ordinance 2009[7] and Recognition and Enforcement (Arbitration Agreements and Foreign Arbitral Awards) Ordinance 2010.[8] Ultimately it took the shape of an Act of Parliament, namely, Recognition and Enforcement (Arbitration Agreements and Foreign Arbitral Awards) Act, 2011(hereinafter referred as Act of 2011). Thus, now the foreign arbitral awards are enforced under the New York Convention through the Act of 2011. At present, Pakistan has two different legislations dealing with arbitration. The Arbitration Act, 1940 deals with domestic arbitration and the Act of 2011 deals with foreign arbitration. In order to consolidate these two legislations a bill modeled on UNCITRAL Model Law (hereinafter, the UNCITRAL ML), viz., Arbitration and Conciliation Bill, 2015 has been introduced

[4]Under Article 89 of the Constitution of Pakistan, 1973 an Ordinance stands repealed at the expiration of one hundred and twenty days from the date of its promulgation. The Government of Pakistan issued successive ordinances to keep the REAO Ordinance, first issued in 2005, alive.

[5]Recognition and Enforcement (Arbitration Agreements and Foreign Arbitral Awards) Ordinance 2006 (Ordinance III of 2006) dated 18th March 2006 and published in Gazette of Pakistan, Extraordinary, Part I, 18th March, 2006.

[6]Ordinance XXV of 2007 published in Gazette of Pakistan, Extraordinary, Part I, 2nd June, 2007.

[7]Ordinance XXXIII of 2009 published in Gazette of Pakistan, Extraordinary, Part I, 26th November, 2009.

[8]Ordinance IX of 2010 published in Gazette of Pakistan, Extraordinary, Part I, 20th April, 2010.

in the Senate of Pakistan on 18th January 2016.[9] As the preamble of the bill (a private member bill) states,

> to consolidate and amend the law relating to domestic arbitration, international commercial arbitration and enforcement of foreign arbitral awards as also to define the law relating to conciliation and for matters connected therewith or incidental thereto.[10]

According to the REA Act, 2011 the designated court for all actions related to arbitration is the High Court.[11] An interesting feature of this legislation has been the statutory provisions regarding inconsistency between the law and the Convention. The New York Convention has been incorporated into the municipal law as Schedule to the REA Act, and Section 8 expressly provides that in the event of any inconsistency between the Convention and the said legislation itself or any other law or any judgment of any Court on the other, the Convention shall prevail to the extent of the inconsistency. This is a most unusual provision. It is a well-established rule of the interpretation of statutes that in case of any conflict between the main part of a statue and any schedule thereto, it is the main provisions (i.e. the sections) that prevail. It is also well settled that any conflict between any treaty provision and municipal law is to be resolved in favour of the latter. Section 8 thus reverses both these rules in favour of the New York Convention.[12]

## 1.1 Arbitration Agreement

In order for an arbitration to be valid it must contain essential elements, viz., present or future dispute, defined legal relationship and consent to arbitration. It must be in writing, valid in substance and subject matter of dispute be arbitrable. However, validity of the arbitration agreement has neither been defined in the Arbitration Act, 1940 nor the Act, 2011. Such validity is examined on the principles of the Contract Act, 1872.[13] Section 10 of the Contract Act, 1872 stipulates conditions to be fulfilled for a valid contract.[14] The enforceability of the arbitration agreement has been

[9]http://www.senate.gov.pk/uploads/documents/1453277461_862.pdf, accessed 10 May 2016.

[10]Ibid., The Preamble.

[11]Section 2(d) read with Section 3(1), REA Act, 2011 ensures exclusive jurisdiction to the High Courts in adjudication of all matters concerning foreign arbitral awards.

[12]Justice Mian Saqib Nisar, 'International Arbitration in the Context of Globalization: A Pakistani Perspective'. http://www.supremecourt.gov.pk/ijc/articles/8/2.pdf, accessed 21 July 2016.

[13]*Karachi Dock Labour Board and Messrs Quality Builders Ltd* PLD 2016 SC 121. The Judgement reads: it must qualify the test of a valid contract in terms of the law of contract. In *Travel Automation (Pvt.) v Abacus International* 2006 CLD 497 the arbitration agreement was evaluated by applying the provisions of the Contract Act, 1872 (of Pakistan).

[14]Section 10 reads: **What agreements are contracts.** All agreements are contracts if they are made by the free consent of parties competent to contract, for a lawful consideration and with a lawful object, and are not hereby expressly declared to be void.

discussed in Section 4 of the REA Act, 2011. Section 4(1) affords a party to an arbitration agreement the right, upon notice to the other party, to apply to the High Court to stay legal proceedings before such High Court on the pretext that the subject matter of such legal proceedings is covered by an arbitration agreement. Further subsection (2) states that on a motion to stay legal proceedings, the High Courts are obliged to refer the parties to arbitration, unless the arbitration agreement is null and void, inoperative or incapable of being performed. There have been few instances where the threshold of nullity or inoperativeness and such criteria has been specified by the court. The express inclusion in the legislation for a provision to stay the proceedings in the event of an arbitration agreement and refer the parties to arbitration process is especially important, noting the fact that there were few instances under the APC Act, 1937 where despite Section 3 of that Act expressly providing for stay of proceedings in respect of matters to be referred to arbitration, Pakistani courts have deviated from statutory direction. A case in point is the decision in *Eckhardt & Company Marine GMBH, West Germany v Mohammad Hanif*[15] where the Supreme Court hearing the appeal from the Karachi High Court decision[16] (which it affirmed) refused to enforce a foreign arbitration agreement on the grounds that it would be too inconvenient and expensive for the Pakistani party to bear the cost of adducing evidence at a foreign forum. The Court's reasoning was based upon natural justice considerations rather than prescribing any test for a *forum conveniens* for a particular dispute.

However, following the REAO, there were a few decisions that emphasized on the enforcement of the arbitration agreement and courts staying the proceedings and referring the parties to arbitration. In *M/s. Travel Automation (Pvt.) Ltd. v Abacus International (Pvt.) Ltd.*[17] the Court held that Section 4(2) … has taken away the discretion of the court to stay the proceeding in terms of the Arbitration Agreement, even on the ground of inconvenience etc. except where the arbitration agreement by itself is null and void, inoperative or incapable of being performed.

In *Metropolitan Steel Corporation Ltd. v Macsteel International UK Ltd.*[18] the Court held that arguments regarding public policy and expensiveness of the arbitration taking place in London as ground for stay of suit were not tenable; further parties to an arbitration agreement could not also plead foreign exchange remittances restrictions imposed by the State to deny participation in the arbitration process.

---

(Footnote 14 continued)

Nothing herein contained shall affect any law in force in [Pakistan], and not hereby expressly repealed, by which any contract is required to be made in writing or in the presence of witnesses, or any law relating to the registration of documents.

[15]PLD 1993 Supreme Court 42.

[16]PLD 1986 Karachi 138.

[17](2006 CLD 497).

[18](2006 CLD 1491).

## 1.2 Separability

The Separability principle ensures that the arbitration clause is autonomous, despite being embedded into the main contract. Both the common law and civil law countries are unanimous on the separability presumption, though with different terms and names.[19] Pakistan's arbitration law also affirmed this principle through judicial opinion. In *Shipyard and Engineering Works Ltd v Messrs General Iron and Steel*[20] the Court held that despite modification and novation of the main contract the arbitration clause, which was severable from the main contract survived. In *Sezai Turkes Feyzi Akkaya Construction Company, Lahore v Crescent Services, Lahore*[21] the Supreme Court observed that despite frustration and repudiation of the main contract the arbitration clause survived.

Further different clauses of arbitration agreement are considered severable under the principle of separability. In *M/s Uzin Export & Import Enterprises for Foreign Trade v M/s M. Iftikhar & Company Limited*[22] it was held that if some provisions of the arbitration agreement are being unenforceable provisions the remaining severable provisions of the arbitration agreement could be enforced.

## 1.3 Arbitrability

The REA Act, 2011 does not enlist matters that are arbitrable under the Pakistan law. However, some guidance on the subject matter arbitrability is available through other legislations and judicial opinion. All those matters that are opposed to public policy are treated as non-arbitrable. An interesting guidance on subject matter arbitrability and public policy has been provided in the decision in *Hub Power Company Ltd. v WAPDA* (hereinafter, the *HUBCO*).[23] The Hub Power Company (*Hubco*) was supplying electrical power to *WAPDA*, the public sector utility, under a power purchase agreement. The agreement had an arbitration clause

[19]Gary Born, *International Commercial Arbitration*, (Vol. I, Kluwer Law International, 2009) 311, 315 He observed that in some jurisdiction it is referred to as separability presumption and in some other jurisdiction as autonomy and independence of arbitration agreement and in some others as severability doctrine.

[20]PLD 1974 Karachi 501.

[21]1997 SCMR 1928.

[22]1993 SCMR 866, in this case proceeding in the civil court was staying in order to enable the parties to decide their dispute through arbitration in accordance with their arbitration agreement, however, a provision of the agreement regarding seat of arbitration was found to be unconscionable therefore the parties was asked to replace it with their mutual consent.

[23]PLD 2000 SC 841.

providing for ICC arbitration at London. Disputes arose between the parties, and *Hubco* wished to refer the matter to arbitration. *WAPDA* opposed this move on the ground that the issues raised by it, which were serious allegations of corruption, fraud and mala- fide, were not arbitrable. The Supreme Court by a majority upheld *WAPDA*'s contention; however the Court noted that the disputes raised by *WAPDA* were not commercial in nature, but presented very serious public policy concerns that were essentially criminal in nature. Other matters which have been held to fall outside the purview of arbitration include, inter alia, minority oppression proceedings under the Companies Ordinance 1984[24] and proceedings for the winding up of a company.[25] Disputes related to income tax disputes, custom duties disputes, excise duties disputes, competition disputes also cannot be arbitrated. In *Ali Muhammad and others v Bashir Ahmad through his legal heirs*[26] it was held that when there is an agreement between the parties to refer the matter to arbitration and the subject matter of criminal litigation is specifically mentioned and made the subject matter of arbitration; the award is opposed to public policy because they deal with criminal case for its prosecution or non-prosecution. This decision was based on the decision in *Gopal Chandra Poddar v Lakshmi Kunta Sha*[27] wherein it was held that an agreement to refer to arbitration in consideration for dropping a criminal proceeding in respect of 'non-compoundable offence' is opposed to public policy. The *Ali Muhammad* decision expressly declared that criminal matters couldn't be subject matter of arbitration.

The Small Claims and Minor Offences Court Ordinance, 2002 specified that only non-compoundable matters are beyond the scope of arbitration. All compoundable offences could, at any stage of the proceedings before the closure of the dispute in Court, with the consent of the parties, be decided by resorting to amicable settlement procedure, including, arbitration.[28] An arbitrator, under this Ordinance is called *Salis*,[29] (Urdu word for an arbitrator). The local laws (administered within the Provinces through the municipalities) also follow similar criteria as the Small Claims Ordinance, 2002. For example, under the Punjab Local Government Act even the criminal compoundable matters can be referred for amicable settlement to *Panchayat* or *Musalihat Anjuman*.[30] It works as a panel of arbitrators.

---

[24]*Pakistan Water and Power Development Authority v Kot Addu Power Company Limited* (2002) MLD [Lahore] 829.

[25]*Orix Leasing Pakistan Limited v Colony Thal Textile Mills Limited* (1997) PLD Lahore 443.

[26]1991 SCMR 1928; *Manzoor Hussain* et al. *and Wali Muhammad* et al. (PLD 1965 SC 425).

[27]*Gopal Chandra Poddar v Lakshmi Kunta Sha*, AIR 1933 Cal. 817.

[28]Small Claims and Minor Offences Courts Ordinance, 2002, s 14.

[29]Ibid., s 2(g).

[30]Punjab Local Government Act, 2013, Ss 96, 97.

## 2 Jurisdiction

The Pakistan law on arbitration reinforces the principle of party autonomy with regard to the choice of forum for arbitration, and this feature finds place in the REA Act, 2011. However, two exceptions could be identified in the law that developed under the APC Act, 1937.

- parties can withdraw from the selected forum if they willfully litigate the matter before the courts. By litigating a matter before the courts, the parties abdicate their right of resolution of dispute through arbitration at the selected forum, and —the doctrine of forum non conveniens, though, it has lost its relevancy after the Act of 2011

Section 3 REA Act, 2011 conferred exclusive jurisdiction on the High Courts of Pakistan to adjudicate and settle the matters relating to enforcement of arbitration agreements. Under Section 4 any party to the arbitration agreement, including a party against whom the other party has brought in proceedings before the court (i.e. respondent) may seek the stay of the proceedings and referral of the matter to arbitration. The exclusive jurisdiction feature has been an important development and a positive feature for arbitration in Pakistan. Legal proceedings are in general to be commenced in the civil, i.e. subordinate courts, and this was the position prevailing under the APC Act, 1937. By directly conferring jurisdiction on the High Courts, the Ordinance has eliminated altogether one level of legal proceedings and, given the unfortunate delays that can plague the legal system in this country, thus greatly speeded up the enforcement of foreign awards.

Under the REA Act, 2011 there has been no precedent regarding the courts in Pakistan exercising jurisdiction in procedural matters like appointment and removal of the arbitrators in a dispute pending before a foreign-seated arbitral tribunal. However, in *Hitachi Limited and another v Rupali Polyester and others*,[31] a decision rendered under the APC Act, 1937, it was held that the procedural questions such as removal and non-removal of the arbitrators is to be determined by the designated court at the seat of arbitration even though the parties had selected Pakistani law as the law of the arbitration. There is no provision within the REA Act of 2011 that specifically addressed this situation; it could therefore be presumed that Pakistani courts could, on application by the party(s), refer them to arbitration, if there is a valid arbitration agreement.

[31]1998 SCMR 1618.

## 2.1 *Tribunal's Power to Decide Its Jurisdiction*

While Pakistan recognizes the principle of competence-competence, i.e., the arbitral tribunal possessed the competence to rule on its jurisdiction or absence of it, such decision of the arbitral tribunal on this point is open to review by the courts. Further, the principle of waiver that specified that jurisdictional questions not pleaded before the tribunal could not be pleaded later in a judicial action was not recognized by Pakistan's courts. The courts refused to accept the principle in instances related to appointment of arbitrators, where such appointments have been made in contravention of the provisions of the arbitration law.[32] The rule on competence-competence principle in the Pakistan arbitration law is differently interpreted for domestic and international arbitrations. In the domestic arbitration under the Arbitration Act, 1940 the arbitrator or umpire does not have the power to rule upon questions of his or her own jurisdiction and the court must decide the same. However, the power of an arbitrator to adjudicate upon his or her jurisdiction has been recognised where the power was granted by statute.[33] The *Hitachi* decision offers some guidance in the context of international arbitrations.[34] The Supreme Court of Pakistan held that insofar as the arbitration proceedings and matters relating thereto were concerned, the same would be governed by the law of the seat of the arbitration and it is those courts that would have jurisdiction. Adopting the rationale of the "seat theory", the Court held that it is only the Courts of that a country where the seat of the arbitration is located which have jurisdiction over challenges to the validity of the award and other aspects of the arbitration.[35]

## 2.2 *Jurisdiction of Tribunals/Courts to Order Interim Measures in Support of Arbitral Claims*

Pakistan arbitration law does not seem to specify the powers of the arbitral tribunal to order interim relief, in the case of domestic arbitration. An arbitrator or umpire may not grant interim relief. Under Section 27 of the 1940 Act, the arbitrator or umpire may make an interim award. However, the interim award would be subject to the discretion of the court to become an order of the court for final enforcement.

Under the 1940 Act, the court has the powers to grant interim relief (Section 41 read together with the Second Schedule). Some of the circumstances where the court would grant interim relief have been listed in the Second Schedule of the 1940 Act and include: interim custody or sale of goods which are the subject matter of the

---

[32]See for e.g., *Karachi Dock Labor Board v Messrs Quality Builders Ltd.* PLD 2016 SC 121.

[33]*Muhammad Aslam Siddiqui and Hasina Begum* (1986) MLD [Karachi] 735.

[34]*Hitachi* (n 31).

[35]Justice Mian Saqib Nisar (n 12) 10.

reference; securing the amount in difference in the reference; detention, preservation or inspection of property or a thing which is the subject matter of the reference; interim injunction or appointment of a receiver; and the appointment of a guardian for a minor or a person of unsound mind for the purposes of the arbitration proceedings.

With regard to international arbitrations, the judicial approach has been to stay away from interference in the arbitral proceedings. The courts have held that where the law of the main contract is Pakistani law but the arbitration is taking place outside Pakistan, it is the law of the seat of the arbitration that governs the procedure and the proceedings of a foreign arbitration, and Pakistani courts would not exercise any jurisdiction in this respect.[36]

The *Hitachi* ratio is an important statement on jurisdiction of the arbitral tribunals. The main contract therein was governed by the laws of Pakistan and contained an arbitration clause that provided for ICC arbitration in London. The Court held that the Pakistan Law governed the arbitration agreement (as embodied in the arbitration clause) too. It may be recalled that Section 9, APC Act, 1937 excluded the applicability of the Act to arbitration agreements governed by the laws of Pakistan, and the said Act therefore, could have no application to the instant case. An interim award issued by the London-seated arbitral tribunal was challenged for validity in the Courts of Pakistan. The pertinent question for the Court was whether the Pakistani courts had jurisdiction to rule on the validity of an award where the seat of the arbitration was outside the country. According to the "seat theory", it is only the Courts of that a country where the seat of the arbitration is located which have jurisdiction over challenges to the validity of the award and other aspects of the arbitration. The Indian Supreme Court had held[37] that in case where Indian Law governed the arbitration agreement, the courts of India had concurrent jurisdiction with the Courts of the seat of the arbitration. The Pakistan Supreme Court in *Hitachi* rejected this approach. It held that insofar as the arbitration proceedings and matters relating thereto were concerned, the law of the seat of the arbitration would govern the same and it is those courts that would have jurisdiction. Pakistani court would not have jurisdiction simply because the arbitration agreement was governed by Pakistani law. However, insofar as the post-arbitration stage was concerned, the Supreme Court held that the interim award could be challenged before the Pakistani courts because the laws of Pakistan governed the arbitration agreement and main contract and the transaction had it closest connection with this country. The court has therefore, taken a view which is intermediary between the "seat" theory and the view taken by the Indian Supreme Court, and it remains to be seen whether this view will be affirmed if Court has occasion to re-visit the issues involved in some future case. The *Hitachi* opinion itself recognizes that, at least in relation to procedural supervision, the courts of the seat of arbitration ought to have competence over the arbitral proceedings. Further this reasoning has been followed

---

[36](n 31).

[37]*National Thermal Power Corporation v Singer Company and others* (1992) 2 Comp LJ 256.

subsequently in *Hassan Ali Rice Export Co. v Flame Maritime Ltd*[38] in the Sindh High Court.

The *Hitachi* decision also held that issues such removal of arbitrators should be determined as per the curial law by the courts of the place where the arbitration is seated. However, the judgment reads, Courts in Pakistan will be competent to go into the questions, whether the arbitrators and/or the chairman have misconducted themselves or the proceeding, while considering the ground for setting aside the awards. There is no provision in the REA Act, 2011 to deal with this situation.

## 3 Choice of Law

Within the ambit of the party autonomy principle, parties are free to choose the law to govern their contractual relationship. This choice of the parties may be an express choice or it can be implied i.e. can be derived from the circumstances of a particular case. The chosen law shall govern substantive as well as procedural aspects of the contract. Parties could also choose different laws and more than one law to govern individual clauses of the contract.

In an international arbitration at least three systems of laws are discernible,

- the law governing the arbitration agreement (also known as Governing law)
- the law governing the arbitration procedure (curial law), and
- the law governing the main contract (substantive law or proper law)

In case where the choice of the parties could not be derived, the arbitral tribunal decides on the question of applicable law by applying relevant laws and rules. Here, the conflict of laws principles has a significant role.

If the parties have not, expressly or impliedly, selected governing law of the arbitration agreement, the court applies the closest connection approach in order to determine the law applicable to arbitration agreement. However, if the parties have selected the applicable law for the main contract then the same law would be applicable for the arbitration agreement.[39] In the absence of any express choice by the parties, the proper law of the main contract by implication is treated as the law governing the arbitration agreement, when the arbitration clause is part of the main contract. The courts of Pakistan have acknowledged the choice of jurisdiction of courts for procedural matters by the parties to an international arbitration agreement, even by implication from the selection of venue of arbitration. Where Pakistani law governs the main contract and a proper law governing the arbitration agreement is not otherwise expressly selected, the 1940 Act would apply.

---

[38] 2004 CLD 334.

[39] *Hitachi* (n 31).

The *Hitachi* decision is the landmark judgment on the issues concerning the applicable laws. On the questions regarding the determination of the governing law of arbitration agreement when the arbitration agreement is embedded in the main contract and there is an absence of any contrary express provision specifying the applicable law, it was held in this case that 'the governing law of the arbitration agreement will be the same which is applicable to the main contract'. In case, where the parties have failed in choosing the law governing the arbitration proceedings, the law of the country in which the arbitration is held would govern the proceedings.

With regard to substantive law, in the absence of an express choice made by the parties, the courts would either apply Pakistani law or settle the choice of law according to the principles of international private law.[40] However, the Act does not empower the arbitrators to act as amiable or decide any matter *ex aequo et bono*. If the parties expressly authorize the arbitrators to act as amiable *compositeur* or decide the matter *ex aequo et bono* then it would be arguable whether such a decision constitutes an award under the Act or would be just a decision of an expert which is unreviewable.[41]

In arbitrations seated outside Pakistan between a foreign and a Pakistani disputant where the applicable law is the Pakistan law, the characterization of the arbitration, whether domestic or foreign, becomes important. Prior to the REAO this situation was clearly defined in §9(b) of the APC Act (the Savings Clause made the substantive law applicable to the dispute the determining factor). The *Hitachi* decision, as discussed earlier, made an attempt to address the feature of characterization of the award in the light of the Savings Clause and held that the substantive law applicable to the arbitration would be determinative of the foreign or domestic character of an award. With the removal of the savings clause in the REAO, the role of the applicable law being Pakistani law is of limited utility in determining the character of an award. It is pertinent to note here that Pakistani arbitration law speaks only about the characterization of the award, and not characterization of the arbitration as domestic and foreign.

It could be stated that the REAO and the REA Act, 2011, by an express omission of the Savings Clause, consciously altered the position of character determination away from the choice of substantive law and towards other factors, such as the venue of arbitration i.e. a more territorial approach has been adopted.

---

[40] *MA Chowdhury v Messrs Mitsui OSK Lines Limited* (1970) PLD SC 373; *Light Industries (Pvt.) Limited, through Chief Executive v Messrs ZSK STICKMASCHINEN GmbH through Attorney* (2009) CLD [Karachi] 1340; *CGM (Compagnie General Maritime) and Hussain Akbar* (2002) CLD [Karachi] 1528; *Masood Asif v United Bank Limited* (2001) CLC [Karachi] 479.

[41] Rizwan Hussain, 'International Arbitration in Pakistan' (2012) Key Law Reports. http://papers.ssrn.com/sol3/papers.cfm?abstract_id=2597551, accessed 21 July 2016.

## 4 Recognition and Enforcement of the Foreign Arbitral Awards

### 4.1 *Definition of the Foreign Award*

Section 4 of the APC Act specified that a foreign award was enforceable in Pakistan as if it were an award made on a matter referred to arbitration in Pakistan. Section 5 stated that a foreign award could be filed in any Court in Pakistan having jurisdiction over the subject matter of the award, if there was no arbitration agreement/clause. In other words, for purposes of enforcement, a foreign award was placed on the same footing as a domestic award, and if the award survived challenge to its enforcement (as foreign awards almost invariably did),[42] then the Court was bound to pronounce judgment according to the award, and upon a judgment so pronounced, a decree was to follow in terms of the award.[43]

As per the literal meaning, a foreign award is an award that is made in a State, which is not the enforcing State. Having stated that the New York Convention also allows for enforcement of awards that are non-domestic,[44] thereby indicating that there are certain categories of awards that could be deemed as foreign awards because they would not be considered as domestic awards. Van den berg explained the possible composition of such awards.[45] But there is no uniform approach of different countries on the definition of foreign award. In some countries, an award made in a foreign country is also considered as a domestic award and on the other hand, in some countries an award made within its territory is treated as non-domestic award.

The *travaux preparatoires* of the New York Convention shows that Pakistan proposed amendment to Article 1 of the Draft Convention that includes the definition of 'arbitral awards'. The said proposal is important here to know as it reflects Pakistan's intention at the time of drafting the Convention. The proposed amendment read,

"Paragraph 1: Subject to Para 2 of this article, this convention shall apply to recognition and enforcement both of arbitral awards made abroad and of arbitral

[42]Justice Mian Saqib Nissar (n 12).

[43]APC Act, 1937, S.6.

[44]NYC Article I "........It shall also apply to arbitral awards not considered as domestic awards in the State where their recognition and enforcement are sought."

[45](i) an award made in the enforcement State under the arbitration law of another State; (ii) an award made in the enforcement State under the arbitration law of that State involving a foreign (or international) element; (iii) an award that is regarded as "a-national" in that it is not governed by any arbitration law. See, Albert Jan Van den Berg, 'The New York Convention of 1958: An overview' (2008). http://www.arbitration-icca.org/media/0/12125884227980/new_york_convention_of_1958_overview.pdf, accessed 25 May, 2016.

awards arising out of differences between persons, whether physical or legal, domiciled in territories of different states".[46]

It could thus be a derivation that at the Convention Pakistan preferred application of the NYC to awards made within the country involving parties domiciled in different countries.

Section 2, REA Act, 2011 defined a foreign arbitral award as an award that is made in any of the New York Convention Contracting States or in such other States as may be notified by the Federal Government of Pakistan. This definition or determination of the scope of foreign arbitral award is, in fact, adaptation of principle of reciprocity provided for in the New York Convention. The New York Convention gives option to States that it can reserve application of the Convention to only those awards that are made in the territory of another Contracting States. Pakistan has availed this option and thus it seems that Section 2 of the Act of 2011 is not a definition of foreign arbitral award but the manifestation of that option.

In *Messrs Flame Maritime Limited v Messrs Hassan Ali Rice Export*[47] an enforcement challenge was raised alleging misconduct on behalf of the arbitrator for passing an ex parte award and granting the claim of one party without taking into consideration the facts constituting the claim of the other party. A further objection was raised pleading that awarding of interest on amount determined by the arbitrator is against the tenets of Islam, therefore, award cannot be made rule of the court. The Court, on an appraisal of the evidence, ruled against misconduct. On objections that the award was in violation of Islamic tenets, for reasons of awarding interest, the Court held that since the award became final in England it could not be nullified at the enforcement stage in Pakistan. The disposal of second argument on the ground of finality of award is a credible decision that removed doubts on the grant of interest being in violation of injunctions of Islam could be accepted by the court as a public policy ground, as plead by the objecting party.

The law related to the definition of foreign award is, as yet, unsettled in Pakistan's arbitration law. The decision in *Taisei Corporation v A.M. Construction Company Pvt. Limited*[48] (hereinafter, the *Taisei)* is a recent illustration of the mistaken reading of the law, thereby continuing the trend of unsettled law.

Taisei Corporation (hereinafter, Taisei), a company incorporated in Japan entered into a contract with National Highway Authority of Pakistan (NHA) for improvement of Kararo-Wadh section of National Highway-25 in the province of Balochistan. Later on, A.M. Construction Company Pvt. Limited (hereinafter, A.M. Company) incorporated in Pakistan entered into a subcontract with Taisei for carrying out such subcontract works as were specified in the subcontract agreement.

---

[46]Consideration of the Draft Convention on the Recognition and Enforcement of Foreign Arbitral Awards by United Nations Conference on International Arbitration, (item 4 on the Agenda), 16th May 1958.

[47]2006 CLD 697.

[48][2012] PLD 455 (Lah).

It was provided in Clause 19.1 of the general conditions of the subcontract agreement that the disputes between the parties shall be settled initially amicably. In case of no amicable settlement, it shall be decided by one or more arbitrators under Rules of Conciliation and Arbitration administered by the ICC, seated at Singapore. Pursuant to an arbitration process an award was issued in 2011. The claims of A.M. Company except one were dismissed and it was directed to pay Taisei for counterclaims, costs, fees and the ICC administrative expenses.

A.M. Company filed an application under Section 14, AA, 1940[49] in the Court of Civil Judge Lahore against Taisei seeking direction for depositing of the award and other documents to the Court. A.M. Company also indicated its intention to initiate the set aside proceedings of the award. It pleaded arbitrator misconduct, that the award is invalid, contrary to the laws and public policy of Pakistan, unenforceable and merits to be set aside, and that the matter deserves to be remitted/referred to arbitration for reconsideration. Taisei's objections were overruled. It made a civil revisionary application before the Lahore High Court pending the proceedings before the City Civil Judge, challenging the statutory jurisdiction of the CJ Lahore on the grounds that the award is a 'foreign award' under Section 2 (e), REA Act, 2011; therefore jurisdiction to adjudicate matters in relation thereto has been vested in a High Court. The Lahore High Court, seized of the matter, addressed itself to the Governing Law clause in the sub-contract that stated,

> Governing Law: - The law to which the subcontract is to be subject and according to which the subcontract is to be construed shall be as specified in special conditions of the subcontract.The special conditions contain clause 3.2, which reads as follows: 3.2. The Governing Law shall be the law in force at the time in Pakistan.

A reading of the above clause, keeping in mind the forward-looking ratio of the *Hitachi* would have brought it home that this clause concerned itself with the governing law of the sub-contract. The clause was, evidently, discussing the substantive law of the contract, and not the governing law of the arbitration. Hence the award for all purposes should have been treated as foreign award, but the High Court determined the domestic nature of the award on the basis of the substantive law applicable to the dispute in the arbitration. It then decided the jurisdiction for an

---

[49]Section 14 of the Arbitration Act, 1940 reads:

"14. Award to be signed and filed.—(1) When the arbitrators or umpire have made their award, they shall sign it and shall give notice in writing to the parties of the making and signing thereof and of the amount of fees and charges payable in respect of the arbitration and award.

(2) The arbitrators or umpire shall, at the request of any party to the arbitration agreement or any person claiming under such party or if so directed by the Court and upon payment of the fees and charges due in respect of the arbitration and award and of the costs and charges of filing the award cause the award or a signed copy of it, together with any depositions and documents which may have been taken and proved before them, to be filed in Court, and the Court shall thereupon give notice to the parties of the filing of the award.

(3) Where the arbitrators, or umpire state a special case under clause (b) of Section 13, the Court, after giving notice to the parties and hearing them, shall pronounce its opinion thereon and such opinion shall be added to, and shall form part of, the award."

action leading to the annulment of the award in favour of the civil court (Lahore) against the jurisdiction of competent authority at the seat of arbitration, an aberration from the spirit of the NYC that stated that an award could be set-aside only by the courts at the seat of arbitration.[50]

The Lahore High Court did not make a complete and explanatory reading of the ratio of *Hitachi*[51] where it was held that Pakistan courts could receive a challenge to the validity of the award because the arbitration agreement and the Pakistan Law governed main contract, which is not the scenario in the *Taisei* case. Following the ratio of *Hitachi* and the support for the seat theory that was built up in that case, the arbitration in *Taisei* being seated in Singapore, the Courts at Singapore would have been the place to receive applications questioning the validity of the award, or any other set aside challenges. Rather the Court could have advised the respondent, A. M. Company to challenge the award when Taisei made an application for enforcement.

However, the decision of the High Court has set certain interesting jurisprudential trends in arbitration law that need to be critiqued in the context of national and international opinion. The High Court has held that:

1. The High Courts designated to hear applications related to international arbitrations under Section 2(d), REA Act, 2011 are not legally competent to entertain the application under Section 14 of the Arbitration Act, 1940. Therefore, said application if filed in Civil Court under the Arbitration Act, 1940 cannot be returned even if the matter involves foreign arbitral awards.
2. Since the AA, 1940 has not been specifically repealed the remedies under it are not non-existent because of the enactment of the REA Act, 2011.
3. When the parties have specifically agreed that the governing law of the contract is the law of Pakistan the award in question would be termed a domestic Award.

An analysis of these three points reveals that they are self-contradictory. While on one hand the governing law of the contract being Pakistan law made the arbitral process and the award a domestic arbitration, the *Taisei* decision held that since the legislature has not expressly repealed the AA, 1940 therefore remedies available in that legislation survive despite the enactment of REA Act, 2011. Thus, it could be derived from the decision that the REA Act, 2011 is presumed to have been applicable, however, in supplement to the Arbitration Act, 1940.

In the case of *Nan Fung Textiles Ltd, Hong Kong v H. Pir Muhammad Shamasuddin*[52] the High Court examining the scope of the enforcement court's jurisdiction in relation to a foreign award held that since foreign awards were enforced under Section 7, APC Act, 1937, the provisions of the AA, 1940 were inapplicable. Similar ratio could be derived from the decision in *Nan Fung Textiles*

[50]Rizwan Hussain, '*Taisei Corporation v A.M. Construction Co. (Pvt.) Ltd.*—Decision of the Lahore High Court in light of New York Convention' (2015) 31(3) Arbtn Int'l 507, 511.
[51](n 31).
[52]PLD 1979 Karachi 762.

*Limited v Sadiq Traders Limited.*[53] The Court held that since enforcement-related provisions have been inserted in the APC Act, 1937 for foreign awards, the provisions of AA, 1940 were inapplicable. It could therefore be said that the judiciary had clearly articulated the separate spaces of the two legislations, as early as in 1979.

In the *Marines Limited v AEGUS Shipping Co Ltd and others*[54] the Sindh High Court dismissed a petition challenging a London-seated arbitral tribunal's award, as the petitioner made the application under the AA, 1940 and not as per Section 7, APC Act, 1937 that specified the criteria for challenge and enforceability of foreign award.

## 4.2 Challenge to the Enforcement of a Foreign Award

A foreign award may be refused recognition and enforcement under Section 7 of the APC Act, 1937.[55] They are—invalidity of the arbitration agreement; lack of due process in the arbitration proceeding; award being beyond the contemplation of the arbitration agreement; composition of the tribunal or the procedure of the tribunal is not in accordance with the agreement; suspension of award by the competent court; matter being beyond the scope of arbitration; and public policy.

The REA Act, 2011 has aligned the Pakistan law with the NYC. It has expressly stated that the law on international arbitration in Pakistan is the NYC. An example

[53]PLD 1982 Karachi 619; *Avari Hotel Ltd and Hilton International Co.* PLD 1985 Karachi 465—when parties chose a foreign forum for arbitration of their dispute, agreed to apply that forum's rules, then the arbitration contemplated by the parties is not arbitration under the AA, 1940, hence the same would not be applicable.

[54]1987 CLC 1299; see a similar ratio in *Hassan ali & Co. Cotton Private Limited v Poly Cotton, S. A.*, PLD 1996 Karachi 416.

[55]s 7. Conditions for enforcement of foreign awards—(1) In order that a foreign award may be enforceable under this Act it must have- (a) been made in pursuance of an agreement for arbitration which was valid under the law by which it was governed, (b) been made by the tribunal provided for in the agreement or constituted in manner agreed upon by the parties, (c) been made in conformity with the law governing the arbitration procedure, (d) become final in the country in which it was made, (e) been in respect of a matter which may lawfully be referred to arbitration under the law of [Pakistan], and the enforcement thereof must not be contrary to the public policy or the law, of [Pakistan]. (2) A foreign award shall not be enforceable under this Act if the Court dealing with the case is satisfied that- (a) the award has been annulled in the country in which it was made, or (b) the party against whom it is sought to enforce the award was not given notice of the arbitration proceedings in sufficient time to enable him to present his case, or was under some legal incapacity and was not properly represented, or (c) the award does not deal with all the questions referred or contains decisions on matter beyond the scope of the agreement for arbitration; Provided that if the award does not deal with all questions referred the Court may, if it thinks fit, either postpone the enforcement of the award or order its enforcement subject to the giving of such security by the person seeking to enforce it as the Court may think fit.

of such alignment could be seen in the provisions related to recognition and enforcement of foreign arbitral awards. Section 7 states,

> the recognition and enforcement of a foreign arbitral award shall not be refused except in accordance with Article V of the Convention.

One of the important grounds under Article V of the NYC[56] that has come up for judicial interpretation in Pakistan, before and after the ratification of the NYC, in the REAO and the REA Act, 2011 is the ground of public policy.

## 4.3 Public Policy

Public policy has been a method for restricting the freedom of contract for private dealings in view of the larger good of the community.

In *The Official Assignee of the High Court of West Pakistan v The Lloyds Bank Ltd. Karachi and others*[57] the Supreme Court held that where the protective right is not rooted in law but is claimed in the orbit of public policy, the basic consideration must be the avoidance of harm to the general public and to uphold the right of innocence. The duty of the courts is to expound and not to expand public policy, and the doctrine should be invoked only in clear cases, in which the harm to the public is substantially incontestable.

Certain standards in the domain of morality have assumed sanctity on account of their acceptance by general community[58] whether they have been incorporated in

---

[56](1) Recognition and enforcement of the award may be refused, at the request of the party against whom it is invoked, only if that party furnishes to the competent authority where the recognition and enforcement is sought, proof that: (a) The parties to the agreement referred to in article II were, under the law applicable to them, under some incapacity, or the said agreement is not valid under the law to which the parties have subjected it or, failing any indication thereon, under the law of the country where the award was made; or (b) The party against whom the award is invoked was not given proper notice of the appointment of the arbitrator or of the arbitration proceedings or was otherwise unable to present his case; or (c) The award deals with a difference not contemplated by or not falling within the terms of the submission to arbitration, or it contains decisions on matters beyond the scope of the submission to arbitration, provided that, if the decisions on matters submitted to arbitration can be separated from those not so submitted, that part of the award which contains decisions on matters submitted to arbitration may be recognized and enforced; or (d) The composition of the arbitral authority or the arbitral procedure was not in accordance with the agreement of the parties, or, failing such agreement, was not in accordance with the law of the country where the arbitration took place; or (e) The award has not yet become binding, on the parties, or has been set aside or suspended by a competent authority of the country in which, or under the law of which, that award was made. (2) Recognition and enforcement of an arbitral award may also be refused if the competent authority in the country where recognition and enforcement is sought finds that: (a) The subject matter of the difference is not capable of settlement by arbitration under the law of that country; or (b) The recognition or enforcement of the award would be contrary to the public policy of that country.

[57]PLD 1969 SC 301.

[58]*Sardar Muhammad Yasin Khan v Raja Feroz Khan* PLD 1972 AJ&K 46.

the Constitution or not. Therefore, any private dealings that would destroy these standards or adversely affect the development of society or its organisation have to be viewed from this angle and these are the sources giving birth to the principle of public policy.[59]

However, it's been imprecise and varying. For what is anathema to one generation may be harmless to another. Public policy, the Court observed in *Sultan Textile Mills (Karachi) Ltd. v Muhammad Yousuf Shamsi*[60] stands as an exception to enforceability of a contract that was contrary to the general policy of law or injurious to and against the public good or *contra bonos mores* or that had arisen *ex turpi causa*. The Division Bench of the High Court of Sindh the court noted that the problem of illegality at common law on the ground of public policy is the discovery of injuriousness to society. This concept has elasticity as well as impreciseness.[61] Even though the contract is one that prima facie, falls under one of the recognized heads of public policy, 'it will not be held illegal unless its harmful qualities are indisputable…. Doctrine as Lord Atkin observed…..In popular language….The contact should be given the benefit of the doubt'.[62]

In *HUBCO*[63] the Supreme Court has held that when a contract is obtained by fraud and corruption, it is a void contract and according to the public policy such dispute arising out of that contract cannot be referred to arbitration. Such matters, the court held, according to the public policy required judicial findings about the alleged criminality. On account of the alleged criminal acts there did not come into existence any legally binding contract between the parties. The dispute primarily related to the very existence of a valid contract and not a dispute under such a contract. Hence, the Supreme Court upheld the anti-arbitration injunction granted by the Sindh High Court.

### 4.3.1 Principle of *Shariah*

Pakistan's Constitution states that the country shall be the Islamic Republic of Pakistan. The preamble expounds that the sovereignty over the entire universe belongs to Almighty Allah alone, and the authority and powers of the State is to be exercised by the people through chosen representative within the limits prescribed by Almighty Allah. Therefore, certain limits have been put on the law-makers. These limits can be derived from the *Shariah*.

---

[59]Ibid.

[60]PLD 1972 Karachi 226.

[61]Ibid.

[62]Inaamul Haque & Naeem Ullah Khan, 'Jurisprudence of Sanctity of Contracts in Pakistan—A Contextual Perspective'. http://www.pljlawsite.com/2009art12.htm, accessed 25 May 2016.

[63](n 23).

Recognition of an award or contract shall be refused in case if recognition would be in contradiction with the stipulations of the Islamic *Shariah.*[64] Mr. Justice Rana Bhagwan Das, the then Judge of the High Court of Sindh, has held in *Grosvenor Casino Ltd v Abdul Malik Badruddin*[65] that when a foreign judgment[66] sustains a claim prohibited by *Shariah,* it would not be enforced in Pakistan. He elaborated that the injunctions of *Quran* and *Sunnah* specified that all existing laws shall be brought in conformity with the Injunctions of Islam as laid down in the *Holy Quran* and *Sunnah* and no law shall be enacted which is repugnant to such Injunctions.

### 4.3.2 Award Containing Interest *(Riba)*

'Interest' is prohibited in Islam. In the year 1991, interest was declared repugnant to the Injunction of Islam in all its forms and manifestations and consequently, Interest Act, 1839 was directed to be repealed. It was also affirmed by the Supreme Court in *Dr. M. Aslam Khaki v Syed M. Hashim.*[67] However, in 2002, the Supreme Court in *United Bank Ltd. v M/s Farooq Brothers*[68] reviewed its own affirming judgment and set it aside; and remanded the case back to the Federal *Shariat* Court for reconsideration.

In *Messrs Flame Maritime Limited v Messrs Hassan Ali Rice Export*[69] one of the reasons for the objection to enforcement was the award of interest, which is against the Islamic law and cannot be enforced in Pakistan. The single Judge of the High Court of Sindh wrongly relied on the precedent laid in the 1999 judgment despite its being set aside by the 2002 review judgment of the Supreme Court and held that in view of the Supreme Court judgment "the enforcement of interest in Pakistan is repugnant to the injunction of Islam, therefore, the enforcement of interest as awarded would be against the law prevalent in Pakistan".

The contemporary position in Pakistan is that the interest is not unlawful because it is permissible to be ordered by the enforcement court in addition to the award under Section 29 of the Arbitration Act, 1940.[70] However there is a possibility of the Federal *Shariat* Court declaring it unlawful, in a pending dispute before it.

---

[64]Riyadh Arab Agreement for Judicial Cooperation states in a similar tone in the following word: "Recognition of judgments shall be refused in the following cases: (a) if recognition would be in contradiction with the stipulations of the Islamic Shari'a.....".

[65]PLD 1998 Karachi 104.

[66]Under Section 44-A of the Code of Civil Procedure, 1908 a decree of any superior Courts of the United Kingdom or any reciprocating territory may be executed in Pakistan as if it had been passed by the District Court [of Pakistan].

[67]PLD 2000 SC 225.

[68]PLD 2002 Supreme Court 801.

[69](n 47).

[70]AA, 1940s 29—Interest on award—Where and insofar as an award is for the payment of money the Court may in the decree order interest, from the date of the decree at such rate as the Court

Islam acknowledges the rights of non-Muslim to contract in accordance with their own religious practices without taking into consideration the prohibition and authorization of Islamic Laws. Therefore, they may enter into a contract and the resultant award can be enforced between them.[71] However, if one of the parties is Muslim then the Islamic law will apply and such award based on any contract prohibited in Islamic Law cannot be enforced for being against the public policy.[72]

## 5 Conclusion

While the enforcement of the NYC through the REA Act, 2011 is a welcome addition to the Pakistan law on arbitration, there is an immense need to modernize the arbitration law and align it with the global practices like, the UNCITRAL ML. A few features of a vibrant law on arbitration that Pakistan needs to immediately address are

- definition and characterization of a foreign award,
- the role of the courts in foreign-seated arbitrations,
- the status on the principle of competence-competence
- interim relief, not necessarily an interim award, but any order by the tribunal and its enforcement in Pakistan
- a clear statement on the 'concurrent jurisdiction' of the Pakistan courts,
- the characterization of foreign awards,
- powers to arbitrators to decide *a case ex aequo et bono or as amiable compositeur* if authorized by the parties; and to apply the substantive law of any country chosen by the parties, and
- the characterisation of international commercial arbitrations taking place in Pakistan.

It is hoped that the Arbitration and Conciliation Bill, 2015[73] pending with the Senate of Pakistan would consider the above-mentioned suggestions in its statutory revision work thereby enabling a much harmonious legal regime for international arbitration, in a world that is increasingly shifting towards harmonized legal platforms for international trade and commerce.

---

(Footnote 70 continued)

deems reasonable, to be paid on the principle sum as adjudged by the award and confirmed by the decree.

[71]Jalal El-Ahdab, *Arbitration with the Arab Countries* (Kluwer Law International 2011) 52.

[72]Ibid.

[73](n 09).

# Issues of Jurisdiction, Choice of Law and Enforcement in International Commercial Arbitration: A Sri Lankan Perspective

**Saleem Marsoof**

**Abstract** It is proposed to consider in this chapter in some detail, issues relating to jurisdiction, choice of law, and the enforcement in Sri Lanka of foreign arbitral awards. It is noteworthy that the Arbitration Act No. 11 of 1995, which is currently in force in Sri Lanka, applies uniformly to the conduct of purely domestic arbitration proceedings as well as to arbitration proceedings conducted in Sri Lanka involving one or more foreign parties and to the enforcement of foreign arbitral awards. Decisions of the courts in Sri Lanka have emphasized the consensual nature of arbitration and adopted a policy of minimum judicial intervention into arbitration proceedings. The courts also have been supportive of arbitration and endeavoured to assist and safeguard the arbitral process. The chapter will examine the provisions of the Arbitration Act that attempt to deal with certain issues involving conflicts of jurisdiction and the doctrine of Kompetenz-kompetez which seeks to empower the arbitral tribunal to rule on its own jurisdiction. In particular, an effort will be made to examine in some detail, questions involving jurisdiction that arise in the context of section 5 of the Arbitration Act, in comparison with the law and practice that exist in other South Asian jurisdictions. The choice of applicable law has always been a problem that has confounded arbitral tribunals when dealing with cases that have cross-border connections and connotations, and it is noteworthy that the Sri Lankan Arbitration Act recognizes the concept of party autonomy in regard to choice of law. An attempt will be made in the chapter to show how Sri Lankan arbitral tribunals and courts have dealt with issues arising from competing norms of national law as well as foreign law. Prior to the enactment of the Arbitration Act in 1995, there were many issues pertaining to the enforcement of foreign arbitral awards. While the Arbitration Act has resolved most procedural issues regarding enforcement of foreign awards, there remain many grey areas, particularly in regard to the concepts of arbitrability and public policy, and the interpretation of the

S. Marsoof (✉)
Supreme Court of Fiji, Suva, Fiji
e-mail: saleemmarsoof@gmail.com

S. Marsoof
formerly of the Supreme Court of Sri Lanka, Colombo, Sri Lanka

© Springer Nature Singapore Pte Ltd. 2017

S.R. Garimella and S. Jolly (eds.), *Private International Law*,
DOI 10.1007/978-981-10-3458-9_19

enforcement provisions of the Sri Lankan Act, which seek to give effect to the international obligations that arise from Sri Lanka's ratification of the New York Convention on the Recognition and Enforcement of Foreign Arbitral Awards without any reservations. Recent decisions of the Supreme Court of Sri Lanka have dealt with some of these issues, which will be examined, in detail in this chapter. An attempt will be made in the chapter to explain how Sri Lankan arbitral tribunals and courts have dealt with issues arising from competing norms of national law as well as foreign law.

**Keywords** Sri Lanka arbitration law · Arbitral tribunal · Jurisdiction · Enforcement of foreign awards · Public policy

## Introduction

Sri Lanka, is a unitary republic situated to the south of the Indian Peninsular, which by reason of its shape, size, location and character, has been long described as the "pearl of the Indian Ocean". Sri Lanka has a rich tradition of alternate dispute resolution through the "*gam sabhava*"[1] going back to two thousand five hundred years.[2] This tradition was embedded into the Arbitration Ordinance of 1866[3] and the Civil Procedure Code of 1889.[4] The said Code contained provisions empowering the courts to refer any dispute for arbitration, and also provided a special mechanism for enforcing arbitral awards.

In 1995, the Arbitration Act (hereinafter, SLAA)[5] was enacted with the objective of regulating the conduct of all arbitration proceedings that take place in Sri Lanka, other than industrial,[6] co-operative[7] and investment[8] related arbitration.[9] The SLAA repealed and replaced the Arbitration Ordinance and certain provisions of the Civil Procedure Code.[10] The SLAA was greatly influenced by the UNCITRAL Model Law (hereinafter, the UNCITRAL ML)[11] with a few provisions fashioned on the

[1]"*Gam Sabhava*" means "village council", and was a body of elders of the village who gathered from time to time to attempt the amicable resolution of disputes.

[2]A.R.B. Amarasinghe, 'Sri Lanka Arbitration Act' in K. Kanag-Isvaran & S.S. Wijeratne (ed.) *Arbitration Law in Sri Lanka*, (ICLP 3rd Ed. 2007) 9, 13.

[3]Arbitration Ordinance, No. 15 of 1866.

[4]Civil Procedure Code, Ordinance No. 2 of 1889, s 676–698.

[5]Arbitration Act, No. 11 of 1995.

[6]Industrial Disputes Act No. 43 of 1950.

[7]Co-operative Societies Act No. 5 of 1972.

[8]Board of Investment of Sri Lanka Law No. 4 of 1978.

[9](n 5) s 2(1) r/w s 48.

[10](n 4) Ss 693–698.

[11]UNCITRAL Model Law on International Commercial Arbitration, 1985—UN doc. A/40/17, Annex 1.

draft Swedish Arbitration Act[12] and the New York Convention on the Recognition and Enforcement of Foreign Arbitral Awards, 1958 (hereinafter, the NYC).[13]

The hallmark of the SLAA is the concept of 'party autonomy', enabling the parties to select not only their arbitrator or arbitrators,[14] the seat or place of arbitration,[15] the rules of procedure to be followed by the arbitrators,[16] and the "rules of law" to be applied in determining the substantive dispute before them.[17] Concepts such as severability of the arbitration clause,[18] minimal judicial intervention in arbitration proceedings,[19] the independence and impartiality of the arbitral tribunal,[20] finality of the arbitral award[21] and efficiency in the recognition and enforcement of arbitral awards[22] are recognized by the provisions of the SLAA. Sri Lankan courts acknowledge that arbitration proceedings are "consensual in nature and private in character."[23]

**Structure of the Chapter**
This Chapter attempts to provide a Sri Lankan perspective on jurisdictional, choice of law, and enforcement issues that arise in the sphere of arbitration. After a brief introduction to Sri Lanka's arbitration culture, this chapter would first focus on conflicts of jurisdiction that may arise in arbitration. It is followed by a discussion on the conflict of law issues with regard to choice of law in international arbitration. The chapter concludes with a discussion on the recognition and enforcement of foreign arbitral awards.

## 1 Issues Relating to Jurisdiction

Just as a court of law derives its jurisdiction from the Constitution or some empowering legislation, an arbitral tribunal derives its jurisdiction from the parties to the dispute through the mandate set out in the relevant arbitration agreement. By choosing arbitration, the parties manifest an intention to exclude Courts from both

[12]Arbitration Act, SFS 1999: 116.

[13]The United Nations Convention on the Recognition and Enforcement of Foreign Arbitral Awards (New York, 10th June 1958).

[14](n 5) Ss 5–7.

[15]Ibid. s 16.

[16]Id s 17.

[17]Id s 18.

[18]Id s 12.

[19]Id Ss 4–5.

[20]Id s 10.

[21]Id s 26.

[22]Id Ss 31–35.

[23]Saleem Marsoof, 'Judiciary and the Arbitral Process' in S. Marsoof & N. Wigneswaran (Ed.) *In Pursuit of Justice* (Colombo: Kamalasabayson Foundation, 2008) 33, 35.

the conduct of the proceedings and the resolution of the dispute. It is ideal for the courts not to intervene in arbitration proceedings except to support and facilitate the arbitral process, as the clash of the two jurisdictions can altogether frustrate the arbitral tribunal.[24]

Jurisdiction must exist if a valid award is to be rendered by an arbitral tribunal, and it is essential that issues relating to the jurisdiction of the arbitral tribunal are determined at the very inception of the arbitration proceedings. Any objection to the exercise of jurisdiction by an arbitral tribunal must be taken up at the earliest possible opportunity, because "long participation and acquiescence in the proceedings precludes a party from contending that the proceedings were without jurisdiction."[25] In order to facilitate this process, the SLAA expressly empowers an arbitral tribunal to rule on its jurisdiction "including any question, with respect to the existence or validity of the arbitration agreement or as to whether such agreement is contrary to public policy or is incapable of being performed."[26] This provision, however, does not preclude a party from challenging the jurisdiction of the arbitral tribunal before the High Court, but permits the proceedings before the arbitral tribunal to go on pending the determination of any such question by the High Court.[27]

The initial question considered in any investigation of an arbitral tribunal's jurisdiction is whether there is a valid and binding agreement to arbitrate any particular dispute. As court noted in a case where the question arose as to whether the guarantors of the obligations of a lessee were bound by an arbitration clause contained in the lease agreement to which they were not parties, "an agreement to proceed to arbitration being an agreement in derogation of a party's right to have recourse to a Court of Law, there must be specific consent expressed by the plaintiff in writing, if his claim against the guarantors too is to be submitted to arbitration before action is filed in court."[28] Hence, in ascertaining whether an arbitral tribunal is possessed of jurisdiction, two essential issues arise: (1) is there a valid and binding agreement to arbitrate? (2) does the dispute referred to an arbitral tribunal fall within the scope or ambit of the agreement to arbitrate?

An agreement to arbitrate might take the form of an arbitration clause in a contract whereby the parties agree to settle any dispute that might arise in the future, or a "submission agreement" by which a reference to arbitration is made after a dispute arises. The latter form is used where the dispute relates to a contract that did not contain an arbitration clause or in a non-contractual situation such as when a tort or *delict* is committed.[29] The SLAA requires an arbitration agreement to be in

[24]UNCTAD, *Dispute Settlement: International Commercial Arbitration*, 5.8 Court Measures, 3 (2005).

[25]*Ranin Kumar, Proprietor, Messrs. Pharma Chemie v State Pharmaceutical Corporation* (2004) 1 SLR 276, 281 [de Silva J.].

[26](n 5) s 11(1).

[27]Ibid. s 11(2).

[28]*Uduwara & Others v L.B. Finance Co. Ltd* [2004] 2 SLR 151, 153 [Amaratunga J.].

[29](n 5) s 50 defined an agreement so as to include an arbitration clause and a submission agreement.

writing[30] but does not require that the parties sign the agreement. It provides that an arbitration agreement shall be deemed to be in writing "if it is contained in a document signed by the parties or in an exchange of letters, telexes, telegrams or other means of telecommunication which provide a record of the agreement."[31]

The jurisdiction of an arbitral tribunal may be assailed on the basis of non-compliance with the formal requirements applicable to the formation of the agreement and on grounds such as mistake, forgery, fraud or duress that affect the genuineness of consent.[32] Jurisdiction of a tribunal may also be challenged on the basis that the agreement to arbitrate is illegal.[33] In *Jafferjee v Subbiah Pillai,*[34] it was held that a contract that was illegal at the time it was made would not be considered legal if the law changes before the date set for performance. Where the illegality relates to a contract in which an arbitration clause is contained, a court would endeavor to give effect to the arbitration clause by applying the doctrine of 'severability', which is enshrined in the Arbitration Act.[35]

An otherwise valid arbitration agreement may be deemed incapable of conferring jurisdiction on an arbitral tribunal if the dispute is not capable of determination by arbitration or the matter in respect of which the arbitration agreement is entered into is contrary to public policy.[36] The question whether a particular dispute is arbitrable, could arise in a wide variety of cases such as those involving violations of securities regulation,[37] anti-trust or unfair competition,[38] insolvency,[39] and dissolution of partnerships.[40] However, the only instance where an arbitration agreement was successfully challenged on the ground of non-arbitrability in Sri Lanka, was in an action filed in the Commercial High Court in terms of sections 210 and

[30]Ibid., s 3(2).

[31]Id.

[32]*Sheikh Brothers Limited v Arnold Julius Ochsner and another* [1957] UKPC 1.

[33]*Soleimany v Soleimany* [1999] Q.B. 785.

[34]54 NLR 505.

[35](n 5) s 12, specified "an arbitration agreement which forms part of another agreement shall be deemed to constitute a separate agreement when ruling upon the validity of that arbitration agreement for the purpose of determining the jurisdiction of the arbitral tribunal." http://slnarbcentre.com/downloads/ARBITRATION-ACT.pdf, accessed 21 July 2016.

[36]Ibid. s 4.

[37]*Rodriguez de Quijas v. Shearson/American Express* 490 US 477 (1989); *Philip Alexander Securities v Bamberger* [1997] EULR 63 (1996) CLC (1) (757).

[38]*Mitsubishi Motors Corp. v Soler Chrysler Plymouth Inc.* [1985] 473 U. S. 614; *Eco Swiss China Time Ltd v Benetton International N.V.*, 1999 E.C.R. I-3055; *ET Plus S.A. v Jean-Paul Welter & The Channel Tunnel Group Ltd.* [2005] EWHC 2115 (Comm.).

[39]*SONATRACH v Distrigas* 80 BR 606 (D. Mass. 1987).

[40]*Soysa v Ranasinghe* 16 NLR 222.

211 of the repealed Companies Act of 1982[41] in terms of which the court had "the power to impose upon the parties a just and equitable settlement".[42]

There has been no case in Sri Lanka where an arbitration agreement or an arbitral award was set aside or refused recognition or enforcement on the ground that it is contrary to public policy. In *Light Weight Body Armour Ltd. v. Sri Lanka Army*[43] the Supreme Court of Sri Lanka observed that the concept of 'public policy' encompassed "fundamental principles of law and justice in substantive as well as procedural aspects".[44] In its decision in that case as well as in *Hatton National Bank v Kiran Atapattu and Another*[45] and *Kiran Atapattu v Janashakthi General Insurance Co. Ltd.*,[46] the Supreme Court expressly declined to base its decision on public policy when other avenues were open, and observed in the course of its judgment in the latter case that "while the dynamism of the concept of public policy cannot be denied, it is important to exercise extreme caution in applying the concept."[47]

An arbitral tribunal that has not been validly constituted cannot lawfully exercise jurisdiction. Thus, making a second reference to arbitration while a previous award pertaining to same dispute stands valid,[48] and the failure to adhere to the qualifications or disqualifications of arbitrators stipulated in the arbitration agreement, could give rise to jurisdictional issues as much as the failure to appoint the number of arbitrators stipulated in the arbitration agreement.[49]

An arbitral tribunal cannot lawfully exercise jurisdiction if the dispute referred to it does not fall within the scope of the agreement to arbitrate,[50] or the ambit of the legislation, treaty or convention that provides for arbitration.

It is significant to note that the NYC and the UNCITRAL ML have been influential in preventing courts from frustrating arbitration proceedings. Pursuant to Sri Lanka's national obligation under the New York Convention to recognize an

[41]Companies Act No. 17 of 1982. This Act has since been repealed by the Companies Act No. 7 of 2007, which is now in force, and the corresponding provisions of the new Act that deal with complaints of oppression and mismanagement are Ss 224 and 225.

[42]*Aitken Spence & Co. Ltd. v The Garment Services Group Ltd.*, HC (Civil) 02/2003(02) decided on 28.5.2003 reported in K. Kanag-Isvaran & S.S. Wijeratne (n 2) 361.

[43][2007] BALR 10.

[44]Ibid. page 13 [Tilakawardane, J.].

[45][2013] XX BALR 45.

[46]SC Appeal 30–31/2005, 22.2.2013 . http://www.supremecourt.lk/images/documents/SC_Appeal_30_05_Final.pdf, accessed 01 January 2016.

[47]Ibid. [Marsoof J.].

[48]*D.M.G. Ukku Banda v Rahatungoda Co-operative Stores Society Ltd.*, 58 NLR 68.

[49]*Merchant Bank of Sri Lanka Ltd., v D.V.D.A Tillekeratne*, SC Appeal No. 43/2001, 25.9.2001; reported in K. Kanag-Isvaran & S.S. Wijeratne (n 2) 317.

[50]*Oberoi Hotels (Pvt) Limited v Asian Hotels Corporation Ltd.* SC.L.A Application No. 28/2000, 25.11.2002; reported in K. Kanag-Isvaran & S.S. Wijeratne (n 2) 259. See also, *Hatton National Bank v Kiran Atapattu and Another*, SC Appeal No 38–39/06, SC (HC) L.A. Appl. No 32–33/06 HC/ARB/1890/04.

agreement in writing, under which the parties undertake to submit to arbitration all or any differences which have arisen or which may arise between them in respect of a defined legal relationship,[51] the SLAA specifies

> Any dispute, which the parties have agreed to submit to arbitration under an arbitration agreement, may be determined by arbitration unless the matter in respect of which the arbitration agreement is entered into is *contrary to public policy or, is not capable of determination by arbitration.*[52]

Sri Lanka has also attempted to comply with its NYC obligation to ensure that its courts *shall*, when seized of an action falling within the purview of the Convention, at the request of any party to the arbitration, "*refer the parties to arbitration*, unless it finds that the said agreement is *null and void, inoperative or incapable of being performed.*"[53] Section 5 of the SLAA states that

> Where a party to an arbitration agreement institutes legal proceedings in a court against another party to such agreement in respect of a matter agreed to be submitted for arbitration under such agreement, *the Court shall have no jurisdiction to hear and determine such matter* if the other party objects to the court exercising jurisdiction in respect of such matter. (*Emphasis added*)

It is noteworthy that sections 4 and 5 of the SLAA, in seeking to resolve conflicts of jurisdiction between a court of law and an arbitral tribunal, do not entirely follow the corresponding provisions the NYC and the UNCITRAL ML in two important respects. Firstly, the SLAA does not empower Sri Lankan courts to consider whether any arbitration clause relied upon to object to jurisdiction of court is "null and void, inoperative or incapable of being performed", and has focused on maintaining mutual consistency between sections 4 of the Act and sections 32(1)(b) and 34(1)(b) of the Act, by excluding from the purview of the obligation of courts to recognize and enforce arbitration agreements, only those agreements that are contrary to public policy or are non-arbitrable. However, while sections 32(1)(b) and 34(1)(b) refer to the "public policy of Sri Lanka", section 4 does not qualify its reference to "public policy" in that manner, and may open its doors to the public policy of the country in which the arbitration agreement was entered into (*lex contractus*) or even "transnational public policy".[54]

Secondly, the SLAA does not expressly provide, as does the NYC and the UNCITRAL ML, that when a party invokes the jurisdiction of court notwithstanding an agreement to arbitrate the dispute, the Court should refer the parties to arbitration. The SLAA provides that in such an eventuality, "the court shall have no

---

51 NYC, Art. II(1).

52 (n 5) s 4 (emphasis added).

53 NYC, Art. II(3). The UNCITRAL ML, Art. 8(1) is to the same effect.

54 The phrase "transnational public policy" refers to the fundamental values, the basic ethical standards, and the enduring moral consensus of the international business community. The phrase will catch up violations of human rights (such as racial, sexual and religious discrimination), *bonos moros* (including corruption, terrorism, genocide and sexual abuse of vulnerable persons) and breaches of rules of natural justice.

jurisdiction." This has resulted in actions filed in Sri Lanka notwithstanding the existence of an arbitration clause, being dismissed by courts without considering the consequences such dismissal might give rise to.[55] This propensity of Sri Lankan courts might cause injustice to a party if after an action is dismissed to compel arbitration, the arbitral tribunal finds that it does not have jurisdiction with respect to the matter, and the cause of action gets prescribed or time-barred in the meantime. In *Elgitread Lanka (Pvt.) Ltd v Bino Tyres (Pvt.) Ltd*,[56] the Supreme Court adopted a more enlightened approach in a case in which it overturned a decision of the Commercial High Court to overrule an objection taken to the jurisdiction of that court on the basis of section 5 of the SLAA, as the defect in the arbitration clause which referred to a non-existent arbitral institution could be overcome by utilising the procedure set out in the Act.[57] The Supreme Court held that in the light of Sri Lanka's obligations under the NYC, it was bound to recognize the agreement to arbitrate, and that the Commercial High Court had no jurisdiction to hear and determine the case on its merits. The Supreme Court then went on to consider whether in all the circumstances of the case it was appropriate for the action to be dismissed or merely stayed, and observed that the neutrality in regard to sanction found in the UNCITRAL ML and the NYC has been preserved in section 5 of the SLAA and that the Commercial High Court enjoyed inherent power "to decide at its discretion whether to dismiss action or stay proceedings".[58] In the course of its judgment, the Supreme Court observed as follows:

> In some of these cases, particularly where there is an international element, it may well be that there are concurrent judicial and/or arbitral proceedings in more than one jurisdiction, and cogent reasons may be advanced to justify the continuation of such proceedings, but in making its decision, a court will also take into consideration the need to avoid multiplicity of proceedings with the accompanying risk of inconsistent judgments and arbitral awards. Many principles have been evolved by the courts all over the world to deal with such issues of great variety and complexity. Apart from such issues, difficult questions could also arise in regard to public policy and arbitrability, which have the potentiality of rendering the arbitration agreement and / or the ensuing arbitral award unenforceable, a factor that should be taken into consideration in deciding whether an action should merely be stayed or dismissed.[59]

For the purpose of discharging Sri Lanka's NYC obligation of giving effect to arbitration agreements, a Sri Lankan court, will not hesitate to grant an anti-suit injunction to restrain foreign Court proceedings, which are in breach of a prior

[55] *Ocean Wind Maritime SA v Gujarat Cheminex Ltd*, [2012] 2 SLR 35 It is noteworthy that s 7 of the Arbitration Ordinance, (n 3) was differently worded and did require a court to refer the parties to arbitration. See *Gordeon Frazer & Co Ltd. v Jeean Marie Losio and Martin Wenzel*, [1984] 2 SLR 85.

[56] [2011] XVII BALR 130.

[57] (n 5) Ss 5, 7.

[58] (n 56) 140 [Marsoof J.].

[59] Ibid., 141 [Marsoof J.].

agreement to arbitrate.[60] Although in *The Golden Anne*,[61] the court was mindful of not committing an "unacceptable infringement of the prerogatives of the foreign Court", in *The Angelic Grace*[62] Millen LJ commented that "where an injunction is sought to restrain a party from proceeding in a foreign Court in breach of an arbitration agreement governed by English law, the English Court need feel no diffidence in granting the injunction, provided that it is sought promptly and before the foreign proceedings are too far advanced." While Sri Lankan courts are likely to apply the same reasoning, it is unlikely that they will transgress into the territorial sovereignty of a country that is not party to the NYC.

Subject to the above constraint, an arbitral tribunal may by way of interim measure order that a party to an arbitration agreement should refrain from taking any further steps in parallel court proceedings, whether in Sri Lanka or otherwise.[63] It is noteworthy that although the UNCITRAL ML[64] recognizes the right of a party to an arbitration agreement to seek interim measures from a court before or during arbitral proceedings, the SLAA[65] only provides a mechanism for interim measures ordered by an arbitral tribunal to be enforced through the High Court. In *Backsons Textile Industries Ltd. v Hybro Industries Ltd.*[66] the Court of Appeal upheld an order of the District Court to grant interim relief pending the constitution of the arbitral tribunal, but in *K.P. Projects International Pvt Ltd v. National Water Supply and Drainage Board and another*[67] the High Court took the view that the correct procedure was found in Art. 143 of the Constitution,[68] and accordingly clarified that the Court of Appeal had the jurisdiction to issue injunctions by way of interim measure pending the constitution of an arbitral tribunal.[69]

---

[60] *Pena Copper Mines Ltd v. Rio Tinto Co Ltd* [1911] 105 LT 846; *Aggeliki Charis Compania Maritima SA v. Pagnan SpA The Angelic Grace* [1995] 1 Lloyd's Rep. 87.

[61] *World Pride Shipping Ltd v. Daiichi Chuo KK, The Golden Anne* [1984] 2 Lloyd's Rep. 489.

[62] (n 60).

[63] *E-Systems v Iran* Case No. 338 2 Iran-US CI. Trib. Rep. 51 [1983] Interim Award dated 4th February, 1983; *SGS Société Générale de Surveillance SA v Pakistan* ICSID Case No. ARB/01/13. See, Michael Black and Rupert Reece, 'Anti-Suit Injunctions and Arbitration Proceedings' (2006) 72 JCIA 207.

[64] UNCITRAL ML Art. 9.

[65] (n 5) s 13.

[66] C.A. Application No. 51/97, C.A Minutes dated 28.4.1997, K. Kanag-Isvaran & S.S. Wijeratne (n 2) 355.

[67] HC (Civil) 546/2010/MR (unreported) *Contra, Swiss Singapore Overseas Enterprises Pvt Ltd v Ceylon Fertilizer Company Ltd* CHC 652/2010/MR (unreported).

[68] The Constitution of the Democratic Socialist Republic of Sri Lanka, 1978, Art 143 provides: "The Court of Appeal shall have the power to grant and issue injunctions to prevent any irremediable mischief which might ensure before a party making an application for such injunction could prevent the same by bringing an action in any Court of First Instance".

[69] Althaf Marsoof, 'A comment on interim measures and arbitration in Sri Lanka', [2012] *Neetham* 22.

## 2 Issues Relating to Choice of Law

To the theoretician, international arbitration can be a wonderful subject offering a variety of choice of law issues, far more than those occurring in comparative proceedings before a court of law.[70] Issues such as, which law governs the agreement to arbitrate, the individual reference, the arbitral procedure and the substantive liabilities of the parties, could arise in the course of arbitration or judicial proceedings, and the answer may vary depending on whether it is approached from the perspective of the arbitral tribunal itself, or that of a Sri Lankan or foreign court.[71] In international litigation, the law and procedure of the state in which a court functions will generally be paramount, but as far as substantive rights are concerned, the position in the English common law which is also the Sri Lankan court practice[72] is that they will be governed by the law of a particular State, which is determined to be the proper law of the contract or other obligation on which the action is based.

In regard to the proper law of the contract, party autonomy plays a major role, and the common law rule, as explained by Lord Wright, was that

> … provided the intention expressed is *bona fide* and legal, and provided there is no reason for avoiding the choice on grounds of public policy, the intention of the parties as to the choice of law prevails.[73]

The choice may be express or implied. An implied choice of law may be inferred where a contract contained a clause providing for the submission of any dispute arising therefrom to the courts of, or arbitration in, a particular country,[74] but in *Bangladesh Chemical Industries Corp. v Henry Stephens Shipping Co. Ltd.*,[75] Lord Denning MR stressed that though an arbitration clause is of the "very first importance" it is not necessarily conclusive in regard to whether the parties intended that the law of the seat of arbitration designated in that clause is the proper law of the contract. Where however, the parties have not made an express or implied choice of law, as Senanayake J. opined in *International Science and Technological Institute Inc. v Rosa and Another*, the proper law will be "the system of law with which the transaction has the closest and most real connection".[76]

---

[70]Michael Pryles, 'Choice of Law Issues in International Arbitration', in Cheong, Lai, Beng and Loon (ed) *Current Legal Issues in Commercial Litigation*, (1997, Faculty of Law, NUS, Singapore), 105.

[71]Ibid., 106.

[72]*International Science and Technological Institute Inc. v Rosa and Another* [1994] 2 SLR 233, 239; This will not include English legislation and EU Regulation such as Rome I and II that apply in England.

[73]*Vita Food Products Inc. v Unus Shipping Co. Ltd.* (1939) UKPC 7 (Lord Wright).

[74]*Hamlyn and Co v Talisker Distillery* [1894] AC 202; *NV Kwik Hoo Tong Handel; Maatschappij v James Findlay and Co* [1927] AC 604; *Makender v Feldia AG* [1967] 2 QB 590.

[75][1981] 2 Lloyd's Report 389 [Lord Denning MR].

[76](n 72) 242.

In regard to action related to torts or delicts the English common law did not recognize party autonomy[77] and initially favoured the *lex fori* with a few decisions applying the *lex loci delicti*, but failed to "establish a satisfactory method of dealing with tort problems in the conflict of laws after over a century of trying."[78] In Sri Lanka, there is a dearth of judicial authority on the subject and Sri Lankan courts and arbitral tribunals sitting in Sri Lanka are more likely to follow the principles of English common law while developing the same to suit local conditions.[79]

The SLAA has attempted to minimize conflict of law issues by giving greater impetus to party autonomy. The Act contains explicit provisions in section 24 thereof for the determination of the law applicable to the substance of the dispute between the parties. Section 24(1) of the Act provides that an arbitral tribunal shall decide the dispute in accordance with such rules of law as are chosen by the parties as applicable to the substance of the dispute, and goes on to clarify that any designation of the law or legal system of a given State shall be construed, unless otherwise expressed, as referring to the substantive law of that State and not to its conflict of laws rules.[80] In this context, three points deserve to be noted

- the reference to "rules of law" in Section 24(1) is sufficiently wide to permit the parties to select either a national law or even transnational rules of law such as the *lex mercatoria* or the *shari'at* as the law that would govern the substance of the dispute.
- unless the parties have otherwise agreed, the designated national law does not necessarily include rules of conflict of law such as *renvoi*, which may be part of that law.
- rules of general justice and fairness or trade usages may only be applied by an arbitral tribunal in the determination of the dispute where the parties have expressly authorized it to do so.[81]

It is important to emphasize that the law applicable to the arbitration agreement will not necessarily be the same as the law applicable to the substance of the dispute, as was pointed out by Saville J. in *Union of India v McDonnell Douglas*

[77]Thomas Kadner Graziano, 'The Freedom the Applicable Law in Tort—Art 14 and 4(3) of the Rome II Regulations', in John Ahern and William Binchy, *The Rome II Regulation on the Law Applicable to Non-Contractual Obligations: A New International Legal Regime* (Martinus Nijhoff, Leiden, 2009) 113.

[78]John O'Brien, *Conflict of Laws* (2nd Ed. Cavendish, 1999), 381. See also, *The Halley* (1866) LR 2 PC 193 (Selwyn LJ); *Phillips v Eyre* (1870) LR 6 QB 1 (Willes J); *The Mary Moxham* (1876) 1 PD 107 (Sir Robert Phillimore) *Machado v Fontes* [1897] 2 QB 231 (Lopes, Rigby LJJ).

[79]*Lily M de Costa v Bank of Ceylon*, 72 NLR 457 at 469 [H.N.G. Fernando CJ] 495 [Weeramantry J.] *Kodeeswaran v Attorney General of Ceylon*, [1970] AC 1111; 72 NLR 337, 342 (PC) [Lord Diplock].

[80](n 5) s 24(1).

[81](n 5) s 24(4).

*Corp*[82] where his Lordship drew a further distinction between the law applicable to the arbitration agreement and the law governing the arbitration proceedings.

In determining the validity of an arbitration agreement, an arbitral tribunal sitting in Sri Lanka or a Sri Lankan court would apply the law to which the parties have subjected the arbitration agreement, or failing any indication on that question, determine the question according to the law of Sri Lanka.[83]

In Sri Lanka, therefore, there can be little doubt that the law governing arbitration proceedings seated in Sri Lanka will be the *lex fori* and the SLAA expressly reiterated the same by stating that the provisions of the said Act shall govern such proceedings.[84] This Act empowers the parties to agree on the procedure to be followed by the arbitral tribunal, including whether the arbitral proceedings should be institutional or ad hoc,[85] and the admissibility, relevance and weight of any evidence.[86] Unless otherwise agreed upon by the parties, the Act provides that evidence before the arbitral tribunal may be given orally in writing or by affidavit and the tribunal will not be bound by the provisions of the Evidence Ordinance.[87]

## 3 Issues Relating to Recognition and Enforcement

Prior to the enactment of the Arbitration Act, arbitral awards made in Sri Lanka were enforced in terms of the provisions of the Civil Procedure Code,[88] and foreign awards were enforceable only to the extent permitted by the Reciprocal Enforcement of Judgments Ordinance.[89] The latter Ordinance defined the term "judgment" to include an arbitral award if such award has, "in pursuance of the law in force in the place where it was made, become enforceable in the same manner as a judgment given by a court in that place."[90]Apart from the fact that the provisions of the Ordinance applied only to an award "whereby any sum of money is made

[82][1993] 2 Lloyds Report 48.

[83](n 5) Section 32(1)(a)(i) and Section 34(1)(a)(i); Also see *Dallah Real Estate and Tourism Holding Co v Ministry of Religious Affairs (Pakistan)* [2010] UKSC 46, [2011] 1 AC 763; *Habas Sinai Ve Tibbi Gazlar Istihsal Endustisi AS v VSC Steel Co Ltd* [2013] EWHC 4071 (Comm); [2014] 1 Lloyd's Rep. 479.

[84](n 5) s 2(1).

[85]ICLP Arbitration Centre was set up in 1996. Sri Lanka's oldest arbitration center is the Sri Lanka National Arbitration Centre (SLNAC) established in 1985. In 2015, an International Arbitration Centre was set up at the World Trade Center, Colombo, with a view of promoting international commercial arbitration.

[86](n 5) s 17.

[87]Ibid., Section 22.

[88](n 4).

[89]Reciprocal Enforcement of Judgments Ordinance No. 41 of 1921.

[90]Ibid. s 2(1).

payable",[91] the need to prove that the debtor was resident or carried on of business in the place of arbitration or voluntarily submitted to the jurisdiction of the tribunal,[92] and the requirement of reciprocity[93] were major constraints on enforceability.

The NYC sought to mitigate such difficulties in the enforcement of arbitral awards. When Sri Lanka ratified the Convention, it did not subject its ratification to either the 'territoriality' or 'commercial' reservations.[94] The SLAA specified

> A foreign arbitral award *irrespective of the country to which it was made*, shall subject to the provisions of section 34 be recognized as binding and, upon application by a party under section 31 to the High Court, be enforced by filing the award in accordance with the provisions of that section.[95] (*Emphasis added*)

It is noteworthy that Section 50 of the SLAA has defined a "foreign arbitral award" to mean "an award made in an arbitration conducted outside Sri Lanka, the defining factor therefore being the seat of arbitration.

Part VII of the SLAA contains provisions for making applications for the setting aside of domestic arbitral awards[96] and the enforcement of domestic[97] and foreign[98] arbitral awards. The designated court for making such application for is the High Court as defined in the Act,[99] Further the Act requires the High Court to consolidate any application for enforcement of an award with any application for setting aside the same award that may be pending at the same time, thereby ensuring that the two applications are dealt with together. The SLAA does not allow any appeals against an arbitral award on the award's merits, and in fact declares that, subject to the provisions of Part VII of this Act, "the award made by the arbitral tribunal shall be final and binding on the parties to the arbitration agreement."[100] The decisions of the Supreme Court in *Light Weight Body Armour Ltd. v. Sri Lanka Army*[101] *Kristley*

---

[91]Id.

[92]Ibid. s 3(2)(b). See also, *Prins Goonesekere v Associated Newspapers of Ceylon Ltd.*, [2000] 3 SLR 122.

[93]Ibid. s 6.

[94]See Alan Redfern, Martin Hunter, Nigel Blackaby, Constantine Partasides, *Law and Practice of International Commercial Arbitration* (4th edn, Sweet & Maxwell, London, 2004) 440–443. See also, S. Marsoof, Recognition and Enforcement of Foreign Arbitral Awards: Some Salient Points (2005) LCLR 27.

[95](n 5) s 33.

[96]Ibid. s 32.

[97]Id, s 31.

[98]Id, s 34.

[99]Id, s 50. This court is not the same as the Commercial High Court established by virtue of an order made in terms of s 2(1) of the High Court of the Provinces (Special Provisions) Act, No. 10 of 1996. *See, Vanik Incorporation Ltd., v L.D Silva and Others* [2001] 1 SLR 110 and *Elgitread Lanka (Pvt.) Ltd v Bino Tyres (Pvt.) Ltd.*, (n 56).

[100](n 5) s 23.

[101](n 43).

*(Pvt) Ltd v. State Timber Corporation,*[102] *and Kiran Atapattu v Janashakthi General Insurance Co. Ltd.,*[103] illustrate the positive judicial attitude of Sri Lankan courts towards arbitration. Sri Lankan courts, therefore, would not "second guess" the arbitral tribunal, particularly on questions of facts.

Seven grounds are enumerated in section 34(1) of the SLAA[104] as grounds upon which an application for recognition or enforcement of a foreign arbitral award may be refused. These grounds are in *pari materia* with the grounds set out in the NYC[105] and the UNCITRAL ML.[106] These grounds have been held to be exhaustive, and it is trite law that no other grounds may be invoked.

## 3.1 Invalidity of the Arbitration Agreement

Recognition or enforcement of a foreign award under the SLAA may be denied if the arbitration agreement is invalid according to its parties-chosen governing law, or failing any indication as to the law to which the parties have subjected such agreement, under the law of the country where the award was made.[107] Such invalidity could also arise from the incapacity of a party to the arbitration agreement due to death, dissolution or insolvency.[108] In deciding whether a party suffered such incapacity, a Sri Lankan court would be governed by the law applicable to the party at the time and place the incapacity is alleged to have occurred, and in *Kristley (Pvt) Ltd v. State Timber Corporation,*[109] although the Supreme Court took the view that the impact of the de-registration of an Australian company during the pendency of arbitration proceedings in Sri Lanka had to be considered in the light of Australian law, the need to decide the matter was obviated by the re-registration of the company during the pendency of the arbitration.

## 3.2 Violation of the Principles of Natural Justice

Violations of the rules of natural justice, such as the failure to give the party against whom the award is invoked proper notice of the appointment of an arbitrator or of

---

[102] [2002] 1 SLR 225.

[103] (n 46).

[104] (n 5).

[105] NYC, Article V(1) and (2).

[106] UNICTRAL ML, Article 36(1).

[107] (n 5) 5 s 34(1)(a)(i). Compare s 32(1)(a)(i) for a domestic award.

[108] Ibid.

[109] (n 102).

the arbitral proceeding, or preventing such party from presenting his case, may also result in the refusal of an application for the enforcement of an arbitral award.[110] In *Merchant Bank of Sri Lanka Limited v Amarasiri De Silva*,[111] the Supreme Court held that even the failure on the part of the arbitral tribunal to serve on a party a copy of the award could give rise to a good ground for refusing enforcement of an award.

## 3.3 *Excess of Jurisdiction by the Arbitral Tribunal*

Excess of jurisdiction of the arbitral tribunal, such as where the award deals with a dispute not falling within the terms of the submission to arbitration, or it contains decisions on matters beyond the scope of the submission to arbitration could be a ground for refusal of recognition and enforcement of the foreign award.[112] In *Oberoi Hotels (Pvt) Limited v Asian Hotels Corporation Ltd.*[113] the excess of jurisdiction occurred when the tribunal considered the contents of a letter sent by one party to the other after the commencement of arbitration proceedings and made an award which included some matters arising from the said letter, and the Supreme Court affirmed the decisions of the High Court to sever the legitimate part of the award from the part of the award that was in excess.[114] In *Hatton National Bank v Kiran Atapattu and Another*,[115] the tribunal permitted one party to raise issues that were not within the ambit of the dispute adverted to in the arbitration agreement and proceeded to make an award in excess of the scope of the arbitration clause. The Supreme Court, in limiting the award to its legitimate scope, observed that the facility of severance;

> … allows a court to sever the parts of the award that deal with matters that were submitted by the parties for determination by the arbitral tribunal from the parts of the award that relate to matters not so submitted, to enable the decisions of the tribunal on matters falling within its mandate to be recognized and enforced, while the parts of the award which go beyond the scope of the submission for arbitration to be set aside.[116]

[110](n 5) s 34(1)(a)(ii).

[111][2001] 1 SLR 220.

[112](n 5) s 34(1)(a)(iii).

[113]*Oberoi Hotels (Pvt) Ltd v Asian Hotels Corporation Ltd.* reported in K. Kanag-Isvaran & S.S. Wijeratne (n 2) 259.

[114](n 5), s 32(1)(a)(iii) proviso, this being a domestic award.

[115](n 45).

[116]Ibid., at 55 [Marsoof J.].

### 3.4 Constitution of the Arbitral Tribunal Not in Accordance with the Arbitration Agreement

A foreign arbitral award may also be refused recognition or enforcement where the composition of the arbitral tribunal or the arbitral procedure was not in accordance with the agreement of the parties or, in the absence of such agreement, was not in accordance with the law of the seat of arbitration (*lex fori*).[117] While the situations in which a tribunal may not be properly constituted have already been considered in some detail, it must be stressed that an enforcement court may not be inclined to refuse recognition and enforcement of an award where the affected party has not taken objection to the jurisdiction of the tribunal without delay or has acquiesced in the proceedings.[118]

### 3.5 Award Not yet Binding or Has Been Set Aside

Recognition or enforcement to a foreign award may be refused if the award has not yet become binding on the parties or has been set aside or suspended by a court of the country in which, or under the law of which, that award was made.[119] An issue of considerable difficulty, which Sri Lankan courts have not yet faced, is whether a Court should invariably refuse enforcement if the award has already been set-aside in the country where it was made.[120] While the language of the Sri Lankan Act shows that a Sri Lankan court may have a residual discretion in this regard,[121] such discretion has to be exercised with caution.

### 3.6 Non-arbitrability of the Subject Matter

Recognition or enforcement of a foreign arbitral award may be refused for reasons of subject-matter non-arbitrability, by which is meant that the subject matter of the

[117](n 5) s 34(1)(a)(iv).

[118]*China Nanhai Oil Joint Service Cpn v Gee Tai Holdings Co. Ltd.*, 20 (1995) YCA 671.

[119](n 5) s 34(1)(a)(v).

[120]In *Hilmarton Ltd. v. Omnium de treatment et de valorization (OTV) Revue de l'arbitrage* [1995] 20 YCA 663, a French Court enforced an award that was set aside in Switzerland, and an American Court did the same with an award that had been set aside in Egypt in *Chromalloy Aeroservices Inc. v. Arab Republic of Egypt* 939 F. Supp 907 (District of Colombia 1996).

[121]*See, Quinhunangdao v. Million Basic Co* [1994] 19 YCA 675, (Hong Kong No. 7 sub I) wherein the Hong Kong High Court declared that it retained a residual discretion to grant leave to enforce in any case.

dispute from which the award emanated was not capable of settlement by arbitration under the law of Sri Lanka.[122]

## 4 Public Policy

Recognition or enforcement of the award may also be refused for being contrary to the public policy of Sri Lanka.[123] Under Articles 36(1)(b)(ii) and 34(2)(b)(ii) of the UNCITRAL ML, contravention of public policy of the enforcing jurisdiction has been an accepted defense against the enforcement of a foreign arbitral award. This provision would be invoked where the "enforcement could violate the forum State's most basic notions of morality and justice." As Lord Donaldson MR put it, it has to be shown that there is some element of illegality or that the enforcement of the award would be clearly injurious to the public good or, possibly, that enforcement would be wholly offensive to the ordinary reasonable and fully informed member of the public on whose behalf the powers of the State are exercised.[124] The parameters of the exception of public policy have been explored by almost all jurisdictions faced with the enforcement of foreign arbitral awards. The notion has been criticised as been too subjective and protective. However its value lies in the need to reconcile business efficacy with notions of good conduct and morality.

It is however, noteworthy that as was observed by Tilakawardane J in *Light Weight Body Armour Ltd. v. Sri Lanka Army*[125] unlike in the case of the first five grounds discussed above, where the onus of proving the ground relied upon to resist the recognition or enforcement of a foreign award is on the party so resisting, in regard to the sixth and seventh grounds, the Act permits the High Court to come to its finding *ex mero motu* whether the subject matter of the dispute was non-arbitrable or the award is in conflict with the public policy of Sri Lanka. On this reasoning, the High Court might take cognizance of a mater not raised before the arbitral tribunal, despite *dicta* to the contrary in *Kristley (Pvt) Ltd v. State Timber Corporation.*[126]

---

[122](n 5) s 34(1)(b)(i).

[123](n 5) s 34(1)(b)(ii).

[124]*Deutsche Schachtbau - und Tiefbohrgesellschaft mbH v. Ras Al Khoimah National Oil Co.* [1987] 2 Lloyd's Rep 246. See also, *Re an Arbitration between Hainan Machinery Import and Export Corporation and Donald & MccArthy Pte Ltd* [1996] 1 Singapore LR 34 46.

[125](n 43) 12.

[126](n 102) 242–244.

## 5 Conclusion

From the foregoing discussion, it would be seen that two factors have significantly influenced the minimization of conflict of laws issues in choice of law and jurisdiction strands in the sphere of arbitration in Sri Lanka. The first, of course, is the SLAA, with its elaborate conflict avoiding provisions, inspired by the UNCITRAL ML and the NYC. The second factor is Sri Lanka's mixed legal heritage, which encompasses a common law built on a Roman-Dutch law foundation, which constitutes the residuary law of the land,[127] while allowing the principles of the English common law to hold sway in commercial matters. English common law principles were introduced into Sri Lanka by a series of late 19th century codification statutes such as the Sale of Goods Ordinance,[128] and by the Introduction of English Law Ordinance,[129] the English Law for the time being applicable in the United Kingdom was incorporated by reference into the Sri Lankan legal fabric, to determine disputes in specific areas of the law such as banks and banking, corporations and partnerships, agency, life and fire insurance and maritime matters (including marine insurance). The second factor has been an effective help in minimizing conflicts with regard to choice of law and jurisdiction in international arbitration, thereby making the path for enforcement of foreign judgments and foreign arbitral awards a better-administered process.

[127] *See*, L.J.M Cooray, *An Introduction to the Legal System of Sri Lanka* (1992).

[128] Sale of Goods Ordinance, No. 11 of 1896.

[129] Civil Law Ordinance (also known as the Introduction of English Law Ordinance) No. 5 of 1852.

# Private International Law Issues in Intellectual Property Law in India

**Vandana Singh**

**Abstract** International contracts include matters related to intellectual property and require private enforcement i.e. legal measures taken by private parties. Such legal measures are based on the territoriality principle and determined by the law of the country where the suit is instituted. A vibrant private international law, which recognizes the expressive and constitutive capacity of judicial decision-making, can make contributions to the system well beyond the resolution of private disputes. In the traditional system governing issues related to intellectual property, national courts have had very little role to play in the construction of international intellectual property law. Litigation involved only national rights as explained within the municipal law on intellectual property rights; courts were reluctant even to adjudicate claims involving foreign intellectual property rights, leading to serial national litigation of multinational disputes, often on the basis of the similar right, guaranteed according to the municipal law system prevailing in that forum. However, it did cause national courts to take cognizance of matters having cross-border implications leading to the entry of private international law into the rubric of intellectual property rights. This chapter attempts to present the Indian position on the grounds that explain Indian courts' jurisdiction in cross-border intellectual property disputes; the laws that govern the ownership, validity and infringement of IPRs and the difficulties with regard to enforcement of foreign court orders.

**Keywords** Transnational contracts · Intellectual property rights · Jurisdiction · Territoriality principle · Applicable law · Enforcement of foreign judgments

---

V. Singh (✉)
USLLS, Guru Gobind Singh Indraprastha University, New Delhi, India
e-mail: vandana19singh@gmail.com

© Springer Nature Singapore Pte Ltd. 2017

S.R. Garimella and S. Jolly (eds.), *Private International Law*,
DOI 10.1007/978-981-10-3458-9_20

## Introduction

Benefiting significantly from globalization, innovation and the emergence of information and communication technology cross border trade and commercial relations are no longer confined to traditional contracts but also to various aspects of Intellectual Property Rights (hereinafter, IPRs) as well. The expansion of international trade, commerce and foreign investment has inevitably caused many intellectual property related disputes involving foreign elements.[1] A trans-national contract, often, provides for management of IPRs and such concerns that may arise from their management; it may include dispute resolution that may require private enforcement i.e. legal measures undertaken by private parties for the enforcement of their IPRs. Such legal measures are based on the territoriality principle and determined by the law of the country where the suit is instituted. The protection of IPRs in two countries may not be based on the same terms and conditions, leading thereon to a possible conflict of laws scenario. States have resorted to multi-lateral and bilateral treaties to address issues related to resolution of trans-border IPRs-related disputes. Evolving a regime of private international law rules exclusively founded upon the needs of intellectual property rights is a recent phenomenon and few institutions and international fora are making efforts in this domain.[2] In India, apart from accession to the treaty regime in public international law, little effort was directed at content development through law-making efforts.

## Structure of the Chapter

Addressing the venn diagram of IPRs and private international law could begin with its contextualization within the basic principles of private international law that apply in trans-border intellectual property disputes with the help of international treaties for intellectual property within the domain of public international law.

In the first section the chapter contextualizes the law on IPRs within private international law, under which it discusses international law regime of Intellectual property and its development. It summarizes the legal and institutional framework concerning the enforcement of Intellectual Property Rights in India, including a discussion on the treaties and Conventions that India is a signatory to in the context of private international law. It also discusses the international framework especially the harmonization efforts in this inter-disciplinary space by institutions like the American Society of International law (ASIL) and Max Planck Research Group's CLIP.

[1]Masato Dogauchi, 'Jurisdiction over Foreign Patent Infringement from a Japanese Perspective in Consideration of the Hague Draft Convention on Jurisdiction and Foreign Judgments in Civil and Commercial Matters as of June 2001' (2001) 44(1) Jap. Annual of I L 35.

[2]For example, the initiative by American Law Institute and CLIP (Conflict of Laws and Intellectual Property principles developed by European Max Planck Group (2004), Munich, established in the year 2004, submitted final text in the year 2011. http://www.imprs-ci.ip.mpg.de/_www/en/pub/home.html, accessed 12 February 2016.

In the next section, the chapter narrates the Indian law—statutory provisions and judicial opinion—on jurisdiction, applicable law and choice of law concerns, and recognition and enforcement of foreign courts' orders and judgments in trans-boundary IPRs-related disputes.

The chapter concludes with a few suggestions for strengthening the legal regime in this domain in India, and especially exploring the possibility of arbitration as a dispute resolution mechanism, a feature that is gaining increasing acceptance in other jurisdictions.[3]

## 1 Contextualizing Intellectual Property Law Within Private International Law

Private international law concerns itself with the legal principles that govern the trans-national interactions of individuals, 'legal persons' of different States. Trans-national disputes related to personal status, property and contracts are resolved through rules of private international law sourced within decisions of municipal law courts.[4] Judicial opinion significantly contributed to this knowledge domain, supplementing the minimal agreement that existed between countries, till recently, on many issues that often arise in trans-national disputes. Many countries, within their municipal law systems, have addressed possible conflict of laws scenarios, yet the diversity that layered such address has increasingly become evident in recent times, with increased interactions trans-nationally. In India the applicable personal law relating to these matters is determined by the religion of the individual concerned, whereas in most of the countries in which there is substantial presence of Indian nationals do not have personal law based on religion and a unified civil code applies to all persons residing there.[5] The content of private international law thus remains in large part a function of national rules on the topics of jurisdiction, choice of law and recognition of judgments.

While private international law also has the nature of public international law as it has content derived from treaty obligations of States[6] intellectual property regimes are regarded as primarily utilitarian in their aims and policies. Thus, it is not surprising that the policies of private international law should generate some friction when they are required to interface with the rights and principles that are

[3]William Grantham, 'The Arbitrability of International Intellectual Property Disputes' (1996) 14 (1) Berk J I L 173.

[4]Ministry of External Affairs, Government of India, 'Private International Law in India'. http://moia.gov.in/services.aspx?ID1=69&id=m6&idp=59&mainid=2, accessed 10 January 2016.

[5]Ibid.

[6]Ademola Abbas, *Complete International Law: Text, cases and Materials*, (2nd edn, OUP 2012) 7, 8.

decidedly public in character. In the domain of the law relating to intellectual property private international law rules are formulated and applied against the backdrop of public international law.[7]

## 1.1 The Regime on IPRs

The bulwark of the international law relating to IPRs comprises of few significant multi-lateral and bilateral treaties. The oldest amongst them is The Paris Convention on the Industrial Property Rights of 1883.[8] The substantive provisions of this WIPO-administered Convention are related to the principles of

- national treatment—the principle that require each member country grant the same protection of Industrial Property to nationals of other contracting states that it grants to its own nationals;
- right of priority—on the basis of a regular first application filed in one of the Contracting States, the applicant may, within a certain period of time apply for protection in any of the other contracting states; and
- common rules—most of the international convention lays down certain common rules that all Contracting States must follow.

There is no provision related to the regulation of those intellectual property disputes that are different from general contractual and commercial matters. There, however, are a few multilateral and bilateral instruments for regulating Intellectual Property matters like the Berne Convention, 1886,[9] the Madrid Agreement, 1891,[10] The Hague Convention for International Registration of Design, 1925 to simplify and streamline overall administration of the international design registration system[11] and the Patent Cooperation Treaty, 1970.[12] The Berne Convention Article

[7]A brief introduction to IP law and the WIPO within the context of private international law was discussed in "WIPO Forum on Private International Law and Intellectual Property", (2001) Geneva, WIPO/PIL/01/4.

[8]The Madrid Protocol of 1891 complemented the Paris Convention for the Protection of Industrial Property, 1883. It was revised at Brussels (1900), Washington (1911), The Hague (1925), London (1934), Lisbon (1958) and Stockholm (1967), and amended in 1979. As of 15th May 2004, the Paris Convention had 164 signatory states. http://www.wipo.org, 'Treaties', Intellectual Property Protection Treaties, Paris Convention.

[9]http://www.wipo.int/treaties/en/ip/berne/, accessed 10 March 2016.

[10]http://www.wipo.int/treaties/en/registration/madrid_protocol/index.html, accessed 10 March 2016.

[11]The Hague Agreement, 1925 on registration of Industrial design 1925, was revised in London (1934) Hague (1960) Additional Act, Monaco (1961) Complementary Act Stockholm (1967), Geneva Act (1999). http://www.wipo.int/treaties/en/registration/hague/, accessed 10 March, 2016.

[12]The patent Cooperation Treaty as amended in 197 and in 1984.

5(1) and (2) discussed national treatment; indirectly though, the principle of territoriality and choice of law could be implicated.[13]

The final addition to the international regime on intellectual property law is the Trade Related Aspects of Intellectual Property Rights (TRIPS) Agreement[14] at the end of the Uruguay Round negotiations of the General Agreement on Tariffs and Trade (GATT). The TRIPS Agreement includes provisions to harmonize substantive intellectual property laws of the member countries by establishing minimum standard of protection for different types of intellectual property in each territory[15] including provisions for its enforcement.

Part III of the Agreement contained provisions for enforcement of intellectual property through civil, administrative and criminal proceedings. Through accession all member countries intended uniformity of the legal regime; however, the agreement does not specifically address matters involving cross-border litigation, such as recognition and enforcement of foreign injunctions.[16] The Hague Conference categorized intellectual property into two groups—industrial property and copyrights. With regard to industrial property it was considered necessary to apply the rule of exclusive jurisdiction for the matters related to registration, abandonment and revocation, whereas copyright has been considered, in general, to be subjected to ordinary rules of jurisdiction.[17] However, the questions related to cross-border infringement of intellectual property cases were not dealt properly in the draft text. While the laws governing intellectual property are diverse, owing to the fact that such legal regime is derived from the sovereign rights of the State to regulate, there are some common features in these legal regimes that have gained universal acceptance.[18] One such common feature is the principle of territoriality and the understanding that the rights in intellectual property do not extend beyond the territory of the sovereign that has granted the rights in the first place. The

---

[13]5(1) Authors shall enjoy, in respect of works for which they are protected under this Convention, in countries of the Union other than the country of origin, the rights which their respective laws do now or may hereafter grant to their nationals, as well as the rights specially granted by this Convention.

[14]TRIPS, annexure I C of the Marrakesh Agreement Establishing the World Trade Organization, 1994. http://www.wto.org/english/docs_e/legal_e/legal_e.htm#agreement, accessed 10 April 2016.

[15]Sung Pil Park, 'Harmonizing Public and Private International Law: Implications of the Apple versus Samsung IP Litigation' (2014) 7(2) J of East Asia & Intl L 351.

[16]Marketa Trimble, 'When Foreigners Infringe Patents: an Empirical look at the Involvement of Foreign Defendants in Patent Litigation in the US' (2011) 27(3) Santa Clara Comp. & High Tech. L J 499.

[17]Graeme B. Dinwoodie, 'Developing a Private International Intellectual Property Law: The Demise of Territoriality' (2009) 51(2) Wm. & Mary L. Rev. 711, 718 Courts of the State that grants or registers the industrial property shall have jurisdiction to entertain claims invalidation.

[18]Yuko Nishitani, 'Intellectual Property in Japanese Private International Law' (2005) 48 Jap. Ann I L 87.

supremacy of territoriality principle particularly in case of intellectual property is due to presence of connection between sovereignty, property rights and territory.[19]

The principle of territoriality has been determinant factor of jurisdiction and countries have, within the municipal law, legislated their intellectual property system as was necessitated by their internal economic, political and cultural factors pushing towards globalization.[20] As a result there are a large number of pluri-lateral,[21] multilateral,[22] regional[23] and bilateral treaties[24] as well as unilateral measures (which may include recognition and enforcement of foreign judgments). That as a whole conforms a global network of intellectual property that results, at least, in a minimum substantive path of harmonization of domestic intellectual property systems.[25]

## 1.2 Indian Legal Regime on Intellectual Property

Post Independence, the Indian State has initiated efforts for increased protection of IPRs in India by heralding changes at legislative and policy level. India is a signatory member to World Trade Organization (WTO) since 1995 and to comply with the minimum standards of WTO. The Indian Parliament has amended the existing laws in relation to intellectual property and also enacted new laws in compliance with the WTO-TRIPS provisions. The contemporary legal regime on intellectual property in India includes The Patent Act 1970, (as amended in the year 2005)[26] Trade Marks

---

[19]Peter Drahos, 'The Universality of Intellectual Property Rights: Origin and Development'. http://wipo_unhchr_ip_pnl_98_1, accessed 24 April 2016.

[20]Mariano Municoy, 'Allocation of Jurisdiction on Patent Disputes in the Models Developed by the Hague Conference in Private International Law: Asymmetric Countries and the Relationship of Private Parties' (2004) 4(2) Chicago Kent J of IP 342, 348.

[21]Pluri-lateral agreement, as distinct from a multilateral agreement, is of much limited scope, with all its signatories having a common understanding of the subject-matter. In a multilateral treaty there is a wider scope for reservations, which is not the feature in a plurilateral agreement.

[22]Paris Convention and WTO TRIPS.

[23]NAFTA, 1994 (North America Free Trade Agreement) and ARIPO, 1976 (African Regional Industrial Property Organization).

[24]See for example bilateral treaty between US and Jamaica, "Agreement Concerning the Protection and Enforcement of Intellectual Property Rights between the Government of the United States of America and the Government of Jamaica", Kingston, 1994.

[25]Municoy (n 20) 349.

[26]In the year 1856 the Act VI of 1856 on Protection of Inventions based on the British Patent law 1852. The Act was modified in the year 1859 as Act of XV. To meet the demands then British Government passed the Patterns and Designs Protection Act, 1872 amended in the year 1883, 1888, 1911. After independence the Indian Government enacted The Indian Patents and Design Act of 1911. The 1911 Act was amended on the recommendation of Mashelkar Committee report in the year 1972. After signing WTO-TRIPS during transition phase the Indian Patent Act was amended thrice 1999, 2002 and 2005 respectively to be in line with provisions of TRIPS.

Act 1999 (as amended in the year 2010),[27] Designs Act 2000,[28] The Copyright Act 1957(as amended in the year 2012).[29]

Certain newly recognized branches of Intellectual Property gained statutory protection in India through: Geographical Indications of Goods (Registration and Protection) Act 1999,[30] The Semiconductor Integrated Circuits Layout Design Act 2000, The protection of Plants Varieties and Farmers Rights Act 2001 and The Biological Diversity Act 2002.

Further, India is also member of the certain World Intellectual Property Organisation (WIPO) administered multilateral treaties and conventions[31] in the area of Intellectual Property.

## 1.3 *Hague Conference on Private International Law (HCCH) and India*

Intellectual property rights are granted through State actions and are limited to the territory of the State that granted them. Therefore, if a State other than that which granted or recognized the IPRs attempted to exercise jurisdiction, it would create an unreasonable interference with the State that initially granted the rights that is subjected to the instant dispute.[32] However, trans-national commerce brought to fore the scenario of IPRs and Private International Law interacting in the space of property law, law of contract, principles of tort and application of territoriality principle for resolution of IPRs-related disputes. However, in the absence of a comprehensive treaty various instruments referencing provisions of private

[27]The Trade Mark Registry was established in India in the year 1940. To comply with the provisions of WTO-TRIPS the Trademark Act, 1958 was amended in the year 1999 and in the year 2010.

[28]The Designs Act 2000 replaced the Designs Act of 1911 following accession to TRIPS.

[29]The Copyright Act, 1958 was amended in 1983, 1984, 1992, 1999, and 2012 to fulfill international obligations.

[30]India enacted the GI Act, 1999 (enforced in 2003), to protect the unique products whose uniqueness is attributed to its geographical origin.

[31]India is member of: Budapest Treaty on the international Recognition of the Deposit of Micro-organism for the purposes of Patent Procedure, 1977, Paris Convention for the Protection of Industrial Property, 1883, Convention Establishing the World Intellectual Property Organization 1967, Berne Convention for the Protection of Literary and Artistic Works 1886, Patent Cooperation Treaty 1970, Protocol Relating to the Madrid Agreement Concerning the International Registration of Marks-Madrid Protocol 1989, Washington Treaty on Intellectual Property in respect of Integrated Circuits, 1989, Nairobi Treaty on the Protection of the Olympic Symbol 1981, Convention for the Protection of Producers of Phonograms Against Unauthorized Duplication of their Phonograms 1971.

[32]Benedetta Ubertazzi, 'Intellectual Property Rights and Exclusive (subject matter) Jurisdiction: between Private and Public International Law,' (2011) 15(2) Marq. IP L Rev. 357, 361.

international law related to IPRs-related disputes[33] have only reiterated the need for a coherent body of rules addressing the adequacy of this domain in a globalized environment.[34]

While it remains a truism that conflict of laws rules in many jurisdictions demonstrate diversity, it is also another truism that there have been many institutionalized attempts to work towards harmonization and unification of Private International Law especially since the last century. The guiding objective for such efforts has been the intention to achieve a harmonized legal platform in a specific area. Commercial law space has seen much success with a combination of international, regional, inter-governmental and private/academic institutions working towards achieving this objective.

Foremost amongst such institutions is the Hague Conference on Private International Law (hereinafter, the HCCH) working from 1955 for the progressive unification of the rules of private international law.[35] It has a membership of 80 States and one Regional Economic Integration Organization (European Union).[36] India joined the Hague Conference in 2008; the Joint secretary within the Ministry of External Affairs has been designated the responsibility to represent India in accordance with Article 7 of the Statute.[37]

At the HCCH India is bound by the following Conventions which have implications for IPRs-related issues:

[33]For example under Article 5(1) of the Berne Convention principles of 'territoriality' and 'choice of law' can be inferred. Article 5(1) states "authors shall enjoy, in respect of works for which they are protected under this Convention, in countries of the Union other than the country of origin, the rights which their respective laws do now or may hereafter grant to their nationals, as well as the rights specially granted by this Convention".

[34]Graeme (n 17) 713–714.

[35]Few of the Hague Conventions that significantly impact trans-national commercial contracts are

Convention Abolishing the Requirement of Legalization of foreign legal documents 1961

Convention on the Service Abroad of Judicial and Extrajudicial Documents in Civil or Commercial matters, 1965

Convention on the Recognition and Enforcements of Foreign Judgments in Civil and Commercial Matters 1971

Convention on the Taking of Evidence Abroad in Civil or Commercial Matters 1970.

Convention on the Law Applicable to Products Liability 1973

Convention on the Law Applicable to Agency 1978

Convention on the Law Applicable to Contracts for the International Sale of Goods 1986.

[36]Details of the membership of Hague Conference. https://www.hcch.net/en/states/hcch-members, accessed 10th March 2016.

[37]The Joint Secretary in the Ministry of External Affairs is the nodal officer for facilitating India's participation at the HCCH.

1. The Convention on Abolishing the Requirements of Legalization of Foreign Legal Documents, 1961 obligates acceptance within each Contracting State of public documents like administrative documents, notarial acts etc., executed on the territory of other contracting States.[38]
2. The Convention on the Service Abroad of Judicial and Extra-judicial Documents in Civil or Commercial Matters, 1965 is applicable to all civil or commercial matters involving instances of transmission of a judicial or extra-judicial document for service abroad.[39] India acceded to this Convention in 2006, and it became enforceable on 1st August 2007.[40] The Convention provides for the channels of transmission of documents (judicial and extrajudicial) of one Contracting State to another Contracting State for service in that Contracting State. It addresses only the transmission of service, not the substantive rules of the process of service.[41] The Convention also requires the member states to designate a central authority for administrative work and for receiving requests from other member states.[42] In India the Ministry of Law and Justice, Department of Legal Affairs is designated as Central Authority under the Convention. The convention's frameworks for delivery of extrajudicial documents are effective in its function and requests are executed within two months.[43]
3. The Convention on the Taking of Evidence Abroad in Civil or Commercial Matters, 1970 establishes methods of co-operation for the taking of evidence abroad in civil or commercial matters. The Convention provides for the taking of evidence (i) by means of letters of request, and (ii) by diplomatic or consular agents and commissioners These Conventions provides effective means of overcoming the differences between civil law and common law systems with respect to the taking of evidence.[44]

---

[38] HCCH (n 36).

[39] Article 1 of the Convention, The convention adopted a recommendation in the year 1980 on information to accompany judicial and extrajudicial documents.

[40] Shambhu Sharan, 'India: Process of Services of Summons in India Under the Hague Convention'. http://www.mondaq.com/india/x/433154/International+Courts+Tribunals/Process+Of+Service+Of+Summons+In+India+Under+The+Hague+Convention#_ftn1, accessed 12th June 2016.

[41] Outline of convention under Hague Agreement. https://assets.hcch.net/docs/f4ccc07b-55ed-4ea7-8fb9-8a2b28549e1d.pdf, accessed on 23rd May 2016.

[42] Id, Article 2.

[43] Ibid.

[44] https://assets.hcch.net/docs/ec1fc148-c2b1-49dc-ba2f-65f45cb2b2d3.pdf, accessed 10 March 2016.

## 1.4 Contemporary Initiatives

Recently, there were a few initiatives towards developing a content of private international law for intellectual property.[45] Towards regulation of cross border intellectual property disputes in 1990s, the United States collaborated with the HCCH to attempt harmonize the rules for international jurisdiction and enforcement of foreign judgments through an international treaty. The Judgments Project could not find much headway due to the absence of consensus between the principal negotiating parties including EU and US. In 2003, the International Association for the Protection of Intellectual Property adopted a resolution proposing rules on jurisdiction and applicable law in intellectual property cases.[46] In 2007, the American Law Institute adopted the ALI principles on Intellectual property.[47] Further, the Max Planck Institute in Munich initiated the CLIP project (Conflict of Laws in Intellectual Property) and formulated CLIP principles (hereinafter, the Principles) in the year 2011.[48] These Principles were expected to serve as a template for national, regional and international legislators.[49] These Principles aim to provide independent advice to European and national law region.[50] They discuss the matters related to international jurisdiction, the applicable law and recognition and enforcement of foreign judgments in the field of IPRs.[51] Principles related to jurisdiction, covered under part 2, are broadly arranged in the following categories: general Jurisdiction, special jurisdiction, prorogation of jurisdiction, and exclusive jurisdiction into:

General jurisdiction is vested in the courts of the State where the defendant has his or her habitual residence.

Special Jurisdiction relates to rules that allow jurisdiction of the courts outside the defendant's forum. Courts at the place of performance of the contractual obligations could be applied for exercise of jurisdiction. If the contract has as its main object the transfer or license of an intellectual property right, the characteristic obligation is performed in the State for which the transfer or license is due. Infringement claims can regularly be brought in the courts of the State where the infringement occurs or may occur, unless the activity cannot reasonably be seen as having been directed to that state, or the defendant has not taken substantial action there. Special jurisdiction also

---

[45]Graeme (n 17) 719.

[46]International Association for the Protection of Intellectual Property (AIPPI).

[47]The American Law Institute, *Intellectual Property: Principles Governing Jurisdiction, Choice of Law and Judgments in Transnational Disputes* (Chestnut, ALI Publishers, 2008).

[48]The draft principles has been prepared by the European Max-Planck Group on Conflict of Laws in Intellectual Property. http://www.imprs-ci.ip.mpg.de/_www/files/pdf2/Final_Text_1_December_2011.pdf. It was established in 2004 to discuss issues of intellectual property, private international law, jurisdiction and enforcement.

[49]Principles on Conflict of Laws in Intellectual Property, Part I, Purpose and Scope. http://www.imprs-ci.ip.mpg.de/_www/en/pub/home.html, accessed 24 April 2016.

[50]Ibid.

[51]Id.

includes an exception to the general rule on the extent of jurisdiction in the context of the territory of the State of the forum court. In case of infringement through the internet media, for example, the Principles state that courts may be competent to adjudicate upon foreign—and even global—infringements, if the acts causing the infringement do not have substantial effect in the defendant's State (or States) of habitual residence, and if the defendant has either substantially acted in the forum state, or if the harm resulting from the infringement in that state is substantial in relation to the infringement in its entirety.

Prorogation of Jurisdiction ensures supremacy of the principle of party autonomy by allowing for courts designated within a choice of court agreement to exercise jurisdiction exclusively.

Exclusive jurisdiction relates to disputes having as their object the validity and registration etc. of a registered intellectual property right. Courts in the State of registration have exclusive jurisdiction.

Principles related to applicable law are discussed within Part 3. The law of the State where the protection is sought would govern the existence, validity, scope, and duration of an IPR.[52] *Lex fori* would be the applicable law regarding the procedural matters.[53] Article 3:103 stated that where possible parties could choose the applicable law. *Lex protectionis* would be the applicable law for disputes related to the initial copyright ownership, transfer and co-ownership. Regarding Contracts and related questions, Article 3:501 emphasizes upon the principle of party autonomy on choice of law, and proposes that default rules to be made to address the absence of party choice. The principles also suggest for the application of the law that has the closest connection to the contract. Regarding infringement and remedies, the *lex protectionis* would be the applicable law; *de minimis* rule would determine the existence of the infringement—the infringement could be found only in that protecting country where the defendant substantially acted, where the substantial effects of such action were felt, or the country to which such activities were directed.[54] Part 4 of the Principles discuss recognition and enforcement of foreign judgments. Article 4:201 specified that a foreign judgment would not be recognized if it were from a court that did not possess jurisdiction according to the Principles. The grounds for denying recognition and enforcement of a foreign judgment include manifest incompatibility with the public policy in the enforcement jurisdiction; serious violations of natural justice principle; if the judgment is irreconcilable with an earlier judgment between the same parties given in the requested

---

[52]Id, article 3:102: *Lex protectionis.*

[53]Id, article 3:101: *Lex fori.*

[54]Ibid, article 3:602; see also, Rita Malulionyte, *Law Applicable to Copyright: A Comparison of the ALI and CLIP Proposals* (Edward Elgar Publishing, 2011) 146.

State, or another State, if the latter judgment fulfilled the requirements for recognition and enforcement in the requested State.[55] CLIP, however, was critiqued as being rooted in European legal thinking.[56]

From a legal perspective, the harmonization of rules applicable across different regions and jurisdictions has not taken place; further existing laws in different jurisdictions have very little similarity, much less shared and common understandings.[57] Given the differences in law, substantive as well as procedural, among countries, there are significant concerns about the undesirable consequences of having overlapping jurisdictions in instances of consolidation intellectual property cases. Litigation of intellectual property rights could involve a variety of proceedings depending upon the nature of intellectual property-related violation that has been alleged. There could either be proceedings relating to the infringement of intellectual property rights, or proceedings concerned with registration, revocation and validity of rights. Finally, there are proceedings that have their source in a breach of contract or proceedings concerning the ownership.[58]

## 2 Private International Law and IPRs in India

Statutory provisions specifically focusing on IPRs-related issues with a private international law connection are absent in India. However, a reference was made to the jurisdiction of the Indian courts under Section 62 of the Copyright Act. The statutory position on jurisdiction of Indian courts could be exemplified through this scenario

> An Indian author agreed to write a book for foreign publisher who is having business in country A and B. If after the publication, the office in country A refused to make payment, or if there was an infringement of the author's copyright, which country's courts would possess jurisdiction?

In such circumstances the Indian court may exercise jurisdiction u/s 62 of the Copyright Act, a significant departure from the norm that the choice of jurisdiction should primarily be governed by the convenience of the defendant.[59]

[55]Annette Kur, 'The CLIP Principle—Summary of the Project'. http://www.win-cls.sakura.ne.jp/pdf/29/22.pdf.

[56]Ibid, 06.

[57]EdouardTreppoz, 'International Choice of Law in Trademark Disputes from a Territorial Approach to a Global Approach' (2013–14) 37(4) Colum. Jour. of L and Arts 557.

[58]Marta Sender Pertegas, et al., Judicial Cooperation in Matters of Intellectual Property and Information Technology, Scope of the exclusive jurisdiction in intellectual property matters under Brussels Convention/Regulation. http://www.ulb.ac.be/droit/ipit/docs/excljurisd.pdf, accessed 21 July, 2016.

[59]*Caterpillar Inc v Kailash Nichani* (2002) 97 DLT 304.

## 2.1 Jurisdiction

The Brussels Convention, 1968 has, through Article 16.4, provided for exclusive jurisdiction concerning proceedings on registration, revocation and validity of intellectual property. Courts of the Contracting State in which the deposit or registration has been applied for, has taken place or is under the terms of an international convention deemed to have taken place, shall have exclusive jurisdiction. Being an exception to the general principle of jurisdiction that was founded upon the defendant, a restrictive interpretation was required. Within the Brussels I Regulation this restrictive interpretation is found in Article 22.4 and was confirmed by the Court of Justice in the *Duijnstee* case.[60]

Apple and Samsung Electronics were involved in multiple suits in many jurisdictions for the alleged infringement of Apple's intellectual property by Samsung Electronics. The disputants however agreed to a choice of forum in the US Court and withdrew all the other litigation in other jurisdictions citing reasons, amongst others,[61] for the purpose of avoiding parallel proceedings. For disputes like this one no tribunal in the world asserts its extraterritorial jurisdiction, as it could possibly be categorized as exorbitant jurisdiction. Russell described exorbitant jurisdiction as jurisdiction validly exercised under the jurisdictional rules of a state that nevertheless appears unreasonable to non-nationals because of the grounds used to justify jurisdiction.[62] The Apple's case reaffirmed the challenge of defining jurisdiction in intellectual property. In India, the rules of jurisdiction pertaining to intellectual property-related disputes and also the generally applicable provisions have been clearly stated in three legislations: The Copyright Act, 1957, the Trade Marks Act, 1999, in specific IPR-related disputes and The Code of Civil Procedure, 1908 (hereinafter, the CPC).

Section 20, CPC[63] enabled an Indian court to assume jurisdiction over a suit if the defendant actually and voluntarily resided or carried on business, or worked for gain, at a place within the jurisdiction of the court, or where the cause of action, or a

---

[60] *Duijnstee v Goderbauer*; ECJ 15 Nov 1983.

[61] Park (n 15) 354.

[62] K.A. Russell, 'Exorbitant Jurisdiction and Enforcement of Judgments: the Brussels System as an Impetus for the United States Action' (1993) 19 Sycse. Jour. of Int'l L and Comm. 2.

[63] Subject to the limitations aforesaid, every suit shall be instituted in Court within the local limits of whose jurisdiction-

(a) the defendant, or each of the defendants where there are more than one, at the time of the commencement of the suit, actually and voluntarily resides, or carries on business, or personally works for gain; or

(b) any of the defendants, where there are more than one, at the time of the commencement of the suit actually and voluntarily resides, or carries on business, or personally works for gain, provided that in such case either the leave of the Court is given, or the defendants who do not reside, or carry on business, or personally work for gain, as aforesaid, acquiesce in such institution; or

(c) the cause of action, wholly or in part, arises.

part of it arises.[64] Unlike western countries, Section 20 placed extended emphasis on the cause of action and the connection between the disputes and the forum.[65]

To the general rules of jurisdiction in India available under section 20, CPC, the specific intellectual property legislations under Sections 62 of the Copyright Act[66] and section 134(2) of the Trade Mark Act[67] carve an exception. In matters of intellectual property infringement, the plaintiff has been provided additional jurisdiction option; he could institute a suit in a court within whose jurisdiction he is based, irrespective of the place of business of the respondent or cause of action's place of occurence. The expression "notwithstanding anything contained in the Code of Civil Procedure" used under Copyright Act does not oust the applicability of the rule of jurisdiction contained under section 20 of the CPC but it is an additional remedy available to the plaintiff.

In *Indian Performing Rights Society Ltd. v Sanjay Dalia*[68] the Supreme Court held

---

[64]Vandana Singh, 'Report on India' in Toshiyuki Kono (ed.) *Intellectual Property and Private International Law: Comparative Analysis* (Hart Publication, 2012) 625.

[65]*Banyan Tree Holding Pvt Ltd. v Murali Krishna Reddy* (2010) 42 PTC 361 Delhi—jurisdiction was decided on the basis of place of business and not on the basis of actual residence.

[66]Section 62 of Copyright Act: Jurisdiction of court over matters arising under this Chapter.

(1) Every suit or other civil proceeding arising under this Chapter in respect of the infringement of copyright in any work or the infringement of any other right conferred by this Act shall be instituted in the district court having jurisdiction. (2) For the purpose of sub-section (1), and "district court having jurisdiction" shall, notwithstanding anything contained in the Code of Civil Procedure, 1908, or any other law for the time being in force, include a district court within the local limits of whose jurisdiction, at the time of the institution of the suit or other proceeding, the person instituting the suit or other proceeding or, where there are more than one such persons, any of them actually and voluntarily resides or carries on business or personally works for gain.

[67]Section 134 of Trade Marks Act: Suit for infringement etc. to be instituted before District Court-

(1) No suit–

  (a) for the infringement of a registered trade mark; or
  (b) relating to any right in a registered trade mark; or
  (c) for passing off arising out of the use by the defendant of any trade mark which is identical with or deceptively similar to the plaintiff's trade mark, whether registered or unregistered, shall be instituted in any court inferior to a District Court having jurisdiction to try the suit.

(2) For the purpose of clauses (a) and (b) of sub-section (1), a "District Court having jurisdiction" shall, notwithstanding anything contained in the Code of Civil Procedure, 1908 (5 of 1908) or any other law for the time being in force, include a District Court within the local limits of whose jurisdiction, at the time of the institution of the suit or other proceeding, the person instituting the suit or proceeding, or, where there are more than one such persons any of them, actually and voluntarily resides or carries on business or personally works for gain.

Explanation—For the purposement was delivered s of sub-section (2), "person" includes the registered proprietor and the registered user.

[68](2015) 10 SCC 161.

> the provision of section 62 of the Copyright Act and section 134 of the Trade Marks Act have to be interpreted in the purposive manner. A suit can be filed by the plaintiff at a place where he is residing or carrying on business or personally works for gain. He need not travel to file a suit to a place where defendant is residing or cause of action wholly or in part arises. However, if the plaintiff is residing or carrying on business etc. at a place where cause of action, wholly or in part, has also arisen, he has to file a suit at that place.[69]

The judgment provided an additional forum to the plaintiff to institute a suit wherein it either has its head/principal/registered office or branch/subordinate/ancillary office. A summarization[70] of the judgment provides the following principles as guidance on understanding the legal provisions on jurisdiction.

1. A suit can be filed under Sec 62 of the Copyright Act and Sec 134 of the Trademark Act at the place of the principal/registered office/branch office of the Company if the cause of action does not arise within any of these places.
2. If the cause of action arises *only* within the principal/registered office of the Company, the jurisdiction of all branch/subordinate offices before which cause of action does not lie would be ousted. This was the exact scenario considered in the present judgment.
3. If the cause of action arises within the principal place of business *and* a branch office/s, the plaintiff has the discretion to choose either of these forums. In such circumstances, the jurisdiction of all other branch offices before which cause of action does not lie would be ousted.
4. If the cause of action only before a branch office/offices, the jurisdiction of other branch offices before which cause of action does not lie would be ousted. However, in interpreting what are the relevant branch offices to be considered, reliance can be placed on the judgment of the Hon'ble Supreme Court in *Dhoda House*[71] which states that there must be some correlation between the branch office and the 'essential part of the business' i.e. the branch office within which the cause of action arises must have some correlation to the cause of action, and not every branch office is to be deemed relevant for the purposes of considering the same.[72]

Recently the Delhi High Court in *Ultra Home Construction Pvt Ltd v Purushottam Kumar Chaubey and Ors*,[73] held that the general jurisdiction provision contained in the explanation of section 20 of CPC has been read into section 134(2) of the Trade Marks Act, 1999 and section 62(2) of the Copyright Act, 1957 for the purpose of isolating the place where the plaintiff can be said to carry on business. The intellectual property statutes were never intended to operate in the field where the plaintiff is having its principle place of business at a particular place

[69]Ibid, para 47.

[70]Arun C. Mohan, 'Shedding Light on IPRS v. Sanjay Dalia'. http://spicyip.com/2015/07/guest-post-shedding-light-on-iprs-v-sanjay-dalia.html, accessed 01 June 2016.

[71]*M/S. Dhodha House v S.K. Maingi* 2006 (9) SCC 41.

[72]Arun (n 71).

[73]F225 (2015) DLT178.

and the cause of action has also arisen at that place so as to enable it to file a suit at a distant place where its subordinate office is situated though at such place no cause of action has arisen.[74] The Court opined that such interpretation would cause great harm and would be juxtaposed to the very legislative intendment of the provisions so enacted.

The ratio of the above two decisions enables a derivation that, in IPRs-related disputes courts at the plaintiff's residence or place of business could also be approached. It is submitted that Section 20, CPC and the Trade Mark Act, 1999 and the Copyright Act, 1957 are *pari material* (two laws relating to the same subject matter that must be analyzed with each other) as stated in the *Ultra Home*.[75]

Indian courts have not addressed the issues of jurisdiction in the circumstances of trans-border matters therefore not dealt with the concerns of private international law. A 1994 decision in the case of *Phoolan Devi v Shekhar Kapoor and Ors*[76] was the only reported instance of a private international law concern being presented to the Court. The petitioner approached the court for injunction against the screening of movie "Bandit Queen" on the ground of infringement of right to privacy and residuary rights under section 57 of the Copyright Act. Defendants contended Indian courts couldn't exercise jurisdiction abroad as foreign decrees must relate to an actionable dispute in the country where enforcement of the injunction is sought. The court without answering the specific question of jurisdiction restrained the exhibition of movie on the ground of right to privacy. Hearing an appeal[77] against the injunction order, the Division Bench of the Delhi High Court discussed the private international law position on jurisdiction. The appellants citing a Supreme Court decision in *Suresh Jindal v RizsoliCorriere Delia Sera Prodzioni T.V.S.P. A.*[78] pleaded that the apex Court while holding that it possessed jurisdiction to order injunction on exhibition film outside India in the interests of justice, it however refrained from making such orders taking note of the difficulty experienced in enforcing such orders.[79] Quoting extensively from judicial opinion and scholarly opinion[80] the Court ordered the appellants to take affirmative action abroad with regard to exhibiting the film, while permitting them to seek remedies in other countries that could possibly exercise jurisdiction. This decision was an important example of the Indian Courts attempting to enjoin parties to an ordained method of action, abroad.

While a forum selection clauses (FSC) could ensure certainty to transactions and disputes, the application of FSC remains controversial in intellectual property disputes. The American experience leads to a derivation that interpretation of the

[74]Ibid, para 17 [also refer, Arun (n 71)].

[75]Id, para 21.

[76]57 (1995) DLT 195.

[77]*M/S. Kaleidoscope (India) P. Ltd. v Phoolan Devi And Others* AIR 1995 Delhi 316.

[78]AIR 1995 SC 2092.

[79]Ibid, para 7.

[80](n 78), paras 17–22.

FSC with regard to non-contractual claims has largely been towards interpreting such claims on the intention of the parties, however appellate courts have not developed a consistent methodology with regard to the scope of FSC to non-contractual claims.[81] In India in *Modi Entertainment Network v W.S.G. Cricket Pte. Ltd*[82] the Supreme Court held that the parties to a contract could agree to submit to the exclusive or non-exclusive jurisdiction of a foreign "neutral" court. It clarified that such contracts are an exception to section 20 CPC, which stipulates that parties cannot by agreement confer jurisdiction upon a court, to which the CPC applies, if such court does not have jurisdiction otherwise.[83] However this was not a case pertaining to Intellectual property matters and going by the general trend, courts in India may not accept the validity of jurisdiction clause to deviate from the principle of territoriality.

## 2.2 Choice of Law

In a trans-national IPRs-related dispute the primary question is the nature of rights involved. A commonly accepted practice is that proceedings related to the registration and validity of intellectual property rights are subject to the exclusive jurisdiction of the state where such registration or deposit was applied.[84] States grant registration after an examination of the substantive and formal requirements through the competent authority, therefore dispute on validity of registration shall be decided by the granting State.[85] This reasoning is based on the principle of territoriality. Objections have to be made to the registering authority of the granting State.[86] In trans-border disputes of infringement of intellectual property this is generally regarded as a tort and subject to ordinary jurisdictional rules, the same as contractual disputes on transfer and license of these rights.[87] For choice of law the concerned court must ascertain the place of existence of intellectual property,

[81]Eric S. Sherby, 'A Survey of Appellate cases Constructing Forum Selection Clauses in Intellectual property Disputes' 15. http://www.americanbar.org/content/dam/aba/events/international_law/2013/05/law_business_andsociety-usisraelglobalrelationships/survey%20of%20appellate%20cases.authcheckdam.pdf, accessed 4 July 2016; See generally *Global Seafood Inc. v Bantry Bay Mussels Ltd.*, 659 F.3d 221, 225 (2d Cir. 2011).

[82]2003 AIR SCW 733.

[83]Anoop Narayanan, 'Cross-Border Disputes and Neutral Courts'. http://www.majmudarindia.com/pdf/Cross-border%20disputes%20and%20neutral%20courts.pdf, accessed 4 July 2016.

[84](n 59), (n 60).

[85]Yuko Nishitani (n 20) Article 22(4) of the Brussels-I Regulation; article 16(4) of the Lugano Convention; Article 109(1) of Swiss IPRG; Article 12(4) of the 1999 Hague Draft Convention.

[86]For example in the case of *Novartis Ag v Union of India*, (2013) 6 SCC 1, the validity of registration of Patent and its objection under Section 3(d) of the Indian Patent Act, 1970 was initiated before Indian authority.

[87]*Novartis AG v Union of India* CIVIL APPEAL Nos. 2706-2716 OF 2013.

ownership, content and limitations of the rights. IPRs are therefore always located in the country that granted the rights and infringements are to be deemed such according to that law.[88] In most of the countries the determination of the initial owner of the intellectual property right is made on the basis of the principle of *lex Loci*. However, in case of copyright initial ownership of the work is determined through the principle of *Lex Protectionis*. ALI and CLIP taking note of digital environment and certain non-registered intellectual property rights advocated this principle. Scholarly opinion argued that there is a need to build upon such exceptions, particularly in cases of infringements facilitated by Internet transmissions.[89] For cross-border copyright infringement, proper law could include the law of the place of the upload of the work, the law of the author's residence, or the law of the country of the initiation of the infringement etc. With regard to other areas of intellectual property rights the inclusion of public policy dimension makes it difficult to deviate from the territoriality principle in the area of choice of law.[90]

## 2.3 Recognition and Enforcement of Foreign Judgments

The process of trans-border recognition and enforcement of judgments is associated with a number of difficulties that are not unique to intellectual property cases.[91] This phenomenon is true of the law on IPRs as well, despite harmonization through international treaties.[92] The Brussels Convention regulated the jurisdiction of the contracting states and the recognition and execution of foreign judgments, by the Contracting States at European Union. It ensured an autonomous system of jurisdictional rules that applied for intellectual property disputes as well.[93] Brussels Convention has been replaced with Brussels Regulation, with no change in the regime on the recognition and enforcement of foreign judgments.[94]

---

[88]Alexander Thunken, 'Multi-State Advertising over the Internet and the Private International Law of Unfair Competition' (2002) 51(4) ICLQ 909.

[89]See, Graeme Austin, Private International law and Intellectual property Rights: A Common Law Overview (WIPO Forum on Private International law and Intellectual property, January 2001, Geneva. www.wipo.int/edocs/mdocs/mdocs/en/wipo_pil_01/wipo_pil_01_5.doc, accessed 97 August 2016.

[90]Ibid, 14.

[91]Samuel P. Baumagartner, 'How Well Do U.S. Judgments Fare in Europe?' (2008) 40(1) Geo Wash Intl L Rev. 173.

[92]Trimble, (n. 16) 499.

[93]Paul L C Torremans, 'Jurisdiction in International Intellectual Property Litigation: The Courts start Struggling with the Brussels Convention' (1998) 2(3) Edin. L Rev. 337.

[94]Brussels Convention has been replaced by the Brussels Regulation (44/2001/EC). http://eur-lex.europa.eu/legal-content/EN/TXT/PDF/?uri=CELEX:32001R0044&from=en , accessed 4 July 2016. The recast Brussels Regulation has been in force since January 2013, it only applies to legal proceedings started on or after 10 January 2015.

One of the grounds for refusal of recognition within the Regulation, which is of particular interest in intellectual property matters, is the principle of exclusivity. Article 35 of the Brussels I Regulation a judgment shall not be recognized if it conflicts with Section 6 of Chapter II, establishing the rules of exclusive jurisdiction.[95] Exclusive jurisdiction is ascribed to the State where the disputed IPR has been granted. Public policy arguments are often resorted to refuse the recognition of judgment.[96] It is an important exception for enforcement of a foreign judgment.[97] Scholarly opinion has been supporting a restrictive interpretation of public policy to intellectual property-related disputes.[98] In *Eurosensory v Teimann & Blind Equipment*[99] a Dutch court granted a cross-border injunction in summary proceedings that was to be enforced, among others, in France. In first instance, the President of the Court of First Instance of Paris had registered the Dutch judgment for enforcement. On appeal, the French company claimed that the recognition of an extraterritorial judgment was contrary to the pubic order in France because it would not be possible to obtain a similar provisional injunction in summary proceedings under the French law. The Court of Appeal rejected this argument and recognized the Dutch decision. In the case of *Renault*[100] the Court held that a judgment of a court of a Contracting State recognizing the existence of an intellectual property right in body parts for cars, and conferring on the holder of that rights protection by enabling him to prevent third party trading in another Contracting State from manufacturing and commercializing in that State such body parts cannot be considered to be contrary to public policy.[101]

Many countries, especially the European Union, for example, enforce the foreign judgments through the responsibilities derived from accession to multilateral conventions. India, however, is a signatory to only a few—Warsaw Convention (as amended in 1955 by Hague Convention), The New York Convention, 1958 related to Recognition and Enforcement of Foreign Arbitral awards (hereinafter, the NYC), amongst others. While the Hague conference on private International law has codified the rules on enforcement and recognition of judgments,[102] India is not a signatory. In India the foreign judgments are enforced through domestic legislation,

---

[95]Ibid, Article 35.

[96]Recognition and enforcement of judgments in intellectual property matters. http://www.ulb.ac.be/droit/ipit/docs/Recog_enforcem.pdf, accessed on 4 July 2016.

[97]Marketa Trimble Landova, 'Public Policy Exception to Recognition and Enforcement of Judgments in Cases of Copyright Infringement' (2009) Scholarly Works Paper, 40(6) IIC 642. http://scholars.law.unlv.edu/facpub/564, accessed 03 July 2016.

[98]Pertegas-Sender, M., *Cross-border enforcement of patent rights* (Oxford University Press 2002) 200.

[99]R.D.P.I.1995.18.

[100]*Regie National Des Renault SA v Zhang,* (2002) 187 ALR 1 (High Court of Australia).

[101]Ibid.

[102]Convention on the Recognition and Enforcement of Foreign Judgments in Civil and Commercial matters. https://www.hcch.net/en/instruments/conventions/full-text/?cid=78, accessed 4 July 2016.

the CPC and the Arbitration Act, 1996. CPC is considered to be the central legislation for the enforcement of foreign judgment. Sections 13,[103] 14[104] and 44A[105] specify the law on enforcement of a foreign court order. No judicial statement has come from Indian courts on recognition and enforcement of foreign intellectual property judgments.

The existing jurisdictional system inhibits efficient dispute resolution and enforcement of the orders in IPRs-related disputes. There however are some innovative suggestions. In a German case of *Keg Technologies, Inc v Reinhart Lainer*,[106] the Court while dealing with the recognition and enforcement of a US

---

[103]13. When foreign judgment not conclusive.

A foreign judgment shall be conclusive as to any matter thereby directly adjudicated upon between the same parties or between parties under whom they or any of them claim litigating under the same title except-

(a) where it has not been pronounced by a Court of competent jurisdiction;
(b) where it has not been given on the merits of the case;
(c) where it appears on the face of the proceedings to be founded on an incorrect view of international law or a refusal to recognise the law of [1][India] in cases in which such law is applicable;
(d) where the proceedings in which the judgment was obtained are opposed to natural justice;
(e) where it has been obtained by fraud;
(f) where it sustains a claim founded on a breach of any law in force in [1][India].

[104]14. Presumption as to foreign judgments.

The Court shall presume upon the production of any document purporting to be a certified copy of a foreign judgment that such judgment was pronounced by a Court of competent jurisdiction, unless the contrary appears on the record; but such presumption may be displaced by proving want of jurisdiction.

[105]44A. Execution of decrees passed by Courts in reciprocating territory.

(1) Where a certified copy of decree of any of the superior Courts of [***] any reciprocating territory has been filed in a District Court, the decree may be executed in [3][India] as if it had been passed by the District Court.
(2) Together with the certified copy of the decree shall be filed a certificate from such superior Court stating the extent, if any, to which the decree has been satisfied or adjusted and such certificate shall, for the purposes of proceedings under this section, be conclusive proof of the extent of such satisfaction or adjustment.
(3) The provisions of section 47 shall as from the filing of the certified copy of the decree apply to the proceedings of a District Court executing a decree under this section, and the District Court shall refuse execution of any such decree, if it is shown to the satisfaction of the Court that the decree falls within any of the exceptions specified in clauses (a) to (f) of section 13.

[4][Explanation 1—"Reciprocating territory" means any country or territory outside India which the Central Government may, by notification in the Official Gazette, declare to be a reciprocating territory for the purposes of this section; and "superior Courts", with reference to any such territory, means such Courts as may be specified in the said notification.

Explanation 2—"Decree" with reference to a superior Court means any decree or judgment of such Court under which a sum of money is payable, not being a sum payable in respect of taxes or other charges of a like nature or in respect to a fine or other penalty, but shall in no case include an arbitration award, even if such an award is enforceable as a decree or judgment.].

[106]No. 1:04-cv-00253-RWS (N.D.Ga. Oct, 28 2005).

judgment in a patent infringement case illustrated a few suggestions for enforcement of foreign judgments. A reciprocity agreement could be an interesting option. Further where there is a public policy taint within the foreign judgment, the principle of severability could be applied for enforcement of the valid and enforceable portion of the judgment.[107]

## 2.4 *Arbitration in IPR Disputes*

Owing to the difficulties encountered in enforcing foreign judgments commercial arbitration is increasingly becoming an alternative for adversarial method of dispute resolution like litigation, especially when involving parties from different jurisdictions and possible issues of conflict of laws. Arbitration as a private and confidential procedure is increasingly being preferred for resolution of IPRs-related disputes. In 2014, the World Intellectual Property Organization Arbitration and Mediation Centre revised its arbitration rules. Arbitration of IPRs-related disputes is not possible in India as they are characterized as non-arbitrable commercial issues. The Bombay High Court in the case of *EuroKids International Private Limited v Bhaskar Vidhyapeeth Shikshan Sanstha*,[108] held that disputes regarding infringement of intellectual property rights can be exclusively tried by Civil Court since it ceases to exercise right in rem which cannot be arbitral dispute. The arbitrable intellectual property issues cover commercial aspects of the contract related to terms and conditions of license, assignment etc. In the case of *Chokhi Dhani Resorts Private Limited* v *Essem Recreation*,[109] Rajasthan High court held that any dispute or difference arising between the parties out of or relating to the construction, meaning, scope, operation or effect of contract are arbitrable in nature.[110]

---

[107]France and Spain included the award of punitive damages within the law though it was in conflict of public policy of the state. http://www.tomeika.jur.kyushu-u.ac.jp/procedure/procedure-cases-judgments%20JAIL-PDF/2-030_SUPREME_COURT_JULY_11.1997.pdf.

[108]2015 (4) Bom. C. R. 734.

[109]2014(1) CLT 534.

[110]US, Canada, Australia, Switzerland and some other European countries have allowed the arbitration of all Intellectual Property Disputes. Their laws amended accordingly to implement properly ADR method in IP disputes. On the other hand China, France and India permit arbitration of all issues except questions related to validity of particular Intellectual Property.

## 3 Conclusion

While it is interesting to explore the possibility of a uniform set of private international law rules in intellectual property to have a global standard,[111] it is also pertinent to ensure that such global standard would not leave space for countries to develop their own law.

The discussion of IPR involving cross border elements in India depicts absence of clarity on basic issues including enforcement-related concerns. Childress, speaking in the context of the US observed that conflict of laws-related problems could be minimized by adopting the principle of comity—a court in one country may apply the laws of another country by virtue of comity.[112] This seventeenth century born doctrine at the time of emergence of nation state in Europe[113] is yet to be recognized effectively by Indian Court in IPRs-related disputes.

While there have been no adjudicated disputes involving conflicts of law in IP-related disputes in India, theoretically it could be inferred that cross border IPRs-related disputes could be adjudicated through a classification of international law—customary international law, or general principles common to major legal system, and through a combination of judicial and legislative interpretation.[114] Owing to the difficulties encountered in enforcing foreign judgments in trans-national intellectual property disputes commercial arbitration is increasingly becoming an alternative for IP-related disputes resolution.[115] Intellectual property disputes have a number of particular characteristics that may be better addressed by arbitration than by court litigation.[116] As it is increasingly becoming evident that the territoriality principle is not significant help in determining the ownership of IP rights and other contractual rights[117] matters related to licensing and assignments could be resolved through arbitration without entering into complex issues of Private International Law. While it was earlier understood that IPRs being granted by national authorities, disputes regarding them could not be arbitrated, it is increasingly being understood that like any other private rights, they are now arbitrable. The utility of arbitration as a dispute resolution mechanism is of significant value in intellectual property-related disputes because the award of the

[111]Trimble (n 16).

[112]Donald Earl Childress III, 'Comity as Conflict: Resituating International Comity as Conflict of Laws' (2010), 44(1), U.C.D.LRev 14.

[113]Leo Gross, 'The Peace of Westphalia: 1648–1948' (1948) 42 (1) AJIL, 20.

[114]Graeme B. Dinwoodie, 'International Intellectual Property Litigation: A Vehicle for Resurgent Comparativist Thought?' (2001) 49(2) AJCL, 429.

[115]Jacques De Werra, 'Arbitrating International Intellectual Disputes: Time to Think Beyond the Issue of (Non) Arbitrability' (2012) 3 Int'l Bus. L Jour. 299.

[116]Why Arbitration in Intellectual Property Disputes. http://www.wipo.int/amc/en/arbitration/why-is-arb.html, accessed 10 May 2016.

[117]Francois Dessemontet, 'Party Autonomy and the Law Applicable to the Arbitrability of IP Rights and Licensing Transactions' (2013) 5 Intl l Bus. L J 421.

tribunal would be enforceable in most jurisdictions across the world, as any judgment of the court of that jurisdiction, courtesy, the New York Convention, 1958 on the Recognition and Enforcement of Foreign Arbitral Awards. Any right that a party can dispose by way of settlement should, in principle, also be capable of being the subject of an arbitration, since, like a settlement, arbitration is base on party agreement. As a consequence of the consensual nature of arbitration, any award rendered will be binding only on the parties involved and will not as such affect third parties.

# Part IV
# Private International Law in South Asia—The Way Forward

# Private International Law in South Asia—A Few Pointers for Harmonization

**Bruno Zeller**

**Abstract** This chapter summarizes the narratives related to Private International Law within the South Asian region. The chapter attempts to critically appreciate the narratives discussed in the preceding chapters. Further the chapter attempts to chart a course of action for revisiting the existing legal regime in the personal law and commercial law spaces. The chapter presents a dual strategy for the law reform effort. It suggests accession to international conventions in this space, especially the important conventions of the Hague Conference within this space. Importantly, the chapter suggests strengthening the regional harmonization efforts, exemplifying through the efforts of similar organizations in other regions. The chapter suggests that harmonized legal platforms in trans-national private law can be achieved through concerted regional efforts and organizations like the SAARC could effectively contribute to the regional harmonization of the law affecting cross-border contracts. The chapter concludes by suggesting accession to the international conventions rather than embarking upon exclusive regional efforts alone.

**Keywords** South Asia · Private International Law · Cross-border contracts · International Commercial Arbitration · CISG · OHADA · Harmonization

B. Zeller (✉)
Transnational Commercial Law, University of Western Australia, Perth, Australia
e-mail: bruno.zeller@uwa.edu.au

B. Zeller
Faculty of Law, School of Law, Murdoch University, Perth, Australia

B. Zeller
Zelman Cowan Centre, Victoria University, Melbourne, Australia

B. Zeller
Australian Institute for Commercial Arbitration, Panel of Arbitrators—MLAANZ, Melbourne, Australia

B. Zeller
Institut fur Anwaltsrecht, Humboldt University, Berlin, Germany

© Springer Nature Singapore Pte Ltd. 2017
S.R. Garimella and S. Jolly (eds.), *Private International Law*,
DOI 10.1007/978-981-10-3458-9_21

The editors of this book chose an imminently important topic namely private international law and organised the theme not only in particular distinct but important areas of laws but also geographically in South Asian countries. It is rich with useful material and is unique as not much research—if any so far—has focused on South Asian countries specifically covering topics of cross border disputes in diverse subject areas.

It is true to say that except India the other countries are not part of important economic standing but comparative studies are of importance wherever they are conducted to understand and appreciate global efforts to create uniform laws. This is specifically important as the South Asian countries belong to the common as well as civil law families. In addition, smaller countries could gain from the experience of their neighbours and undertake law reform to help improve the ease of doing business and thereby foster increased economic growth.

This book indicates changes which are on foot and hence it will contribute to an understanding and implementation of law reform in South East Asian countries. Three important areas which are not only economically but culturally important are flagged as warranted research—jurisdiction, choice of law and enforcement of foreign judgments, which includes arbitration.

The first contribution discusses issues emanating out of South Asian countries but are decided in the UK. This will indicate the benefits but also the negative aspect that issues specifically in family law are decided without the necessary cultural background being one of the deciding factors. The second essay examines the choice of law issue from the point of view of arbitration and points to the unique fact that arbitration is less bound to rigid rules but allows arbitrators—depending on the choice of procedural rules—discretionary power to determine the governing substantive law.

An issue that has not found much traction but at the same time cannot be ignored is The Hague Convention on Choice of Court Agreements. Besides Mexico and the EU no other country has signed the convention and at this stage it is doubtful whether the Convention will ever be successful. Arguably it does not harmonise the law effectively in relation to court agreements and careful contract drafting will overcome any problems this convention attempts to regulate.

The Afghan contribution on choice of law in personal status, property and contract law is most interesting as it relies on the civil law aspect namely the Afghanistan Civil Code. It offers an insight into laws that are at variance with the common-law system specifically as it is practiced in India.

The contribution from Bangladesh correctly notes the importance of the selection of proper law and forum for settlement of disputes specifically if the judgement needs to be enforced in a foreign jurisdiction. The paper traces the unsettled aspect of an enforcement of a foreign judgment in the context of the State of Bangladesh regarding matrimonial, adoption, corporate, property disputes etc.

A further chapter discusses the cross-border divorce regime in Bangladesh noting that the available divorce procedure obviously is different for Bangladeshi and non-Bangladeshi procedures. The paper describes the differences and difficulties encountered by non-residents specially if they are married under Muslim law.

Fittingly the next paper outlines the public policy consideration in matrimonial remedies in India. It allows the reader to understand the interpretation of matrimonial issues within Hindu law. One of the "big issues" in India is the reluctance of courts to recognise foreign judgments and that irretrievable breakdown of marriage is not a ground under Indian law to grant a divorce. The conclusion is that Indian law is not in tune with many other jurisdictions.

Cross border surrogacy has become not only a human but also a legal problem as specifically couples from advanced economic countries such as North America are drawn to the Indian continent. It is not surprising that challenges specifically in private international law are common to regulate issues such as parentage and nationality of children and hence need to be regulated. This chapter demonstrates that urgent work by international organisations is required to harmonise the law on surrogacy.

The next chapter closely follows the theme of protecting children not only in surrogacy issues but also in inter-country child abduction. The author notes that international marriages are common and hence the issue of one parent abducting the children is a reality. The issue of which country has competence in hearing abduction cases is a crucial issue. The Hague Convention on the Civil Aspects of International Child Abduction serves as the comprehensive body of law that first establishes which country has the right to adjudicate custody. The chapter attempts to define the issue of "wrongful removal" within the international context as well as in India, which is not a signatory to the Convention.

Nepal only recently felt the need to develop a framework on private international law as before the *Sabina Pandey* case private international law was only sparingly used. The chapter—using *Sabina Pandey*—as the centre point of the discussion sheds light on the new development in Nepal in relation of enforcement of foreign judgment in Nepal.

The next chapter focuses on the problem of inter-country child abduction in the context of the law in Pakistan. The chapter focuses on the quality of the domestic Pakistani private international law capacity to deal with the issue.

The argument based on the increase of child abduction is focused on a growing trend of cross cultural marriages and the issue that woman suffer from discrimination is not conducive to find a solution in the short term. The author argues that a divorced woman is left with no legal option in Pakistan once the child or children are taken abroad and hence authorities in Pakistan ought to put their mind to solve this problem.

The next two chapters discuss aspects of Private International Law in Sri Lanka namely divorce and cross border child abduction. In the context of cross-border divorce and the the author concentrated on the three main issues, namely, jurisdiction, the choice of law and the enforcement of a foreign judgments. The discussion also takes into consideration international conventions governing divorce matters.

In the chapter on inter-country child abduction, the author noted, firstly, that Sri Lanka is a signatory to a few key Hague Conventions on private international law related aspects without having significantly embraced them. The author explains that this is due to the unique position of Sri Lanka in relation to religious, political and traditional values. Secondly, the author specifies tha has enacted the Civil Aspects of International Child Abduction Act of 2001 and the chapter offers an extensive of the pre-legislation and post-legislation legal position in respect of child abductions.

The contributions from Bangladesh focus upon commercial issues, namely — enforcement of jurisdiction clauses in commercial contracts and international commercial arbitration. Bangladesh has adopted the UNCITRAL Model Law into the Arbitration Act, 2001 including the capping of the courts' involvement in arbitration. The paper specifically addresses the fact that the direct or indirect supervisory role of Court over the arbitration process that is still in the process of development.

The next contribution specifically analyses and builds on the above contribution namely the enforcement of foreign award in Bangladesh. The author specifically highlights the recommendations for law reform to prevent any interventionist attitude of the judiciary, to expedite the cross-border resolution of disputes and thus to promote international trade and investments.

The book concludes with two contributions from India one on issues of intellectual property issues and the second one on Indian practises in relation to international commercial arbitrations. The author specifically addresses the proliferation of the international multilateral and bilateral treaties related to intellectual property and private international law and its applicability in India.

The other chapter from India addresses the interplay between international private law in relation to the seat of arbitration, interim measures and choice of law and the ever-present public policy exception as to the enforcement of arbitral awards. There is a chapter in the book discussing the Sri Lankan law on international Commercial Arbitration elucidating the features of the Sri Lankan Arbitration Act related to jurisdiction, choice of law and the enforcement of foreign arbitral awards in Sri Lanka.

## 1 Discussion

The chapters in this book touch on private international law issues in South Asian legal systems. The problem is that South Asian Association for Regional Cooperation (SAARC) is not a recognised trade block but has increased interactions among the independent municipal systems. It is not comparable to the ASEAN trade block which is a political construct with economic integration based on a Free Trade Agreement nor is it a construct modelled on OHADA.[1] This book highlights the diverse but crucial subject areas affecting the region specifically:

- jurisdiction,
- choice of law, and
- foreign judgments/arbitral awards.

The issue is whether harmonisation of important issues would be a solution to assist in cross-border facilitation and hence reduce the risk and add to increased trade. Issues of human rights including child abduction and divorce are a subject which will arguably not attract harmonisation efforts as culturally there is too much of a gap. At best, it can be argued that enforcements of judgments with SAARC should be granted and be prioritised in discussions among member courts and governments.

[1]Organisation pour Harmonisation en Afrique du Droit des Affairs.

Whatever the issue the point is that a selection of a forum as well as a choice of law is important but not easily achieved. In the end, at least one party must deal with a foreign law. The only way to overcome this issue is if a harmonised law governs—as an example—the contractual relationship between the parties.

Several mechanisms are available to harmonise interregional laws. The obvious point is to ratify the Vienna Sales Convention (CISG) as well as attempt to foster interregional law reform on a governmental level.

## 1.1 The CISG

Currently 84 countries are party to the CISG and the only two major economies not having ratified the CISG is India and the UK.[2] It is surprising to read that India has not done so and the reasons given are not always demonstrating that the opponents to the accession to the Convention have understood the mandate of the CISG. After all it is always possible for an Indian buyer or seller to have to deal with the CISG if the governing law is the one of a contracting state. If the law of China is the governing law it includes the CISG unless specifically excluded. The important issue is that most of India's trading partners have ratified the CISG and it would also not be uncommon if arbitrators apply the CISG if no governing law is specified.

It needs to be understood that the CISG is in effect a compromise between civil and common law principles; the legal profession must be aware of the advantages and no doubt disadvantages of the CISG when drafting contracts. One anecdotal fact appears to emerge mainly in the United States where law firms have been sued because the contract drafters could not explain properly why the CISG was excluded except we have always done so. Universities have a major role to play in the dissemination of information to the legal profession to make sure that the relevant knowledge is made public. One issue arguably has been put to bed namely whether the CISG should be expanded. The Villanova Conference in 2013 emphatically rejected the notion of an expansion of the CISG through the proposed Swiss initiative at the 45th meeting at UNCITRAL.[3]

The real issue is that courts and counsels have not yet grasped the fundamental issues and advantages of the CISG. It has been argued correctly that an introduction of a convention or soft law into a legal system is difficult if "nobody knows that it is there, [therefore] the new law has little capacity to shape behaviour."[4] This is certainly the case in Australia as the interpretation and application of the CISG exhibits a clear lack of applying the underlying principles of the CISG. Arguably this is mainly due to a

---

[2]See http://iicl.law.pace.edu/cisg/cisg.

[3]See as an example K. Loken, A new Global Initiative on Contract Law in UNCITRAL: Right Project, Right Forum? (2013) 58 Villanova Law Review 509.

[4]Gordon, J., and Rosett, A., "United States" in Bonell, M.J. *A new Approach to International Commercial Contracts*. Kluver Law, London (1999) 388.

lack of appreciation of the interpretative mandate of the CISG pursuant to Article 7 but also a clear lack of understanding of the implications of Article 8. This is a scenario of significant concern as contract interpretation "[is] the lifeblood of commercial law."[5] To study the developments in Australia can be a lesson for SAARC countries once the ratification of the CISG is on the political agenda.

## *1.2 Examples of Regional Organizations*

### 1.2.1 OHADA

The OHADA solution is not an option for SAARC as it requires the creation of a supranational court to deal with litigation emanating from harmonised laws.[6] The point to note is that the Uniform Act on Commercial Law has been modelled on the CISG and the Uniform Act on Arbitration on the UNCITRAL Model law.[7] As it can be seen the CISG is not only a convention it is also a source to harmonise sales law within a trade block.

### 1.2.2 The EU

In addition, the EU also provides a lesson in the inability to harmonise laws in a specific area. It is obvious that EU regulations are binding on EU members but some of the regulations have embedded clauses allowing a member state to exempt itself from the regulation. The UK is an example at hand on this issue. The EU does have a supranational court namely the European Court of Justice. However, looking at the efforts of the EU to harmonise contract law the conclusion is that it has been a failure.

The question of regional harmonisation has not found traction and can arguably be dismissed as not being superior to a simple acceptance of the CISG.[8] The efforts in the EU in drafting a common European Contract law should be a lesson to be learned. Several major attempts have been made starting with The Principles of European Contract law (PECL), the Common Frame of Reference (CFR) and now

[5]Calnan, R., 'Construction of Commercial Contracts: A Practitioner's Perspective' in Burrows and Peel (eds) *Contract Terms*, (2007) 17.

[6]See B. Zeller, Mining Projects in OHADA: The Legal and Judicial Climate in G. Moens & P. Evans (eds) *Arbitration and Dispute Resolution in the Resources Sector—An Australian Perspective*, (Springer Publishing, 2015) 231 ff.

[7]Ibid., 237. See also F. Ferrari, CISG and OHADA Sales Law in U. Magnus (ed) *CISG vs Regional Sales Law Unification*, (Sellier European Law Publisher, 2012), 79 ff.

[8]See for example B. Zeller, *'The Development of a Global Contract Law. Still a Dream?'* in UNIDROIT (ed.), Eppur si muove: The age of Uniform Law—Festschrift for Michael Joachim Bonell, to celebrate his 70th birthday, (UNIDROIT, 2016) 1179; and B. Zeller 'Regional Harmonisation of Contract law—is it feasible?' (2016) 3(1) *J of L, Soc. & Dev.*—UNISA, 85.

the Common European Sales Law (CESL). Much work has gone into the drafting of the three instruments and what can be said is that UPICC overshadows PECL and the CFR and no doubt CESL. It can be confidently stated that all three instruments will collect dust on a shelf.[9]

### *1.3 The UNIDROIT Principles*

As the CISG is only a sales law and not a contract law any discussions on an uptake of the CISG arguably should include a discussion on the UNIDROIT Principles. As Kronke, as early as in 2005, noted,

> What we see looking at the two instruments – the CISG as the mother of all modern conventions on the law of specific contracts and the UPICC as the (inevitably) soft-law source of modern general contract law – are neither competitors nor apples and pears. What we see is and even more, potentially, a fruitful coexistence … [T]he UNIDROIT Contract Principles are, obviously, complementary in that they address a wide range of topics of general contract law which neither the CISG nor any other existing or future convention devoted to a specific type of transaction would ever venture to touch upon.[10]

As noted above an introduction of a Convention is never easy and requires a legal system to prepare itself adequately to successfully integrate—in this case—the CISG. To that end lessons from other countries are valuable. Another point needs to be noted namely the introduction of soft laws. An opting in option is never successful unless the parties understand the importance of the soft law and it has been promoted or drafted by industry sources as was done in case of soft law instruments like the INCOTERMS and the UCP. The UNIDROIT Principles have been referred to by arbitrators and judges to assist in the interpretation of contractual problems. But in the end, it is left to Conventions and domestic law to govern contracts and their potential cross border issues.

## 2 Conclusion

The question is what can SAARC learn from the global experience? This article has demonstrated that the biggest roadblock in an internationalisation of contract law and other cross border issues is the inability or reluctance of the legal profession to engage in a rethink and hence move away from a past knowledge base. It has been demonstrated—and history has shown that to be true—that the shortcut to a proper

---

[9] B. Zeller, Harmonisation of International contract law—dream or reality? Paper presented at the 2015 UNCITRAL Emergence Conference to be held on 30 November 2015 at University of Macau, Macau SAR. To be published by Comparative Law Journal of the Pacific (CLJP).

[10] Herbert Kronke, 'The UN Sales Convention, the UNIDROIT Contract Principles and the Way Beyond' (2005) 25 J.L. & Com. 451, 458–59.

understanding of global developments—and in this case the CISG—is via the judiciary. This has been aptly demonstrated in *Perry Engineering v Bernold*[11] where the court noted,

> … there is a further complication that the Sale of Goods (Vienna Convention) Act 1986 (SA) applies to the dealings between the parties but the relevant provisions have not been pleaded in the plaintiff's statement of claim. The statement of claim has been drawn up on the assumption that the South Australian Sale of Goods Act applies. This seems to me to be fatal to the plaintiff's ability to proceed to judgment based on damages for breach of contract.[12]

Hence training of the judiciary is a far more effective and a cheaper alternative in the introduction of change. Above all it has been demonstrated by past efforts that regional harmonisation has not found traction and can arguably be dismissed. OHADA as an example has shown that if the political will to harmonise laws with a region is present it can be achieved. Also, the drafting an uptake of the Cape Town Convention is a lesson in law reform and is eminently useful in copying the approach when law reform is on the political agenda.

In the end, it will assist reducing costs not only for business but also for courts specifically in SAARC where variations within the region are still great. The papers in this book illustrate the variations well and should be given priority by courts and governments as a foundation to law reform within the region.

---

[11]Australia 1 February 2001 Supreme Court of South Australia [http://cisgw3.law.pace.edu/cases/010201a2.html].

[12]Ibid.

FSC
www.fsc.org
MIX
Papier | Fördert
gute Waldnutzung
FSC® C083411

Kolibri 360 GmbH
Ferdinand-Jühlke-Straße 7
99095 Erfurt, Deutschland
produktsicherheit@kolibri360.de